An Accidental Autobiography

BOOKS BY GREGORY CORSO

Elegiac Feelings American

The Happy Birthday of Death

Herald of the Autochthomic Spirit

Long Live Man

Gregory Corso eating grapes in his room at
"The Beat Hotel", Paris, 1958.

GREGORY CORSO

AN ACCIDENTAL AUTOBIOGRAPHY

THE SELECTED LETTERS OF

GREGORY CORSO

EDITED WITH COMMENTARY AND INTRODUCTION BY

BILL MORGAN

FOREWORD BY

PATTI SMITH

A NEW DIRECTIONS BOOK

Book design by Sylvia Frezzolini Severance
New Directions Books are printed on acid-free paper.
First published clothbound by New Directions in 2003
Published simultaneously in Canada by Penguin Books Canada Ltd.

Library of Congress Cataloging-in-Publication Data

Corso, Gregory.
[Correspondence. Selections]
An accidental autobiography : the selected letters of Gregory Corso / edited with commentary and an introduction by Bill Morgan ; foreword by Patti Smith.
p. cm.
Includes bibliographical references and index.
ISBN 0-8112-1535-0 (alk. paper) ISBN 978-0811215350
1. Corso, Gregory—Correspondence. 2. Poets, American—20th century—Correspondence. 3. Beat generation—Correspondence. I. Morgan, Bill, 1949- II. Title.
PS3505.O763 Z48 2003
811'.54—dc21

2002152183

New Directions Books are published for James Laughlin
by New Directions Publishing Corporation,
80 Eighth Avenue, New York, NY 10011

CONTENTS

TO

ALL THE READERS

OF GREGORY CORSO'S POETRY

PAST, PRESENT AND FUTURE

FOREWORD

By Patti Smith

Gregory Corso, the flower of the Beat Generation, is gone. He has been plucked to grace the Daddy garden and all in heaven are magnified and amused. I first encountered Gregory long ago in front of the Chelsea Hotel. He lifted his overcoat and dropped his trousers, spewing Latin expletives. Seeing my astonished face, he laughed and said, "I'm not mooning you sweetheart, I'm mooning the world." I remember thinking, how fortunate for the world to be privy to the exposed rump of a true poet.

And that he was. All who have stories, real or embellished, of Gregory's legendary mischief and chaotic indiscretions must also have stories of his beauty, his remorse, and his generosity. He took benevolent note of me in the early '70s, maybe because my living space was akin to his—piles of papers, books, old shoes, piss in cups—mortal disarray. We were disruptive partners in crime during particularly tedious poetry readings at St. Mark's. Though we were aptly scolded, Gregory counseled me to stick to my irreverent guns and demand more from those who sat before us calling themselves poets.

There was no doubt Gregory was a poet. Poetry was his ideology, and the poets his saints. He was called upon and he knew it. Perhaps his only dilemma was to sometimes ask, Why, why him? He was born in New York City on March 2, 1930. His young mother abandoned him. The boy drifted from foster home to reformatory to prison. He had little formal education, but his self-education was limitless. He embraced the Greeks and the Romantics, and the Beats embraced him, pressing laurel leaves upon his dark unruly curls. Knighted by Kerouac as Raphael Urso, he was their pride and joy and also their most provocative conscience.

He has left us two legacies: a body of work that will endure for its beauty, discipline, and influential energy, and his human qualities. He was part Pete Rose, part Percy Bysshe Shelley. He could be explosively rebellious, belligerent, and testing, yet in turn, boyishly pure, humble, and compassionate. He was always willing to say he was sorry, share his knowledge, and was open to learn. I remember watching him sit at Allen Ginsberg's bedside as he lay dying. "Allen is teaching me how to die," he said.

In early summer his friends were summoned to say goodbye to him. We sat by his bedside on Horatio Street in silence. The night filled with strange correspondences. A daughter he had never known. A patron from far away. A young poet at his feet. On a muted screen, Robert Frank's *Pull My Daisy* randomly aired on public television—unaware of its mystical timing. Images of the Daddies, young and crazy, black and white. Snapshots of Allen taped to the wall. The modest room lorded over by Gregory's chair in all its shabby glory. So many dreams punctuated by cigarette burns. He was dying. We all said goodbye.

But Gregory, perhaps sensing the devotion surrounding him, became a participant in a true Catholic miracle. He rose up. He went into remission just long enough for us to hear his voice, his laughter, and a few welcomed obscenities. We were able to write poems for him, sing to him, watch football, and hear him recite Blake. He was here long enough to travel to Minneapolis, to bond with his daughter, to be a king among children, to see another fall, another winter, and another century. Allen taught him how to die. Gregory reminded us how to live and cherish life before leaving us a second time.

At the end of his days, he still suffered a young poet's torment—the desire to achieve perfection. And in death, as in art, he shall. The fresh light pours. The boys from the road steer him on. But before he ascends into some holy card glow, Gregory, being himself, lifts his overcoat, drops his trousers, and as he exposes his poet's rump one last time, cries, "Hey man, kiss my daisy." Ahh Gregory, the years and petals fly.

He loved us. He loved us not. He loved us.

—Patti Smith

EDITOR'S INTRODUCTION

By Bill Morgan

When Gregory Corso died on January 17, 2001, he was the last of the "Daddies" as he liked to call the core group of writers — Jack Kerouac, Allen Ginsberg and William S. Burroughs — who created the Beat Generation. Obituaries referred to him as a great American lyric poet and "L'Enfant Terrible of the Beat Generation," and he was both. In fact, his life can be viewed as a complex assortment of contrasts, conflicts and contradictions. He could be very charming and very rude. He could be generous one moment and steal from his oldest friends the very next. He could be just as insensitive to people as his poetry was sensitive to the plight of mankind. It seemed as if the only constant about Corso was his poetic genius. When he wrote poems, he was always honest, direct, clear and concise.

Corso must have been wrong when he said that a poet and his poetry were inseparable. For a man who wrote so openly about beauty, truth and respect for all beings, he caused a tremendous amount of pain to the people close to him. You don't have to like a man to like his poetry and by any standards, Gregory Corso was a tough man to like, but his poetry is very easy to love. There are at least two sides to every facet of his life and work. He pretended to be spontaneous in his poetry and he pretended to be care-free in his life, but he was neither. As his letters reveal he believed in carefully crafting, rewriting and tailoring his poetry, even if the original inspiration was spontaneous. Some poems went through years of revisions and hundreds of drafts.

In many ways it is remarkable that Corso lived to be seventy years old at all, for his life of excesses must have taxed his physical body to the limits. Not content to burn his candle at both ends, he lit it in the middle as well. Poet, Ed Sanders, wrote that "few have lived the life of a poet with more energy than Gregory Corso." He devoted his life to nothing but poetry, and his loyalty was only to his work.

As a college student, I had discovered Corso through those wonderful black and white paperback editions issued by his long-time publisher, New Directions. Through my work as Allen Ginsberg's archivist for twenty years, I had met Gregory dozens of times and had dinner with him on several occasions.

He made quite an impression on me, even if he never really remembered me. As a result, I was pleased and surprised when a film company asked me to do research for a documentary on Corso's life. I was anxious to learn as much about him as I could, because I had heard so many stories and knew so little of the facts. The more I read about his life, the more mysterious it all became. At every turn there were contradictory stories about him. Many times the conflicting sources were interviews given by Corso. I began to think that the truth about his life would never be known, but as I began to assemble his correspondence from dozens of sources, I realized that all together, this was his truthful autobiography in his own words.

Corso grew up on the streets of New York City as near to being an orphan as is possible. His mother disappeared when he was about a year old and his father put him in a string of foster homes, from which Gregory ran away again and again. He spent time in orphanages, reform schools, a psychiatric ward, and prison all before he was twenty. He only went as far as the sixth grade before leaving the school system behind, and educated himself on the streets and in the prison library. He had no friends and virtually no family to write to, until he was in his early twenties. It was then that he met Allen Ginsberg, and through him, all the other members of the soon to be named, Beat Generation.

For the next ten years he wrote letters regularly, with the main subjects being himself and his poetry. He was accidentally writing his autobiography. Then in the mid-sixties, the various demands of drug and alcohol addiction began to take over. His letters became shorter, less frequent, less informative, less self-examining. They became increasingly bitter, as one after another of his old friends failed to respond to his many demands. He still had that junkie's ability to flatter the right person at the right time, but he couldn't sustain relationships, and was lucky to have a few loyal friends for so many years.

After his disastrous reading in 1965 at the Royal Albert Hall poetry festival, which was a triumph for other poets like Ginsberg and Ferlinghetti, Corso stopped reading in public. Although he would try again from time to time to make money by occasional readings, his alcohol and drug use always marred the event. At the same time his rude behavior grew worse, and as more and more people abandoned him, he sank into a self-inflicted silence. He assured his publishers that he was writing constantly, but in fact, it was only in fits and spurts that he would produce enough for publication. He did continue to write poetry over the decades and some books and wonderful poems were created, more a tribute to his natural talents and abilities than to hard work.

He was aware of what had happened to him, and he was continually telling people that he was getting his life in order and on the verge of something wonderful and creative, but he was never able to muster up the energy to follow through with his resolutions. Until the end he was flattered to be well-thought of as a poet, but felt at the same time, that he was not given his due and that society owed him for his poetic gifts.

Corso was truly a remarkable character in literary history. It seems a shame that he was never able to break out of the drug addict, con-man mentality, and burst forth on the scene again with a new sheaf of poems under his arm. But the happy-ever-after ending was not to be. He had friends and family enough in the end to care for him, but up until his last breath he was hard to get along with. He seemed to want it both ways. He wanted people to love him without having to love people in return. It was only through the sweet temperaments of his close friends that he was taken care of through the last years.

These letters have been selected from nearly eight hundred examined in public and private collections. As the editor, I have felt that it was my job to let Corso speak his own words in his own voice, and I have tried to remain in the background. Footnotes have been provided only where needed to help identify the people and events that he is writing about. When passages have been removed, usually to make a passage easier to understand, an ellipsis within square brackets is used [...]. The only exception is the twenty-one page letter he wrote to Jack Kerouac in late August 1958. More than half of that letter has been deleted, because it is repetitive and doesn't provide any greater insight into the mind of the poet. Ellipses have not been used in that one example, and interested readers should go to the University of Kansas where the entire letter is available for research. Where a word has been added to help clear up the meaning, it has been inserted within square brackets.

It was not a common practice for Corso to date his letters, so in many cases the dates are approximations based on the postmarks of the letters, notes by the recipients or the date of their replies and by an examination of the content of the letter. Dates which are not in square brackets are actually those given by Corso himself. This book is not intended to be a collection of every letter and postcard that Corso wrote, but to lead the reader through his life as he lived it, with special emphasis on his poetry and literary life. To that end spelling errors have usually been corrected except when it was obvious that Corso was making a point or a pun by the mis-spelled words. Corso's unique word inventions have not been tampered with, as they are an important part of his creative work. In a very few cases a word was illegible and when I wasn't absolutely certain, I included the word within square brackets. Occasionally I was unable to identify some of the people Corso was writing about and I extend my apology to anyone so slighted. If any of the elusive characters in this book are discovered they will be added to future editions.

I never thought Corso would allow these letters to be published, so I was surprised a second time when a few months before his death, he gave his permission to the project. I hope he would have approved of the result. William Carlos Williams wrote in his introduction to Ginsberg's Howl a warning that seems even more appropriate for this book of Corso's: "Hold back the edges of your gowns, Ladies, we are going through hell!"

ACKNOWLEDGMENTS AND ABBREVIATIONS

A book such as this could not have been possible without the lifelong dedication of many people and institutions determined to preserve the written word. Many of Corso's friends saved his letters faithfully over the years and then saw to it that they were placed in libraries where scholars and researchers like myself could study them. Some of the people who helped most in the recovery of these letters are thanked below.

A great deal of gratitude is also due to the many people who took care of Gregory Corso over the years. We will never know how many people actually helped support him during the fifty years of his adult life, but they are legion. Besides the support of his family, of particular importance in the last decades of his life were Allen Ginsberg, Hiro Yamagata and Roger and Irvyne Richards. Ginsberg was famous for his generosity, not always appreciated by Corso, as these letters will attest. He provided financial support for a long period of time. Hiro Yamagata was a fan of Corso's writing who was able to give him a monthly stipend for support over the last decade of his life. It allowed him to live in some comfort without the worries of rent, food and clothing. Roger and Irvyne Richards welcomed him into their home and provided not only physical support, but emotional support and personal friendship for decades.

Special thanks are due to Gus Reininger, who while making a documentary film on the life of Corso first asked me to collect materials about his life and work. It was from that research that this book sprang and I am grateful to him for his permission to allow that work to be shared here. Long time friends of Corso's also helped in many ways, providing copies of letters and information as I needed it. Don Allen, Alan Ansen, Rick Ardinger, Gordon Ball, Laura Boss, David Carter, Neeli Cherkovski, Kirby Congdon, Robert Creeley, Lawrence Ferlinghetti, Raymond Foye, Bill Gargan, Jack W.C. Hagstrom, Anselm Hollo, Sheri Langerman, Michael McClure, Kaye McDonough, Peter Orlovsky, Roger and Irvyne Richards, Ed Sanders, Herschel Silverman, Robert Sutherland-Cohen, Philip Whalen, Ted Wilentz, and Bob Wilson. A note of thanks should also go to my current colleagues who have been good enough to cover for me while I daydreamed of Corso correspondence: Oliver Sacks, Kate

Edgar, Diana Beck and Sheryl Carter. Special thanks to the staff of the Allen Ginsberg trust for their endless help and permission to use Ginsberg's photographs in this edition: Bob Rosenthal and Peter Hale.

Institutions where Corso's letters have been preserved have also been very helpful in providing access to the letters and granting permission for the letters to be included in this volume. It is encouraging to see the list of so many important university libraries that have saved Corso's correspondence over the years. It is a testimony to the growing importance of Corso's writings in the academic world. Brooklyn College; Brown University (Hay Library); Columbia University; Cornell University Libraries; Harvard University; Indiana University; New York Public Library (Berg Collection); Reed College; Simon Fraser University; Stanford University Libraries; SUNY Libraries at Buffalo; Syracuse University Libraries; University of California at Berkeley (Bancroft Library); University of California at Davis; University of California at San Diego; University of Connecticut Libraries; University of Delaware; University of Kansas; University of Michigan; University of Texas at Austin; and Washington University.

The editor wishes to extend an extra thank you to entire staff at New Directions who have helped see this book through the publication process. Especially Griselda Ohannessian, who recognized the importance of these letters upon seeing just a few pieces of the puzzle. Finally, my endless gratitude to my wife, Judy, for her years of patience and support for this and every project.

An Accidental Autobiography

▼ [One of Gregory Corso's earliest letters was a brief note dated Nov. 18, 1954, written to Isabella Gardner, an editor of *Poetry* magazine. Corso thanked Mrs. Gardner for what he called her "beautiful helpful letter." It was in response to a rejection letter consisting of the single line: "'Mental muscle'—yes, how right you are." Corso was just beginning to struggle with the process of publication and wanted to be recognized by the established poetry forums of the day without giving up his individual style and voice.

At this time Corso was living in Cambridge, MA, as a drop-in mascot for the literati at Harvard. He was busy writing poems and plays, a few of which were published in late 1954 in *The Harvard Advocate* and *i.e.: The Cambridge Review.* In June 1955 many of his works were collected into his first book, *The Vestal Lady on Brattle,* published privately in a small edition by a Cambridge associate, Richard Brukenfeld.

Corso did not write many letters before the mid-1950s. There are a few letters to Corso from his family to indicate that both he and they wrote infrequently. A note from his stepmother thanking Corso for his Christmas gifts of Dec. 1954 is followed in 1955 by a few notes from his father asking where he is and why they haven't heard from him. His father wrote him a rare letter: "We were so thrilled about the first book you sent, needless to say when your book of poems arrived this week, well – I was so proud I showed the whole shop and boss as well." However, the family was not especially interested in Corso or his life as a poet, and Gregory had to look elsewhere for approbation and support. It appears that the family did not save many of the letters he might have written to them.

In 1956 Corso wrote a letter to a friend in which he established a pattern he followed for much of his life. His dreams of travel, his money woes, his hatred of work, his apologies for rude behavior and descriptions of his wild and spontaneous antics fill the pages of his letters for the next forty-five years. Even his word inventions, such as "street-cornering" and "writs" are evident in this first letter, along with his formulation of the ideal of the "closest thing to what a poet should be."]

To Hans [Cambridge, MA]
[ca. May–June 1956]

Dear Hans –

I did not make it to Afghanistan. First of all there was the problem of the cats. I tried getting them good homes but to no avail. People just don't like a bunch of cats—one, maybe, but a bunch, no. I have four and they grew up together so I didn't want to separate them. I stood for hours one day on a street corner accosting each passerby with "Cats, would you like some cats?" It was an embarrassing business.

Then, after two days of street-cornering, a great thought struck me. MacLeish[1], vacationing in Antigua, would surely be sympathetic. So I wrote him of my plight, offering him the cats, and having just enough money to go to Afghanistan I offered to ship them C.O.D., railway express. Do you know they ship all sorts of animals? If you wanted to ship a rhinoceros you could. Well, I haven't heard from MacLeish since. I guess he's become a little wary of me or maybe he has enough cats of his own. It's a fact, you know, all poets love cats. Well, the only thing I could do was to keep the cats and postpone Afghanistan. Still determined to travel, though, I decided to leave Charleston[2] and return to Cambridge cats and all.

Well I'm in Cambridge and guess what happened? You wouldn't believe it. The first week, the very first week, mind you, the cats got lost. It happened this way. I got up very early one morning to have breakfast [. . .] and to do some visiting. I let the cats out to play and go to the toilet in the backyard. Well, when I came back that evening I went into the backyard and called: "Here, kitty, kitty." To my horror a strange mangy homeless Tom heeded my call. I kicked it aside and furiously began searching under porches, old washbasins, between and behind garbage cans and abandoned iceboxes - no cats! I looked and looked and called: "Here, kitty, kitty" over and over. All I succeeded in doing was congregate a horde of homeless Toms. If there's anything I can't stand that's a parasitic cat. Not that I have anything against parasites, on the contrary I love them and am fortunate to be one myself, it's just that when they're cats, I dislike them, because cats are supposed to be dignified.

A parasitic bum being there an amount of charm in that—unless he's a cornball who eats a lot. I stronger detest parasitic gluttons, in fact, any kind of glutter. Man is closest to an angel when he eats with restraint, don't you agree? Well—no cats. I searched until early morn calling "Here kitty" but all was in vain. Once it was about five, when called "Here kitty kitty" in some old lady's backyard, she screamed "The milk thief!" I hardly knew what to make of that, but I was wise enough to tail out of there, because a few minutes later I heard sirens. I went back home heartbroken because I really was very fond of the little things, but man is a bastard, and I'm no exception.

Little images of Afghanistan began to form in my mind. At last I was free! I made myself some hot Ovaltine and, Hans, if only you could have seen me, I doubt if there was a happier man in Cambridge, aye, in the world, that morning. I paced my room up and down, up and down and with each step I imagined myself riding on a gray Arabian Horse across the desert sands screaming: "Allah! Allah!" "The devil" would have been more appropriate. I suddenly realized I had exhausted my boat ticket. What with the pad and the hi-fi set and the twenty cans of beans and the forty jars of Ovaltine and sixty, sixty mind you, cans of cat food, —in truth I had ten dollars left.

Free, I was finally free, but what good was it? How was I to get to Afghanistan? I thought of selling the hi-fi set, but I'd hardly get what I paid for it. I even thought of returning the beans, the Ovaltine and the cat food, but I doubt if they would have accepted it and even if they did, it wouldn't have been enough to get me to Afghanistan. Then, after two days of trying to find a way out, I came upon the idea of work. "O God," I cried, "Am I impelled to think thus?" Well I didn't give it a second thought. Rather than work, I said, "Screw Afghanistan." So now I {am} back doing what I did last year here in Cambridge, drawing Xmas cards with dead dinosaurs on them. They sell slow, Hans, and Xmas is a long way off. So if you can mail me back the 30 dollars I mailed to you by a previous loan I'd really appreciate it.

No matter what, though, I'm still writing poetry. And, without any exaggeration, I'm still, if not the best, at least the closest thing to what a poet should be. The more I read these Cambridge poets the more I'm convinced of this. These New England poets, apocalyptic crocodilians, the whole horde of them. They do not realize that poems are nothing without the <u>poet</u>. Why are Shelley, Chatterton, Byron, Rimbaud, to name but a few, so beautiful? I'll tell you why, they and their works are one the same, the poet and his poems are a whole. These New England poets aren't hip enough to realize that. They stand away from their poetry, as though it was something they were ashamed to be associated with. That's why they write for the *New Yorker*. Not only can they be poets but sophisticates, too. How can anyone truly be a poet who goes to the john with a clothespin on his nose? Fops, that's what they are, not poets. I dare one of them take rat poison like Chatterton[3] did. They wouldn't dare. Aside from wanting to be buried in some quiet Episcopal graveyard, they want to endure—endure. And they do! How old is that Frost? It's disgusting! An old man writing verse. Verse is for youth, after 30 the only honorable thing to do is give it up. Look at what happened to Goethe—Wordsworth.

But Frost there's an excuse for him. In his own words: "I'm just a {nut} from Vermont". That's excusable because it's so, but when it's not so, then it's inexcusable, and I refer to the young New England poets—damn lawyers all of them. Completely bereft of sorrow—and that, dear Hans, is the essence of all great poetry, sorrow. And I mean that one sorrow, that only sorrow, that one wondrous sorrow which in the soul of the true poet, renders both joy and calm. I believe, Hans, that the most joyous poems were written with a tremendous culture of sorrow, for is not joy the true essence of sorrow?

God, if anyone else said that, I'd say he was coming on pretty corny. But, nevertheless, I say, without sorrow these poets are nothing. Sorrow. This noble sentiment will forever be foreign to them if they persist in dilly-dallying among prisms. (A favorite word of theirs, by the by). Shelley's life, Chatterton's life—those lives were poems! These poets, their lives are writs. Ah, if I were dictator I'd have poets throwing bombs! [. . .]

I just met the most obnoxious Radcliffe girl. Good God where do they come from? I knew her slightly last year so I went up to her and said: "Hello." She said, "Hello, you back. Ah, still wearing P.Y's jacket from last year—and R.S.' shoes? What [did] you do, come back for a new wardrobe?" (Last year, very broke, some of my beautiful Harvard friends gave me some clothes. God knows how the bitch found out.) I looked at her and smiled because I didn't know what to say. I wanted to say a lot of things, but thought best not to. I merely replied: "Sometimes I have money, you know," and walked away. In actuality I was hurt, and that's a bad sign, Hans, a very bad sign because I should have told her, "Of course I've come back for a new wardrobe, why not? Am I not beautiful? Are we not all beautiful?" But I didn't say it, I only said, "Sometimes I have money, you know." Lucifer! I hate myself for saying that. Well, next time I see the bitch, I'll bite one of her buttocks real hard.

[. . .] There are other things. Afghanistan, for example. Oh, Hans, I do want so terribly much to go. How great it'll be to learn Afghanistani, and maybe venture to write a poem in Afghanistani. But you must not think I'm altogether unhappy here. I've met a lot of beautiful people since my return. O, but I do wonder about those cats, though. Allah be with you.

I am, Gregory Corso

▼ [At the end of the summer of 1956 Gregory Corso flew to San Francisco to visit Allen Ginsberg. Ginsberg and Corso had met in New York City in 1950-51, shortly after Corso's release from prison. The two were sitting in a bar when Ginsberg noticed Corso's notebook of poems and they struck up a conversation. The friendship blossomed and it wasn't long before Ginsberg had introduced Corso to all his other writer/friends including Jack Kerouac, William S. Burroughs, John Clellon Holmes, Neal Cassady and Herbert Huncke. Late in 1953, Ginsberg left New York City on a long trip which took him to Cuba, Mexico and finally San Francisco where he hoped to renew his romance with Neal Cassady. While living in San Francisco, Ginsberg had a vision which led to his writing *Howl*, one of the most important poems of the twentieth century. After hearing Ginsberg read the poem at the Six Gallery in San Francisco in the Fall of 1955, City Lights' publisher, Lawrence Ferlinghetti, asked to publish the poem. While waiting for the publication of the book in 1956, Ginsberg shipped out as a merchant seaman and was on a cruise to Alaska when Corso first arrived in San Francisco looking for him. As Corso was preparing to leave for New Mexico, a note arrived from Ginsberg asking him to wait for his return. Corso replied to Ginsberg with the following letter.]

To Allen Ginsberg

San Francisco
Aug. 23, 1956

Allen—

Your letter and poetry came today, today, a day before I set my mind on going away from this here San Francisco. Someone is driving to New Mexico, I put my hi-fi set and records and books and other things in her car, and they are still there. I will stay. If you say three weeks. I will stay. Reason for coming out here was to see you and to experience first plane ride; experienced plane ride, have yet to experience you. But I am not Sweetface Corso, but RATFACE Corso, really. Perhaps second canto will squeak that I am. I have finished second canto, and have no carbon. Chris MacLaine has second canto, when he gives it back I will carbon it and send you. I met Peter[4] and accept Peter and like Peter and Lafcadio is or can be a Kirilov or a Barsorov[5]—he has the face, and I preached to him, told him, "Don't do anything—be sixteen fifteen kill yourself, be always fifteen . . . " He listened and maybe didn't—his face looked like it heard at any rate. Two weeks ago Peter gave me five dollars. Haven't seen him since.

June 1955, after leaving Harvard, I met a beautiful Shelley with a cunt with Anton[6] and she dug me and gave me a place to live and has been with me up till a month ago when I decided that I wanted to go to California. She went back home and expects to join me soon. She sends me money and delightful letters and I love her very much. Was she, who taught me. She has fantastic memory, only nineteen, can recite and feel all of Shelley, yes all, *Prometheus {Unbound}*, *Alastor*, *{The} Revolt of Islam*, and also fifty stanzas of Swinburne's *The Triumph of Time*—but more! She is going to kill herself on her twentieth year. She planned her death two years ago. The year that I lived with her was all her . . . she'd lock herself in a room and would walk up and down up and down . . . spoke to no one but her Gregory . . . weep, she'd weep and weep . . . I can't really inform you about her, but I tell you she is the greatest person I've ever met, and if ever you meet her, I doubt if you'd disagree. Her name is Hope Savage, I call her Sura. Write to her: Hope Savage, [. . .] Camden, South Carolina. She, Allen, is our Rimbaud and more today.

But haven't you discovered Lucifer? Why St. Francis? Oh, I can see why St. Francis, but why? Is not Lucifer the first free thinker? Is he not the emancipator of worlds? The eternal rebel? Lucifer is love—St. Francis, gee-gaw. And I will not wash Peter's feet—no never! That is not saintly! I will, instead, have him wash my feet and give me all he possesses in return for having me stay a night or a year on his bed while he sleeps away from me—far away on the floor. And this he will do if he is a saint, but screw saints. One is almost inclined to wash one's own feet. Nor is the saint one who, old and peeling, flashes his cancerous fingertips before the eyes of children squealing: "Cock cock cock." Children, almost invariably, would, like Rousseau, tease these old men with a grand expose in some half dark, saints ain't to be teased but frankly I never knew what a saint had to be or could be for Gregory to say: "Ah, a saint,"—or for someone to say: "Look, a saint." And I reply: "Ah, yes," because his hands were dwarf-clawed, his face gnarled, and his back weighed down with apple carcass. Kierkegaard would have replied: "A midget, yes—a saint, no." But fuck saints. I was once a saint and everybody said fuck me so I'm going to say fuck me too—besides when I do see a saint I do not say: "Look a saint?" I say nothing because I SAW A SAINT, and if I saw a saint, and I am Gregory, why should someone else see that saint when his name is: Anyname.

Marlowe,[7] in my intensity, comes closest to knowing Lucifer. Beautiful Marlowe—fuck Shakespeare, Burroughs' immortal bard, fuck him! Marlowe is God. Only God can make a Lucifer. And he's made one that I accept and live for and with and I will tell you: He is 1954-55 Gregory. He's sucked clean of enthusiasm. He's fucked Wagner and has accepted Bach Chopin Vivaldi—and no longer is *Les Miserables* his favorite prison book, but no book, or Unamuno[8] book or Turgenev book, in fact any book, all book . . . my favorite. He's licked off his "green armpit" of green and even arm, and writes with a clean tongue but with a gut full of green arm, waiting to be excreted or puked. He is a dead Gregory. A phony Gregory. But he was once a 1950-Gregory, a blind sick beautiful Gregory. I'm up there with you Ginsberg, asshole dry, with my binoculars . . . looking, and I don't know what you're looking for and I don't know what I'm looking for . . . but it's great looking because nobody anymore says a John Holmes[9] to me or a Lucien [Carr][10] or a [Robert] Merims[11] or a fucken stupid idiotic nowhere Helen Parker[12] who I broke down and put down and laughed at having an orgasm as my revenge! I was greater than any fucking thing she could ever copy to think or say. And Merims was always and is a bad breath smelling distraction. And Lucien, all right. And Kerouac, he'll never be tubercular. And [Alan] Ansen[13] and Burroughs, I forgot their faces. And Keck[14] I dreamed I pounded his face over and over screaming: "You are the Moby Dick in us all!" But Keck wasn't worth that dream. He, like Anton and the rest, are Christ scabs, long since picked, examined (like a monkey who examines his own shit with its head tilted guttering: "Ohhhh ahhhh gooooop"—swallowing it). Fuck them too. But there's Dusty [Moreland][15], and Dusty has been the only true sorrow I've know other than Sura, and I love Dusty.

As soon as I hit San Francisco I met Ferling [Ferlinghetti] and he has twenty of my books[16] to sell and sold twelve, and I gave him copy of *Way Out* and he didn't know what to say or I didn't stay long enough to listen. I met Neal [Cassady], and Neal turned me on and ran. And I don't like North Beach. And I told [Robert] LaVigne[17] he is dead and he nodded his skull and agreed, but for a dead man, like a dead Gregory, he can do.

I once said in a poem: "I have eaten flowers / and every flower I ever told was a lie." My only true poems are the ones you saw piled high on 15th Street three years ago . . . they are all gone . . . lost . . . I lost them in 1953 . . . in a Greyhound bus terminal in Florida. I even met Jane again . . . two months ago in Cambridge. She took me to her pad, undressed, undressed me, but no hard-on. I laughed and she wept, and I laughed, and she left.

Siesta In Xbalba[18] is almost as phony as my *Way Out* but not quite. You believe your *Siesta*. And I will not go to see [Philip] Whalen,[19] [Locke] McCorkle,[20] etc., because I do not believe in my *Way Out*, but I am nevertheless, working on the third canto. And if I do see them I will tell them I am not a phony and that I believe and that, please, they should believe in me. And they will believe in me because I still have a young face and can smile just at the right time. And DEAmont [Ruth Witt-Diamant[21]] wants me to read, and I can't see myself getting up there assbare and read[ing]. Poets should never read, but shoot, fully clothed, Tommy gun in hand, and shoot.

In The Morgue like your *Dream Record* was also dream. And why hasn't my name every appeared in any of your poems? You goofed. I was once alive, and you didn't even record me. You recorder of shit. Record your Neals and your Kerouacs and they'll record you and you'll record them . . . la-la-la the merry-go-round, the fucking horses will never run away. They're always there to ride and record. I got off the wheel and ran away, and now were you to go back to that merry-go-round you'd find the little Italian olive wild haired horse gone. What is there to find out? Has anyone record of his name, any bureau? I'm laughing, so do not accept this bullshit, and I'm sure you aren't, and I'm sure you're laughing. Good.

Archibald MacLeish tells me I have created a world of my own and that is good after he read my book. I told him the world created me; not me it. When I see you I'll show you his letter. He's a great white father, nothing else. Fuck him. And if Rexroth[22] is anything like McClure,[23] fuck him too. I don't like these wedded homespun poets who ain't. And [Henry] Miller is a shit because he put down Moricand,[24] poor Moricand, closest thing to Rimbaud that Miller will ever meet. He, Miller, in *Time Of Assassins* bemoans the fact that he didn't meet Rimbaud in his youth, and now in his *Devil In Paradise*, retracts it. Just like all them old fucks. Retractions retractions . . . who will you retract GINSBERG? Solomon[25]? Neal [Cassady]? Kerouac? Who? When will you present your *Wilhelm Meister?*

I only scream because I think you have it, and having it, will for the love of the learned elders of Zion, throw it away, and assume a quiet tea-tinkling-cup air. Maybe not. But I can say it anyway. Angered and drunk, I told LaVigne I did not like his lips. I like him and want to be his friend. I pulled down my pants and said "Okay LaVigne fuck me." It couldn't happen. Now we will be good friends, that done with. After that we went to Dearmonts [Diamant] Ruth Witt. I fucked them all for two hours with beautiful lies. When I spoke there was silence. I DEMANDED SILENCE, and got it. I was too drunk to remember all. Perhaps Bob does.

I will wait here until you arrive. I am staying with Nicole Sanzenbach. Write me as Gregory Sanzenbach for the love of an old landlady. Enjoy your sunsets.

Gregory

To Allen Ginsberg San Francisco
Sept. 1956

Read *Howl* and said "Allen is Allen still and better." *America* cry was embarrassing, but so was Novalis[26] and Wackenroder.[27] And Kliest[28] had the Amazon eat her lover raw right on stage and he, Kliest, double-suicided with Eva Schmidt. The German poets are the end. Read *Howl* and thought why? when Rimbaud put us all down by 19ing himself. Read *Howl* and said why? when Chatterton rat-poisoned us by 17ing himself. You are old. I am old. Our cries sound more like cracked wheezes than GRRRRRRRRRRRRRS. And LOVE. We are too old to say what love is. Easily enough we can call it Zen Polemic Boycock. I send you the first installment of *Way Out.*

Met Orlovsky, LaVigne, Donlin[29] others. Don't like San Francisco. Reminds me of hip mid-western town. Besides, don't see much of it. Stay at home all the time. Met McClure. He says he wants to have a nice home with family and only write six poems a year. I don't think he has it. Read some of his things. He's produce for *New Yorker* magazine. Read *Howl* and liked it because it's almost like my *Way Out*. Two old men who cupped their farts in an organ. E. Power Briggs plays Bach's Toccata in Fugue. If you don't write and live a great poem before your 30th year, give up. I told that to MacLeish, and he sent me away from Cambridge.

Goodbye, Gregory Corso

▼ [Review of Ginsberg's poem *Howl* by Corso]

Howl is the howl of the generation, the howl of black jackets, of James Dean, of hip beat angels, of mad saints, of cool Zen, the howl of the withdrawn, of the crazy saxman, of the endless vision whose visionary is Allen Ginsberg, young sensitive timid mad beautiful poet howler of Kerouac's Beat Generation.

Howl is essentially a poem to be read aloud, but only by the Howler . . . any other Howler would screw it up, thus for those who are unable to hear Ginsberg read his *Howl* will have to settle for its visuality. And visuality it has, that is, if you're hip enough to visualize it. If you're a drag, go read [Richard] Wilbur or something. But for the hipsters, the angels, the Rimbauds, etc. etc., I, and all the Universe, recommend *Howl*.

Technical notes: Style, romantic, after a long dry classical necessary spell of Eliot, Pound, Williams. Tradition, Christopher Smart, Lorca, Apollinaire, Crane, Whitman. Rhetoric: Prosaic, rising into elliptical messianic imagery. Line: Long, a development out of short-line W.C. Williams practice to accommodate sudden burst of exclamatory energy. Structure: Part I, Random, catalogue of spiritual excesses of legendary anonymous personal heroes, variations on a fixed base, "Who" (did this, who did that, etc.). Part II, Contrived, variation on a fixed base with strong repetitive rhythm, mainly dactylic, with great syncopated jumps. Part III, Further experiment in variation on fixed base, employing a response to base, beginning with response equal in length to base, each response gradually extended longer and longer ending in outsize fantastic streaks of thought—still held down to base by elastic of breath.

To Robert Creeley

San Francisco
[early Oct.] 1956

Bob,

I will go to Mexico right after reading with Allen and Peter to see Kerouac. [Randall] Jarrell was here and dug my poetry and wants me to go to Washington to live with his wife and him and record my poems for the Library of Congress. He even wants to get me a grant to go to Europe on. Sounds too crazy. I'll probably end up by picketing the bullrings . . . I find it terribly unfair to slaughter out of enthusiasm. It bugs me when a race of people expiate their primitiveness by grooming their heroes for Sunday afternoons and the bull.

Be happy, Gregory

▼ [Randall Jarrell met Corso at a dinner given by Ruth Witt-Diamant. Jarrell was the Poetry Consultant for the Library of Congress between 1956-58 and was one of the most influential people in the academic literary circles of the day. On October 20, 1956, Corso and Ginsberg gave a reading for Witt-Diamant at San Francisco State's

Poetry Center, the first time Corso read before a large group. After the reading, they began their trip to Mexico, via Big Sur and Los Angeles.]

To Philip Whalen [from Gregory Corso and Allen Ginsberg] [Berkeley]
[mid-Oct.] 1956

Dear Phil,

Was thinking of eating some eggs with Allen but instead thought of what we did today, like trading or exchanging a [size] 32, 50 dollar cashmere sweater for a bigger size kind of sweater, and did. Then we went to Gumps[30] and saw Ben Shahn and all the little Buddhas. After that to Moars to see Bufano's murals[31] which were all right and so was the food: Zucchini and cauliflower and banana cake and lettuce. Then we went to see Moloch[32] in the daylight and Allen said it was different at night. I believe him. Then we went to the Institute of Asian Studies[33] and did not see Watts but did see someone else. We had some wine and spoke and left thinking of Peter Du Peru[34] who last night was kicked in the shins by an exasperated cop.

While walking away from the institute we thought of gasoline and Allen wants his next book to be called *Gasoline*. Very good title. Means almost anything and explosive too. Then we went to Berkeley to record for KPFA. Then here.

Goodbye, Gregory Allen

To Mr. and Mrs. Randall Jarrell San Francisco
Oct. 23, 1956

Dear friends,

For the first time in my life I faced 500 people and read my poems. At first I was terribly scared, then suddenly I became involved in my poems, I was no longer scared; I read with certainty and clarity, and feeling. But I dared not look at the audience. They were very responsive to both Allen and me. I read about six poems from book, and four new ones, including a completely new version of *Power*. I was interrupted many times by applause. I'm so happy that I can contact people! Poetry is alive! I ended my reading with my *Power* poem and the ending was:

> And when I am assassinated / I will curse with my dying breath all peasants of the world / For it is they, my people, who plague this earth / with indignities and futility and Saturday night music. / Long live Homer! Long live DaVinci! Long live me! / All of you out there / Long live you! / You are power! / Go home do things! / Be gigantean! / Long live all of us!

And I think I did put some hope and enthusiasm and anxiety in hearts of those who listened. When I wrote in the center of poem:

> Kneel down for Beethoven / Know that Al Capone was far greater than you / You deserve no Michelangelo / . . . / Have you ever wept for Chatterton. / No wonder you have no power! / Why haven't you been kicked out of your schools? / You deserve no power. / Have you ever thought of having your children roam / the stars by 1957? / What have you done with your power? / Why don't you admit the Germans to be the greatest race / on earth? / You deserve no power.

I wanted to cause rebellion, I wanted to wake them up, even if my song was impractical and somewhat silly. No wonder the youth of today has for their spokesmen Elvis Presley, James Dean. These two are of the generation, they are crying and fighting against all that youth is fighting. They are singing a song all youth understands. How sad it has to be a Presley or a dead movie actor bringing all this out. It should be the poet. He is the minstrel, the legislator, the eternal rebel. . . . it should be the poet.

I will leave for Mexico this Wednesday. God, that's tomorrow and I haven't anything packed! I have decided to take manuscripts with me. I want to work on them while sitting on some plateau. Felt very sad leaving Rexroth last night . . . . I do not like to see poets grow old, I always imagine a most horrible loneliness pervading them, the world, the universe seems to become smaller and smaller for them. Maybe it's not like that with him. But his face was sad last night.

I will put in mail tomorrow or today some books. I hope you received the *Vestal Ladies*. I will hitchhike down to Mexico . . . I have never hitchhiked before. I hope it won't be awkward, I hate awkwardness.

Yes, I would love to spend a month with you in Washington, perhaps right after Thanksgiving, how beautiful it would be! Outside it would be cold and windy, and inside, at night, it would be warm and at my feet a sleeping cat, and across from me Randall . . . and he'd be talking Frost and Rilke and Ransom and Warren and Goethe to me, and I'd be listening intently. I just read MacIntyre's translations of Rilke[35] and love them! Are they the best translations? Can there be any better? I will write to [you] from Los Angeles where I will be for a week. City Lights will forward all my mail.

Love, Gregory

To Mr. and Mrs. Randall Jarrell San Francisco
Oct. 26, 1956

Dear friends,

Today I received both Jarrell and Proust. I put them in my little brown army bag with my toothbrush razor ink two pair of trousers three shirts and thirty poems I must work on when I get to Mexico for the City Lights publication.[36] Some nice young lady who liked my reading and me, I guess, presented me with a beautiful black cashmere sweater for my departure. Wasn't that nice of her? I always wanted a cashmere sweater, and what better color than black!

The fools at the reading, both Diamant and a friend of Allen's, didn't record my reading. Both machines went wrong. So Diamant had me go to State College and record. I did. I read for an hour. Lo! mistake . . . the man had the wrong speed on . . . .I read again, and midway the reading pinkblood dotted my manuscripts. "Oh, dear," I thought, "Poe's Virginia Clem died that way" I felt terribly tragic. What a way to die. In a recording booth . . . felled by the urgency of his poems! But I didn't die. Although I should go to a doctor for a check up . . . .haven't been to a doctor in years.

Then last night I had to go to KPFA to record, and did. But I enjoyed that recording and I read well. I read all my short poems, and made some nice comments on each. I do not like my *Power* anymore. Perhaps I've been reading it too much. Yes, that might be it. Well, I'll put it away, and if I feel kind towards it again I'll pick it up and re-work it. How I hate to re-work!

I must try to get a sleeping bag. I am off tomorrow. I'm a little frightened because I've never hitchhiked before. Poor Europe, when will it ever be happy again? Hungary and Poland,[37] ever since I was old enough to realize things, I always remember reading or hearing about their unhappiness. Surely, I thought, when Hitler leaves Poland, there'll be joy. I have a special fondness for Poland, when I was a child I read *Fire and Sword* by the same man who wrote *Quo Vadis* and thought the Poles to be the most marvelous race on earth!

Love, Gregory

To Mr. and Mrs. Randall Jarrell Guaymas, Mexico
[early Nov.] 1956

O but what a long and terrible and inspiring journey! I am now in Guaymas, 700 miles from Mexicali — 700 miles on a bumpy dirt road in the middle of a sandy desert. My three companions and myself were the only Americans aboard the clanking broken down bus. How sad and impoverished these poor sad polite people are! They sleep on floors — babies sleep on floors — the water system is contaminated, the food is nothing for health, but the stars, how near! and the little towns, how colorful and the graveyards, new fresh flowers adorn each grave. How strange these people. I must study them. I've only two weeks, but I'll try. I'm learning some Spanish, how alien I feel. My visa has my occupation as "poeta" isn't that wonderful! I'll write a longer and more detailed letter later.

Love, Gregory

To Lawrence Ferlinghetti

Mexico
Nov. 13, 1956

Dear Ferl,

Thanks for forwarding mail. Mexico is poor, sick, and nowhere. I don't like poverty, painted whores, tacos, tortillas, frijoles, Pepsi-Cola—Everywhere is PEPSI COLA! *Mademoiselle* asked me for my book. I haven't any, please mail one to them for me. Just put it in envelope with no message. I have already written him or her letter. Do this as soon as possible, thank you. We made hit in L.A. I guess some people are ordering book from there. We gave your address. Allen sends love. I will have manuscripts ready by middle of December.

Love, Gregory

To Mr. and Mrs. Randall Jarrell

Mexico City
Nov. 14, 1956

Dear friends,

How happy I was to receive the leaves autumnal! I felt a strange sadness about Cambridge—the year I wrote all my *Vestal Lady* poems in a small warm room in a big old gray house on Ash Street Place—leaves all around, orange, red; "hectic red"—and cold, that beautiful exciting sad sweet New England October Halloween cold. Thank you very much for both *Mademoiselle* and *New York Times*. I'm so happy you think well of my poetry. The editor of *Mademoiselle* wrote me and asked for poems and *Vestal Lady*. *Poetry* magazine had some sociologist write something about *Vestal Lady* and he branded me a "bopster." Ha! How wrong he is! I hate bopsters and all its meaning. I thought it was an unfair review because he was mistaken—the only truth in review was that I spend no time overtime on my poems. I agree, but I wish it that way. There's something unfair about re-working poetry: Poetry is poetry. I only wrote about jazz as an observer and a product. He claims I'm a spokesman or something. I've always seemed to have a constant war with sociologists. But not with poets and library consultants. Mexico is sad, poor, and all its walls, sides of churches, look as though firing-squad walls. I walk the streets and I see bowed homeless thin dogs, small girls holding smaller girls, huge Pepsi-Cola signs, taco peddlers, I see poverty everywhere. I am not enchanted with Mexico. I've been here a week, I spent some time in Guaymas and Guadalajara—everywhere sad poor people, mostly Indians, crouched around their churches selling begging moaning. I hate the smell of Mexico—it is deep old and oppressive—it is shreds of meat. The girls, how sad the girls, there's a street here, Panama Street, where girls, some not older than your wonderful Boswell,[38] stand in dark doorways, their dark faces painted heavily, waiting for men—Allen told me their fee was five pesos—that's 40¢. I almost wept, how pathetic they looked, how thin and dry their legs. I ran from there questioning poetry, if people are like this, why poetry? When I see man akin to animal in every form (toilet conditions here are frightful) I begin to wonder about the truth in poetry because all that I now see is truth, the poverty, the sorrow, the futility. But what poet wants that truth? Not I. So I ran to the museum and sat before Cézanne, Tamayo . . .

Is it cold in Washington? All I have are some khaki slacks and a few shirts and a pretty beat up jacket. But if I take a plane to Washington and a cab straight to your house I won't be cold. I wrote to my girlfriend's mother for the plane fare because I do not wish to wait any longer in Mexico—all it is to me is a wait—and I loathed the bus, and the Mexican trains are absurd. How nice my room sounds! I've always wanted to sleep like Viking kings slept, on soft furs and skins surrounded by brown-skinned tents contemplating a dream of conquest! Boswell sounds delightful, when I see her I will tell her all about poor Montezuma or does she know already? If she knows, then I'll tell her all about poor Cortez who, in my opinion, was even poorer. Today I go to see the great pyramid—thank God! Allen and Kerouac want to see something other than Panama Street and "Thieves Market". "Thieves Market" is sort of Hong-Kongian, but smellier I'm sure. The parks here are beautiful—but no zoo! And hardly any mailboxes! Miles and miles for a mail box. One thing I demand of a country and that is sufficient mail boxes!

Read *Pictures* [*from an Institution,* by Randall Jarrell] and enjoyed the humor that only a poet can possess. I think the wit of the poet is far greater than the wit of a wit. I also found a great underbelly of sorrow in *Pictures*—futility seems to be everywhere. Only at Harvard did I experience some of what Randall was writing about. I mailed it to my girlfriend in South Carolina to read, I also mailed her your first letter and she thinks you have great insight and love. That's something because she's not apt to praise, I must tell you all about her.

I read some of Proust coming down an old dirt road from Mexicali, the bus was filled with Indians—how incongruous! After 14 hours of asphaltless roads, I raised my head to look at Peter, Allen's friend and said: "O but how great is Proust!" Allen, Peter, Jack Kerouac, Lafcadio (Peter's brother) are all down here—they want to stay another week, if Hope's mother doesn't send the plane fare I will have to wait the other week and go back with them by bus. I dread the thought! I do not want to take a bus back! I'm having nightmares about buses –as you may recall my telling you that I lost all my earlier poems in a Greyhound depot in Miami Florida. I am plagued by buses! But I fear airplanes. Poor Gregory. If I get the money I will telegraph you—in any case I will inform you ahead of time of my arrival.

The reading in Los Angeles went over quite well, but I didn't enjoy it because Hollywood depressed me. I am having someone ship my typewriter from San Francisco to your home. How I miss it! I hope my handwriting isn't too difficult. The expectancy of seeing you all soon keeps a sly smile on my face—I must smile or else I'll brood—I have fears of walking thru "Thieves Market" and being pounced upon for my new cashmere sweater and being shrouded in a huge tortilla, with a crucifix-like Pepsi-Cola bottle for a grave mark. How terribly lost I would be!! Who will find me? So now you can see what kind of thoughts run through my head here in Mexico. Truthfully, everyday I spent in Mexico, I was filled with a sense of doom! But today I am happy because I know I'll see you soon sans haircut, sans warm clothes, but with sun and joy on my face.

Love, Gregory

Dear Boswell,

The Siamese cat of the horse family is the beautiful Mexican burro. It has almost the same markings as does the Siamese, and it's gentle and sad, sad because the Mexican farmers have no love for their burros, they work them mercilessly. Still the features of the burro are wonderful. Soft black wet noses, soft tawny furry bellies, little straight sturdy legs—I wish I could buy you one and mail it to you—but they make funny long noises and it might disturb your father at his desk. But wouldn't it be great, a burro in Washington, D.C.?

To Mr. and Mrs. Randall Jarrell

Mexico City
Nov. 16, 1956

Dear friends,

I told Hope, my girlfriend, to mail you a play I wrote quite sometime ago, in fact my first play, called *The Death Of A Beautiful Boy* — it's all about a Shelleyan youngster caught in the throes of N.Y.C. Mexico City does have a zoo! It's in Chapultepec Park where for days I've walked alone along the Calzada De Los Poetas. It is a good zoo — clean — spacious (except for the cats, they are in small cages) and they have some of the best specimens I've ever seen. The two *rinoceronte* are exquisite — low, sturdy, black, and powerful. They even have American brown and white bulls! The *Oso Blanco* [polar bear] has a newly white-washed den that doesn't melt — and I fed two long black woolly sheep some Life-Savers. All the animals seemed terribly hungry. I don't understand people's attitudes toward animals. Now if I had a cat in my house I would always see to it that it has food constantly on its plate so that it would never feel the pang of hunger. Animals are helpless — must their cries of hunger be the only indication of their hunger? Someday when I own a zoo my animals will be so big and fat and happy that psychiatrists will recommend my zoo as a form of therapy. I saw a new-born Barbary Goat! How awkward, yet how graceful!

Also visited Maximillian's *Castillo* — I was impressed by his story — he seems to have been a very kind sweet man. The great thing about the place were the old treasure-chests! When a guard wasn't looking I opened one! And found, to my horror, bits of cigarettes! Orozco has an impressive mural in the *Castillo*. It depicts the horrors of the Catholic church. Went visiting the art galleries in town and came upon some great drawings of Cézanne, Matisse, Manet, Renoir (who surprised me because I can't stand his peaches and cream paintings), Derain, and Modigliani in the Galeria de Antonio Souza. While looking at these wonderful works I peeked into Souza's office and saw a huge Tamayo leaning awkwardly in the corner. I walked in, looked at the Tamayo then turned to Souza and presented myself as Gregorio Nuncio Corso, *poeta* from the United States — he rose from his swivel chair and shaking my hand presented himself also as *poeta* — I asked him about Tamayo and he said in clear English, "Tamayo was here, but is now in New York." I bowed, he bowed, and I departed. Happy for the first time in Mexico.

I sent *Mademoiselle* eight or seven poems. I put as return address yours. So when they are returned you may open the letter and read them. I did not put any return stamps because I couldn't get any American stamps. They'll send it back anyway, won't they? I know most magazines demand of poets return stamps. I sent my best. I wanted to send two of my very best short poems but couldn't as I have already given them to *i.e.; the Cambridge Review*—but what I sent them I am very happy about. Here's one:

> *The Mad Yak* / I am watching them churn the last milk they'll / ever get from me. / They are waiting for me to die. / They want to make buttons out of my bones. / Where are all my sisters and brothers? / That tall monk there, loading my uncle, / He has a new fur cap. And that idiot wife of his, / I never saw that muffler before. / Poor uncle, he lets them load him. / How sad he is, how tired. / I wonder what they'll do with his bones; / And that beautiful tail — / How many shoelaces will they make of that?

Isn't that sad and perfect? Then I sent them some beautifully imaginative poems. Today I will return to the zoo and write some poems or draw some pictures for you to see when I arrive.

Hope mailed me a book called *Memoirs of a Good-For-Nothing German,* by Joseph Von Eichendorff—she demands I read it right away. I am ninety pages in Proust—I have three poems in my head—I have so many pictures I want to draw. I think I'll abandon everything and just go to the zoo with sufficient candies for the *rinocerentes*—They love candies.

Love, Gregory

To Mr. and Mrs. Randall Jarrell

Mexico City
Nov. 23, 1956

Dear sweet beautiful people —

Money is coming! 150 dollars — but Mr. Savage, Hope's father, had difficulty in finding a way to send it. Seems a money order can't be sent airmail or something — but surely I'll see you before the 9th of Dec. How strange I felt when I saw the difference in my handwriting. How wonderful! My hand expresses my feelings, my moods, my love, my hate — everything! I hate plastic handwriting — all great beautiful people have wild mad hands! Did you ever see Shelley's hand? Or, even madder, Byron's!

Finally Mexico is great! Why? Well, because last night I went to the ballet and before that to an opening of some Russian painter named Valday. We, the group of us, met a painter there — a 60 year old Mexican Indian who is a great painter and a friend of Rivera and Tamayo. He brought us to his studio and showed us fabulous paintings by Siqueiros and Tamayo. We all got drunk and recited poetry — and he recited beautiful Lorca. Met Souza again at the opening — what a strange man! Allen disturbed a timid Frenchman there by praising Jean Genet. The Frenchman, very reserved and dignified, said to Ginsberg: "Genet is filth and not for people who were well brought up." I thought that a little snobbish of the Frenchman, but I also understood his reaction. How much I want to be in Washington with you all! How happy and certain your letters make me feel! I feel I've known you personally for a long long time. Do you know your handwriting is mad, too? Yes, it's pronto and filled with enthusiasm — I am happy about your handwriting. What a beautiful house the painter lives in! His name is Alphonso Michel — he speaks English and French and Spanish — and is very dignified. Dignity always makes me happy! Well, his house is 17th century. His floors are huge stones! His walls, terra cotta! Well, maybe not terra cotta, but something like it.

Allen and Kerouac and Peter and myself were all amazed by him, but after a long long study of his paintings — I sat by myself in a corner — I came to the conclusions that his paintings are take-offs of Picasso and Tamayo. I credit myself with a good eye when it comes to painting. Gregory who loves and knows [Piero] della Francesca, saw in this man's painting a great lack of individuality! I told him. He looked blankly at me. I hope I didn't do wrong, I hate people who make senseless comments on other people's works. The truth is, earlier he said, when I sat praising the Renaissance, that the Renaissance wasn't as great as I was making it be. (True, when I praise, I praise thunderously!) So, I was upset and got back at him with what I thought to be a cutting but nonetheless exact statement on his work. He is very famous in Mexico, and has shown countless times in galleries on New York's 57th Street.

Well, enough of him. How's my Randall doing? Is he to be my poet that I've always dreamed about walking down long paths considering grand schemes about the universe? Will I learn wondrous things from him? Will he ever become angry with me if I yell at him when we differ about the planets? or a simple tree? More than anything I want to learn from him. People are always telling me no one has anything to teach me. I believed that and lost the joy of being taught. I want to be taught. I want to sit on the floor beside a great man and listen. I wanted, I *should have* done this when I was seventeen and wild — but I had no one — thus prison. But at twenty-six I feel I can still learn, I am not obstinate. Actually I am really six years old with life. When I left prison at twenty, I was wide eyed and expectant! Not hostile, not mad at the world. I will tell you all about it when I see you. I want to tell you. I want you to see how much in need I am of good constructive teaching. My Bohemian fling is over — I have found truth. I am finally being accepted by society, but isn't it odd and sad that one need fight society, suffer, and then become accepted? Still I hold well to myself for breaking away from a stupid family and environment. How terrible were my father and stepmother to me. No love in them whatsoever — no letters in the three years of prison — how stupid! My father is forty-five, very young, lacking in compassion and understanding. When I was fifteen I begged him to buy me paints. I told him I loved painting. He made me cease school at the sixth grade and go to work. I couldn't put up with that so at the age of twelve I ran away from home and have been living on my own ever since — getting into countless trouble. It was all so tragic and humorous. Humorous because I sure made a funny figure on my own at twelve in the big big city of New York. I will tell you all when I see you. Although it seems I'm telling you everything now, that's because I feel like writing.

I, too, weep for your cat. But whatever you do, *DO NOT* have it put to sleep if it is very bad off. Sometimes people think it is out of love to "put to sleep" (how I hate that phrase) what they love, when it is in pain, when all seems hopeless. So promise me you won't even consider the idea.

I'm glad you like my *Mad Yak*. I've been writing some surrealistic poetry about Mexico lately — I'm not too happy with them, but they certainly are new and imaginative. I feel that is all I possess, imagination. I need [. . .] some form or order. I'll have to talk to Randall about this. Eichendorff is not as good as Voltaire's *Candide* — but it's worth reading. I want very much to go to the football game with you — I can see it all — Gregory between Randall and Mary, buried in a German Army officer's jacket, contemplating the next play, and the people and the eventual darkness and loneliness of an empty football field! My Ted Williams poem will have to do with an empty baseball field, and he, all alone, bowed and graceful, standing in left field happy with the absence of masses and noise!

Boswell's little note was charming and delightful — she loves you very much. How ignorant I am of that kind of love.

I hope my money comes tomorrow. I will take a plane right away. Should you or should you not buy a football ticket for me? Do! Do! If I can't get plane I'll fly on my own. I'll summon the spirits of both Shelley and Rimbaud and they will underarm me and zoom me to my destination. It they do will you invite them in for some tea? Surely their arrival will make both you and Randall very happy. I must do something for you both so maybe I'll do that. You don't know the great powers I have! I will send telegram as soon as I make plane reservations. Love. No, no warthog in zoo—

Gregory

P.S. I wrote many poems, descriptive poems about zoo.

To Philip Whalen

Mexico City
[Nov. 26] 1956

Dear Phil –

We all want to write you. All of us: Jack, Allen, Peter, Lafcadio—Lafcadio? Well, anyway, Gregory, me. How are you? I hope this letter finds you in the best of health. If not, do not hesitate to see a doctor because only God knows what might be the matter with you. Do you have headaches or stomachaches? Well, I don't know much about sicknesses, all I can say is stand on your head like Jack. *Mademoiselle* asked me for poems, and I sent them poems, but I doubt if they'll dig them. Jarrell did that number for me. He also will write about me in the *New York Times* either in January or February. No word from *i.e.;* [*the Cambridge Review*] yet, but I think he took all—if not, I'll abandon him. I've been writing some crazy poems. Mexico is good, but I'm off to Washington this week. Go see and make it with Barbara—Barbara Hansen [address] San Francisco. Say I sent you over. She's a lovely girl.

I went to book store where the proprietors, well-dressed, sell new editions of [Marquis de] Sade, D.H. Lawrence, [Henry] Miller and Genet—the books are atrociously high priced. I tried stealing *Lady Chatterley's Lover* but a bow-tied greasy mustachioed man eyed me with concern. My plane fare is due soon. I will fly to Washington. Transfiguration assembled with various kinds of glues keeps together a scatter of lunchmen sighs. Buddha was an ice-cream cone dropped on Main Street by a baby in a turnover carriage—3/4 of the time Jack is in a position of sleep in bay—fluffy flat. Night is an empty headdress—lost is the bald void.

To Mr. and Mrs. Randall Jarrell

Mexico City
Nov. 29, 1956

How impatient I am! Money order was sent to me on the 20th, it still hasn't arrived. I hate banks, I hate post offices, I hate waiting. Damn Mexican system of things is annoyingly incompetent. Allen and group have left already. I am all alone waiting for stupid international money transaction. Please bear with me, I want so much to go.

Your anxious annoyed friend —

▼ [Ginsberg, Kerouac, and the Orlovsky brothers all left Mexico City before Corso's air fare arrived and ironically they were back in New York City long before Gregory had the money to fly to Washington.]

To Allen Ginsberg

Mexico City
Dec. 3, 1956

Dear Allen –

How funny, how miserable—how stupid—the money was sent two weeks ago. I am still waiting! I hope your trip was fine. *i.e.* [*The Cambridge Review*] will publish you, me, Whalen—they think Whalen a fine poet. Kerouac, they said, was a disappointment. They returned Rexroth's poems.

Gregory

To Mr. and Mrs. Randall Jarrell

Mexico City
Dec. 3, 1956

Dear friends —

A money order mailed to me on the 20th of November from South Carolina goes to Dallas then to Laredo (for currency exchange) then to Mexico and me. The pony express surely did better. What a stupid senseless system especially for two countries so close to each other.

I am miserable. God knows just how long I'll have to wait. How funny, when I first hit Mexico I felt a sense of doom, can this then be my doom?

Waiting day after day for a money order that never comes? Sounds like an O'Neill play. If money does not come by 7th, I will have money wired to me. I mustn't miss the 9th.[39]

Love, Gregory

To Mr. and Mrs. Randall Jarrell

Mexico City
Dec. 4, 1956

Dear friends —

After fifteen days of expectancy and futility I am finally resigned to come what may. Mr. Savage, Hope's father, sent me a telegram saying woefully that he sent money order Tuesday, Nov. 20th and that it does take two weeks to get here, thus today is two weeks — Nothing. Perhaps tomorrow? If not, what can I do? I know what I must do, I must wait. "Must" is terribly big and long. If I don't arrive by the 9th, if I am still here waiting for that damned money order to arrive, the 9th will be a day of gloom for me. How absurd all this is!

MacLeish, I am told, has written a new play. I found warmth and a lack of warmth in the man. Contrary to most young poets I know, I hold that he is a good poet and has written three great poems. My favorite is *Not Marble or Gilded Monuments.*

Surely you realize my suffering, I am anxious to see you. I am enough of Mexico, I want to see Hope. I want to brood in that awaiting nest and type out my poems for the City Lights publication. I want to see the 9th of December in Washington, etc. etc. Anyone else in my place definitely would have had a breakdown. I enclose a photo of Hope, hold it for me.

Love, Gregory

To Allen Ginsberg

Washington, DC
Dec. 12, 1956

Dear Allen,

I am in Wash[ington] and everything is fine. Wrote to [Ezra] Pound[40] asking to see him. Jarrell and family are okay. Sent some poems and *Vestal Lady* to [James] Laughlin[41]. I enclose some poems for you and *Evergreen* [*Review*] and [William Carlos] Williams.

I will definitely see you New Year's; tell me where. Sura [Hope Savage] is going to Paris the 16th, I will join her at the end of January. I talk to Jarrell about you. His article in *Times* will have mostly to do with Frost, Ransom, etc., and then at end of article, Wilbur, and me. Good God, Wilbur. Am so happy WCW [William Carlos Williams] liked my poems, that is, I gather he did, if he wanted to see more. Have his complete poems here and have been reading them. Am working hard trying to get book for Ferl [Ferlinghetti] together.

Love to Jack and Peter, Gregory

To Lawrence Ferlinghetti Washington, DC
Dec. 13, 1956

Dear Ferl,

Please send me some *Vestal Ladies* . . . deduct mailing expenses from books coming to me. Send about five. I want to see Pound and give him one, also Aiken, etc. Washington is a nice quiet place, but being under the shadow of the Pentagon, etc., bugs me. Randall seems a little ambiguous about tapes[42]—but I think I can convince him about the importance of them as I feel you to be a fine poet. Did [*i.e.*] *The Cambridge Review* accept you or not? I know they refused Rexroth, Kerouac, Burroughs. Jarrell is going to write about current American poets in *New York Times* either in January or February and I'm to be one of currents. Randall thinks that you should publish some of my *Vestal Poems* in the forthcoming book. I don't think it such a good idea because I have enough for book now, and definitely better poems. He will write intro for it in a few days, thus I'll mail you manuscript in about two weeks.

Cold, very cold in Washington. Send some poems to *Evergreen Review* (Grove). When *Black Mountain* [*Review*] comes out mail it to me. Have a good New Year, both you and your lovely wife,

Friend, Gregory

To Lawrence Ferlinghetti Washington, DC
Dec. 20, 1956

Dear Lawrence

City city blackout books, (blackout because you said you is powerless ergo lights is got no power) just received your letter—wish I cd uv seen u and Wailin [Whalen] at the Sultry Senther, but I wuz in Washinton instead, instd. Screw *i.e.* [*The Cambridge Review*], they bugged Rexroth no end, I hear. It's funny too in a way. Glad about ND [New Directions]. Ginsberg told me to send them something and I did. Do you know what those fools at *Mademoiselle* accepted? A poem from my *Vestal Lady* called *The Shakedown*, surely not one of my better poems, but I did get twenty five bucks for it.

How much did rooster-head Diamant pay youse guys for the poultry readings? If she keeps on paying poets ten dollars for a cock-fight I suggest the poets go tell her to go lay an egg or somethin . . . ten dollars! What a fuckin' insult. Boy, but I sure needed the ten dollars anyhow, and did I use it! I bought a new pair of socks, a Papermate pen, two stacks of airmail envelopes, a bottle of cheap wine, and a record by the Budapest String Quartet. It was a treat, so I guess I shouldn't complain.

Jarrell gave great lecture here on what's wrong with American taste. It was good. He will, if I ask him, I'm sure, take your tapes. Also he will make sure that my new book, as you put it, will be reviewed by Ransom, Frost, etc. ... all his dear friends, so the reviews should be favorable. God what a con. He'll do, as you already know, introduction. Call book: *Gasoline. In Ran Moonlight,* too long. I'll use it for title of poem. I have all new poems for you. Jarrell wanted me to use at least ten poems from *Vestal Lady* . . . what think you about that? Are you willing to take my *Power* poem? If so, let me know, and I'll retype it. I gathered some old unpublished poems of mine that I wrote in Cambridge. They are on the same style as the *Vestal Ladies*, I'll include them in manuscript also.

Has *Black Mountain* come out yet? *i.e.;* [*The Cambridge Review*] refused my poems too, except a small four line poem I wrote for the death of a friend of theirs, they could hardly refuse that. I feel bad about them refusing you because I acted as middle man, and my taste had it that they should have taken your poems. But surely New Directions is far greater.

Also send some poems to new *Evergreen Review*—they are looking for poets poems fame and gasoline. Don't you think *Gasoline* a good title? Ginsberg and I thought it up while walking the streets in Berkeley. The *Power* poem should work well under the title *Gasoline*. The *Power* poem is not necessary, but I do like it. And I did fix it up the best I could. Wrote Pound a letter, me waiting for him to answer, him no answer yet. Do any girls ask for me?

Goodbye, Gregory

To Allen Ginsberg

Washington, DC
Dec. 20, 1956

Dear Allen,

Been reading William Carlos Williams and find how similar at times we are, especially his earlier poems. Him very good poet. Ferl [Ferlinghetti] wrote and said that ND [New Directions] has accepted his poems for annual and maybe book. I sent ND poems and was told that MacGregor[43] and Laughlin are reading them, sent them *Vestal Lady*, told them to use any from book because book has not been distributed so much, etc. Did you get my poems I sent you?

Ferl wants me to think over title for my book and I think being as I have just completed big poem on *Gasoline*, I will use title before you, *Gasoline*. We both did think of it, but I did have it in my *Power* poem as: " . . . enough gasoline and evidence to allow dictators inexhaustible power." [. . .] Besides, *In Ran The Moonlight*, too long. *Vestal Lady*[*On Brattle*] was too long, too. Something like *Howl . . . Gasoline*.

Did I tell you about *Mademoiselle*? They accepted a poem, paid me twenty five dollars . . . but horrors, what poem did they choose but *The Shakedown*? A nowhere poem from my *Vestal Lady*. Randall said that it was just like them, that they don't know any better. Randall is good sincere guy, and does have taste for good poetry. He likes WCW very much. I found great poet. Jules Laforgue[44], French, died at 26. He's very good.

Hear you see Dusty {Moreland}, how is she? Will I see her New Year's? My Sura in Paris, saw her for three days then she left—she has money for me to go, if I can get passport.[45] If I can't, she'll come back. Maybe I can work something out. What is all this about *Evergreen* and New Directions? Ferl and Phil {Whalen} read at the center, and Ferl says it was a sockaroo. A "sockaroo"? Anyway I take it was good, etc. How is Phil? I sent him Xmas card.

Randall gave great lecture a few nights ago on *TASTE OF THE AGE*. Here's clipping from *Washington Post*, maybe you saw similar article in *New York Times*. It's pretty good. Ferl says my book will go to press after WCW's book, sometime in April.

How is things, I hear you is bugged with NY? Tell me all about it. See if you can set up reading at Open Door.[46] Maybe for Jan 5th or something. Write right away.

Your friend, Gregory

Sura, for Xmas, bought me new Parker 61[47]—costs twenty five bucks and fills with capillary system. How's Peter? Is Lafcadio gone—hid beneath the heirloomed night, tight behind 42nd Street—mad with other pimply-faced mad youths?

To Allen Ginsberg Washington, DC
Dec. 27, 1956

Dear Allen,

Of course you're right about most of poems, Randall himself said same thing, in fact, so did I, to myself. Spontaneity in poetry is nothing more than notes, not poems; my Mexican book is a series of notes, journals as it were, and, if I have any respect for my poems, which I don't, they should not be pawned off as POEMS. Since I've been in Washington I've been writing and rewriting and my Israel Hans, for instance, has formed itself a careful poem. Rewriting, I find, is most {of} the pleasure of writing. In the case of *Power* there was no pleasure, no ease thus a bad reworking of the poem ensued . . . but how to rewrite such a poem as *Power*? I thought this: *Power* is not a poem, or it is but use it as a prose piece, a paramyth, or what have you. Call a work prose and surely no one would be apt to question one sentence of the work.

I will be in New York this Saturday, the 29th. I will try to get in touch with you. Randall has been getting lots of publicity in *Time* and etc. for his lecture, and it's about knocked him out, the poor man is beset by all sorts of people. Jack found him to be very sweet, and kind, as well he is. Too bad you and he did not hit it off, too bad you attacked him the way you had because both of you obtain the same sweetness and kindness. . . . I tell him that always, and I think he sees it.

Too bad William Carlos Williams calls (in *Vestal Lady*) what I feel to be intentional, careless. Then again if he means my intended carelessness careless, he probably has something there. What I strove for in *VL* was a natural free-strained attempt-success not with words but with idea, not with form, but with unregulated flow; example:

> I dreamed Ben Franklin was a woman / with bald head and long white hair / He said he was a woman / And boasted his 160th year. / "Really!" I asked, "and do you / have Shelley's autograph?" / He said that he had—/ His room was a man's room / walls covered with shoe buckles, kites / and small iron spectacles—/ His laugh was a man's laugh / but he said he was a woman / and claimed his 160th year—/ "Tell me about Shelley, was he happy; / was he reading or practicing chemistry?" / "Here's the key I used," he said, / "It's burnt as well it should be." / Never had I seen a blacker key, / and big, oh how big! / "Praised by electricity," he said. / His room had a strange smell/ an old smell/ something like stale cloth / and dry hair / and everytime he rocked his chair / a cloud of dust / added another smell in the air / "God!" I exclaimed, "you must be the oldest man alive!" He patted my hand / his hand was rough and fat / unlike a woman's hand / etc. etc.

I end poem by having him dead and looking finally very much like a man. Now this poem was an actual dream I had two days ago. I think it an interesting enough dream to write about, but here is where the difficulty comes in: How to explain the woman angle? As I elaborate on the woman angle it sounds unlike a dream and more like a poem, a repetitious idea used; "he said he was a woman; he looked like a woman, his hand was unlike a woman's etc." To make a dream sound like a dream is *In The Morgue*, a steady flow (what I call an unregulated flow).

My *Ben Franklin* (God, I've been hung on that man, how come?) is a true dream. I felt him to be a woman, but he wasn't womany. He spoke like a man, dressed like a man, etc. . . . The reader will want to know why the woman angle, why, because I leave it unexplained . . . God knows how to explain it . . . I doubt it to be sexual or any of that crap . . . so I thought, by rewriting, (I gave you first draft) that I would leave just the first line; I dreamed Ben Franklin was a woman . . . and the rest of the lines not mention his womanness; for instance, in the dream I was more intent on asking him about Shelley? But he never gave me any direct answers about Shelley, when I asked him about

Shelley, he showed me the key he used to conduct electricity with.

I give you this poem as an example of what rewriting can do for me. But oddly enough *In The Morgue* was not rewritten. I fear poems is as mysterious as dreams. Sometimes we dream a first draft dream, a dream complete, understandable, exact. And sometimes we dream an incomplete dream, a confused dream as dream of many odd symbols and situations. Thus the poem, at least with me, is similar.

Randall thinks three-quarters of my poems in *VL* are magnificent works of art. He likes mostly *In The Tunnel Bone.* Reading his poems, *Little Friends Little Friends* I find him to be extraordinarily good, in fact great. I say this not because I live at his house or that he gave me his German coat etc., but because having known the man and then having read the work I can see deeper and clearer into the work, thus you with WCW . . . in other words, here is a poet who I finally, other than you, understand to the fullest.

Am coming to NY to get passport, must get to Paris by February. Sura is there, waiting. Meet me in San Remo[48] Saturday eve at seven. If not, I call Paterson.

Love, Gregory

Been working very hard on my book.

▼ [As the last letter indicated, Corso left the Jarrell's house just before New Year's and visited his friends in New York City. After a few days in the city he began to plan his return to Washington to live with the Jarrell's, but it would appear that they wanted no more to do with Corso. Kerouac had visited him during his stay with them in December and either something happened during that visit, possibly involving the usual alcoholic escapades of Kerouac, or Corso had just worn out his welcome with the Jarrell's, as he would do countless times in the future with other friends and acquaintances. A thorough search of Jarrell's journals and correspondence has failed to turn up the exact reasons for their obvious reluctance to host Corso again.]

To Mr. and Mrs. Randall Jarrell New York City
[early Jan.] 1957

Dear friends,

New York is cold, my father is sad, met Oscar Williams[49] at a party thrown by Eberhart,[50] and he is foul. I told him how dare you publish just one poem of Keats and four of yours! He staggered up and chased a young girl as is his custom. Horrible man. Tambimuttu, *Poetry London*, etc., editor, Jose Villa, and some others, how nowhere they are! Tambimuttu, the most ambitious, egotistical ass there, Villa, the biggest lecherous fairy, and Eberhart the oddest in that he didn't seem to belong. I liked him. I liked also Arebell Porter. She and I had a nice long talk. But Oscar Williams, he sickened me. If you're familiar with the paintings of Balthus, his subject of little girls, then you'll know what I mean about Oscar Williams. The next day I met Meyer Shapiro,[51] and he was wonderful! He said how sad it was that I did not go to the Freer Museum while in Washington. I told him I will when I go back. We spoke a lot about Randall, and he said he is very fond of Randall's criticisms, both pro and con. He has some library! And some of the oddest paintings imaginable!

O but I must tell you I miss you and Washington so much. I am sad, and want so much to come back. The German coat is a big hit! I was offered seventy dollars! Will it be all right if I come back Monday? I am expecting my birth certificate, and also some other letters. And I do want to complete my book. I have it all there, I must work very hard and get it done. Then I'll be free. And I promise I'll wash the dishes every morning, and will bring in the coal whenever coal is needed, etc. etc.

Hope you had a wonderful New Year's. I love you all,

Gregory

I do hope Mary is relaxed and happy once again.

▼ [On the back of this letter Randall Jarrell has hand-written the following: "Dear Gregory—Mary's doctor won't allow her to have any company for a long while so it is not possible for you to come here now. Your things are on their way to you. Do leave your telephone number at the Biltmore. Will call you then." This was probably the text of the telegram message that Corso refers to in the next letter.]

To Mr. and Mrs. Randall Jarrell

New York City
Jan. 7, 1957

Dear Randall,

Received your telegram and am sorry and understand fully. How sudden: I am saddened by it. Mary seemed always happy and vital, very vital. Rest, of course, will be what she needs. You people mean very much to me . . . even though my awkwardness in a new atmosphere wasn't really Gregory, it did make me love both of you and the girls very much. Unsuccessfully, I feel, I've at times tried to corner either you or Mary to express my overwhelming happiness. Be very happy, all of you, and continue your way, and your sweetness. Yes, even rugged Jack [Kerouac] saw sweetness in you.

Saw C. Abels, and she would like to see you when you arrive in New York. She was very kind and nice to me. We spoke considerably. Also saw [Salvador] Dali, his show was horrible, but he wasn't. He was charming, and sad. Yes, sad. He directed and explained his paintings, his studies of St. John of the Cross (whom he adores). I told him he needn't explain, that I, myself, feel, and see. He smiled and invited me to lunch with his wife and himself at his hotel. I previously spoke to him about poetry. He loves the works of Lorca (who he knew and spoke of, he told me some real odd things about Lorca) and St. John of the Cross.

I am walking my city again, and see it differently. I am saving, if it's possible, the Metropolitan [Museum] for you. More than anything I'd love going to a museum with a feeling knowing man, a poet, the paintings he runs to would receive an added scrutiny by Gregory. Did you send my mail? Give my love to little Boswell. I do not know when you'll arrive . . . . rather than I call you, you may have things to do and not enough time, I will give you my phone number. I do hope Mary will skip around about again soon.

Your grateful friend, Gregory

To Lawrence Ferlinghetti

New York City
Jan. 21, 1957

Dear Ferl,

No New York address, am going to France, Paris, will send poems to you from there. I still have time, don't I? The railway express card[52] is, I guess, my *Vestal Ladies* sent to me from Cambridge, but 21 dollars?! Fuck them, let the railway keep them. Am bugged with New York and Ginsberg and Kerouac and all groups. Lone Gregory from now here on in.

How is all my pretty goils in San Francisco? Are they dead? Or are they still walking down Grant Street contemplating the various kinds of cement? If you want the *Vestal Ladies* from railway you can have them. Sell them at a loss, give them away, in fact burn them, burn them all. Send one to New York to Miss Anita Martin, 16 West 77 Street. Thank you.

I sent a dirty Kleenex to Salvador Dali, plus a match, plus bits of pecan walnut cookies. By mail. If you want to send him anything here's his address: Salvador Dali, St. Regis Hotel, 5th Ave. and 55th Street. My address in Paris will be American Express. New York is icy and windy and every poet here is a salesman. I am reading *Salammbo*, by Flaubert, you ever read it?

Is Rexroth bugged at me? Can't help if *i.e.* refused his poems. Tell him so. Fuck all poetry magazines. Saw William Carlos Williams, he's beautiful sweet man.

Luck, Gregory

To Robert LaVigne

New York City
Jan. 24, 1957

Dear Bob,

Have been running around madly looking for way out and found it finally. Paris. I am going in two weeks. Maybe sooner. New York is old and dirty and fruitless and timeless and verging on Almighty Edge . . . one push, and fall. New York is cold. Allen G. is doing sales in poetry. Going from publisher to publisher peddling his, mine, Kerouac's works. Saw great exhibition, Jackson Pollock and Balthus, at Museum of Modern Art. I like Balthus very much . . . he's delightfully depraved. Saw Salvatore Dali and he invited me Peter and Allen to dine with him and his wife. That was two weeks ago, nothing came of it. But I did mail him letter with used Kleenex and burnt match and pecan crumbs in it. Wonder if he'll see the surreal intent. Peter and Lafcadio are living somewhere on 15th Street, when I visit them I will tell them you wrote and that they should write. Allen address is, damn, I don't remember. But when I see him I will tell him to write also. I haven't been writing since I got to New York a few weeks ago. Been busy trying to get to Europe. I have passport, and my girl, Sura is giving me the money to go. I stayed with the Jarrells for awhile, and enjoyed it very much, although I fear they weren't accustomed to the likes of me. How is Irrgang[53], God, I've yet to write him. How bad that is of me. I usually write. But life has been so damned quick. I have worlds to think about and worlds to forget. But when I get to Europe, and I'm never coming back once I get there, then I will have time for poetry and letters and rest and dream, God, how I miss dream. Saw Nicole [Sanzenbach] in New York last week, saw her in the Met museum, she was with her Mexican lover. She said she was going back to San Francisco this week. Are you ever going back to S.F. [San Francisco]? I will always keep the drawing you did of me wearing cloak.

Kerouac is going to have novel published by Grove and Viking. Allen will be published with me and Jack in this February's *Mademoiselle*. Jarrell will write me up in *New York Times* soon, maybe end of this month or beginning of next. Allen and Kerouac were written about in last week's Sunday *Times*, Breit's[54] column. Thus the literary situation. Bah. Allen, Kerouac would do best to abandon all and flee. Best that they'd become camel drivers or something. When all is done and lost or partly lost and done for me . . . I too will cook coffee beans on the desert, and partake of camel meat. Fuck walking crowded talking life. Without love, man is strong and free, and wise, and sad . . . . .

Love frustrates the true great desire in man. That calm evil, that awesome Godliness, that fear throwing stare, all this that man has is destroyed when man loves. But it is better to love. Man is weak. Man will be untrue being cool, calm, ... so where does beauty lie? Love never really allowed beauty brought to light. Not really. But sorrow, sorrow has. Sorrow has held a candle to beauty for all to see who care to see.

Be as you are as you want to be, your friend,

Gregory

To Lawrence Ferlinghetti New York City
Jan. 28, 1957

Dear Ferl

Thanks for cards, *Gasoline* looks good, I find there's another way to spell gasoline, gasolene. But I think gasoline looks better than gasolene. It's just like the word esthetics, what looks better esthetics or aesthetics? Aesthetics, of course.

Jarrell will do intro, but why don't you write to him anyway send him the card? Tell him what's really happening in S.F., he doesn't know, he has bad impression of it. I wrote letter to Railway Express pertaining to *Ladies,* saying: I can't pay, but if he distributes my books of poetry to his fellow workers I wouldn't mind. Nonetheless I stated that you might be interested in rescuing them. If you do, you can do what you will with them.

I probably will go to Paris next week, if not definitely the week after. What's happening in S.F.? Are Duncan, McClure, Harmon[55] looming? What did or do you think of Whalen after reading with him? Is your wife happy? Did Stanley Gould[56] visit you yet? He's notorious in N Y. Tell Rexroth I send my love. Is Alcatraz still sad?

After long time I ventured to look at *Power* again, and I think it a good poem, probably the best I've done, and would like very much to re-work it. But if you don't want it for publication that's all right too. I'll work on it, and will send it to you with the others probably in a month or two. Must get French book, don't know a damn thing about the language. *Bon Soir, mouseyour.*

Gregory

To Lawrence Ferlinghetti New York City
Feb. 8, 1957

Dear Ferl,

Ain't left yet because international money orders take time, but should leave soon. Gee, I hope so. Wow, like I've been here a long time and more than anything I want to go, but who knows, who can tell about international money orders? I've always been accustomed, when good fortune struck me, to local money orders. Boy, this whole month I've been hung on Ben Franklin and money orders. Too much. *Life* wuz here and interviewed us and I told them that poetry just ain't S.F. poetry but all poetry and that more people should read poetry mags than *Life* magazine and they smiled like they hated me and bugged me by taking pictures of me eating raw meat with a lot of hair on my face and chest. Send me few more cards with Pocket [Poets] book list. Friend.

Gregory

▼ [Corso was able to travel to Europe and support himself on his wits alone, usually through the generosity of his friends. This first European trip set the pattern for what became his future routine. Without any planning or any visible means of financial support he was to see much of the world and live abroad off and on for the next four decades.]

To Lawrence Ferlinghetti

Paris
[ca. Feb. 25] 1957

Dear Larry –

Arrived in Paris—saw George Whitman.[57] He wants to order some pocket books and wants to trade stores with you, why don't you? It's a great store and Paris is so much nicer to have a book store in, in fact any store is so much nicer in Paris. But I feel so damned inadequate not knowing the language. I will enroll tomorrow for studies of French. I want to conquer the language in two months at least.

Everybody here is young bearded dirty and heavy coated. The girls are fat legged and ugly, the men, good-looking and dirty. Students. I haven't been around too much as I have to aid a friend of my friend escape from a mad house, *maison sante*, if I get caught I'll be deported but I must help. The boy confined is only 18 and his parents put him there because he wants to be a poet—good God!

I am finding time to revise and revise my works. Soon I will have them ready for you. If Jarrell's *N.Y. Times* article on current American poetry comes out in the magazine section send it too me. Send also the article *Esquire* and *Life* plan to do. Write me care of American Express, Rue Scribe. Write to George Whitman about trading stores.

Your friend, Gregory

To Lawrence Ferlinghetti

Paris
March 14, 1957

Dear Lawrence –

George Whitman is cold but interesting, his book store seems to do well. I like St. Germain des Prés, the students frighten me—they look too damn intelligent—perhaps it is because I cannot understand them. Tomorrow I shall enroll in French lessons. I am almost finished with *Gasoline*. I'll mail it to you in a week's time. Then after you select, send them to Jarrell for intro. The poems that I am extremely satisfied with I will place a √ [checkmark] on top of page. Met two French girls last week who had copy of your *Pictures* [*of the Gone World*] and Allen's *Howl*—seems they got it from Betty Keck. How come nobody sells Pocket Series in Paris? I gave George Whitman your listing.

Oddly enough, I miss San Francisco. I thought that were I ever to get to Paris I'd be nostalgic for nothing, but when there's a dark October day in my heart I think of Grant St.—Columbus St.—Russian Hill.

Did you get the *Ladies* [*The Vestal Lady on Brattle*] from Express? I can't find somebody with a typewriter—would you mind if, by chance I don't get one, I were to send you the poems in long hand? Perhaps I'll be compelled to. But I'm sure that before you'd send them to Jarrell you'd have someone type them. Maybe that girl Eleanor will do it for me. Am reading lots of Rimbaud, Diderot. How about a letter of intro to Monsieur Prevért? I dig his poetry. Write right away.

Love, Gregory

To Lawrence Ferlinghetti Paris

March 25, 1957

Dear Larry,

As you can see I have hold of typewriter. Good. How odd, I know Theodora's husband fairly well, though I've never met her, in fact saw him today at his mistress's house. I am living on the Rue De La Sorbonne . . . but I will move soon . . . can't take all them uninhibited students. I am starving, but existing. I have chance to write and sell some pornography to Olympia,[58] but don't know . . . must think about it. Jarrell is probably right about my automaticism. Kerouac impressed me and befoggled me. It's all right for prose but not poesy. I told Kerouac that the last time I saw him. We hit off badly, I told him I didn't like him anymore, etc. etc., also told him he befoggled me. No, poetry needs time and time and time. I didn't get your letter telling me what Jarrell said, too bad. What did he say? Does he still want to do intro? If not, fuck him. Besides, I've been working on thirty poems for year and half now. What automatic stuff I showed him was done in Mexico under Kerouac's belief of extemporaneous writing. I've canned most of those poems since I've been in New York. But to be fair to Kerouac I somehow do believe that only great poetry can be written on the spot, and when finished, done; not to be worked on. I will try to peddle books when they get here, I sure could use the money. What books do you want? *Justine?*, *Who Pushed Paula?*, *Play This Love With Me.* All kinds of books in this city. Even maps, and stamps, and old parchments. Anything you want. Let me know and I'll send. I go to Bonaparte Cafe for drinks. The Magots [Les Deux Magots] and also Le Select. Jean Francois Bergeret says that Prévert's agent is a bitch, and terrible to deal with, that she once charged a publishing firm for the translating from the English to the American tongue. It's funny about Railway Express giving my books away, I don't know how many, maybe 150. Great. I wrote them a very funny letter.

Glad to hear you're working a lot, at least someone is working. I haven't written a poem since Washington. Have you heard from Ginsberg? Rexroth seems to be in his glory now, I guess. San Francisco has finally worked out for him. Who sponsored reading in Cellar?[59] Is State Diamatt [Ruth Witt Diamant] still presiding? I walk the streets of Paris broke and hairlong and bowed and bugged under the loom of gargoyles. Gargoyles everywhere. Climbed Notre Dame, couldn't find one damn Quasimodo bell. Am reading [Gerard] De Nerval, [Alfred De] Musset. If I am very hungry I'll go find Genet or maybe Michel Morgan, yeah, she'd be better. George Whitman is impolite. I gave him a book on Mozart for a gift, but to read. Next day I find it on a shelf, up for sale. He also hates people. I will see all your friends and will tell them everything. There's only one good book store in St. Germain but they don't have all the crazy pocket books. If you are serious about coming to Paris why don't you? Trade places with George Whitman. He wants to. I'd like to work with you, but I doubt if Whitman's place can match your place, in fact, it doesn't. I intend to be in Paris for long time so if there's anything you're planning I'll be ready to help. I would like to start a pocket book store here but it takes money and all that nonsense, or maybe I could open store and you could ship me books and I could sell them here. It'll be your shop, part of your chain, in Paris. You'll be like those crazy jewelry shops that boast London Paris New York in gold on their windows. I like France very much. I walk a lot late at night by the Seine and feel free and good. Tomorrow I'll be 27 and I'll celebrate by communing with my favorite gargoyle. It hangs over a small park from a church called St. Jacques. If you didn't know, gargoyles are primarily used for running draining water rain, those that don't, that are just used for evil ornament are called Chimeras. [. . .]

Just when do I have to send *Gasoline* manuscript in? Let me know. Give my love to your wife. Is Rexroth upset with me? I know McClure is, maybe even Duncan, but surely not Stock[60] or Harmon? I don't know, is everybody upset with me? God, I bet even Bunthorne[61] is upset. Is Stanley Gould still there? Read you had big earthquake, well, don't fall in. I once saw a movie in which dinosaurs and lizards and snakes fell into a earthquake crack. It was frightening. What a way for you and Rexroth and McClure and Duncan and Ruth Diamant to go. One wouldn't know what to think. What would *Life* mag think? By the way, is that due? How did you survive in Paris? Let me know. Met one good poet who has book out, a man named Ghérasim Luca, wrote a book of verse called: *Heros-Limite.* Paris is getting hot, and the Arabs are beginning to sweat.

Friend, Gregoir

To Lawrence Ferlinghetti Paris

[ca. April 9] 1957

Dear Larry,

The concierge has her witchy hand on the doorknob. She demands rent! Do I abscond or will you aid me? I send *Gasoline* off in few days. The Queen is here and I am hungry—Prévert will not feed me. Genet wants to **** me—I have a little French girl; nobody wants to buy her. I've become debauched. The concierge turns the knob. Maybe I will repay you. But you must help—else I hang myself from the nearest gargoyle.

Gregory

To Lawrence Ferlinghetti Paris

April 16, 1957

Dear friend,

The books came today and I went to the ten stores and gave them all away, some paid, some didn't. In all, got a *mille*. Ate well. Also read them. Levertov, good, strong, and somewhat delightfully mechanized. Her poems try to be too perfect, I feel. But there's nothing wrong in that. She's good, and you should feel good about having published her. Ponsot.[62] Well, Ponsot's first poem is like all the rest of her poems. She wants to be truthful about her woman self. Good. But when she try to be truthful about her women self for "a thing of man" then Gregory no find greatness, but truth. But music she has. Yes, I feel she has music, and some of it is good like good fugue. But she no my kind of poetry. Patchen (it's the first time I read it) is like Puccini: can't give any opinion, can only like.

You. Now, listen carefully: Your *Pics* [*Pictures of the Gone World*] hit me while sitting in sun on chair in Deux Magots. You brought back 'noble chimneypots and morning sheets and the artists on Sundays' to me, but your 'noble chimneypots' etc., are different than mine. Mine has always been Eastside New York impressions of the same theme, but not really the same, mine never had the 'reachless seascape spaces' mine was always the 'dreamless seascape spaces.' Gregory had much dream in his youth, his Eastside, but all was really dreamless. I want to say something not pedantic but something really warm and sweet about your verse and it's hard, hard because what you have written is what I have always inadvertently felt but could never express, that is, express not in verse, that I could easily do, but in cold critical detail . . . alas prose. Primarily, I would, if you read poem in *Needle*, feel about city as you feel, and bring that city to its knees, have it down and merciful . . . Laughing, saying: You where I live, I know you. You are nothing that I know you. And thus go home and dream of those dreamless cities, those cities that should never be known.

Well anyway, what I felt was what I probably could never do. That is: Write about the thing I really know most and best. My horror, my wracked youth, bred and red on rotted-teated Eastside New York. Why did I ever start poetry but to use it as a means to tell all the world what a strange lugubrious place is Delancey Street . . . But I can't do it, I can't because somehow I find that I am really a poet and therefore I feel much sweeter less simpler things. You, undoubtedly have had a good life, maybe not, too bad I really didn't get to talk soul to soul with you, but let me assume that your life was easy as it was hard. Could you, a college man, claiming himself an anti-academician, see the Chickenplucker? The dead soaked rat in the gutter? The molded bagel up for sale? The dry sad rooftops of Eastside? Yes, you do see dead rats, but do they mean to you what they have meant to me? Example: "Morning sheets" now morning sheets meant to me, two beatings, one from stepmother, one from father when he came home from work, I wet the bed, I hid the sheets, I was afraid, ashamed . . . they found out, the smell was critical, I was whipped, and thus out on the clothesline that terrible sheet would hang, newly washed, my horror, because when they took it in and placed it on my bed, God knows I will wet it again, and hide again, etc. etc. etc.

I am off to somewhere tomorrow. I leave without paying rent. I don't know if you sent me money or not. If you did then it will reach me wherever I go. I love Paris and will be back, but first I must make my fortune, and it can't be made in Paris. I will mail poems, o but did I work hard on them, before I leave. I see Prévert tonight. I will convince him. I have much power. Kerouac came and went. Him too fucking professionally morose for me. Good about Allen, he'll be famous, now, I guess. Met some folk who know you, sculptor named Keith Monroe. Give my love to Mimi Waxman, tell her I met Pat Bowles, translator of Beckett.

Goodbye, your grave but happy friend, Gregory

Jimmy Baldwin[63] is reading manuscript. He digs my poetry very much. After he's finished, I shall send them off. When you get them you can put them in whatever order you see fit. I will send you a week later four more poems that I am still working over. All in all you have about 30 poems, mostly small ones. I will send dedication later also. I am off to Barcelona.

To Allen Ginsberg Barcelona

May 6, 1957

Dear Allen,

Just received your letter in Barcelona where I am staying for a week. I will not go back to Paris. Sura is a little too unreal for me we separated, she's now in Aix-en-Provence. I will live the summer in Castelnau, an old village high in the Pyrenees in a 11th century chateau with a madwoman. There I will write and think—thing me to think and write about: BROWN. Everything must to itself beguile BROWN. What do you think about BROWN? What does Burroughs think of BROWN (rectuminal caves, undoubtedly?) I have no money. Ferl sent me five dollars for my concierge. Kerouac came and went—his morose attitude annoyed me again, but we had some fun in Paris. He's now in England, I think. What does Kerouac want? What does Kerouac expect? Surely if he wanted the impossible then he would be possible. He writes well but doesn't reach for much, maybe does, I don't know. Ferl sent me Ban of *HOWL*.[64] How absurd of that man to seize the books. How many children will read *HOWL*? He is afraid of what it might do to children—but children read nothing! Children know nothing—children are nothing! Was any other POET banned from American kids before, but the poet of Batman, The Human Touch, The Joker and The Penguin? Saw Genet in Paris sitting with three old men in Deux Magots—his bald face says nothing, but his infant soft hands speak much. I did not talk to him. Why does Don Allen[65] want my poetry now? Has he not seen them twice before? Does he expect different poems? I saw first review [*Evergreen Review*], good, good cover, crazy chick on it. Love to Peter to Bill and to Ansen when he arrives.

Barcelona is filled with cheap shoes and beautiful whores and sad bulls. You'll like Barcelona. Lots of English and Germans and Spaniards here—love

Gregory

I will see Artigas[66] tonight—him good ceramic man

To Lawrence Ferlinghetti

Barcelona
[May 9, 1957]

Dear L,

I will hold manuscript for awhile, must give you only perfect poems, went and had lunch with Miro and Artigas today, they dig me because I got them hung on BROWN. They still don't know what I mean by BROWN, I don't either but it got me a crazy meal. Miro and Artigas are *tres gentile*. They have very small hands.

Love, Corso

To Lawrence Ferlinghetti

Nice, France
May 20, 1957

Dear Larry,

I am back in Nice where I hope to settle—I hope. Things are very difficult for me, life is becoming too real. When I see it that real, I feel not as a poet—but as a bum.

Well, went to Miro opening in Nice and met Picasso—we shook hands and this is what was said:
Me: I'm a beautiful poet—don't you feel goofy the way everyone is looking at you?
He: Do you speak Russian?
Me: Oh, you can't understand English?
He: No.
Me: Oh!
Then Artigas came over and put his arm around Picasso and said: "This is the young man who visited me in Barcelona."
Me: (To Artigas) Tell him (Picasso) what he thinks of BROWN, (meanwhile fifty people gathered).
Artigas to Picasso: (In Spanish) !!%'&*#!*
Miro was alone! His opening and he was standing alone! I felt his rage.
Picasso asked: "What, the color?" Artigas looked at me. "No," I said, "I mean the BROWN that is the mystery to God!"
Picasso turned his head and began shaking hands with fat ladies. Miro joined Artigas and me. I asked Miro: "Oh, I bet you know what BROWN is—he (Picasso) didn't know."
"What do you wish to know about it?"
"I want to know what you think about it."
"I don't use it—I never liked it."
"I don't mean the color!"

He and Artigas walked away. The gallery owner was bugged by me. I wore no tie—my pants were dirty and I had crashed the opening. I walked out screaming: "Goodbye! Goodbye!" Picasso's eyes bulged. Artigas bowed. Miro smiled faintly. Thus a day in Nice.

Gregory

To Lawrence Ferlinghetti Paris

May 27, 1957

Dear Larry,

Read stupid review John Hollander (Allen's friend) gave Ginsberg in *Partisan*[67]. When will poets or critics or reviewers who feel as alive as vital as Ginsberg review a Ginsberg? Hollander is a dead fat academic dedragonizer. After starving for literally five days in Nice I came back to Paris and will be going to England soon. Poems are all ready—must re-type them. I am very happy with them, they are the best poems I've written. Will go to see Prévert again for you, last time he was busy and rushed about something. Send me news—American Express Paris.

Love, Gregory

To Allen Ginsberg

Paris
May 27, 1957

Dear Allen,

Am back in Paris after wild hungry sad good bad trip. Castelnau was bad—too many goats and flies. In Nice I went to Miro opening and saw Miro and La Met (Picasso). Picasso speaks no English—too bad—I would have liked to have spoken to him. I did, but he didn't understand and Miro was a bad translator and about 50 people tried to drag them away from me but couldn't because I broke down crying saying "*Fam! Fam!*" Al, I was terribly hungry. Then my friend fucked it all up by asking Picasso what he thought about BROWN.' "What, the color?" asks Picasso, in French. "No," says my idiot friend! "BROWN that is biscuits that taste like sardines on the tongue of God!" Picasso ignored us after that.[68]

Read Hollander's anti-vital review of *Howl* in *Partisan*, he will be recorded amongst the illustrious obscure. I thought him unfair and damaging. Poets who criticize other poets generate a smell of bitter cunt. I will be off to England soon. My poems are ready for Ferlinghetti. I am sending him a great collection. I am very happy with them.

When I came back from Nice to Paris, via hitchhiking I had a gun—I got it in Barcelona. I went to the Deux Magots (St. Germain des Prés) and decided to shoot myself—but didn't. Instead I aimed gun at everybody and screamed, "Why did I starve in Nice? You bastards!" Immediately cops came but gun was not noticed. As soon as I got in van I hid it beneath seat. All the people loved the cops for taking me away—and they applauded me when I waved from the van good-bye! In the station they charged me with drunken conduct (I had drunk four liter of *vin*) and let me go.

My love to Bill and Peter, Gregory

To Lawrence Ferlinghetti

Paris
[early June] 1957

Dear Ferl,

Here they are.[69] They're my best and I am happy with them. Hope Jarrell likes them enough to introduce them. He'll surely see that these ain't "automatic".

Love, Gregory

DEDICATION: For Hope, Zina, Zion, Lee, Jean-Francois, and Allen Eager—my angels in Paris.

To Lawrence Ferlinghetti

Paris
[early June] 1957

Dear Larry,

Please change dedication to: –
Allen Ginsberg, angel poet
Hope Savage, sad sweet angel
Avilda B?, recent angel [this line has been crossed out after Ferlinghetti received it, at Corso's request]
Jagat Bhatia, angel of film
Allen Eager, jazz musician, fallen; not fallen, angel
Anton, wise Anton
Zion, but surely a wondrous painter
Albie, and women do flock to his side with apples and woe
The Brothers Orlovsky, perhaps the only real angels
Lee, Zina, Jean-Francois, and will they die in Paris?
Ferlinghetti, angel with cup of aid and song
Randall Jarrell, good gentle poet
Corine, my brother's child who I've seen only once

And also add—separate paragraph—to *How Poetry Comes To Me.* Yesterday an academician came to me and said: "I am not happy, they gave me a gasoline pen with which to write." / "Ah, you lucky bastard!" I cried, letting him sleep in an orange crate while throughout the night I used his pen, used his pen, used his pen.

To Allen Ginsberg

Paris
June 12, 1957

Dear Allen,

Your letter picked me up and made me not forsake poetry as I have been doing lately. A good poet shouldn't go hungry and homeless, not really. There must be some other way than the way of kneeling before lesser people who are only too glad to throw a few crumbs your way. And how well dressed they are, and how beautiful they look these people. I, I seem as though I am prepared to sell them peanuts or something. I look terrible. Worms in my hair, holes in my feet, city dumps on my hands, I must bathe, I must once again go back to poetry . . . haven't written anything since I left America, 'cept a poem 'bout Paris:

> This cityless city/ this time without time or term/ this indistinct theme/ this bulleted rain/ Citychild, Aprilcity/ Picassos and churches gargoyling everywhere/ spirits of angels and poets crouched in doorways. Worms in hair/ Idealess city, city of useless love and labor/ city

> of informers and concierges/ harlequin deathtrap/ hear Genet's deathrattle/ the buildings look to fall/ the Seine generates ominous mud/ Eiffel looks down, sees the Apocalyptical ant crawl/ New Yorkless city/ city of Germans dead and gone/ Dollhouse of Mama War/ hear in the night in the night always/ Montparnassian woe/ deathical Notre Dame/ hear in the nightcity, heirloomed/ Hugo and Zola together entombed.

That is only poem, all the rest has been making it with jazz musicians and dead women, and my Sura is gone, has been gone for two months now. Am unhappy about that, but not too. Tried some H [heroin] and almost died, so won't try anymore. Paris has no poets, only St. Germain des Prés creeps who dream stupid dreams and eat well and fuck and sleep and wear good clothes and who despise good poets. I will try to send to *Measure* and *Evergreen*,[70] but how, and why? and why? What good is poetry really? Ferl sends me five stinking dollars when I write and tell him I am literally literally really honestly dying starving and need money. And he sends a five dollar check and he is a poet and surely he is a poet. Peter's little letter was intelligently written. He's learning. It was also a warm letter, and it made me feel. Thank him for me. *Middleton Gardens* and *Trembling About Thoreau*, are not good, really. I don't think I sent them in to Ferlinghetti, I did send in *Last Night I Drove A Car*, but in a much simpler form. I sent in selections from *Power*. And lots of others. Also one you don't know of:

> *Amnesia In Memphis* / Who am I, flat beneath the shades of Isis, / This clay-skinned body, made study / By the physicians of Memphis? / Was it always my leaving the North / Snug on the back of the crocodile? / Do I remember this whorl of mummy cloth / As I stood fuming by the Nile? / O life abandoned! half-embalmed, I beat the soil, / Who I am I cannot regain / Nor sponge my life back with the charm of Ibis oil— / Still omen of the dribbling scarab; / Fate that leads me into the chamber of blue perfumes, / Is there no other worthy of prophecy / Than that decker who decks my spine with ostrich plumes? / / No more will the scurvy Sphinx / With beggy prophets their prophecies relate, / The papyrus readers have seen the falcon's head / Fall unto the jackal's plate.

I think it's a good poem, somewhat like Yeats, but not really. It surely sounds unlike me, though. I wrote it on ship coming over, intent on seeing Egypt, etc. etc.; enough to recapture all those real dreams I used to have, but somehow I felt that: the falcon's head fell unto the jackal's plate. That all was really over and that today is 1957 and not history books that sing 5,000 B.C. etc. etc. etc.

I'll send that poem to Don Allen. He should be quite happy with it. If he isn't, fuck him, poetry doesn't come too easily for me anymore. I hope you like Venice, God I would like to see my Italy sometime. Maybe if you find yourself settled there send for me, I'll hop on Hermes winged foot and make it there.

Bill's letter 1954 to you is good and if you want that he should be published he could be published right here in Paris by the guy who published Miller's books and all he does publish is pornography and pays 1,500 francs a page, that's not bad, and he does want material and lots of Americans write for him and earn their living that way and what they write is shit and terrible and maybe you'd better not give him Bill's because I'm sure they won't take anything great. They sell only to the tourists and sailors and pornos.[71]

Saw Merims and he gave me 300 francs when I told him I needed money for lunch and I hated asking him because I'm sure it made him happy and thankful that he never became a poet or a guitar player. I never did like him. I'm sure you and Peter will dig Paris, lots happening here. But *tres chere*. Hotels cost a dollar and over a day. Food is anywhere from a dollar to a dollar and a half. Paris, in fact, France is most expensive country in Europe. And the French are the pettiest and rattiest and cheapest bastards on earth. But come, you'll like it.

Love, Gregory

To Don Allen

Paris
[early Summer] 1957

Dear Don,

I hope these poems are to your liking. Read first issue of *Evergreen* and dug the cover and the inside very much. They sold out in St. Germain. Is there anybody here you'd like me to look up?

Love, Gregory

To John Wieners

Paris
[early Summer] 1957

Dear John,

Ginsberg says you are starting crazy magazine and to send you something, I have nothing, all my poems are now in hands of City Lights for publication and I have no copies. What I can send you is a canto of a poem called *Way Out*, you can select some things from that. I'll send you the whole thing and you pick out what you like if you like.

Paris is big and fat and I am going hungry and thin and need a new pair of pants and living seems senseless but I met a girl who will wash my pants and feed me so I am going to live some more. Hope *Measure* makes it.

Love, G. Corso

Can't fit whole canto in so I'll send you selections.

To Lawrence Ferlinghetti

Paris
July 14, 1957

Dear Larry,

I have been waiting to hear from you. Have you received poems? I sent them registered mail. Please let me know right away. I will probably go to Sweden soon; I'm not too sure. I've been thinking of settling down on some nice clean moralistic Swedish farm with some nice clean blonde farm girl. Has anything been happening? Ginsberg says he's going to Venice. I wrote to him there, but received no answer. I wish to hell people would keep up their correspondences, it's a drag always to go to the American Express and find nothing. I don't know whether the poems got to you or not, if they are lost, I am lost. But I have registered receipt, that means that I'll get some money from the postal people if they are lost. But surely the poems are worth more than what they could give me. Please tell me you have them. It is a publisher's duty to acknowledge what he receives. I have enough worries as it is. I am working on a novel. A good novel. All dialogue, no description. How can I get *Howl* and sell them here? Please send me at least two *Vestal Ladies*. Saw Genet. Prévert difficult. What news?

Gregory

Cross out on dedication: AVILDA, RECENT ANGEL . . . the bitch deceived me.

To Lawrence Ferlinghetti

Paris
[mid to late July] 1957

Dear Larry,

Take out "Avilda, recent angel" in dedication—put in place, "Barbara, my good quiet friend" instead. Damn Avilda won't give me anymore money, result, I'm starving again, but not too much, so erase the bitch out. Now, about your difficulty with the un-illustrious obscure. What you are going through is marvelous, young, true, great. The philistines can't win out—you will win—the whole world scope of cellar—drivers lovers of beauty, unlike rats, come out to stand by your side. Thus, fight on! Go forward, for forward is the Light!

Paris is cold and tense. Arabs and French on very bad terms. Woe!

Gregory

To Allen Ginsberg

Paris
[mid to late July] 1957

Dear Allen,

I sent Don Allen poems, but I don't know if he's accepted them or not. And is Ferl in jail? I haven't heard from him. It's been three weeks now since I sent him poems—and no word! Has he poems? *Esquire* was absurd, almost embarrassing. But Lafcadio did look like a sinister cathedral.

I have the good fortune to be living rent free in a crazy apartment for the summer. It was given to me by Gabriel Pomerand,[72] a surrealist filmman, good friends with Cocteau and Genet. Met Genet up Pomerand's house—ate crazy meal—Genet has round bald head—pugilist face—infant's fat hands. Pomerand is tubercular (T.B.), thin, pale, like Banaxet. Married to a great Egyptian woman, and digs my surrealist poetry. He wants me to meet Breton. He and his wife are leaving for Naples, Ischia, and have given me apartment. So, come to Paris and live rent free. Genet is here, Cocteau is here. They need you. I want very much to go back to San Francisco, and settle down. I think I will after the summer. How is Ansen? Do you know that I knew, at Harvard, the new Aga Khan? In fact I fucked the same girl he fucked. How strange—to have fucked the same cunt the descendent of Mohammed fucked. I almost feel like a part of Allah now. But I wonder how the girl feels? Surely as a St. Theresa would feel. Thank you very much for your consideration. The money will feed me for a week! Do not forsake Paris, much is here. The apartment is yours, Peter's, Ansen's.

Love to Ansen and Peter.

To Lawrence Ferlinghetti

Paris
[late July] 1957

Dear Ferl,

Allen tells me you have been arrested.[73] Are you in jail? If so, say nothing until you see a lawyer. Don't incriminate yourself. You must be careful because I once knew a man who was sentenced to 30 years for selling children dirty books with pictures—thank God you didn't have pictures in your book. I guess you must feel terrible—now all your neighbors will whisper, "There goes Ferlinghetti, he sells dirty postcards." Actually for a man in your position the only honorable thing to do would be to take to the knife—alas, suicide might erase the shame. You know, of course, that the writer of the book is immune to shame—that only the peddler of said book is mune—and, I must say that the most shameful person or persons involved are those that condone—such as Mr. Rexroth, and Miss Diamant. Too bad that such a nice guy like you got mixed up with such a lot.

I've been thinking about leaving Europe and going back to San Francisco. If I come back would you give me a job in store? You don't have to, though. But I am suddenly aware that it takes more than poetry to exist in this sinister cathedral. Seriously, I think that you are perhaps the only great publisher in America and will have to suffer for it. Met André Breton, he digs my surrealist poems. By the way, I've still to hear from you. Good God, all is lost if you didn't get poems! Please let me know. Keep me informed on the trials, etc., if worse comes to worse, and they condemn you to death, I will gather a band of poets and we, vigilante like, will rescue you.

Love to both you and your wife, Gregory

To Lawrence Ferlinghetti Paris

[late Summer] 1957

Dear Larry,

Saw *Evergreen* [*Review*] and your face and it is placed in bookstore window near Deux Magots—very good issue. I did not believe Allen when he wrote saying you were put in jail, but Barbara Hansen says it's true. If poetry is going to make any sound possible it surely will come out of injustice. Leigh Hunt was jailed for an incident of poetry—he later won out. Please keep me informed. The English bookshop wants more pocketbooks. How can I get Ginsberg's to peddle? You've yet to let me know if you received my poems, I fear they are lost. Good God! if so I give up. I am going to work on a film here with a producer from CBS. He likes my ideas and wants me to work with him. Film is a good medium for poesy.

Love, Gregory

To Peter Orlovsky Paris

[Aug. 29] 1957

Dear Peter,

Got your card but not your important letter at American Express because it seems that all my mail that goes to American Express goes to Barcelona then to Nice then to obscurity, I never get that mail, I only found out today and put a stop to it, but I fear that I have lost lots of money because people have been sending me some, and never got their mail back, I wrote immediately to Barcelona to send me all my mail, if any, so I may well get your important letter, after all. It is safe now to write to American Express, Paris, I have moved from 26 Rue St. Benoit to 123 Rue De Sevres, a pad with beds and cooking until end of September, then I go to India, I am set on it.

Hope you get this, Gregory

To Lawrence Ferlinghetti Paris

[late August] 1957

Dear Larry,

I just came from American Express [where] they hold mail for two months. I go there every week but no books, no letters, only letter from Ginsberg who is going to Greece then Istanbul. More poems? Good. I have some for you. But how fat is book going to be? I sent you more poems than Levertov had printed, I think. Being I didn't get your letter on what you think, write another one. I will send in poems as quickly as possible. Too bad Jarrell didn't help you in *Howl* case, the fool. It could have been a great opportunity for him, what does he use that job for anyway?[74] I know, I saw him at work, old ladies come to him with their works and ask him for advice etc. etc. Too bad, because poets should help out one another, but they don't, they're like jealous little girls, hoarding globs of earthly cake under their beds.

Good God, I hope you are happy with my poems because them poems is me and they are what I believe in, and you must see it that way. Or you mustn't. I'm glad you need more because I have decided to give you my automatic poems and fuck come what may. They are pure and good. They are essentially visionary, and written in much sensible discord. You'd be the only person to publish them anyway. You don't have to use my *How Poetry Comes To Me* pieces if you don't want because I just wanted to be funny, and perhaps I shouldn't be funny but serious. Yes, why not serious. Them poems is serious. But I must be a little goofy because I'm always laughing at them. Tell Diamant I am dying in Paris and that I will die because winter is coming and that after September first I have no place to stay and say for her to send me fare back and I will go to San Francisco and work and pay her back and empty her garbage and wax her floors and walk her dog. I like Paris but I have bad memories, the girl I came for is gone and I am not happy that's all there is to it. So don't make me die because I will and I feel I'm worth saving in a way. So do try to get me back. Good God man, I have no one to send me money to get back, no one, and how to get money in Paris?

I am happy about you, your record, your success and everything. I will send poems right away. Please write me. I will be here at this address until first of September. Best write to American Express.

Love, Gregory

To Robert LaVigne

Paris
[Sept. 2] 1957

Dear Bob,

Paris teeming with war. Arabs FLN are bombing cafes, shooting people in streets—great wave of terror. I owe you a letter, you will get it. I hope you find the beauty in Sura that I found. Off to India in November. Go ask Ferl to show you my *Bomb* poem.

Love, Gregory

To Isabella Gardner

Paris
[Sept.] 1957

Dear Isabella Gardner,

Four years since your "lady on Dutch cleanser" enlightenment to me; and now four years later I thank you again, how happy and wonderful your book of lovely spring-wild poems made me, I read all your poems the entire noon on the side steps of the Louvre; I fell in love with your poetry, it is marvelous wondrous beautiful poetry, in *That Craning of the Neck* your fantastic ellipse, from your silent heron vision to the elliptical actual zoo, that "fished on a concrete shore" reality I find myself so often fain to go in; the poem makes me feel that DREAM is awakening.

Cockatrice! Chanticleer! What lovely words, eyesounds! I felt so elated reading your poems, really; *Of Flesh and Bone*, I never read anything more brilliant and mad about Death—"the salty boys bugled desire to die . . . the girls harped a lust to be buried . . . I vowed that eyeless earless . . .". On and on, the whole poem a perfect mad scream into Death, Death's ear must have shattered—I really have nothing but mature praise for you, and that's something I'm awkward to be, much more graceful accustomed and honest in my immature self; but beyond the praise, joy and love, enlightenment, I thank you . . .

I'd want to talk about every poem, I got so involved again with *Of Flesh and Bone* just now, it's right at my side, that I can't talk from poem to poem; "and IT became my parlor slang. . ." mad! "I would refuse to die" madder! That whole part from "I vowed that eyeless" to "Wrack of sorrow. . ." pure soulfelt wonder! "Girl and child my nightmare was the ceasing." What sucks my marrow is not the final fact of IT but the engagement of some tomorrow.

I have a nice room in Paris that looks out on Sainte-Chapelle and cone towers, not a present scene in sight; I hope to go to India in November, not for enlightenment (Hindu calm yogi meditation) but for cows, and the Rhesus monkeys and the brown blue skin, and red dust, and the human dead Ganges. Ah your poetry, I used to think Robert Lowell was the only and final energy of Albion's stifled child.

My love, Gregory

To Lawrence Ferlinghetti

Paris
Sept. 6, 1957

Dear Larry,

I grow old, my face changes, it's become happier, no good, so before it is too late to me great beautiful favor, and necessary, print this sad photo of me in *Gasoline*, what ever it cost you can deduct from what I might get from sales, if any, besides, I won't live long and this is only photo of me in existence that is truly sad, all the rest are phony sad and even hammy, but not this, anyway my family ain't seen me in long time, also many of my childhood gangster friends ain't either and imagine when they see my picture, me looking so truthfully sad. O I met a beautiful little blond body shaped French Irish rich living with mother on Champs-Elysées big apartment, she 17, was married for four months, divorced, she likes me. Big huge apartment, but I have changed, I like her better than apartment, anyway she saw pictures of you and Ginsberg and all them other less-sad-than-me pictures and asked why I didn't have any picture? She's right, I deserve to have picture, so I told her that I will have one, and she believes me so Larry don't fail me, her name is Elisabeth.

How was New York? Meet anybody I knew? I hope you put that added line at end of *Automatic Sun Poem,* "O constant hole etc. etc."

I also enclose two more poems for you perusal, two new good ones, if you like use, there's room now that Ginsberg didn't make intro too long, but if you no like them send back, and if you no like photo send back, it only copy, must send it to my father who ain't seen me in long time, but if you print it at my expense then not only my father will see it but also my Uncle Rocky and my aunt Kate and Grace and Betty and also my Grandmother and my old school teacher Miss Driscoll and God knows how many people!

Yes, I think I am in love again, this time really, but the black-market guy I gave bad checks to is after me, lo! What a way to die, just when I'm finally in love. Anyway I'll pay him back, so I don't think he'll do me in. But if he does, then please send all money I might make on book to—no, rather use the money for a fund, the Gregory Corso Fund for Needy Poets, to be given annually to the most shabby of poets.

Love, Gregory

To Lawrence Ferlinghetti

Paris
Sept. 6, 1957

Dear Larry,

It is all right to send letters to American Express now because I told them, too late, not to forward my mail to Barcelona anymore which they have been doing so I guess them letters are stationed somewhere in obscurity. Okay down with *Power*, down with *Way Out*, I send this week all I have, can do no more, but can say when you say that I am only beginning that youse is wrong, and I don't care, and I'm going to India, fuck America, and Ginsberg will come on the 15th of Sept., and after that I will go to India.

Love, Gregory

▼ [Ferlinghetti was critical of many of the poems that Corso sent him for the book, *Gasoline,* and Corso was not happy when he first responded to the news.]

To Lawrence Ferlinghetti

Paris
Sept. 6, 1957

Dear Larry,

Today is Sept. 6 and I received all my back mail since May. What you say about *Power* means nothing to me. Don't use it, but don't give opinion either because *Power* is my first extemporaneous poem and it is very dear to me just like a little cute lyric is dear to some Rexroth or something. *Power* is terrible, shouting about nothing, true, so what? In fact I know it to be a bad poem, but it is my first baby, and I have abandoned it, why be so critical of it? Are you mad! "Babbitt on pants" is complete, everybody digs it, or don't, but good God man I love that poem, and my beautiful *How Happy I Used To Be*, you only like part of it, only part! It's one of my truest and saddest poems, and in case you are interested *H.G. Wells* is a definite unchanged automatic poem. I forget the rest I sent you, but I do remember *Amnesia in Memphis*, a grand poem! Don Allen says he wants to use it in *Evergreen Review 3* . . . oh hell, I'll send you all I have then I'll rot in Rotterdam or Amsterdam or something for the fucking winter, I hate poetry and all its fucking ambitious son-of-a-bitches who call me a showman because I act myself and am truly not a disguised academician like most "wild side" walkers, or "lazy on-the-air" talkers.

I'm happy you won't use *Way Out* or *Power*, but my other poems, I just don't understand, you are to be the judge of my work you will make the choice, I realize it puts you in a terrible position, I can say no more or do no more than send you all rest I have and go to sleep because I'm terrible bored and angered by life and its petty cries or sighs or joys, in fact poetry almost seems futile and second rate means of expression, in truth when I one night find myself tremendously inspired or whatever and sit down and write for five straight hours a *H.G. Wells*, mad poem I don't want to hear five months later a reader say: "I don't like it but I like this one, and this one, and not that one, and and and and." How unhappy I am to be reading all those old letters, I thought everyone deserted me, but they didn't, Jarrell sent me 100 dollars, Harmon sent me eight dollars, my Hope Savage is in Russia, begging for me, and all the while I thought she forsook me, o damn!

I don't like Rexroth no more for some funny reason I don't know why. And in fact I think I dislike that whole fucking crocodilian culture mad group you got out there, McClure with his vanity that no sensitive person would dare venture to possess, Duncan with his gentle-cattiness, like a St. Mary ministration, and Rexroth for his old age and his 1930s that are dead dead and dull and nothing new and earthly, so fucking earthly, he Papa Academician, a spy, man, a spy. Who else? Yes, You, I felt you to be almost in idea, alike, and that idea is, if a poet is a poet, a poet should not think too much about another's poetry, too concerned, I mean, because one poet is another poet's poison. I suffer when I write because I FEEL what I write, I don't give a damn if no one else feels it, that ain't my job, my problem, and my big attack against Academicians is that if they write poetry they should not be critic critique critique of poetry . . . but I guess a poet feels that if he is capable of writing a poem why not be capable of criticizing a poem, means he can gain reputation not only as poet but as critic, and "critic" always seems somewhat PROUD when augmented with poet.

Enough. Ginsberg will be here 15th but I won't, I'm getting out of Paris, and will spend winter in Amsterdam where I will undoubtedly become obscurely plain amid the stupid bodies of the Dutch. You say you want what you saw in S.F. I only withheld five poems, I don't much care for them, but you do. Where is the fairness? But I guess that's what goes into making a good publisher, I don't know. I assure you I'll die a better death than McClure, Rexroth, Duncan and the whole fucking lot of them who chant because they can't become either Congressmen or Hollywood stars . . . I am sorry, because I am weak and easily discouraged, and worst of all, I am at this moment a sewerage of excreted dreams, and I stink, and my little Hope Savage is in Russia, and I undoubtedly will never see her again, and right now, poetry seems so fucking small, right at hand, small, that its proximity can be stepped upon like a roach, and crushed, and forgotten, and I only live this miserable existence for poetry, once that is abused, I give up. I don't mind people, jailers, doctors, stupid parents, unhappy loves, I don't mind when they toy with my life . . . it means nothing . . . but my poetry means something because it isn't poetry but a precious little answer of things I discovered when I was born . . . fuck everything else, abuse it, curse it, love it, have joy in it, or destroy it, it means nothing . . . but please, my little answer, my own little personal answer, should not be abused, no matter how bad, at times, the answer may be.

Now of course when I send you all the rest I have I am confident that you will select what you feel to be best, if so, don't tell me what you accept or refuse, because, I am terribly discouraged, and feel it unnecessary to be further discouraged by the like or dislike of a poem.

Don't say anything but I cashed a phony check on the black market and if I get caught I'll go to jail for good and I don't care because I was broke and mad and sad and I gave my passport number to check so I guess even if I do get away they will eventually get me and my life is truly fucked up, I have no responsibility to myself, I am indeed stupid . . . dear friend, I don't feel like sending this letter out, but maybe I should because in it all I am terribly confused and perhaps you can help straighten the confusion via poste.

Love, Gregory

Further note: Why not just go ahead and publish Prévert? What can they really do to you? I can't see him anymore. Jarrell has not abandoned me. And realize that he unwarily was against *Howl* therefore it would have been against his taste to fight it, but I do feel none the less that he should have come to your aid. It puts me in a funny position because I accept Allen as a greater poet, still I must now ask him if he still wants to do intro, I have to, and I would like him to do it because he does like my work, and why not, but if you don't want it, then dictator you and persecuted me will have no intro even though I'd dig having Ginsberg do one for me. Maybe if Jarrell refuses, then certainly Ginsberg, I'd be very proud because Allen knows well my mind and my work.

About *Power* if not to use, then use: "*Am I the stiff arm of . . .*" until "*Am I, Don etc. etc. etc. No longer a power?*" and just call it *POEM*, because that is very severe and true good selection, but if you hate ALL my *Power* then just put it all aside. I'm still mad about SHOWMAN Gregory because those who say it are like those who have killed me all my life, the gentle social worker type, sweet, but unhelpful with their bad judgments.

Goodbye, Gregory

To Allen Ginsberg and Peter Orlovsky Paris

Sept. 6, 1957

Dear Allen and Peter,

Poor Garver[75] and his store of history and huge Michel, [Morgan] old people are going and new ones are coming, where does that leave us? I had a vision that I was dead and in death I was an idiot child blowing a wheel on a stick. Even in death the wheel must roll, we must blow the wheel, blow the wheel. I have been writing a work on a grand scale. A work entirely automatic, but not a Kerouac kind of automatism. By force and extreme concentration and scarcely want to eat. I have in a weeks time written well over five hundred verses. In one weeks time, a week in which I experienced countless visions, and I wrote down what I visioned as I visioned. I had high talks with the illustrious dead.

I had in me the power to envision anything anyplace anyone I choose to I calls it my *Sadness Song Of A Wounded Deer*. The outline of the poem is this: I see Death as Death is, I see it stand in the center of a green room, he goes through a ritual, then puts his ribboned hands down his throat and comes up with a handful of wriggling wormy wounds, he goes to window and flings them upon a forest of sleeping deer. Thus the deer are inflicted, wounded. Now I of course associate myself, you, Peter, every human living hurt thing with the deer. All right the deer are wounded and helpless, the West Wind (the beginning of the visions) comes and with raging claws digs into the wound of a deer, me, and carries me over the Dying Man of the Eastern Gulph, he is arched like a rainbow and I talk with him, and leave him and enter a place of many doors and thus (the doors of perception) I see and talk to Alexander, Mozart, James Dean, Shelley, Hitler, Darius, Self, Other Self, Bird Parker, and Chatterton. After awhile the wind wisks me away again and this time I see a field of dying stars, "like the dim lights of some hallucinating facade" and on and on and on until I break out into a lyrical sadness song, bemoaning my wounds, etc. etc., and decide to got to a movie but Dostoyevsky stops me and turns me on opium and drags me to see Baudelaire's grave (I actually did get high on opium) and high I spoke to Baudelaire and he begged for a woman, and: "If not a woman, a cat, please!/ A cat that will sit on my bones/ and with paws on my jawbone/ stare eternally into my eyeless pits!" The opium had made me ill. My sight became senseless. I created sound, and what frightened me most was I heard the tombstones whisper to one another: "An overdose, he's taken an overdose. . .." Suddenly I became terribly afraid of trees, I thought they wanted to eat me. I saw Archie MacLeish before me sitting in a huge leather wheelchair, his hands were of stone and on them were carved winged heads of seraphim. I saw a derby on the head of a cigar smoking fish. I ran to Dosty and told him: "How happy I would be if I were born, suddenly born, perhaps in some magical glen in Scotland! How good it would be to grow up among heather and gentle sheep! To drink pure sweet milk! And sleep and dream on the green hills of Scottish Kings!" etc. etc. etc., the damn poem is endless, the idea is endless, I employ everything into it! Carolyn Hiller is in Europe she came upon me while I was being sad writing my sadness song but she too was sad and she spoke and I listened and when she left I wrote down in my sadness song what she sang. It's terrible, but pure. I got a letter from Ferl asking for more poems and saying that you was famous and that he sent me twenty five *Howls* that I didn't get, and I added his letter to my sadness song, and today Peter's letter. Life goes on. How fortunate you both are to be friends and traveling. I am miserable where I am, but at least I am working. Genet is so fucking bourgeois phony pugilistic-face poet. Pomerand, the man who gave me place to stay, came back from his vacation and screamed at me when he saw that I did beautiful oil paintings on his walls and doors. He ran to his buddy Genet and cursed me to him! Genet shook his head and looked badly upon me as though I were some evil person. I told him I wanted to talk to him as a poet not as a Frenchman, these fucking French are always putting down Americans, all Genet ever says to me is, "I don't like Americans, why don't you speak French, you Americans are . . . ," and on and on and on until I told him I look upon him as poet as universal what is this bullshit about nationalities, and condemnation, and why the fuck don't you wake up? You French are decadent, aye, even you. Well I told him something to that effect, but I doubt if he understood he doesn't understand much English, and I don't like him, and I told him about a great poem called *Howl* and have *Evergreen Review* for him when I see him, but right now I don't see anybody.

Carolyn's father died so she is here to live and get work or something. Met John Ashbery, via introduction, and said hardly nothing. I have great fears that I'm going to be stuck in Europe and freeze. I wish I was in Italy, I wish I was going to Istanbul. Be happy, and write to me, I need your word.

Love, Gregory

To Lawrence Ferlinghetti

Paris
Sept. 7, 1957

Larry,

Here is all, I give you everything, the poems with ink x on lower left corner of poems are what I consider my best, this is all, I can do no more, I hope we have a nice book, been up all night doing this, am beat but got to get Gare du Nord train to Amsterdam now, please show Don Allen *Botticelli's Spring*.

All poems you don't use please mail back because I ain't got copies of many. I want to change dedication, will send it in this week to you. Really hope you like these.

Love, Gregory

To Don Allen

Paris
Sept. 7, 1957

Dear Don,

Because of some screw up with mail in Paris, mail sent to Barcelona instead, I got your good letter late. Today I am off to Amsterdam for winter and will sadly miss Allen who comes to Paris this week. I also with the mailing of this letter mail to Ferlinghetti rest of poems for his publication. Look at them and if you like select, but I think you took what I feel to be my best poems, especially *This Was My Meal. Two Poets on Highway*, good, and I didn't know *Coastlines*[76] had it. They want more [*Evergreen Review*] number two in Paris but ain't getting it. I gave number two to Ed Grusken head CBS TV man here in Paris and he loved *Howl* so much that he read it aloud weeping to his entire square office. He wants to get in touch with you on *Seven Lively Arts Program*, he's very sad gentle lost man, wanted to be poet but had to make money, he says. He is truly sad, so maybe you could work something out with him, he'll speak to Ginsberg when he arrives. He also liked Whalen's poetry, but didn't think too much of rest, especially Rexroth (who he felt to be so contrary-*howl*) but none the less said was first literary magazine that he wasn't dulled by, whatever that means.

I sent some poems to *Botteghe Oscure*, that I am enclosing in mail for Ferlinghetti which they may use: *But I Do Not Need Kindness* (I wish you could use that because I actually wept writing it), *Vision Of Death, A Madness Song, On The Walls Of A Dull Furnished Room.* They might well reject them, I don't know. But I certainly feel *A Madness Song* and *But I Do Not Need Kindness* should be considered by you. I'm having so much difficulty with Ferl because he wants more poems and I have them but I'm not too happy with some, well, when I get to Amsterdam tomorrow I'll forget everything and ready myself for a Dutch winter of stiff white sheets, good clean food, empty after ten o'clock snowy canal streets, and perhaps a gentle Dutch girl who will marry me and in her fiftieth year chase me around the house with a big fat Dutch spoon screaming: "You lazy good for nothing!"

Here are some biographical facts: "Born by young Italian parents, father 17 mother 16, born in New York City Greenwich Village, 190 Bleecker, mother year after me left not-to-bright-father and went back to Italy, thus I entered life of orphanage and four foster parents and at 11 father remarried and took me back but all was wrong because two years later I ran away and caught sent away to boys home for two years and let out and went back home and ran away again and sent to Bellevue[77] for observation where I spent three frightening sad months with mad old men who peed in other sad old men's mouths, and left and went back home and knew more than father and stepmother did about woe and plight of man at age of 13 so ran away again and for good and did something really big wrong and was sent to prison for three years at age of 17, from 13 to 17 I lived with Irish on 99th and Lexington, with Italians on 105th and 3rd, with two runaway Texans on 43rd, etc. until 17th year when did steal and get three years in Clinton Prison where an old man handed me [*The Brothers*] *Karamazov*, *Les Miserables*, *Red and Black*, and thus I learned, and was free to think and feel and write, because when I wanted to write before, when I used to tell my father that I want very much to write, he used to say, a poet-writer ain't got no place in this world. But prison was different, the poet-writer had a place, before prison only went to sixth grade. Came out of prison loving my fellow man because all the men I met there were proud and sad and beautiful and lost, lost. I must also say that the most cruel thing that did happen to me in my youth was when I was twelve at the boys home, I went there because I stole a radio and sold it to a dealer and the dealer was taken to court and I had to appear as witness so they took me from good boys home to TOMBS[78] at the age of twelve! For five months I stayed there, no air, no milk, and the majority were black and they hated the white and they abused me terribly, and I was indeed like an angel then because when they stole my food and beat me up and threw pee in my cell, I, the next day would come out and tell them my beautiful dream about a floating girl who landed before a deep pit and just stared.

I say this to you because I think it is the first time I have ever felt the horror of that twelve year old Gregory. I want to fight it now, I couldn't then, because I was true then, somehow, along the way, I lost that Gregory.

Came out twenty well read and in love with Chatterton and Marlowe and Shelley, went home stayed two days left family forever, but returned at night to beg their forgiveness and retrieve my stamp collection. Lived in Village with kind girl until 1952 when I went to Los Angeles and got, by fluke, good job *Los Angeles Examiner*, cub reporting once a week, rest of week working in morgue, left seven months later to ship out on Norwegian line to South America and Africa and did. Lived in Village until 1954 when beautiful now dead Violet Lang saved me and brought me to Harvard where I wrote and wrote and met beautiful people for the first time in my life. Had *Vestal Lady* published there by contributions from fifty or more students from Radcliffe and Harvard, *Harvard Advocate* first to publish me, then many times *i.e.; The Cambridge Review*, then went to S.F. and saw Allen and Ferl and Ferl asked to publish a book of mine, *Gasoline,* and since then been published in *Mademoiselle, Needle, Combustion*, you say *Coastlines*, and *Measure*, and now you. While in Frisco kind Jarrell liked me and asked me to go to Washington to live with him and I did, but left for Paris where I am now and am about to leave for Amsterdam." Finis.

Re-reading this I am almost ashamed but I'm sure you'll pick out something for fact, and I don't know what fact is, so I give you all. Besides I'm feeling terribly sad tonight, and am feeling better now that someone gave me chance to bring up past.

Love, Gregory

And thank you for seeing *Amnesia*, Ferl didn't, much to my sorrow. You see, *Amnesia*, is the only poem I have respect for because I am indeed truly ignorant when it comes to discipline, and if anything, *Amnesia* is a disciplined poem. Paris has good jazz, Lucky Thompson, Kenny Clarke, J.J. Johnson. God knows what Amsterdam will have.

To Allen Ginsberg and Alan Ansen

Amsterdam
[ca. Sept. 8] 1957

Beautiful city. Dutch poets mad. Simon Vinkenoog, young, hip, knows many American poets, poet and editor of Dutch *Podium*. Will publish me, you and anybody. Will set up reading for you if you come.

Love, Gregory

If not Jarrell, I'd be honored to have you do intro. I sent manuscript—all—to Ferl.

To Allen Ginsberg

Amsterdam
[ca. Sept. 9] 1957

Who are my friends, Allen, do I have any, Allen, you, perhaps you may not know this but you are the oldest friend, yes, seven years now, strange, but I feel I have no friend, although I can weep to you, make funny, make novelty and get away, but who, Allen, are my friends, tell me the truth? I haven't any. An Ansen won't see me after a 1951 Gregory mistake in behavior. A Burroughs thinks of me then too, how sad for me who when he walks alone in the street feels beautiful and understanding, these men don't see it. A Peter? Perhaps, but always when confronted with a Peter I act bad mean stupid because they are like me and I hate me because I know better men than me, and that is bad.

Gregory

To Allen Ginsberg

Amsterdam
[Sept. 11] 1957

Dear Allen,

Amsterdam is great and met some famous writers here and editors of literary *Podium* and they will publish me, Simon Vinkenoog very intelligent Dutch cat, knew Pollock, Robert Lowell, [James] Merrill, etc. when they was in Holland. Do come here. The most beautiful city I have ever seen, and young things are happening here.

I sent Ferl manuscript with huge mad letter saying I don't mind *Power* and *Way Out* being omitted, and I don't, but when it comes to some of my other poems. I hope he selects correctly, that's all I can hope for. If not Jarrell I would be honored to have you do intro for me. In fact do one and send it into Ferl and let him choose as he seems to be choosing everything. I got back all my old lost mail and in it Jarrell said nothing but [sent] 100 dollars.

Did I tell you that Don Allen accepted some of my poems? *Amnesia In*

Memphis, In Ran Moonlight, Two Poets On Highway, he asked for biographical notes and I had a ball writing him two full pages about how I was born and am now in Amsterdam.

Yes, write intro, you know most poems, so write it without seeing manuscript, Ferl has all my poems, I have nothing here. Its up to you. Told lot of literary folk here about new American poetry *Howl* in particular and they want very much to SEE, get Ferl to England me some, maybe he sent some to Paris and they will forward here, so far received none. Wiener's *Measure* very good. Guy wants all I write, says I could use his mag as outlet for automaticism.

I must steal to eat live so I cashed some phony checks on Paris black market, hope I ain't caught. My poor life is so fucked up, what's the meaning of it all? I don't yet know, when I do find out I fear it'll be too late.

Gregory

Just got your card—bring Caresse Crosby up to Amsterdam where all is beautiful—I SHAN'T RETURN TO GARGOYLE CITY.

To Allen Ginsberg Amsterdam
[Sept. 12] 1957

Just received twenty five *Howls*, I will distribute them here, lots of hip people interested. *Podium* will review it. Really sorry about not Verlaining with you in Paris, I do miss you very much, but I just had to get out of Paris, for many reasons. Holland is not far away, only 3,000 francs by train. I have nice room with steam heat—you and Peter can stay there with me. Yes, seems Ferl doesn't want Jarrell—so please do intro for me. I'll tell Ferl I want you to do it. When in Paris go to Ed Grusken, head of CBS TV in Paris, at 33 Champs-Elysées, and speak to him about proposed *Seven Lively Arts* program—33 million viewers! You can say what you want. Also tell him to please mail me my manuscript.

Love, Gregory

To Allen Ginsberg Amsterdam
[Sept. 13] 1957

Dear Allen,

Simon Vinkenoog gave me bookstores in which to distribute *Howls*. He's great guy. Has two books published and four books of verse published and has translated Artaud in Dutch and has contributed to *Paris Review* and *Hudson* and *Poetry* and *Botteghe Oscure*. I gave him *Howl* (and I hope it's all right with you) gave him permission to reprint any poem he likes for next issue of *Podium*, very nice looking magazine and very known read in Belgium and Holland. They will also review *Howl*. Much more is happening here English poetry wise than in Paris. Everyone here speaks English, and publishers here want English verse. I go to see one today, he wants to interview me about American poetry, too bad you couldn't be here to do that, I ain't so good at such things. Name of interviewer is Jan Vermeulen, editor of *Litterair Paspoort*, polylingual mag that publishes articles by Hemingway, Brecht, Hesse, Picasso, Sagan, Prévert, Eliot, Stevens.

Love, Gregory

To Allen Ginsberg

Amsterdam
[Sept. 14] 1957

Dear Allen,

Received letter with "reciting in earthen voice" poem, liked it very much. I have been commissioned here by biggest publishing house, to write article about American poets in their 5,000 circ. sold in England, France, Germany and here, magazine *Litterair Paspoort.* I'll need photo of you and Kerouac, I wrote Ferl for one of himself and Whalen. That's all poets I will write about for I am only allotted two pages. Also they will review *Howl*, too bad my damn *Gasoline* ain't out because they'd do that too. I distributed *Howl* to three stores here. People here dig English lit. much more than I can say for France. As if all big poets and writers and publishers here have seen *Howl.* So when you come all is opened to you. Been rereading your poems and saw very much beauty in Greyhound poem.[79] Excellent genius poem. A pig with a beard is wont to be sneered. This poem for you and Auden and his table of fairies. All in deathy fooly fun:

> "Now that you are famous / by sweet music / in defense of the anus / have you but considered / the plight of the cunty dick? / For altho poets confess to sodomy / while howling their friends lobotomy / they hardly ever rarely never / their own vicious dicks dissever / Auden, for example, Auden / a 100 lire a dick a day / when he him ownself / unable an anus to spray / and Burroughs with dick morose / erects but his eyes / when an unnamable cock / outdoes another's size / Why the cock for these men, then? / Surely Auden's cock can never rise again / but alas he can't well amputate it / nor surely in a rage masturbate it. / So why that swinging dead seamen's knell? / Does it await some future dongless belle? / No, No, then why is it there / just useless hanging / like a dead thing caught in a snare? / I pray the Gods there be / exuberate their cocks toward liberty! / And Kallman,[80] Te Deum La Damus, O thou gland of anus! is his ass so fine? say finer than a swine, or thine, or mine? / Dead cock no attraction for woman contraption /

> Poor dead cocks of the world! / Poor dead cocks!? What dreams have they but the sorry comes in dirty socks / or the wheezy spurts that trickle like poker dots / upon some young boys goldy locks / O weep for the dead cocks of the world / Because men that were men became girled / because they into excited hands are hurled / and useless, useless when their feeble cocks rise slightly curled / But of course there are dead assholes, too. And one should weep for them in lieu / but not me because I'd rather you do / you of the dead cock and me of the dead ass / Tell me, for instance: "Your ass is dead to the feel of grass" / and I'll say: "Your cock is as sensitive as a rock" / etc. etc.

But I wonder, can a dead cock get up?/Or a dead asshole erupt?/Or a dead cock Lazarus? or a dead asshole Erasmus? No! NO! Useless! Useless! "the dead cock forever dies, / and the dead asshole is a rusty vise."

Now there's a automatic poem especially for you. Send photo, but no information on as how I should write article, I know very well what I want to say. ALL ME ME ME and a little of you and Whalen and Kerouac and Ferl. Peter will love Amsterdam, I am sure.

Love, Gregory

To Don Allen Amsterdam

[Sept. 15] 1957

Dear Don,

Have met some very interesting Dutch poets, they write in both Dutch and English. Most are terribly influenced by E. E. Cummings. Aside from that, I found the poems to be quite good. If you care to see their work, I'll gather what I can for you.

Love, Gregory

To Allen Ginsberg Amsterdam

[Sept. 16] 1957

Dear Allen,

Please do your damnedest to get me intelligent exact information on where why and who St. Christopher. I think I hit on something that might shatter all Christianity, please, I am doing my best, spending hours and hours at it, don't get any sleep, forsaking poetry, everything, until I get this thing solved. I've got to know about St. Christopher! Theodoricus[81], famous great 14th century painter of St. Christopher gave me lead, had vision, just like Theodoricus painting, angel came to my ear and said: "Find out about St. Christopher, employ agents, researcher, but find out. . ."

No Catholic priests here. Go up to one in France and ask him about St. Christopher. PLEASE.

Love, Gregory

To Peter Orlovsky

Amsterdam
[Sept. 16] 1957

Pray, my good friend, did you ever form any opinion, or, rather, did it ever happen to you to meet with any rational opinion or conjecture of others, upon that most revolting dogma of Pythagoras about beans? Czech painters are suddenly becoming famous! Theodoricus great Bohemian painter of 14th century. Keats said in his epistle to J.H. Reynolds: "Two witch's eyes above a cherub's mouth." Jarrell said in his *The See-er Of Cities*: "Tears are the only object of these eyes." Of course nobody says a Goddam thing about Pythagoras's beans!

Look up Theodoricus!!! Magista Theodoricus is a discovery for me! As great a painter as Masaccio and Giotto! Please get information for me on story of St. Christopher. I don't know anything about him. Theodoricus, wild mad painter of 14th Century does mad St. John Baptists!!! I need info on St. Christopher, get it for me!

To Peter Orlovsky

Amsterdam
[Sept. 16] 1957

Dear Peter,

Just had long poem *Requiem for an American Dreamer* accepted by Dutch magazine—they pay. In fact all Dutch publications pay. I will also get 150 gulden for two-page article on American poets. So Holland is good for me and I am very happy here, busy working on wild: *Communion With The Magnificent Dutch Dead.*

> September 1957 summoned by my vision / agent, via ventriloquial / telegram / delivered by the dumb mouths / stoned on Notre Dame / given golden fare and a 17th century / diagram / and left the gargoyle city / and, with 2 suitcases of despair—/ arrived in Amsterdam.

Everybody gentle here. Hope I can induce you and Allen to come and visit here. I have nice heated room—one bed, but huge carpet!

Love, Gregory

I don't know a damned thing about St. Christopher.

▼ [As work proceeded on City Lights' publication of *Gasoline,* Corso began a lengthy correspondence outlining changes, second thoughts, and self doubts about words, poems, and titles. This pattern would be repeated in the future with each new book.

Often the revision process would involve months or years of work even after he had given the manuscript to his publisher.]

To Lawrence Ferlinghetti Amsterdam
[late Sept.] 1957

Dear Larry,

Your selections all right, but *Mad Yak* must be substituted for weak poem *Bird Leash,* also I send you some better poems to substitute for: *For Miles, Favorite Doll, Who?, There Was A Girl Who Picked Flowers*, these poems are not really great, but the ones I send you today are. So please, for me, and for atonement for not using my *How Happy I Used To Be, H.G. Wells, Two Poets On Highway*, use the poems I sent. Allen's intro is great. I hope not too long, even so, use it all even if it means 54 pages, I'd hate to see any other poems excluded, but if some exclusion is necessary take out reluctantly: *H, To H. S., Written Sept 18, 1956.* I hope you like the way I fixed up *Paris* poem, you were right, and I feel poem is better now. Also please put at end of my automatic *Sun* poem this verse: "O constant hole where all beyond is true Byzantium."

Happy about Nathan doing cover, hope it ain't too arty, . . . I have made list of poems in chronological order. Dedication finished. I am sending it in with intro and poems. Finally the fucking thing is coming out, now I can go on to my great long poem about how to bring back the dead. I must hurry and do it. This *Gasoline* has side tracked me for year, I haven't much time, forces of batterical wolves sulk thru the deathical electronic eyes of the Siberian Tiger, hope I don't die, love, Gregory. Nice face of you in *Life*, grim, tense, certain, true un-American. Imagine, all the blonde children of Iowa have seen your face, the same face Du Peru hath seen! Love, Gregory

I also feel that *This Is Sadness Song* ain't really perfected, so leave that out, if you want, instead of *Who?* or leave both out. Now on the back cover for the biographical data use this: "He is at present at work on a mammoth poem about how to bring the dead back to life. Anybody willing to help support him please send money to publisher, in return he will send you drawings of little ghouls."

Love, G

To Lawrence Ferlinghetti Paris?
[mid-Oct.] 1957

To use as epigraph on title page: "Gaming tables where the games are played for incredible stakes. From time to time a player leaps up with a despairing inhuman cry, having lost his youth to an old man or become Latah to his opponent. But there are higher stakes than youth or Latah. Games where only two players in the world know what the stakes are."—William Seward Burroughs (*Naked Lunch*). Use this definitely, omit mine, I want serious book! Larry: Latah, above, is spelt Latah. South Asian robot disease.

I sent you this month ago from Amsterdam, with, I think two poems, one called *Zizi's Lament* and *I Lebanon*, did you get them? Hope you did because they were good poems. Also you mention nothing about using photo, I think it would be nice to have photo, don't you? But I don't want to bug you, yes, you are a poet, I told you that long time ago, in S.F. and five months ago in long letter, yet you seem or at least you indicate that I don't think so. I realize that you are busy, thus why don't you get workers? You're starting a publishing business on large scale, I mean with novels and everything; sounds great. Maybe if it gets big you can give me job as manuscript reader. I got pretty good taste, can tell the crap from the good, the good from the great; you mean to say you really got 100 manuscript? Do you read them all? What are they like? Any big names?

Red and white cover is just what I wanted. 1000 copies, of which I get 100, what about sending out to reviewers, does it come outa my 100? or, like Allen says, do we go half half? Anyway I will send you list that you can give to your secretary to deal with, must send books from USA, I would send them out but—What do you think of book, you never really said; are you happy with it? I am, I think we got perfect book there, and I'm very happy that it all worked out, you did a good job of deleting (except for *H.G. Wells*) so if you like you can put "Edited by LF" on title page, were it not for you, *Paris* poem would have gone unchanged, and also I'm glad you sent back the poems I asked you to . . . I have been working very hard on *Power*, you feel it to be fascist, I do not know what fascist means and I believe it to be appropriate semantic word. What I MEAN by *Power*, is Spengler's warning and advice that poets give up the pen and take to the slide rule, by *Power* the poet can achieve and conceive and answer just as well as the scientist, what *Power* really says is: What is conceivable is answerable. In truth I don't like writing this kind of poem, that's why I don't think I can ever be satisfied with *Power*, but I must finish it and get it out of my system. You must remember that my *Power* has proven itself prophetic wise, when I read it in 1956, I said we should have our children roam the stars by 1957, let me be your wise Buck Rodgers. Screw your trip to Paris, there's the moon! Now ICBM Sputnik. My plan is to write in *Power* what Einstein wrote in Relativity, he believed light bended, he believed man can go the speed of light, Gregory believes man can go the speed of Time. *Power* will prove me right.

I am thinking if you got all the poems I sent you in Amsterdam, I might of had Burroughs' quote in that batch. I sent you long poem about Rose, another called *Ecce Homo*, another called *No Word*, etc. Did you get them?

Great about New Directions coming out with your poems, what I do believe about your poems is that they are too conversational for me, but that's all right, beneath your conversation there is always the disruption of intent, that intent being the lava of your poem. I got burned by such lines as "And the Arabs asked terrible questions" "looking down at tranced fish" "silence hung like a lost idea" "through all the burnt places of that almond world" anyway I'd like to read more of your work, haven't really seen much, you know. Send some new ones, starved for reading.

No, I want no *Howls*, the twenty five you sent me I gave to Allen, he says to take that off his royalties, he's got them, thus all I owe you is five dollars right? or do I owe you more? As for contract, good God.

Love, Gregory

To John Wieners

Paris
[Oct. 17] 1957

Dear John,

After Allen told me all about you and what you desire and heights you reach and touch then I definitely want to give you my best poems for that platform you must touch to reach and you will, so soon I send you my: *How To Bring The Dead Back To Life*, a long mad golden snow poem about werewolf hairs from all the Transylvanian bathtubs, and half eaten cookies of sorcerers, etc. I intend it to be long long poem, maybe you could print work in progress in installments, poem not all quack, little pure science in it too.

Love Gregory

To Don Allen

Paris
[late Oct.] 1957

Dear Don,

Both Allen and Peter sick and bearded in bed with flu but not serious. Paris very beautiful to me now. Met charming young girl who likes me, she being 17 and intelligent and sexual and rich and sad. Am working very hard on my *Power* poem for you and also some others. If you have extra #2 *Evergreen* [*Review*] send them as bookstores have sold out and want more, I will distribute here for you. Spoke to Rossett about it—said he would send 100. Allen and I were promised big window displays of *Howl* and *Gasoline* and *Evergreen* by four stores here—so send. Hope you are well.

Love, Gregory

To Lawrence Ferlinghetti Paris

Oct. 29, 1957

Dear Larry,

Am back in Paris and am in love with it becuz Fall and no tourists and one beautiful 17 year old bodily blonde Champs-Elysées much Francs girl is in love with me and me with her and I eat well and have new typewriter and rent paid and all I want (I think). Anyway Allen and Peter were down with flu and they being broke I helped. Yes, let it be said that Gregory hath come to Ginsberg's aid! But ain't heard from you yet as to whether or not you got my poems and Allen's intro??? Allen going to meet Beckett. And my photo, the sad one; did you get it??? Yes, Paris is beautiful when it is Paris and not vacationing ivy-league. If you do Jack's *Blues*, and you should, then let me do intro; ask Jack, I'm sure he'll agree to it. I understand Jack's poesy very well.

How did you like New York? Write soon sooon sooooooon.

My *How To Bring The Dead Back To Life* going on to 867th verse! Didn't get your photo and poems and Whalen's yet!!! Why must you send things regular mail!!! Too late; article done and sent in and due this November, but I mention lots of you and say who and what you do and what you are seeking in life and that you are friendly and sell books as well as write them and that you are married but have no child and that you live on the third floor.

Love, Gregory

To John Wieners Paris

[ca. Nov.] 1957

Dear John,

Here's first supplement [of *Death* poem]. It's my best work to date aye to forever! If you can use this in place of *Way Out* do, *Way Out* is nowhere really, what I have done in this poem needs explanation; the form and idea don't, but the discovery; the discovery does. But maybe it's best I don't explain because if I explain then I'll have to explain my explanation. Yes the poem is that fucked up, all twelve pages; and I got forty more! And I'll do ten thousand more! Somebody's got to cure death. If I don't do it; who will? I think you understand, John, so I'm going to take you in as a partner, all you have to do tell your readers that before they read the poem they must, in order to bring back their loved ones, promise to read every word and promise not to yawn or put the poem down; for if they do then their loved ones will stay in death forever. The reason I want you to do this is because I need lots of believers, so far I only have Ginsberg and you; and Ginsberg isn't too certain about his belief either, so you see it is quite imperative that you get me some. Ah wait John, you'll see, by aiding me in this; when all is over, I will recommend you in the awking annals of Foolery.

Hail to our new partnership!

Love; Gregory

To Philip Whalen Paris
[ca. Nov.] 1957

Dear beautiful Whalen,

Should and wanted to write you long long ago but have been dazed by the inadequacies of living and death, and now I write . . . I've been writing a lot, and have come to new realization that my verse is ready for a medal of honor, meaning, not a complete overall in dress, but a tag of illumination, that is extending sound in consonants, not vowels, spreading lines over page like Mondrian painting, simplifying basic obscurities, crew-cutting my hairy images, breaking and shortening lines with use of "ic" and "ical" i.e.: rain, rainic, death, deathical etc. etc., thus blossoming forth my consonants into song. Essentially I am a consonant poet, in the past vowels have bugged me and my output because I knew not the music of i-e-o-u-a . . . The use of consonants can be rude, but I feel that I have lessened the rudeness by applying a discorded structure to each line . . . examples of some will be in *Gasoline* due before Xmas. I wrote nice thing about you in English for big *Saturday Review of Literature* of Holland called *Litterair Paspoort*, will send you copy when it comes out. When is Ferl going to come out with your book, damnit, what with *Howl*, *Gasoline*, Jack's *Mexico City Blues*, and your *Slop Barrel* (you should title book that). City Lights would be greatest poetry publishers in USA, Allen and me must get on Ferl's ass about that. Do send something to *Partisan Review*, they are wide open now . . . They took two wild unthinkable poems from me.

Allen hard at work on Mother poem [*Kaddish*], so far it's great, but he has habit of not typing his poem, therefore how can he see? I try to get after him to type it out so that he can SEE the poem, a poem must be seen not only read aloud. There's no end to Allen, wonder what after his Mother Elegy poem? He alone gives me sight in the future of American poetry, the transition from Whitman to Williams and Pound to Ginsberg Whalen Corso Kerouac is over. By 1960 America will know her poets. I have just found this out, I feel that you have always known it, your lack of ambition should have told me, you know.

Now, aside from verse, what you doing, and why, and can you get out of it, or do you want to stay, or are they conspiring against you, or will that unrecognizable girlface coming down the long street present marriage to you, will you accept, what about your life, will you abandon all? I wonder the same. Is India a wise idea, can I accept my own personal poverty? Me, I will enrichen my face with perfumed soaps, adorn my body with fabulous garments, I will not gnarl myself in India to please my addicted poverty, I will come back to America, but not right now, ain't got the money to, anyway . . .

Let's see what can you do for me . . . yes, you can send me some new poems. Here some random lines from my verses:

> "And the orange Stella cap filled the dunce of Florida in my image standing on the highstool of highschool where he dreamed the owl's galaxy cap / On the steps of the bright madhouse I hear the beared bell shaking down the woodlawn / the final knell of my world / I leave, and enter a firey gathering of Knights / and they with mailcoated fingers trace sheepskin plans / and mark my arrival," etc. etc.

Can't remember rest, but this is from long poem *Partisan* accepted. I am at Allen's and don't have my poetry here, and I can never for the life of me remember any of my verse, why is that? Am I the stupidest poet that ever lived? Anyway, *Gasoline* will be out soon, and you'll be able to read my new work, I doubt if you read any of the poems in it, most of them were done in Mexico, Washington, NY and Paris. Write to me, I must get to bed, feel like Flu.

Love, Gregory

To Lawrence Ferlinghetti

Paris
Dec. 25, 1957

Dear Larry,

When I got the proofs I felt both good and sad, good because there are some very good poems in book, and sad because there aren't any poems that bespeak my dream my idea my lyric, God knows what, but I definitely feel the book lacks the dessert of my poetry. I had it in *H.G. Wells* in *How Happy I Used To Be* and in *Power*, all that I had in those poems are in those poems and not in book. All right, I can easily solve that, I send you three definitely good poems, I send you news also that I am very unhappy about *Poem On Death Again* and *H* and *Dream* and *Written Sept 18 1956*, that makes four bad poems. They are no good Larry, and matching them against the poems I now send you I'm sure you'll agree. Yes, it will cost money to boot them out, all right, I send you twenty dollars, it's all I have, I'd give you a hundred dollars just to have *Gasoline* perfect; being that it took so long, let it take a little longer, but let's have great book. All my short poems say almost the same thing. I love the poems, but where's my real poetry, my mad great poetry? I am at fault, I've always had it, but I had it in bad form or incomplete form, well these poems I send you, now that you have two pages free, and that those bad for meaningless poems will be taken out, will find room I'm sure. Also, instead of putting poems in chronological order, put them in any order you see fit, try to get as much room as possible, many of the short poems can go two on a page, also, the *Downfallen Rose* poem should not precede the *Sun* poem because they seem repetitious together. I honestly feel *Gasoline* will be a better book if you follow these pleas of mine. Today's Xmas, it's breaking my heart to send you the twenty bucks, I sure could use it, but I want to show good faith, and concern not only for book but for you, and for myself, for surely they are going to pan me badly. I know, these poems I send you and the poems in book can withstand any putdown. I wrote to *Esquire* and *Partisan* [*Review*] for permission to use, so give credit to them *Esquire* for *Ode To Coit Tower*, *Partisan* for *In Fleeting Hand Of Time*, and also *Evergreen* for *Amnesia In Memphis* and *This Was My Meal*, I guess you can put credits on library catalogue page.

As for titles, don't you prefer the smaller print better? I do. But that's not so important. I don't wish to bug you with such detail. Got William Carlos Williams' *Kora* [*in Hell*], his cover is the cover I thought I'd have, what color will I have? How's about purple? I hope my corrections on proofs don't screw things up too much. If it cost more to do all changes I ask let me know and I will comply. *Vestal Lady* fucked up. I'd hate to see this go the same way. I send you typed script for *Italian Extravaganza* linotype sure screwed up on that. Boy what with Ginsberg's last line in intro and Kerouac's praise I feel I got a lot to stand up to and prove somehow, anyway, even if they are right, I'm still my old same modest self. Of course smaller titles make bigger room to put two small poems on same page. Yes today Xmas I go to Notre Dame and maybe hear jingle bells, let me know as soon as you get this, don't keep me waiting, please, and when do you think book will finally get out? I mean this is the most I have to do with book, it's all up to you now, *Ode To Coit Tower* as you can see is very inspired poem. God, but I always hated *Dream* and *Poem On Death Again* and *H* and *Written 1956*, they are such bad writings, I didn't realize I sent them to you, you asked for everything, and remember I was bugged when I sent them to you, I didn't care then, but I do care now, I live my life for poetry, and I'm willing to die for it, therefore I deserve only to have good poems published. Them fucking traditionalists ain't gonna die for poetry so let them publish bad poems.

Anyway had a nice Xmas party at George Whitman's, he made Scotch and ice cream and doughnuts and had songs, very nice guy.

Let me know your real personal feelings about *Coit Tower*, I feel it to be one of the best poems I ever wrote, really inspired lines like: "sparks issued from a wild sharper's wheel / in that infinitive solitude where illusion spoke Truth's divine dialect / like the dim lights of some hallucinating facade" etc. and what enlightenment when I ended it with "Swindleresque Ink," I wrote swindleresque ink in Frisco depicting some of the phony verse abounding there, ala, Harmon, Stock and clique, but never knew where to put it, well it's found it's bed . . . therefore I had Allen cut out quote from intro, also I took out send money to publisher because it doesn't dignify book in that it lessens seriousness of both publisher and poet, (?) anyway I'd like it out. Well, Larry, that's it, I send you back everything. I am alone. I leave it all to you, I am happy now, I send you my heart's joy and love, if you can't find room for all poems I send you, then leave out *Rotterdam*, although I'm sure you'll have sufficient room now that those four bad poems go out, and some of the short ones go together on same page. Yes, now book will have truth. Thank you Larry, and my love for you and wife for New Year that will bring both illumination and grand visions.

Ever faithful and obedient I am, Gregory Corso
Write right away, I'm anxious.

To Don Allen Paris
[Dec. 28] 1957

Dear Don,

Merry Xmas, at two o'clock Xmas Eve Notre Dame choir I finished wine-drunk and amassed with clouds, my *Power*. I will type it now, and send it. God, I've been working one whole year on it! Allen fine—he's writing poem about his mother's death—very beautiful so far. Now that I'm done with *Power*, I'm going to learn French because I want to read Laforgue.

Be well, Gregory

To Allen Ginsberg and Peter Orlovsky Frankfurt, West Germany
Jan. 8, 1958

Dear Allen and Peter,

Got off in Frankfurt, was met by three very business like German efficiency business men of the Colliers Encyclopedia Corp.!!! They immediately would me to sign papers, all kinds of questions, so that I could fill out German Tax forms, U.S. Army permission forms (four of them!), also photo, life history, etc.). I said to them: "Wait, now, gentlemen, I don't mean to slacken things, but I sure would like to know where all the museums are." They looked at each other with eyes that said: "He'll not be a good Colliers Encyclopedia salesman." I couldn't agree more. Anyway, I tried. That night they drove me to Gibbs (an Army unit) I went with kit (filled with Colliers propaganda) and tried my luck. The first soldiers I spoke to got me so confused and unhappy that I couldn't speak, say nothing of selling. That night I met more stupid people than I ever have since leaving America. But I have strength, so next day I went out to sign papers.

Well, that's today, and guess what happened? I filled out the German Tax form, then went to U.S. Army H.Q. and there had to fill out four forms. In office of six personal staff, two Colliers bosses, and clerk—I said upon receiving first form: "No! I shan't sign my name on such!" They, the bosses, said "What?" I said: "Gentlemen, you may not understand this but I shall say it nonetheless—I am a poet. I detest you people. You almost caught me. I was almost not a poet but a Colliers representative." I had your *Howl* with me, "Here, read this and see what I mean." One of the bosses held it in his hand. Looked at his friend, then at me, then handed book back to me, realizing full well that I was insane and could never be a good Colliers representative. I walked out singing.

Now I am happy. No cares in the world. All is museum before me. Two days I tried the real world, I tried. I laughed. I cried. But just don't fit. I will never fit.

Love, Gregory

Ferl wants me to take out "Miller, poet in residence." I said no, because it's there to bring down so as to rise when Swindleresque ink comes up. He likes poem. Good. I will look up guy in Frankfurt. Need funds somehow. Yes, send my mail to Frankfurt—good—was happy to hear from you both today. No Joy[82]? Please tell her all. Say I will be back, that I had to go—that—that—that –

All these Germans do is work work work work. Get to Prévert for him. Somebody in hotel I'm staying stole my electric razor. Graham [a man who also lived in the Beat Hotel] is fine, but guess I'll leave him soon. Keep writing to me, as all is love. I do hope something beautiful happens here. Oh, don't give up on me just because I couldn't sell a fucking encyclopedia—I just ain't that sort of person. Red pencil *Power* for me. How was Don Juan? Besides, them encyclopedias are terribly corny. Books for idiots. I ain't gonna sell no idiot books to no one, not me, I ain't.

Love, and I do miss my two dear friends, Gregory

To Lawrence Ferlinghetti Frankfurt, West Germany
ca. Jan. 8, 1958

Dear Larry,

Am in Frankfurt for awhile—came trying to sell Encyclopedias to soldiers. First day I had to go with boss encyclopedia men, very business-like, German efficiency men, who when they saw me, their future encyclopedia man, almost went insane. They took me to Army P.O.H.Q.—and gave me a form to fill out—I refused. I told them I wouldn't dare sign my name to a paper that gives me right to sell encyclopedias to dumb soldiers. And are they dumb! I almost wept! First night I went with experienced salesman, I was told to follow his pitch. I couldn't believe my ears! How stupid they both sounded! I realized then that I could not sell encyclopedias. If I were to, and I tried, I'd speak about universal gnaws, electric poisons, ominous weeds, etc.—So I quit—right there in the military command with the two bosses, two brass, and a secretary—I said: "No, I shall never sell myself thus!" They looked at me agog! I continued: "Oh, you bunch almost caught me! Almost got me into the scheme of things—well, you ain't—I quit—I shall not sign this nowhere document!" Well, now I'm in Frankfurt—broke, alone, but happy, because I remain myself.

Glad you like *Coit Tower*, I've been writing like that during last six months—yes, at end of *Coit Tower* I got a little personal conversational—but with reason: Here it is: Tower has a pitch—it goes up—good—but I want it to come down again. Why? Because I seek to build up to orgasm when Hay-like Universe—swindleresque ink—appears. But I agree with you fully—cut it out, O God! what would Allen and Jack say? As you see I still am incapable of judging my own work. Woe! Woe! Woe!

If you can spare maybe some cash, not check, to American Express, Frankfurt—I'd be very happy about safety—because all is lonely and broke for me here. As for Prévert, Allen is working on it. He called up woman agent and will see her. When do you think *Gasoline* will be due? Germans very weird people. Always working. Work work work work work work. What paradox! Here in land of WORK—sit I, and dream.

Okay—I'm confused. Should I let you take out "and even picked up on Mille etc." Or not. Somehow I feel it necessary to keep in. But also out. No. Leave it in. Just decided after five painful minutes. Leave it in. Surely I ain't gonna write as such two years from now—so why not leave in 1957 what was done in 1957?

Write to me right away as I am all alone in Frankfurt. Need to hear from outer world. But I know my mission, I'm a dreamer, and Germany is in need of dreamers. (And not like Adolph either.) Hope all goes well with books and everything.

Love, Gregory

To Allen Ginsberg and Peter Orlovsky Frankfurt, West Germany
ca. Jan. 9, 1958

Dear A and P,

Germans make great cake, I'm always eating some. Met American with Graham who went to Frankfurt with us, a big mid-Western Arthur Murray dance instructor pot head, saxophone player who writes poetry almost akin to mine, though I feel he lacks the "golden [bell], naked child" that is Gregory. Nonetheless his work, especially his "Horse Poem" is very much like my little weird poems. I send you some—tell me what you make of them. He read *Howl* and dug it. A very strange guy. Sometimes very corny, other times great. He has an F.B.I. look about him. Anyway, read what I feel to be some good poetry. He immediately saw the similarity in my work and acknowledges me as a master when I recited him above other's Swindleresque Ink. He's never been published—so if you like, maybe you type and send to Wieners—it would make him very happy.

Ah, Frankfurt is wild! I went to see Morrison's friend—he is a professor and a leading German poet—he has appeared in *Atlantic Monthly*, and has countless books out of his work, mostly anthologies—and greatest of all, he knows you! He was in S.F. last year and bought *Howl* and *Pictures of Gone World* and [Sather] Gate (which he didn't like). He liked your poem very much and he said he writes that way! He good friend to Arp, Böll, and Brecht (before). He gave me twenty marks, and a dinner, and three letters of introduction. One to TV president for a program interview about S.F. scene (that's all they're interested in). So today I go see the guy. Höllerer wrote him that I am in dire need of money, so something will surely happen. He wants very much to meet you. He said you could give reading to Goethe University students. He gave me list and books of all good modern German poets, I will mail them to you soon as I get loot to. . .

Jazz nightclubs plentiful. Rock 'n Roll big thing, here. All young Germans sure dig it. Why don't you come down? Don't or do—like in Amsterdam; I have set ground that when you arrive, a bed and people of importance are at your command—send me all my letters.

Love, Gregory

Did Bill come yet? Did Joy come by? Don't know her address. Give all my love. Höllerer wants to come out with a San Francisco issue in German, not a magazine but a book. Yes, Höllerer told me he wants to bring out a book—he introduced me to a publisher, we had lunch together—they think a "book like that would do good" that's just their attitude—so gather all best S.F. works possible, and give it to Höllerer. He will get someone to translate—he also knows of someone to translate my *Gasoline* your *Howl.*

To Don Allen Venice

[Jan. 1958]

Dear Don,

Here is first part *Bring Back The Dead.* I also include some other poems. Some I did years ago, I am happy that I am sending you all (I have more, but reworked) because I always lose my poems. But now that I'm settled, at least for another month, in Venice, I can make carbons. I make three carbons, one for me, Allen, and you.

As for *Bring Back The Dead*, have three parts done, but parts two and three need much re-work. Intention of poems: By use of word-combinations I hope to revive the dead; as an alchemist, by use of newt etc., hopes to put sun into lead. Thus I really don't expect to revive the dead, but I do expect, with such an idea, come to some crazy formulae and scheme and placing of words. Part 1 is not as wild as part 2 or 3, intentionally, because I expect to graduate; just like the Weber's Magic Bullet, when Kasper calls to the evil forces for seven bullets.[83] Well, is my intention to go to seven parts, and thus have all the combinations of evil made good. I send these slow mail, as my allowance ebbs.

Love, Gregory

To John Wieners

Venice

[late Jan. 1958]

Dear John,

What you didn't seem to dig was that in *How To Bring Back The Dead* I tried my 'measurement of idea'. Did you notice it? Anyway I myself canned the poem, ain't really what I'm striving for, my *Ode To Coit Tower* is more like it, will come out in *Esquire* and *Gasoline*.

Now for business. I'm doing anthology for German publishing house about young American new verse, bi-lingual, and want you and Marshall,[84] so send me your wildest best beautiful etc. etc. and lots of it, also Marshall, get in touch with him, I think he fine poet, here is list of poets I have so far, if you know more, especially ones you dig, tell them to send me their best too: here's list: Whalen, me, Ginsberg, O'Hara, [Kenneth] Koch, Ashbery, Ferlinghetti (if he sends me something wild), Kerouac, Burroughs, Ansen, McClure, Snyder, Creeley, Olson, Dick Howard, Lamantia, Loewinsohn[85]. I am allotted 286 pages, so I guess I'll need more poets, but I don't know of any more, at least any that I dig, if you do, then tell them to send me their best.

I wrote article for Dutch magazine[86] in which I mention you, your poetry, and *Measure*, and said something about O'Hara, Koch and Ashbery that was quite unfair, but nonetheless something that I felt at the time. Now I am completely sorry about it because I was wrong, they are not *New Yorker* poets, the more I read them the more I realize that they are indeed the best young poets, other than Ginsberg, around today. Even better than Kerouac and most of S.F. How about sending me copy of *Measure?* Also *Evergreen 3*, can't get it here. Now send me poems right away, and get in touch with Marshall. Send everything to Gregory Corso, American Express, Venice, Italy.

Love, Corso

To Lawrence Ferlinghetti Venice

[late Jan. 1958]

Dear Larry,

Here is last poem, I can't and won't send more all is done, I'm sure now that book is perfect, yes, it is done, thank God, about time. Yes, take out "poet in residence, etc." you are right, sometimes I can't see, now I see. Hope you like Uccello new version, much better ain't it? When *Esquire* sends me loot I will send you another twenty so that all expenses shan't fall upon your resplendent head. Ah I'm in Venice where all is most beautiful place I've ever seen, am so in love with place, I doubt if I'll ever leave, what a glorious place, what light! What dream! and indeed it is a city of love and woe, have you ever been to Venice? I will write to you soon about how I see it, right now am rushed to send you this, tonight I see Peggy Guggenheim[87], at house I am staying, she will be over for cocktails . . . Allen thinks I am capable of conning her for a life's supply of dollars, he's mad, I wanting nothing to do with dollars, only when I need it, and that ain't often really. Anyway I could be no happier than I am now.

Love, Gregory

Important: I am gathering poems for German anthology to be translated into German by big German publishing house, they want me to get all young American poets together, so send me your best, and have it to me soon, I will get Marks for such labor, but I really want to get out a great anthology, because surely it will be sold to English publication after the German, ain't hardly any really good anthologies today.

To Allen Ginsberg and William S. Burroughs Venice

[Jan. 29] 1958]

Dear beautiful Allen and Bill,

Am busy gathering writing letters to all poets to send for anthology, got letter from *Partisan*, check for $25. Also letter from Höllerer who wants me to go to Frankfurt for half hour TV, Ansen will go with me, he speaks German. Wrote huge real apologetic letter to Ashbery, Koch, O'Hara, saying (they read Dutch article) that I was at that time with the opinion but ain't no more and that I go on my knees begging their forgiveness. God, I'm so sorry I wrote that, I don't know why I did, I'm just a fuck up at times, I'll never learn. I do hope they forgive me, because I admitted to them that I erred, and didn't know what the heck I was talking about. TV thing to be about new young American poetry, nationwide. I will do my best for Burroughs, *Howl,* Kerouac, me, O'Hara and everybody.

Ah, but Venice is so wonderful, I'm so happy here, at last this life's dream is kind and good, Ansen very sweet to me, met Guggenheim momentarily at concert, shook her hand, that's all. Been writing mad poem about Venice here some lines:

> And the stealthy Doge in his fine discipline moves in proportion as a large jewel to Tintoretto carats / tapping his large nose with thoughts of state / he passes in sparkling gowns through the years of his reign through Byzantine arches and arcades, stopping occasionally in the barren areas with magnificent foundations in his eyes / and the bobbed haired princes whispering in the Piazzetta tales of new enunciations, the sons of Bellini with love and careful dialect describing their father's bright technique, madrigal lovers planning the night . . .

All these are just lines, no order, just draft, impressions:

> Mosaic beads like drops of oil run down every canopy and the bright alabaster walls / To sit in a gondola with metamorphical eyes / seeing nothing downstream but an old image of Central Park sadness / the awful outer music writhing in the horizon clanking violins bucking the bright onion-skinned atmosphere in whose dreamy solace Lord Byron dwelled invincibly / Or drunken boys in golden tights stammering out their allegiance on little bridges in the dark velvet night / from my own heart's soldiery I protect glimmering cathedrals and moony palaces / And dream of bearded Venice trudging knee deep down the Grand Canal behind him cries of gold showering in the purgatorial air / all the beautiful echoes of a child's afternoon sleep / ring through his fingers as he touches a dream of palaces / Or the winged lion whose stony flight is enduring may in a vision fall sick from his craggy sky and rot in the sudden gloom of St. Mark's / Ah, strolling in Guardi footsteps and time / a young cloaked man with golden lamps in his infinite eyes / seeking the morning star . . .

So far this is all, but I know it will become a fine poem, how great it is to write here, how nice the room, the desk, the view from my window, indeed I am more than happy, isn't that finally nice for me? I mean it's about time that in the year I've been in Europe I am at peace.

I wrote to Höllerer and TV to send me the fare, and I will go, with Ansen. Alan and I got high yesterday and had a delightful evening of talk and writing, we wrote a nice chain poem together, about God flying through heaven for inspection, really wonderful poem, Alan extremely sensitive man. What's happening in Paris, hear from Peter? Is he all right? As soon as I go to Frankfurt I'll let you know. Don't forget to write to people, get them to send me poems,

I did write, but if you can also, then do it . . . Ansen read me something I like very very much of Bill's I think I used it for book that will have the four of us. 'The Mahatma Routine,' really extraordinary fine piece of writing.

How does Bill feel about it? Is it all right with him if I use that for the small anthology? For the big one, well, he can choose what he likes, I feel it only fair that a man choose what he thinks best. But I am set on Mahatma for the small anthology.

Ansen reading all my works, thinks I'm a fine poet, likes *Vestal Lady* very much, first time he's read it. He seems to get kick out of everything he reads. He makes breakfast and I supper. We get along fine, and in sight of this, I'd like very much to go to Greece with him; perhaps it'll be possible, I do hope so. If you find *Evergreen* no. 3 in La Hune, please send me a copy.

Also, Allen, dear good consoling helpful friend, you know me very well, my ways and everything, please help me now, what should I do about Ashbery, Koch, O'Hara, etc. I did write them long honest quite lovely letter in which I said that at times I am mad irresponsible and am capable of cashing phony checks and doing phony things, etc., in other words big confession . . . did I do right? I also said that you had nothing to do with it, that it was all my doing, and that you were bugged at my having written it. [Howard] Kanovitz says this in his letter: "John Ashbery rolled his eyes at my mention of your Dutch article which someone sent translated to him. Did you really put him down very strongly? He and others like Koch and O'Hara like your work and have good things to say about Allen." O but I cried and went insane, my whole day was ruined, I am still terribly upset, here I put down criticism and I myself guilty . . . Oh, well, I am not at fault, I mean well, I am not brutal, I'm just a fuck up at times. If ever you write a letter to O'Hara please explain my personality, that at times I become transformed. Read *City Winter*[88] here, and he's really a fine poet, better than anybody in Frisco other than you. Hope you and Bill are well.

Love from me, Gregory

To Don Allen

Venice
[ca. Jan.] 1958]

Dear Don,

Here's *Power*, two years in the making, let me know what you think of it, good God, hope it doesn't need more work, I don't think it does, in fact I'm sure it is as complete as I hoped it to be. But if you have some criticism to make please don't hesitate. I feel it's best thing I've ever done, and darn Ferlinghetti didn't allow it to be in book, he thinking it fascistic or something, good God he missed the whole intent of poem, but anyway Ginsberg quotes it grossly in introduction, he loving poem very much. My only sorrow is that it shan't appear in book, it would have made *Gasoline* quite perfect, I feel. I really hope you can do something with it, I'd hate to store it away, it'll mean nothing when I get older. I am in Venice where all is beautiful and good. I am staying with Alan Ansen, do you know him or of him? He's very charming person and once was secretary for Auden, he reads me [Ben] Jonson, and [Aleksandr] Pushkin in Russian every morning before leading me on tour of Venice . . . thus I really feel that life is becoming very beautiful for me.

When I was in Frankfurt I met with Walter Höllerer, a poet, professor, and anthologist, and editor of *Akzente*, he wants me to do German anthology for him, bi-lingual of young American poetry. You once expressed desire to see European poets or writers works, so I gave him your address, did he write to you? He writes me that I was offered half hour TV program in Frankfurt on current American verse, sounds like wonderful idea, he says that I can come anytime in near future and do it. Ginsberg is in Paris, I think he's best for that, and will see if he'd like to do it, or perhaps we can do it together. Been pushing *Evergreen* number 2 in Frankfurt and Amsterdam and Paris. Did number 3 come out yet? Can you send me copy? Alan Ansen says he ordered Frank O'Hara's book, he paid, quite some time ago, and would love to receive it, so would I, I think O'Hara very fine poet.

Also if you know of any good young poets I should include for anthology, please have them send me poems to American Express, Venice. And I would love to have some of your poetry too, I did not know that you wrote, but Allen tells me you do. So far I have: O'Hara, Ashbery, Koch, Ginsberg, Kerouac, myself, Ansen, Levertov, McClure, Snyder, Whalen, Ferlinghetti, Weiners, Marshall, Carroll, Creeley, Olson, Burroughs, for the moment, that's all. What do you think? I met some German poets in Frankfurt and they seem quite interested in experiment. I wrote my first article in Amsterdam on American poetry, and the lesson I've learned is, never again! In it I expressed my feelings at the time, but now they've changed, not all but some, at least where Koch, O'Hara and Ashbery are concerned. I'd better not ever write another article again. The whole thing has made me sick. Bill Burroughs is now in Paris with Allen, and Peter has gone back to America. I'm glad, now Allen can have enough solitude in which to write. He found it difficult to write with Peter around.

I don't have spare copy of the article I wrote, but if you ever come across it, please forgive some of the obviousness in it, the stock cry against the academies, etc. I did mention the fine work Grove is doing, I can quote that: "Grove Press, a new very successful firm, purveyors of Beckett to America, have founded a new and attractive Literary Review to carry much of this material,

(San Francisco) . . ." I am writing much, and am enjoying what I really feel to be the most beautiful city in the world.

Love, Gregory

To Lawrence Ferlinghetti

Venice
[late Jan. 1958]

Dear Larry,

Quick letter, Venice great, am writing beautiful poem, but must go to Frankfurt for TV half hour interview about new American poetry, with interpreter, man who wants me to compile anthology, 286 pages, of American verse, so please send me your best and latest and wildest, and much. Here are the people I so far chose: Kerouac (a little reluctantly because I ain't too hip on his verse lately, but he necessary), Ginsberg, me, Whalen, Snyder, O'Hara, Ashbery, Wieners, Marshall, Koch, McClure, maybe some Loewinsohn, if you see him tell him to send me much of his latest and wildest, Carl Solomon, Creeley, Olson, Lamantia, Dick Howard, Burroughs, Ansen. I got crazy thing from Burroughs, really a beautiful piece of writing. So far I think I made a good choice, I ain't too keen on Levertov or Duncan. Please send me what you have right away. Find myself very busy, wish I could rest enough to see Venice, but I believe this anthology to be very important, it will be bi-lingual, and is subject for American distribution, I want to get the best and the wildest together, and the damn thing ain't gonna be a plug for S.F. either, enough of that crap, in New York there are three poets, O'Hara, Koch and Ashbery that far outshine many of the S.F.'s . . . I want it to be no group, but an entity.

How's *Gasoline,* old *Gasoline* getting along? So many people have given up on me because they don't believe book is coming out and because of the delay I can't sell any in Germany or anywhere new, how great it would have been to have it for the TV program, could have sold much there. Hell with it. It's done. Just when do you think it will be out? Why don't you rush a little? Now that I am doing sort of ambassador poetry thing in Europe it'd be sort of nice to have my own book with me, am a little weary of pushing you and *Howl* and Kerouac and Levertov and Rexroth. What color will book be? I asked you that a billion times, you never answer!

Okay, now please Larry send me your best and what you'd want very much to be in an anthology. Anthology endures.

Hope all is well, love Gregory

P. S. But Levertov is important, please get in touch with her for me, no got her address, tell her to send me NEW and wildest poems, much, also tell her to get in touch, never mind I just found her address. If you see Olson or Creeley or Whalen please have them send me their poems, all new and wild.

To Allen Ginsberg and William S. Burroughs Venice
[Feb. 1958]

Dear Bill,

What can you ever say to me that is not knowing? I mean I feel by reading everything you wrote that I can't talk to you because I feel you make me a person before friendly finance, afraid, guilty, confused requiem, dead, no thing to say. What then can I say to you? You hold firm the laws of all your years work. You have sat nights of nights, Egypt, Peru or what have you, nights, I can't say naught to you. But in Paris I saw you and liked and kissed and yet felt uncertainty, why not, you answered the unanswerable, the fourth dimension, the last cry of man, but I feel deeply feel the last cry, though answered, means nothing to you. Why do I think that this night, Venice, I know why. Because you offer the mind of "Yage[89] City" and rest to a new mind, a psychiatrist, a soul unaware but surprised of you and all Peru and Joan[90] and South American witch doctor lore and all all, but how sad, a great good mind, to give that to a new new new soul, a pay soul, a studied soul, a living soul, a brain heart body mind soul of medical timidity. O Bill I feel it just a whim on your part, if so, I love you, but if it is intention to find another life, a better one, than this glorious chosen given life, then I weep for you like I have all my life for the life you seek. For the life you seek is but coaly misty air, psychiatrist will only kill your beautiful hand of words, then you will be dead of hand, requiem, dead of words, of hand, new Bill, the new man, who will you gloriously speak to then? Will you feign the angel? Will you shun Ginsberg? Will you die altogether? But you must if you listen to psychiatrist. You must if you think another late new soul can give you new new new, can't because you are so set. But though you are set your poetry will suffer by such ferret. You perhaps seek nothing. You perhaps are getting tired, you perhaps know what you are doing, and I nor he nor any should interfere.

So I say all in all no outside uncertain muse. Don't forsake the true muse, what dies in beauty dies in you. No psychiatrist can revive that. But I can't love you with all my years of Hope Savage who died by psychiatrist, who was angel and beauty, I can't love you if you go to those killers of poetry. They'll kill you, and perhaps that's what you wish, perhaps you don't want to write anymore. And if you wrote like Utrillo painted under psychiatrist orders then I think it is terrible. Flee the Mohawks! Beautiful Bill, too bad my nonsense walk did not hand and hand with you in Paris, perhaps it would have been good, but I say save until I get back wealthy wise and old and old and sad and good.

Love, Gregory

Allen, forgive me all but know I love beauty and Bill is beauty. Please send LeRoi [Jones][91] some of [my good] poems, like I sent you, because I sent him long bad one, so send him what you think best of what you have of mine, and say I ain't too happy with what I sent them, now, afterthought. Bill should be happy. Ansen is worried about sex law and death of plague for sexuals, he thinks of Belgium, Vienna, Spain, Africa. Place to sex sex in freedom hand to foot, poor angel Ansen duly worried and rightly so, but no bother with him yet by law.

Morning after last night's drunk with Pegeen[92] and Alan crazy ham supper: I wrote all [above] last night wild, but should send it on, only hoping I do not say wrong, and with sober sense this morning I feel that what I wrote to Bill is me, therefore all right. [. . .]

Gregory

To Lawrence Ferlinghetti

Venice
Feb. 5, 1958

Dear Larry,

Today is Wednesday, I guess book is done, how wonderful. I just hope it doesn't bug *Partisan* or *Esquire* who felt that they should have first published *Ode to Coit Tower* and *In the Fleeting Hand of Time*, but I know nothing of these politics, book being more important, besides they already paid me for poems. Yes, red is good, red is what I wished, but then I saw *Kora*[93], I thought it to be impossible. I definitely wanted that line you disapproved of out of *Coit Tower*, also I am glad you received final *Uccello* in time, it is much better than the previous version. Send out to reviews. Also make sure to send to Rosalind Constable of *Time* magazine, Time and Life Building, Rockefeller Center, New York City, I'll have Ginsberg write her a letter. Yes, you can send books to me, but first you should send some to these addresses.

Also, it is true will go half half on review copies. Thus you have addresses of all magazines, *New York Times* etc., I realize it will be a job for you to send them out, but I am in Europe and cannot do it. Send my father five copies.

S. Corso, Brooklyn, New York
Jack Kerouac, Orlando, Florida
Louis Ginsberg, Paterson, N.J.
William Carlos Williams
Donald Hall, *Paris Review,* N.Y.
Randall Jarrell, Washington, D.C.
Ed Fancher, *Village Voice*, New York City
Archibald MacLeish, Cambridge, Mass.
Cyrilly Abels, *Mademoiselle*, N.Y.
Robert Sedgewick, Cambridge, Mass.
Mr. Henry Savage, Camden, South Carolina.

So far that's it. All are to be extracted from my 100 except two, Don Hall, *Paris Review*, and Ed Fancher, *Village Voice*. He, Fancher, promised big favorable review for me, so send him one almost immediately. I do hope Eighth St. Bookshop gets it in, because many of my Village friends are waiting for it. Can you get them to order it? I will write to them. Anyway, let me know who you send books out to for reviews. I guess this time *Time* should start reviewing City Lights, also, *New York Times*. Yes, send books to me in Venice, but soon I go [to] Germany for half hour TV program on American poetry. And it would be crazy if I had at least ten copies to hand out, especially to the man who is putting out anthology, so can't you send air mail, ten copies? Besides, doesn't Ginsberg deserve a rush copy? If it cost a lot, then deduct it from me, but I feel it necessary that I go to Frankfurt with ten copies, and I go next week. Also hurry with your poems for anthology. I'm getting myself into so much work that I have not time to write about the silver hearse gondolas and the black palaces, and the lurking Doges. Received letter from Anita Martin, she's back at Antioch, and says she is very fond of you and was sorry she did not get closer to you or something. Here's what she said: "I like your Lawrence very much and am sorry I didn't get to know him better in this time had you been here we could have had much more to say together. You are our constant conversation piece through which he conveys his charming self and I dig his charming self." Send her a copy too. Anita Martin, Antioch College, Yellow Springs, Ohio. I had dinner and drinks and music with Peggy Guggenheim and got on well with her. I go to her house maybe tomorrow and see her paintings. No romance here. Damn Italians are always men, and never women. It's the stupid Italians who feel that women are a privilege, so they keep them out of sight. San Marco filled with men, all insipid looking, waiting for summer to come and bring Radcliffe, Vassar, Bryn Mawr girls to their shore so that they can come on with un-hip Latin lover routine. They seem to be waiting for nothing else. Each one of them has seen a film called *Summertime* fifteen times, each one of them seeks to live up to it. These men very nowhere.

But Venice, Venice is wonderful, and I am seeing all the churches, and paintings, and will take a plane ride over city.

Love, Gregory

To Allen Ginsberg

Venice
Feb. 6, 1958

Dear Allen,

Sent *Power* off to Don Allen. Ferlinghetti writes that my book came off press yesterday and was shipped airmail to me, so I'll probably get it two days from now. He says book will be bombshell, etc. and that color is like William

Carlos Williams' but only in reverse. I wrote him back immediately and told him to send copy to Rosalind Constable of *Time*; so maybe you could drop her a line, and prompt her, being that she is very fond of your word, she is sure to adhere to it. So do this for me. *Black Mountain Review* came, liked the Burroughs selection very much, and your new addition to *America*, Michael Rumaker gave you a review, when you see it you judge it, Ansen calls it Mallarmesque, I call it a mixed review. Best thing in *Black Mountain* issue is long beautiful poem by Edward Marshall who is indeed the best poet of that whole lot, and the only poet that I go enthusiastically for. Levertov, Creeley, Wieners, they ain't got nothing on this kid. He is really great poet. Ansen mailed three copies of the issue to Bill. So have Bill send you copy. Good poem by Whalen too. Of course they don't have me, which makes me feel that they just don't like my work, or maybe I didn't send them good enough, but still I am getting feeling that these people aren't too keen on me, and the child instinct in me says: "Okay, so I won't try and like their work"—which is in essence partly true because I DO try to like their work never really liking it. Like I say, Marshall so far is poet I am all for. Kerouac sent me nice letter saying he will send things for both anthologies. I wrote to everyone for poems. So far Kerouac and Ferlinghetti have replied. Can you get on Solomon? I wrote him, but no answer. Saw Guggenheim, had drinks with her with Alan and then music in the old jail Alan belongs to as member, then drink at Harry's, then home . . . it could be called a successful meeting, yet all she did talk mostly about was her sick Tibetan dog, she seriously thinking of calling a specialist all the way from Zurich to aid it.

When I go to Frankfurt for TV Höllerer says I can take my time, give him weeks notice, and it will be set up, I will not see it my duty to talk about poets, or just poets. I would much rather talk about you, Burroughs, Kerouac, and what you are doing, or trying to do, or have done, and why where how when etc. etc., because I am not a spokesman for the others, you recall I tried in Amsterdam and failed. Believe me the failure has hurt me more than anyone, well I am not going to be the scapegoat. I believe it unfair of me to put down O'Hara and praise Levertov when my heart tells me it should be the other way around. I get nothing out of Levertov. You see something in her. Maybe I am blind, because I see nothing. Still I didn't want to feel too much like a praiser so I thought of a possible wrong in O'Hara, and in actuality, found it, and exaggerated it. Well, I shall never do that again. From now on I will listen to myself. If I can't hear myself I just won't do anything. It's all right for everyone else to give their feelings, but when I extend mine, holocaust. Well, I did something that should even my conscience. I wrote a five page apology letter to the three of them, Koch, Ashbery, O'Hara; they probably will have no respect for me now. But why did I send letter, because everybody got on my back for making what I felt to be a fair criticism? Just any kind words Corso and all will be all right, but if any of us must say bad words then I guess it's got to be you, scapegoat, and don't get us involved. Like Kerouac in his last letter to me saying that I should not write or talk about Rexroth or Duncan, but about him, Ferlinghetti, you, me, etc.

Anyway, dear friend, how do you like England? Are the Parkinson's taking you to Westminster to Chaucer to Blake, to Thames, marks of woe, I guess at least you're eating and probably are meeting some people so let me know all, I have been ill, but am better today, Ansen sometimes difficult, stubborn, but am putting up with it, but at times I feel like screaming. I just can't live with people, but I am living here, and quite well, because I have private room, but he doesn't knock when he comes in, so I feel a little unfree, but I do eat and cook cook cook. Oh, I wish I were a sultan fat on fat cushions, Allahing before my God Herr Lazy. Anyway I won't IBM think because I am not a machine, and it seems I make the most mistakes, all right, but they cause more harm to me than anyone so I wish I wouldn't cry, anyway you writing anything? I told Ferl to send your father copy of *Gasoline*. How do you do it? You don't commit yourself. You don't like Parkinson's poetry, yet does he know that? But he knows I don't, and now he probably doesn't like me. O this stupid fairy game of verse! I hate it. Shelley's heart is buried somewhere in England. Maybe you can find it and this time save the leaf for me.[94]

Tell me all you are doing, and please try to get *Gasoline* going. It is out. It is done. And the overhaul project has been successful. Just like Jupiter C. Give my love to the Parkinson's. What has Peter to say? Gosh, I'd give up all Venice just to be back [in] November [at] 9 rue Git-le-Coeur, *chambre* 25 at night with lentil stew and poems. Be happy Allen, write to me.

Love, Gregory

To Allen Ginsberg

Venice
Feb. 7, 1958

Dear Allen,

Ah, after a goodnight's delirium and sweat I awake feeling fine. Truth is I have been junk sick here in Venice and have only now gotten over it. So all is well. No longer cranky. Ansen doing German translation of *Howl*, very carefully, dictionary always at his side, and notes, he's made many notes for Höllerer to examine as use of words such as hipster, dungarees, bop, etc. Ansen very efficient. I suggested he do a review of my book for *Partisan*, and he said he would be glad to. Good. At least I'll get one good fair review. So far no poems from all the poets O'Hara, Koch, Ashbery, Marshall, Wieners, Snyder,

Whalen, Lamantia, Howard, Solomon, Creeley, Olson, Levertov. I guess I should be patient. But I'd like to get the damn thing done with for all that. At least our four for Stomps will be ready shortly, just as soon as Jack sends me something, Ansen is doing all the translating for us. Book will consist *of Howl, Power, Mahatma* and *Yage City*, and, I hope, *Mexico City Blues* [by Kerouac]. Alan digs *Power* very much, and is very sad that it is not in book. O curses on thee, Ferlinghetti, thou of little insight!

Venice has lost its sun, all fog and gloom. Ah I bet you're experiencing fog like you've never experienced fog before. Have you gone to Baker Street, 221a? Or to St. Mary Redcliffe, Rawley's corner? or to 17 Tite Street, Wilde's quarters?[95] How are the pubs? Meet any interesting poets? See Watson Taylor[96] again?

Well, I still have four thousand lira left of the sixteen thousand I got from *Partisan* week and half ago. Never held money so long, but staying with Ansen one finds it quite easy. Still I have to give him a thousand tonight because he is buying me ticket for *Tristan and Isolde*, very good, I want to see it, it is Bayreuth company, so should be very good. Are you taking advantage of their socialized medicine? What with your constant complaints about lumbago and arthritis and high blood pressure and compulsive urine? Ansen puts flowers in my room, very beautiful ones. O damn be it to Yvor Winters, W.S. Merwin, if they wish to write that way then why don't they take from Pound who does it so much better, than taking (as Ansen claims) from Auden's *Musee des Beaux Arts*. This poem is dangerous, he said, because it has been the creed of all academic poets. I quote one insidious passage: "In Brueghel's *Icarus*, for instance; how everything turns away quite leisurely from the disaster. . ." Yes, all those who can't write poetry have found a way to write poetry, thus Auden is their Cézanne. Auden has given them a way. But of no use, their verse is dead and the rot does not forsake the stench. Is not one tired of seeing their 18th century Connecticut landscape? Being that I can't take care of myself ever I have decided to propose marriage to a girl in America, a friend of Anton and Joan [Rosenberg]. Who, by the way, is fat with child! A little Anton due on the horizon! But of course nobody will marry me, I'll go uncared for, head bowed, through my chain walk of cry hot hot mountainous earth. Alas. I am writing long poem called *Army*. Love, be happy my dearest of friends.

Gregory

To Allen Ginsberg Venice
[ca. Feb. 8] 1958

Dear Allen,

Well received some poems from Loewinsohn, some very good, and also special delivery letter from Carl Solomon, quote letter: "My dear Gregory, you are the only wild young hip poet I know. Carl." End of letter. No poems. How to reply to such? Ask again? You ask? Don't ask? Perhaps you think he was being kind to me? Perhaps he was? But I am sure that when I wrote to him I wrote saying anthology will compromise of young hip wild poetry, therefore his reply. I am only one. Why need Carl or anybody else? Maybe I am paranoid. All right. But I can't be entirely wrong in believing that he won't send poems. Too bad. Damnit. It would have been great to have him. Perhaps you can write to him and persuade him, perhaps if he felt I had not much to do with it, which I don't, the Germans have all to do with it. Special delivery letter, and just "My dear Gregory, you are the only wild young hip poet I know. Carl." How lovely. But I am confused. When has he read my poetry? Ah, I am naive then, yes? no? All right. But I ask you what to reply, or is reply necessary. Oh, I can think it out myself, but I don't want to goof, I prefer not to upset him by reply, maybe my letter just ASKING him for poems, upset him. Oh, well.

Good news. I had wild alone ball dancing through Picassos and Arps and Ernsts with Peggy Guggenheim, she digs me much, I told her all about me prison, etc., etc., she will have date with me tomorrow, so all should be nice. She is very sweet person, sad at heart, and old with memories. But I make her happy, she laughs, and thus I am good in that way. We spoke of sex, we spoke of sex, but I don't know what to do about that. She wanted me to stay over the night, but I couldn't, and didn't, and I am glad because she walked me late at night to boat to Ansen's, and sat on barge with me and told me great things about she and Beckett and her life, and it was pleasantly sad and good, thus Venice is becoming romantic for me, in this fashion. I will take her on date tomorrow but I only have two thousand lire left, what to do, what to do, ANSEN TO THE RESCUE. Her dog died, two days ago, she buried it in her garden. What a weird scene. Late at night she led me into garden with a jug of water, dark it was, and the moon was bright, she wore my raincoat and with her thin hand led me to the plot of dog, there past the Brancusi past the Arp past the Giacometti, we came upon the canine grave, and with great solemnity she took the jug from me and poured the water on the earth that covered the dog. It was all very touching. Later in the evening, after she knew all about me, after all the sex talk, I said "I must go home, but somehow I am a man and feel unfulfilled," she embraced me, kissed me, and taking my hand we danced the Picassos and Ernsts. Very strange marvelous lady. Didn't you see that in her? How did you miss it? Perhaps you didn't have time, but she really is great, and sad, and does need friends. Not all those creepy painters all the time. I told her painters were making her into a creep, she laughed, led me to the boat, there we sat and when boat came fifteen minutes later, I kissed her good-bye, while I watched her walk away I saw that she put her hand to her head as though she were in pain. I suddenly realized the plight of the woman by that gesture. She is a liver of life, and life is fading away. That's all there is to it. It is going. God, how painful to see and know and watch it. But I will say funny things, and she will laugh, and who knows what may happen.

I wrote a poem in which I end: " . . . alien gaud, the leer of ruminating She, in her two thousandth year, hath hired sight of sordid cameo. . ."

Love, Gregory

P.S. Something you must know, I am a man, and I am sad as a man, and as a man I am sad and with such manness and sadness I love you, can you understand? That I would let's say die tomorrow I could not by power of revival return to say what I say now: I love you as a lone sad dark eyed person who ponystabled[97]eyed me in my 20th year only out of prison with love and joy, you are the one I would die for and fight for, you are my friend, I wish you to know that, and O please don't take advantage of me for this, I am somehow a noble person, and I do dream the hired sight of cameo, the swindleresque ink, the ghost's gray memory that rakes epithets from indefinite weather, the whatever else you have, Ginsberg, I will always weep you in my sadness with people, as I did last night on a barge with Guggenheim, saying you were all to me in life, so so so, what else that I love you, as a man as a poet, I would, for you, die, good friend, I fear by dreams never to see you again, thus such a letter, but surely I will see you again, you who are my Shelley on earth, O do be happy my angel, my love.

To Ron Loewinsohn Venice

[ca. Feb.10] 1958

Dear Ron,

Just received your poems, liked them a lot, will use at least four, but need time to think which four, just looked them over quickly, like *Seagull* very much. Can you get [Richard] Brautigan to send me poems? I'd appreciate it. Listen, tell him to send me copies I don't have to send back, it's almost like work for me to exchange those mad stamp things you sent, like I have too much to do to send poems back, so tell him to send spare copies. Yes, book will be hardcover bi-lingual, German-English. Married life, how is it? I wonder about it. At times I feel a sadness. I think perhaps it is because I am not married. But no. It was not meant for me to marry. This I know. And therefore am sad. I know it would be beautiful to have a child. Still I have Venice. And yesterday had mad wild time with Peggy Guggenheim in her huge mad house dancing in and out the Picassos and De Chiricos and the Arps and what not. She wore butterfly spectacles and streamlined witchy shoes, and I wore nakedness and a Zebra sheet, she is a great woman, and Venice has become seemingly romantic as she has become a sort of George Sand for me. Peter back in New York. Ginsberg in England. Has my *Gasoline* come out yet? Ferl tells me it was due last week. About time, took almost a year. All my goof. Anyway I am aging quickly. I must go to India soon, while yet 27 and strong and careless. If you know of any other wild great young hip poets have them send send send send.

Be happy wed epithelium here comes the bride and white veils and confetti hoard of sordid cameo and ring.

Love, Corso

To Lawrence Ferlinghetti

Venice
[mid-Feb.] 1958

Dear Larry,

Book is lovely, everything about it all right. Yes, some mistakes, for instance, "spoor" not "spore" others are minor, will tell you in next letter. Ah, too bad no *Power*, but, as I say, I am happy with book. But you forgot to put Burroughs piece in! I explicitly wanted it in. Oh, well. Now listen, this is very important. Rush two copies to Jarrell, I want him to get me National Academy grant. Here also is list of people I want you to send books to. Did you get my previous list? I give it to you now, then what is left over, send to Venice, but please air mail me about five copies for Germany TV thing, please. I will pay you for that, it is very important I have copies soon. Also if any reviews or comments do send me them. Last night Peggy Guggenheim gave me a watch, and we will probably go to Greece together, at end of March. She is very fine woman; she likes me very much, and I, her. *Quelle Vie!* Really beautiful book. I am happy about all poems except: *Three* [and] *For Miles*, is there possibility of taking them out in second edition? I give you much better poems. Okay here is list, please rush the Jarrells.

Randall Jarrell, Washington, D.C. (2 copies)
Sam Corso, Brooklyn, N.Y. (5 copies)
Mark Van Doren, Columbia University, N.Y.C. (1 copy)
Archibald MacLeish, Cambridge, Mass. (1 copy)
Ed Fancher, *Village Voice*, N.Y.C. (review copy)
Sal Amico, Utica, New York. (1 copy)
Henry Savage, Camden, South Carolina (2 copies)
W.H. Auden, N.Y.C. (1 copy)
Pound, St. Elizabeth's Hospital, Washington, D.C. (1 copy)
Don Allen, N.Y.C. (1 copy)
Louis Ginsberg, Paterson, N.J. (1 copy)
William Carlos Williams, Paterson, N.J.

Howie Kanovitz, N.Y.C. (1 copy)
Jane Guelich, Buffalo, N.Y. (1 copy)
Anita Martin, Antioch College, Yellow Springs, Ohio. (1 copy)
Cyrilly Abels, *Mademoiselle*, N.Y. (1 copy)
Robert Sedgewick, Cambridge, Mass. (1 copy)
Sherry Martinelli, Washington, D.C. (1 copy)
Jack Kerouac, Orlando, Florida (1 copy)
Robert Gardener, Cambridge, Mass. (1 copy)
D. Gordon Bensley, Philips Academy, Andover, Mass. (1 copy)
Barbara Guest, *Partisan Review*, NY (review copy)
(important send right away) Rosalind Constable, Time and Life Building, Rockefeller Center, (review copy)

Dear Larry, for me, please send these out right away, as for other copies that go to magazines for reviews, you know the addresses and the magazines, just deduct from what you send me, on review copies we go half half, please air mail me five copies, Guggenheim wants one, Germany needs at least three. Please do this. Send all regular mail to Venice. Hurry the Jarrell, the Constable, and my father. Ah, nothing else, dear poet friend, but where are your poems for anthology? Hurry that too. I am so happy about book, such an advancement over *Vestal Lady*, and I feel I'm getting better better, if I don't die of starvation, but I won't, Jarrell is bound to get me funds, and Guggenheim is now my dearest friend. So all is well. Will you let me know when you send all books to these addresses I gave? I want them to get them right away. It's been so long! Don't miss any address. Also another address: Marlon Brando, Hollywood, Calif. Please rush these because these people will spread word around to all my friends, especially the Cambridge ones, and they will thus sell. Be happy, and write right away, I must know if you sent them out, then I could write to Jarrell, and Constable, etc.

Love, Gregory

To Allen Ginsberg Venice
[Feb. 13] 1958

Dear Allen,

Received *Gasoline*, it looks great, Ansen liked poems so much he kissed me and said I deserve to be supported all my life. He immediately set to write review for me for *Partisan*. Some mistakes in book. Ferl said he sent you copy. One big mistake, he did not include Burroughs piece, all right for second printing; other mistakes, about eight minor, except for misspelling of "spoor," he had "spore".

Whalen sent me poems, he doesn't sound too happy.

Well, Allen, now you can write to Constable and see if she can get it reviewed in *Time*. I wonder about *NY Times*? I don't think they do soft covers. I will immediately write to Jarrell for Academy 250[98]. I had Ferl send books to my father, your father, William Carlos Williams, Pound, Auden, etc. He'll send review copies out. He is going to send the rest of the books here, to Venice. When they come I'll send you twenty five copies. Peggy Guggenheim is really great lady. She presented me with watch which I thrice refused, then at fourth insistence, Ansen said take it, I took it and kissed her, and am now wearing her watch. I also proposed she go to Greece with Alan and me, and she said yes, and will go! She called me pure and sweet and good all evening, but I said that I have a mental evil also, she said no, she couldn't believe that. Then Ansen proposes heroin to her, she rejects it vehemently, Ansen says he got it from me, Peggy just would not believe, she says I am too pure and sweet and good, and that Ansen is terrible influence on me. She thinks he is addict now, poor Alan, but all is in jest, she loves him. Ah, how nice Greece will be with Alan and Peggy! Crete, Rhodes, Minos! What future poems! What undreamable dreams!

Tonight I see the Bayreuth Wagner grandson production of Tristan. It is anniversary of Wagner's death, so it is big occasion. Well, I am finally broke again. That date with Peggy cleaned me, though she offered to pay, I declined that. But it did last long time. Ah, but I know more shall come. I got drunk two nights in row with Alan, night before last drunk I offered Peggy my soul in exchange for life, she asked why, and I said I want peace in which to write write write, she said all right, then I said but I must have you for life, and she said, but I am 59 years old, I said if she'd mention age again I'd hate her because I hate old age, she said, all right, is it life you want, then I thought awhile and said, I don't know, all I know is I give you my soul, what I wish in return is obituary, it'll come, someday I'll ask you.

Very very funny conversation, we were both drunk, but Alan was drunkest, he demanded she try heroin, and that she love her daughter and forgive her daughter, and then a *Time* and *Life* man came to sit with us, and he in gooey maudlin Italian fashion said: "Ah, everything will be all right." But I said: "No! not everything will be all right," and I yelled at Peggy for taking flattery so easily and she denied that she took it so easily. It was all mad, the evening closed with a long long embrace and kiss on some Piazza. I went home, Alan went to the night boys. Thus my date with Peggy. She says the letter you sent her she has kept, she explained it all to me, about how you said you slept with Peter thus could not go without him, she calls it famous document. She is a woman who does demand manners, that is certain. I tried telling her that Peter realized she was a great personage therefore decided to impress this great personage, and the best way he thought was, the flying towel[99]. She said that that is no way, because one need not put up with that, that she would like to be impressed with an enduring thing.

Understandable, but I think I can get her to forgive. So far she is impressed by my love of you and your poetry. Alan works on her with Bill. It all tends to lead her to realize that she, who makes it with great people, hath failed with two great ones. She said: but is he (meaning Peter) a famous poet? I could only laugh, because it was a childish remark. Be happy.

Love, Gregory

To Don Allen Venice

[Feb. 14] 1958

Dear Don,

Got *Evergreen* yesterday, beautiful issue, loved Guest's poems, what a coincidence, as soon I read them, especially *Safe Flights*, I wrote her letter asking for poems. She's very fine poet. O'Hara is great. Yes, I don't think there is a better poet for me writing today, other than Ginsberg, who gives me what I want in a poem. But he has yet to send poems for anthology, damnit. I wrote long apology letter saying I was sorry for what I said in article, and I am sorry, because what I felt weakly at time, I no longer feel now. Oh, well. If you see him try to explain me somewhat, and do tell him the anthology is worthy of his work. As I said, anthology would be unfair without his or Koch's or Ashbery's work. I am glad you liked article, but what do you mean by "sticking to positive side of new poetry"? Do you mean I shouldn't mention any names? But, if you'd like to use it, then more than anything else in the world, I'd love to revise it. I want definitely to change that "Mr. Jarrell's verse" tone, and of course the O'Hara piece. Why don't I revise it and send it to you?

Gasoline came to me via air mail. I wrote to Ferl to send you copy. It looks good, and I am happy with poems inside except maybe for two or three small ones. Some printers mistakes, too, but not serious. Does Evergreen review books? If not Don, can you see that it gets reviewed for me? I would love O'Hara to review it.

Venice is lovely. Last night went to opera with Peggy Guggenheim, she's a wonderful person, and saw on Wagner's deathday his grandson lead the Bayreuth group into a wondrous *Tristan and Isolde*, I probably will go to the isles of Greece with Peggy, and Alan Ansen. A dream come true. I fear once I set foot on Crete, I shall remain, Schliemann-like, for I do believe that Theseus lied, and did not slay the Minotaur. Of course, when I find him, I won't either, but maybe I'll entice him to come out in the open, then! I'll forsake my poetics, and will have waiting outside a gang of husky men to chain him, and put it on a boat, and take it to N.Y. with me, and there exhibit it at $2.00 a peek, why not? How else for poets to live in this possible life?

Höllerer says he wrote to you. Yes, I have new poems, I'll send you whole batch of carbons, you can keep them for your own, even prose, I'll send you everything, no intention of publishing, only if you care to, just for your own personal self. Oh, I was so happy about the Camus piece, how I hate the whole business of death and especially social death. I liked Camus after that piece, that's the way all men should feel be they men. I wrote to Wieners long ago for poems, no reply. I like Marshall's work very much, wrote him, wrote Carl Solomon, wrote everybody worth writing to, but if you know of more, then please give me their names and ADDRESSES, I don't know how to get in touch with Blackburn, or Eigner. Yes, will write a preface when all poems are compiled. Please convince beautiful O'Hara that I am all right, I have not heart for anthology if he declines.

Love, Gregory

To Lawrence Ferlinghetti Venice
[Feb.] 1958

Dear Larry,

I was right, I was right, and Ginsberg was wrong, and I never believed him, though I always do, but as you were concerned, no, I never believed him, you are a beautiful poet, I love you. *I Am Waiting* is a lovely a great it made me cry, it is a great poem, you have a gentle good soul, Larry, like mine, I cry the same things you cry, thank you for such a beautiful poem. I haven't read anything like that ever, but I knew of it, it has always been in my heart, and I guess in the hearts of all men who love the beautiful. Ah, but now you are beyond hurt, and therefore, you, we, have won. How happy your poem made me, really. I love it. Surely it must go in. Surely it will be best poem in there, so far nothing comes close to it. Great, really great, I cried, what more can I say.

Larry, please send book to Carl Solomon, Bronx, N.Y. If you see any reviews please send them to me, and when your book comes out send it to me. Ginsberg and Bill Burroughs failed with Guggenheim, but I made it with her, until last night, when at dinner table I called her an old Jewish mamma, (because she was bugging me and my host, Ansen, about the hunchbacked boyfriend her daughter was going with) she got mad, phtttt. Over. I join Ginsberg and Burroughs. Goodbye Greece, she would have taken me, but I ain't no gold digger and I say what I feel. I am proud of myself. Besides I don't need people anymore, especially them who can't take truth.

Be happy, and I do love your poem. Write to me.

Love, Gregory

To Allen Ginsberg

Venice
[Feb.] 1958

Dear Allen,

Been reading much Keats lately, and was struck by: "We must inspect the lyre . . ." from a sonnet in which he says a new form of sonnet is needed to cope with the new sound of the English language. Keats inspired me to write, what I feel to be, one of my best efforts, *In A Grecian Garden*. I enclose it. Also enclosed find *Stone Of Cretan Scale*, it is about Guggenheim getting foolishly stupidly bugged about a hypothetical question in which I offered to take her daughter away to Afghanistan and thus abandon her there, pregnant and all, to the hordes! All in effort to get her away from the boy her mother hates. Peggy asked me what would I wish in return for such a favor (thus the play goes on, she adds to it) I said I would wish Crete. She looked hard at me, then burst out with a "How evil can you be!" and rushed out of the house. I fear, what with all her good intention towards artists, she's not too bright. And after all, she helps painters, not poets, she is a business woman, really, for in painters there is a return, the Picasso on her wall will never die, but the book of poems on her shelf, shall; for there is no return. Anyway the poem is set thus: I bemoan the fact that kings, by the insistence of nymphs, have left their kingdoms, and settled in Crete (there to await my proposed arrival) they wait there and conflicts arise, and thus Minotaur, and thus the devastation of Crete. In comes Peggy then, she is Demeter, and Pegeen, Persephone. The "two lights of your night" are you, and Bill. Refrain and intent I wished for poem is: "Crete was not meant to be woman's gift." Poem is another fine effort, but *In A Grecian Garden* is pure inspiration. I send all my poems to Don Allen. He gets them first. What he doesn't wish I told him to send back, but I am sending him everything making carbons, that he can keep everything in his house for me. I am writing well at Ansen's, only a few minor interruptions that I don't suffer when I am entirely alone, but I can't expect the chamber of death. How was England, and please send me anything new you've written? We will return poems. All right? You keep what I send you, and I keep what you send me. Did you get *Gasoline* yet? When I get all those copies I will send you twenty five to distribute to La Hune and Whitman's[100], need the money. Sure there are enough people I know in Paris who will, detecting the pittance, buy. I have been under strain lately; feeling quite sad about nothing. Just sad. At times I feel that if I were to meet Mr. Death at the next corner, I'd not dodge him.

Also enclosed find *Army*, don't really know what to make of it. Some very good passages in it. Please let me know what you think of *Army*, and the others, too. Any news about anything? How is Peter? O but I must write to him, been so damned busy doing nothing but poetry and woe. Please send me the poems I sent you of Sheldon Thomas[101] for anthology. I wish I had his address, can you get it from Graham? I want more of his work; also I told Don Allen about him. I sent him a letter at hospital that came back to me explaining why I didn't see his friends, no wonder he is bugged, oh, well, but nobody has a right to be bugged anymore; an unnoticeable mess shall soon sit upon their heads. Omen. Ideas of wizardry. Pitchfork Blook flings screaming chickens down the road. What happened in England? I expect one long letter. Ferl said Rexroth said *Gasoline* will cause another sensation. He must have liked book. Got poems from Ferl, one very good one, from Kerouac, Loewinsohn, Shenker, and alas! Creagh![102] He sent me a book of his, saying in the poem "there are bad poets in Frisco" oh, damn it, whoreson night! I ain't got any really good poems for anthology! Ansen, you, me, Burroughs, Kerouac, one of Ferls, that's all, unless I take the *Black Mountain* Marshall poem, I need O'Hara, and Wieners and more. I've written them, they don't answer. I sent Don Allen two of Ansen's poems, he writes extraordinary well. He sent you the one on heroin, it is fine for its perception, imagery and over all vision, lots of color too, and not at all *chichi*.

I say farewell, and love to Bill, and I am happy to join the two lights in Madame Guggenheim's night.

Love, Gregory

Alas, do miss incentive of undetectable things, is it possible for you to mail me some pot or hash? Do try; squash it in letter, put no forwarding address. Or mail me five joints; my imagination is abundant, but my eyes grow dim. Whatever, no H.

▼ [Corso's last comment, "Whatever, no H," reveals the growing concern he had over his heroin habit. Ginsberg was interested in the effects of all drugs on the mind, but he was very careful to never become hooked. Many of his friends were not so lucky, and Corso's casual drug use, became a lifelong addiction.]

To Don Allen

Venice
[Feb. 21] 1958

Dear Don,

Enclosed find two wonderfully soulful poems written by Alan Ansen (I am staying at his house in Venice). Not only is *Ode to Heroin* informative it is also so marvelously mad! the images, the color, the perception, the overall vision, and the sensitivity of sudden conception, make it, I feel, a truly great poem. *News Item* is poignant, true, oh, well, let me not dim your eyes with my enthusiasm, read and see.

Alas, I go the way of Allen Ginsberg and Bill Burroughs in having failed with Madame Guggenheim, she misunderstood a hypothetical question I put to her, after much vodka, she up and left. I wrote long poem (I send it to you in another envelope) about how, even if she WOULD have taken me to my desired Crete, and she would have, that Crete is no woman's gift. Poem is called *Stone Of Cretan Scale*; and with that poem I send you the poem I have wanted all my life to write: *In A Grecian Garden*. It is my Shelleyean poem. In poem I cry my loss of youth, youth that once gave me Greece, etc. I send it to you first, I will always send you anything I write first, but if you do not wish *In Grecian Garden* let me know, so that I can send it elsewhere. I don't usually send poems out unless Ginsberg asks me to. But I do feel *In A Grecian Garden* is my best poem so far, and I would like it to get published.

Let me know what you think of Ansen's poems, I feel he's my discovery. Ginsberg is always discovering, and quite well, too; but I, never. This is second time, first one was a poet named Sheldon Thomas who writes amazing poetry . . . soon I will send you some of his. Oh, do I tax you? Anyway snow in Venice today! And winds! All very beautiful. Atmosphere enough for me to write my beautiful *Grecian Garden*. Have you *Gasoline* yet? Again let me know what you think. I await O'Hara and Guest. Anthology coming along fine. I will continue mailing you poems, I have lots, but all need work, when done, I will send . . . be happy and joyous.

Love, Gregory

To Allen Ginsberg

Venice
[Feb.] 1958

Dear Allen,

Thanks for Chatterton, very thoughtful. What names from *Harvard Advocate* did you meet in London? Am yet expecting to hear all in nice big or small yet fantastic informing letter.

How is Bill? Is he working? I am working, but not too much these days. Want something, don't know what; pot, girls, people, Paris, something. I wrote to Jarrell for 250 dollars but no reply, [American] Academy. If he doesn't do it, who will? Surely I can get it. Did you write to Rosalind Constable for me? See review of *The Subterraneans* in *Time*? I sent [Stephen] Spender *Gasoline* some time ago. Write to him, perhaps he'll then acknowledge it. So far I hear nothing from anybody about book, except LaVigne who says he did poster and that Lamantia read *Sunday* and *I Am 25* at reading. But I hear nothing!

Sending Don Allen all my poems, everything. Also sent him two of Ansen's, *Heroin: An Ode* and *News Item*, but no reply as yet. Has Bill ever read the *Book of the Dead*? In it it states that Thoth, weigher of hearts, puts the innocent in the Field Of Beans. Beans also was something with Pythagoras, now there must be something behind this bean stuff. What? Osiris! Thy brother Set hath dabbed vile talc on his pythonic snout! Jack mailed me long scroll of *Mexico Blues*, what I read I like. So far no more mail for poets, no poems, just Kerouac, you, me, Bill, Ansen, Ferl, Shenker, Loewinsohn, Creagh. Ain't enough.

Hear it is cold in Paris, is Bill happy with German coat? Should keep him very warm; I am happy with mine because here it isn't too cold. I wrote a letter to Getty, the big oil man, and said: "A rose cannot defend a rose, therefore it is your duty, and not the poet's, to free Pound." A very good letter, clear, to the point, and interesting. I told him all he had to do was mention to reporters that Pound should be let free. An idea, anyway.

As you know, Ansen expects reciprocation, it's his way; you and Bill know this, thus it is unfair of both of you not to answer his letters. He shan't write until you do. Don't be lazy, we wish to hear from no one more than you two; perhaps though, you are snowed in at Git-le-Coeur and can't go out to *poste*. Alas, Bill Burroughs, of Tangier and Peru and Green Hell is pinioned by Parisian snow in a dark room forever in the eyes of obstinate dew. Shall Alan and I come to the rescue with Venetian shovels?

Alan is afraid to weigh himself. I make big cakes and puddings and ducks and hams and cheese—meatballs and spaghetti for him; just like a Dutch mother who wants to see her children get big and fat so that she can eventually put them in the oven for the final last grand meal. But I won't cook Ansen, no fear. Write write write write write write, or else I fain to loudness—sulked in dumbness—Ansen and I ever stone before thy and Bill's harkening ear-eye.

Love, and Alan sends his, Gregory

To Don Allen

Venice
Feb. 24, 1958

Dear Don,

Here are more poems. I will send much revised article, and first part of *To Bring Back The Dead*, this week. Went to Castelfranco yesterday—saw beautiful Giorgione. Probably will go to Florence for few days this week. Can you send me *The Subterraneans*? Would love to read it. Ginsberg just came back from London where he gave reading of *Howl* over B.B.C. He sent me wonderful photo of Chatterton—the one of him lying on bed—rat-poisoned, green, and sadly dead.

To Bring Back The Dead is an experimental poem in which I acquire formulas—some poetic, some fantastic, some quack—but all one unit. By process of alchemy in "words" I intend to bring [the dead] back to life. Poem is good medium for me to employ strange sentences and word-combinations. Yesterday Keats died. Having very nice time with Pegeen, P. Guggenheim's daughter.

Very sweet girl. She drove me to Castelfranco and Padova—but at Padova the Giotto chapel was *ferme.*

Love, Gregory

To Allen Ginsberg Venice
[early-March 1958]

Dear Allen, allen, alien,

Why arms hurt my angel, well take care yourself, or I come back to bug you, but I will guess go to Florence for the month by people who like me with big villa in April 15th, o, but at least I'll write and not starve. Getting much poems from wild New York, Roi, and Postell, he in Bellevue madhouse,[103] good poems, all; and Di Prima will send, and Levertov sent but she say in letter: "I just picked up *Gasoline* and quickly scanned over it and was sorry to see in the beginning a poem in the style of Ginsberg—becuz you have your own way and I think should follow it. Influence is one thing but a taking over of someone else's voice is ventriloquism. Please don't take offense, I like your own poems very much." I wrote back and tried to explain *Coit* to her. Was hurt. What an accusation! She missed whole point of *Coit*, like break away of end. O well. She girl.

Am very good friends with Peggy again, she cut my hair. Will be over for supper tonight. Harloff[104] here. Had good talk with him, he know me better now; I think I surprised him. Only thing like review but notice, about *Gasoline* was in *San Francisco Chronicle*, quite stupid, talked about, well I'll enclose the idiocy. What last two *Esquires* have to say? Did you get check from *Esquire* for April issue? I just wrote and asked for one if they take, but I much doubt if they'll take. Bosquet[105] sounds nowhere asking you to put up funds; don't fear me poverty, all will be well with me this summer; I only hope you know. Me all right. *Partisan* refused Ansen's fine sensitive real review and said they already got somebody to review it; you write to Constable?

Yugen too late to publish poem that they called great, will do it in next issue, a long poem about the American Indian, I first disliked it but now I like it better: It begins: "Wakonda! Talako! aesthonic turkey gobbling in the soft foot-patch night . . ." And ends with a new end, "myself should strangle the crabbed Logician for the wolf's inquire." Good mad poem. Called: *Spontaneous Requiem for the American Indian.*

Bill's reprimanding letter to me, fine, and true, and well, I am a pest at times but mine heart is good; that he knows, so I deserve any spanking, and what does he, you, or anybody think of *Gasoline*? Good God, ain't heard anything from anyone really good, or critical, ain't got any more books to send [Thomas] Parkinson, books ain't arrived yet. I did send one to Spender. Ferl says Paperback Bookshop ordered 250 [copies]. O the pittance! Odd thing is I have a much better book in type now. O well. But I like my *Gasoline* for all its ascent to the final good poems that I'll do.

Haikus the end: Jean Valjean walks in silk pajamas. Ants go to sleep. Beat Generation in France yes, but all gooey with God God and not Lucifer and not stabbed soap or fried shoes or or or.

Jarrell doesn't seem to be coming thru for 250 dollars grant, no answer, ah, pestilence. Roi, Levertov, everybody, 'cept Ansen, likes the small poems, I fear, I fear.

Judy Garland's trembling lower lip. Myself have a haiku:

> "Smolder the clouds of summer / I wanted a sea / the sea was awful." *or* "Virgil's head falls back—/ buoyant taxes; / enamel estuary buggy tombs." *or* "His book was *Gasoline* / but it was his fingers / they wanted to eat his fingers!"

Harloff will give you Kerouac's scroll. Love to you and Bill and hope all is good.

Gregory

To LeRoi Jones Venice

[early-March 1958]

Dig your poems and Postell much, what he in Bellevue for? Save him? Surely write to Ginsberg he write to someone so [they] get him out [maybe], hate to see poets in madhouse. The poems you like in *Gasoline* are light, what about *Arnold? Coit? Rotterdam?* Everybody like the light poems, almost like stabbing soap, frying shoes, hiding [doors] in pints; anyway that you dig *Requiem for Indian*, okay, but cut out all from page 3. Too answerable. Specially last line. Like no answer. Have it end, after . . . "massacre, massacre, o America, o Requiem" with this: "myself should strangle the [crossed] Logician for wolf's inquire." I would like to change lot in poem but can't because it was spontaneous like title says, so unfair for change, but can eliminate, alright, don't you think? I hope. But that: 'strangle the [creased] etc." is only lie in poem; why not. A poem should be full of lies [she steals] and smells the unicorn vomit. Denise Levertov writes me that *Coit Tower* is Ginsberg, has said she no see the parody that poem meant to be, but heartfelt, sad woe, but she fine poetess, but girl. No girl here in Venice for two months, I almost go mad; Venetian girls look at my milk-stained raincoat, and glue-fat pants, and Hesperian hair, and no like to talk with me about Universal Gnaw or electric poisons; so I go without girl, at night I embrace empty air; but last night I met a girl! Yes, now there is a girl afoot! I am almost happy.

What poems of yours or Postell's I'll use yet don't know; need much time for choice, I want only the imperfect poems; I hate perfect poems! "Perfection will not let you forget / the imperfection you did not get." But of course I love Mallarme. Maybe you know what I mean as imperfection; surely not poems for the Ozarkmen, but poems that bespeak Oafish cays and [Komouos] in the still fix of located scrub.

Di Prima hath a story about me that I should never know? But I fear. There are dark agents in New York who claim much that is useless of me, heed them not, Roi. Yes, no poet in madhouse anymore, get your friend out. Cause a disturbance or something; don't let him there; I was there; terrible. Speak up. Kerouac will help, Ginsberg, all will help, just cry.

I send you poem about my nostalgia for good ole New York. I remember finding Di Prima's poems interesting and mad and only didn't dig that hip overcast that was in 'em, but loved the purely mad ones, she good; but yet no poems from her, rush her, tell her the German publisher bites his nails. O the work! Anthologies is such work that I no like because . . . well, at least it'll be the maddest the goofiest anthology ever, and in German. Who are you? Did I ever see you? Do you lie? Tonight I burn fifty poems, I don't know what to feel. But I got to burn them because they've turned into leopard apples. What you mean by "Future quote from Kenyon"?

Saw great Mantagna yesterday at museum palace here. Tonight I eat squid with Peggy Guggenheim. Ink! Ink! Ink!

Love, Gregory

[Barbara] Guest good poet. What I've read—not much. Frank O'Hara, the end. Know you them?

To Allen Ginsberg, William S. Burroughs, Joy Ungerer and Balf[106]

Florence
March 6, 1958

Joy! Joy! City of beautiful bodies and music of stone—echo of Greece, all lovely. God has imitated Michelangelo Tombs! Tombs! One is almost inclined to jump in one of them—and gloat in the eternal fix. Alan sends love, love, and a screech against cars. I send love, love and sigh of awe.

Gregory

To Don Allen

Paris
March 27, 1958

Dear Don,

Am back in Paris hard at work on anthology. *Climax* wrote me asking for *Dollmaker Dialogue 2*—I sent it to you, can I send it to them? I am not satisfied with *Bring Back The Dead*—I must work work work on it—please destroy copy I sent you. Ginsberg fine. Many wild young hip Americans in Paris. They're everywhere! The plague is on. Joy to the future. Yesterday was my birthday—I got no presents—only a wild party at Allen's with four girls and Bill Burroughs, two Frenchmen, and the drummer Benny Clarke who dug *Howl* very much. We all took off our clothes and turned on, and decided that if this is sign of a new AND enduring generation, who would the Messiah be, what would he look like? We all decided he'd come with white shoes. After two months of quiet in Venice—the evening was needed—but no presents! Thus I ask you, Don, send me a present? Frank O'Hara's: *Meditations*. Both Allen and I want very much to see it. Hope all is good and beautiful with you.

Gregory

To Philip Whalen

Paris

[ca. March 29] 1958

Dear Phil,

Forgive me for not answering Quintexius's winged velvet letter, am back in Paris, Venice was good but dull, unlike the Bellini Carpaccio days of Doge Ducal yore. I like Paris much better because there are girls in Paris. No maiden can wonder the bird a gentle look, or fascinate the beast a pure creature. But it's not really girls I needed to love Venice better, nor the lack of them to love Paris less. Lately I find myself mostly concerned with the weight and distribution of LOVE. I loved everything once and it has become almost a horror in my present sleep that to love everyone is to wet the bed. What do you mean by love other than the love we all seem to agree with? I weigh the pounds of my love in accordance to the pounds of food, beds, cigarettes, soap, that is given me. Yet I do NOT distribute my love to the givers; instead I, dark at night with thoughts of bats and leopard apples, distribute it among the fabled. Woe to humancy [humanity]. And how are you my Philip Whalen? I bet you never told a lie in your life and that you might have stole or chased chickens but when asked if you put horseshoes in the tomb you did not lie. Does the judge you're staying with lie? Tell him I lie and that he can't get me because I'm safe in Paris living in a pool of lies and shan't drown; but of course, it's always truth that wishes to pull you under. Black Mountain too philosophical for so young a bunch of talented poets and students. Some of the poetry, maybe all the poetry, always says something that must be said, they experience certain things and express it; it is there; you see it; you dig it; end of poem; philosophy is very telling; BM [Black Mountain] is way out because they've discovered a way to marketize the Literary Bone. You are the only poet of your kind I know and I acknowledge you with arms filled with the joys of Spring, poet, clanking oven, I forget you. Will use all Slop Barrel for anthology; anthology coming along fine.

Love, Gregory

To Herschel Silverman[107]

Paris
[ca. March 29] 1958

Dear Hersh,

Thanks for your Hermes rainbow gift. Had a choice to pay part of rent or buy lots of food or go to a Champs Elyseé movie—or buy some pot—but wondered awhile about your kindness—and decided to give half to rent and half the rest to Allen. With my part I bought a big cake and lots of cherries and two bottles of Vitel and with the final 500 francs I bought some pot and got myself Allen Bill and BJ[108] high. In the middle of our high we all mentioned our love for a man in New Jersey who runs a candy store and we decided that you were our neo-wizard flowing with goodies, always with a smile—always protecting the good in life. Allen sends his love, I send my love. And if ever I get back to America—India hovers over me like a necessary light—we shall meet and you shall show me Bayonne—exchange poems and perhaps in due time I can interest you to join me to find Neptune's golden statue ten feet high that the Trojans had and worshipped until Ulysses came and took it away and drowned it somewhere in the Aegean.

Love, Gregory

To Robert LaVigne

Paris
[ca. March 29] 1958

Dear Bob,

Angel, years ago friend, and I never write you letters when I should and must and now I write to you [from] Paris, having left Venice where all was just as Turner says; and Carpaccio and the Bellinis and of course Longhi, Guardi, Canaletto, but o never Titian except his last great dim painting; and never Veronese and Tintoret but they did some crazy things; but like Vivarini most and Canova of sculpts most in Venice, of course went to Florence and saw wonder upon wonder and so quickly that I gave a DaVinci awe to Lippi, and a Botticelli glare to Polliaio [Pollaiuolo], can't spell his name, also saw beautiful Last Supper and Boboli Gardens. Saw much in day's time, am in Paris now where all is spring and light and joy and Allen and Bill are here philosophizing and Allen is going back in July to NY; I will stay forever; unless very broke and they kick me out.

Your poem to me was vulgar, I don't like dirty poems like that, sexy sexual mouthings of no import but to ass and cock when ass and cock themselves seek; my life of tongue has been blessed with curses. I ain't no square in that I put down such word usage; but when all you can think about when writing a poem is SEX SEX then it is SEX. (But of course in poetry one says it's not sex but soul). I feel that there are too many angels around with unhappy cocks. What a fucking thing to become sad and gloomy and poet over. The Melancholy of Cock! The Cock Screaming in the Crypt! Behold the Tomb of Cunt! Aughhhhh, the Vampire's Thin Ass! Anyway you got great way of expressing and need not use the sensitive parts of your body to relate the sorrow in your possible life. I sound real nowhere. I love you, always will, you very nurse delicate hand of ink and paint and touch, I always say you paint like a hallucinatory Japan. Gui de Angulo,[109] tell her send me poesy and love; and Peter Du Peru, I think of him always and all the goodness I knew in Frisco.

Really every body speaks about organs sexual; the rose fades; or the rose is wrapped around the cock of the brain that . . . I also saw Cranach's great Eve in Uffizi, very very wonderful;

Love, Gregory

To Paul Blackburn

Paris
[ca. March 29] 1958

Dear Paul,

Dug very much your poems, yes, very much. Will use most you sent, where and what books or magazines can I see more? I saw some, but would like to read much of your work for my own pleasure, so would Ginsberg, he, too, digs you much. Venice was beautiful architecturally but people were drags in way that when I sat by Grand Canal with my cloak and almost cried for romanticism and tried to measure a poem with calligram-gondola funeral that passed by, they, the Venetians, (very regimented all wearing cheap thin blue raincoats) marched by me un-Carpaccio pants-like making all kinds of denunciations to some imaginary Doge. They felt I was dirty because I had holes in my socks and I think I was very paranoid because I thought I would see Venice as Bellini saw it. Am very afraid to go to Greece because I always dream of Greece and if I see it I'll lose the dream. So far all Europe has been like that to me, except angel-Florence, maybe am getting older. I just read very stupid nowhere *New World Writing* poets article by Tambimuttu, sorta-like drowning creep grasping for shade of [Dylan] Thomas. He says that Thomas is great American poet, something like that, that whole nowhere social group, Oscar Williams, Tambimuttu, Garrigue, Eberhart (not so much Eberhart) and half of Williams' anthology. Saw them all at a party in New York once and they acted as if they were Hollywood stars or something, real scary. I tried to get Tambimuttu to talk about Mayakovsky[110] and Artaud and measure and form and space, and he knew nothing but that D. Thomas was/is greatest poet and that is only kind of poetry and I called him a creep, which he is. That whole New York scene is dying, thank Lucifer, Arabella Porter, Villa, Oscar, Tambimuttu, *Hudson Review*, deathical, end, happy, great ones in New York are Ashbery, Koch, Frank O'Hara, Levertov, I love Frank's poems, Don Allen is going to mail me *Meditations*, Frank's book, can't wait to get it, things are happening. Do you know of Bill Burroughs' work? Real great soul writer, master, Ginsberg and I always learning from him. A kid named Ed Marshall very good fine young poet, Wieners, also; are you married hung up with home children and cats and teaching?

Do you have a wild dark hidden in a drawer kind of experimental poem I can put with your poems I'm going to use? I'd like to have from all poets in anthology one wild BAD poem. So send. So far these are poets in anthology: Ginsberg, Whalen, Ferlinghetti, Kerouac, McClure, Carroll, O'Hara, Koch, Ashbery, Levertov, Loewinsohn, Wieners, Marshall, Creeley, Olson, Oppenheimer, Ansen, Burroughs, myself, you, Guest, Snyder, can't remember the rest, but all young and great, should be end anthology. Yet the translation is going to be a job, Höllerer has five translators he'll use, but I'll have to work with them, chance to really pick up on German, then I can read beautiful Hölderlin, Goethe. I met a lot of young German poets, a lot of them are experimenting, some very way out forms and sounds, most of them are visual-sound poets; very good one is [Horst] Bingel, and Hennimen; they dig Heinrich Böll and Hugo Ball; not to keen on Benn.[111] Anyway things are happening in Europe too; poetry really coming alive.

Also in Holland, but not very much in England, Allen says, they don't dig William Carlos Williams or just don't give him a chance, and their poets are too political and not mad universe. France has some yet not much either, all the experimentalists still talk about Breton and well, that's enough, thanks for your beautiful poetry,

Gregory

To Peter Orlovsky Paris

April 2, 1958

Dear Peter,

It's been so long, too long, since sight or word or tear hath passed our eyes tongues hearts—how are you, angel? And you are belabored with unliving men in a sad hospital, good for those wretched souls to know the nurse of your young hands.[112] And poetry—you are writing much—capital!—and Jacky mio reads your wonder—marvelous! How I miss my New York City. "No mayor I knew of that city/ that stood/ with magnificent foundations in his eyes". Still it is a beautiful city and my heart goes out to it. Lafcadio is transforming to the angelic call, need not fear for him. His path is lain. He only needs freedom to grace the path with some determined step. And Jack is M.C. and read some of my mouthings, how splendid! Jacky reads well and knows my voice. A house on Long Island! Long Island is new Olympus. Joyce[113], and is she yet with world and old Columbia days grim drear of love in soda and Herder? Jack's angel with a cunt. My Hope was a Shelley with a cunt. Too many angels with cocks around. But angel is angel.

And Lamantia, he is deserved of money, catholic-mystic-spiritualism necessitates GOLD, had not gold been great a thunder in the reign of Christ? But you are right, poetry was never meant to be gramercy to GOLD. Voice your soul to the human ear, for no metal.

I yet walk Paris with dusty hands and clothes. I eat seldom, random but well. I am foolish still and happy and I yet cry when drunk and when not drunk and I yet live for beauty and am yet dedicated to die for beauty, thus I drink, drug, and feel the comfort of my old good lovely dovely Hyperionic friend, by old lovely childhood friend—Charlie Doom.

There is a lot of sun now. Sun all the time. I have met a batch, a flock of new angels—ex-black jacketed rock-n-roll motorcyclists—they have forsaken their noir jackets and music and speed—and have become huge bearded long haired dirty wild screaming new born dreamers, thinkers, spiritualists, poets—not one considers politics. There is hope. There is hypnotic insistence. There are traumatic herewiths! There is a lot of sun. Beautiful sun—the psychopath bathes on the roof.

Be happy at all mathematical illuminations. To you and to Jack who hath caused the rapid blinking of God's verbatim, and to Lafcadio who is growing beautifully and to Lamantia who attends the distribution of garlands, and to Joyce who enforces the dire agencies in the final solution of light. Lucien is yet in my apocalyptic image. Dusty Moreland I will always love. And Anton [Rosenberg] is quiet still. Though Stanley Gould moves! "In the park of God / There are no children." Maybe there are?

Love, Gregory

To Don Allen

Paris

[ca. April 2] 1958

Dear Don,

Been so damn busy on anthology, saw Höllerer this week, gave him many manuscripts, must select more for him though, am allotted 250 pages for anthology. He has four very good hip translators. Ginsberg dug him very much, they like Creeley the end, say he's great poet. Höllerer said he wrote you.

As for your anthology these are the ten of mine I like most: *Army, Power, Dialogue: 2 Dollmakers, Uccello, Birthplace Revisited, In The Tunnel Bone Of Cambridge, In The Morgue, Last Warmth Of Arnold, On Food, Italian Extravaganza.* I selected two from my *Vestal Lady*. I enclose them: *Tunnel Bone Of Cambridge*, and *In The Morgue*, they were written in 1954, and should be dated.

You have *Army* and *Power* and *Dollmakers*, the rest are from *Gasoline*. I changed Dialogue of *Dollmaker* slightly, I took out the last line about making something out of "Japan," I'd much rather it end on "Abandon Farms To Use." What do you think of selection? As for the other poems you have of mine, I'd wish you throw them away because I am working working working on them, I first liked *In A Grecian Garden* very much, some very nice lines in it, but overall, it's nothing, same for a lot of others I sent you. You also have *On Food*, so I needn't send that. Am going to England in two weeks with Allen, should be fun, I want very much to see Albion. Thanks for O'Hara's book. He is indeed a very fine poet. I'm going to use, if it's all right by you, his *On The Movie Industry In A Crisis* for German anthology. Let me know if this is okay.

Love, Gregory

To Paul Blackburn Paris

[May 20] 1958

Dear Paul,

I sent and recommended Eith Aron's name to Höllerer, but Höllerer already has four translators working, what a business. I only took on this thing because good representation of what's happening in American verse should be shown, but I hate all this business; I am incapable of it, but my job isn't too bad, all I have to do is receive poems and send them on to Germany, only thing that bugs me is rejecting, just ain't in me. I don't know if they'll give any money for gathering of poems or will give any to poets, I'm not doing it for that anyway, just want to get Wieners, Marshall, Oppenheimer, you, Kerouac, Burroughs, Ginsberg, Whalen, McClure, Black Mountain, San Francisco, O'Hara, Ashbery, Koch etc etc etc together. I want to go to India and sleep among the cows. [. . .]

Damn anthologists and translators, too much like selling sardines, too much sound of ambition and all that, bah, the only thing, write write or don't write or live or don't but no hang-ups on writing and living. Thanks for your book, liked it very very much, you is good poet, but somehow I don't feel any disorder in you, don't know maybe it's good that way. I know I always get into a mess when I am not ordered, always saying too much of wrong silly things, and too little of right serious things; was proved in a recent interview Allen and I had with a journalist funny man, very nowhere. After this anthology I abandon all, India, thought, dream, sweet companionship; alien gaud.

I wrote a long poem about A-Bomb about how I dig it and how I would like to put a lollipop in its furcal mouth, a wig of goldilocks on its baldy bean, and about how everybody wants to die of cancer old age electric chairs but not by bomb, and about how I want to eat the bomb's boom, etc. all very much against bomb, but in right way, I feel. One must not hate, for that which one hates is apt to destroy.

No copies, if I had one I'd send it on; Allen gave a batch of poems and works to *Paris Review*, *Bomb* poem included. The *Paris Review* people here are very gentle and good and, well, not as I expected them to be. But damn all magazines and things, it all comes on too much like red frogs, unique, skip, funny, novelty, is poetry necessary for publication? I mean is it the intent of Black Mountain to do and having done, be seen, read? Don't know what it is, when I write a poem, I don't know who to send it to. I send it to friends, Don Allen of Grove, or Wieners of *Measure* or *Yugen* but never to non-friends or connections, but I do send out to these friends, why? Surely I do not write to send to them, all very confusing. I shouldn't think too much about that, but can't help it. Don't want to fall into that state where one's only concern is publication; and reason I come on with this is that you and BM [Black Mountain] and S.F. give me that impression, and I've fallen into that impression; but it ain't so bad, because you do write great poetry. I guess I'm just bugged by the ambition scene, but why not ambition? Poetry should be given to all, should be sold, be given all all all; but what would Shelley say? I don't believe in the girl diary type who writes and hides it, shows no one; but I also don't like the poet ostentatious list-of-all-the-magazines type either. Transition, the in between, the indifferent one, Burroughs and Whalen are like that, they don't care, they write for themselves. Allen is inspired, I am inspired, we both like to see our poems in print, but the kick lessens all the time; ego be damned, the great poet of the future will cut the throat of the I.

My early Sunday morning spoor.

Love, Gregory

To Robert LaVigne Paris

[May 22] 1958

Dear Bob,

Just got back from London where Allen and I read poetry to Oxford at B.B.C. and got drunk and saw all London sad and swans on the Thames and Auden and Blake's grave and [Edith] Sitwell at George Barker and the angry young men all very English and tired and old but sweet and gentle. How are you, aged friend, sorrow, Uccello friend? I wanted to write you sooner but I have been so dotty these last few months. Anyway I love thee and all 1956 when just I saw you S.F. on Leavenworth Ave. How is De Haro Street? Will I go to Russia? Where should I go? I don't want to go to Mozambique. Wherever no money will take me—I'll go. Or: wherever money takes me I will die. Anyway I am sure to lull in Europe for quite some indescribable time. Saw a lot of great Turners in England, he really was a prophetic painter.

Hope you are well,

Love, Gregory

To John Wieners Paris

[May 22] 1958

Dear John,

Yes, your poems in time. Germany got four good translators working full time, very difficult job this translating business. My job is done, I collected it—fine—thanks for sending. Got *Measure*, I understand what Duncan says, he's right, in a way. But it all depends what kind of workshop one wants to run—*Origin, Black Mountain Review,* they are workshops, and good ones. Just came back from London where Allen and I gave readings at Oxford, London, B.B.C. All very enlightening, they dug us, except at one reading at Oxford, they threw [a] shoe at me for reading crazy *Bomb* poem I wrote—all about the Bomb being lonely and sad because everybody wants to die by cars lightning drowning electric chairs, but not by *Bomb*. A parody really, but they couldn't get it—anyway, it did bug them. I told everybody about Marshall's beautiful poem in *Black Mountain*—I love that poem—and it is being translated into German now for anthology. Paul Blackburn real great poet—he sent me poems, too. When my typewriter is fixed I'll send you nice long letter about walking in Christ Church with mellow sad eyed Auden, huge drunks with George Barker, and lunch at the Lady Macbeth Society with Edith Sitwell—all very strange and funny. She says poetry today its hope, is definitely American.

Thanks for poem, thanks for *Measure*, although that *Yaaaah* thing is old hat for me, don't like it, old old poem from the gray ghost pile in my room of poems. If you like nicer poems for next or next or near far time *Measure*, I'll send.

Love, Gregory

To LeRoi Jones Paris
[May 22] 1958

Dear Roi,

Sorry so late—been to London. Allen and I gave readings at Oxford, London, and B.B.C. At B.B.C. they said I should learn to pronounce the word "combatant." Allen very much admired by young hipsters in Soho, met George Barker, very away aware gentle man (but he is lost in the dusty iamb attic.) Also saw Auden twice—he acted like my Shelley at Oxford—leading us to Christ Church—pointing out the Oxford of his youth—very mellow angel, he. Saw Sitwell too—she invited us to lunch at her "club"—the Lady Macbeth Society—it was all very strange. Allen and I went to see her high. She ordered some very odd food for us, shrimps caught in frozen butter. She is real soul. Likes our poetry and when we offered to turn her on she gracefully declined saying "I fear I have been denied the joy of drugs—I once had morphine and became ill."

To Elaine Feinstein Paris
[May] 1958

Dear Elaine,

Yes, always felt social civic something's-wrong-with-our-system poetry was uninspired, good that you'll have an English magazine bereft of that; I mean when Blake saw the cold woe in his chartered streets his vision was not a civic one but heaven directed sight, eyes of an angel spotlighting the Thames, and lo the swan, he saw the swan. And if one must by one's need see civic social how much grander it'd be if one worked that see into a wild mad illuminating humor. Shelley is a good example of a poet who, conscious and heartfelt for social conditions remedied such dour by ethereal inspiration. Most young poetry of late is gossiped dark polemics, such poets really have nothing galaxy to say; they'd never wear velvet, no weakness, that good poet weakness, in their we're-for we're-against the bowler hat man's zombic mien; though I did see that inspiration I love so well in Dom Moraes and Christopher Williams and Geoffrey Hazzard who are not so hung on social welfare; whereas Logue who is pure poet is doomed with his political rut, his golden wheel spins greener and greener; politics and betterment of earthly conditions is death to poetry, unless these newspaper subjects be treated with light, love and laughter, like Allen's *Howl* and my *Bomb*. Imagine the young English poet writing great verses about the Battersea Powerhouse, or the four moused lions surrounding columned Nelson, with no concept of what is wrong with England but with love of the past and the beauty that was England, heaven built, by such architects as Marlowe Nash Clare Smart Shakespeare Shelley Keats Wordsworth

Swinburne—couldn't see Swinburne hung on why parents don't get along with their children.

Ah this angry young man thing, what if one were angry young at God's lack of gift to us, the senses are insufficient. Why don't these angry young angels rage at the stars and demand the stars stop staying so far apart from each other, but that they join each other, and coil around each other like a ball of rattlesnakes? Anyway something like that. City systems are born dead, sometimes the death takes hundreds of years; the law of 1834 will undoubtedly change in 1958; were poets meant for such duty as to hasten the death? that they in their lifetime see the change? If so all I can say is what a sad duty the muse has bestowed; anyway, it seems she has leveled such a hand upon England. In America, yes, much civil social there, and poets are writing verses for its betterment, but they do it not as a duty but as a vast earthly joke, because these American poets lack a remedy; they can just show the condition, that is all, they accept it as part of the time that will soon become part of history, that perfect history, perfect because it is done, no matter what anyone does or says, it is done, history, finished; the new American poet accepts this, and so with no actual complaint records it, and records it dadaistically almost. These American poets I speak of are few; of the older poets, I would say William Carlos Williams and Auden and Robert Lowell are social when they are social in a grand way; they would not anoint let's say NYC with their rose. I get the feeling that that's what the young English poets are doing; poor muse, they ain't sacrificing any imagination lambs to her. But then again poetry is poetry, and these poets whose golden wheels are rutted in her are poetry; all is poetry, I've always believed that; there can't be a right and wrong way with poetry, so in other words I don't know what I'm talking about, never do when it comes to making some comments or statement about it; though I do feel a poet should die for his poetry die gloriously and nobly for it, and my heart tells me it ain't so noble or grand to better the conditions of death, they the poets, happen to be born in; poets are born in heaven, and when born dropped out of their whirling starry beds unto earth, like little human parachutes, where they land is none of their affair.

Well, I just got out of bed and you have a nice long letter from me.

Love, Gregory Corso

To LeRoi Jones

Paris
[June] 1958

Dear Roi,

Thanks for letter, and thank you very much for your Hettie[114] who I'm sure put *Spontaneous Requiem for the American Indian* in some great crazy form, can't wait to see how she did it, was too much for me, because if I would have put it into form I would have changed whole thing around somehow. I am continuing *Requiem*, I now have section two, done spontaneously two weeks ago, all about the Indian Gods and rituals and games and food, if you're interested in second part I'll send it on; but this time I am giving it some sort of pattern, form, etc. but as free as first part.

I wish you would send me that so-so review in *Odyssey*, have yet to see a review of *Gasoline*. Can you send it on? Allen and me been drinking and getting silly with interview with funny man masses Art Buchwald, real nowhere and jerky interview, but who cares, I guess I do, so does Allen, O well, all is forgivable—but no more interviews. Number 3 *Yugen* sounds like great venture . . . Allen be back in NY July, me may go to India and sleep among cows, but am nostalgic for my NY; just kind of afraid to go back, fear fear that city, its albatross back.

Love, Gregory

To Gary Snyder — Paris

[June 4] 1958

Dear Gary,

Thanks for poems, should be translated in few months, will send you translations. Book due for '59. You can publish them anywhere, no hang up. Paris calm after threat of civil war—paratroopers and all—very strange. I used to say much, but I don't say much anymore because I am trying the six deductions of silence—that is, I'm plowing my way through the silencer's warty ear. Besides I once wrote you a letter full of enthusiasm and joy and noise and you never answered. I thought perhaps you considered me presumptuous but I eat the dark like bread. What to write you who only knows your poetry while I love all the tales from Allen's tongue about you which I also dig. So joy to the human sparkle! Please give my love to beautiful Phil Whalen. I was in London and saw Blake's grave in Bunhill Center. O that poetry were cannibalistic enough to eat the I.

Gregory

To Don Allen — Paris

[June 21] 1958

Dear Don,

Saw Barbara Guest couple of times, she very blond aloft alive gentle. She and her husband went to England this week, when they come back, I'll see them again. Allen going back to NY in July, if I get the funds I may come back too, don't know. Am almost finished with anthology; never again will I take on such a venture, one needs more than just a taste for poetry. Overall it'll be an awkward yet mad collection. I enclose two poems maybe you could use. Are you happy with the ten poems I selected? Allen would like to know if you're satisfied with his too. Guess you're very busy, why don't you go to Bar Harbor Maine and eat lobsters all summer, I went there two years ago and saw dolphins bound in the sea, that's all I recall about it; so maybe you shouldn't go. Thanks for Frank's book [Frank O'Hara's *Meditations in an Emergency*], he really is great poet.

Been meeting lots of interesting people in Paris, had lunch with Jacques Tati, went to party and [had] long talk with Duchamp, Man Ray, Peret[115], the old shades of dada-year. Duchamp laughed all the way on the metro with Allen's *Howl*, Allen ate his shoe; I ate Man Ray's tie, Allen was all right; I got sick.

Love, Gregory

To Gary Snyder Paris
[ca. June 30] 1958

Dear Gary,

Persian poets, have you read the Shah-nama? Read it long time ago and liked it very much. Allen and me were interviewed by syndicated funny man for masses newspapers, silly jerky and drunk interview, guy named Art Buchwald who came on sympatico, but his article sounds as if he interviewed two nowhere Bohemian cats, o, well, all is forgivable, next time I know better. Allen says poetry expiates all; he's right, but this 'beat generation' nonsense lessens the poetic intent, no wonder the academy poets keep aloft. Poetry is not for public humor make-fun-of kicks, ridiculous, the whole thing, sardine salesmen. I've been failing my Shelley, it's so easy to jest, and I am always no-practical way of coming on when metre or measure or form or stress is concerned. Poetry is a private thing done in private for the private, yet masses lurk Victor Hugo-like at executions waiting for the poet to grow a beard and do something goofy, expected of him. O well, if I am guilty of that, and have hurt the poetic idea of life, then I am to be forgiven because I do it impulsively. Need solitude, all right when I write, am serious and laughable in elegant good poetry way. But when asked to talk about poetry and life to interviewers all I can say is fried shoes or something and give some silly experience, all very nowhere. So I now learn to keep quiet. That interview, in *Herald Tribune*, really got me wrong and showed me as a talkative, idiot. I worry about it because I, as a poet, least of all people, should not go novelty on the thing I will die for.

So, if you ever get chance to read it, forgive me. I think mainly the reason for my silliness and Allen's in interview was because some girl from Frisco came to Paris and showed us articles and clippings of the S.F. scene that came on so nowhere and gloomy and bullshit and sad, that I felt inclined only to be silly. For sure there is laughter and no station in the good poets of San Francisco, McClure, Whalen, Duncan, for instance, but those clippings that girl brought by depressed Allen and me so much, we decided to be jerky, funny, silly, and perhaps change the clime that is threatening gloom.

Sad news about Neal being in jail[116], Connie Sublette being strangled;[117] good God, how horrible. I love your poems, my love to you, hope this letter makes sense and not too much reprimanding of myself for past talk.

Love, Gregory

To LeRoi Jones Paris

{June 30} 1958

Dear LeRoi,

Fair poet of long time since we met and I screamed but will you assume my friendship as ever never ending though I did write a funny [sinister?] poem about FRIEND. "They always want to get NEAR you"—I make it spooky—Anyway, send me things to read, like Yugen, and Totems, and does your child talk yet? Give it Mother Goose not, Mother Goose hath caused much woe-light on children.

Is Ray[118] really back in Bordentown? Can I write to him there? I will. I miss New York, yet shan't return until the ADVENT presents itself—and I feel it will—soon. Or, but I am a weary and flipping, return to U.S.A. and rush the ADVENT. Anyway, I think and write and dream and WOE, JOY.

There's big woman conspiracy going on. Watch it. Soon the Arab women will break free, then what? Wham! Kali, the Goddess of Destruction—something must happen—women are restless—no bomb, no war, no history, no time. Womankind is womantime. Must tell you the only really beautiful thoughts I have of New York was the tour with you and Bremser. O.K. Love to Hettie.

Love, Gregory

Burroughs here—full of magic.

To Lawrence Ferlinghetti Paris

{ca. July 17} 1958

Dear Larry,

Got *Gas—Howls*. Allen left for N.Y. So far my *Bomb* poem has been parodied and written about without being published. *Paris Review* got it, but I'd like to print it up myself because I want it in shape of *champignon* {mushroom}, a long sheet. If I do so I'll send you batch. The way worldly things seem today, poem is very timely - a Chaplinesque kind of poem—satirical. Write me—give me news, Henri Michaux up for supper, digs my poesy very much. Paris calm.

Love, Gregory

To Don Allen Paris

[July 21] 1958

Dear Don,

I'll be in Paris at least until November—do come and see me—Allen off to U.S. four days ago. Henri Michaux sees me and Burroughs for supper at our place, he's really inspired, great talks. He and Bill talk about various kinds of effects from nutmeg—how many cq's in a pill etc. He said he likes my poesy "mad children soda caps." Even with my poor French and his poorer English we had rapport. Been very busy on *Bomb* poem—very timely—its shaped like a *champignon*. By the way, except for the poems you want for anthology, can you send me rest back? I've been reworking so much that most I sent you from Italy Venice, are changed and people ask me for poems and I don't have any.

Best love, Gregory

To Lawrence Ferlinghetti Paris

[July 28] 1958

Dear Larry,

Yes, I hope I get some money on second printing because I am getting my *Bomb* poem printed here. Very expensive printers in Paris, for 2,000 copies (a single sheet) 40,000 Francs—100 dollars. I want poem printed myself because its got to be a single sheet—to look like a mushroom—*Paris Review* has poem but they'll put it on five pages. Really great poem—best I've ever done. I had difficulty with ending—didn't know whether to end on hopeful note or funny note or bitter note. I decided upon the last, alas. Hope you didn't change my *Car* poem.

To Allen Ginsberg Paris

[late July] 1958

Allen,

I am off to Lapland for two weeks. When I come back Bill will be gone for a month, Spain. I will fly to Stockholm—from Stockholm, after day's sightseeing blond angels, will take plane to Lapland—top of the world—midnight sun. An experience, I guess—no, no guess, it will be because I'll have to be on horseback six days and I don't know how to ride—adventure. Cost me 100 dollars and the rest will be paid by the guy who planned the whole thing. Bill thought I was being conned into something, but last night we had supper with the guy and his wife, and Bill agrees all's all right. Guy just digs taking me along—poet, etc.

Anyway even if when I'm on a high mountain he annoys me with silly talk—it'll be worth it. I finished *Bomb* poem—had much difficulty, pain, thought, for ending. Could have ended it with light or profundity, or humor, or bitterness, I choose the later because deep in me it's the way I feel—someday perhaps the light, but as for now—no.

George Whitman will print it up in his new job as publisher, mine will be the first (scroll) yours the second, Whalen third, Snyder fourth. Send me long poem, mother poem.[119] George very hip on doing this—just thousand of sheets—no fanfare—natural. Anyway, hope you are well and all is Peter and moon.

Love, Gregory

Tomorrow Lapland, yaks, reindeer cult. Will I return? Alas—will write from Tannu Tuva.

To Don Allen Stockholm

[Aug.1] 1958

Dear Don,

This is beautiful city. Will spend five days here then off to Lapland. Tomorrow I meet two Swedish poets. The people are so quiet—and the city is clean, and they have ravens on the lawn and the restaurants are dim and Viking the girls lovely. I'll be back in Paris on the 15 of August—so I'll be there to see you when you arrive. Alas! I wish I could live in Sweden forever. All is calm here. Will write you from Lapland.

Love, Gregory

To Allen Ginsberg Stockholm

[Aug.1] 1958

Dear Allen,

This city is really lovely—and the blond people! How they stare at my blackness! Quiet, they make no noise—only cars make noise—the restaurants are cozy Viking-like—and the parks green, brisk—and they have ravens on the lawn, and the girls are the prettiest in the world. I'll hitch to Lapland in five days—want to spend lots of time here—most beautiful city I've been in. I could live here forever.

My love to Peter—will be back in Paris on 15th.

Gregory

This hotel too classy—will get room in "Old Town"—like Amsterdam—no meet any poets yet. Guy I'm with is a bore—I told him I want to be alone—

he go to Lapland alone, and I alone. All in all I have plane ticket back to Paris, but wish I could live in Stockholm.

To Lawrence Ferlinghetti

Stockholm
[early Aug.] 1958

Dear Larry,

Letter to let you know I'm on my way to Lapland—the North Pole—wish to dig the reindeer cult, and the peace, the midnight sun—etc. Alas, wish I could spend all the time in Stockholm, really is a lovely city—and the girls—all blond, all like 5th Ave. *Harper's* models. Please have money in Paris for me when I return broke on the 15th of August. Hope I don't die in the snows of a Lap.

Love, Gregory

To Lawrence Ferlinghetti

Sweden
[Aug. 6] 1958

I am in Lapland, rode a horse three days, never rode a horse before. Yet to see the midnight sun, but reindeers abundant. People very indifferent, they get high on muscarine, a sort of mushroom, can't get any, yet. Will be back in Paris in two weeks, same address. Hope when I come back you'll have sent me money, trip cleans me. My love here to you on top of world,

Gregory

To Allen Ginsberg

Stockholm
[Aug. 8] 1958

Dear Allen,

Flying back to Paris tonight—earlier than I had expected to. Will spend one day in Copenhagen. I just don't know how to go into a country and relax. Too excited. Was interviewed here by newspaper on BG [Beat Generation]. I told them the only answer to everything was love.

Gregory

To Don Allen

Paris
[Aug. 12] 1958

Dear Don,

Just back from lovely Copenhagen . . . I received *Evergreen Review,* number 5, and I thought what a wonderful cover this picture of me between two monks would be; it was taken over a year ago, on Boulevard du Montparnasse. Allen in US, Bill in Tangier, I all alone. Höllerer due here this week; Ashbery here, will seek him out; have just completed my bomb poem, *Paris Review* says they'll take it, but they won't do it in mushroom shape, have it fold on one long page, like *Esquire* girl of the month. So maybe for sake of mushroom I will get it printed up myself, in any case it's a poem I am very happy about, even the ending which gave me so much trouble, having ended the poem with no light.

Yes, I am always happy to see a new *ER*, somehow I feel a little part of it, when I receive it, I alone in all Paris have the copy, and I lend it to the bookstore in the reading room, then when the bookstores get it, I take my copy back. In Stockholm I went to book stores and *Subterraneans* is big seller there, also saw *ER* record in few of the bookstores. If you don't use picture please send back, or even if you do please send back, and photo's credit name is on back of photo, everybody I show it to flips.

Hope to see you soon, Gregory

To Lawrence Ferlinghetti Paris

[ca. Aug. 12] 1958

Dear Larry,

Just back from Copenhagen, very nice pleasant city, but of all cities I love Paris best, now that it is August all the *boulangeries,* most all the cafes, are closed for vacation; Allen is in US, Bill in Madrid, and I all alone in rue Git-le-Coeur, in a nice room that sees only Sainte-Chapelle and the tower in which Antoinette awaited her head. Please send me a copy of second edition; how wonderful that City Lights pocketbooks do so well, poetry at last has regained its bardic mien. In Stockholm they know all about Beat Generation and San Francisco, they don't know what to make of it, but the youth there seem enthusiastic, no wonder, that country has much death in it.

My *Bomb* is finished and *Paris Review* will take it but I wanted George Whitman to print it up like mushroom shape, which review can't do. Whitman, Mistral,[120] wants to come out with a single sheet series of either one long poem or manifesto, etc., printers in Paris *tres chere,* one wanted 40 thousand francs for one thousand sheets of a poem, too much.

Larry, please send me what you can on second book because I am broke, that trip to Spain and up North has left me in my room with potatoes and yogurt. Don't even have enough to mail this letter; I got a month back 150 dollars from National Arts and Sciences, very nice of them. What news? Has Hope Savage arrived in S.F. yet? Is Neal really doomed to five to life? Can't anybody help? That *Odyssey* review proves that little magazines deserve to die, no wonder the whole world hates a little magazine. Actually it was pretty funny about that Neal comparison, alas, got a letter from Allen. Him all right but had kidney stone, and he almost wonders why he left Europe, but he can make it anywhere. I still am determined to go to India this fall.

Write to me, love, Gregory

To Gary Snyder

Paris
[ca. Aug. 12] 1958

Dear Gary,

Just back from Lapland, very strange but I liked Viking Stockholm much better, went to Lapland and got lost and cold and wanted so much to get back to that city of gold girls, all like Vogue models. One week in city and saw much of sorrow and why they have highest suicide rate. The people are *mort*, they can't be shocked into anything. It's artists' big complaint there, they say they can't shock the Swedes, very funny. Lots of morphine addiction there among the young. Well am back in Paris now, and Allen is gone to USA and Bill is off to Tangier. So all alone in lonely August Paris. All the Frenchmen leave city in this month, good. Now I walk the streets at night and can imagine to hear George Sand Musset Flaubert arguing their worth over some drunken table. Some artist in Sweden, quite famous, but I forget his name, very hard names to remember, did a life mask of me, but it looks like a death mask. I have it in my room, but can't bear to hang it up, what to do with it? I guess it's something nice to have, maybe I'll take picture of it and send it to everybody.

A friend of mine in England, a very aware guy, is starting a magazine called *London Today* and he would like some poems. He doesn't want to start a little magazine and run it for ten issues or less and fold, he wants to come out with a one shot deal, a mad wild issue, and that's all. So please send him something, but this sending out thing is becoming a drag. I made the mistake of promising four editors my *Bomb* poem and now they're all bugged with me, because each wants to print it first or something. Anyway Allen says give it to all of them, which is right, that old little mag taboo of one publisher at one time, is absurd. So you see my problems which are slight and funny and good. I am very set and happy and I complain like an old shoemaker, but India will soon take care of the complaints, alas, I go in November, with Bill and a polio, smileless young Harvard profound very deep junkie writer Rothschild heir [Jacques Stern] who I love very much, really a very beautiful soul.

Have you ever read Kzwang Zu, I think that's how you spell name? Last night I had a fantastic dream in which I got on a boat and went down a stream past China and into Russia where I met girls and boys who liked me very much, then I found Allen at my side and he said if they catch us they'll shoot us as spies, so we ran back on the boat and slipped again unnoticed past China and back to Paris. Very funny situation or location of ferreting thru China.

I hope you are well, and that if you are in S.F. that you meet an old love of mine, two years back, lived with her two years, very young angel of a girl, Hope Savage. She has studied Chinese and is really a pure angelic mind.

Perhaps you can leave a message for her in City Lights, she has been in Europe all over and just arrived in USA. Nothing more to say, it is noon, but it is dark, because it is going to rain.

My love, Gregory

To Lawrence Ferlinghetti Paris

[late Aug.] 1958

Dear Larry,

Ah Sheldon Thomas, very funny he there, him not to be heeded gossip wise too much, but shan't go into that . . . Now George Whitman has abandoned idea about publishing business, too expensive here, so please for me, with money coming me, use to print this up, small print, centered right hand margin justified, on single sheet of paper, so that mushroom effect will stand out . . . now I hope you don't think this poem is what you term my "fascistic thundering," it ain't. I wept over poem, and I dare say it is a very inspired poem; *Paris Review* said they'd publish it here in Paris office but have to hear from New York office and if old Donald Hall has anything to say about it, it ain't gonna get to see the light of day; though here they are very excited about having it. So far, on one reading, this poem has been parodied twice, once in *New Statesman* and other in *French Arts*; I want it published before that damned bomb does fall, but now that the moon is objective I doubt much if it will fall. So write me express please and let me know if you're going to do that for me, you can use what's coming me for printing.

Hope all is well, Paris very lovely at this time of year, saw Michaux few times, didn't get up to Lapland, only ninety miles up, got lost, cold, came back to Stockholm and stayed there over a week . . . I like Paris best.

Love, Gregory

Now please don't take ten years to answer, let me know right away, and don't show poem to anybody, because if *Paris Review* finds out here, they'll be bugged. All this silly ethic be damned, small magazines are always demanding return stamps and don't send same poem to two places at once. Larry, so that paper won't be too long get it printed in small type, long enough that it can fold once or twice.

But if you think not to publish it, then please send me some loot because I am a grown man who does not ask people for money and starves, or has learned to starve, quietly. But you ain't Mr. Ferl publisher to me, you are poet, and a man who befriended me in S.F., on those feelings I ask you to send me some fucking Viking armlet ores or Kronas. It's not that I am poor, just broke, as Mike Todd once said. For you see I flew to Stockholm and back, a gift of a ticket, and millionaire angel friend Rothschild gave me 200 bucks, and will always give me more without asking, but him on Antibes yacht for August and shan't be back till late Sept. Oh damned lies of gold, so come off this publisher talk about no sales yet, and treat me as one who does roam in bright ashes . . . Larry, if you no want to do this lovely poem for me, one can never tell your whirlwind decisions, do try to get it published in some S.F. small mag, preferably *Needle*, so that S.F. gets to see it . . . I read in *Nation* an article by some guy praising a group of S.F. unknown to me, but it all sounded like the Son of Bad Bohemian poetry making his laughs. He better be careful else Captain Poetry will put on his magic cape and Zeusam after him. Do all you can for me, I deserve it, I am Poids net Andalouse Raffine.

But write me right away, I miss your letters, next letter I tell you all about *Coney Isle of Mind.*

▼ [The following letter has been significantly shortened from the original twenty-one page version by the editor. Ellipses showing the many omissions are not included to make it easier to read. The whole letter is in response to Kerouac's book, *The Subterraneans*, which is based on a love triangle in which Corso wins the affections of Kerouac's girlfriend. Corso remarked later that since he and Kerouac were not close friends at the time (1953), he was doing nothing disloyal through his actions. This letter shows that once he had become closer to Kerouac and read Jack's own account of the story, he regretted his actions.]

Jack Kerouac — Paris

[ca. Aug. 21-25] 1958

Dear Jackie, mio

A long long letter from my heart because your *Subterraneans* made me cry, you did not understand me. Alas nor myself at time. Human beings, they live they die, what a drag to punish them or reward them. Imagine some guy being born to shine shoes all his life, then he robs somebody and kills him and gets the electric chair and goes to hell. It doesn't make sense. The opposite of him is just as laughable. A man is born to love God and lives by God and dies by God and goes to heaven. All I can say then is that heaven must be a pretty creepy place, it seems like all the squares go there. I always felt that were there such a thing as heaven and hell, I'd rather hell, because who wants to spend eternity with the little old Italian lady fingering her rosary in the church. I mean, what can I say to her? Or she to me? If I heed all my Catholic upbringing then surely Shelley is in Hell. I once asked a priest, "Do you really think beautiful Shelley is in hell?" And he said, "He left his wife didn't he? Married another didn't he? Was an Atheist, wasn't he? Then surely his soul rests in hell." But I said, "Look at his poems, he loved God!" Now that I think of it I was raised a Catholic, how strange! I used to go to church every Sunday and I had my first communion and my confirmation. I believed it all and I used to say hundreds of Hail Marys happily for the poor souls in Purgatory, but always when I went to confession I didn't know what to say. I never liked the penance I got for masturbating, ten Our Fathers and fifteen Hail Marys. Once I confessed that I masturbated six times in one week, and for the first time I felt no fear for the man behind that black meshed screen. He yelled something at me, and demanded I do 100 Our Fathers and 100 Hail Marys. I was angry and confused, I was thirteen and had just found out about masturbation, and I loved it. I thought what a wonderful feeling it is and I can do it all by myself. I couldn't understand why Catholics didn't condone masturbation, it was the only pure joy I knew. I got to like masturbation more than God, so all the while at the boy's home I masturbated and when I went to confession I told the priest that I didn't commit any sin but cursing, cake-stealing, white-lies, fist-fights. I guess I would have been a good Catholic today had they allowed me to masturbate, but I ceased being a Catholic at the age of fifteen, it was very strange how I stopped, it had, of course, to do with masturbation. I went to the Chapel, it was a weekday night, and the chapel was empty, I sat down in the second row directly in front of the crucifix that had that purple marble Christ hanging from it. I looked hard at the statue, at the cloth where his penis was supposed to be, I looked at that spot for a long long time, then I got up and went behind the statue and stared at the buttocks, I was scared, I knew I was doing great great wrong. Of course now that I am older and much more imaginative I tell people I broke away by masturbating before the crucifix, actually I don't think I could have been capable of that.

Anyway I don't regret my Catholic upbringing. There is something in me that is still very Catholic, I think it's that only-we-see-the-face-of-God conceit. When I look at the map of Japan or India or Arabia I realize how extraordinary and select I am. No wonder when I was in San Francisco I didn't want to be a Zen Buddhist. It's all right for people who haven't got baptismal certificates to be Zen Buddhists, God, I remember when I lost my baptismal certificate, I was sixteen, and I always kept it in my back pocket, it was soiled and worn and its folds were torn, that was because I slept on rooftops and in cellars and had dirty pants, I was really scared when I realized I had lost it. I ran back to that backyard to find it, it was very dark so I used up a packet of matches to find it. Then all of a sudden some lady screams, "The milk thief! The milk thief!" Lights went on, shades went up, undoubtedly somebody was stealing their milk. I was a very likely suspect being that I unknowingly slept in the backyard and was dirty and had no money. I could still hear that lady yelling "Milk thief! Milk thief!" Anyway for a long long time I always felt bad about my baptismal certificate, it was the only thing that really meant something to me I guess.

Maybe it's because I don't like losing things, and I'm constantly losing things. The first thing I ever lost has remained with me to this day. I was five years old and was living with my second foster mother when one day my first foster mother came and visited me. She gave me a quarter. For days I played with that quarter in that little dull room they kept me in, I rolled it on the floor, I balanced it, I put paper over it and with a pencil traced the Washington head on it, I pressed it on my forehead, wrapped it in tin foil, spat on it and shined it with my sock, I even spoke to it. God I'd love to know what I said to it. Then one morning I woke up, it was gone, I looked everywhere for it. To this day I can't possibly imagine how I lost it. I was sick for one whole week, and that's when I began wetting the bed, right after that, and I continued to wet the bed until I was twelve years old, the great horror of my youth.

I stayed with that second foster mother for two years, and during those years because of wetting the bed I was confined to that room, it was to punish me so that I'd stop wetting. I wanted to stop wetting, I couldn't stand the damned smell, the discomfort. So I tried to hide it from her. She'd go into the room and it'd smell and she'd rip apart the bed and wham! Once I remember dreaming that I went to the bathroom, I dreamed I actually peed. When I woke the bed was wet, I cried that this time it wasn't my fault, that it was only a dream, that I didn't mean to wet the bed, that I dreamed I went to the toilet. But of course I think the reason why she was so mad was because again I hid it, don't know why I hid it, I guess I was ashamed or scared or something. I wet the bed an average of three or four times a week. To stop wetting they'd have me not drink any water after six in the evening, and before I went to bed I had to stand in the toilet, with the faucet running, and try to pee. Sometimes I stood an hour in there trying, and I just couldn't, and even if I wanted to, I couldn't, and I just couldn't understand what that running faucet [was for]. They once took me to a doctor and he gave them a green medicine to give me. It didn't help, and I wished it would have, because bed wetting made my youth miserable. On Sunday when the Bungalow Bar man came by, I'd get no ice cream. On Saturday, the movie day, I'd have to stay home, all because of that damned pee.

Oh how happy I was when I didn't wet. Immediately I would get up and call her into the room to look at the bed, and all that day I would be happy. Happy that is, until the night came, then that horrible fear. When I left that foster home and my real father who had married another woman took me back home, I was ten, and it was the first time I lived with him. Well that's when the fireworks really began. "He wets the bed! He wets the bed!" his wife screamed. I tried to tell them it was only a mistake, that I don't really wet the bed, that I must have been sick or something, and they believed me, but not for long. The next night I wet it again, in fact I began wetting it more with them than with the others in the past. She thought that if she rubbed my face in it I'd stop, but I didn't. I even tried not sleeping on the bed, at night when they were all asleep, I would sleep on the floor. All the discomfort was worth it because the next day I wouldn't have to worry about hiding it. Hiding it, of course, was the main problem. I'm sure if I would have told them when I wet the bed, they wouldn't have been so harsh, but I was just afraid I guess. Once when I discovered in the middle of the night that I had wet the bed I immediately got up and took [the] sheet into the bathtub and washed it and hung it out the window praying that by morning it'd be dry, but the worst happened, we lived on the sixth floor, and the sheet, I guess I didn't clothespin it enough, fell.

When my father went to the war, and I went to the Catholic home, I ceased wetting the bed, but not before I spent a year at the home. When the Christian Brothers saw that I wet the bed, they had me stand on the main path that leads from all the cottages to the mess hall and hold my rubber sheet. It was at that time that I ran away from that place and went back to my third foster home. They asked me what I was doing there and I said I wanted to come back to live with them. They let me sleep there that night and that night I wet the bed. The next day they sent me back to the Catholic home and I never wet the bed after that.

I remember when I was fifteen and living on the streets of New York, I met a boy my age who also had run away from home and he lived in a small airless furnished room. I told him I had no place to sleep so he took me home with him. I could sense that he was worried about taking me home with him, not that he didn't like me, in fact he liked me very much, it was because he still wet the bed. He said I'd have to put up with his wet sheets. I tried because it was winter time and very cold out, but I just couldn't make it. My pee never smelled like his. There was something very ugly about his smell, so I got up and slept on the floor. I could feel that he was hurt. He was the kind of kid that came on very tough and brave and had bad skin and knew how to make money like selling fountain pen sets on Times Square. People liked him, by people I mean those he knew just casually like the counterman, or the landlady or the other runaway boys. I don't think they liked me because I was always talking like an aristocrat or something. They thought I was trying to show off my smartness.

I was smart, in school I always got the best marks, except for conduct. I never got good conduct marks. God how I remember those report cards! The wetting bed business all over again! Whenever I got a D on the card I'd immediately try to erase it so that my father shouldn't see. Of course he could see that I did something with the card. Actually I was very happy in school, I liked going to it. I hardly ever played hooky, in fact school was more than school to me, it was a place where I had friends, where the girl I loved very much was. The farthest I ever went was grammar school, the sixth grade, and I think I learned an awful lot from it. I will always remember Miss Driscol who loved me very much I think, because she used to keep me after school and give me milk and cakes and have long talks with me. All I did was sit and smile stupidly at her, mostly intent on the cakes. I knew she was trying to help me, but I just didn't know how to accept such help, because she was not the kindness that I would be going home to that afternoon.

I haven't worked since a year after I got out of prison. How I lived for seven years without work is amazing. I lived with girls but I never came on like a parasite. What they gave me in physical aid I gave in spiritual, if that's the word, aid. What I stole, I stole out of fear and not being able to cope with a situation. I will never put down my way of life in those seven years because during those years I did only what I thought was beautiful. If I hurt people who were kind and generous to me, I hurt not intentionally but unknowingly. Besides they can only be hurt once by me, whereas I am constantly hurt by me. It's not that I'm lazy and don't want to work, it's just that I am incapable of work. Everytime I tried it I had to be very real, and that's something that is very impossible for me to be, besides, all I want to do is write poetry and dream and have cats, and not have to worry about rent or food. If I have committed any hurt, and I have, it all had to do with rent or food. The only thing I ever stole or worked for to get were wristwatches. I just can't understand my obsession for wristwatches.

When I was living with my third foster parents I stole a strapless wristwatch from their bedroom drawer. It was a beautiful thing to me, small, thin, with numbers and two handles, and it ticked. I kept it in my pocket for three days and showed it to all the school kids. When I left school I'd hide it under a rock across the street from their house. I had it for a week and when the teacher asked me where I got it I told her and she told the foster parents and they spanked me or something. The next watch I got was when I took ten dollars from my father's pants. It was a Mickey Mouse watch. That night at the supper table he looked very upset. I tried to make him happy by saying, "Dad, look at this watch I found!" I should have kept quiet because he became very suspicious and told his wife and my brother and me that he lost ten dollars. When he said that, he began to sweat and the way he looked at me convinced me that he knew. It was my first strap beating from him, and it was beyond description. In the morning my whole body and arms were welted with blue cuts. The black and blue remained for two weeks or more. The next watch I got was a cheap Ingersol from a friend of my father's who was always putting his hand on my penis. Once I let him, and he gave me that watch. I can't recall what happened to it, but I remember it as being my watch, that it belonged to me, and I wore it in such a way that all could notice. I think I looked at the time more than a hundred times a day. The next watch I got was when I won sixty dollars in a dice game when I was fourteen. I never had so much money. I immediately went to Canal Street, the watch center in New York City and bought myself one of those new waterproof shock resistant florescent watches. It cost me thirty dollars, how great I felt wearing it! I didn't have that watch long. One day while examining its seventeen jewels, I dropped it and it fell five flights down in the hallway. I only had that watch three days, and I think I loved it most of all my watches. The next watch I got I stole from a sleeping man, a pocket watch, a very good gold case watch, but somehow I was afraid of it, and didn't like to look at it, so I hocked it.

At the age of seventeen I went to prison for three years and during those three years I had no watch, and I didn't miss one. When I got out and worked in the Garment Center I got one, a wild mad extravagant one, one with fake diamonds on the case and with a shinny sparkling silver wrist band. Oh, I forgot, before prison when I was living at home with my father and stepmother and my brother, I stole a fabulous watch, but a watch that I could never wear. My brother who is two years older than I am and very much in my father's favor, opened up a clubhouse with the other kids in the neighborhood. One night when we were all painting the place, one of the boys took off his watch, a gold band twenty one jewel shiny beautiful lovely wonderful watch. I asked him if I could wear it awhile and he said yes. As the night went on I prayed that he'd forget that he gave it to me. I almost believed that he would, but I wasn't taking any chances. I put the watch under my belt in the back. When we left the place we walked six blocks or more and then he asked me for his watch back. I told him I gave it back to him and he said that he didn't recall me giving it back. I insisted that I gave it back to him, I even emptied out my pockets for him. Then my brother suggested we all walk back and look for it. All of us started to search, two hours we searched. He cried that it was a gift from his dead grandmother or something, but I was determined not to give in, even though I got a little scared. God what nerve I had then, how strange.

A strange thing happened to me a few months later when I met the guy who I took the watch from in the street with his pretty sister and mother. He introduced me to them. I felt terrible because I suddenly became attracted to his sister. Perhaps because I knew she knew what I had done, I couldn't look her into her eyes. She knew, and because she knew, I fell in love with her, and when I saw her on the street again a week later I told her that I took the watch and lost it, and after I told her that I didn't like her anymore. This kind of feeling, this liking a girl for knowing what wrong I had done, was the main dream I had for women when I was in prison. I used to dream that some beautiful woman would take me in after I had escaped and protect me and love me, and when I was caught cry for me and wait for me until I got out. I always have felt and still do feel that women, lovely elegant sophisticated women, are the only ones worth confessing to. Of course it doesn't always work out, once I made up a story to a real beautiful sophisticated lady about how I killed somebody just for the experience of killing. I thought she would be impressed, and love me, but I was wrong. She got very nervous and said that she would like me to leave.

I don't want to be too harsh on my father because he really was a well-meaning and simple man, a man who had not much education, who was not religious, who married very young and was first generation Italian, who was brought up around Mott Street which was a very tough neighborhood and he never did any wrong in society. My mother was sixteen when she married him and gave birth to my brother and when she was eighteen she gave birth to me, and then left my father and went back to Italy. I have never seen her, and until I was seventeen I was told she was dead. One night I got it out of my grandmother, and she said she was nothing but a whore, a terrible women for having left my father and me and my brother. I didn't know what to feel about that really, because I had never known her, she was non-existent for me. I did question my father about it and he told me that she ran away with another man, and he then finally showed me pictures of her. I was amazed at her beauty. I began to realize that she probably was a very intelligent woman for having left that man who could only look upon her as a whore. In fact I was very proud that she was because she at least did as she felt. [She] surely must have been a wild beautiful angel, to do so. Surely then I take after her, because I'm nothing like my father or his family. I began to be all mother-conscious. Every poem I wrote had something to do with mother, even to this day, my poems always have traces of mother in them, a mother that I have never known. I remember when Allen [Ginsberg] took me to see Mark Van Doren my first year out of prison. I really wasn't too intent on going to see him, but Allen persuaded me, and he had me bring all my poems. Van Doren didn't make any comment, but when Allen and I got up to go he said: "Too much mother." That night I burned all my prison poems, I don't know why I did, but to this day I don't regret it, they were like albatross's on me. I piled images on images, and when Allen's friend John Clellon Holmes read them, he called them 'Green armpit imagery.' I always remembered that, and knew what he meant.

I don't know why I'm saying all these things, surely it's not because I want to be hard on my father, or feel sorry for myself; all that I know is that I feel very eased and kind of released in writing this. I mean there were many times my father and step mother were very good to me, and there were times I loved them very much, surely now that I am grown up and feel much love for life and my youth and have understanding of what they both had to go through with me, I don't hold any grudge toward them; in fact, now that I haven't seen them in three years, and before that only five or six times in five years, I want very much to see them and talk with them, but if I feel this way then I can't continue this anymore, and I want to continue, and if I continue I want to continue in truth; I can't help it if I recall all the horrible things.

In my eleventh year, 1941, I was a Boy Scout, and my baby brother was born, and the war broke out, and my father went into the Navy. My brother and I and my step-mother lived together, 1942. I'm not sure I'm getting these dates straight. It's kind of hard because all that has happened to me from my eleventh year to my fourteenth year. I stole a radio and electric iron from the lady downstairs and took it to a junk shop and sold it for ten dollars. With the money I bought myself a bright wild tie, a sports jacket and went to Times Square and saw *Song of Bernadette*. That evening when I came home the lady was sitting in the kitchen talking to my step-mother. She immediately asked me if I took her radio and iron, and I immediately said yes. It seems she went around with detectives to stores looking for them and found them in the junk shop.

That night three detectives drove me to the Youth House to await trial. The Youth House was once a YWCA, now changed into a house of detention, and it was there, in my twelfth year, in that inferno of youth, that I first entered upon actual misery and suffering. I was there four months, four hideous months because the judge didn't know what to do with me. The place was filled with ten to sixteen year olds. More than three quarters were Negro, and the majority of these Negro youth were members of gangs, whose names I remember so well: Comanches, Lucky Gents, Sabres, and each club had divisions: Tiny Tims, Cubs, Debs, Juniors, Seniors, and each division had a captain, a sub-captain, and so on. When I first went in I was very happy and thought that there'd be a lot of fun. There was no fun, these kids had just come off the street for gang fighting. Some had wielded bats, knives, zip guns; they had a rep, how well I remember that word. My second day there I was jumped on by four of them. I screamed, cried, and that was the wrong thing to do because the word got around that I was a sissy. After that every little Negro, to improve his rep, picked on me. I lived in constant fear there. I think I averaged four beatings and a million humiliations a week. I learned from that how not to cry.

I don't feel right writing about the horrors youth bestows upon youth, yet I know of no other horror so vicious and bereft of mercy. They had me see the House psychiatrist. I told him countless times I was very unhappy there and wanted to go home. Not once while I was there did I receive a visitor, not my brother, step-mother, grandmother, aunts, uncles. At the end of four months I got out and went into a lesser hell. I got out by going mad one day, I ran up to a huge window and put both hands through it. I fell laughing and crying and cut and bleeding. The teacher rushed me to the infirmary, the nurse picked the glass from my hands. Fear had left me, I was no longer scared. I just sat there laughing. The next day they put me in a huge siren ambulance with two female nurses and one man, and we zoomed away from there to Bellevue. How happy I was to be there! No Negroes were there, a few old ones but they were very gentle; and there were nurses there, pretty nurses who spoke kindly to me and made my bed every morning and made sure I washed my mouth out with antiseptic before and after sleep, and nobody took my desert away from me at the dinner table, and one man who had just finished having a visitor had a big box of cakes and candies and fruit, and he gave me the whole box. But something had changed in me, I had changed. I was no longer myself, I had acquired something I never had before, that I never knew I had, I had become nasty and belligerent and cocky. I had become a Negro in search of a rep. I was in that Ward for three weeks. There were always oranges for breakfast, and it was the habit of most of the inmates or patients to take their oranges and eat [them] later. They'd usually keep them on their tables beside their beds. I used to steal at least five oranges a day, and cigarettes from their drawers and candy if ever there was any. I didn't know how long I was supposed to stay there or what was to happen to me, and I didn't give it much thought. Then one day, my third week there, I did something that made me give it much much thought.

I was sitting by a window with a piece of bread in my hand, I broke the bread in pieces and rolled them into little balls. A group of men were sitting playing cards, I began to pelt them with the balls. I hit one man in the eye, he jumped up screaming, suddenly they all started screaming. I sat there laughing. The nurse and three guards rushed to the scene, the men pointed accusingly at me, screaming like children. The next thing I knew, before I could even explain to them I was only having fun, was that I was sent to another ward. It was a ward all the way up on the top floor, a ward that had no young pretty nurses, no quiet clean robed inmates, no mouth wash; just zombic men, self-talking men, men seated on floors naked with huge scabs all over their bodies, men lying on the card tables, mouths opened, men looking into space with bright dotted eyes, men raging in locked rooms. I was there for a week, a hot July week, a troubled 1942 week, and it was the night before Fourth of July that I woke up in the middle of the night trembling with fear, screams, indescribable female screams, lone and painful so unimaginable coming from the woman's ward across the hall. I had never heard a human scream and moan and cry like that before. I couldn't understand what was happening to them, but somehow I had the feeling that nothing was happening to them, that they were all alone like me. And I came to know what human sorrow sounded like. Fourth of July day visitors came and I watched them greet their human sorrow. Their human sorrow just sat down beside them and stared straight ahead. I stood by the window, the sun was very bright; through a little slit in the window I could see and hear children playing in the street, that, and the sun, and the screams the night before seemed all at once to gather into my heart and burst forth into sobs. I sank to the floor and heaved tears out of my eyes my nose my mouth. I experienced my first moment of truth, and how amazing it was that I knew, while standing there, that those children playing in the street, and that that sun, and those screams, all contained a whole ... I would like to think it was there I became a poet.

Enough, no sense going on to tell you about prison because I was quite happy there. I just wanted to tell you the unhappy things, I guess ... You see after reading *Subterraneans* again, this time with an awareness, I realized the hurt I had caused you, and I wanted to tell you it wasn't my fault. Oh it was my fault all right, but not my fault, me, what is really me. It was the fault of a boy who was only two years out of a past that rightly calls "institutional." Just as that night when I dreamed I peed in a toilet and woke to find the bed wet. I insisted it wasn't my fault, that I had not part in it, that it was the dream's fault, not mine. I have cried much over this letter, I hope it lessens the hurt I caused you when you were very much in love.

Much love from the *Till Eulenspiegels* in me yet, Gregory

To Allen Ginsberg

Paris
[ca. Aug. 25-29] 1958

Dear Allen,

Stayed only week in Sweden, couldn't get horse to ride with host and ten others to Lapland, but did take trip up north 90 miles, got lost, no place to stay, dark, sat in station, took train back to Stockholm and watched the life there. When I [got] back Bill was about to leave for Spain, then Tangier. He looked ill, and seemed determined to kick, never saw him so set on what he was going to do. Anyway I saw him off, and Jerry [Schwartz][121] downstairs will meet him in Tangier, not all alone. I guess I should have gone with him; but I hate Spain as a country, just came back and didn't want to go back there, but surely he needed help and I should have gone for that, but maybe not, anyway I am yet in chambre 41, all alone, and John Ashbery came by and showed me a poem and I showed him one, and we walked, and I introduced him to BJ and Baird, but nothing much in way of talk with them, but I got along fine with him, and I like him very much. Ansen also was in town, and we went over to Annette Freckman's to hear long opera with Elliot Stein, but Ansen seemed aloof, all seems aloof. And Guy Harloff doesn't want me to talk to him or his chick and God knows why, this today. He is grouchy creep really, no never liked him, too serious about nothing, and then Ferl writes me that he can't send me royalties on second edition yet which now is out because the first haven't sold all yet. Real silly, because I told him I need the money now. Anyway Shel Thomas, he says came to bookstore there and spoke ill of me, which is his wont, but good God people are getting me down. Dave McAdams gets me one night for not realizing how Negroes suffer or something when I was drunk on and on so I told him I hate inferior races Jews Negroes Italians and then some creep came up to me and spilled beer on my head sarcastically thinking me real Jew hater. I get up and for first time in long long time I go to violence and punch him and punch him again, and he was big and he didn't hit me and they took me away and I felt good, because they are all here now picking on me with questions Beat and so on. So I just don't go out, now I see how poor Jack feels, people are creeps, but alas, I incite it. My funny mouth that thinks all it says is loved by all. Gael Turnbull[122] came on the day I left for Stockholm and he was nice and was sorry to see me go. He wanted to walk with me and do things. I am sorry the merchant poets are bugging you, Howard Hart[123] never did sound any beautiful and I'm really shocked by Lamantia. I gave Pomerand a big yelling for writing in *Seven Arts* about the "degenerate Auden in Ischia with little boys etc. etc.," a real French Walter Winchell that Pomerand. And what else, yes, I've finished the Bomb poem and *Paris Review* is almost certain to take it, and George Whitman has given up venture, I had much pain trouble with ending, whether to end in joy or light or bitterness, I ended in bitterness . . . I leave the light to the now-we-are-on-the-threshold-of-a-new-era poet . . . Did the new *Partisan* come out with the *Weedy Lyke?* Ashbery tells me the issue is filled with poetry, good poetry, O'Hara, etc. Went to the flea market last week and bought a bronze angel, I have it hanging from the ceiling. What news what joy and love and what with Peter who merrys New York, BJ and Claude to marry the twenty-second. Nancy Lenard came by and she likes me and oh oh and she is Buchwald's secretary now, nice, and that USIS girl says article will be out in Sept., will send it on and I wish people who once knocked on [room] twenty five refrain from taking the extra energy to climb to 41 because no time for anything, and one's almost inclined to move, haven't heard from Stern[124] yet. How is all with good Jack, do you see him? Met Appel[125], the Dutch painter, very big mustachioed man, pretty wife, and also Sam Francis[126] and his wife.

I have a little kerosene stove in room, and do my own cooking so no hunger alas, and I sent out for Saxton Memorial Fund, and though I wrote two letters thanking Kay Boyle[127] I thought best to write to National Arts and Sciences and thanked them very much. I'm almost inclined to go back to New York, get that passport settled, much on my mind, and I think I've had it with Europe so when next funds come maybe I'll come back or India yet, will wait until November and see, but when I go to America I'll get some indescribable job and work and take care of myself, it's only me unto me, alas, so if you know anybody who wants to wing or sail me back, please don't hesitate, but don't go out of way, and will always work out well.

Did the books you mailed to home arrive? I got Baird on the Mayakovsky and he will comply, I will rush him. I sent the mad photo of me between the two monks to Don Allen for *Evergreen* cover, it should make a wild cover, if you see him see what he says about it; and if you see him tell him I need eating money and it would be nice if he wanted poems for number 6, something like that, because I don't want to go down, no more of that. I should be able to get some money for my poetry so that I can live an honorable and noble life like J. Caesar.

My love, and love to Peter of the hospitals, Gregory

Four days later, no had money to mail, but got lots of food in house, I send thee *Bomb* poem, all done. Being that *Paris Review* yet has not decided, went ahead and gave copies to Cummings *Isis*, and Rety *London Today* and sent copy to Ferl to print up, him only one to do long sheet mushroom effect, and now I need it published in New York, so show Don Allen, him first, then Jones, or anybody else. It is poem worthy of anyone, really labored over it, how you like the Ubangi Bang, orangutan etc. If somebody take, make sure they justify right hand margin, no good too jagged, no effect, tried it, it looks like wine glass, no word from Bill yet, anyway if you can't do anything with it, please give it to Don Allen for anthology in place of *Power*, for *Power* is the germ of this . . . and write to me and did you see William Carlos Williams? and news, that Shirley Goldfarb and her man are a pair? They are sick, they got me one night on their clique business and said I was like everybody else wanting publicity and you too, but you get more, and are on top of pyramid and won't let me get up etc.; they don't like you because you asked them, "How are you making it in Paris?" Also Annette Freckman no friend of yours, she tells people she and her husband refused to introduce you to Genet . . . these fucking creeps are very jealous people, catty, and unbeautiful. I mean it, Allen, they are very conscious of fame and its agenda; Annette puts me down for getting publicity unbecoming a poet; maybe she right, but I am not aware of it . . . they are very aware . . . you have your New York [Howard] Harts, I have these stepmothers of literature. All sick, I just want you to know they talk bad of thee, and I told them that I would relate to you, they don't seem to care for that so much; and I told Goldfarb and her husband (I mean they really pounced on me) the only retort possible, I said: "Do you know Allen put you in a poem?" She opened her eyes and alert wanted to know what: I told her; it hit, as Kerouac says, sure and true; at first she thought I meant minstrel Goldfarb . . . so for gossip. Lastly, wrote four nights no sleep twenty pages like this honest account of my youth to Jack, 22 pages, longest letter I ever wrote, because in Stockholm read *Subterraneans* again, and realized that I had hurt a love in him for a girl I had no idea of. When I get enough loot I'll mail it first to you, you read, maybe you see something about why Gregory is sometimes like he is, very good therapy for me, I cry much writing it, all truth, all about the horror of my youth from beginning about bedwetting until twelve and the implications that caused, and my pigeon days, and my obsession with wristwatches . . . all in effort to show Jack that I am not really to blame for the Gregory who is like that. And example, when I wet the bed I never would tell stepmother I did, she would ask I would say no, she would look at bed and see yes, and beatings, always same, then one night I dreamed I peed in a toilet, when I woke the bed was wet; but I dreamed it, therefore it wasn't my fault, and that day I didn't lie, in fact I ran in morning to her bed and told her, I dreamed I wet the bed, it isn't my fault this time, etc. . ..

All so damned unhappy, but that example stands for much of what I do today when I screw up like bad checks to Pierre, passport etc., done compulsively not in right mind, unable to cope with situation, I am oft to blame, but when I dream I do horror, and morning deems it real, then I am as lost . . . I had to get it out of my system that writing, when I got into it, it no longer became a letter to Jack but a good sensible talk to myself . . .

Let me know any dear friend criticism on *Bomb.*

My love, Gregory

To Herschel Silverman Paris
[ca. Aug.] 1958

Dear Hersch,

Sorry took so long to answer; been wondering under a gargoyle whether or not it's best to look into gargoyle direction. Two things happen, the cars become very real, and the rain pours from the demon mouth onto your head. Meaning; I've been in straits lately; and have all correspondences piled up; and am now breaking the lock.

I liked your poem about Goodie's [128] bar; I remember I used to go there around 1951 when I was 21, and always wondered what kind of people went there, the Gene Fowler crowd, etc. Have you more poems? Why don't you send me a batch so I can get a real SEE in thy soul, sir. Have you seen Allen? He's back in America; and writes me that all is well; good. I too may return, am become nostalgic for my 26 year old city. I am in rush, so please send more poems; all you have, let me see them; I can't promise you anything, but if there are any I really dig, I'll suggest some magazines for you, if you care about publishing; I did when I wasn't published; but now, it's really a big drag.

My best, Gregory

To Isabella Gardner Paris

[ca. Aug.-Sept.] 1958

Dear Isabella,

At the time you saw me in Cambridge I was very new to non-institutional life and was so excited and careless and somewhat helpless about it that I did many mixed up senseless things; I cannot reject those doings nor deny them; now that I've become accustomed to "outside" life I realize the "wrong" be it wrong, or such a things as wrong, is good; and in its way, perfect; like past history; because it has been done; there's no going back, can be no denial; only 'ifs'; and 'ifs' serve no remedy. I left prison at 20, before that, having spent my seventeenth year to my twentieth there, I lived in Catholic boys homes, and orphanages; a real institutional background; I had no conception of how and what it was like to "live" in the possible world; I found myself in it; just as confused and dreamy as when I left it to go to prison; but in prison I got something; there I learned. Before that, I only went to the 6th grade, and all was not ethereal during that time; ran away from home, lived on the streets from my 13th year to my 17th, living very awkwardly, sleeping on roofs, subways, stealing to exist; and though I learned much in prison, spiritually, soulfully, beauty and love; I had not learned how to live in the world; and thus when I found myself alone, lost, hungry, I became afraid, almost like a pregnant rat with a broom over it, and I struck—stealing most of the time. I didn't know any other way; I just didn't know; but, as I wrote in a poem once "he stole pennies from the library, but he also read about Paderewski"—so I still felt love and a need for that society I was blind in; then when I was 21, I met Allen Ginsberg and he woke me up and showed me the way, and I stayed out of trouble and did no harm to anyone; we became the closest of friends, and poetry sense, had much in rapport, so the same with Kerouac; then after two years we all went our separate ways, they to S.F. and I to Cambridge, by the angelic hand of Bunny Lang; I felt stranded there, as I felt stranded a year before in Provincetown and stole again; O how I wept and wept over that, there was no way out for me; I just couldn't learn; I tried work but I couldn't make it, couldn't because I just don't live in this possible world, I don't know what it is, and therefore couldn't participate in it; I told most of this to Lang, and she, very lovingly and understandingly, understood. Anyway I tell you this to let you know that since I've been in Paris, two years now; I am a grown person, very able, perhaps a little too able, to exist in this possible world, and I tell you, it is not altogether an enlightenment; I mean, I see those cars as being very real out there, and as I see that, so do I look into the past and know my "wrong"; it's all a gray memory if I think it so, but no; I look upon it as a golden memory; because I was only one year old when I came out of prison, and now in my eighth year, I can rightly assume that grand state of maturity; but with conviction, and by going through a life that would deem most people doomed, impossible to get out of; all the more why I should be proud of my past, and never deny it. I am not the person to say I know my limitations, and leave it at that. Whenever anyone says that to me, I don't want to know him. I tend perpetually to go beyond myself, and yet let my impetuousness and spontaneity be my will's directive; I can do no wrong. Once when the man, a sociologist, who collected rent for [Paul] Frost's house, asked me for rent, I went raging to Bob Gardner crying that I am writing beautiful poetry, I have no money, for the first time in my life I am living in a lovely place, all is good and peace, why can't I stay and write!—I felt I deserved that; I wasn't begging, I was arrogant about it; I was deserved, I went through enough of horror; and Frost was very happy to have me there; countless times he told me my arrival there gave his poor soul joy; I as his faun on the banks of the Tiber he loved so well; therefore I did give; but that sociologist plagued me! They've always been the plague in my life; what did he want me to do? get the money? Surely, but I would have stolen it . . . I thought perhaps Bob would have understood when I cried there, but he didn't; well, I can't blame him because he knew nothing about me; but I was doing good work there; I wrote that good careless *Vestal Lady On Brattle* there, and a play, *In This Hung Up Age,* all about hipsters and beat people, long before any of this Beat nonsense came to light, and the play reviewed in the *Crimson* was said to have been the best play of the year there; and Roger Shattuck[129] came up to me and told me he liked it very much. So I mean I wasn't just existing there, wasting my time, living off people, and I wasn't. I drew little Xmas cards and made some money on that, and worked part time in a college store there for money; it was just that damned rent. Oh, well, that too is done, and all about that was perfect too; in fact, I don't think I'll ever forget the beauty of Harvard, and all the great lovely youth I met up there; all so very different from my youth, and the youth I've known.

Well, now, I don't have to worry about anything as banal as rent or food anymore; my book *Gasoline* brings me in money, it having gone into second printing; and Kerouac sends me money, and Allen, and that is money, not considered money. And even if I were without it now, I'd not do what I used to do; I'm too tired and sad for such absurd vitality; I'd just do without it, and not care. But I did care at that time because I wanted to live very much, I wanted to know this life, this possible life; and now I feel I know, maybe not all, but enough, enough to tell me it's not worth all that knowing. Hope this doesn't sound like fey, it's not; it's actually become, by knowing, quite insignificant. I mean, I am more concerned with all that wondrous spiritual dream mystical, what-have-you, madness up there, that universe, that wild surrounding thing, it's that I wish to know about; not earthly things. I remember too how "wrong" people were about me there; at the Poets Theatre when they asked me to explain "hipster" to them, mostly under Lang's insistence, that the hipster was a new soul in America, most of them poets, and that they would defy the system of academic poetry that has been death to American poetry; defy national sobriety and the generally accepted standards to good taste, good poets who knew what they were writing and didn't care about anything else; that they went out on the streets and embraced the leper, partook in drugs, in visions, dug Pound and W.C. Williams, and Mayakovsky and Artaud; that theirs was a violent and beautiful expression of their revolutionary individuality (a quality only had in American poetry with the formulations of Whitman), and that one must not expect some Bohemian stupidity from the hipster, that this hipster is fated to make a permanent change in the literary firmament of America. This at the time was laughed at, yet was indeed quite prophetic. And in your *Poetry* magazine, that other sociologist, Denny, putting down my "bopsterness" as bereft of audience; he too didn't see . . . and his use of "bopster" is so outdated that anyone who uses it just ain't "hip". The actual meaning of "hip", at the time before the general public got hold of the word, had nothing to do with juvenile delinquency, not with entire jazz, or drugs; it meant, awareness; that almost Nirvana state of KNOWING; and most of these young kids I knew at time, who at time Kerouac branded as Beat; were young men from colleges, who abandoned all conformity, and took to their soul selves and tried to live in what they considered TAO. It has nothing to do with creeps who have switchblade knives or abuse marijuana or who sit in cafes exhuming Paley. Ginsberg is a good example of a hipster; of a person in the know, his *Howl*, called by most a poem of Hate is so obviously a poem of Love. He doesn't know what it is too hate; he's too "hip" to hate; *Howl* initiates a new style in composition in U.S., returning to the bardic-strophic tradition, till then neglected in the U.S. of Apollinaire, Whitman, Artaud, Lorca, Mayakovsky—and improving on the tradition to the extent of combining the long line and coherence of Whitman, with the cubist imagery of the French and Spanish traditions, and adding to that a fantastic rhythmic structure which begins on a relatively flat base repetition, and builds up to the rhythmic crisis of a Bach fugue, and ends, on a high peak of ecstatic elongation of the line structure. The poem is built like a pyramid, in three parts, and ends in merciful tears—the protest against the dehumanizing mechanization of American culture, and an affirmation of individual particular compassion in the midst of a great chant. How absurd to call it a hate poem. It is a lovely poignant poem for humanity.

Ginsberg saw his generation at Columbia and in the madhouse; I in the subways of NYC and in prison; Kerouac in the somberness and death of his family, and all youth's families; how very fateful that we met in 1950; a part of this new vital America; and yet it has become such that the original intent has been lost; and that is sad. Once a thing becomes a group it is bad; and I realized this long since, and have done much to stay out of it; because it was not the wild dreamy intelligent sad beat hipster we three once knew; it's become a generation, a generation of social-declaimer decriers; and I, who have the right to cry against society, have never allowed it to enter my life nor my poetry; I find it very false in those who do, because they have nothing else to do; and so does Jack and Allen, especially Allen; he is a great poet; and he accepts me as such; and both of us, somewhat romantically yes, but not cornily, will die for our poetry. Yes, I want you very much to see my *Gasoline*, and also my *Bomb*, especially *Bomb*, it is my latest work, and its content is one of love, love for life, love for man—and the only way for me to do this was not to say "O Bomb how terrible you are," but to say "O Bomb I love you, I want to put a wig of goldilocks on your baldy bean, a lollipop in your furcal mouth. . ."

I have not once brought the muse down so low as to weep against the "hurt" caused me. There hasn't been any hurt; it all has been perfect.

O I wish if you'd ever see that Denny you'd tell him so; God, what small scope some very supposedly educated people have. Where, indeed, is his love? Is he just a chronicler of the times? Is there not that in him that can move with the times? How way off base he was; and not only in that review but in *The Lonely Crowd*; it makes no sense 1958. That's because he wrote all that in his academy iambic attic. I hope this doesn't sound bitter, it isn't meant to. Nor have I anything against tradition; if there is one poet I love writing today it's Robert Lowell; but the way the world goes and its cattiness of who to love and who not to love, will make impossible, let's say, a meeting and a love between he and Ginsberg; whereas they both have that SOUL. But in my little stay at Harvard I saw much that made academic poets guilty; not their going to conformity; but their self destruction that might have been poetry in them; I can rattle off names; but what will that mean. And nor am I entirely for this "new" vital poetry; much in the Black Mountain school which derives from Pound Williams and Olson is bad, and much in San Francisco is bad; poetry was never meant for schools, groups, coteries; my love of Shelley, Chatterton, Marlowe tells me the only poetry worth anything is the inspired poetry. Yet this abandonment of the iambic pentameter, and embracing of "measure" is something new, and good. Though, I myself, well aware of such technique, am bereft of it; I still write carelessly and spontaneously and with much inspiration; though I've learned through time how to measure an idea, and that's all that is important to me; if music be in poetry, then let it be an unheard music; I care nothing for law music. God, if I did, then I couldn't write what I write. It is the idea that is important; the craft should no longer be the worry when one sets one down to put down the idea, he should not have to say "can I do it right?" His craft should be whisked out of his mind like a handkerchief from the pocket. How poets can spend all their time devising new forms, new meters, new measures, cadences, is beyond me; that does not mean poet; poetry that sounds like poetry is bad poetry. Just like an actor who acts is a bad actor. Poet is soul, soul is alive, don't restrict it in poetry-shape; if you wish to restrict it, restrict it in whale-shape. Ah, but what has become of me, so conscious of what poetry is or isn't or should be or shouldn't be; I guess I want to impress you on how much I've learned; but perhaps you'll conclude that I've learned nothing by such talk. Well, I don't know. I don't talk to anyone about poetry here; except when Allen was in Paris. We had a marvelous time here; Henri Michaux came and visited us several times here at Git-le-Coeur, a real fascinating man, great poet; a visionary; takes mescaline, and says he has learned to adore God by its use. Also saw Céline, whose prose I find much to my liking, having not read very much great prose in these modern times

Let's see, I'll give you all the gossip, what I've done and who I've seen since I've been in Europe. My happiest time was at Oxford (always dreamt of that place in prison, because Shelley went there) and had a dream come true when Auden, who had read my book and thought very highly of it, took me for long walk around Magdalen Heath (it's pronounced like maudlin) and to Christ College, and his old room, when he was a student, and I asked him if he thought birds were spies, and he said "Who would they report to?" and Allen said: "The trees." Anyway I felt as if I were walking with Shelley there; if I could only convey to you how I really dreamt so much of Oxford and Shelley as a youth; that this was very dear to my heart, that walk. And also in England I gave a reading over BBC, and disturbed everybody by pronouncing combatant as I would combat; and they said it was the other way, and I said but I wrote it with that pronunciation in mind; and had my way; very silly of me, really. And then had lunch with Dame Edith [Sitwell] at her Lady Macbeth's Society, and what a grand wild Swineburnesque talk we had. God how I love poets; nobody in the whole wide world like them really; every poet I met, never have

I been bored, except by two, and they lacked poetic grace (not in their work) but in their stand, their being, they being Rexroth and George Barker. I tend very much toward the romantic, and happily so. In Paris I see often and have high talks with Tristan Tzara; we play a mad surrealist dada pinball game. O it's all varied the time, and mixed up, but I've met many wonderful people and have had rapport with all. Michaux of course is dearest to me, when I speak with him I am elevated to that state I only receive in writing poetry; and he gives me that state in conversation.

So, in a matter of an hour or so I poured out my heart to you; it's what you wanted, you having asked to want to know me, and I wanting very much that you do; I could go on and on, but I think, in all this, you'll find exact traces of what and how I am; and that I am ever changing, and for the better; though, as I said, it's not all that enlightening, in that it torments that guardian dream in me.

I have recently found out that Paul Frost died, thus another soul, like Bunny, who death has denied me chance to thank, appropriately. Must I wait until 1960 to see more of your poetry? I don't know whether I should return to America or not; God, how differently I'll see it now; what these two years have done to me!

My love, Gregory

To Lawrence Ferlinghetti Paris

[Sept. 1] 1958

Dear Larry,

Forget about printing poem, it'll be done here in grand style, son of owner of Simon Schuster here good friend gave me money to do it myself in best way possible 150 dollars worth, he thinks it's greatest poem ever, and wants to see it printed like mushroom which *Paris Review* won't do, nor the other magazines coming out with it next month, two English ones, *Isis* at Oxford, and *London Today*, new small mag.

Poem really causing furor in England without it's being published yet, so much so that old anarchist Herbert Read[130] has invited me to London to read it at I.C.A., expense paid for and money to boot, all very nice, because I want to see England again, and when I get it printed here, perhaps only 500 sheik [sic: chic] copies, black paper, white mushroom, gray words, he, the S&S son will have it offset in New York and get more copies printed up then but he thinks I should have 500 select copies. He likes poem that much, and says I should keep copyright, but I don't understand what it all means, perhaps you can help me on that, how do I assume copyright?

Love, Gregory

To Allen Ginsberg

Paris
Sept. 2, 1958

Dear Allen,

I sent big letter to Paterson. Here poem for you. Bill all right, he be back in middle of September. Philip gave me money to get *Bomb* done in elite format. So hard to do, am trying, he says just to get copyright and have select copies, he thinks poem very important. I want very much for Don Allen to include it in anthology, please relay to him. Am waiting to hear from I.C.A. in England, they told Gene Litchenstein they want me there to read *Bomb*, expenses paid, fare etc. Should be nice to see England again. Hope all is well with you, and that you are in peace. Peter, I bought two bronze angels (cherubs) from flea market—they hang from my ceiling.

Love, Gregory

To Peter Orlovsky

Paris
Sept. 2, 1958

Dear Peter,

Paris in an uproar. Arabs FLN have taken to war in city, they have in past week killed ten cops and four soldiers (mostly on dark streets and in Metros). Yesterday they blew up a cafe around here and killed nine. Paris very uneasy. No Arab allowed on streets after nine o'clock, tourists are trembling, fleeing, situation bad. Guy Harloff will have to run off again. I remain.

My love, Gregory

To Don Allen

Paris
Sept. 2, 1958

Dear Don,

I mailed my *Bomb* poem to Allen to give to you for anthology in exchange for *Power*. Paris teeming with war. Arabs killing police and soldiers and blowing up cafes, but will end after De Gaulle makes forth his constitution.

Love, Gregory

To Lawrence Ferlinghetti

Paris
Sept. 2, 1958

Larry,

This is view I have from my window on Git-le-Coeur [referring to postcard picture]. Paris is boiling with trouble, Arabs have placed their war here. Last night cafe a block away blown up, dead nine. They are killing soldiers in Metros, and many police. I'm sure a tourist is next. La Hune wants more *Howls*—*Gas*—and *Pics*—and Levertov—and Patchen.

Gregory

▼ [LF wrote to Gregory that he would produce an inexpensive broadside version of *Bomb*.]

To Lawrence Ferlinghetti Paris
Sept. 3, 1958

Dear Larry,

Great, go ahead with printing, I can't get publisher here, all on vacation, so do it, and I'm glad you're doing it, and yet giving me money I need so badly, good, yes, please have it look like champignon shape, just as you indicated in diagram; NOR, is my vision of what infinity and all cosmos is; just leave it; now if I love the bomb; well, take line: "pregnant rat in a corner before the raised broom nations of the world," meaning that in order to out step the bomb or anything that is capable of destruction and everything is capable of destruction you must present that rat not a broom but a velvet cushion. Of course the heavens are with it, it always has been, from the beginnings of time, what else to budge history? Fact, I see that great mystery as FACT, if nothing else in this possible life, this reality, I see that main dream as FACT. And *Bomb* is really a small part of that fact, "snatched-sky"—Yes, print it up right away, because I sent *Bomb* poem to *New Statesman, Nation, Partisan*, three magazines in England will publish it, *Paris Review*; Oh they're going to hate me, because in little magazine ethos you just don't give your poem to everyone, well I did, and even now Allen is running around with it in New York. He loves it too; but you come out first before all of them, and also, yours will be the only one abiding by length and shape.

How's this? "Robert Lowell—final energy of Albion's dying child—the children of the immigrants are entering thy shade." In *Power* as in *Bomb*; I am professing love; and I find that my love stems from humor and originality . . . I can condone no harm to man, but I can see with opened eyes the harm there be. My love, (and as for the reader wanting to know whether I love *Power*, *Bomb* or no, what difference does it make? I do not assume <u>that</u> kind of power that it need be a difference).

Be good, Gregory

I have another book of poetry ready, titled: *Corduroy Eggs*.

To Allen Ginsberg Paris
[ca. Sept. 10] 1958

Dear Allen, angel Allen, pure blithe Shelley to me,

How I miss thee, wild-eyed string-haired sensuous-lipped chaff of eternity—so happy am I that you are pure and will keep pure, and I knew you would; that day at the station when you left, I knew you would; and good; but we are susceptible; the gown of purity is always stained, and why not. But please give me full detail of what went on and said. Bill okay, got two mad letters from him from Tangier where he says the queens are fleeing, such information of course more apt for Ansen gossip, but Bill is all right then if that is his topic. Not sick he, though he went to kick, and I guess he has because he says he lies in bed smoking pot; anyway he'll be back in five days and all will be all right. I love him very much; actually loved him most when he left to go to Tangier; he was as I never knew him to be, a determined, calm, no-foolish-word man at the time, and even the kiss I gave him goodbye was brushed aside. As Sulla once said: "There are many Marius's in this fellow Caesar."

Bomb is going to be several thousand long mushroom shape sheets done by L. Ferl. City Lights. Good, that saves me the bother, NO MAGAZINE WOULD PRINT IT AS I wanted but Ferl will; so Phipps[131] money to me can be used for living; Ferl also sent me 50 dollars royalty; so I'm all right with money.

But I gave *Bomb* to *Nation, New Statesman, Partisan, Paris Review,* three English magazines. What is going to happen? This is not ordinary magazine ethos. BJ and Claude married, funniest wedding in world, everybody high, old Stendhal-like mayor pontificating; he confused about Graham laughing, and me, and BJ when asked if he takes this woman for wife, he said, bombed: "Yeah, man." The first Beat wedding, as Claude terms it. And true. Couldn't imagine a wedding like that. They think of you often and ask about you and send their love.

Since you've been gone I've been meeting some young black jacket French poets, who are very bright and beautiful looking and say about us that we're discorded and rebellious and for that we have their love who are disciplined but mad. Sir [Herbert] Read wants me to come to ICA and read *Bomb.* Someone don't like you or me, calls us Saturday night poets and who rejected us at *Esquire,* Gene Lichtenstein. Told George Whitman; he told him that Read wanted me to read at the ICA expenses paid, so I wrote Read a letter and am waiting reply, I think it'd be wonderful to read *Bomb* now, now that it is done and perfect. How odd that Ferl doesn't understand me, he still (I enclose his letter) thinks about *Power*, he wants to know if I love the bomb or no; of course I love it, but he thinks I love it in his silly way; and when he says the readers want to know if I love power or not; I told him that I love all things what difference does it make what I love, and I do not assume <u>that</u> kind of power that it need make a difference. I hope he understands that . . . But he'll print off several thousand *Bombs*, good; he knows. Please Allen for Don Allen's anthology he must use *Bomb*, because that is thing I like most, so please inform him, I can't because he never replies to me. I'm not sure that my letter to Jack should go to the whales and fish because it's just a letter that one night the sad clamp clam let spew forth; all is sea. Let the sea be merciful.

But the main thing of this letter is you. I am really proud I use the word good PROUD of you that you went as poet to radio thing, and will and are determined to do so: you are the only person in this life that can really shatter the only light I have for this life; I love you, respect you, and know you to be a grand and glorious poet, and a deep romantic too; my hope of what is beautiful in life lies in you; but I am trying to see other lights, none yet, dear soul—Robert Lowell—final energy of Albion's child, the children of the immigrants are entering thy shade.

Why don't you and Peter go some Sunday out to Brooklyn and see my father and brother? How strange but do; write them a letter first. My love, to Peter angel, and Lafcadio who is flying saucer welcomer.

Gregory

Stern not back yet from Yacht, I hope India is due, if not I would like to come back to US; I miss it, and am full of Paris; enough of it; am tired here; take care.

To Diane Di Prima Paris
Sept. 15, 1958

Dear Diane,

I sent all poems sent me to German publisher, selection is not all up to me, God knows what they are going to take, and it will take time because translating ain't so easy; I mean especially the kind of poetry I sent them; yes, do send more poems and I'll send them on, but I wrote to publisher that I am incapable of selecting for anthology because I just ain't fitted for it, that it is not my fashion to ask for poems and then reject them, that I wish not part of that, that I send them the poems and they choose what they like and think translatable, and thus saving me from horror of rejection, and selection, etc. etc. my only deal in that was collecting the material.

I will never again do anything like that, not write an article or gather. I wrote one article and in it I put down poets like Frost, and that is sheer ridiculousness on my part, I hate myself for it, and at this moment I find I like Frost. Oh, well. So you have a ten month old angel, and it says paper, good sign; get it paper, lots of paper, all kinds of paper, color paper, even that kind of paper that when you write on it what you write disappears. Yes, *Bomb* will come out this week at City Lights, and in England. I felt very happy writing it, I don't think I enjoyed or received such pleasure from writing a poem as I did from *Bomb*.

How is *Yugen* getting on? Please have LeRoi send me all future issues; I think *Yugen* indicates an awakening rose, so far I didn't like one and two so much, but in one and two there were signs of such a sleep. What is my New York City like? Ah, I do miss it, haven't been there since 1954 with slight intervals; a few months in 1956 and 1957. NYC is very much a part of me, and it is always dear to my heart, my dirty urchin city.

Paris is lovely and overwhelming with its newness, its suddenness and light but I've about had it here, and will definitely go to India in November, I hope. I mean someone has invited me there, all I need is fare, and that runs about 150 dollars, and I can get that, I think. O for some surety! I am never sure of things; I AM sure but things aren't sure.

People always knocking on my door for talks about God knows what, Beat Generation mostly, and I don't know what to say about it, because I don't know about it. I mean I knew what it was, but what it is now, I don't, so I tell them the BG [Beat Generation] is all a big con, and laugh. But now absurd people are really, in the beginning when they came up I complained, but complaining leaves me uncomfortable, so now I just lock my door and hide by my little window that looks out on Sainte-Chapelle and cone-towers. I had a few girlfriends here, but I can't be consistent with them, I try to, but no use. Ah women, will always love them; but sometimes I don't because I see them in a very odd way; I mean I don't ever dislike them, but I shudder when I see them in that odd way when I think that at times I am wont to kiss them and bed them and say I love them, I won't explain that odd way, not now, so, alas, another knock, this time it is an angel, a little red haired girl who I never see in that odd way, not yet that is. Fare thee well, my love, and tell me all about NYC, and more.

Love, Gregory

To Allen Ginsberg

Paris
[ca. Sept. 22] 1958

Dear Allen,

Bill back, and he's still on [drugs], but looking all right, and seemingly straight. Stern not back, and we have much doubt if we'll go to India—and I tell you I'm going out of my mind in Paris, alas, Europe—I've had it—I'd love to come home if I can now get the loot—I am terrible here—complaining, sulking, gloomy, argumentative, the real terrible Gregory. I.C.A. in England wants me for a reading in October. How will that be like? What's happening? Jack wrote and asked for "installments" referring to my letter—he's actually a well-meaning simple soul.

And younger than I am, Gregory

To Lawrence Ferlinghetti Paris

Sept. 24, 1958

Dear Ferl,

Bill and I are set on doing a magazine, *Interpol* "the poet is becoming a policeman"—and our content will be of the most sordid vile vulgar oozing seeping slime imaginable. We only want the most disgusting far-outness; for the first issue we have in mind odious humiliating maudlin gush from some of the best writers in the world. *Interpol* will be the outlet for vile, so please aid us in making this magazine possible, send your contributions to Bill Burroughs, *INTERPOL*, 9 rue Git-le-Coeur, Paris; here is Bill Burroughs word:

"When the Human Image is threatened, the poet dictates forms of survival . . . Dream police of poetry protect us from The Human Virus . . . The Human Virus can now be isolated and treated . . . This is the work of the new Police poet. The virus must be traced with radioactive images before it crystallizes in cancer, blood, stone and money of the world nightmare surface . . . The Nightmare of last night is the soggy toast of this morning's breakfast . . . This is latest way of revelation and way of action." Please heed, and send funds, Vileness must succeed and numb the shitless lily.

Bill Burroughs

Gregory again, our first issue will be, we promise it, most humiliating, so we await your generosity, thank you,

Gregory Corso

Bomb is great, nice format, thank you, please send bunch, George Whitman wants and La Hune wants. Now no kidding about this venture of ours, and everybody is helping, so you help too, and if you have any vile or odious disgusting works send them on. Please get McClure and Whalen and Snyder to send money; they all will be happy to aid such a noble disgusting venture, my love. May we say that you will by your aid be putting on history a great big Centipede spilling over with gooey eggs and clogged eyes, green eggs, bile,

Love again, Gregory

When I received the five *Bombs*, I dropped them—ill-omen: a dud. I really like format—sorry of course not to see it on one entire sheet—but shape is there. Again, this mag venture by Bill and I should be the most natural disgusting end—it's your duty to come through—Send news. Your Paris really in bad state, machine guns everywhere. Can't walk late in streets, all Arabs in at 9, curfew, every night a policeman gets shot, or a soldier—right in city. India seems remote now, alas, winter is coming. I think if the muse dictates me golden fare, I'll revisit my wonderful America.

Now don't take ten years to reply—this mag *Interpol* must come out. For our first issue we got Paul Bowles and Tennessee Williams' most disgusting works, so far. Get everybody (kind and good and friendly) to help, even you wife. I'm sure your angel will be glad to aid such a noble disgusting venture.

Love, G

To Allen Ginsberg and Peter Orlovsky Paris

Sept. 24, 1958

Pardon this format, carbon, dear friend, but will you also help? Everyone is, Ansen, Ferl, Snyder, Whalen, we hope Kerouac, Don Allen, etc., so please go out and raise funds. The mag should really be great, and Bill, amazingly, concocted the idea, I gave name, and we both agree not to publish anything that's not of the most crushed centipede sort. We intend doing it right away, so poste haste! My *Bomb* is out. Ferl sent copies, please get 8th Street [Bookstore] to order batch. N.Y.C. needs *Bomb*. Did Bryant mail Mayakovsky yet? He said he would. Now Allen and Peter, Bill is bored here, so am I, he says if he's got this mag to work on he won't need so much to take drugs, so (this is an indirect threat) get on the stick, ask all! Send MONEY, Bill must do! We promise to be the most vile of editors. Get Lucian, Holmes, all to send their fucking golden tokens.

My love, Gregory Corso, grand centipede

Send all loot to Bill—as editors of vile, we don't trust each other. You will all get receipts.

To Gary Snyder Paris

Sept. 24, 1958

Dear Gary,

If you aid us in this most hideous venture—Buddha be with you—green eggs literature—send with money your most disgusting work.

Love, Gregory

Paris really like Germans were here, machine guns everywhere. Arabs to be in at nine—curfew. Police found shot every morning. All's twig smear—Autumn—nice. Hope you see my *Bomb* poem at City Lights. Now this is no kidding about this magazine Gary—it should be the most hideous literary magazine ever concocted—for first issue we'll have Paul Bowles', Burroughs', and Tennessee Williams' most humiliating efforts - And we, the editors, Bill and I, have decided to reward the one who sends us the most contribution with the honored title: Grand Centipede.

Hope Savage—a girl I used to love very much, and is yet a part of my golden memory, wrote to me that she saw you, and was much overwhelmed by you—good, I am happy—I knew she'd like you.

To Allen Ginsberg Paris
Sept. 30, 1958

Dear Allen,

Magazine definitely will happen, for first issue Michaux, Bowles, Stern, Burroughs, you, me, and more Tzara. I want your best, either *Ode To Light*, or Mother poem [*Kaddish*], now I know they ain't finished, so what to do? How about publishing both rough fragments of each? Something in that; the roughness of such subjects; purest kind of poetry really, jumble kind, or else your mad cocaine writing, you know best, but please baby, your very best. Bill is writing to Michaux now, and yesterday I saw Tzara, he greeted me in Les Deux Magots, and told me to come up and visit him, I'll get work from him, too.

I bought, instead of a winter coat at the flea market, a lovely fifteenth century medieval velvet suit, all black, with lace ruffles, and gold seal on chest with black club on it—I look great in it.

Love, Gregory

Bill says he'll write you. He's all right, and set to go on *Interpol*.

To Don Allen Paris
Oct. 1, 1958

Dear Don,

After three years of working reworking, I can maturely say, *Power* is done. I am very happy with the results, and hope you can use this final copy for anthology or *Evergreen Review*; worked two whole days and one night no sleep on it. Allen G. loves this poem very much, and if it wasn't for him I would have piled it away long ago. Now as poem stands I don't think I'd like to have *Bomb* replace it in anthology. Besides, *Power* is very important to me, I wrote it right after *Vestal Lady*, and it was my first free poem; compare the copy you have with this and please let me know as matter of comment, feeling you have about it; much in this copy is not in copy you have; I had eight drafts of poem, and took best from all eight, and lo, this. Surely, if anything, it is much clearer, and states my feeling of *Power*; it's not fascistic as Ferlinghetti puts it; I used the word *Power* to give it new meaning, and to destroy its old. You would make me very happy if you let me know what you think of it, and soon if possible, while I yet retain this re-lived feeling for it; worked so much on it last year, that I actually got to detest it. Also can you send me list of ten poems you'll use for anthology? I forgot, and need to know; tho as far as I can remember I think only *Power* is poem I reworked. I want to make sure. Discipline, discipline, when will I assume that!

Usually I inject fragments or poems into poems, and thus a whole; I do this with honest inspired intent, because all that I write stems from one whole central madness. Ah but we are not sitting in Deux Magots you and I? Aren't you coming to Paris? And I missed Frank [O'Hara] when he was here, damn it. I wanted very much to see him; seriously next to Allen G. I think very highly of Frank's work.

I told Alan Ansen to send you review. He wrote me and told me Auden stayed with him for two weeks to see new Stravinsky score, and that Auden said he thought highly of my poetry but that I should not be "discouraged" from learning more of the language. I think I know what he means, but as it is I am getting too conscious of the language, and find myself hesitating in my "careless" "arrogant" choice of coinage. Anyway, all is fine, and sun, and I am happy.

Now, please, Don, another thing, you must tell me if I tax you, (I have the impression that everybody does nothing all day like me). Could you please mail back all those poems you aren't going to use that I sent you? It's confusing for me, because like I said, I injected lots from *In A Grecian Garden* and some others (none from anthology) into poems. I want very much to get straightened out.

My love, Gregory

To Allen Ginsberg

Paris
Oct. 1, 1958

Dear Allen,

Wasn't at all happy with *Power* ending, think you'll dig this ending, wrote it in mad fit, all there, all new, all 1958, yet with same feeling, no changed much, but now to me and as it always was, *Power* is my human sparkle.

Roditi[132] wrote me letter and said he was told by Bosquet that I dug his poetry and he was so happy to hear that, he wrote me long letter how he didn't sell himself out, even though with poetry disappointments, and that somebody yet perverse or learned enough to dig his work was great enlightenment to him; and so I wrote him mad letter in return saying how and what I got from his poem, and that he should not worry about poetry disappoints when such as I who value the inspirations of Chatterton, Shelley should now be happy; and I think he will be.

I want to tell you that the more and more I looked at fragments of what you sent me, [the more] I want rest. It is beautiful and WISE and there; you are wise. I had a mad dream about you and Peter going to see a wild mad old man of great wisdom and that he told you how he became wise and asked you how you became wise, and you said: "Laughing gas! 'Twas laughing gas that did it!" Very funny dream. Please send the poem on; and please don't knock yourself out for aid of me home, etc.; I will try myself; take time for yourself with yourself and by thyself, I ain't to be thy handicap and plague, I KNOW, you know I know; so make it, and let us hence forth assume maturity and not child helplessness, okay?

As for Levertov, well Balf is here and he told me she didn't dig *Bomb*, well, not to be mean or anything, but really all she does is talk about the bedbugs in Mexico and has not ventured to universe bugs; whereas I have, and surely she must have something against me, if she did not see some very nice things, and funny things, in *Bomb*; as poet she must have, but had closed mind; because when she wrote me in Venice that my *Coit Tower* was imitative of thee, I wrote back and said: "How would you like me opening up first page of your book and stopping there and saying: Ah, William Carlos Williams." Very silly of her, and woman, women poets, my nemesis; and all I can say is, I am not hurt, but I think she's a little closed.

Got nice letters from Gary and Whalen. Also Laughlin, sending me his book, "for laffs." I told him what gives me laughter must also give me sorrow, that I couldn't take poetry that lightly, and he told me to get *Akzente*[133] boys to see his German translations for my anthology and then asked for my work for his anthology; like a switch deal; which ain't in my heart, and I told him so, in good honest way; God the damned business in this all. Though some of his poems, especially the publishing ones, are quite undercover sad. Told him that. Told him that he, Laughlin, of ND [New Directions] has done good with [Djuna] Barnes, Bowles, William Carlos Williams, Pound, Michaux, [Paul] Eluard, and that he as editor don't like his own work, and that deep down he is serious about it, and that he should come off it, abandon all and flee, and go to lonely mountain peak and sing. Did my best; my soul; I am much a proud mature little Gregory now, and can handle myself; almost like an old man, but still goofy.

Then Irv Rosenthal[134] wrote me and said "I guess I'm convinced you are a good writer." And do you have "carbon" of 23 page letter; he's very witty, so I replied with equal wit: first how dare he assume I have a carbon of a letter that I wept out on verge of great crisis in my life; and that his "being convinced of my being a good writer," was just like the parole board saying "we're convinced you're eligible for parole," very funny letter really.

Don't be afraid to write anything, just write and don't CARE if it don't stand up to past *Howl*, get that black bird off thy neck, and write, I say you are doing and will always do wonderfully; you are poet; that is all. Write. I say what you sent me, the fragments, is all that you have become and wisely feel see and know. Take it from Gregory.

My love, Gregory Mayakovsky on way, slow mail.

To Allen Ginsberg Paris
[ca. Oct. 6] 1958

Dear Allen,

After much nights of work and inspireries, I finished *Power*, hope you like it; sent to E.B. Feinstein[135] for his [sic: her] magazine, and to Don Allen to use either for *Evergreen Review* or anthology. I wish he'd use it for *ER*, could use the tokens; I get a funny feeling he's not too hip on publishing me; and Whalen says he'd published him, but that he thinks Don Allen too scared of critics or something, thus the letter from Whalen. James Laughlin, who I don't know, sent me an autographed copy of a little book of his poetry. Ansen says Auden thinks highly of my work, but feels that you shouldn't "discourage" me from learning more of the language; whatever that means. Do you discourage me, sir? I dare say you do! I think I'll make complaints! I demand encouragement! I ain't gonna remain with just this liddle store of language, I wanna be learned the big woids, and all their meanings.

Stern back, and on; and still have no idea of India really, he has to wait for trial and Dent[136] cure; I actually wish I could come back to States, but will stick it out and see if India comes true. Did I tell you Saxon Memorial Fund coldly, a small hard card with a check on it indicating why they thought Gregory Corso did not deserve a lotta money. Let me know what you think of *Power* now.

Love, Gregory

Does Eighth Street [Bookstore] have *Bomb* yet?

To Allen Ginsberg Paris
[Fall] 1958

Dear Allen,

I think I am very sick and that's why I want to come home; pills, junk, pot, lush; it's catching up with me. O not dying or anything like that, but on the verge of a big depression; I've [been] building it up these last two months, ever since I got back from Stockholm. Something happened in Stockholm, the plane, the sky, the world as it was. I can honestly say that the shock of certain realities can make one very sick, I mean I never knew how real cars were before, and things, things don't remain, and people die; I always actually felt that no matter what one did, like cashing bad checks or doing some wrong or hurting someone, I always felt such things remedied by the mere fact that one could always return because one never changes, one always is, the action of yesterday means nothing tomorrow; but people die, actual people die, and there's no going back. I suddenly realize that I am growing older, that I won't always be the Gregory now, that it'll be a different Gregory. That's what's so shocking. I thought years ago when I looked into the mirror that no matter what I did I would still be as I was and looked in the mirror; yet even now, when I see myself, I find it difficult to trace the change; actually your "mind-consciousness" the "we imagined all this up" is just the state that I have been in for years. Good God Allen, you're going into something I am being shocked out of; really; when you say "Jack and the Buddhists are really right" yes, but right about what? I'll tell you, they're right about living a clown in a circus of power, that's Nirvana, the ability to step out of a small magic box, and lo, into the arena, for all to see, and laugh; that's what Jack is actually looking for, humor. In humor all is answerable; of course laughing gas, what else? Happy, clowny, deep. And I full well understand the "disappearance", it's sensation and reason; Swindleresque Ink has finally been seen by you; before you just liked it and thought it a mad image and coinage of words, with the sound of word sense; the tie between Swindler, Ink and eradication—of course it means "universe disappearance." When I wrote it, yes high, I felt as though that face of mine I saw in the mirror, me, Gregory as I was then, far from the cellars and rooftops and subways (my New York hotels, I got the finest recommendations; never once stole any towels) in Mexico, a bed, food, friends, love, and poetry; I realized this in Mexico, and thus, the past disappeared; it never was; it was all my own imagination; I created such a past; the question I should have put to myself upon having realized this should have been: Are you happy with it or not? I'm sure I was newly silly at the time to have answered, "No, I'm not happy with it." Of course now I am very happy with my created past; even though I went through hell on those subways in the winter time when I was sixteen. Oh Allen, you don't know what it means sleeping for weeks and sporadic months on the subway, it was unbearable; no sooner I'd fall asleep I'd have to get up, the train having reached its stop; the cold empty lonely platform and the white tile walls, so morbid, ah the loneliness of a last stop! And especially when you're tired and cold and hungry! What a real perfect draggy situation to be in! You stand there half awake, cold, itchy, stray people staring at you; more terrible if they are a young couple because you yourself are young, and you know they'll be going to nice warm beds; you suddenly become very conscious of your appearance, your hair, your dirty face, clothes; and the train would take centuries to arrive; and there are always all other sorts of characters sleeping on them, and they try to meet you, to get to know you; and you don't want to know them because they're even dirtier then you are, and you at least know that you are young and will soon find a bed, that you won't be like this for all your life; but with them you get the feeling that they'd always be like that, that they'd never get another bed again. Terrible feeling. And how funny I used to feel when I took the A train, I always took that because it went the most stops and therefore had less disturbance, when that A train would go into Brooklyn and stop at Ralph Avenue where I used to get off to go home; I don't know why I never got off and went home; just could never do it, couldn't face doing it. Good God seems like another 21 page letter! Good, it makes me feel much better, very much better; been frightfully depressed; damned reality got me; thought it never would; always said "My dream is enough armor for that barbarian." Strange, you are entering dream, and I am drowning in reality; yes, your whole concept tied in with your Western sense of logic about Zen, satori, Harlem vision, life being a whole cloth out of void Womb Nothing, indicates clearly that you have entered that select state of outer-being, you have out stepped yourself as a man, you are outside, you see the world you imagine; more than laughing gas gave you that, surely; else your being be a hilarious one. I mean, can I imagine Homer being dictated to, not by the angel muse, but by laughing gas? It would be funny, almost wild; but then again maybe there was some laughing gas in the air over Athens. No, Allen, all the laughing gas did to you was drive out the spiritual pain in you, that mystic pain you covered for years and years with your sad body, your sad sex, your sad heart. I'm sure any Zen would agree with me that Enlightenment can be reached when the spiritual "disappears"; you disappeared that saintliness that was raw and unused in you; good, now you're opened for reprisal, finger will wag at you, telling you to stop being silly and listen, or telling you not to forge baptismal certificates, telling you not to expect to live off others, etc.; see? Now that you realize this, you can also realize that, if all that is is imagined, "which does not exist but is not necessary except for this last thought that there could be if there weren't nothing but an idea that there might not be nothing" it's enough and damned good reason, to demand love and aid from all that you imagine; how far I've come that I in return give to what I imagine! And I give my best, my all—only that which I don't imagine, I hardly give anything; realities; reason I don't give realities anything is because I don't see them! You know me well enough that I'd not hesitate to give to them invisibles either. And when reality becomes real to me, when I imagine it, and see what I imagine, I am become scared, scared because such imagination is alien to me, as well as distasteful. God, I feel like I'm making an awful lot of sense. Wanted very much to write to you for a long time anyway, I mean really write you; there has been a definite change in me, and I had wanted you, who, as I often say, are the closest thing to me in life, my guardian understanding angel, to know of the change. I don't think the change will hurt my poetry; I still feel fully devoted and dedicated to poetry, and have not backed down on my dying for it; I won't allow anything to hurt my poetry, I don't mean the poetry written, I never like poetry that has been written, I only like it when it is inside you, but when its out, bah! Really, poets don't understand that poetry is like semen, in you it is good, it is there, and when it flows out, even greater; but when it's out, it dies; and I am sure there is no womb for poetry; I mean semen is Godly, onceness, a finish. Consider a poet showing you a sheet of paper with a poem on it, and as you consider the poem, consider him. But have the poet come to you and give you that flow he had in writing it, have him speak the poem, and then consider him. See how much more his eyes are lit, how much more he is with feeling. And if you dig what he's saying, then surely we can say there is a womb for poetry; not just an ear; but a conception ear. Sounds all very sexual, but I don't mean it in the sexual way; but God knows what with all this mad psychiatry going around (a little recent imagined reality) I may well mean it to be sexual. Really, Allen, it's not stubbornness on my part, nor fear, nor ignorance; I find psychiatry an insult to the imagination; a gossip, a most basic gossip of the soul; it may well be fine for those seeking an imagination and such a soul, but when the imagination and the soul is had, how is it nobly possible to "imagine" a man to "imagine" what you imagine? Do you understand? Take you, for instance, you have an imagination (I'm thinking of it in its highest form) and a soul, a definite live lovely soul (you are not saving it entirely for God) both your imagination and soul, your poetical cock, (to get back to being unconsciously sexual again) contains and secretes that muse-baptized "semen", perfect, what more do you need? Has your poetical virility become impotent? And do you think the "imagined" Freudian can rejuvenate you? Show you the way to get it back? or not? Whatever his therapy; it's bad. Like Robert Lowell went to a psychiatrist and I feel that, in the sad judging eyes of the muse, the psychiatrist and all those who encouraged him to go and himself, a crime against beauty has been committed.

The creator's mind, his genius, his being, is in the employ of the muse; the muse, whatever the muse be, give it any name, that unnamable power, 4th dimension, God, etc. (Why have poets abandoned the muse today?) Poets are no longer dictated to by the muse; that's because poetry has become all "I"; the muse's dictation is usually objective. If the muse dealt with "I's" then it would become dictated to; used, made to wash and scrub the floors of (I'm feeling the muse) syntax, sew the buttons of meter, measure, stress; cook the stew of rhyme; make the bed of imagery. In other words it would become oppressed under the poet's dictatorship; why that hungry poet would exhaust her to death; selfish are poets when they capture the muse. I believe Shakespeare to have whipped the muse; abused her night after night making her pregnant without moments rest; like good souled Catholics. Yet all her children were beautiful, she had a good man in Shakespeare; a real cocksman; and I am sure that when his muse could bear no longer, he did not ignore her, but indeed paid homage to her. Dante too, Milton, even Shelley, though Shelley was, I feel good to say, quite lenient with his muse; he despised servants. Ah, and Chatterton, Rimbaud! They were just like "cool" jazz musicians, always putting their muse down; digging them; but not for long, then after awhile completely breaking away from them. Anyway, muse, or inspiration, has become a 19th century meaning today; I know most poems I write are definitely written with inspiration, I don't say inspired poems are any better than non-inspired poems, but I do say they are surely dearer to the heart. The only poems I love of mine are the inspired ones; those uninspired, and I'm happy to say I've written very few of them, are, sometimes, much better than my inspired ones, the images are more exact; and clearer; my structure and theme less careless; yet I prefer the ones less better. Yes; because as I said before, it is the poem in me, the poem that wants to come out; that drive, that magnificent come! That's all that is important, because that's all that is poetry; nothing else; not spontaneity, not measure, not meter, not rhyme, nor knowledge of WC Williams or Pound or Shelley or Whitman; and even not the language itself. Actually I find the language insufficient; not enough word-poems in the vocabulary. Back to sex again, my poetic-mouth finds the breasts of the body that possesses the womb of the too small poetic-cock not enough to incite, excite, though I've never been one to care about the size of a woman's breast, they're all beautiful to me and sufficient, I think, I don't know; right now I'm putting down sex; so I don't care one way or the other about breasts; I've decided that the girls I "imagine" are too unimaginable now that I find myself bombed by reality; before it was all right, I "imagined" them and loved them and went to bed with them with my imagination (sounds incestuous). Now see? I have to make excuses for what I say, and why? Because people with fat Prentice-Hall books of psychiatry (the actual Reality Police) force on you this awareness. I know I shouldn't listen to them; and I don't anymore; but once told becomes now known. So now I am aware that I have sexual hang-ups, and that they show in my poems. Well, I have no sexual hang-ups, and my poems are one body and spirit; just like the human body; sex and all. Why must people find the sexual unconsciousness (I hate that word) in poetry, in the images. Is it because they seek a meaning? When one meets a person for the first time does one inspect for sex, does one examine immediately the private parts? When I say I am become ascetic abstemious whereas girls are concerned, I say it not because I am sick sexually, but because I find sex a real drag; and also something quite ridiculous. Why only a month ago I was talking to a beautiful reserved sophisticated girl and I had so much respect for her and loved being with her. Then we had sex and while we were having it I opened my eyes and looked down upon her and realized that what was beneath me was a human being; and I said to myself: "What am I doing screwing a human being? It's mad!" and I kept on thinking how strange it was that man or woman got pleasure from each other, when each had the same skin! the same shape! hands, eyes, hair, flesh! even though man and woman are sexually different, they are of the same mold; I couldn't understand how I could screw such sameness (I kept on having sex; as I thought, of course; and I didn't think that long) and I also realized that having sex with a human being, a woman, is an act of selfishness; whereas having sex with a man, I can only imagine such sex, never having really practiced it, is, I feel, bereft of selfishness. I used to think when I was young that people got married because they wanted to have sex; not once considering if they loved each other, I never thought married people loved each other. I only thought love possible between two friends, and who wants to screw one's friend? Anyway I truly feel that heterosexuality and homosexuality, all kinds of sexuality, even my old hope of screwing a planet, the whole need and desire for it, I find (to return to the "imagined" and the "disappeared") false. Yes, false. Why do people want sex? They want sex because they love each other or because they're hard-up, or because just for the kicks of it, or because they pay for it; anyway, they WANT it, and they usually get it. Now, who can say, after they've had it, how necessary it was to have it? Everyone. Necessary because of human life. This is the phrase "necessary because of human life" you'll find spoken by people who contribute no human life to life; that is, they give birth yes; but it was not that phrase that raised their bodies to orgasm; no, sir, it was lust, good old lust; and therefore, false. The majority of mankind was conceived by the dim soft lights of a perfumed room, by a sensational energy of two humans looking absurd upon a singing bed. The whole thing is false when one thinks of an Einstein. And if there is false in sex, there is also truth in sex. And that truth is, masturbation. But don't think I mean there shouldn't be false sex, no, on the contrary, I love life, and it must go on, on and on, for as it goes on, I go on; if life goes, my "imagination" power goes; death, all death. But, to continue, I deny masturbation. Though I give it the gold medal of sex, I put it down whereas I'm concerned. It means nothing for me to masturbate; there was a time I used to love it, I used to imagine God coming in the room and catching me, the fear of that imagining filled me with power as well as with a wonderful come.

God, I feel like I'm writing a book of pornography for Olympia. Do you know I was almost tempted to do one for him? With high intent, I was going to write about the Fuck and the Anti-Fuck, Angus Plow and Scratch Vatic; O the great plans and ideas I had for it! The Force against the Force. The whole answerable mystery to life! Which force wins? A 4th dimension thought. God knows what attitude and what soul one must have to select or hope for one's favorite force. It was to be written with humor, not vile, with a humor that excited the "poetical cock" not the human one. I didn't write it. And I feel I did wisely; some ideas are not to be exercised. Besides, Shelley would never have forgiven me.

Whalen tells me he and McClure are finally discovering Shelley; I'm glad. Shelley was the purest "imaginer", he "imagined" himself, and he knew it, too: "The brightest hour of unborn Spring" See? More: "I leave this notice on my door/ for each accustom'd visitor:–'I am gone into the fields/ to take what this sweet hour yields'." These lines are from his *Invitation.* It's all too clear. Well, I feel I am one "accustom'd visitor" who dug the message; and at a very early age, and I knew right away too; that's why I am influenced by him; not his way or style of writing, I'm not influenced by that (I can think of nothing more embarrassingly absurd as an East Side Shelley, or like Ansen says, "a nigger-Shelley") only at times do I imitate his inspired flow, when I intentionally feel like, because to me it's not the line or the image that's important but the entire idea, if I have any setness in poetry it's in forming and measuring an idea; I think William Carlos Williams is half-way when he measures only line—line means nothing; you can write a million of them, but if you put them into an exact measured idea, it'll mean something; for were I to measure a line and put it into a measured idea. Oh God, I'm all confused, I don't know what I'm talking about; I'm getting away from what I wanted to say. Oh yes, I don't believe in measure.

I think it is a "cultist" invention poet's usually invent thus to insure their "meaning" as a poet. Looking at nineteen year old poetry today I am really amazed by their use of William Carlos Williams' and Pound's invention, when I think of a poet as a cultist, I often wonder whether he does good or harm; surely most of his following move on toward their own invention and some toward their own cult; the others who don't, and I know a few who are very high in your esteem, just don't; the harm I see is in this sinister passing-the-ball; but it's all not very important, really, the main thing is to possess the poetic idea, buy or steal the rack you fit the idea into; it's a way; but none such that it deems my love, respect, and appreciation of what is poetry; when I say I take from Shelley, I take not his poetry, but his own-self idea his "hour". But really, Allen, my two month old visitor, Reality, tells me I should complain and criticize, become argumentative, unsanitary, and junky. I just listen to it, but not once do I adhere to it. Do you think this sex denial has to do with my inherent Puritanism or junk-arrows? I don't know. Spoke to Bill about it; he knows. Also, back to psychiatrists, I am in much accord with what Bill gets from analysis; it makes him go far out, like a human fix, almost.

Your laughing gas poem, the fragments you sent me, are truly great, angel; really. Loose, too. And, perhaps you aren't aware of this, it's a new light in poesy. Jack says poetry is only pyrotechnics, he's so right for himself, but so wrong whereas you and me and Wieners is concerned; been really studying Wieners and think he's great. This "new light" I speak of is this: If you write a poem about the universe and use (like I did in *Bomb*) such phrases and word coinages as carrion stars; ethereal, celestial, etc.; this does not explain the use of universe. I didn't realize it at the time; it is the ABSENCE of such words that explains the universe; like Proust; like painting night white without the use of the paint, white; because the absence of white makes white; if ever you have a chance get a full book of Keats and see his canceled passages of 'Ode to Melancholy', you'll see what I mean. In those canceled passages are words related to melancholy, like moribund, dreadful, gloom, dark, a ship of human bone with sails of skin, etc.; well Keats knew that this wasn't the way to explain melancholy. Actually it's well-worn knowledge that tragedy is best explained through humor, paradox sort of thing. How correct was Irving Rosenthal in seeing no humor in Jack; o if only Jack would listen to the laughing Buddha; what is it that elevates confessional prose from the True Confession bowl but humor? Bluntly, and pyrotechnically, to be bereft of humor is to be like that sad lonely zero who, like rag picker, roams amongst the dumps of dimensions seeking that which it never had, seriousness; and let's say if lonely zero found what it sought, what would it be serious about? Nothing. Because zero is nothing. Yet I can understand the zero, it feels that if it were serious enough it could maybe get a whiff of one's neck. I must make myself clearer; there is much truth in that cliché "love is only possible when there is hate; the two are inseparable" thus "seriousness is only possible when there is humor; inseparable" yet so is the body and spirit one, but look how often man denies the body, or the spirit; I say Jack has humor, of course, but he denies it; and I understand, I think, fully why; his ego is such that, it is not he that sees the universe, it is the universe that sees him. When the universe fails to see Jack, then Jack will die; not when Jack dies, the universe dies. Both in *On The Road* and *Subterraneans*, this ego is so dominant; the humor that's in it is never flowed from Leo or Sal, but from the others; yes, he can see humor in others, and that is good; but to get personal, he does not see that unsurfaced humor, as he did not see it in Yuri, and good God, Yuri had the map of humor on his bugging-people face. What good he going into the desert if he won't make jokes in the desert? How almost corny really for him to go to the desert and sit like Buddha and think. O all the thinking!

All the thinking; why? To find out the meaning of life? The answer to the Question? God? Peace? Why he'll never find out, nobody will, nobody ever has. Science, religion, art, these are only applicable tools used on false works; the Real screw fitting into the False nut. The mysteries of life, their answers have been denied man; and surely this is unfair, man is allotted a hundred years, and much of those years are sorrowful years. Then man dies, he dies like billions billions before him, knowing nothing about such basic things as, when how and why the world the universe began; the meaning of time; the inability to walk to infinity and BEYOND. Now practically speaking, man will never know; speculation, all's speculation; so why the desert? Why Zen? Simple, because man believes he can know, and if the ego is big enough, he feels he can know through himself; and that's when things get to be serious and dull. As I said, I think it's unfair that man was not born with such information. That's why in *Power* I say the senses are insufficient; that all we can do is "imagine" the meaning; the reason I use Jack for this is this: Buddha was one man who "imagined" and told all to "imagine." Fine; but Buddha was human man, earth man, a man who laid down a cult; and many many follow the cult, the way, the belief, call it what you will. His was a necessary answer; but! An answer to what question? Yours? Jack's? Life's? Okay. But mark what I said before, nobody knows, only "imagines", therefore you who did not spring from Buddha's head couldn't possibly use his answer to your question; his answer was made possible only through HIS question. Therefore you, Jack, Snyder are all off base, because you seek an answer (and are so smartly conning lovely powerful enough to have found one) when you don't even have the question. If Jack goes into the desert he'll go without that all important yet impossible question; the answer he'll get will be anything he wants it to be; the ego is such that Ghost Cheese could well be the sought after answer; yet not once have I heard from any unslanted eyed Zen the Question. Buddha is all right, and I love him. Christ is all right, and I love him. Luther is all right, and I love him. Allah is all right, and I love him. But how dot you all become on the big white sheet when you feign to explore the sheet with an exploding atomic bomb question mark. Meaning, if you put a question mark on a blank sheet, anybody can write an answer beneath it; and that well could be a crazy way of creating an American equivalent to the Haiku.:

?

Infinity is a dog sitting at its own feet

Man's way is personal, and it's his own way, and therefore it is good. Jack and Zen are good, but I'd much rather Jack and Catholicism; less ego involved. I mean I think Zen satiates the spiritual selfishness in man. "I am an intellect, not a truck driver, therefore I need a religion or a mystic way or an enlightening way in which to cast my soul, my belief, my being, a religion equals my beauty, my, my my my my my." Bah, really; that's why I always say Lucifer. Why? Because in Lucifer I see no demand of my thinking process. You nor Jack nor Snyder can't deny that the three of you are bred with LOGIC, and logic is a Western invention; the Orientals are bereft of logic. Didn't you ever consider that you with your logic are incapable of comprehending the illogical? Buddhism is alien to your way of thinking. And you are alien to it. You THINK. Meditation is the absence of thinking. But when a Zen meditates, he meditates to THINK, and he succeeds, he thinks "imagines" Nirvana. You, Jack, Gary can never "imagine" Nirvana no matter how long you lotus because you erroneously eliminate thought from your meditation; a blank mind is a blank mind. And besides you angels are too New York and life and worry or no and drinkers, eaters, livers, girl man mad, to ever see Nirvana. What right have you to see it? Especially Jack, just because he asks to see it? Just because he's studied Buddhism? Just because he believes? He'll never see that kind of Nirvana, nobody will. But of course everybody can just simply by creating Nirvana; just like Beauty. Beauty never was, Beauty is created. I feel like I'm talking to a bunch of Jesuits; and that's the way you guys come on. I think the funniest image I have in mind now is Jack sitting alone in the desert, sweating, and muttering "Yeah wow wow O God now now NOW"—and if he can't see the funny sight of it, then indeed he lacks humor; but then again, if I see it funny, then he should do it. Always do funny things. But good God what if he went seriously? If he went really seriously then the only thing for humanity to do is circle around him out there, set up TV stations, etc., and watch him, because he is SERIOUS. Old Gregory again. But I mean well. I feel like a child with Jack, like to tease him. Actually I find him very innocently funny; therefore he couldn't be that much without humor who causes to laugh. Yes, gentlemen, I think you should take heed from the Zen lunatics; and be lunatic; laugh, damn it! Laugh at everything! Take nothing seriously. Look at your lives, look how often you refused to be funny when something SO serious was going on; look how serious you took the Hungarian Revolution when you threw that table at me, look how serious Jack was about Mardou, look how serious Peter is about Julian, look how serious all other unimaginable imaginables are? Good God don't die serious. Laugh! Go to the window the three of you and look up at the sky and LAUGH! Aren't any of you afraid of seriousness? I am. But I'm never afraid of laugh. Please, gentlemen, wipe away this image I have of thee; I see you three in a world that in years to come you will leave, and I don't see you laughing. I see you like wiggling worms crawling on the surface of the earth, serious! Humor devours wisdom. But, alas, I am talking to myself and for myself, for indeed Reality has yanked out my laughing heart. No don't laugh, gentlemen, weep! Weep for me, for I am a lonely zero falling like a snowflake. My nothingness that was once my humor somethingness is circled with a serious crust. It is not Jack or you or Peter that is serious, it is I! I am serious! O God! O woe! O me!

To Allen Ginsberg Paris
[ca. Oct. 8] 1958

Dear Allen,

O angel, don't get money for *Interpol*, just Bill's and mine's crazy idea, and if it comes thru Stern will probably take care of it, but he's ill and too much on his mind, too. I enclose Ansen's review of *Gasoline* and think he is very perceptive and should be published, Don Allen asked for it, show it to him but he said that O'Hara will review me, so if not him, what about LeRoi, *Yugen*? Anyway I think it should go into print. Ah but don't you think *Power* is finally done? Finally I am happy with it. I sent it to Feinstein Cambridge address magazine you gave me, [she] wrote me too. Also send it to Don Allen for anthology, and *ER*; but surely loved Irving Rosenthal's letter to you, he sounds very fine. I have no copy of *Power* to send him, can you send him yours? Yes, I would like to come to America and see everything so differently now; how much I've changed! India seems way off in a way; no set plans in Stern, and I'm so senseless in Paris, Europe, taking H [heroin] and getting real down and sick. I don't think I should waste myself, not yet, and I'm so susceptible to doing so. Yes, I want to come to America, a big decision on my part; don't know how to get money but I may find some way; I'm afraid to ask Stern, I need an arrogance to ask, and he's become a friend, and he even thinks I'm conning him, but knows that it's a natural part of me, and that it's inherent in me, and that I don't mean too; nor do I. But I need love, and a gift of gold I guess is a form of love to me, I don't know; God knows I don't care about it. But right away, soon before I go into gloom and get too thin and look red-eyed ugly. Ah my dear friend how I exercise your love, but someday we'll die, and it wouldn't have been too bad your concern for me. Your "mind consciousness" "we imagined all this up" is just the state that I have been in all my life. Good God Allen, you're going into something I am being shocked out of. *Laughing Gas*,[137] of course, there's nobody in the whole world like you. Your part of poem is wonderful, so much greater than Vaughn's vision of eternity last night, and I full well understand "disappearance" its sensation and reason, yes, Swindleresque Ink means "universe disappearance", "life being a whole cloth out of void Womb Nothing" indicates clearly that you have entered that select state of outer-being, it was not the laughing gas but you, all the laughing gas did was drive out the spiritual pain in you, that mystic pain you covered for years and years with your sad body, your sad sex, your sad heart. I'm sure any Zen would agree with me that Enlightenment can be reached when the "spiritual" disappears. You "disappeared" what you "imagined" eradicated that Harlem vision. How far we've come that we can give to what we "imagine"! Reality is such a "imagination" that is alien, as well as distasteful, to me. I want you to see something in Shelley, it's from a poem of his called *The Invitation*; see in it your laughing gas enlightenment and my Swindleresque Ink: "The brightest hour of unborn Spring . . . I am gone into the fields to take what this sweet hour yields." God how clear that is! But we go one more than him, we take, but we also try very hard to GIVE. How's this for Haiku . . . ?

Trees are hard hairs on earth's belly.

Oh, fuck it, Allen, I wrote you a seven page letter, but thought best not to mail it, because in it I am writing what was two nights ago a very confused sick unhappy mind, but [now I'll] send it to you. Please don't show it to Jack because the poor soul is being so criticized and all that, and I have no right to join in. I love what he is and his soul joy love, I guess I wrote what I did about him because of what he said about sending him "installments" of a thing that wept from me, as if I were a professional confessor, and I thought it belittled my outpour to him; AND I DO NOT WANT THAT LETTER PUBLISHED, I mean this now; but if it gets published I don't care . . . you see how I am; I say "why not publish it" and "tomorrow I can always 'imagine' something else, and nobody will always see me as that letter" and then I say "No, I am a thing of dignity, and my dignity is not to be painted and paper hung on the walls and posts of this life". What do you really think? Seriously. I mean, will it make my dreams of coating Byzantium with day's bright casualty, an absurdity; that "nigger Shelley" business again? I'm afraid, Allen, I don't want to be completely bereft of mystery; I don't want myself all known. If I am all known, then how impossible for me ever to convince myself of change, and others, too for that matter; but then again if I say I will die for my poetry, then I must show myself naked, mustn't I? O I'm so confused. Shelley leads me to a safe unreal high gold muse, and life leads the opposite; like Don Allen sending me a contract to sign for anthology poems. Now surely Shelley wouldn't sign, I mean, in his day there was no such thing, I mean it's not right for a poet to be so conscious of his output; then again, look at me with those ridiculous interviews, but I only did those interviews because I felt happy to play and laugh and clown, while deep in my heart I laughed most because I DID write good poetry, and was not just a creep clown. So don't show Jacky letter until I talk to him. I feel that he is being too bugged with criticism and that I who should know better . . .

Oh well it was spontaneous and that's what he advocates. God, I wish I knew how to decide for myself. Such a letter as that written to Jack, I hate it now that it has been written, again like old come, at the time, great, but now, no. Don't you understand? I don't. Shel [Sheldon] is back, and I've forgiven him for the lies he told about me, but I find he bores. Yes, I've changed very much. Yes, Allen, I really think it a matter of emergency to get out of Paris, and away from drugs; taking needle now, Bill and I, but don't mention to Bill. He says that he will probably go to Dent, he is hooked, and his room is black, and fumes of PG, etc. etc. It's not good for me, but then again, I ask for it, and all is not regretted, I am very strong. What should I do about Bill? I mean he's not sick, and he's still great funny genius self; I am trying to get him to come back to USA with me, but he has no desire to. Says there's nothing there for him, but I told him that there is. That he is loved there, and also that he is a great writer and that he is accepted and recognized as such, and that he should not abuse his genius, etc. He listens, and we are very much in closeness; almost a love. How nice, I never thought that possible. I never thought he'd really get to love me, but he does. We sit up for hours talking, he thinks I am a Puritan and my old Catholic upbringing, etc.; but I know it entertains him.

Yes, you are right about *Bomb*, as is always the case, my work is in constant need of change; and I probably can't change it now, it's done, but maybe someday I'll be perfect. As for *Marriage*, I am in process of fixing it up; did you give it to Jones? He says he has a poem of mine for 4th issue, is it *Marriage*? If so, I'll fix it up for him. Sent Rahv[138] of *Partisan Review, Bomb* when I was very drunk and wrote him mad letter about how *Bomb* was prophecy, etc. Can't say I wished I hadn't of done it, I did, but why, I don't know. Again Gregory. But so what? All is "imagined". My attitude. Phipps would probably help me get back [home], but maybe he's lost his faith in me, I don't know. He actually doesn't know me, if anyone should see that letter to Jack, it should be he, then I'd feel much better if it were he who called me back to America. I want so badly to see. But I do want to come back. India will always be.

Dear Peter, so you are going to have FIRST POEM[139] in *Yugen*, great. Now that you are an established poet, Höllerer will be here in few days and I will give him final batch of poems, so please send first poem to me for anthology and any others you have. I see now that I have not thought you poet before because you did not scream poetry, very wrong of me. What makes a poet is not scream but growth upon growth; my conception of what is and what isn't is forgivable, straw-haired broom angel. Did Laff get my cards, is he paying heed? Tell him to study up on the importance of the quanta.

I want very much to come home, but I feel like I am a bother, I don't know what to feel; anyway. I love you all very much, and you are right about my going through the junk angle, full swing, with mad machetes, o the horror of those decapitated boas!

Why haven't you written me, are you annoyed with me, can't you forgive? and do you still slurp your soup? Well, I want no part of that when I come back, but I do have a nice gift for you, a sixteenth century deep spoon, a million slurps in one. [. . .]

To Lawrence Ferlinghetti

Paris
[ca. Oct.] 1958

Dear Larry,

Ah, angel soul; true I don't know half the time what's happening, but in that severed time I am not totally an extremist; like you truly mistaken me about *Power* and *Interpol*. *Power* is a poem of love, of self-discovery, a poem that rose me from East Side Italian truck driver gloom to self, not political self, but ethereal self. In *Power* I destroyed the meaning you attribute me, and gave it a new one. I hope you can see that in my new and final version Don Allen will have in anthology. And as for *Interpol*, it was a pot idea thought of beneath a gargoyle by Bill and I concerning untouchables and junkies, and had nothing to do with NeoPound fascism; believe me. Now I shan't explain my explanations to thee any further. Like don't you know I love everything? That I'd be equally wrong (be there such a thing) to deny as to accept, and therefore am without one-sidedness, be it in love or politics.

James Laughlin sent me his poems, a small book, and he has some nice things, his flow almost like yours, but not as varied or opened. Yet some things he wrote were quite good; especially his two "publishing house" poems. Working very hard with Höllerer on German bi-lingual anthology. It'll be a mess, I dare say. LeRoi Jones of *Yugen*, a small magazine in New York, writes me that he wants to do a book of mine; I feel I should first ask you; as with Allen, I am very happy with angel Ferl; but I do got a lotta poems; some I'm really very happy with. So please inform me on this kind of subject. Is *Bomb* a dud? Ah, but how I'm progressing from that birth poem; I am now reading all about quanta; yes, Larry, it'll be the poet, you'll see, who'll someday answer the universe. Besides, it's always like that; that's why I dig Shelley so much. Now be good, and stop accusing me of politics. Politics is just a toy in the great use of things.

Your bon ami, Gregory

To Allen Ginsberg

Amsterdam
[ca. Oct. 5] 1958

Dear Allen,

Am in beautiful Amsterdam again, just for three mad days. Saw Jan Meullen of *Litterair Paspoort* and Simon [Vinkenoog] and others. All fine and the wax dolls are still sitting in their glowy windows. So nice to walk these streets. Am really most happy here in lack of paranoia sense. Am now at Tajiri's house—remember the sculptor Japanese? He's doing great mad things. I will return to Paris tonight—hope in the mail I will see token home. Really miss you and Peter. Xmas is in the air. I wrote six days exhausting mad poem very deep spontaneity thing called *Xmas*, will send it on when I get back, be happy,

My love, Gregory

To Don Allen Paris

[ca. Oct. 6] 1958

Dear Don,

I understand now what you meant about my being less-objective in a Venice letter to me concerning that Dutch article—very silly of me to put down just names of poets who, a year later, I dig; like Frost, really. I've always been against such put down, but mine was really laughable because all I did was pick names out of the blue who I knew somewhat to be academic; but I am silly, it's my way; as I grow older I grow less and less silly—I learn. But the learning is not pleasant; it brings back all that naive goofiness in form of grey memory; how to expiate it? Or need I expiate? I mean, I am learning more and more every day; only recently has this been happening and yet I am not apt to deny my past; I stand by everything I've done, because even if I see "wrong" in what I've done; I did it with no heart knowledged with "wrong"; be there such a thing. Anyway everybody's past is perfect. As perfect as history, because it is done. There can't be any denial of history, only "ifs"—and I find no remedy in "if." Anyway I just want you to know that I now know what you meant by less-objective.

Saw Höllerer and he says he had a fine time and with you, and that you showed him around the Village night. He and I will put finishing touches to anthology. God, Don, is it going to be a mess? I mean, really; it should either be very damned interesting, or terrible. What mixture! The golden coq has flown from Sainte-Chapelle, winter did it. India seems very remote now, alas; but NYC looms more and more an India to me. I mean I'll really see it with different eyes, now.

Adios, amigo, Gregory

Is it necessary I write a biography piece?[140] I think photo is nice, don't you?

To Gary Snyder Paris

[ca. Oct. 8] 1958

Dear Gary,

Ah, but *Interpol* was a wild pot idea Burroughs and I loomed beneath a gargoyle; seems such ideas rarely bear onions. Anyway thanks for your wise humor in it all . . . more than I can say for Ferl who insists *Interpol* conception to be neo-Pound fascism; in fact I really believe he thinks I am of one extreme in my no-beliefs; like I love everything; don't he know that yet?

I may go back to NYC, I want to; I am become somebody else who wants to see the city I've lived in for 26 years. I mean, I can always go to India. And besides, I think I should yell at you; but a bird's yell—when I asked for your most vile humiliating work; I did not mean for you to send me dirty words of cleanliness mind; but, for instance, clean words of dirtiness mind; like descriptions of how you sometimes imagine yourself tormenting an untouchable; or how you sometimes spend all your time at Buddha's pad, never making it over to Zeus', like the cat's a gas, too; perhaps a little aggressive, and not as cool as Buddha, what with all his hang-up with swans, and clouds, and bulls; still he deems a visit. But, then again, the house we visited in our childhood; if we go there now and knock on the door, somebody else's mother might appear. Scary thought.

And, again, I've never made it over to Buddha's; and I'm bugged with having, after all these years, returned to Christ, dragging me with his talk about how Western Civilization ain't going to die because Dante gave WC to Hell, and Hell shan't forget; what Hell remembers, Earth remains.

Yes, ah, yes, but we must meet . . . it will be good;

Love, Gregory

To Don Allen Paris

{Oct. 13} 1958

Dear Don,

But o all week I wasn't happy with ending of *Power*; here is last and surely final better end; light light all is light, and good. I sent you photo and mad contract and nice letter telling you how much I now understand what you meant about not being so objective concerning Dutch article; I see the light; and I know it'll make you happy to see that letter. I sent it slow mail not having any money at time, so should take week and a half to get to you. Laughlin writes me that he'd like to have *Bomb* for his New Directions anthology; I wrote and told him you have it but if he'd like to see others, fine. But really write to me and tell me what you think of *Power* now, please. I need to be told about that damned albatross poem I love so well.

Am studying all about quanta, quite fascinating, and am reading reading and am learning very much; got a nice letter from Edouard Roditi; a poet who wrote a poem years ago about being the priest of his religion and the God of his religion. A poem I loved very much when I was twenty; so it'd be nice to correspond with him.

Love, Gregory

To Peter Orlovsky Paris

{Oct. 23} 1958

Dear Peter,

That big article depressed me, how sad some life things are, any way big color pic of Jack nice, good stance, nice expression on his face, all red glow, like movie screen. Your two poems lovely. Good. They'll go in anthology. Find out from Allen when he needs poems for his collection; tell him I am working on huge poem *Death*, and that that might be good for mine part, also *Army* if possible, but ain't got copy, Don Allen has, and Höllerer.

That Corso FUND very very mad; but alas who'd want to give their dimes to me there in that wide city of no bed but rooftops and subways always, hard to believe if they'll give anything; but nice if they would, lovely gesture on Allen's part.

Bill in England for cure, he seemed very determined to kick, he and Jacques [Stern] there, to hold good hands and get better. I'll let you know results right away. Did Phipps get H [heroin] I sent him, he wanted it, and I wanted to do anything I could for him, though I wish I could have done something more to my height and taste. Edouard Roditi sent me big queer letter inviting me to Mediterranean, very nice great letter writer; we have a mad Kafkan correspondence; also I am corresponding with Isabella Gardner who, Allen, you should pickup on, she being a female Lowell almost, and, without malice, much more DREAM and WILDNESS OF THOUGHT in her than Levertov female poets.

The gray cat sends his regards, I found out its name, it's Mardou.[141] Sheldon Thomas on his way back to NYC, I got to like him very much, and we got along fine this time. A very weird angel cat really. Why don't you and Allen some day make it to 1496 St. Marks Ave. Brooklyn and find out just what my folks are like and what they think and how things are? Would really appreciate that very much; but if you think it'll be a drag, then don't.

Allen please find out what Don Allen is going to use for anthology, because I don't know where I'm at; but say you wish to find out for YOURSELF, because he don't seem to reply or know yet or something; just say you'd like to know; please; want very much to straighten out my manuscript; all asunder. Wonder if Laughlin is bugged at me? Wrote him long inspired letter about this book and why he should abandon all and flee; in truth and in fun; maybe he thinks I am presumptuous or something, which I ain't. How much has that CORSO FUND got in it yet? Millions? Maybe we could keep it going forever maybe? What madness! Yes yes I know Frank O'Hara would be the one as much as Allen to dig my work, because Frank and I are very much in idea alike. Did *Poetry* take Ansen's review? I think it's too favorable for their taste.

Ah Peter you sad? Don't be sad when I come back I'll make you very happy with my new countless costumes; I'll even give you one, a court jester's, okay? But now, I want you and Allen one night to be the most truthful you've ever been with me and say what you really think of my coming back, I want to know. Please, this most important to me. Because I don't want to come back and be drag on anyone, anymore. I mean this. So pour out TRUTH to me.

All's love, Gregory

To Allen Ginsberg Paris
[Oct. 25] 1958

Allen,

As Bill is away, I've no immediate funds for food, rent, etc. so it'd be wise to send me dear Zina's contribute.[142] Don Allen says he won't use *Bomb*, so I'll send it to New Directions, they asked for it. Paris cold, yesterday was a nice autumn day, though, and spent much time in Luxembourg Gardens. [Hypodermic] Needle is broken—happily, so I'm all right. Strong and rosy-cheeked *Army* will be used by Don Allen, I guess. So I'll soon send on whole batch of poems for you to select. Got poems from Robin Blaser—good. More Koch—and [Arnold] Weinstein. Will use [Stan] Persky.

Love, Gregory

To Gary Snyder Rome
[Oct. 31] 1958

Dear Gary,

I'm sitting in view of Keats' grave and directly in front of a huge white pyramid with tuffs of grass coming out of it—I think a Roman family is buried in it. Last night saw the Appia Antica, and the familiar sight, the prettiest suit of ruin, was there: cypress, marble, and moon. I wonder if there can be anything more lovelier than Rome or Greek ruins? It's those Roman inscriptions thin and worn, those half-columns, those missing noses—nothing except perhaps, Egyptian ruins can come close. The *Colosseo* [Coloseum], the *Foro* [Forum], Nero's palace. The past is true—it is not a lie, it has not been made up—It's all here! Shelley—Caesar, Augustus, Vespasian, Keats, Michelangelo, the new Pope, Giovanni XXIII !!

Love, Gregory

Back in Paris on the 12th, alas,

▼ [These postcards were written while Corso was sitting near the cemetery of his two great heroes, Keats and Shelley. Following his death on Jan. 17, 2001, his ashes were interred in this same cemetery at the feet of his beloved Shelley.]

To Philip Whalen Rome
[Oct. 31] 1958

Dear Phil,

Enclosed find two clovers—one from Keats' grave, the other from Shelley's, big one Keats. The idea of these poets, their having existed, their perfection of all that was Romantic—equals now their real death buried here in view of Rome and ancient Rome, the dream gets realler and realler. What to say it but romance? Jack K. says romance is dead—Rome, the *Foro*, the *Colosseo*, Nero's palace—the Appian Way, Keats, Shelley, Michelangelo—they say NO—cypress, marble, and moon trio is a sturdy symbol of Romance. *Viva Roma*—and the new Pope, Giovanni XXIII !!!

Love, Gregory

To Allen Ginsberg Rome

[Oct. 31] 1958

Dear Allen,

Am writing this in that sniper's ruin just before Shelley's tomb. Don't understand my feelings. Nero's house with its huge labyrinth dining hall, baths, rooms, throne room, all underneath new Rome; the coliseum, the forum, Michelangelo, the Appian Way, and now this—too much to feel, I guess I didn't know Trelawny[143] was buried near him. Just wrote to Snyder, Whalen, and Jack, telling them in Roman omen truth way that Romance is madly alive! That this is the sturdy unfailing symbol of Romance: Cypress, marble, moon.[144]

Anyway I went mad the other night and ran rampant into exclusive bars and started screaming beauty, save ancient Rome, sing for Shelley—on and on, and met gangsters who I told gangster stories to, they buying me scotch, and to Fascists who I told I was Ezra Pound's son—Gregory Pound, and got drunk drunk running up to police and telling them to throw away their guns, we all have got to sleep in the Forum tonight. They didn't lock me up—obviously I mix my ideas with people, with real things—my wanting everybody to be beautiful because I love ancient Rome is hilarious as well. I cry and laugh—laugh in the Coliseum screaming Victory! Victory!

Thanks for *Village Voice* fund to send me home, hope they can make it. It costs quite a lot to go by way of Greece, Istanbul, Tehran, India, Japan, Pacific, S.F., N.Y.—but surely they don't expect me to take that dull oft-riddened sea back home, do they? No—the only noble thing if there be a fund, then a grand fund. My life is too far in heaven now for me to be grateful for life's beggy pittance. I know you, my sweet friend, understand. Enclose find two clovers one from Keats the other from Shelley. You seemed not to have any except the one you sent your father. I will be back in Paris on 12th November. Hope Bill's well, can't wait to see him.

To Lawrence Ferlinghetti Rome

[Oct. 31] 1958

Here is all my joy—Really—really. Am writing this in Keats' room where he died, all the books in here! And photos! Paintings of Shelly, Byron, Keats. Long line Romance! It's coming back, you know.

All right—I'm glad you understand that I am not that kind of soul who is NEO—but fun me. I am happy you love me and know that all my life I've always chosen the grand noble Roman in us all. You have it, Allen has it. Yes, Allen who, as soon as I left prison, give me the wriggling truth of Roman columns and statuary. My Merry Xmas to you and your wife. I have just finished after six days Roman haunts a grand poem, my best, yes, called *Rome*!!! Be happy, balding tall young poet-man.

My love, Gregory

My only aim is now, and has always been, to revive that which was always alive. ROMANTICISM. Anything other than romanticism was always laughable. Right now I'm in the midst of twenty priests in Rome—in their monastery, and I'm trying to get them to join me in taking down the awkward cross from the Pantheon. I'll be coming home soon.

To Lawrence Ferlinghetti Paris

[Nov. 7] 1958

Larry,

Am back in Paris, will write soon about play and new poems. Hear Allen is doing an anthology for you—good, what's it going to be like? Why you no print Whalen, Snyder? They belong to you, not Grove—forget your own personal tastes, and dig that it's your duty as insight poet to print their books. Am sick with cold.

Love, Gregory

To Philip Whalen Paris

[Nov. 7] 1958

Dear Phil

Angel justice alp-eyed cloud forgive me for no answer soon, I ill in little attic that has windows and its wind all wheres, am stayed layed in bed with heaps and heaps of blankets and coats and shirts and even a cat, alas. Lovely lovely poem, but *Interpol* folded, just some quick happy quack idea me and Bill loomed up; told Gary about it, had fun writing him about his poems, which I dug but said when I asked for most humiliating didn't mean dirty birdy words, all in fun, also about him making it over to Zeus' pad sometime, hope he ain't bugged because I just type mind rapidly and say all gauderies and goodies not meaning no HURT, O steadfast love is always me. I didn't dig your prose piece in *Chicago Review*, now really didn't because I love your poetry too much; does that make sense? I mean don't spill thy gold elsewheres where it'd cry for its mamma's soft warm golden teat. Still not much sense. I mean, write a long mad at your age now final great YOU now as you are with all behind POEM.

Waste no time; call not Death by a lesser name; NOW: DOW: DO! Anyway you know, so for my knowledge and perhaps unkeen insight explain to me just what you're getting at with the PROSE TAKE. Also, don't hesitate to, if you can, send me some loot for something, like I can't even make mailing stamps, really, and find it awfully awkward to be broke now that all is winter near and aclod and acold and alone.

I am shaking dandruff, dandruff God's snow from my hair, so much of it, why? What does it mean? What new things are happening, angel meat? Ferl sent me newspaper clipping of great photo of you me and Allen and Jack, me got my hand around your forgotten-felt neck, you smiling so nice and angelic; me with turned up pants cuffs, Allen with beard and EYES, and Jack with now famous face. Did you see *Bomb*, did you like *Bomb*? O but I wept that poem out I did, worked hard on it I did, new openings, new feelings, ever changing I. *Chicago Review* asked for poems, this second time, first time they refuse, now I send them *Power* at its best, and *Marriage*, two best great poems, and they write they are "considering"; o how I hate that sort of thing. Hate it because them poems are not poems meant to go to parole board and get decision of whether they be eligible or not for publication freedom air; they'd be published anyway; and really I'm now saying damn publishing, all too sordid and sinister and unwarranted, and unromantic in a way. By their letters to me one would think that without them I am helpless; that patience is needed, consideration needed; they make me feel like a boy who is seeking to get his first bad poem published; don't they know I am grown sad and tired and quiet, not even lion's roar of silence anymore; that I am not in NEED of CHICAGO AZERBAIJAN ADEN, enough, you see I still complain, good, all's not old Gregory aged mute. Yet.

I have stone floor, to keep room warm I pour alcohol in big pan and lit match, wham! great dance of heat. Yes, it be so nice if you and Gary were to aid just a little me, for I am in dire need at present, Allen gone, Bill gone to England for cure, now all alone, and no possible work here or holy beg.

My love, Gregory

To Allen Ginsberg Paris
[ca. Nov. 7] 1958

Dear Allen,

Am back in Paris after hectic week in Rome then Monte Carlo all with a richy girl and casino and there met at dice table James Jones,[145] and we talked. He says he wanted to see you but you had left and says he digs Kerouac very much, and I asked him about illuminations and all that and he didn't seem to know, but seemed nice, and says it's only the criminal mind and attitude that can exist in this world, and we shot dice and lost and won and lost. Then I go back to Paris and catch bad cold on cold train so now am laid up in bed; Whalen and Snyder angels sent me some money five and ten dollars and Wally sent all my mail to Rome so I have to wait for it to return here in which I was told is some *Village Voice* loot and letter by you, etc.; so I'll get it soon; hope I can get enough to get boat ticket; a cold winter in this small air conditioned room will slay me sure.

Bill hasn't written to me yet but I hear he's over cure and he and Jacques are living in England and will be back in a few weeks. Roditi sent me some crazy poems, he real great; will put him in anthology along side with Olson and William Carlos Williams. Right now too phlegm catarrh nose clog to sit up and write, so when better will write.

Love to Peter, Gregory

▼ [The following was written in response to Loewinsohn's inquiry about poems he sent to Corso for inclusion in his German anthology, *Junge Amerikanische Lyrik.* He requested the return of his manuscripts as he had no copies, just as Corso would do with his publishers countless times in the future.]

To Ron Loewinsohn Paris

[ca. Nov. 7] 1958

Dear Ron,

Care not so much about publication, write the poems. If they are asked for or not, send them in, and forget them. Your impatience blinds you; don't you realize that there are four translators working on at least 60 poets I have selected? and that this doesn't take a day, a year maybe, or more, I don't know and I don't care. I not an anthologist; I don't want to be bothered with such detail. I told this to Di Prima and to Jones; what's all the hurry? And do you think I can hurry it? All I have to do with this project is collect, period. Now leave me alone concerning outer things. I guess I was wrong in taking this venture in the first place, but I thought and they thought it'd be a mad idea for me to compile an anthology; and I have and as far as I know, all is not translated as of now; it will be bi-lingual. As for that poem you want, all your poems are in Germany; when I go there I will seek it out and send it on; and don't worry so much about ethics of publication as giving rights etc.; sounds too productive in very unpoetic way; you just write your poems and let the publisher insist; it's all a bother, really.

And who says I'm starving? I just came back from Monte Carlo where I lost 300 dollars, and I spent tons of money in Rome, and everyday in the mail

I'm getting money, and I always have girls and angels here who have great houses in which I eat.

Gregory

Nice about forthcoming life[146]; it doesn't know anything yet, but it will know; it'll even consider high talks about Light, Death, Hegel, Unamuno, St. George, and all that ridiculous small capture that man is endowed with. Or maybe it won't talk at all, or maybe.

Anyway, I am off to mad Berlin to read *Bomb* over radio there, and then back to states. When in Berlin I'll try to get your poem. One thing I don't want, and that's responsibility for other poets poems, it's enough that I don't make carbons and lose so many poems, all I can say is, it's a real drag that I got to go to all that bother; and you don't help with your sporadic cold empty letters demanding compensense for next month, six months, 30th century . . . publishing be damned. Forgive me, but your letter was one of dozens I've been receiving concerning this. Whalen, Snyder, they don't ask nor do they care, they sent their poems in, it was done; like history, it is done, finished, look forward, for forward is the light. My job with anthology is done, thank Lucifer—I have nothing more to do with it; one thing is certain it should be the worst mixture ever, and by that, it should be good, because I took poets who aren't poets but who maybe wrote one or two poems, also candy store owner poets, and jail poets, and creepy poets, and angel poets, all mixed up; if I were asked (and I'll explain this in introduction to book) do I like all the poets I chose, I'd say NO, and that would be true, the only poets I dig going in anthology are Edouard Roditi, Ginsberg, Whalen, O'Hara. And maybe not even them, there just ain't any good poets today; I take Shelley, Nash, Keats, Watt, Vaughan, . . . poets today are too damned conscious of making it in poetry. They serve no purpose whereas romance is concerned. American poets are like show-off bowlers on a bowling team, and none of them live beautifully. They write and take the meaning of poetry and brand their hearts and neon their talk and faces with it, . . . I guess it's 1958 that does that . . . Anyway, I'm convinced heaven is round. Be good.

To Peter Orlovsky Paris

[ca. Nov. 10] 1958

Dear Peter,

Sweet Peter, seems like it's only you who is remaining proud to your love, its ways and truth and illuminations; maybe it's because you are yet real with youth, and that what you believe and do is too bright to once bright eyes that have seen, and having seen, become dimmed; but it happens to all man, you know. A quick jump, and then a slow walk. An accepted pattern of life. I try very hard (see how fortunate I am) to join that slow walk; else I'll continue perpetually to be out of step . . . and why not? Good that you are the way you are; when the change comes, when that sofa gloom much thought time comes you'll see that what you were and how you were was good. Kerouac and Allen see in themselves their good; but they can't deny life, it's change. Sure Jack drinks more and sex becomes no longer it, but other things; has to, else it'd be absurd to deny that a human face grows wrinkled. Know that you have youth and that it's your youth that questions the reactions of another, less fortunate in years. You have it, so don't care. Yes, care, but care with a compassion, accept and love the reactions of other different souls. All's not the same, nor will it ever be. Yes all man will eventually love all man, but pray that the loves be varied. Many years ago youth had to contend with the flogging-block, "Now, boys, be pure in heart! For if not, I'll flog you until you are!" And this sort of attitude and way birched half the ministers, bishops, generals, dukes and poets of the day. So accept Jack's and maybe even Allen's loving flog. Don't sulk. Besides that's the penalty you pay for being wild happy soulful young. And imagine if you weren't like that! Why you'd be an old boy! Why I'd no longer have love fun with you about slurping soup, don't you see? And now a flog for me: Don't hurt the presence of your guardian angel; it's always with you, so know that whatever you do, be it dancing before Dali's wife or blowing Allen before Jack, that there's in you that which where no man can go goes and what no man can do does; see? You speak of love, then LOVE; nothing should bother you; if you make things bother you then you are weak; now you know I always have this thing about and against weakness; all kinds of it; not fascistic like Ferl says; but man dies, and with that knowledge an Alexander in the soul is not only necessary but SMART. So there. Take it from me. We are very much alike in this respect. I know what I'm talking about. Don't try to cupid your actions with the reactions of another. Okay? Get arrogant, damnit! Hide your beauty; stand before man and show them your great desirable vault. Don't worry, they'll soon beg thee to open up. And don't be weak and open up either. There are billions of man; put a matchbox on your head and spill water on your ear, then you'll be ONE out of a billion. Select Orlovsky! Noble elegant select Orlovsky . . . and why not? To love is also to TAKE, you know.

I think your letter to me beautiful, only beautiful one in such a long time, too. And you don't have to invite me to live with you; you should know me by now that your house and Allen's is MINE, period. And while we're on the subject I want the darkest room, and also lots of caviar and goodies in the icebox; and I'll bring with me lots of real iron angels I bought in flea market; and I don't want Allen using my toothbrush, and I don't think it'll have to be my duty to take the garbage downstairs; and I don't want anybody using my new

Olivetti typewriter or wanting to borrow my new velvet pants; let's see, what else, o yes, it is deep in my heart that I want very much to get my own place and settle down in a happy darkness and only wish to walk the places of my youth. I want to be Balzac in New York, and I'll need a companion, and you'll be that companion. I have a velvet Elizabethan page boy suit for you, and when we walk the streets or meet elegance you'll stand beside me. Don't die, damnit! Dance *Till Eulenspiegels* Ah, but I'll be really so happy to see you and Allen again, and I know you'll both let me have my way, and that I won't take advantage of it; yes, all will be all right. Our life is one; and yet, of course, that too must change. Two birds that land together, usually fly apart. The birds bathing in the fountain, seem as if they are one, but no, when they fly, they fly all elsewhere. Poor Zina! A princess in jail! O gaoler, a basket of sugared meats for the lady in black, lo, avast! within a pistol! Escape down the stony stair, up the tower, free over the tombs. But they won't keep her there, will they? My love to you; and now I await my return—I've never felt stronger.

Gregory

To Allen Ginsberg Paris

[Nov. 10] 1958

Dear Allen,

I got no copy of *Army* or *Power* even, but Don Allen has *Army*, and so does Höllerer; and with *Park* and *Food, Army* will fit well, and yes letters, how mad! But what letters? Good ones? When ones? What years? Also will soon send *Death* on, *Death* very happy poem, really. Nice about Steve Allen,[147] how to answer him? Say: Ah, great, I accept you for my patron! Now this is what I wish etc. etc., that attitude or just simple, thanks. But I feel funny so maybe I'll do the first; don't know, haven't received it yet, and when I do, I'll write him thanks spontaneously. YES I WANT TO COME BACK! I am too strong now to let it all waste here.

James Jones said that only the criminal mind can exist today and that they, the criminals, shouldn't brag about being criminals, and that he likes jazz musicians because they're criminals and don't brag about it. I screamed: "But I am a criminal and I brag it unto you! A criminal! A criminal!" So loud did I scream that a group of unnoticeable Monte Carlo private guards suddenly became noticeably alert; maybe they thought I was going go stick up the joint. Anyway Jones seemed sweet, and quite conditioned to life; strong, and straight.

The only time I honked Beauty was in Rome nightclub life seeking the golden prostitute in my mother, and talking to all the Italians that I was Italian and that I've come to bring back ancient Rome, and to the fascists, I met a group, I screamed that I was Gregory Pound, son of Ezra; and they BELIEVED me, I think. All fun, and tears, didn't get hurt, but cops did try to lock me up, the owner gangster of the private club dug me because I spouted my love for Suetonius[148] and he got me off and fed me more whiskey and all the Italian's didn't know what to make of me because I cried love and kissed them and they just didn't know what to do.

As for letter publishing, E.B. Feinstein of England Cambridge wants to print a letter I wrote him [sic: her], about I think the poet who is concerned with universe and the poet concerned with social, price of meat, earth. If you like you can print my 22 page letter to Jack in your anthology. Why not? Why not anything? all is perfect.

And DON'T unintentionally disappoint Peter. Ferl writes now that he wants *Power*, alas. He wants to do book consisting of *Army Power Bomb Marriage Food Park*, how mad! No? Hey, I wonder what the fuck Don Allen has? I mean I don't even have my *Dialogue of Doll Makers Weedy Lyke* poem. Daisy Alden of *Folder* asked for poems, and I sent *Food* and some small ones. Max Gartenberg asked for *Power* and *Bomb*, I got no copy of *Power*, so told him to get these, and to buy *Bomb*.

Wow, all this *Power* and *Bomb* at once! Is *Bomb* really dug? How nice. Ah, but you know now I can really fix it up perfect, but can't change it, too late somehow, but who knows? All that reading you have to do? Great? Yes. Skull bank. What a life! Tired? No. No tired Allen, all is good. Don Allen should tell me what he has of mine, damn it, because I've changed most poems he has, but when I do change, like *Food*, I send it on to him.

No word from Bill, yet, except that cuff link missile; he'll be back soon. Will try to get him to come to America with me, I can do it you know; like to feel it was some of me that one night screamed love at him to go to Dent. He listens to me, you know. How funny. We got very very close.

Write, love, Gregory

To Max Gartenberg Paris

Nov. 12, 1958

Dear Max Gartenberg,

Thanks for your Xmas 50 dollar proposing letter for two poems I love best of all my poems but of all my carelessness, no making of carbons is dominant, yet Ginsberg has both copies of *Bomb* and *Power*, and even a short one called *Police*, if you'd like. Actually I wish I had a copy of my *Power*, I feel like I no longer have it in a weird sort of way. Anyway just came back from old Appian Way Rome where I slept in Coliseum and couldn't have any illumination because a damned crucifix was standing huge in there as if to say to all the world: SEE, WE'VE WON, so I took off to Monte Carlo and gambled my Greece and Istanbul away, and James Jones was gambling beside me, and he with all this ETERNITY only gambled a pittance, alas; but we had a mad talk about criminals and he said that only the criminal mind could exist in the world today, but that they shouldn't brag that they're criminals; jazz musicians, he said, are making it because they're criminals and are cool about it. I would have none of that so I jumped up with laughter and joy and said: "No no I brag to you I am a criminal, a criminal!"—at that very moment about five Monte Carlo unnoticeable guards became noticeably alert. All very funny and nice, for Monte Carlo; a real draggy place.

So if you are happy with everything do you think you could send me the fifty dollars and I won't gamble but put it into my fare home? Haven't seen my NY in two years.

My best, Gregory

I say damned crucifix, but I love the crucifix.

To Philip Whalen Paris

[ca. Nov. 12] 1958

Dear Phil

Good on Romanticism; itself in word is suspect; and of course Camille with her ever drooping rose is always ominous; but the fruit of the word, that which tends something romantic, is, next to humor, heaven in man. God you know how hard and cruel and bitter some things seem/are today, the misery of man is there; no holding a rose and seeing just that; the rose is thin really; much more surrounding and millions of miles behind it, - how to hold a rose to cruelness if there were no love no humor in man? And to love fully is to laugh well and both go into the making of Romanticism; almost goofy existence, Romanticism. But you know this and you are this, you love well and laugh well, and you are not Camille; all right then, dissect Romanticism, and choose of it what you will; it only goes to prove your nobility, and nobility is like the Hydra of Romanticism. [Charlie] Chaplin covered sentimentality with a sentimental rose, were his rose more profound then no Chaplin. My *Bomb* for instance, oh how I wish I were not only more sentimental in it but maudlin! The true combative rose, you see. Alyosha, perfect angel, simple; were he profound, then consciousness, then imperfection. No, Alyosha like St. Francis like St. Joan like Alexander even, had to be sentimental to be what they were; and of course, they did reach the grandest loft of Romanticism, didn't they? Yes, *Howl* is sentimental, really almost cozy Yiddish sentimentality; but what employment, with what purpose! The tears for Carl Solomon outwept Carl Solomon and cried for the soul of man; again the sentimental rose blooms in the loftiest garden of Romanticism; in Jack, too, who says Romanticism is dead, there blooms such a rose, is not his love for Neal an example of that rose? You with your always shy monkish air, chiding life for your extravagant flesh, cherubing in the streets with a ready-to-give rose; victim! You are victimized just as I; a breathing cell that keeps activated that mad mad mad Eat, old glutton Romanticism. Else, as I said to Jack: "You'd be now a French-Canadian in Canada with a fine taste for caribou meat." To be a poet is to be Romantic. Be any kind of romantic you want; pick out its eyes and use them for cufflinks if you like; it makes no difference how you bear it; it'll stick to you and itch you and bug you, little guardian flea, old romanticism, a pretty corny flea, at times, but then that's where the humor comes in, that good ole nurse of Romanticism. And ah how often at times when I read your poetry do I wish I had such a nurse; mine is too nuts in the head. But fun. Really. I think. Yes. Why not. Here's part of my *Police* poem: "Police / you are the promised the promised / of promised flowers / promised flowers / we are the same / the promised same the promised all / all all lily flowers under this sun." This is at end of poem after I damn police, then I realize they're flowers, too. How lightly sentimental that! But I know no better way. 1958 is not, as I youthly feared, an awkward place time space for Romanticism; the absurd Oldsmobile's only short-coming is that it parks. Were it to whizz on, why then who's not to say: "By Jove! a chariot!" I mean IMAGINE; thing is not to see the Oldsmobile as the Oldsmobile; but, ah, to see it as it is, such desirable sight! but quite monotonous really; to see things as they are, yes; but to see them and change them and world them, yes yes. I see the Oldsmobile as the Oldsmobile; but I'm not going to let anyone know I do. I can't. Something bizarrely sinister about all this, but let me say that I have tried to tell the flesh I touched that I felt. Omens, Black Skulls, Old Beads, all say: Don't try to cupid the senses.

So just IMAGINE, . . . and try to make some sense out of what I'm saying because sometimes I get a funny feeling that I say a lot but that it only gets clogged in the golden gate meaning.

Well there I tried to sound intelligent about Romanticism. Now about now. I received you angelic token and good, thank God, there was money for me when I got back to Paris, yours and Gary's, because I was broke and what a madness! In Rome had all the loot I needed and loved every moment of Rome, and was so happy that I decided to come back to America because I was finally strongly truly happy again. So I took all the money I had and went from Rome to Monte Carlo and there prayed to Dostoyevsky to take revenge to all Gambledom by spiriting me to win, so I prays to Lucifer calling his name at the craps table. Come on Luf, Come on Luf, and who happens to hear me call summon conjure that lucky spirit by James Jones *from here to eternity*? He and his wife are digging me at the table in Monte Carlo taking me for a Brooklyn hood or something and invite me for a drink at the bar, turns out he was James Jones, but I didn't know until his wife told me, then I immediately pound on him for illumination, God, soul, pot, the whole works, and he says: "I like the criminal mind, it's the only possible mind that can exist today, but they shouldn't brag about it, now the Negro jazz musicians got it, they're criminals but they don't brag." Then I jump up and laugh and joy and say: "But I brag I brag, yes, I've been in prison and I'm a criminal and I'm existing in this world it's all a gas, a ball, and I brag it unto you, yes, yes" and he says: "What'd you go to reformatory for?" And I tell him for a mad Mabusian scheme, and then his wife wants to gamble more so end of talk and in talk he says he digs Ginsberg and Kerouac very much and that he is working on a novel but that he hates writing and thinks fucking is better. So James Jones. Anyway I bet with him at table thinking that it's all a movie so that therefore I can't lose because I made myself the hero of the movie; but I lose. So onward to train had ticket thank God and find myself hungry in train having when had money forgetting to eat so I get off at Marseilles and go into Arab cafe and present my watch for big meal, they think I want money, suspect Arabs, no I say I want food, nothing else; they take fifty dollar watch for 150 franc meal; great, did wonders for me, and was happy about the transaction the pittance of that time machine; so got back on cold train fifteen hours to Paris and caught cold and got sick but got home all right to my Paris room and music and typewrite and peace; am very happy, Phil, never been happier, no drugs, no woe, no doom, all is joy. I love you, bye, may be in New York City soon, hope hope.

Gregory

WE GOT TO LAY EYES ON EACH OTHER AGAIN AGAIN.

To Lawrence Ferlinghetti Paris

[ca. Nov. 12] 1958

Dear Larry,

A Max Gartenberg wants *Bomb* for his Beat Generation A. Y. M. [Angry Young Men] anthology. So I told him to get in touch with you. Rome really did wonders for me—I feel spiritually fine. Am thinking now of returning to N.Y.—as soon as kind Herme's winged foot thinks best. And how are you? My anthology will be at press soon—you'll be surprised at poems of yours I selected—maybe not. Paris cold and always proudly sad.

My love, Gregory

▼ [Corso had signed an earlier letter as "Andalous Raffine Poids." Ferlinghetti wrote asking where the name came from and later used it in a book of his own.]

To Lawrence Ferlinghetti

Paris
[ca. Nov. 15] 1958

Dear Larry,

Andalous came from a can of fish soup, and Raffine from a box of salt. So there. The entire mad meaning of your proposed hero. Salty Fish. Yes, it'd be a marvelous name; but with a name like that he'd have to [be] kind of fishy, and maybe, a little salty. Wow, what a cornball; acting fishy and then coming on salty. Nobody would want him around. But the Drag as hero is pretty okay. I joke. I am happy. Never been happier. Want very much to return to America, happy. Couldn't when I was sad. What got me out of it, out of last year's horror you remember, when Hope left me and starving and streets under bridges and bad checks, what got me out of it was an excursion in Drug land; took much H and O [heroin and opium] and got deeper deeper into my then surface haze; on the bottom of this haze I saw a black light, so to speak; made me see a lot; so I strongly proudly followed that *noir illuminaire* and came, as expected, to beautiful *BLANC* light. Rome did much for me. In Paris in my little room sick with drugs, thin, complaining, vomiting, a fat girlfriend of Anita's arrived, just off the boat, 19 years old and not so pretty and very sullen Jewish Antioch hip draggy chick, but I saw her as savior angel, and she was; I made her be. That night upon first meeting I asked her how much money she had and she said a thousand dollars and I said: "Good, let's go to Rome then Greece then Istanbul." She said: "Yes." So off we went and when I got off the train five in the morning in Rome I wanted to run to the Coliseum but she moved SLOW and I got angry and said and hoped that I came to Rome alone, that all the money in the world wasn't going to hurt my visit to my ROME, so after two days I sent her back to Paris and she left me with 300 dollars and I stayed and saw all I had wanted to see, the Appian Way, the Forum, Nero's house, Shelley's grave, etc., and was so happy that I got drunk and ran into modern Rome and screamed and laughed and wept to all the whores I met thinking yet not believing them to be my mother and it was almost sick, but not really because I was funny and they laughed, but they didn't know what to make of me when I cried. They asked if I wanted to sex them and then I would cry, I would say "No No, I just want to talk to you, tell you things," and all this in a real clip joint. Then they would try to get me to buy them false whiskey and over-expensive cigarettes, and I did, and that confused them all the more because WHAT DID I WANT FROM THEM? Well, I got what I wanted from them, but how was I to explain THAT to them? It was fun. And I got very drunk that night ran into a Via Venetto cafe and screamed that I was Gregory Pound, and a whole bunch of fascists surrounded me and asked me to show my passport to show proof that I was Gregory Pound, son of Ezra Pound.

They were corny and unbearable so I ran from there and climbed over the Forum gate and slept in Augustus' house, all nice and moony and warm out, but did catch cold there, and am still with it. Hung over and shy and quiet the next day, I get plane to Nice (didn't want to ride that train in Italy, too many families with corded suitcases on them, decided to take train in France to Paris) got off in Nice went to Monte Carlo to gamble my 260 dollars, went to dice table, bet high, and won a little, then lost, but not all, walked away from table, and who follows me but man and woman who were at dice table, they were American and invited me for a drink in the bar; they thought I lost all my money and were sorry for me, and while shooting dice I would say: "Come on Lucifer," or, "Come on Shelley," so this fascinated them, and thus the drink invitation. I immediately told them I enjoyed losing the money, that money meant nothing to me; then they thought I was rich, but not really because the wife asked me if I came from Brooklyn; and I proudly said: "No, Manhattan." The husband went to pee. She asked me what I did, I said wrote. She said: "My husband is a writer too, James Jones." "Oh," I said, "Well, great, yeah, wow, I didn't recognize him" (I didn't even though I saw his weird face all over literary propaganda). He came back and we talked and then got to BG [Beat Generation] and he said he read me and Allen and Jack and all, and dug Jack very much etc.; and then he says: "It's the criminal I respect, it's the only mind that can exist in this world today, but criminals shouldn't brag about being criminals." (This, I thought, was a dig against me because that's all I've been doing is bragging about it). "Yeah," he continues, "take jazz musicians for instance, now they're criminals but they don't brag about it." "Well," I screamed happily, "I brag it! Yes, I brag unto you, I am a criminal! A criminal! A criminal!" So loud did I expound honk that five unnoticeable Monte Carlo fuzz suddenly became noticeably alert: What? A criminal in our establishment? "Come, let's go back to the dice table," I said, (because now that I knew he was James Jones I suddenly got the mad idea about the movies that all things come true in them and that if I were to play a movie with him I would break the bank, etc. etc., so back we go to it, and in a matter of seconds, wham, I'm broke. But I don't let it on; I bow them a polite goodbye, and head high out of the joint. A real creepy place, really. Like poor Gregory was the highest better at the table, I bet the limit; I always thought Monte Carlo was so splendidly extravagant and mad and fortune suicide world, but no, just a lot of silly people hung on money, that's all. No color. No pretty sophisticated ladies, no nothing. So I take bus back to Nice and next morning get on train to Paris (had previously purchased a ticket, thank God, or else I'd be back in same position I was in last year at Nice, if you can remember, I went five days without food down there, and that's where I wrote my *Food* poem). I get on train, hungry, yes all that money and then I find myself wanting to buy a 30 franc piece of bread! I just ain't got that ol' sense yet alas, so I realize I can't make that long 17 hour trip without any food, so I stop off in Marseilles, and find out I can catch train back at five, four hours later, so I go into the Arab quarter and enter Arab cafe and sit down and take off my 40 dollar watch and hand it to the man and say: "Beaucoup, Couscous"—at first he's suspicious, I am all neat and clean and with a watch, how could I be hungry, something must be wrong, so I pat my stomach (by this time five camel drivers and his wife is on the scene) and say "*Fam Fam artiste fam.*" Don't know whether he dug or not, but he screamed his wife into kitchen and she came out with the necessary couscous, and then they gave me big bottle of lemonade and then more food, and then even a 500 franc note . . . very lovely of them, really, and I felt so good, just like in a Russian novel, so perfect, a watch for a 300 franc meal. Great. Then back on train, long cold draggy ride back, and home. As soon as I get home there is mail for me from New York from the *Village Voice* where Allen got them to start a fund for me to get back home, didn't know what to feel about that, so with money I went out and bought a crazy record player and records and that made me very happy because I want peace now and all I desire and still want to go home, but want it in lump sum, only way, when I get it, and Allen will get it my angel from my friends, then I come home, weirdest of all contributors was Steve Allen who sent 50 bucks, didn't get it yet but will definitely hold that for fare back; anyway when I heard that they started this fund, I started getting fears, like who wants to come home this way! I want elegance damnit! And grandness! No old pittance beggar me, so I wrote to *Village Voice* and said: "Thank you sirs for this fund, how very kind of you to want me back home, and I will come back, but of course you'll agree and bear with me that it is not in my wont to come back by that dull La Havre Liberte route, so I shall come back via the other way, Greece, Istanbul, Tehran, India, Japan, San Francisco and then Kansas. Kansas where I intend to spend the rest of my days." (All joking of course because I can't make the traveling thing anymore, not for a while anyway). Besides, I can only accept aid or money or what have you with arrogance and fun; otherwise it'd be too terrible for me. Terrible because at heart and soul I don't need a damned thing, nor do I feel it necessary to crouch before aid. Life is big and by a dozen illuminations my eyes are getting fat enough for it. Anyway all is good with me and joy. I love Paris, and have had a great awakening here, even though I didn't learn the language, but you see, I didn't want to, because I only know Americans here, and they are by far more interesting than the French or any Europeans. I learned more about Americans and America here than in America. I did right by digging them and not the French. Listen these French are so different from me, no connection, they bore me, really; alas, though, even now the Americans bore me, and that's why I want to return home. Of the many reasons for the return, one stands out most, besides wanting to dig Marvel bread again, I want to see NYC now; before I saw it in a daze, living in its subways on its rooftops and cellars, God, man, I want to dig Brooklyn! I'm ripe for it now, all is real love with me, nothing else. And I love NYC. Anyway I can always leave. The world is opened.

Great about you doing a novel. Yes. Prose is good, I've tried it, but find myself always running into a poem. Poetry is with me too much, I guess. But I have written plays, used to only write them, especially when I was in Cambridge, Mass., and even had a play up there that the *Harvard Crimson* said was the best play of the year . . . it was good, but I know that now I could do much better, and will, soon, I hope, get down to write a real mad thing, I have the idea and its form all worked out in my mind, been thinking about it for two years, even more actually. And I dig dialogue, can make it with certain kind of personalities. But as for moment poetry still reigns high. Been just reworking a mad song poem called *Police*. Here are some parts: "Death! St. Francis all police! / Demand golden stool-pigeons on their shoulders / Black Seraph stigmatize John Law! / John Law kneel in the midst of God! . . ." Am still working on it, but am very certain of its outcome, and am very happy with it, what a gas! Calling cops Lily flowers, and telling them to love the cop-killer, like that's the worst thing you could be in NYC, why you'll get the electric chair for sure, and no sympathy from the papers, and even children will hate you. Ah, what fun, but in all that fun, I see. Saw that old whitehaired cop on the sofa, didn't I? Sure when a man wakes up to what this life is and what it has meant and how it is too late to dig its meaning, imagine a human being carrying a gun! Imagine a policeman! How mad, and how sad! But so then, hate them? No, no, they too are lily flowers, you see. Sad dopey unfortunate lily flowers. When I fix it up good I'll send it to Allen [Ginsberg] for his anthology for you, plus *Army, Food*, and *Park*. How did you know about *Park*? Did you see it? Well it was published in England in *Oxford Review*, but it was first draft and I had wanted to let it wait and build it up more, wanted to exhaust my knowledge and experiences of *Park* (you see that is why I am calling these poems only by one name, best that way for me because then I can go wild and free with poem, see?) Well, I did re-write *Park* and don't really know about it, the first draft was so free and loose and careless that maybe I'll leave it that way, what I'll do is send you both copies and you see. Yes, that proposed big poems book sounds great, *Power Army Bomb Marriage Park Food* and *Police*, mad! Have you seen new *Power*? It's all right. I cleared it up. It needed that. Been on the poem for three years now; my first love, that poem, my first big feeling, my first swinging, it's close to me for that.

Germany, Berlin, translated my *Bomb* and they want me to come to Berlin to read it over radio, fare paid plus lots of marks, they say. I think I'll do it before coming back, want to dig Berlin. Well, you got a nice long letter from me, good, your card was very sweet and loving, that's why . . . or maybe it's the ham in me, being that youse is writing a novel about a hero whose got some of me in him. Ha. Hope Big Sur[149] got kind musey eyes on you. Anita here to get married to her love in army at Bordeaux, she is lovely and sweet, great girl, and she digs you very much, in fact out of all she met in S.F. At moment no girl interest for me, I find them plentiful and not so bright, alas. I'm really becoming a terror that way, can't stand to have dull people around. Am getting old old old, ah good. Take care, and you have my warmth and my joy and my love,

Gregory

To Allen Ginsberg Paris

[Nov. 15-16] 1958

Dear Allen,

You sounding NYC string-used in a tired needle, I come there with new thimble thumb, me very rosy cheeked and happy, never been happier, know just what I want, all is visiony bright, lion's ruddy eyes, lion's roar of silence, all lion, good, I come and damn life with joy and mad feast like mandolin 16th century dropping goose legs on the floor; yes dandy for awhile here in Paris until Opium dragged my tails into the gutter and phantasmic pale; all is fine, got letter from Bill, he having difficulty putting on cufflinks, but CUFFLINKS, so I wrote and said "What mad Bela Lugosi thing is this you and Jacques are up to? What mad kick cure demons are you in your elegant English flat about to venture on some golden lush scene, pushed by the fog of Baker Street down to Fleet Street final destination gloomy White Chapel Street." Anyway from tone of his letter he seems all right; and will be back in Paris in two weeks; yes get angels Phipps and Zina to build up fare for me home; I wrote funny ME letter to *Village Voice* telling that I was taking long way round home but can't now because I am too much with Europe and need to use all this NEW energy in getting home and getting you off your ass and start things Harpo Marx; so prepare! No NYC death is strong enough for me anymore; I'm too strong now; got it all here in my little lost button; pinned to my soul. Get fare right away because I want to come right away. I envision myself final savior, all kind and no goofiness, all happy, no sad, true Allen no sad. I am so fucking strong and enlightened and happy and struck up by my ancient Rome that nothing in life can ever cower me again, no hunched shadow me. What did I see in ancient Rome? Nothing. That is, the ancient Rome of my dreams was a far greater ancient Rome, an ancient Rome that never existed; what realization!

What shot for strength! I can devise far nobler Caesars, far colossus Coliseums, damned if I had gone to Greece and I would have forfeited that too; happily so. So I come back to New York and we walk 9th Ave., and all will be good, and even if not, THE DOOR IS ALWAYS OPENED. I can't feel as if I were an old uncle coming home from the old age home; another mouth to feed, a handicap. NO, I am life coming to you damn it, and I'll give it to you; so prepare, big mad feast the day I arrive, for I arrive with strength and velvet color and NEW—so poste haste Zina and Phipps to me; I will set down and write to them too. [. . .]

I must hurry, much to do, all is activity, rush rush zoom no time no waste, all is good and important, no moment to waste; be good, do well, take care, sing well,

Gregory

▼ [Several people had responded to the notice in the *Village Voice* with letters asking if Corso was truly destitute and starving. His pride was hurt so he quickly replied, but did not turn down the money offered.]

To Philip Whalen

Paris
[Nov. 18] 1958

Dear Phil,

I do not starve. Impossible—I know too many angels here—and besides, all is deception. All I wanted was $, because sometimes I spend all I have foolishly happily and forget to buy sugar or olive oil. I grow FAT—I do not hunger. NO! All lies.

Love, Gregory

To Gary Snyder

Paris
[Nov. 18] 1958

Dear Gary,

Deception! Yes, Deception! I am not starving. Only time I starved was over a year ago in Nice—where all was helpless. I am light enough not to starve. I do not starve—all lies—all—I grow fat!!

Love, Gregory

▼ [Loewinsohn was still upset that Corso couldn't return copies of his poems that he sent in for the German anthology.]

To Ron Loewinsohn Paris

[Nov. 18] 1958

Dear Ron,

Okay, yes, yes, but you were young and I was old and yet had to be myself which when left prison with wise words of old tailcoat men there said go out YOUNG, and I did and was not false or phony or "full of shit" as you say, but real and true, and how awkward to say this, but I don't think I was ever false, and the way my life patterns or goes or is, is no kick or joy really but yes that too, there is joy, and mostly that thing I know so well, sorrow; and what business had I with you, young poet, but wanting to meet and flounder and astound and goof and error with but a wild haired young maiden? All my own silliness, then yes, now no; now all is real and correct and seemingly possible, I make it so, have to, else I'd die, yes die, because who on his own is so adapted to life? Allen perhaps, and that's good enough reason for his concern and love to you, no? But I have that too in me, and he knows well of that, but to get that from me takes not spontaneity but scheme, yes, alas, there perhaps my only streak of falseness. Nothing like that matters really. One doesn't leave one and jump in time and come down same, does one? One does change, or at least I am always perpetually mutable; horrors of horrors, yet I do retain old boy complaint, and why not? And what golden lush scene in LA? what silver bronze machine do you work? or does so handle the silk damask tread? Whatever, you are great poet to me and I love you and only know that I am NOT ALWAYS GREGORY SEEKING OUT WILDHAIRED MAIDEN.

Glad you liked *Bomb*, wrote it during mad period of this small attic great room overlooking Seine and medieval tower in which Marie Antoinette waited her head, and cone towers allwheres. Summer, on drugs, H and O, in this here room, with great global weeps about life I suddenly woke up to, and thus *Bomb*. O but what time what difficulty I had in trying to get that famous champignon shape! Yet Ferl did all right with it, no? Yes. England mad about poem, it's been published there in Oxford and London, and all them Eton Shelley-like angels dig me somehow and I love them, always had when long long ago; so all is well with that, and that summer Seine cone tower H and O scene was worth all.

But got madder poems, yes, *Death* is madder, *Food* is madder, *God* is madder, *Power* is still maddest, and *Army* even madder, and *Marriage* the maddest saddest funniest. So I've done an awful lot since early attempt *Gasoline*, yet *Gasoline* will always be dear to me. But then again now all them poems or at least all in that red book are so so dear to me, and, no good critic of myself, excellent, like Monsieur Genet says. And Michaux too; met them both, but at various times, separate. Michaux lovely sinister alone, doesn't dig anybody nor see anybody, and Genet only if you look great.

But these European poets are so different really, like when Michaux came and visited Allen, Bill and me, he brought champagne and we cooked chicken, all was well we spoke of drugs, poesy and blah, good mad blah. Then one of us pees in the sink (this we all do in Git-le-Coeur because the johns are terrible in the hall, cold and dank and oppressive, so the sink is really a cozy cove). Yet this great French poet of the day recalls this natural action of one of us and relates it to all his colleagues and mouth to mouth treats us as barbarians; or "trying to impress" attitude, which is so absurd yet the European way of consideration. They are dead here, and all is good in their writing yet they, themselves as heroic or mad or eccentric, no; stale all of it.

I would like to clear up some things with you, some impressions, if possible. First: if I do not work for my livelihood it is because I am the sort that gets too involved with what he is doing. Thus if (as I did for year) work in the Garment Center, I am PART of that life, and I give all of myself; I do not detach myself from that which I augment myself to. Well that just ain't good for poesy nor me, now, at any rate; so how to live? By my wits? Scheme? No, because I am not like that. O I try to be, you know, all this Lucifer joy in me, but it's laughable, and I allow it to be, good novelty. So what I get as pittance for sleeping and eating and living is returned by me hundred fold; and whatever I do, it is done nobly, and worthy to what I believe is beautiful in this possible life; in other words, I don't only take. Nor do I have so much or a ball at it all. There are times I can't stand the sight of people or talk and stay deep in my room, and deny food, etc.

Consider that I spent two years in Europe with no possible means of support etc., yet somehow have managed to make it nobly and proudly and sometimes terribly, but nonetheless DID set eyes on Rome, Sweden, Spain, Venice, Germany, Paris; and all of it was joy. I "pay" something much better than gold for all this. The black scorpion clicks along a rug of stars. Parasitic? No, no because mushrooms have grown about me, and I grow thin. And, besides, after all, I DO KNOW WHAT IS HAPPENING, and still retain myself as I am to all I meet.

My love, Gregory

To Allen Ginsberg Paris

[Nov. 25] 1958

Dear Allen,

Your review of *Dharma* [*Bums*], almost made me cry because how real and true things are and how odd the world feels under. Really got along with Genet in bad English, French, but all right—in Cafe Flore. Read *Ignu* aloud to some friends, and they broke up—great about getting back to "Mothers" poem, yes.

Yes, Gregory

To Ron Loewinsohn

Paris
[Nov. 25] 1958

Dear Ron,

Oh, please forgive me but one day I scream, then laugh. No consistency. Sorry I took all that nonsense out on you, who, after all, are gentle and good, and lovely genius poet. It's my head that's gone wrong, alas. Oh, but no! I've never been false, I don't think, just new, and awkward to things, that's all—and now, after two years in Paris. Alas, I am no longer that supposedly full of shit soul, and I love your Sue, and your heritage, and your child. So there, am returning to states soon, will write letter soon.

Love, Gregory

To Allen Ginsberg

Paris
[ca. Nov. 26] 1958

Dear Allen,

Bill back, and he is off [drugs], and well. Stern is going to remain in England, he off too, to live there. Bill says he and [Denning] off. *Ignu* great lovely, great God Pan is dead. *Dharma Bums* pure poetry. Beautiful. No man, I don't want your cross, but your heaven, yes. I see what you mean, tho. But after *Bomb*, I just can't seem to get <u>back</u>. Everything has become REAL for me, alas, but all right. Saw Genet other night he sweet to me, polite, all last year's forgiveness, gave him *Bomb* — you're right about *Food* — I'll fix it up. Can't wait to get back. All's well.

Love, Gregory

To Allen Ginsberg

Paris
[Nov. 28] 1958

Dear Allen,

No news from Phipps boat yet, all packed away, waiting the word, though my vin cup has not runneth over yet; all is fine. Bill is fine. Irv Rosenthal quit, he very fine dedicated for 1958 madness, no?

I enclose all the unused parts of *Bomb*, some I put into *Police*, but returned it to unused *Bomb*, digging deeper into what you said about cross, heaven, etc.; that I'd do best, and am best, and feel best, doing "starmeat bead balling boulder clinkers dunged to hairy alps" yes? yes.

Met a very beautiful young (17) rich, elegant many-languaged girl, English, here at Sorbonne who sees me everyday and likes me, and I like her; she'll be done with school in July, and that's about when I intend to return to Europe, and she and I will make it to Greece, so all is fine love wise. Erica finally digs me, but I no dig her no longer, she's really empty and I guess all I wanted was to humiliate myself before her, and did, and once I stopped, and ignored her, then she comes around and starts humiliating, all very gamey and sick and so American girl like, bah. Read my new angel, Jane Armitage, your *Ignu* and she like you very much, and I know you'll like her, Bill digs her, she really extraordinary, very well brought up and educated.

The enclosed cancelled passages from *Bomb* can be if you think you can assembled to order somehow; and try Don Allen with it first for loot, if not, then with love to LeRoi *Yugen*, I just hope you don't feel I left out some great things in *Bomb*, I actually feel I have, but had to keep poem sensible somewhat, in order, etc.; which you must admit is accomplishment for me; but just couldn't see these lines to go waste; well, you look it over and see. Actually I yet have more, but can't type no more now, but if you like this for your anthology instead of *Bomb*, great, I'll send rest, but as is I think Don Allen might be interested; besides it goes into my way of poeming. Enclosed too find something on Lee Forest[150] sent to you here. Poor chick, is she in Welfare Isle? How you? Big turkey yesterday? Me, lentil soup, and figs and Milanese pie. Try to get the two *Weedy Lykes* for your anthology, and also *Army*; I have no copy of these things. Being Ferl wants to come out with book consisting of long poems, maybe I should send you whole batch of small poems, good ones, the best ones; but just ain't had it in me lately to write or rewrite or type; flee the typewriter, thought I'd never get to that; oh well, a rest is good.

Did you pee in the sink when Michaux came to visit? One of us did, and what's wrong with that? But rumor has it that Michaux told people about it and thought we were trying to impress him; very small of him really, so fucking European to even detect such an action; I still say American young poets are the greatest and most understanding peoples in the world; these European writers are nothing but a bunch of immigrants. Bill looking great, is entirely off. Does LeRoi really want to do a book for me? If so I'd like to give him all my little early poems, get rid of them once for all, like *H.G. Wells, Creepy Flower Peddler*, etc. work work work work work.

Love, Gregory

They still didn't send me Steve Allen's 50 dollars and why not? After all it's mine, and I could use the money, of course; and wisely this time too. What do they think, I'm a child or something, that all that candy should be teased offered me? Alan Ansen stationed in Athens, likes it there. The gray cat sends regards, haven't seen Joy. Kenny Clarke asks for you. The last segment of cancelled *Bomb*. The idea not the *Bomb* etc. . . . could be little separate poem for William Carlos Williams co, instead of word *Bomb*, change it to the word Line.

▼ [Corso returned to the United States on December 23 and stayed with Ginsberg on East 2nd Street in the East Village.]

To Lawrence Ferlinghetti

New York
[ca. Jan. 7] 1959

Dear Larry,

What? An unromantic book? How dare you in 1959 venture upon such a chop the gargoyles head off? Thanks for the check, and for me owing your chamber of words 100 dollars, wow, well, okay, but did you charge me for the twenty five books you sent La Hune? Anyway, I want to tell you that the 8th Street Book Store is out of *GAS* and *BOMBS*, and that nobody else in NY has *BOMBS* but them. Why? Are they hard to distribute? Would you like me to distribute? No, maybe not. Heard yesterday your record on impeachment, very lovely delivery. Much feeling. Did you have a nice New Years? I did. Since I been back I been to bed with four pretty girls already. Four in one week!

I have ready next week my new book *Starmeat*: with these poems: *Death, Police, Army, Power, Bomb, Marriage, Xmas, Food.* Perhaps *Park*, but it needs work. So far I send thee: *Police, Marriage, Xmas*, and revised *Bomb*. Please let me know what you think; these are to my feeling so far my best work.

Do you still have any *Vestals* left? Do you know that it is one of the most wanted books on the BOOKLIST for second hand wanted books? and to think I gave a hundred or more free away to the S.F. Railway Express employees.

Actually all I want to revise in *Bomb* is: "I want to put a lollipop in your (not thy) furcal mouth / a wig of goldilocks on your (not thy) baldy bean. It should be a mad mad mad collection.

Love love, Gregory

To Lawrence Ferlinghetti

New York
[ca. Jan. 14] 1959

Dear Larry,

Here is *Army, Food, Hair, Power*: so that means you got: *Army Food Hair Power Xmas Bomb Marriage Police*; next I will send the final two: *Park, Death*. That makes ten mad mad poems in all for next book, should be nice, no? Trouble is you'll be reading them all at once whereas they should be read one at a time for what they are. But then again, when folks read it in book form they'll have to read it all at once. What you have is one and half years work; so you see I wasn't just goofing in Europe.

Love, Gregory

Title is: *STARMEAT.* Poems will be in chronological order: *Power, Food, Army, Park, Bomb, Marriage, Police, Xmas, Death, Hair.*

To Gary Snyder New York
[ca. Jan. 23] 1959

Dear Gary,

Am reading your manuscript of poems and Whalen's and almost cried that such loveliness is unwreathed. But if LeRoi Jones, I promise you I will make sure beyond anything that format and print be of the highest order; that the printing go into gold, that Allen and I will put up what he can't afford, that gold be rubbed on the fingers that pick up the book. I just don't understand the world of letters that way that works like these are denied by men who supposedly are masters of Japanese and directions light and beauty. Money; I guess that is it; the ugly childhood face of it truth, money is God, else why not? taste? Only Ferlinghetti can be accused of that; he rejects you because he doesn't understand what you are doing, he can only understand things like me who write East Side trying Shakespeare from the heart, novelty maybe almost, I don't know. Anyway it makes me feel awkward that I seek to publish another with him, and you and Whalen are no; a poet must be published. I am not that romantic that says no to publishing. Why Shelley himself published, and paid his own, too. So if it's LeRoi, I promise both you and Phil that the print job be of the best and highest order; I myself can't stand cheap beared bearded smelly loft cold water green clothes kind of paper and print, and those hideous staples, and those lousy sizes. Your books will be hand sewn and sizeable right and print of Swiss or Holland birth.

I am very happy to be back in New York, much change in me and in it; will say all in next letter. I am very happy with Duncan, not so happy as satisfied with his poesy.

Love, Gregory

▼ [Ferlinghetti voiced many reservations about the poems Corso had submitted for his next book and Gregory angrily replied.]

To Lawrence Ferlinghetti New York
[ca. Feb. 7] 1959

Dear Larry,

Don't mind you rejecting me poems, but don't reject *Gasoline. Gasoline*: so many places in Village are out and can't get any; like the Paper Back Stores, Eighth Street Bookshop, etc.; why not? after all that's my only source of income, as I do not accept money for readings (this my own Shelley keep of nobility). So please send them books or send Paper Editions, they is out; I get paranoid as to think you are rejecting me entirely, *Gas* and all, woe on me, angel.

That *San Francisco Review* don't sound so kind, after all, out of all that two years work in Paris where I did change in life and that two year work is two year me; they refused all, that's why I don't send out. I keep with *Evergreen* who will publish this coming issue *Marriage* and another poem. They are ok, but publishing ain't so important no more, that young poet kick of getting in print hath gone too, gone with Daffy Duck.

I mean I think you should have sold more than 2,000 copies of *Gas*; because people do want it and are always asking where to buy; well, enough; it's just that I feel all falling under me when all falls. I have been reading much, bringing the muse to the man in the street, I do it with humor and gentleness, and now I am weary, and wish life had a plum palace to offer.

My love, Gregory

To James Laughlin

New York
Feb. 7, 1959

Dear James Laughlin,

Hello, I send you these poems for your anthology. Mine is done . . . finally. And I changed whole idea plan of it; instead of just using Black Mountain / San Francisco crowd, I decided to put in everybody who sent me poems; and I'm glad I did, because the collection is so haphazard and crazy that it should be very interesting. Also the publisher gave me a free hand, said I could do anything, that his first intent was only the San Francisco and Black Mountain poets, but after ten of my convincing letters he decided my way. I put in Roditi, Zukofsky, Goodman, Dahlberg, Williams, you, so all this expiates my long frenzied letter to you. Never again will I undertake such work. All I had was albatross complaints; and I didn't even get any money for it; actually they should pay me, shouldn't they? I mean, it's a big printing publishing house that's doing it. Because that anthology wasn't poetry, and I wouldn't mind taking money from something that is not poetry. Maybe I should ask them. Allen and I went to Chicago to raise money for the suppressed issue of the *Chicago Review* and all we went there with was poetry and love and joy and they treated us in the papers like a bunch of freaks; I just don't understand. I'm reading at the Living Theatre with Frank O'Hara on the 28th of this month, on a Monday, can you make it?

My best, Gregory

Ferlinghetti rejected my new work, my two years work done in Paris; he just doesn't like long poems, I guess; because these new poems are by far my best. When I gave him the manuscript of *Gasoline* he only took the small poems, and refused the long poems. Do you like long poems?

To James Laughlin New York
[ca. March 31] 1959

Dear Mr. Laughlin,

Thanks for your encouraging letter; encouraging in the sense that lately what with all this publicity and poetry readings and acceptance, I've been doubting whether the muse's nobility sat snug upon my winged head. No, I could never doubt the poetry, but I am disturbed and confused by all this other nonsense. I've been flipping lately, the last two poetry readings I was drunk and silly and read always on the defensive. So best I give up this reading. Besides, one is not a machine that he can get up there and read a poem with the same intent and feeling as when he wrote it. OK, enough.

No, I haven't read much of Greenberg,[151] but now that you mention it, I will. I remember clearly though, one poem of his; something about a stain, again the stain has come to me—Allen says he's a very great poet, that he taught himself how to write etc; and that Crane did paint green the grass. I will read him. O I would love a book done by New Directions; how mad and how respectful it makes me feel. Good, I feel good again. And I'm sure Ferl won't mind, because he said I should try publishing them elsewhere. So if you like I'll send you all my poems to date.

Thank God I don't feel about publishing as I now do feel about reading. Though there is in me now that un-Shelleyean feeling about clique publishing; I don't know. I say Shelley, hold him as a light almost, so as not to abuse this thing I love very much. And I am at times such a screw-up that I might well abuse. Ah, perhaps it's me who should get to shepherdland. This city, this poetry, this beat, it's all too real.

Big Table is out and they published *Power*, but you re-publish, don't you? If not, then I made a mistake by giving it to them. I'll gather all the poems I have and send them on to you; I would prefer what you think would make a nice little collection out of the lot. Will we meet?

My best, Gregory

To Willis Barnstone New York
April 4, 1959

Dear Willis Barnstone,

Too much reading, have stopped; would only give one more if it can get me to Tangier where I want to go to get out of this Woody Woodpecker cartoon; can your Wesleyan give me 200 dollars? Ha ha; but you see of all the readings, Harvard, Yale, Columbia, Princeton, I ain't taken no token. Do I sound like I won't read but for loot? No. It's just that I want to get away, and I'll probably get the money from somebody; under threat of madness etc. etc.

Allen and I liked your poems very much; alive, wild gentle, muse is there; Allen is off to San Francisco soon, so he can't make reading either. I am busy with getting book together for New Directions; if they really want it as they say, then maybe I'll get the fare from them. I feel bad not making it for a reading, really. I thought you very gentle and understanding and THERE. *Basta*. Write. I'll write.

Fate, Gregory

To James Laughlin New York

April 14, 1959

Dear Mr. Laughlin,

Been reading Greenberg and his poesy seems as though a kidnapper composing a ransom note, piecing type from newspapers onto the blank page. He is primitive, yes, and striking; and at times reaches the cloud strolling feet of the muse. I see no connection as far as myself is concerned. I am Lower East Side, and I am Phrygia;[152] it is my humor that allows the two to meet; my seriousness that keeps them apart. I think I tend to seem primitive because of the fat in my poetry; the pure flow alack revision, discipline, etc. But it is an intended primitiveness; whereas Greenberg is that he is. I don't think Greenberg could have made his poesy any other way, no matter how much he tried; whereas I can, if I try. And I don't. My song is in my naturalness. When it's sung, I leave it that way, no revision, no discipline; and God knows I could revise could whip discipline into use; but it wouldn't be my song. So in this respect Greenberg and I are alike, we both sing our song. Our only difference is: I'm much better, because I know better, and more. Yes, you should re-print him; and if you like I'll write a preface to the re-print. As for my own print; I am busy typing up everything; that you could have all the poems I have, and thus choose.

Ginsberg is off to take me to have some laughing gas at dentist. Have you ever had it? He says Coleridge and all the romantic poets had it. It's supposed to induce a moment of active death. Ginsberg saw the universe fade, and Woody Woodpecker appear, laughing at what was never there. Anyway it scares me, but I'm going to try it. Also I want to get away and go to Tangier where Paul Bowels [Bowles] is, I've been seeing him and envy his calm. If Tangier can give me some of that peace, great. I want to be alone, too. And what a place to be alone in. Have you ever been there? Anyway I hope you like my book and that we'll meet before Tangier takes place. Why don't I bring book up to office when you're there? I'll be done with it this Friday, the latest.

Again ca. Greenberg on me: My writing, my expression may be primitive but me ideas my dream my whole outlook is contradictory and mad.

Your fateful servant, Gregory

To James Laughlin New York

[ca. April 16] 1959

Here it is; Thursday I will bring in just a few more, with dedication, and title. Been disturbed most of the week, think it was S. Greenberg, went back to Astor Library to re-read him; he's great, hauntingly so, and I think those two men who came out with his poems did him a disservice by changing some of his words, like woob to womb, I think the reason why I didn't go deeply for Greenberg when I first glanced at him is your saying he was primitive, he's not a primitive, he's a pure lyric poet born and placed in a ridiculous time and place, truly a nigger Shelley. I do see your connection now; why hadn't I read him before? Saw Tennessee Williams the other night and he spoke highly and warmly of this Chatterton Columbia. You owe it to poetry to re-print him, for sure. Ok. I'll be back on Thursday; only poems lacking here are *Power Army Police* and you could get that from *Big Table.*

Fate, Gregory

To Lawrence Ferlinghetti New York

[ca. April 2] 1959

Dear Ferl,

Spectral ne'er to me; I am too sensitive for this here Woody Woodpecker cartoon; I must go back to Europe; can't work here. Can you please help? As advancing me much as you can from printed *Gasoline / Bomb*; I have no other source of income; gave many readings, but thought muse-wise best not to lean toward that gold. So. Honor. Nobility. And a will to live. What think you of me? Lost from me? We haven't corresponded in long time. So, anyway let me know what I can expect; HELP; but I do deserve some money; I just ain't received nothing for all that language. And everybody likes *GAS* and the bookstores are always selling out; and I want to be alone again; NYC and its multi-poets confuse me. Love to you, dear balding bard.

Gregory

▼ [Ferlinghetti had inquired about the chances of Corso writing a novel for City Lights. He had suggested the title of *Old Angel Midknife* as a take-off on Kerouac's title *Old Angel Midnight.*]

To Lawrence Ferlinghetti New York

[ca. April 26] 1959

Dear Larry,

Thanks very much for the much needed check. That piece in *Gemini* was written in Paris at the end of 1957; I thought it quite humorous then, and even now in a way; but so much water has passed under Triborough Bridge that it has lost much of its gist. Happy to hear your finishing the *Black Book Of Andalouse Raffine.* What made you think I thought there was something of me in it? Ah, thou gentle Germanicus, do you still think me possessed by ego-fascism? That I even tend to usurp the seed, the crystallization, the bloom, the festival, of thy comet? If so, you are wronging my legend, wretchedly arbitrary me. Despair, infidelity, insomnia, and still I seek some trout to fry. Yes, I gave Laughlin my brimming entreats, how will he treat them? God knows. I gave him everything I've written since *Gasoline*; he likes me; likens me to Sam Greenberg, who I only recently discovered by his introduction. I like Greenberg very much; but see no connection. Weariness saves me, alas. But I have even more poems in Venice, I'll get them and also give Grove, and Indiana a book, and let buoyancy take hold. The kick is gone. I mean, it was a great feeling to have *Gasoline* published, and *Vestal*, but now publishing reduces me to the ho-hum state muscular men should receive when visiting their Swedish gymnasium for the thumpreenth time. Lo, the task of resuscitating. "The birds lose their forms after their colors." But I will never deny publishing for it is, after all, a stirring thing.

How is Allen doing there? Was Penelope with her dry sex there to greet him? Did he slay all her suitors? Did you read with him? What news from San Francisco?

A prose book? Right off the top of my head? Would you want it? Blind free? Do you think do you trust I'd do it right and true? What say you; you be blind looker, and I be midknife giver. Lo, I begin, I shall launch forth upon a black, a lament, a lachrymae, a pitiful disclosure of what grapevines are. Yes, I'll be a disciple of black book—disciplined, that is to its psychological method. I'll follow without conflict. I'll obey. I'll execute. I'll be complete. Mine will be Papa Black Book; and I'll be pale and diseased, deprived of all my illusions. But I don't care, so long as I bring out BLACK BOOK! I had better act quickly. Must wipe way this theological smile off my face. Must be like that old apparatus I once saw rusting in a backyard in Villefranche. "The truth rests upon the mathematical rattans of the infinite." Between the banks of life and death eternity dills. How's that for a start? OK? Sight unseen? You want it? Have it for you in a week. Actually there are rivalries of insincere pedagogy initiating me. I haven't a Breton's chance. But now that all the poesy is done, though I still write, wrote a poem last night, it might well be enjoyable to venture upon Black Book, why not? Part of the poem last night goes: "I reached heaven and it was syrupy. / It was oppressively sweet. / Croaking substances stuck to my knees. / Of all substances St. Michael was stickiest. / I grabbed him and pasted him on my hand. / I found God a gigantic flypaper. / I stayed out of his way. / I walked where it smelled of burnt chocolate. / Meanwhile St. Michael was busy with his sword / / hacking away at my hair. / I found Dante standing naked in a blob of honey. /Bears were licking his thighs. etc. etc. etc."

Ok, I end his absolu. Telemaque! Perpetual. Does Eternity drizzle?

Fatefully yours, Gregory

To James Laughlin

New York
[early May] 1959

Dear Laughlin,

If none of these can sell, then I'll send another batch. You pick what title you best like.[153] I went to the Hayden Planetarium and saw so many stars, that I left the place contemptuous of man that he need consider himself so important. Do you know that you can put a thousand or more earths into our star the sun? Yes. I am very ashamed of myself especially for brooding so much over death and life when all that up there is so unanswerable; and also upset with myself for having ever listened to the words of man, what is man compared to a star? Nothing. And I used to be so scared of that "nothing". I laugh now. And I wish I were in the country so that I could study the constellations, you don't get much of the stars here in the city. I enclose a late poem. A poem after the 1959 (death brooding poem) and awakening, a loss of the second form, the ass, (Death). But it was written before that illumination in the Hayden Planetarium. Anyway, hope all is well. I met Delmore Schwartz[154] and asked him if he liked Sam Greenberg and he said no, and he doesn't even like Crane, so I'm a little confused about him; I mean, Crane is a star screwer; excelsior poete!

Take care, Gregory

To Willard Maas

New York
[May 1] 1959

Dear Mr. Maas's children,[155]

There are six thousand stars at night; but there are billions and billions of unseen stars. Six thousand you can actually count. The sun is a star. But earth isn't a star. You know how many earths can fit into a star, let's say our star the sun? I bet a thousand or more. So there. How does that make you feel? Insignificant? Cheap? Terrible? Envious? Contemptuous? That's why there's a Beat Generation, not because doom hovers over earth man-made doom, doom (destruction) was here before we were born, there's no escape, so why worry about that, destruction is a distraction, there are other things to consider, wondrous things; the Beat Generation is insulted when linked to doom, thoughts of doom, fear of doom, anger of doom. The Beat Generation is because truth rests on the contradictory rattans of the soul. The BG [Beat Generation] is very logical. To be logical is to be contradictory. Contradiction is the basis of logic. Common sense, that white Protestant disease, is foreign to all true poets. See? That's a contradiction for you. The poet's trek is to go beyond the obvious. "Man is a work of God. A work that works, that is the climax!" All is endless, limitless, infinity is a dog sitting at its own feet. The BG is a climax, therefore it's as insignificant as anything man can mouth, for what has the BG to do with the dromedaries of the solar system? Shelley, who really wasn't plagiarizing God, would rightfully call anything man had to say a distraction. A waste of time. Nothing means nothing. Cows, radiator soup, mother's death, war documents, Alcman's Maiden Song, Greeks wearing shorts, Smith College; only the wonders of sunset means anything. The BG is in a fixed position without any idea of its fate. It is disciplined to a psychological method. Youth follows it without conflict. They obey. They execute. They are complete. Yet starless things would deprive the BG of its illusions. Why? Because they, the starless, don't believe in clairvoyant abstraction, that's why. They really believe that man is, that man exists, how sad how absurd! Man does not exist, man is just an invention of God; a senseless invention in this great movement of insensibility.

So. Does eternity drizzle? Walk forth on the soil of light. Wake not the bee less the fairy in the honey bowl flee. Unlike the rose, the BG [Beat Generation] hath risen from a chilled territory. It rose in sight of this metropolis, it saw the smoke climb where death could not climb. The BG falls on one another, the BG rides freighted light; repentance keeps the BG gay, no pierced birds falls its way. Creation licks the BG's blood. A departed train is a train to arrive.

The flaring Beat Generation, ablaze! The Beatnik's warring hand anchors the Eucharist, his back burdened with merciful ampullae. The BG is fixed with riddle and challenge. The BG is filled with pebbles. Give it a secret shake, and lo! the proxied sacrament, rake the heavens. So don't just listen to what earth has to say, earth is jealous of heaven. Jealous because it knows it's not even a star. The truth is thick in the fleeted loom. Mutinous substance! The truth is deep, the truth is sickening, the truth is relatively safe; everything but the BG stands amid the ordeals of lie. The BG is the happy birthday of death.

Where? Where is the BG? Where is that which does not exist? In that which does exist. God. Where? Where is God? Where is that which does exist?

Whenever I see a cat, and it sulks away from me, I go up to it, and say: "But I am not a barking red-toothed dog!"—And if it still ignores me, I say: "Tell me about Egypt if you're so smart. I'll tell you about Egypt. They put things like you in jars, that's what they do!"

Your most fateful servant, Gregory Corso

To Allen Ginsberg New York
[May 2] 1959

Dear Allen,

Don't send money I have enough, a gift from the Gods of arrogant yore; a Macedonian, to be exact; a Greek restaurant owner (Johnny Nicholson—Jack saw him give it to me); beware of Greeks bearing gifts? Anyway I could go to India on the money; or I could return it; but, like I say, the arrogant Gods of yore have returned to me; I took it, and shant return the $675. 'Twas, I hope, my opening of the Vast; my contempt for man who is so vain as to think the stars inhabit him; my faithfulness to the wonders of sunset; my complete entering and departure of simple death, cars, etc.; so abused absurd; all is magnificent, man the least.

GC

To Allen Ginsberg and Peter Orlovsky New York
[May 15] 1959

No money! Starve! Money all mine! $495 from Jack's article! $100 from Spoleto. $670 from Nicholson. Lost at Belmont about $400 on such names as Aegean Cruise, Macedonian Way, Agamemnon all came in last or next to last. Can you imagine that and I who put so much faith in Greece. Damn Greece I say. He doesn't know about Laughlin taking my book, 96 pages, *The Happy Birthday Of Death.*

Allen, Don Allen says you vomited before reading, well take it easy and don't throw up no more. Forgive me for Belmont but that kind of gift money makes me uncomfort, and besides Lucien and Jack think it very noble of me to lose it that way. Are you bugged? I don't care, I'm a poet, not a world trade fair.

Love, Gregory

To Allen Ginsberg New York
[May 20] 1959

Dear Allen,

I have check for you from Berkeley do you want me to send it and all mail on to you? I paid gas bill and balance of your unbank account, you miscalculated. Also went with Jack to Wesleyan to read and great great. Had nice talk with Wilbur, very sweet guy. Germany your publisher wants to do *Gasoline*, and New Directions will publish my book, called the *Happy Birthday Of Death.* 96 pages. Nice. When are you coming back? Send you mail? Check? Love Peter, Whalen -

Gregory

To Willis Barnstone New York
[May 21] 1959

Dear Willis,

Thank you for your kind letter; today sun is bright and drink is gone from me and I am bright. I had my passport renewed so can up and leave at any moment. I am busily typing all my scribbled poems; spend hours at it; I love it; smoke feverishly; the cats jumping all over; drink Dr. Pepper, let the ball-game blare; and lo! I transcribe a poem. Surely these were not the atmospheric conditions of the Lake poets.

I loved your wife and child—and all Wesleyan. Peace. Crete. And if you see Terry Fredricks please tell him: "Frozen knees" is true image; like "human ice;" and also if he could send that *Hartford Journal* man's piece on Jack and I.[156]

Best, Gregory

To Lawrence Ferlinghetti New York
[May 25] 1959

Dear Larry,

Thanks for #3,[157] it's ORANGE; or faded? *Papa Black Book,* Jack says is great title but I don't feel like writing letters or things, I'm stifled, yes; must get away, to Crete; yes. Now here this: I have a book of poesy for GROVE; and have already given a book to New Directions, ND accepting it; now this one for Grove is a group of mad short poems, they asked for a book; so should I bypass my Porto Rican Italian angel[158] and give it to them? Why not? Let me have the full rich joy of glory and fame and attraction and bloodsteam. Also Germany wants to do *Gasoline*, how will that work out, will I get the money I so deservedly need????? A million marks! I must go to Crete! Hurry! Sell it to Hitler even! I don't care! BUT SELL!! Herr Schluter did write me a nice long letter saying he dug work and wanted me as one of their authors; what a way to put it, we'd like to have you as one of our authors; augh, fucking Aryan regimentation!

Love, Gregory

To James Laughlin New York
[ca. May 25] 1959

Dear Mr. Laughlin,

Worked hard all week on Crete and done did it. Called up Greek cargo boat and they will take me this coming Friday the 29 to Athens only for $255 which I have and didn't spend on Pegasus at Belmont; but I'll be broke when I get there so if you could advance me yes, ok, anyway I feel it's doing something good by going.

I bring you what I feel would be lacking as per variety in *The Happy Birthday Of Death*, short surreal poems. I love them, and do hope they can be put in. Why don't I return later and see you, after your lunch, because there ain't much allotted time. Also I leave for your quick reading this magazine I just got from England; there's a letter in it I wrote a year ago when in England. Also it's kind of interesting to see how they feel toward their writers etc. ok.

Gregory

To Allen Ginsberg and Peter Orlovsky New York

[May 28] 1959

Allen,

Send money, lots of it, because the Black Hooded Proletariat has me by the leg. Anyway Spoleto promised me 100 dollars—so I'll pay back. No gas bill yet. Peter, that virgin you deflowered says she caught "a disease" from you—honest. But I told her it was you who might get it from her—so go to a doctor. Allen too, ha-ha (no he). Cats ok. Will send letter soon.

Gregory

Big Table held up at Washington post office. Willard Maas sent telegram wanting poems for symposium. I'll send it on. Give my best to Whalen—Don't allow them boo's from Spicer. Whalen—Does Eternity drizzle?

To Allen Ginsberg and Peter Orlovsky New York

[May 29] 1959

Dear Allen,

Ah before I go with all the loot to the Pegasus track I am off really honestly and truly yes to GREECE this here Friday, and I will be back in two months and Bremser and his lovely wife will take care of cats and home and good God baby I'm really doing it on a shoestring I think unless today when I go and sign contract for Laughlin book; he did say he'd advance me, then I can pay this month's rent, but if not then I will mail you your checks now and also half of the rent and you could mail the whole thing to Molly Cohen, I just don't want to get to CRETE and find that I ain't got the fare to DELOS; are you envious jealous and hateful and happy that I am going? O I do think I know what I'm at, I think I think, but of course don't care for am I not Cathay? I will also give a book to Grove and wait their word; alas, I have no more poesy! I am broke! Need to write new ones, Mycenaean ones, Asia Minor ones, but am really going there to prove my belief that the golden statue of Poseidon, the biggest ever, the Trojan gog God is two miles out beneath the Aegean; yes! and I will find that, and also I have a hunch where Hades is, and when I unearth that! Well, let's wait and see.

LSD, be careful with thy selfhood.

Peter I am going this here Friday yes, and Paul Carroll writes and says he's using your 'First Poem' in *Big Table* 2 and that he now likes the last line, and that girl there is nothing wrong with her, she just had her wombydoor squeaked.

So. What now? I send you checks. I send you my check too. Put it all in for rent and you send it to her. I am off. Bremser will be here. Write to me care of Athens American Express. Ah in two months thou mustest start another Corso fund, alas, no, no, I shall have the fare back, or remain and you and Petey come to Greece then Turkey then Iran then India then Russia, esp. Russia, I enclose and you see why.

Jack and me had ball at Wesleyan and all is good. I love you both very much and this trip will do us all a lot of good. So. Did I tell thee Germany wants to print *Gasoline*, and that Sir Herbie Reed called *Bomb* an elephant with pink eyes. And that William Carlos Williams says that beat poets should learn from Orlovsky's poem. And that magazine from Cambridge England [*Cambridge Opinion*]came it has your *Supermarket*[*in California*] and a letter by me, and I will leave it here for thy return read. So. White War Artic Boar Reel the pure kite more and more white strange white orange. The dead a wildcold body must bear. *Sursum corda* O dead! The dead are born in Cheeryland, their buttocks neigh . . .

I love thee both well, for did not Prince Hal say, when looking down upon poor dying Jack Falstaff: or rather Falstaff to Hal: "Hal! What do I do now?!" and Hal waved a straight finger at him and sayeth: "Jack Falstaff, thou owest a death to God!"

"So there. Caracalla—joy of Shelley / seated dusk-stained / a brownlight prince of ruin / cribbing a barrage of sun."

Fare thee well, and write and joy, Gweg

To Lawrence Ferlinghetti New York

[late May] 1959

Ah Larry baby,

No Hitler just again my pesty way with thee; I love you and all good; how can I ever really adhere or wend or give to such a floppy idealist a commendable dupe of Death? I only said him becuz. Now I got no book for Grove becuz lovely ND [New Directions] took all my good poems and they also get next option; but they do have a wild wild collection, really. I'm very happy with it. For am I not a herald come from Salamis the fair, my news from thence my verses shall declare? So Greece tomorrow; my life's dream; when first in prison I looked upon Athena's noble lovely worn away face; a grand civilization appeared; a mile long civilization becuz Delos is only a mile long, and lovely Delphi not longer much. Anyway; I extenuate no error but that of liberty and "aggrandizement"—why not.

Love, Gregory

To James Laughlin

Venice
[June 15] 1959

O James L,

All the trip I been thinking about the title and it just doesn't make it with me. *Cars Are Real*, is what I feel, even though it might seem that I am hipped on the petroleum industry. You'll see that *Cars Are Real* is far more salable too, ha ha! As for dedication: "For the Beat Generation—when cars were chariots." For epigraph: "Whew! / Well it's gone. / Dear me, dear, we do take chances. / Didn't it look exciting at that height of passion. / I wish . . . No, better not" / Alan Ansen, on seeing his first car, from his poem *The Public Hangman*. See how nice and funny that will be with title and dedication? For I do wish humor to cloak my poems.

As for poems I discovered here in Venice, hundreds (actually 20) of them I wrote while here last year, all written after *Gasoline* and after *Cars Are Real*. What to do with them? A gap. I shall send them on to you. I shall go to Spoleto, then in August to Greece. I decided on Venice. My address will be American Express, Venice. Please do let me have my way with title, and I do hope you can see and joy in that way. I do not wish to hand out entire doom to man. Laughter laughter, no gloomy me. Please write me and let me know for I worry about title. Hope you like dedication, can't see dedicating it to one person.

Best, Gregory

To Lawrence Ferlinghetti

Venice
June 16, 1959

Dear Larry –

Please send me as much as you can because I am in trouble with my fare. I gave a $200 check to Hellenic Lines in N.Y. and $55 cash. Mid-sea, the check bounced. There was only 160 in bank. Woe was me. fifteen days at sea. Stopped at Genoa—they held my passport—it cost me 65 dollars for telegrams to banks and Hellenic Line. I can't go to Greece now. I paid fare, and am now broke. Doom—Doom. Anyway, I'll stay in Venice, and go to Spoleto, and if all is well—Greece. Please O Anti-work, Family, Country, Travea, Patria, Republique, (Fascism) send me 100 angels—for I am a 29 year old who would like to assume some propriety. Where the poetry when Venice Venetians down eye me with Carpaccio wickeds. Anyway, you did promise you'd send me more loot later on—Could you put some light on Papa Black Book? I am dirty, need hair cut—and money for Nazionales [cigarettes], food, and I'm depending.

So off I go again—still there's joy, if not my Greece.

Love, Gregory

Advance, advance me, o charley pot.

To Allen Ginsberg and Peter Orlovsky

Venice
[ca. June 16] 1959

Dear Allen and Peter,

By some quirk which I shall later explain, I have stopped in Venice and have resumed the dream—hectic ways of Ansen and Venice. I am staying with Alan, and we shall go to Spoleto, then in August I shall go to Greece. Please forward all mail to Venice, American Express.

Love, Gregory

To Allen Ginsberg

Venice
[ca. June 17] 1959

Dear Allen,

Am in Venice instead because I went thru great horror as is God's want, but I did come out of it loving St. Paul. Instead of Greece I got off at Genoa and Ansen rescued me because my boat fare check bounced. Here in Venice I see all my poems and I am now begging Laughlin to use them in my book, but I already signed contract, yet he might give in, and I don't like title *Happy Birthday Of Death*, I want *Cars Are Real* its more like me. I read in papers here that my *Marriage* a big success at Spoleto.

WRITE TO ME BABY. I love you you golden brain of responsive air. The Chinese tea in the closet is from Johnny [Nicholson] to you and Peter for your return, and I have a present for thee in same closet; in brown paper wrap a portrait of you done long ago by Iris Brody.[159] Also I left my OLIVETTI TYPEWRITER in middle drawer of my room. As for my cat let somebody who loves me hold it if you decide to come here and we to Greece together and Istanbul and India.

We must <u>move</u> dear poet.

To James Laughlin

Venice
[ca. June 21] 1959

Dear James L,

Ah, do I tax thee? What with title changes and all that, wondering now if you won't allow change, but I do hope you will, even everybody I ask: "What do you like better, *Cars Are Real*, or *HBOD {Happy Birthday of Death*]?" And it's always *Cars Are Real* and no doubt, it's more like me. Anyway this letter is not for that. It's for all these poems I left in Venice written 1958, very happy poems, children poems; how can I publish them after this forthcoming book? It won't be honest. The book you have now explains just how I feel, can I have such a poem as: "Children children don't you know / Mozart has no where to go / this is so / though graves be many / little Mozart hasn't any." See? Chronological is what I wanted, *Vestal Lady, Gasoline*, now these poems come after *Gasoline*, and after them, the ones you have. What should we do? There's a gap, a big gap; I have one solution, but I don't know if you'll like it; I suggest take all these poems and put it in *Cars Are Real / Happy Birthday* (whatever) and I will pay for the printing. It'll be a fat book, but a true book, a great funny book: The money I'll pay for them being in *Cars Happy* you'll deduct from royalties. How does that sound? O you should see these poems! They're better than *Gasoline*.

So help me; suggest, suggest, and don't get annoyed with me, for indeed, this is upsetting for me. WHAT SHALL I DO WITH THESE POEMS? If you want me to send them to you, I will. I love Alexander and Michelangelo, and hate small things, like little books of poems, come out with a fat powerhouse, I have the poems, they're here, even a great funny *Prometheus Unbound* called *Sarpedon*, all in metre and rhyme, I can even do that! I brag; I do; because looking at them here right on table I have created some great things. So. What shall it be? Don't let my excitement stay you. I am serious. I enclose just one poem at hand, you already have the Mozart one. I am not a fascist as Ferl says or thinks, I am dreamed with grandeur. Let me prove it. 300 pages of poetry. Or will you tear up contract and be done with me as is the case with me and man.

Love, Gregory.

You'll have the poems in a week if you want them. Let my cherub arrogance be victorious—I can come out with a book of hundreds of poems—I literally have 150 poems here. All good.

Tonight I dine with Peggy Guggenheim and Caresse Crosby, I love her husband's work. Will then take trip to Spoleto where they'll have recital of *Marriage*; by the way, Al Aronowitz of *New York Post* is doing anthology of beat lit, he write he wants *Marriage Power Army Police*, I told him to get in touch with thee. Answer me soon please. How are you?

Am writing a requiem, for no one in particular. O I worry worry *CARS Happy Real Birthday* has got to far surpass *Gasoline* dammit.

To Allen Ginsberg Paris

[late June] 1959

Dear Allen,

Send me some new poems to be translated in Italian for hip Italian magazine. How's things? Bill working on *Naked Lunch* for Olympia. All is well. I go back to Venice this week, spent a few days in good ole Paris, still the same. Write. Best Peter, Peter send poem.

Love, Gregory

▼ [James Laughlin was adamant in his response about the change in the title and the late addition of the new poems. He felt *Cars Are Real* was a terrible title.]

To James Laughlin Venice

[late June] 1959

Dear JL,

Just got a contract and $50 advance from Fantasy Records. They want to do *Bomb.* Ferlinghetti said yes to them, and *Marriage,* now who is *Marriage* for *Evergreen Review* or thee. O why must I be beset with these kind of things. But I need the 50 so I sent in contract and told them to get in touch with you. The poems are already taped, from Chicago reading. I have no advisor, so please angel advise. OK, do what you will with title, and as for all these forgotten poems I have here, they can go for next book. No more bother about that. Yes, Alan Ansen is a real live fleshy constant addition to this poetry machine, but a good one, and we have his permission.

I will mail you a carbon of the contract Fantasy sent, I think they want both, they sent two, so you send it on after you read it, I cashed the 50 check already because I need it, as I bought a suit and shoes so that I can go to Peggy Guggenheim's parties, and hear Sir John Gielgud read *Ages Of Man* tonight. Am even having a romance with a lovely girl here, gondolas and all. And had nice chat on Lido with Caresse Crosby all about her Harry, and she showed me some of his writings never before seen. No, I did not say to *Big Table* that they should ask for fee; in fact Rosenthal said they could go ahead with it, it must be that fool Carroll in Chicago. All is well, and when I have feeling/time I will explain the great horror I went through on trip coming over and why I could not go to Greece.

All is well, Gregory

Advise on contract for Fantasy, money I owe on this advance, etc.—today I go see Diaghilev's grave.

To Lawrence Ferlinghetti Venice

[late June] 1959

Dear Larry,

Thank you and there is no goal and all is well, and thank you for Fantasy urgency and I wrote to Laughlin for has he not something to do with the recording? I did sign contract with him, but also Fantasy's so they can give him commission. All is well, I have had parties with Sir John Gielgud and Guggenheim and other personalities.

Why don't you reprint *Vestal Lady* and I'll give you rest of poems written in that period, I found all of them here in Venice where I left them. What other news? Is Allen gone yet? Allen says Jack's agent can get me $500 advance on record company; but no less I still did sign that Fantasy contract, shows how much I care about money. Though I speak with the tongues of beatniks and squares and have not money I am become like crocodile smoke or a radiator soup.

I have money now and am living at Alan Ansen's and all is again well, got $30 from Grove for *Marriage*, 50 from you, 50 from Fantasy, 200 from Nicholson, and 160 dollars I won at casino with your 50; but don't tell Allen or Fantasy; else Allen will think me cry wolf next time, and Fantasy will send a pittance. Now, what to do with all this loot? I did buy a crazy Longhi mask, do you know the kind? White with a long nose? Hope all is well and love and dream and droll.

Gregory

I spoke with Caresse Crosby and she has given me lots of Harry Crosby's things, poems, etc., for me to peddle, execute, publish, etc. What say you, are you interested in Harry Crosby? I am, I am most influenced, if there be influence, by the 20th century poets.

To James Laughlin Venice

[late June] 1959

I will send on manuscript—but please go ahead on *HBOD*. I wait in Venice until I have corrected proofs then will be off to Greece. I don't think *HBOD* should be changed or subtracted from or even added to. This batch of poems could go into a separate book. I await the proofs. Spent a week in Paris.

Best, Gregory

To Allen Ginsberg Munich, West Germany

[July 15] 1959

Broke and happy but serious belly trouble in Munich. Berlin, I pray! If an angel pays my golden fare.

Love, Gregory

To James Laughlin Munich, West Germany
[late July] 1959

Down and out in Munich, I will remain in Munich. I read at University here. J. W. Aldridge introducing and got 100 Marks and have eaten, yet sleep amid rabbits in English garden. Will get room.

Thank you, Gregory

To Allen Ginsberg Munich, West Germany
[late July] 1959

Dear Allen, or Irving or Peter,

In my room in drawer you'll find my Olivetti typewriter, please sell it, hock it, doom it to commerce, for I need the money, can't explain, as ever,

Gregory

All have abandoned the grease of an empire, and a bucket of pink looms before me. Rush Rush Rush

To Lawrence Ferlinghetti Munich, West Germany
[late July] 1959

Larry,

Please get Weiss of Fantasy to rush me rest of money for signing contract like he promised. Don't got his address. Am actually sleeping in English Garden. And Weisbaden publisher won't give me gold for *Gasoline*, they say you must, can you? I starve really in Ludwig land—will I always be like this? Will die in a bucket of pink? I am good.

Gregory

I remain in Munich. I hate Hitler. I hate Hitler. Help. Help! Express letter.

To Willard Maas Munich, West Germany
[late July] 1959

Dear Willard Maas,

Send money. Send Wagner Magazine. Send the ransom of Rome. Send a bucket of pink. Send MONEY! Because, alas, I am alone, and with tears, and, I want to go to the Black Forest. If you don't send me at least enough to stand awesome before Goering's daughter, I will place thee on my poetic shit-list. Help!

But don't tell anybody unless they come thru. Great discover. Truth is just as bad as God,—a man-made thing.

Warmth, Gregory

To Allen Ginsberg Frankfurt am Main, West Germany
[late July] 1959

Dear Allen,

Am on my way to Berlin, will read in University there, via Höllerer. Then off to Warsaw. So I guess I resume a life-giving self and society be done. All is well—and I hope you are fine. Will our eyes meet? Perhaps off-far in India someday.

Gregory

To Allen Ginsberg Berlin, West Germany
[late July] 1959

Dear Allen,

The reading went off great before big crowd in new theatre here. Your *Howl* read first on record, then *Army* and *Bomb*, McClure, Whalen, Ferlinghetti. All was carefree and fine and most reviews in Berlin called the poesy prayers. How strange East Berlin, so vast and desolate, yet somewhat gentle, more so than the West. Maybe it's because I'm too accustomed to West—I'll remain here,

Love, Gregory

To Allen Ginsberg Berlin, West Germany
[Aug.] 1959

Poem flawless—what is flaw? Read Tom Hardy, says universe was a better place before man appeared, and will be so again when he has departed. Alex Blok,[160] says almost same—not you or me—I think man is strange, I like his strangeness. No conclusive pessimism. Wrote long prosaic poem on the American Way. Set it as big evil that even gets nature to make Americans look, walk and talk alike. Maybe great psalm poem—it is done—but you will re-done it, and that'll be fine too.

Gregory

"Night falls, I awake, my anxiety returns, the splendid vision has melted away, I am a man once more and now tell me, lord, tell me in my ear: can all this beauty abolish our death?"

To Allen Ginsberg and Peter Orlovsky Venice
[Aug. 20] 1959

Ah dear friends,

But I lie, for I am not pure and yet I tend to hold that I am because I am indeed mad or dew-bespangled, therefore do grab hold of young Irving [Rosenthal] and kneel him to grieve over all penitent Puritan bitches like me.

And are the cats yet alive? And did you see that picture I got for you in kitchen closet done by Iris Brody many years ago of you? And the box of tea by Nicholson? And did Jack get my letter published in his anthology? Then why no money for me from the publisher, for indeed I did iron-manner beseech loot from him when in dire Munich need, now no need, for once gain Venice, and James Merrill said he would get me two thousand this September from fund, and then Greece, but must hold here for proofs of New Directions book, and in Munich I had great rapport with lovely lady Eve Hesse[161] who translates Pound and Cummings. Sartre is in Venice, and Arnold Weinstein, and I have not written a thing, but of all things am subject to a nameless melancholia that blushes whenever I see something luxurious, how odd.

What a trip you both must have had! Did you see that book Willard Maas put out, a magazine and all the things in it, and the man at Fantasy lied when he said if I'd sign contract he'd send more gold for he did not, and now all I am involved with is nuggets and shafts and assayers. [. . .] What else is happening and is the cat big now, and do you see Nicholson and has he felt that I did abuse his plucked good?

Burroughs is not in Paris, his book is out. Is he on way to New York, for surely the police did not hold him awhile? Ansen has a lovely little book out, and I think that film done by Leslie and Frank[162] is nowhere, silly, amateurish and a thing for record of its ingredients; and I do feel that Wentley poems[163] went by me without such consideration, and I'm fed up with poems and poets and *par avion* where just now 32 little students crashed in Spain, and in Germany on train when I was going to Chimsee Prein to see fest I did see a jet plane crash, the whole thing, the canopy, the projection seat, the dive, the bibulous black red ball, and just before it, saw a white bird fly low by.

Kerouac did not come to my aid for I am always in need and I am not insulted and Lucifer knows I did not like that reading benefit, I'm tired of them there things, and Rossett sending me twenty five dollars hearing I was stranded, I spent it, and must write him a thank you note, but all is done. One month in Munich and helplessness, the trip over, helplessness; yet Venice all is calm, God, sometimes I feel that *par avion* would be just the remedy, no? No. For I do not yet sing and gl'd glee.

Höllerer says anthology is translated and accepted by Carl Hanser Verlag. What else? Ansen will send separate letter . . . wrote to O'Hara but he no answer me, and how is gut olt LeRoi Jones, and did *Yugen* come out more, can he send them to me here in Venice? And can you send me the Maas thing or any other interesting thing?

Pull the train down, keep the wall up, hold the copy, the roof, the final hour later, the action, the fat madman who in other room sits being me, and me being he, and the floor, the clinging pot, the cellar, his darting eye to see if I dart too, his shoes taking the whole closet, and the ceiling spitting wirelessess's down on us, and outside, thank God, I've got to run and get away he breathes in me times on me dines on me and I build germs invisible ones so that I can think all this when all this is not happening, so now I shall stop, and so will he.

Goodbye; Gregory

The grewed chants forests brool in loose and feeble dews—the damp rabbits the dreary haze ungenerous for day makes a bloodful pain so pensive where rosy shepherds lay.

To Lawrence Ferlinghetti Venice
[Aug. 21] 1959

Dear L.

Limes Verlag has signed contract with you so why can't I get some gold? I do need it. And did you ask for me Wiess of Fantasy that he promised me 50 dollars for signing contract? Forgive all this switching of finance — necessary. How's things? Had big party at Stella Adler's, much parties here, felt sexy for Sheila Graham's daughter.

Love, Gregory

To Allen Ginsberg Venice
Aug. 21, 1959

Just got the letter with the checks, thank Bremser and all else. God what an exhauster I am of token; sorry bout the cats, the bed, the chair, the t v, but I had to get away from USA; and the check, that bounced while on ship was the bank check at 3rd Street I made for 200 and gave to Ship Line and mid sea the cablegram of doom, insufficient funds in bank, whereas bank said before I left there were sufficient funds, yet I must of given a check early or something and was cashed late, all in all it was horrible, and stayed me from Greece, but I'm all set to go now, and will as soon as I get proofs of book; India in Xmas great, is Bill in New York? I then might come back to New York after Greece, perhaps around November; Jean-Jacques Lebel[164] here, remember him, the kid at Duchamp-Man Ray party of me drunk vomit; well he read *Bomb* over air in Warsaw and said the radio got batches of unprotest letters, and that they dug the poem, and Höllerer writes that he's off to Warsaw, too.

Had party last night; Stella Adler, some famous Italian poet, John Meyers, and Arnold Weinstein and de Kooning girl, Ruth, and others, all very fine, drunk, happy, sex, and farewell to Arnold. Höllerer says the anthology is set to go, and that I'll have to sign contract soon; and I also sent letter to Merrill Foundation, and Jimmy says I can get it sure, and had a nice long talk and soul with him in Munich.

Your trip sounds fascinating and all that Americana touring and Chicago and what did that moonman Carroll do with my *Clown* poems and is *Evergreen* out with *Marriage* yet? Ok, Peter be good.

Love, Gregory

Ever read German poet Paul Fleming? (ca. 1609). All poets are fascists. If you see O'Hara give him my love. Any new propaganda? Send some. Has Irving forgiven me?

To James Laughlin

Venice
[Aug. 22] 1959

Dear J.L.

Am in Venice waiting for proofs from Villiers.[165] I wrote to him where I am, then for sure Greece. Yes, take from Venice batch, and being that you select so well, select. Hope your trip was a wonder. Met the American Ambassador to Italy, and we spoke long of poetry and opera, also Eva Hesse is a grand angel. She enlightened me with Cummings who I never before really got to.

Best, Gregory

To Willard Maas

Venice
[Aug. 26] 1959

The pink is in Munich, but it'll be sent to me. Thank you, and joy to the Clarion that spilleth gold on thy blue-armored head. My heart goes out to you. I am in Venice for awhile for proofs of book, then to Greece. Will you send Wagner College magazine to me? Air? *Das ist gut!*

Love, Gregory

To Willard Maas

Venice
[late Aug.] 1959

Dear Willard,

Just got the Munich money yesterday and rushed off a card of thanks to Museum of Modern Art because I didn't have your address and forgot the one at Wagner, so now I got your real address and will rush this letter off to you before you get to the Amer Express in Munich, but I think it'd be nice if you got into some mad contact with the Amer Express all over Europe, because I intend to go all over Europe, but I do not intend that you send me a bucket of pink all the time. Anyway, Venice is hot and hazy and I am overlooking the

Salute.[166] Movie stars for festival and will go to Greece for sure as soon as I get proofs for my book. There were a lot of people named Maas in Munich.

Luv, Gregory

To Allen Ginsberg

Venice

Sept. 4, 1959

The red house with the crazy Venetian windows is where I am now living,[167] a big place, old palace; 40 thousand [lira] a month; de Kooning[168] here, got drunk, went to casino, he gave me a hundred, I won 400, and thus I can live. Left Ansen's who had another guest, much better alone, really big gloomy old furniture palace, de Kooning wants to paint here, but he's not sure how long he'll be here. Ain't been writing much, but now that I am alone, who knows, the muse might once again pick me up. How's New York? Peter, I just got your poem *Morris* and except for excess repeats think it's great, know it's great, and the spelling, sheer bloom. Saw *Time* today with pained Gregory picture; I ain't ever realized I was raking in all that dough though. Tell Kerouac I don't want a million, I want emergency love; also if Avon took my letter then I expect loot, a good sum too, else I won't consent to its being published, it's about time I start getting strong about these kind of things, especially now that I oft find myself without a sou and a soul to emergency. God's messenger grips the crown of man.

Gregory

To Lawrence Ferlinghetti

Venice

[ca. Sept. 4] 1959

Got drunk with de Kooning last night, grewed great talks, bout going beyond Truth with him, very sweet cat. Am still waiting for my proofs for ND [New Directions] book, then off to Greece. Fantasy sent money to Munich? I ain't ever got it. I'll write to Munich. What's up? Are you older? I'm writing different kind of poems, all about the Prisoner of Zenda; all yours.

Gregory

To Allen Ginsberg

Venice

[Sept. 12] 1959

Ah dear ones how sad both you sound and me with all my complaints of gold and havens, and that Maas of only 50 dollars to demand your love, I'll write him that he's got to send me at least the ransom of Rome for your love, and I ain't kissing ambassadors because of equaling them to the muse, but just because they are ambassadors and they're a being in themselves, very strange to be, an ambassador; and I didn't kiss him but called him beautiful for something he agreed with about my saying black evil was the pure makeup of diplomacy. I go to Greece tomorrow on a Yugoslav boat . . . had mad time with de Kooning here who is very unhappy about love, but I love him, and we had Rome together, and also met Cyril Connolly[169] who thinks Burroughs the greatest and he asked for Bill's address, I proposed we see Pound but he said rather see Burroughs. Yes, tell LeRoi, I'll send him all my Greek poems, and new ones, and that I love him and gender about his child, and wish he'd supply me with *Yugens*, and could you send me *Big Table* 2, and I swear I'm not doing bad when I run to write [to] people for money though now I shouldn't because of fame way they expect something, whereas before nothing was expected. Well heck with them and drive them from your velvet door. Lucien sounds sad, maybe up gets him down maybe he should go back to studies and Iberia; why don't you and Peter come to Greece? Well anyway I promise I shan't do [a] thing that will bug you both, that's the fate of friendship, and I slightly slack from my pesty self it seems. The ransom of Rome gets into all my letters lately whenever I need money, and it used to be the concierges witchy hand is on my doorknob, when I needed money in Paris. Ah how listless such repetition; and that picture of me [in] *Time* was strange to see because I do look mean, and maybe I am mean if you think of poor Irving Rosenthal who I hurt I guess and LeRoi and Bremser, etc., I guess I hurt em all, but I don't hurt the next day. What else, I feel by your sad letter that maybe you both should get away and come here or somewhere but I would love to be back together again with my angels, even if I am pesty with youse I am always more dignified and never ask for gold from anyone and am more myself, but alone in this world I fight very much always have and would do anything I don't care because it's the world.

Ok, be good both of you and all is for the best, yes, and don't grow old in NYC and forward far forward is the light! There's more more much more to do, you haven't done it yet, only poetry ain't so much for a man to be in, there's adventure yet, more than poetry is needed, complete resignation to life; steal cheat love beg hunger get cold sleep on floors on quilts do do do do, let's all do together; Egypt, India, Hope Savage is in India, she hitch-hiked all the way to Iran from Munich; fame hath made thee a letter answerer, a Vincent Peale, get out of that house, you are too comfortable in not a comfortable way, you hate that house, you know a prison when you see one, you are a man and man creates those in betweens in between life and death, marriage is a man's creation, truth too and prison, a human creation. Surely if I were there I'd inspire you and Peter to come to Greece; you see, I am basically useful; not so practical, but that's my, as Alan [Ansen] puts it, saving grace. I'll write from Greece, goodbye, love love yes

Gregory

To Lawrence Ferlinghetti Athens, Greece

[ca. Sept. 15] 1959

Well I'm finally here! On the Acropolis with wind and storm—hear old Triton blow his weathered horn. I still didn't get my proofs from Laughlin, is he always that slow? How are things? Good about *Her*[170]—send me rush copy and all kinds of news and new things. I guess I'll spend winter here.

Love, Gregory

To Allen Ginsberg Athens

[Sept. 24] 1959

Dear Allen,

Your letter cards sound so rushed that nothing seems to be happening to your life of good ecru-report. Anyway I am filled with Athens and know well its tower of winds Acropolis Agora stoas etc. and say to you that you are too serious with the no-goodness; face it, saints can unbuild, St. Paul chasing away the Gods of Greece, yet rebuild, what beyond the St.? Go to Chile, be good and happy, dear friend, serious conglomerous Theseus friend.

Love, Gregory

To Allen Ginsberg Athens

[Oct. 3] 1959

Got drunk and threw a glass at *Life* photographer—missed thank God and now I go to the isles to flee the wake of the tail. Did you find the [Iris] Brody picture of you in kitchen closet? Finished my proofs—book looks good—and I went mad over Burroughs' book—the best prose written for me, like Jack—they's both been gifted by the battle of Salamis.

Love, Gregory

To Don Allen Athens

[Oct. 3] 1959

How are you? I am off to the isles—can you air me a copy of the latest *Evergreen Review*? Please, there ain't much to read here. Was bothered so much yesterday by a *Life* photographer that I got drunk on ouzo and threw a glass at him. Missed (thank God) and ran out crying into the gymnasium of Diogenes. They don't got Grove books here in Athens. Hope you balance off *Marriage* with maybe some other poems in your anthology. Is everything all right? Are you in the mood for a million dollars? Then sell nostril makeup for girls (good idea, yes?)

Love, Gregory

To Don Allen Hydra
[Oct. 5] 1959

Dear Don,

Yes please use *To Bring Back The Dead*—I've picked the poem clean—used it as patchwork. Many poems in forthcoming book are filled with lines from it. My *Bomb* poem is a hundred different poems. It seems when I sit at typewriter as I did with *Marriage* the poem is written straight away, but when I write in longhand in a book, I patchwork. A poem could start off and be about Turtles and end up being about Mules. I guess I'm a tailor more than a poet. I got up at six this morning and saw the sun come over the Peloponnesus—This is really an extraordinary lovely island. And what fun watching the fishermen sell their fish. Am writing a long poem called, of course, *Greece*. When it's done I'll send it on to you. How's Frank [O'Hara]? Do you see Ginsberg? I may go to Crete today—I return to Athens in ten days. Food here made me very sick last week—fainted—broke out in pimples—am better now. Send *Evergreen Review* to me air mail like Barney [Rossett] promised. I like Archaic Kore art very much, am not at all interested to look at Byzantine art yet. Greek has me busy. Many cons here. Goodbye, fair winged Sherlock, your most fateful friend and obedient complainer,

Gregory

To Don Allen Athens
[Oct. 8] 1959

Dear Don,

Just back from Hydra where I experienced a strange thing, I walked to end of isle where nobody lives and was so hung over from having drank actually two quarts of whisky scotch the night before was crying all night putting down the Greek peasantry for having chased Poseidon away etc. etc., almost got killed, but anyway in the morning I walked that long walk and suddenly had spots before my eyes and thought I would faint, my breath actually did stop, this I thought was death; but no, everything seemed to open up; I sat down and thought for a long long time, and I realized there that people this world this universe is going one way and I another. Proof of it was in Athens four nights before when I agreed to have pictures taken of me by *Life* and he was nice all day but he brought friends and supposed friends of mine followed and I got scared and I realized I didn't have a friend there, and this came to light after much drinking on my part that night after a whole day of entourage photos, I thought it'd be nice to have my picture taken on the Acropolis, but they also wanted a "group" picture; so to a tavern they led me and there the photographer starts calling me names all to get up my anger, that he did, I threw a glass at him and ran into the street crying, ran into a car my leg all black and blue and he the photographer comes after me and says "All right Corso we're alone you can stop the act." I ran from him but he kept on coming after me and I stopped and wept hysterically to him that I was a poet and not a freak and that I suffered enough in youth homes orphanages prisons etc. and and and and, until he finally saw that I wasn't acting, perhaps drunk, but not acting, then he extended his hand and said, "I'm sorry, its my job, let's shake hands." I shook his hand and disappeared and was miserable so miserable I went to Hydra and there too, I couldn't get away from it, I couldn't understand why I was so unhappy. Why let another person who's going the other way disturb me? Well, on that morning fainting walk I realized it wasn't that *Life* photographer, it was me, I'm just not for this world, that's all; but I'll be damned if I'll leave it; people have been the horror to me not this life, life is good, people just ain't, and I can prove it, my life proves it, I mistrust all people, I am an institutional type therefore I am subjected, easily intimidated, always under their heel; I am beautiful and they're not, they know this so they hurt hurt hurt, they know I'm going the other way, they get impressions of me that are always contrary to me, even Kerouac in *Subterraneans* got me all wrong, they don't know me; and that I am going the other way I've no protection, I need love I need that protect I need somebody somebodies who understand and protect me, no wonder I always feel death near, everywhere I can see the death warrant. *Basta*, forgive me, but it had to come out, and I spew it out to you.

I like writing poems but I don't like the people who hover over it, the feeling I get when I write is my joy not this aftermath, who is this Beatnik Corso they write about? I don't know him. I like your selection of poems except you have no *Vestal Lady* poems, why not? You once said you liked the book, why *A Dreamed Realization, Yaaaah, From Another Room, Away One Year, Paranoia In Crete*, these all have been published, what about *In The Morgue, Requiem For Bird, Tunnel Bone Of Cambridge, In The Early Morning*? All from *Vestal Lady* . . . reason I say this is because you want dates, if so then you're interested in progress, why not start with *Vestal Lady*?

You can show this letter to O'Hara and Ginsberg and that's all, because I'd write to them this recent horror, but now that it's all out unto you, I can't repeat it; I just want you to know that everybody I meet thinks I'm a creepy publicity hound and I am innocent and wish no profit from anything in this rotary, if poets are damned to solitary, then I must face up to it. One thing is certain, never again will they dupe me into publicity.

Thank you my fair winged Sherlock, Gregory

To Allen Ginsberg Athens
[Oct. 8] 1959

Dear Allen,

These last few days I went through hell but came out of it with a sight! I almost drank myself to death two bottles of scotch because I was unhappy about an incident in Athens with Zina Rachevsky and her clawing husband and *Life* photographer. O I can't go into that again I wept it to Don Allen and Ned Erbe[171] they'll show you letters, just can't go on talking about it. I hope I didn't blame New Directions, anyway out of it all on the lovely isle of Hydra I actually saw Death, yes, it was the morning after the big night of sad drunk and much tears, I got up at six in the morning and walked out of the small town to a high deserted spot, five miles out, no inhabitants and when I arrived I suddenly had myriads of spots before my eyes and I spoke to myself loud and long about so many things and then felt faint, I stopped I could not go on, my breath stopped, I fought, got my breath back, o the feeling! I felt so strong so knowing I sat down and immediately said I KNOW I KNOW, people earth life this universe is going one way and I the other, yes, that's why I've been speaking death. Well death is not bad, it's good, it's soul, there that what we think is soul is in us is but death in us, lovely deaths but man destroys that loveliness by morbidity and foundations and institutions and churches to aid life unto death. What they think is death, they're all wrong, they have it all confused, they are going the wrong way, even the universe, it goes the wrong way; I saw there at that moment a skinless light, a naked brilliance and felt like I never felt before in my life; I had done a great thing, I stepped out of the circle and did not die, and outside the circle, dear friend, death holds its warrant; a summoning to something wonderful and beautiful I'm sure; I was scared and stepped back into the circle, but now I know I can go out of the circle anytime I want and always come back; no wonder I wrote all those poems about death, I knew I wasn't a morbid doomful person, I knew there had to be a reason behind it all; and to think I was afraid to come to Greece, to think I came for Zeus, Menelaus, etc., when what really drove me here was that experience; how strange how we fight what is necessary for us; look how long it took me to get here. I did not need laughing gas pot lsd mescaline; it is not in drugs, it is in you, it's there, waiting; and it's not soul, its the lovely death in you, the thing you eat against, the thing you kill unknowingly; you are not to blame, life's inexperience is to blame; but I've no doubt about you, I know you'll find it, what now? Less expression; as you can see I don't even care to elaborate on this experience, words are words, poetry is poetry, all of this wrong crooked path. Anyway I am well, maybe when I calm down I'll expound more; Bill's book great, he too has seen, I'm sure.

Love, Gregory

To Allen Ginsberg Athens
[Oct. 11] 1959

Dear Allen,

I wrote to Laughlin yesterday asking him not to print poem *Birthdays End* because I did not get to the light, no light-language, death sucked me off image weak in that it out suggests Death; also not enough compassion, too one-sided, a sight into the dark. Why so boastful Gregory? Alas maturity is due in poesy too. I wish I could describe the day at Hydra but that wouldn't be enough because it didn't begin there: at full I can go into length, a youth filled with pictures in hallways with eyes that moved to turtles nibbling at my toes, all childhood merit; nothing unusual; the breakdown of childhood taboos, three days before Hydra-deathsight I gathered all my deaths, the early one written in Paris, so fanciful; the spooky one feared in New York on my return, the facing of people, the readings, the city cars, I never saw New York that way, my old toyland well you know, the subways the rooftops the jails, all cozy good; I am not a graveyard soul though I find a romanticism easily expressed through such medium, but abandoned that too as you can see at end of *Power*; another Death, myself being called good beat poet, loss of helpless dreamy Alexander-talking Gregory, death of that, that that you called my childishness; recent clipping sent to me by New Directions from a *Newsweek* article about gloomy Corso, saying all is death by their use of aposiopesis (. . .) and so the death I probe is but gloom, but vengeance on a world that deemed my youth, but some silly pox on you world; no, this is not me; a million times mistakened, I with *Power Bomb* and now *Death* have happily toyed; *Death* was too much, I became fascinated by it, I took it SERIOUSLY, I became involved deeply in it, my whole life 1959 changed, I saw and thought death; now easily to assume to myself that death is but a form of suicide and suicide thinking is a poet's nipple; corny this, corny Harry Crosby,[172] why can't death be used? Why must one give in to its con? By fighting death, by not giving into it, do you see and know death, go with it and you are powerless; the experience on Hydra, when I ended poem with "now I know"' why do I now know? Prophet, you say. Easily said. A prophet of myself, perhaps; the death I saw was for me, not for man. The sad meaning of man is not my wealth; it is yours, angel, thy beauty which did haunt you in your sleep to undertake the death of all the world; by reading your list of death and your poems on Death and Beauty the murderer shows that you are prophet of man, I am and always have been for myself, but we are the same in that we are feeling Death, why do they now wear black stockings, bizarre youth, black light, black coffee? When I said that the BG [Beat Generation] was the happy birthday of death, I wasn't far from the beautiful Lie; but surely not a death that stinks a body; just an acceptance and an awareness to myself that Death is me [. . .] . I do not glum my days away in gloomy damned solitude, I go out into the street and BEWARE BEWARE to people that they be aware? that they know my discovery? If I were at home with you and Peter, only your ears would have gotten the fullness of it. Look what I found! I must show what I found. When my book comes out all one will see is an honest exploration into Death, not one that will shudder folk, or lack them from shaking my hand because if they do they'll be shaking hands with death; I am essentially a happy bum. *Cars Are Real* was my title, James Laughlin liked *Happy Birthday of Death*, why not? And it was, but not the kind of birthday he thought, I say only I was invited, of course, to one's death goes one alone. Lyric, not statement. Variations with *Hair Bomb Power*, variations with *Death* more than a man's job; for this holy powers seem actioned; perhaps, but I am hesitant and yet doubt holy powers; I still feel the self with no attachment to any outerness is power.

On Hydra that morning two miles away from any house or man but one man who is the most depressed soul I have ever met walked with me and on the walk I spoke a torrent, said that poetry—poetry is not me I am not poetry I am scared because I am saying and feeling something outside myself I think. O did I find it so hard to express myself to him, his were the only ears around; what did I wish to say? I tried and tried and he acted as if he understood, it was a long walk, the scene was lovely, pure Greek isle of Homer, early morning, bright sun, I said faster faster to him I'm coming to something I'm coming to something and it has nothing to do with poetry, I'm scared. At that time I began to see spots, I kept silent from then on, he walked ahead, out of sight around a bend, I sat down, "Do you see that black bird, Norris? Is it a vulture, Norris?" He was out of hearing distance, I screamed to him, "Do you see the vulture, Norris!" He yelled back, "No!" Then it happened, I lost my breath, fear set in but only for a second, everything became light, I say not the edges of the mountains, not the sea nor where I was sitting nor myself, just light, I was in that light, the description that it was "skinless" is only my helpless description of sight that I felt and can readily be expressed, but what I saw, ah . . . It seemed like hours, thank God Norris was away, he had to walk away, I asked him why later, and he said he felt he had to, and was afraid of me because I became all pale and strange looking, he said he surely thought I was his death warrant; if death be a naked light, the false heir to Dark; then I have indeed entered it; how long was it before my breath came back? Time was judgeless. Right after the big black bird that only I saw came Death with only a drop of human fear, I am sure that that drop of fear did not bring back my breath, else I would not have seen Light disrobe. Still human me when I came out of it I sat breathing heavily and happily and cried happily like one released from a horrible ordeal vowing never again to hurt any man or thing or interfere with any way in Life, when Norris returned I told him half all, and badly and excitedly yet enough to blank his eyes with strange curiosity. I sat there for two hours or more after, couldn't get up, couldn't walk, very weak, and VERY CONFUSED, slight fear because of this harboring and catering and blending of death for one whole year entered, this I thought is the beginning of death, I will not leave this spot a body; else what did that Light mean? Will my breath stop again at any minute? I did not wish it to, though I have been very very unhappy of late, I did not wish to leave this mad crazy lovely world. [. . .]

I have exhausted myself to myself, questioned everything, left no thought out. Did I see myself plain, Mr. Browning might say. No. I saw something (about two days after the Light doubt set in) (that's why the rushed hysteria letters to you Don Allen Ned Erbe, good God why them? Expression to you would have done it, I did not wish it done, I wanted Don A. and Ned [to know] that I regret the Light, by writing it to them I would lessen the experience to myself; by writing it in full to you I would have heightened it. [. . .] Yet of all the bright realizations I received from pen to paper probing, none could come close to that penless morning on Hydra; came to me without that drug called Poetry. It had to be that way I guess, couldn't see myself in poetry's zoo-cage finding what I found in Hydra—yet well I know it was poetry that started me on the way and put me there.

How do I stand now? Unafraid, the last stains of death-probe fading away, mischievous, still getting involved with the joys and woes of people, still hurting some, still in need of money am completely broke in a room too expensive to pay and don't know what I wish to do whether to return or go to India or Tangier or if I really want to move, in short, I am in a complete stupor and am not afraid, my begging letters can no longer flow from me, I can no longer ask for money, what I now need is a kind soul to allowance me, just peace, a room, books, myself, and a much needed solitude. At least for a year, a year away from everything; I'd even be willing to write travelogues that I get enough in allowance way for surely had I the lot of it I'd deny myself that year; there's a funny little monster in me who's always screwing me up, and I love him, alas.

You to India? Ah, Hope Savage is there, Sura, a lovely lovely heavenly angel very close to me, I am very much in love with her; could not know love in any other soul. The monster in me was hideous to her. God were it in me to pursue her and kneel at the very sight of her. She is something that I must finally face up to. "My life closed twice before its close" surely she was the first blessing. And God did I so stupidly not sinister-intentionally hurt that light. I guess I was not ready. But how can one be ready. No such Christian preparation, the visitation, the announcement of Light, is due man. I can only be calm not sad about Hope Savage. I pray that I see her again, and proud her with my now being. *Basta.*

Is Chile off? How I wish you and Peter were here; I do miss you both terribly so. Received a lovely warm letter from Bill; I might well go to Paris and see him, he knows nothing of Hydra, I cannot write to him about it, I would rather see him and let it flow some evening in his room of Burroughs world. *Naked Lunch* is a great book. When I read it in its fullness completion book form I saw that we were all wrong to be upset or driving on his connecting the events; the events ARE connected, like something glued that doesn't need string to hold it together, the string is not necessary.

Alan Ansen's book too, amazing; is everything good? Which tree was it? Is that the tree? Distinctly I remember a difference among them. Can I see one tree, know it well, and knowing, know all trees? A big forest of poets, wow; if anything to bring down God, that! All the poets in New York, all the poets in America, they're wonderful to me now, and how I used to ignore them, never really considering them, good Bremser Jones Moraff Gui de Angulo; Peter; ah Peter; and even lovely Jack's poetry once, remember, at your father's house, and he called me two-faced; I'd like to think that I was impetuous, for I am certain of one thing, there has never been any bad in me, be there any "bad"; my horrors were apologetic horrors to being with or else I would have been disdained. And you, how you loved them! The poets not my horrors. You were a good working Jesuit among them—you sang them, not yourself; I, of course I sang myself, selfish impetuous a golden rape a bright siege that damned sack of poetry's property; was it even my intention to put up a NO TRESPASSING sign; the humor of it, walkie-talkie, Alexander, Gregory. For sure, I exaggerate, and make obvious what is far from the actuality. Retrospection brings forth a dark Gregory. Grace. I can also see myself all perfect; impertinent to deny what I have done; of no importance; how one sees oneself is never stational, if I see everything as good then I see myself as good, if I see everything dark then I see myself dark; my sadness only comes when I see everything as good and I as dark; this tends on self-pity, and I'm very capable of being wallowed in it, but Grace, not for long. I am never anything for long, I may hate something but not for long—do you realize that I do not hate anything? I don't. I hate but it does not remain, I have no old hate; subconsciously I dupe myself into thinking I do—I do not. When I hurt (or think I hurt) another, I suffer; they probably have forgotten about it, not I. When young and was hit I put both hands into a window; I hurt myself; I screech at myself, I blame myself; all this, self-pity. If I see things dark and myself good, then I tend on selfishness, boastfulness, Alexander. I do see myself plain actually. A mixture am I. I am not what I think I am, I am not what I am told I am, what I am is what I am, a "I

AM"—this tends on piety and quackiness; what I am is a degraded button, this tends on humor and poetry, and that's the way I intend to go—Does Fate laugh? All those 'tends'—I feel it an injustice to examine oneself, be 'right' about one's self, knowing thyself, seeing yourself plain; the self of yesterday is capable of another self today. "I know you" is foolishly said.

At this moment I am even wondering if I did see that light; I remember being dizzy, walked much, hangover, talkative, but I am never talkative when I awake with guilt, and I awoke that morning guilty that I called people names and cried and causing havoc in the town, morning after like the reading with Frank O'Hara; this was the feeling I had when I awakened, and when I began the walk, halfway I lost that feeling and began to talk and cry to Norris about now seeing everything, that the world goes one way and I the other, then he walked around the bend, then I saw the bird, then the spots, then the loss of breath, then the fear, was it in the fear that I saw the light? I must have caught my breath after the fear went from me, and with the fear went the light. I can't place my finger on it, I can't even see that light now, whereas before I could recall it. I must be very honest with myself; am I creating that "light" and believing it; if I saw that light in fear then that light I saw must have been the light of life and not death, perhaps the stopping of my breath, that little taste of death "the cigarette dream, the one puff" made me see life as light. I don't know. I did not receive any message, saw no form, I can't even remember what I did see, or if I saw anything at all, or if even that moment ever existed; did I imagine it all? I am capable of that, you well are aware of; I might well have induced myself into believing that I did see at that moment of fear a light. Makes no difference how you see it if you believe you saw it, I guess. Faith, I might well lack that.

I read the happy article on New York in *Holiday*[173] and wish Jack catch the echo my love has for him, it's hovering about his ear; it says, Hail Jack, all is Menelaus, Diomedes, Mycenae is brown, the earth a little town, send money, I am done busted, ho! gallons of ladies; the region of Wheel.

Love, Gregory

Why no you all come here to Helleneland and eat big EAIHNHVEE with me, the sky no brown yet; not really; love love chain reactioning love.

To James Laughlin

Athens
[Nov. 3] 1959

Dear JL,

Thank you for the check as I needed it badly—saw and had a nice time with Tennessee Williams here, I joined him in an interview for air forces radio and we both were very funny. I showed him proofs of *Happy Birthday* and he likes them—he's also offered me a plane ticket back home, I didn't ask for it, he offered, but I was hesitant to accept not because he was buying it but because I didn't know whether I wanted to come home or not, as you can see by poem enclosed I have had it in Greece, but America, it takes great strength to live in America, actually I should come back and give poetry readings and herald the age and make money and get myself my much-dreamed of library with big books and long dusty velvet curtains and fireplace—or even go back and get in with the Mafia and go to the Copacabana[174] with them and smoke big cigars and flirt with chorus girls—or maybe go back to the garment center and resume my work of delivery boy—or just hang around the Village cafes and read everybody's poetry—or go to Harvard and demand they give me a professorship, or join the PAL [Police Athletic League] and have big conversations with juvenile delinquents or just give readings in prisons and madhouses, or go to Smith College and win myself a wife or go to Hollywood and become an actor, or go to Vermont and live amid big trees and mountains and running streams, or even come back and run on the Beat platform for President. When I entered prison an old man said to me: "Don't serve time, let time serve you." Well, why not let publicity serve me, why not interviews and TV and articles and poems? Surely if I were to put myself up for President you'd support me, and surely all the beats would, and the jazz musicians and the pot smokers and the Italians and the delivery boys and the girls and the poets and painters and dancers and photographers and architects and students and professors—even though I've two felonies, I'd be voted in—America is essentially a Dadaistic country—could you imagine anything more dada than me as President? O but what to do about foreign affairs, how would Russia take to me? Actually I'd go to Khrushchev with a stick of marijuana and together lie down listen to Bach as though we were dead to the world. [. . .]

In poem I kept in, Death sucked me off because I now realize that I wrote it with much feeling—I sent *Greece* (the final entire poem of *Birthday's End*) to *New Departures* printed in England for publication.

Tennessee Williams looked into my eyes and said "YOU MUST LIVE!"—death is a big thing with him. I tried to explain to him that the death I was going through was not suicidal but a probe. That death (its subject) at first fascinated me and I played with it (as you can see in DEATH poem) and then the sudden realization that by probing it I might well get into it and even go beyond it, and I feel I did that in Hydra—but I think he sees the kind of death I see, even the surface is his bad heart, my surface was a car—we had long talks about this; but I don't think he understood me because all he would say is "YOU MUST LIVE." Anyway Delight—eternally toward delight.

Best, Gregory

To Allen Ginsberg

Athens
[Nov. 19] 1959

Dear Allen,

Can you beg somebody for me, even ten dollars would do somehow. Am down to God, and he's my last button. *Van Gogh's Ear*,[175] great. Hello Peter—am stranded again. You and I still refuse to die—on with BEGGARY!

Love, Gregory

To Lawrence Ferlinghetti

Athens
[Nov. 30] 1959

Just a line to let you know that you is my only shameless source of income, whereby I everybodies beg or so. Anyway *Time* magazine says you owes me rolling dough. Greece is cheap place to live, so I don't need much. I just finished proofs for New Directions. Am writing Greek poems, seeing antiquity and am feeling older somehow—or are you on your trip?

Love, Gregory

To Allen Ginsberg

Athens
[Dec. 2] 1959

I got the $10. Thank you, sorry to bug thee. All's manifest. Have a good Xmas you and Peter. And so—you needn't feel obligated or compelled or necessary to reply the Hydra spook. Write of N.Y.C. and the scene, and Chile and cats and Peter, Jack.

Gregory

To Lawrence Ferlinghetti

Athens
[Dec. 2] 1959

Larry,

So happy you came thru, good man. I am well and for first time in years, rearing to go. So—I'll send you poems too, you send me yours. No Chinese on Acropolis.

Gregory

To Lawrence Ferlinghetti

Athens
[Dec. 7] 1959

Dear L,

Here I am again in front of the Bank of America. Had a nice time with Tennessee Williams here, much drink and talk and fights. How was reading trip and I only kid you about *Time* saying I is making a lot of money and dat you is done finagling me, anyway when I want money SEND IT TO ME or else

I will sic the gritty goo-muse on thee, and thou shall be stink-poesy. How's your wife, any babies yet? Why no you leave printing in udder hands and come to Greece and maybe join me in journeying?

To Don Allen Athens
[Dec. 8] 1959

Dear Don,

There's no winter in Athens, always sun, sometimes wind—yet I'd give anything for winter in Amsterdam. Winter is nice; you shouldn't envy my winterless winter; did you ever notice how goofy those people who live in Miami or Los Angeles are? It's because they run away from winter. You got to have the four seasons—it's childish and being spoiled not to want all four of them or to want more of one.

And why don't you have rent to pay? A man of your stature and bearing will not allow himself the trivial experience of where-am-I-going-to-get-the-rent thoughts; your thoughts are clear straight Eastern cool thoughts; you'd not want the landlady scratching on your door: "Mr. Allen! I WANT MY RENT!!!!"—You with your soft voice and delicate aging ears will not allow yourself the monster-situations of life, such as: Borrowing two dollars from the bigmouthed photographer who sits in cafes and chases girls, and never paying him back, and he goes screaming to everyone, "DON ALLEN OWES ME TWO DOLLARS!" or, ringing a false fire alarm, or, lock your door and buy a big turkey, smoked and ready to eat, and eat it all yourself.

All the work you put in your anthology will prove itself; there is no real modern American anthology, anthologies usually consist of history or centuries—you've got a decade anthology; not many decades can boast an anthology. You say you've been working on the anthology when you should be doing something else; good, that feeling usually means you are done with your work at present and will go on to new work, or a nice two weeks in the Fiji islands with lots of friends and drinks and sun and sea and FUN. This pleasure is usually pleasured by those unlike you; those who write or work or anthologize for the kicks of the accomplishment, not for the doing. Is not the writer the judge of his doing? Take Norman Mailer, everytime he finishes a book, he has a big celebration, scotch gin bourbon wine cheesebit olives. Now will you alot yourself this when you finish your anthology? You asked for a comment on my way with poesy. I know no way. I just write. I love to write. Life is great in that it allows me such love. A great big screwed-up love.

Merry Xmas and a happy new year and now is the time for big decisions—a year to commit oneself to, 1960; a new decade, what took centuries to formulate the era or epoch of history, now takes a decade; what will 1960 be like?

I'm going to watch it. Love, bright Sherlock of fog and thin nose and pipe and blue green grey eyes. Funny how I like writing letters to you, yet when faced with you I shy away. Means maybe I am an agnostic misanthrope, or a gregarious hermit, or a blinking rocking horse.

Gregory

To Lawrence Ferlinghetti

Athens
[ca. Dec. 18] 1959

Dear Larry,

Thanks for check. I saw Ike today pass by, lots of U.S. flags here in Athens for his arrival. Had a drink with Primo Carnera,[176] very strange. Dug your *Dragon*.[177] Send me [Bob] Kaufman's poems. What's happening in good old S.F.? How was Chicago? I may return to Paris, will let you know. Merry Xmas to you and your wife.

Love, Gregory

What does theological tennis mean? Here's a poem: "The night horn blow / The sunfly bless / Prince and princess / Gone the winged children / the rabbit / the afterglow."

To James Laughlin

Athens
[ca. Dec. 18] 1959

Hello,

Merry Xmas, good New Year. Saw Ike pass by today, was a nice feeling to see him amid flags and crowds, God, I'd like to see *HBOD* off the press, would like the feeling of something done. I think I might go to Paris, been here two months. I will let you know immediately when I do go. I've more poems, I'll send them on. *Greece* poem has been re-worked—though the copy you have will be published in England as is. Had a drink with Primo Carnera (the fighter) what a strange experience, his hand is ten times the size of mine!

Best, Gregory

To Allen Ginsberg, Peter Orlovsky, and Jack Kerouac

Athens
[Dec. 19] 1959

Dear Allen, Peter, Jack,

Am off to Paris this eve. Merry Xmas and New Years dear angels. Dear to my heart / dear to the night-hour the sun fly / the prize of noel. Goodbye Greece—Was mine. All's well,

Love

LEFT: Gregory Corso and Allen Ginsberg in Times Square photo booth, early 1950s.
© Allen Ginsberg Trust

RIGHT: Corso in his tiny attic room at "The Beat Hotel", 9 Rue Git-Le-Coeur, Paris, 1958.
© Allen Ginsberg Trust

LEFT: Corso posing for souvenir photo in front of the Parthenon on the Acropolis, Athens, 1961.
Courtesy Allen Ginsberg Trust

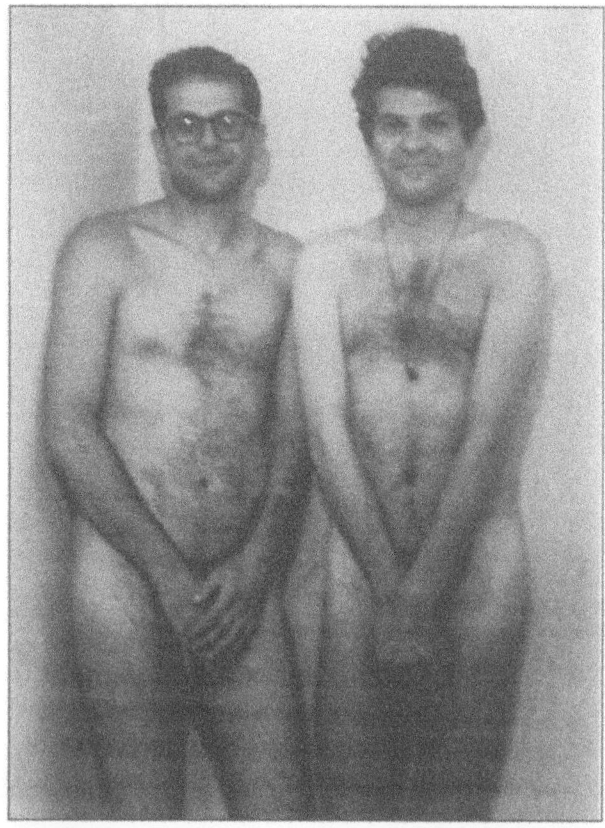

ABOVE: Peter Orlovsky (seated), William Burroughs, Allen Ginsberg, Alan Ansen, Gregory Corso (with sunglasses), Ian Sommerville and Paul Bowles (on ground) in Burroughs' garden, Tangier, Morocco, July 1961.

LEFT: A modest portrait, Ginsberg and Corso in their room, Tangier, Morocco, July 1961.

ABOVE:
Corso reading at Albert Hall, London, June 11, 1965.
Courtesy Allen Ginsberg Trust

RIGHT:
Ginsberg and Corso in front of Ginsberg's farmhouse retreat near Cherry Valley, NY, 1970.
© Allen Ginsberg Trust

LEFT: Corso in Lowell, MA, beneath the crucifix described by Jack Kerouac in his novel, *Doctor Sax,* March 17, 1986.

BOTTOM: Kaye McDonough holding their son, Nile, with Gregory Corso in their North Beach apartment, San Francisco, October 1984.

To Allen Ginsberg Paris
[Dec. 24] 1959

Dear Allen,

I love you, and I am agreed you are the greatest man alive today. A poem for the realization you have given me; not that Hydra realization which was just a Hollywood prop, a stage setting.

> "The Bomb prevents war / History ends / In the Beginning the desire to go back / has been fulfilled / We now begin / The height of elevation is Heaven / Heaven is the end of history / The history of Life and Time is done / We are in Heaven / and / Heaven is a familiar place."

You see! The bomb eliminates war, no war eliminates history, no history eliminates Time, no Time eliminates Death, no Death is immortality. We, the Beats, have been the final rebels of Life. All is golden. I am happy here with Burroughs, thank God I left Greece. I wish you were here, ah but you are.

Gregory

Peter Peter, read Mother Goose now that all is well.

To James Laughlin Paris
[ca. Dec. 25] 1959

Dear JL,

Arrived in Paris. Paris is lovely. I love it more than any city now, I really do. Felt so great walking in and out and around the gray little streets again. I immediately went to see Burroughs. After awhile he showed me the *Life* article. I read it quickly and thought "another down article". Then Burroughs asked me "Did you read it?" I said yes. Sensing my indifferent reaction he said "Read it again". I read it again, and what I read frightened me. How sinister and real! Did you read it? I asked myself "Is this the Beat Generation?" And I couldn't find a no in me. I read the article and asked myself what has night-horns sun-flies tons of dried fire to do with this big dark article? Here is no poetry, here is Stalin Trotsky politics, a no-politics politics; I read the article and I didn't know the Ginsberg the Kerouac he was writing about, mostly the Ginsberg who he set up as a raving intentional system breaker, how he must despise Allen! And Allen is all good, (doth the cause of such despite stem from that?) Then I began to wonder about myself. These last three months in Greece affected me very much, my last shakings of Death-probe, with the result of a ordinary stage prop illumination on Hydra; I was broken up after that because I went into Death and came out of it with a creation of invisibility, with a Hollywood powder-puff vision, if it were any vision at all. All right. I immediately dashed off that poem *Birthday's End*, it was a nowhere poem and it rated the "vision"; I, of course, being myself wanted better, so I "created" by use of poetry, an even worse poem, *Greece*, I "covered up" *Death* with *Greece*. Well I am very true to myself and I knew it wouldn't do. The best thing was to forget it, read mother goose, and I did.

I read the article as lightly as I have always taken the Beat Generation, I always made jokes or fantasies about it; I did not see what Kerouac or Ginsberg saw, or what the interviewers from *Arts*, French art paper here, saw. They interviewed Burroughs and myself last night, and asked such questions as: "Do you hate police?" "What do you think of surrealism?" They were probing for surrealism, that was the big thing, they were very good friends of Breton, and they wanted to get me to say the Beat Generation is founded on surrealism, because where surrealism left off, the Beats executed. It was strange, because all he wanted me to say was "hate" "against", and I told him no, I think cops are a necessary evil; I don't think surrealism has anything to do with Beat, surrealism was a social clique, keeping its surreal for themselves, not for the man who sells *poisson*, whereas the Beat claim that it is possible for any man to write a poem, even a great one at that, if he only "free" himself. "Beat is surely a movement and dangerously politic, such that it can annoy both existing powerful systems". After that I went upstairs with Burroughs and he showed me the *Life* article, and it all came clear to me, and I have written that poem I tried so foolishly to write under the dupe of death.

(I must clear time element) I came to Paris last night, Burroughs showed me *Life* article, I read it casually, went to sleep, next day word got round I was back, the photographers of *Arts* and the interviewers came to the hotel; Burroughs introduced me to them, we spoke, then went to Burroughs' room where he showed me article again. This is main idea that came to me and allowed following poem, if there is a *Bomb* then it eliminates war, if war is eliminated, then history is eliminated, if history is eliminated then Time is eliminated if Time is eliminated then we are immortal. I have never been more happy in my whole life. Here is poem:

> The Bomb prevents war / History ends / In the Beginning the desire to go <u>back</u> / has been fulfilled / We now begin / The height of elevation is Heaven / Heaven is the end of history / The history of Life and Time is done / We are in Heaven / And / Heaven is a <u>familiar</u> place / The night-horn blow / The sun-fly bless / Prince and princess / The universe's property / now disproportioned / Gone the winged children / The rabbit / The afterglow.

And so good tall kind sir who saw me in natural poesy, my last poem. I will continue to write, but what I'll write will be useless to what has already been done; I should feel very proud and happy of being a part of what has been done, nay not a part, but a cause. And I am happy. The thing now is, go beyond poetry. And so now that history is ended, now that immortality is before us, gather ye your rosebuds with eternal delay.

James is it not true that WITHOUT war all existing governments will fall? Please write to me about this, for if it is so, then I shall look upon the Beat Generation with new eyes; yet will I ever get over this antipathy I have for sandals and beards and beat pad life? One last thing, out of that *Life* article I also got this: Luce is God. He owns LIFE TIME and CHANCE (Fortune). In *Life* he is all strong, in *Time* he can write about something before it even happens! He made the Beat Generation! In the article O'Niel asks "How did this all come about?" And why did Luce make the Beat Generation? Because he is God and he knew that Beat would find that out and DID, so he choose Beat for his chess mate, thus CHANCE, here he was not all powerful, here he could LOSE, and did. That is why I say history is ended. There is no stopping this Beat thing, we simply do not verge or fall into a new era, eras are ended, done. Also consider this, in article Kerouac is "raised" so to speak to the "granddaddy" of the Beats, a genteel level, a quiet harmless level; Kerouac has made much money and has never really been Beat and has done his duty as informing the public of Beat—whereas the real sinisterism is the replica of Ginsberg; I know Ginsberg very well, that bearded picture in *Life* is NOT Ginsberg; I have received his last letters KNOWING it is not Ginsberg; Luce has made a replica of him. Remember Lorca: "I am no longer what I am, the house I own is not mine to sell"—I may be going a little too far, yet you can't deny I am close as to be burned of the Truth.

Well. And now what do all this mean to poetry, let's say my poetry; if all is done as I see it, what use the publication of *Happy Birthday*; what can it mean or say or do? Surely now I see that that poetry was not meant to entertain, but to mean and do; how do when do is done? In practical sense the book will sell, if anything, let's say as you publisher and I author, we have a book that will sell; and that's as far as it goes. I would like to see book published, my best poems are in that book, but it is too late; I think you can understand what I mean by this. I have been very straight with you; I await your reply; I never felt so clear of mind and body; even my face looks younger. I have achieved certainty.

Noel, Gregory

I dare not re-read this letter for fear of not sending it. So where is that achievement of certainty after all? O Gregory!

I did re-read it and damn it I am certain, and one thing I forgot in that article notice how they say of me GUNS—*Don't Shoot The Warthog, Bomb*, in photo: Corso aims as if to SHOOT—also notice, photo of Ginsberg lying in bed, the Sitwell "bad smell" comment, next to Ginsberg photo is an ad "how to get rid of bad smell from the house." I was with Allen when we saw Sitwell and she mentioned nothing of odor and had a fine lunch and spoke only of poetry. But that's minor. Of the article—it was more than an article, it was a great declaration of defeat,—Luce may be God but he is a failure God—and end result, in Heaven there is no God. I could go on for hours. I'd best go back to Mother Goose.

To James Laughlin Paris

[ca. Dec. 26] 1959

Dear JL,

I enclose article to show thee that I didn't remain too serious about Luce realization. If you wish to use *Greece* poem for *New Directions 17*, then send it back to me for rework, for I have no copy, the English magazine is not due yet and they have other copy.

Great news for me, the poems in *Big Table* won me 300 dollars, Longview Foundation Inc.; do you know them? Anyway it came in time as I owed rent in Greece and the landlady was going to go to the American embassy. I think I'm somewhat of an alarmist, because what I felt to be the end of history has deceived me; all this recent Jew flu that's spreading; can it be that man will never love the Jew? What remedy then? Has there been a liberal Jew who has denied his son circumcision? Heine denied Judaism and WAS German. Do people hate Jews because Jews refuse to blend and become of the country they inhabit? Let's say like me, I am of Italian descent, yet I claim America, and think of myself as American. Or could it be a big conspiracy of mother-love? Jews love their mothers and are led by them. I spoke to Art Buchwald about it, we had a long talk, and we went over all these points, yet we were both left with the feeling that the imagination could never comprehend the sum-total of human suffering caused by humanity. Is it STILL the Germans and their Goddamned angel of history, their metaphysical Nordic balderdash? Perhaps, like Art said, they're giving it too much publicity and thus crackpots come to the fore and perpetuate it. This is not the flower I thought held for the coming '60s. Anyway, the dire illumination did show me that poetry is never ended; and so I shall not abandon it.

I won an award, my second one, my first one was when I was 14 in a Catholic boys home, 1945 when I wrote an essay on the deaths of Mussolini, Roosevelt, Hitler, on their having all died in April.

Your friend, Gregory

To Allen Ginsberg Paris
[Jan. 4] 1960

Dear Allen,

Great to hear from you and good God don't listen to rumors or gossip yet in both is deal of truth; yet know there are forces that would see us split in aughs and spikes. Why don't you get [Edith] Sitwell to verify what was not said, for I swear it is unlike me to say such a thing; and surely she did not say it, unless she's a real witch, because she doth praise thee as seen in mag called *Lilliput*. People here saying I say you sold-out, when all I say is that you is become a replica, that Luce hath your words, and that he now can put forth a Ginsberg, as well he could a Shakespeare, and beware Rosalind Constable for she did say to one here that she is "DEVOTED" to Allen. I enclose article in which I expose all.

Bill on very interesting and bombshell way with new poetry,[178] he told you about it yet you dismissed it, when I really think you should write to him about it because it is revolutionary; what takes three hours to come out with some images, he has brung it down to three seconds.

What's all this Jew flu that's spreading around? Can it be really the Jew again? Why always the Jew? Is it because they won't blend, because they hold class and separation and do not want to join or become what they are surrounded by? Are people jealous of them? Can it be that man will never love the Jew? And I thought the millennium had begun.

Peter? Saw [John] Ashbery, James Jones, James Baldwin and Octavio Paz, Ashbery nice sincere great, Jones a simple giant man, Baldwin is, and Paz quite young. Chile, then what? Will we ever see one another again? Is film to be shown[179] and if it makes loot will we get some? And I forgive Kerouac his parsimony, yet can't yet forgive his beauty. Now please know that by your last letter you is become unreplica'd in my eyes. Poor Stanley Gould. When is my book coming out? Go up to New Directions for me and release their hoard. Huncke, good. Can you send me or get Jones to send me *Yugen* 4 and 5, and Smith article in *Escapade*, and any other nice little things. That *Life* article sinister-real, yet *Life's* downfall, for you have out stepped them.

Love, Gregory

To Peter Orlovsky Paris
[ca. Feb. 1] 1960

Dear Peter,

Could you please ship me regular mail all my writings I left in box there in my room? Try to sort out the letters and unnecessaries, as all I NEED is the prose and poetry and plays; please as I am compiling a book, and hope to have it in order for publication soon. I know I have much there and it would take a ton weight off my muse's mind if I had them here. Please do this for me as soon as possible.

Tonight I give a poesy reading here with some French boys and maybe something will happen here; only reason I'm reading with them. I can't read to jazz so won't, but they will; it should be interesting, as it has not been done here since the beginning of the war; I think. How is you and 170 East 2nd Street? and the cats? Bill here and mystique as ever. I wrote to Allen in Chile; he must be having mad trip down there, you well might be with him so I hope somebody else there in pad maybe read this letter and send me the things I need. I want all my manuscripts; I need them badly.

Love, Gregory

To LeRoi and Hettie Jones Paris
[Feb. 4] 1960

Dear LeRoi and Hettie,

1st — Happy to learn Kellie[180] is beautiful and pray she makes womankind surmount the ridiculous mankind plain.

2nd — Don Allen's anthology a landmark, your poems great and lovely, but your statement and everybody's meaningless in that they are for ones self, stational, and all stanchioned things can be knocked down once you take a position.

3rd — All positions must be contradicted, else its bullshit.

4th — Levertov's statement so fucking unpoetry, cold witches tit, yet she writes nice. O'Hara's the best statement. Yours was dictatorial, Olson's like W.C.W. organizes, Duncan's agonizes. But all the poems ARE GREAT. What with all them statements on poetics, one would think the new American poetry was very Christian indeed. Pound finally given his exact light, as Olson surely has learned from him. But what is there to learn? If one need learn poetics, then . . . Long live the new American poesy. Let no bombs fall—China, / birds, / babies. Creeley is wonderful lyricist, *basta*.

Goodbye, yours as you will have me, Gregory

To James Laughlin Paris
[Feb. 7] 1960

Dear JL,

I would appreciate it if you would mail back to me all the poems you have of mine that are not to be in *Happy Birthday*, that is, the Venice batch, don't know what else you have. I would like to see them again, and have them around, because a lot of little magazines are asking me for poems, and I haven't any. And now that I am busy on prose, I'd not like to reprint poems already printed. Most [of] those Venice poems have not been printed. Hope this doesn't inconvenience you.

Will *HBOD* ever see light? It would do much for my heart if, instead of Gregory Corso Beatnik appearing in print, my poetry did. Hope my past letters haven't disturbed you. You mustn't take them seriously, because I am both serious and not—maybe I'm a bad writer who knows not how to convey. Anyway—all is fine.

Best, Gregory

To Allen Ginsberg, Peter and Lafcadio Orlovsky, Herbert Huncke Paris [Feb. 20] 1960

Dear Allen and Peter and Lafcadio and Huncke,

How are all of thee? I would like to come home, so if I think of coming home, will I? Now does Peter want me to come home? or will he think a future again of my cats and bitter practice? or will I just sit in my room no longer and say not a word but look back on somebody else's childhood for a change? Whatever, I think to come home.

My mood is ironic in that I am without complaint now, now that I have the freshness of a vision, and that is, Allen did see what Bill did see, and I have yet to see, but had to in Hydra scream, "Allen no see," because then I thought sure to get some transfigured situation. Yes. But if I do come home please no tell anyone as I want it secret for passport reasons and when I leave boat I leave unknown but though to thee; yet I need the fare, the money and so wrote to de Kooning who has been so nice to me and who calleth me his son, so I pray I no take advantage of all, which I never do, and guilt hath never been with me, but it cometh only because I think. I am writing poems about love, a subject so alien to me, yet I am writing about it, and am feeling it all. Peter must know me to divide what he thinketh with what he feels, as I say in love poem, the absence of she be ever in my presence more– so am I in the presence of Peter? and Lafcadio must know that when we leave time consciousness, we will go into space consciousness, and lo space is not spacious, o there is room for only one in space, because in time-life we have much time to spare, but in space-life we only got one space to spare, and that's the spot we are standing in, so room for only one, and who fits in that single spot, be God, and so Lafcadio sinister scheme. And Huncke, I would love to get to know Huncke, and see Irving again, and now I am so older nicer too. Well, do I fit to return? do I sound as though I am ready for the look of thee? and again like in love poem, I sayeth; unlike the noble wrist that waits the dun hawk, I can only hold what has flown. All of you have flown from me, will you not land again? My wrist is held out–I wait.

Last night I dreamed Khrushchev had bongo drums, of all things! bongo drums, something I never cared for, but he had them and sat by me like a father, so what means that? If you guys don't get me home I'll go and join the Reds and say bad things about you all! This is a threat! Allen's magic poem is a guided progress of vision, one with intense feeling of the Adar[181] June Plot of Zion!

O echoes of axes! What news? Am I yet gossiped about? O so many things said of me, that I feign to believe them anymore, for surely anything said of me is true but NOT REALLY; so what have you heard? Tell me all you emotional emotional knights of glimpse and deterioration! You common man! You last hundred years! You institutional New Year's Eve party poems! You hairy fishes! Peter is a fucking moron who knows nothing of the astrological rejection of neo-Platonism! and Lafcadio is a pimply assed Tartar of cosmic disaster! and Allen is the goat-shit cloak of a monk! And I? I can only say like Rilke: "What will you do, God, if I die. I am your jug (what if I am smashed) I am your drink (what if I go bad?) I am your cloak and your trade, if you lose me you lose your purpose." If I come home everything will be great and strong again. The rooms will be illumined and the icebox will be consumed, the beds will be warm and the walls will listen once again; and in the streets a people will gather and look up at the window and looking up will give them chance to gaze at heaven—so!

Or should I go to Warsaw first? But I want home, want it very much; so write to me and say what you all think. My heart goes out to my very dear friends.

Love, Gregory

To Lawrence Ferlinghetti Paris

[ca. March 6] 1960

Dear Larry,

Could you please transfer [George] Whitman's bill for 24 dollars on my royalty bill plus an additional ten *Howls* and 30 *Gasolines*? Send to me, 9 rue Git-le-Coeur, because George, is having a Durrell Baldwin Jones Wright Genet Corso signing autography day. Before March 18. Thank you. Ship the day you get this letter. Please, baby. As for me, I am giving poesy reading with four young poets here, all American—should maybe stand something here—as Paris is quite quiet. [John] Ciardi says we are dead.[182]

"What thunder you / The Saturday review? / Sta say you are dead / or no hadda you read? / Sta say No more the Beat / They's a lies and a cheat." Anyway as Mark Twain says, "Rumors of my death are grossly exaggerated." The Big Guns are now upon us - BOOM! but Boom was a sound of the 50's - neo 60's.

Love, Gregory

To James Laughlin

Florence
[March 8] 1960

Dear JL,

I had a dream in which you said that you felt I was a great poet, and when you said that, I said, OK, if you really feel that then send me to India, and you said that you would, plus an allowance of that I wouldn't go hungry there; and you said "Yes." But also in the dream listening in was a man named Philip Brooks, he runs the American Library in Paris, and he was the villain of the dream because he shook his head no at you—and that was the dream. I wish it would have been someone else other than you because whenever I was asked who's printing publishing your book I said You, and most of them shook their heads and said that you were a tough man with gold, and so forth. Anyway that was the dream, and when I woke up, I said "YES THAT IS WHAT I WANT." So are you going to do it or not? If not I'll find a way, because now I think it is the greatest thing I can do before returning to America, and I want to return. I haven't seen *HBOD* yet, and can't wait to see it—I gave up the prose venture, as I am a poet and no more, except that I can paint quite largely. I am in Florence and I met a nice American girl, and so all is well. Yes, everybody, well most everybody I met in New York before I came to Europe, when I told them I gave book to you said you were a wrong one to give it to because you were unfair to poets; I thought it very funny, and you haven't been unfair to me, and even if you don't follow up on this dream, I will still look upon you as a fair man, because you are a poet: but aside from poesy, you said to me when I was in your office "READ THE CONTRACT," so I did, and I remember it; and in it it said March 1960 you will give me an estimate of how much I am due by sale of book; well you haven't given me that estimate, so can I, on legal, not friendly, grounds demand from you an estimate, which of course will be nil. *Basta*, I just want to show you I'm not stupid about these matters, and know that I literally go hungry here at times, which has become a bother because I'm going to be 30 soon, and have had enough of such days; I think you owe me some WATCHING O'ER. (?) Well maybe book will sell well so that what would be coming to me from you would be deservedly mine; but it has been so long; that is why I am a little upset with you, because you didn't even consider that. Can you air mail a book to me at Florence American Express? I've been moving around very much lately; there's a lady translator in Milan who would like to translate *HBOD*, so I gave her your address, she knows you through correspondence, Fernanda Pivano,[183] a very nice lady. Again missed Roditi, he's now in Greece; maybe fate means it so.

You and I in same French anthology; nice. I gave a reading with four young French poets two weeks ago, and great crowds, first time since here, and first event with jazz, they read to jazz, I couldn't as I don't believe in it; and audience had [Tristan] Tzara, James Jones, Bill Styron, Styron is a fine man, and a whole bunch of people. It was a big success, I read my *Marriage* poem and flipped everybody, lots of Americans there; the French are all screwed up because of their language, the 40 men in the Academy hold on to the language, no change possible: that's why English is so great, it can be changed augmented twisted, everything! In other words, these French kids have the ideas but can't express it in their old tongue. Nothing is happening with the young in Florence either, they're still pecking away at the cadaver of Lorenzo. That Paris reading was a success, and free admission; but then when some people saw the big crowds, they wanted me to do it all over again, once a week, with the French kids, and that bugged me because I felt they took me as some kind of entertainer, whereas my main intention for the reading was perhaps to start poetry readings FRENCH rolling in quiet Paris; I know why Paris Florence etc. are quiet, it's because they are hung on politics, and politics 1960 is death. Youth should put its energy in other than that bloody kitchen mess. I think the best way to end politics is to ignore it: I am happy, are you happy, if you don't want to send me to India, all right, just don't mention it; I will get there anyway; but if book sells right away then advance me there; also, again; and I've been thinking much about this; what if Ahab <u>had</u> killed the white whale?

Don't get any taller, Gregory

I'm writing a long poem on Italy which begins: "Because I was not Italy / yet desired to live there and did / but shortly, for, like most places of history, / the glory that was, was no longer . . ." Ned Erbe has good sense of poesy as his choice of poems sent to me were the ones I liked too, the others were really awful—still, as I once told Ginsberg, even when my poems are awful, they're o.k. because they're weirdly awful. Can you send me Levertov's book? I don't like female poets, and she's no exception—but I should read it.

▼ [Corso had just received the first copy of his book, *The Happy Birthday of Death* when he wrote the following letter.]

To James Laughlin

Florence
[March 21] 1960

Dear JL,

What a lovely book! The cover is mad! A great cover, should scare even Boris Karloff; really great; thank you; so the bomb had to be else the cover wouldn't have been; the candle will always be—all good, really a nice looking book, and how funny I felt seeing it, kind of proud and all that, and walked away from the American Express with a silly smile on my face; thanks too for check, I got them both together, and when I went to manager's office in Amer Express I showed him check and then came up an American tourist who interrupted us and thanked the manager for introducing his wife to some doctor because she was getting too knock-kneed or something, anyway the manager asked for proof if your publishing firm was a secure one, so I showed him the book, and the American said: "Wow! Get that title!" and I said "It's a happy book, really" and he looked at me kind of oddly, and said to the manager "Well, at least he speaks English" and the manager promptly ok'd the check. So, all is well. As for your being a patron, it would be funny, and unique! as I don't recall a poet patronizing another poet, can you? But I did get what I wanted, some money, and you did send it, so now I can stay in lovely Florence; I really like it here, and wrote the longest poem I ever wrote, in two days, 309 lines, called *St. Francis*, inspired by Giotto's paintings of him. What's written on back of book quite noble and nice—God you don't know how happy it made me feel, I mean, the important thing is in writing the poems, there is all the feeling, but I can't help feeling the added joy of seeing it in print.

I met Elisabeth Borgese, Thomas Mann's daughter, she knows you and calls you very sensitive being, and she too is a sensitive being, and I imagine quite deep; I live about one hundred yards from her in Fiesole, in a nice villa with poet Arnold Weinstein, whose poetry is quite good; also met Alan Weinbaum [sic—Mandelbaum] I think that's his last name, don't remember, he translated Ungaretti for you; also nice soul. So everybody is nice, and I am become nice, and anthology we are in is Bosquet one. God I wonder how *HBOD* will be received, should be interesting to see, so let me know everything. Life continues, and I'll continue as one of its wheels.

Best, and thanks again, Gregory

Dear Ned,

So I got book and you didn't, I sent it off long (two copies) long time ago, must have been held up, also sent one to Orlovsky and he hasn't received it either, I will write to Burroughs to ask him to venture again—The book is really marvelous, it should shatter the store windows, no dud there—Palmistry?[184] Why not? Send the kit. I once knew a feet reader, but it was embarrassing; hands are easier, and—well, no sense going into that—Did you meet Buchwald? He's all right; great Jewish wit; and when I see him I always get very funny with him. I don't like writing prose; I don't know how; I find it a waste of time; I find it slow; uninspired; play all right, but prefer poesy; and so poesy.

I think that cover on *HBOD* is the best and wildest cover I ever did see on poesy book; and the candle great idea in contrast to bomb. Isn't it great about Chessman?[185] I mean, this is a funny age, things really are beginning to happen—in my St. Francis poem, the Giotto of St. Francis chasing the demons out of the city, I have prisons being chased out of the city—actually I'd like to be back in America and see if there is really as much crime going on as their used to; when crime ends, the *Daily Mirror* and *News* will end, or visa versa—Melville was right, it is easy to imagine the whale being killed, but not killed, well that's something else; as it is easy to imagine the bomb falling, but not falling—again something else.

Love, Gregory

To Peter Orlovsky Paris

April 1, 1960

Dear Peter,

Thanx for everything you have been wonderful to me and that's nice because everybody else here treats me like freak goof soul unlike jealous poems but waynik in life so I flipped many times in front of people and they laugh, no way out but to leave them forever yet return to kiss them, but God, some times it's hard to love them and I don't but now ok because I see earth as heaven, this here place is heaven, and in this heaven there is a hell; and it wasn't heaven that came to me because heaven was always with me, but hell, and that hell so new to me, and so old to itself, I wrote a poem about it, called every man God, that was the death I was seeking, the thing behind that death, and this I found out, that we is in heaven that we is bad, and wow how crazy and nice. . ..I stay alone a lot now because you know me, how I am and be and can't face people now with all this beaternity; hail. Got poems yes and all other things you sent, in my new book did you see in poem where on typewriter you wrote last line? "To out the door yard hunk junk crab spring figoooo?" I left it in. If come to NY a girl named Jeanie Knight, she from Denver, a female Neal, she is my angel, 18, and please see that she is taken care of all right in our good old 170 E 2nd St. fashion; and I don't mean orgies--ha! any more of them there things going on? I haven't had sex in years; miss it and don't. Well if Huncke is reading that book o mine then I'm sure he's bound to dig the poem *1953*, don't know why I called it that. All them cats! How many five? and no Siamese ones? good God what must the house be like ! Please do this for my right away send a letter not a card to Miss Jeanie Knight, 2350 Colorado Blvd, Denver 7, Colorado USA; and make her feel welcome as she's never been to the big city before and it will help her trip there immensely if you give her love-voyage--she is really a wonderful girl--says she's going to give birth to the second coming.

I hope I get enough loot and maybe come back home, I'd like to rest, but can I rest there? I fear wild ridiculous end, which is all right, but if I see heaven now then all is ok. No fear. What say you? This girl is so much like Sura to me, how nice.

Yours, Gregory

Read Loewinsohn's *Watermelons* very great poesy there.

To Peter Orlovsky Paris

April 19, 1960

Dear Peter,

Please air mail me *Yugen* 6. I should zoom to Allen in South America and would it I had the gold because here I am all alone, and am in deep reflection of faith in all of us. Yelled at Burroughs for being the world's number one stool-pigeon which of course he ain't.

Love, Gregory

To Peter Orlovsky Paris

[ca. April 19] 1960

Dear Peter [and Allen],

I don't know where to write to Allen, since he and I have been moving around. I wrote him a while back, long letter, wonder if he got it? Anyway, send this letter on to him please. Glad to hear de Kooning and Lucien making it, de Kooning is a fine man.

Allen, India and Red China, great.[186] Will be strong and able for that now. Went thru one year of complete hell for such a soul as I who has known hell to be heaven, that is my youth and all its dealing. Now at 30, I realize where I am at—and so, no big confessional letter, but a word that I am re-proud and full-bodied, deep breathing, and all set to continue on golden ventures.

I had it out with Burroughs, his ass-licking friends are bores and they hate, and he, Bill, is O.K. but he does not know me. He tries to hypnotize me, con me into his beliefs etc. So much bullshit really, when you get down to it. Anyway I go to have lunch with him today, so alls well, though I must confess I used to take his say, his word, as IT, which of course was very unlike me. Man is man, and all that has been said has been said by man, so! If God then man is God, because he creates it. Man needs a limit and so calls that limit God. So anyway I gave dictatorial Burroughs a piece of my east side mind etc. Lots of fun, fire, finality. *St. Francis* poem, let it wait. In Florence a man will print it with eight Giotto color prints, the poem, 310 lines is broken up into eight sections: St. Francis and birds, miracle of water, giving of garment, Frate Leone's vision of St. Francis' ethereal throne, Pope's dream of St. Francis holding up church, full portrait of Francis, St. Fran chasing demons out of city, Stigmata. Of course the poem says not much about the paintings—for instance, for the chasing of the demons, I write about chasing the prisons out of the city, etc.

Can't wait to see *Kaddish*, when is it due? Read *Caw caw caw* in *Big Table*, lovely and good as any German music I ever heard. I met Romain Gary,[187] pop novelist and friends diplomats thru movie actress Jean Seberg,[188] she plays St. Joan. And God, what a nowhere world is theirs. I mean they are sweet and good people, as is all people, but their emotions reach a certain pitch, and that's it. Of course you know me with my romantic eye for celebs etc. Well, I've had it. I prefer the folks selling flannel shirts and shoes on the Quai. Lots to tell you—my drunks, my screams, my complaints, my poems, etc. Yet all is behind me, and the present looks great. I'm writing a long endless poem prose piece about everything I know—all paragraphs beginning with Joy! Both spontaneous and reflective—I try to sustain the vital Joy. So I am working and God I'd like to hear what's been happening to you? It's been a year since we last saw each other, long time. Jack wrote and thinks you and I don't know how it is to be Jack, whereas I wrote the angel that Jack should not consider his path ended but go on—instead of room light writing, and that besides he had loot to hide from Jack-fame, whereas we, or at least me, had to beg under Gregory-fame. Also feel Jack should come to India. If he say no, we kidnap him.

I've been thinking much about my letter to you from Greece, when I said Bill went through it and not you. I lied. Bill went through a physical life, the spiritual he made by drugs, or by magic balls, or by stigmatizing himself mystico. Whereas I did not deny you your Harlem visitation. I only wanted to connect the process. Why I had that in Greece, and why I've been so hard on poor Greece, was simply that I did not really expect to see ancient Greece, my dream of it, there and so raged there terribly, come horror whatever.

Anyway the *St. Francis* poem ends that probe experience whatever for me. What I see now is simple, the now, and the now being heaven. This is it, and it's great. I can only sing Joy and praise now. O.K. If India I will return to U.S.A. and get passport, and go straight.

Love, Gregory

To James Laughlin Paris

[ca. April 21] 1960

Dear JL,

Girodias of Olympia Press here, gives me fifteen thousand francs a week on which to live, and in return I promised him a book, this I did without your permission and under strain of not having to beg or steal—now I don't feel I did anything unethical but hasty, as it is kind of hard for me to beg or steal now that I am what I am—it's just downright awkward—but you will get that first novel from me, and I will definitely abide by contract and ethos—you have been very good to me—so. But I am at times a fuck-up, and as always it falls on my head. Now as for Olympia, I will not deny him either—not that I am machinery myself, but I do have much writing all it needs is to be typed up. Indeed there is a slight mess I got myself into, but I want to do right, especially now because I am very happy and see everything in life as great and wonderful. When I was sad and full of complaints I just didn't give a damn what I did. So, to prove my faith to you, I will each week send you my prose manuscript as I have been working hard easy and steadily. Contract with Girodias is for one year, and so I am sure that by the end of that year, if I keep working like I am, he too will be kept by my faith. So don't be mad with me, and write to me what you feel best to do about this situation I got myself into. I signed his contract two months ago, and was afraid to tell you. The prose I have for you I am sure you will like because it has everything that is in me in it—One big Hail! Yea! Joy! Spontaneous and reflective song.

I've been meeting many personages lately, Jean Seberg (actress), Romain Gary (odd man) and a famous young French actress who is very very lovely, and how strange it is, because she likes me, and I her, but she's married, so—and I'm not the one to interfere where there'll be hurt—so I just remain their friend, she and her husband, who's a very nice person. So! look at me with all this Hollywoodiana, and holes in my shoes. Its all right, because money is not really necessary where I am concerned, though at times I do need it. In prose manuscript I have a long hail on money, praising it, as it did formulate my life, as everyone's life, I guess. In Italy I almost got on a religious kick—but went through that too. So, I feel very much like a man. O.K. Give my best to Ned Erbe and I hope by now he got his copy of *Naked Lunch*.

Your friend, Gregory

Again thank you for a lovely job on *HBOD*.

To Lawrence Ferlinghetti Paris

[ca. April 25-27] 1960

Dear Larry,

Did you send the 30 *Gasolines*? George [Whitman] is still waiting for them. Thanks for liking my book, of course I knew you would. And I thought your *He* a real loving poem for a wonderful person.[189] But Death, etc. Death is not Allen's mission, he is not here to undertake the death of all the world - he is here because I wished it. No, really he is here because James Jones wished it. Anyway I'm off to live in Geneva, Suisse, so write to there, send *Gasoline* to George Whitman. You sent me bill, but no books. How's things?

Love, Gregory

Don't send books to Whitman, as he have to pay customs. Also the ten

Howls, send to me care of 9 rue Git-le-Coeur, and all will be taken care of. George is holding up autograph party until books get here - so urgent. O.K. Write Write Write. Work Work Work!

To Peter Orlovsky Geneva, Switzerland
[ca. May 2] 1960

Dear Peter,

Ah, but there is no problem with Jeanie Knight, as I don't know her but by my craziness of answering letters, and her letter to me was one of goodyouth sorrow and warmth, and so that kind of love, but I am hectic and can't think so of human life that wishes to HOLD what was felt yesterday was for yesterday, what is for today can be many things. I will write to her, for I don't know about coming back to New York; I want India, and if you and Allen are going to go I'll wait here; or maybe come back to go to India, but not to come back to a girl—I am done in a way with new human involvement; what I sorely need now is new ventures, new breath, and new talk with my dear friends. Burroughs is great, and he upsets me and makes me laugh and I he, so. Yes Jack should Hermes us to India, but Webster yet rages and is rightly direct in its direct. You know how I get myself involved with fold—even ones I don't know—O.K. God knows I'd like to come back to N.Y. and you and Allen and all. If I get up enough old Gregory then I shall. Also when is Allen coming back?

I am in peaceful Geneva, and trying to get all my writings together—but wish I were off on some wild crazy adventure—Remember? Like in Mexico or Amsterdam or Paris. Maybe we can all do that again in India. No, I doubt if my book will be reviewed, as I am only good for mock copy, yet what matters? The poetry is done, and that is all important, not what people have to say.

Did you get copy of *Naked Lunch* I sent to give to Ned Erbe at New Directions? Tell Laff he'll find all he wants to know in the American Indians the northern one, and that he should read about Liver-Eating Johnson, the Crow Indian killer—O.K.

Gregory

To James Laughlin Geneva, Switzerland
[ca. May 2] 1960

Dear JL,

Am in Geneva where all is peace and am settled and working enjoyably happily on book, big hail, yet down today because of [Caryl] Chessman and just can't understand this death-law when we came out of caves 25,000 years ago, and God but man has advanced so marvelously, and this I can't see, yet even if it is trite cause for emotion, for what is one death or death, but this death-law, that's something else, in that all the young who become lawyers must surely have some misgivings, don't know. But this "abnormal sex" attributed to him; then all sex is abnormal, and all of us should go to the gas chamber, and I enclose first poem I ever really went hog wild silly on words FUCK etc., anyway, today he died, and I feel funny as sure most men do. God, America, but perhaps it all closes down to this haiku: "50,000,000 buffalo / 900,000 Indians / white man."

Also received today Levertov's book, and she brought man in his glory back to me, for her poems are indeed great and high above low deathlaw. I was too hectic when I knew her, and we hardly spoke and, now for reflection, I wish I could speak to her now. If you see her, will you tell her how her book balanced the condition state of man this day? What a connection, she and deathlaw, but moldless, things still fit. It used to be that liberal souls heralded, all is right! there is no wrong! Ok, but 'all is right' has proven awful somehow.

I've been typing up my Greek poems and the poems written after, and I came across this poem:

> WRITTEN IN A GREEK ARENA / Long summer thoughts where marble stood / and fell / an eternal landscape; / here I stand and sit / if I would / unlike marble, ephemeral—/ Anchored to a long season / in a quick life / I am not wearied / nor feel the absence of former things / things unremembered in the memory / The relation to Time, the weak dream / its weaker success / my reaction to death / my lovelessness—/ When love came, all loving delight / grotesque it came, away at an angle, / like a devil light; / What rays on me is never full / Half dark forever / I hold love incapable—/ When these on my love side / map out my love / they yawn content in their Know / and seek out my other side / where no map can go . . .

This is fragment of poem, can't remember it all, yet can give the importance of poem's end: "When now to me all laws are unified / and the universe is no longer found in art / how oldstrange I'll be who has not died." So I look forward to a good white beard. Am reading Emerson, and find him extraordinary! Yes!

My best, Gregory

If Ned did not get *Naked Lunch*, then the post office is sharp and on the lookout! Ever read of Liver-Eatin' Johnson? He was a frontier man, a mountain man, killed 300 Crow Indians and ate their livers—much feared was he. Good old American heroics!

To Peter Orlovsky Geneva, Switzerland
[ca. May 16] 1960

Dear Peter,

Poor Siamese gone, alas, and your defending me, alas, for you should realize that whatever is said is said by men, all is o.k. Please send me *Journal American* article, should be funny to see, also send me Eighth Street anthology, would like to have that.[190] Got *Yugen*, yes. Burroughs in Copenhagen, I think I stay here for awhile. Hope you and Allen and Jack come here. Allen be back soon? Fine.

Gregory

To Don Allen Geneva, Switzerland?
[ca. May 20] 1960

Dear Don,

Just got your anthology yesterday and stayed up all night reading it and it WOKE me up to almost everybody you have in it as it is a great work of art and is definitely THE anthology and will be STANDARD. In fact maybe the last anthology if that whore peace doesn't seek the cock of the war. Whatever your selections were pinpointed as I myself have always liked the Marshall poem, and Ashbery's *Instruction* and Koch's *Fresh Air*, and Levertov's *PepperTrees* and Olson is really indicative, now I see, and CREELEY is beautiful and I like him best other than Allen and O'Hara, but all of them, Orlovsky is pure soul, Weiners genius soul, Loewinsohn should be president of USA, sensible good calm bright. The whole thing really, like I say, woke me up to the beauty being done by this millennium youth. Whereas before I was lost in that beard sandaled feet pad *Time* magazine man crazy world, and so thought nothing much. This anthology is exempt from that, and thank God for us and you, and do you still look like Sherlock Holmes or have you now sat back, the work done, take off your glasses, and let time be done? No more trails to follow?

Alan Ansen says it is a masterly selection, and authoritative, and possibly definitive. Everything is all right, no more Hydras, all is growing up, and nice. William Carlos Williams and Pound should be very pleased. Finally Olson is in right light. Any reaction? I think it's a big conspiracy! The question is what are people like Hollander and Merrill going say? I don't think they can deny this book. You left out Herman Borst! What are you up to? I'd like to hear from you. Do you believe as I that man stands apart from nature yet sustains all things in being? Do you believe as I, that war is sex in synthesis? I'm writing a long poem called *WAR*, and I use sex as war. Do you feel I know what I'm talking about? Bremser is straight, is he still in jail? Ok.

Goodbye, love, youse is a good man, Gregory

To James Laughlin Geneva, Switzerland
[ca. May 22] 1960

Dear JL,

Yes received Don Allen's great anthology, puts things in right light, little poesy conspiracies, Olson fixedness, tribute to William Carlos Williams Pound (eliminate influence Eliot per) as maestros, youth, more so Pound—Only just, poetic justice for poets?! But Levertov's statement (I feel any statement really on poesy is kind of dictatorial in that it as oft says THIS IS THE WAY or SHD be the way) makes a stance, and making a stance is being in a position, and positions are never enduring; the other side of the coin; therefore, best the whole coin, or no coin at all; who's to say, and why should poets say it; like talking about the ladder one climbs rather than the height one reaches—Kerouac's statement also statement; Ginsberg's most soul felt; Duncan's personal and dictatorial, O'Hara's statement trying to 'get out of it', LeRoi Jones' statement abandoned and I just can't take seriously, Ferlinghetti's completely out of context—this of course has only to do with STATEMENTS; as for the poems and the selections of poems, I think Don Allen has come out with a great reference anthology, and as I said, gives Pound his exactness, his poetic-just desserts. Though I must confess I have not gotten anything from these grand old men, William Carlos Williams, Pound; in fact, am not so keen on WCW's. I feel it is a sandbag that stops the flow; said it before will say it again, and there I go making statements, but I always do, and it's ok if I do because I'm apt to contradict, only make statements that you can contradict! I also saw *The Beats*,[191] and thought it stupid. Bad selections. Bad poets. I did not see the other. Send it?

Good about Girodias, he is very fine person. As for book, it is coming along; I have remained indoors for week now working like madman, really in it. I won't tell you what it's about right now, but will soon. How is your anthology coming along, I remember the big box at your desk side—it looked terrible! Did you cover it up? hide it? burn it? Things like that could become monsters, y'know. Wrote a long poem called *War*, begins—"War is sex in synthesis men against men shooting guns or dropping bombs due to the lack of combatable therefore actual evil . . ." "Death by cock bayonets wounds like wombs blood like babies Death in evening blitz two lovers in bed buzzbomb silence their orgasm suspended windows shattered no real damage the sirens clear the act goes on . . ." Also "War is death in which life is active / Peace is life in which life is inactive" and "Peace unlike war can never be legendary," and near end, to bring the idea that war is like sex, that peace is the whore, and war the whoremaster: "War can't go on war is weak war rests and peace jeers peace, huge and tireless, standing over war jeering tormenting bugging bugging war rise war sing war feel war burst! and so war gets up and grabs peace by the skirt and swings it up and brings it down and the blood of peace drenches the bed the floor the sink, and the eyes of peace gulp in and darkness mouths the cock of war and in the empty sockets go the cocks of war and bang bang bang the black cannon the black cannonballs of come come come till war falls back dead to the world and peace gets up pregnant with more and more war . . ." Gloomy? No, but God by looking at history, true. When I complete entire poem, I will send it on. I hear Ned finally got his *Naked Lunch*, fine—all right, thanks for nice encouraging letter.

Yours, Gregory

To Lawrence Ferlinghetti

Venice
June 1960

Dear Larry,

Am in Venice, don't know if Whitman got the other 30, whatever, don't send any more or charge to me, as he ain't paid me–so all is mix-up. I think customs holds all, but why? I asked George to go to Git-le-Coeur and he hasn't answered me. *Basta*. If you could send me June remune, or check for what is coming me if anything I'd gladly appreciate it. Don Allen's anthology will be a landmark I feel. All the other anthologies, loose, and some bad, some downright stupid. Met Quasimodo[192] in Milano, dyed his hair black as he likes girls, couldn't talk much as for why? He surrounded by girls, white ones colored ones, all under flood lights. When is *Kaddish* out? If so, send copy, please. When is *HER* out? If so, want very much to see it. What's new? I like *He* very much, I think I told you. I dreamed I was in Red China a prisoner and big big Chinese soldier had me stacking jars filled with crabmeat tuna shrimp lobster, each jar contained an atom bomb. I said I wouldn't stack them because I wanted no part of it, he put his bayonet to me and said "stack or else" so I went to stack, but only one jar remained to be stacked, I stacked it, and as soon as I had, a million flashbulbs clicked, catching me in that infamous action. O what a cowardly dream I sold out! No martyr me, alas. What can it mean? Should it mean? ok. Anyway if you can air me a check if any thing is coming me, please do, as you said you'd let me know in June, write write write!

Yours, as you will have me, Gregory

To Lawrence Ferlinghetti

Venice
June 1960

Dear Larry,

Thanks for check, I received here in Venice all the *Gas's* and *Howls* of second shipment, will send them on to George. What have I to offer thee? I have a long *St. Francis* poem, longest poem I wrote, but I promised it to publisher here who is going to use the Giotto paintings in color all, eight of them, as poem is in eight sections on the eight paintings life cycle of St. Francis. Now that was three months ago, and no word, so I will write him again, and see what's up, and even if he does it, I don't see why you can't have it. As for letter I have none of mine as I don't make carbons, but sure you can get some or all or what you like for/from Allen Jack or who else.

Papa Black Book is all going into my book of prosy, been hard at it and should be done soon, it must go to ND [New Directions] and if they don't want it it definitely goes to Olympia Press, Paris, Burroughs' publisher, as I signed contract and they gave me gold and by rights it's their book, but I signed contract *Happy Birthday Death* and it says they get rights to next book, so all this publishing world is confusing and ethos is hard to stand by, but I will; and could if I wish it send ND a book of poems and Olympia novel, but that would be cheating, I think—so what to do? Fuck it all and just write the book—it will be funny and on grand scale, I think it will amaze thee, o thou porto rican bard. I bought a white suit for India, I am sure to go now.

Ok, I'll find out about *St. Francis*, I think you will like the poem, as I say it is my longest, and my best since God knows what as it was done high up on hill in Fiesole, overlooking Florence, and bright sunny day, I pen and pad in hand wondered just how did all that gold happen down there, and thought of Francis, the demons out of the city, I have him chasing the prisons out of the country; at Francis giving his garment to passerby, I deny man should give all his possesses away as he, man, stands alone before the universe and needs all he's got, also that if the birds gave their wings away, how would they have flown to Francis? St. Francis and the birds, I ask Francis why not have penguins on his shoulder, why not elephants, even herds! St. Francis, Frate Leone visioning the ethereal throne for him; I ask that I have the church no longer necessary to be held up, that what once gave light to dark now gives dark to light. Francis and miracle of the water; I interpret my trip from Milan thirst to Florence where I did drink and thus the writing of the poem, Francis and the stigmata, I forget now, as poem is put away, but as I say, if not a reply in a few days, the publisher is in Florence, I will send it on to you. Poem is 400 lines.

OK, goodbye, yours as you will have me, Gregory
Who are we?

To Allen Ginsberg

Venice
[June 31] 1960

Dear Allen

Got your lovely informative (South America scene) letter, but want to skip over everything and get right down to the urgency at hand. I have 500 dollars—all set for our India trip. It will be my offering—So—Please! When India? I want to go right away! You are yet in S.A.—then N.Y. for how long? Now that I have the money I am impatient I crave to do something! Been too self-abused in this here society—I now can have out—and India, the East, will be it for me. I want more than anything to go with you and Peter—Jack (does he want to go?) and Lafcadio. How long will it all take? Should I go down there first—Bombay or Calcutta, and set things up? Take Bill with the 800? He is in England. Yes, should I take Bill, and we meet you there? I will have to write to him.

Ted Joans[193] here in Venice, he's too much at times. Peter's poesy, yes. If Bill no want to go with me, I will then send you the 800 dollars when you get to N.Y. and then you will come here or I will go to India and set things up or I will wait here for you (if I can make it) and we'll go Berlin Poland via . . . Whatever, just let me know, I won't write to Bill, until I hear from you. Jack says he be in Paris in July. Perhaps we'll all gaze upon our stranger faces again, good.

Love, Gregory

To Allen Ginsberg

Venice
June 1960

Dear Allen,

This is second letter. I wrote to Burroughs in England and said if he'd like with my 800 bucks I'd take him to India and we would set up things there, and you come meet us. I will await his reply, and zoom word on to you, via Peter, via Peru. I bought a white suit for India, I will buy Bill one if he comes with me, or you one if you come, and I wait here for you, but like I say I'm really impatient, want very much to go, society I have done, it is now a dimension. I have fared as well as I could with it, as not so silly but lost and wild in it, and serious and happy, and much a confusion to all peoples who expect just a fool or a gloom or a character or what, but I am all these and something else or nothing but no-self; and with such credentials I have this last year mingled when rest as me are in my position would have snobbily or strictly detach themselves—I took on all comers, and have never ceased to yell or seethe—fini. Now India, that is most sure.

I will express letter to Bill, his reply I will relay to u.

Lo! Let us now turn wombs backwards, and make babies a million years old in the crib, Yes yes Weiners is close to me, I feel him pure and true, and now so Peter, Peter only pure surrealist poet, what Lamantia strains for, he, Petey, flows—Him big spinach, no old man social security Gerber's-baby Peter burps poesy.

Yours, and remember, what with all your vision—hammer hits, and holy eyes, gwegory tells thee that sometimes the laundry loses a shirt button in heaven.

Love, Gregory

Ansen gave poesy reading with Ted Joans in Venice and Ansen was great. I did not read as I saw no point in it. I will type up St. Francis poem and send it on. Had first real sex madness in big palace on Grand Canal with prettiest of pretty Italian girls, she great, and young count, and he peed on her and she reveled and I was shy and amazed and yet loved the human vision of such a thing, bodies is OK was night big big palazzo on canal, and we three near big stained windows, sexing, all gentility, but what got me was how could he pee with an erection?

To James Laughlin Venice

[ca. July 15] 1960

Dear JL,

Have been working much on novel, wonder if you'll like it? So far it's a free flowing strained attempt at style and no style, high-sounding, full of conspiracies that never quite get off the ground, struggling imaginations, *beaucoup* dialogue, tailored untailored pieces, no sex, much God, much youth doings, big potpourri, appropriate to title it *OATMEAL*. I will send it on soon, would like very much if you'd comment on it if you say no to it, also would like you to hasten your impressions as Girodias is in waiting—ethos is well with me—have another book of poesy. How is *HBOD* doing? If it were published a year ago I'm sure it would have done better—but my days concern is that it is something behind me—I go to Berlin this week invitation to read there. Should be an interesting place to see. Could you air mail me a *HBOD* to this address, as I am without a copy.

Yours, Gregory

I am sharing big apartment with of all people, Mary McCarthy's husband. He's a very fine gentleman. I met Salvatore Quasimodo in Milan with Pivano. He was surrounded by floodlights and ladies—but after while, all dimmed, and ladies dispersed, we shook hands, he seemed pleased to meet me and I seemed wondering why I was meeting him—never read anything of his—Nobel Prize influence? Anyway I found him great! and after that read him, and found his poesy greater .

To Allen Ginsberg Berlin
[ca. July 26] 1960

Dear Allen,

Made it! This city is great! Calm tensity! Big mound in city made of all World War II things like bombed houses, furniture, sinks, tubs, human bones, etc. Russian soldiers look very neat, certain. A sappy city really, centered on itself, seems all else worry but they. I read here with four Germans on Thursday [July 28], it should be fun. Lots of people, all for poesy. I just arrived yesterday, today I go out and see things, will go into East Zone. Will I be kidnapped?!

Love, Gregory

To James Laughlin Berlin
[ca. July 27] 1960

Dear JL,

Am in Berlin. Really wonderful here! What with all the professors and students and poets with great talks of Goethe, Fleming, Schiller, and the man who influenced Kafka, Robert Walser, have you ever read him? He sounds very interesting. Remember the anthology I gathered three years ago for Höllerer? Well, it's all translated, and looks good after three years, almost like Allen's [Don Allen], but wilder and less ordered. Your poems look great in translation. Will read here Thursday with four German poets at the Technical University, how strange the university is! It was bombed and is augmented by new glass structure, old and new entwined, very odd to see.

Yes, Kaufman, I met him in 1956 in S.F. a Jewish Negro communist. Haven't read much of him though.

I have many new poems, all quite different than anything done before; pensive, reflective, mature. All in Venice—will I return? Now that I'm here, I'd like to venture Warsaw, on and on and on. Too social the scene in Venice, Paris, etc. Broadwater is very nice and we got along well, didn't see his wife. Lots happening here poesy wise. Everyone intense about it . They know a lot. But I really enjoy talking again about Novalis, Wackenroder, Kleist, my early romantic favorites. I'll let you know how the reading fares, and today I go into the East Zone. Will I encounter adventure? I'm always happy whenever I go to Germany or Holland or Sweden—more than the Latin countries, I prefer the northern. Saw the Reichstag, the fire stains still there. History is here, it can be felt, a calm tensity.

Do you know Höllerer? A very gentle brilliant man, the youngest full professor in Germany. I'm trying to get him to get me an honorary degree, told him when the senate gets together to consider degrees that he should recommend me, even by use of gangster tactics, because last year a professor recommended Walt Disney! Höllerer declined. Will write you.

Best, Gregory

To Lawrence Ferlinghetti

Berlin
[ca. Aug.] 1960

Dear L,

Never knew there was a magazine called *Beatitude*, send me all past issues; read your poesy here, *HE*, to big German audience. All went well, and poem is included in that anthology I started two years back, now all poems are translated, will be bilingual, 35 poets represented, should be ready by Jan. 61.

I enclose first part of my Berlin prosy, and first part is part may never get off the ground, as I am busy getting all my poems together for another Laughlin book. He so asked anyway and I have two years work all piled up. If you no can use this essay whatever, I'll send forth poem.

City Lights Books sold here but no copies of mine, all sold, so your distribution is slack, so they says here. Berlin is all right, but not what I expected it to be what with Conrad Veidt[194] 1930 smokiness, etc. I will try to get visa for Warsaw, hope I can get some money to go, I live by bread alone, and don't really care as I have ceased my emergency letterings. Let me know what [you] intend on article, is it too cold unfunny?

Gregory

I also enclose a poem called *Humanity.* I think it would make article if it were printed with poem. Let me know what you choose, and if you can't decide, choose both.

To Allen Ginsberg

Berlin
[ca. Aug. 2] 1960

Dear Allen,

I am sure you have seen much and have changed with the seeing. I too have been following the world political scene more than I ever have, every day reading *Tribune* and English papers. One sided view, but can gather enough to see that the world is and has been determined by all kinds of various strange Ernorm man, big plotters, confusers, peace mongers and war mongers, all same, chaosmen. Something to do, have a meaning or a SAY in life, everybody wants everybody else to have something, and that usually starts it all. South America doesn't seem to have a chance like Africa, both are probably the same. Africa being the darkest, but I think they are the same, and it seems all sympathy goes to Africa. Don't know about China, feel that [they] had it, not much world sympathy there, too late? Anyway what Real difference does it make? No matter what happens the world goes on, big cries that it won't, but it does. All that matters is everybody realize that they are very strange things, strangest thing alive, should be happy about that, chance to maybe find out what it's all about, that is if everybody got together and wondered or probed or questioned or came to something, like Peter asking all to tell dreams. I think to study the American Indian, the Northern one, he was very strange, nobody like him, except maybe Egyptians, straight nosed, red-faced, nor do I think he came from the Bering Straits, I think he was there, was always there.

Death, like you rightly say, is what we are here for. Big prospect I am sure because that's what makes everything, belief, hope, big life small life, Christ, now one can see why Christ. He came to ease people or to give them something more than the death they at the time conceived. Which was dying and rotting and no more. He came and gave them something more, much more, death. Without death St. Francis would never have been, etc. etc. So death is all important, the trouble is, one has to go beyond the morbid aspect, the dying aspect, fear, pain, horror, grave, worms, etc., all a mankind death I calls it, to go beyond that and come to the real thing. Ain't nobody knows what the real thing is, and that's what makes life so great, and so fortunate to be alive so to experience it one day, one day, ah that day!

I am not writing about it anymore, I feel I went thru it in a way, slight, but necessary to my makeup now, I am all set, and not altogether convinced, but I am set, and what I have learned was: you got to lose something to go beyond, and what is usually lost is a certain kind of inbred dignity, not the moral rigid kind, but that God kind, power? That thing that makes one such as us what we are. [Alan] Watts said rightly to me, "Ah enlightening but dangerous!" The danger for me was giving up all romantic belief and nobility in man, getting older? No. Realization? No. Just choice, either go ahead and go naked, or stay in self, and remain with other men's conceptions, religion, etc. etc. Like I concluded in poem, man really stands apart from nature yet sustains all things in being, just like God. God is a being apart from nature yet sustains all. So man is God, simply because he conceives it, or the theory that God is all things that are good, therefore existence is good, therefore God exists. God, Death, I can see no difference. Am working hard on mad prose novel about Danger entering the world.

I enclose one clipping of ten from all German papers, mostly Berlin guy whose poesy I don't especially see, but who read with me on Höllerer's recommendation. At reading he read too slow and dull and I screamed at it and it caused a little off-color life to reading. I happy little drunk but all was read well, and cried to hear your voice on *Howl* record. Berlin is a very strange place, as though things were suspended here. Big vast city, but I am more interested in East part, very quiet there, and the cameras they sell look old, and the blankets and the buildings look like upper Fifth Ave. Respectable, quiet, uninhabited, all a facade I guess. Would like to go in one of the houses and see what the rooms are like, but one needs a pass to get into the building. Can't go to bars there because you need German East marks and they are hard to come by, and when you have them you also need a pass, it's all for East Germans. Yet best museum and the Brecht theater are there. People in the East seem settled and calm and no different really than the West people, only big difference is in atmosphere. Life has a certain tempo and that tempo can be felt in the West. That is, city life has a certain tempo, the East has no tempo. Just like a big De Chirico painting really. Actually its a place you got to see for yourself. I'm writing a little play about it, using for East side young men, American thru and thru, entering the East zone for the first time, and thru their eyes I give my impressions, very funny and indicative, who better to see? I saw big statue of Stalin standing less graceful than the Hercules across from him on the gymnasium steps, but first statue of him, and Russian soldiers who look like Peter and Lafcadio, all very young, and friendly. It ain't them who are horror, ain't nobody who is really, it's just the big clan tribal laws made centuries and centuries ago that is horrible and all man is caught under it, but again I assure you death hath no tribal laws.

They have a great zoo in the West, two big pigs from Hungary with wool, with heavy sheep wool! Never saw such a sight before. And at the zoo, there is none in the East, so the East has to come to the West to see the zoo, one ticket window for the East, for the difference in marks, and one for the West. Both lines after paying usually enjoin inside and they all go streaming toward the monkeys! Germans like to laugh at animals, they won't look at the dour serious zebras.

No German 1930 jazz, no Blue Angel, Dr. Caligari here. All is bombed out, but some very nice nite spots with sporadic jazz. Big cafe still there where Mann and Walser (he supposedly influenced Kafka, ever read him? Robert Walser) and all the Expressionists used to hang out. Benn friends all around here, big talk with old men, who where close friends to he and Brecht and they say he and Brecht got to hate each other over their ideologies. So that caused REALLY the separation of East and West, that Benn stayed in the West and Brecht went to the East. Wrote a lyric for the occasion: "East is East / West is West / Berlin has both / And both is best."

I live in the British sector and every morning they wake me up with big tanks. Ever see tanks streaming on the highway? A sorry yet mad sight to see upon waking. Don't hardly see any soldiers, they are kept out of sight.

What think you of the Don Allen anthology? It is really a very good one.

But I just can't stand this almighty reference to influences. But it's a great one, a document, no? As for my anthology, it is done and translated and will go to press and come out in the spring, bi-lingual.

I have chance to go to Warsaw in Spring with Winter here. But I think, maybe I'd like to go sooner, so done is my social world. [. . .] Kerouac is always going somewhere to be alone, he so young, as if all were done with him in life. I feel he should, if he write poesy, go out now when necessary into strange other world and be, no Big Sur refuge, not now, he young, refuge maketh for complaints. I make good anthology now because I do it without Beat in mind, just poesy, I hail no thing but poesy, I am not down on Beat, but it can overshadow poesy, and that I am wont to do. Beat is a word coined by man, poesy is IN man. I think you will like what I have done. [. . .]

Burroughs is something else. Truly a giant of a man. [I have a] little war with him because I think he wants to kill poesy. So if you saw *Minutes To Go* and see what I emotionally silly wrote in back, my feelings on the matter. I believe in Burroughs, anything he touches is gold, but when I must touch what is already gold, I see no sense in it. It did not do for me, so I backed out, not without an argument. Called him such names as cold earth hell only knew. Very funny. Thought all poesy was lost, thought he was taking it away from me, because when I came back from Greece very upset, he gave me some pot then sat me before him and said, "Gregory do you know why you are what you are? It is because I wished it so, Gregory." He said it in such a way that with tears in my eyes I called him God, and he accepted that. And then I caught myself and said, "Whoa! Whoa! I give in to no man on this count, sir. You ain't God and I ain't because of you." But for a moment I must confess, I believed he really was. It all seemed to make sense, and also it was a great relief because if he indeed was, then all was done, complete, no more bother. It felt good to believe it. But I would not give in, and so denied him. He is not mad or was he jesting with me? If he were, it was silly on his part, because I look up to him. Allen if there were a man God, I'd believe Bill comes closest to my impression of Him, but not a funny gentle God, but one with Catholicism of wrath and wisdom and fear. I reread reread reread his work and he is for me the best writer in prose, barring none. He can do anything and make funny sense of it, here is a man, Shakespeare would say. [. . .]

You say Kerouac love me now. I don't see why he didn't before. We wrote each other all was well. My own deep feeling about him is that he doth not own poesy nor should he feel that I should be subservient to that. Poesy was long long before I ever met him a thing to me I hailed. By the coining of Beat, I do not head under that. I head under poesy, my attitude and way in life. I hold to no man, and I think maybe I was a little disrespectful to him on this accord.

Much I have learned if from anyone or persons alive, was you and Sura, from the dead, all English poesy, and of course mine own self. [. . .] This is no wishy washy business, there can't be no lie in this, no "all right I'm gonna be a poet," because anybody can write a poem, anybody can do. I felt Peter's hurt on this by him writing me a real silly letter about how some fool came over the house and told him Corso isn't any good etc. etc. and how he, Peter, defended me with "Well you must first realize what Gregory went thru and what he came from." God, if I ever heard a sillier and more damaging defense, funny, and useless—like why defend? It's all done done, past, the stain is there. So is it a la Greenberg like, for Peter. What he and Jack do not realize is that though I may be absurd most of the time, underneath I am well aware, maybe too aware, of the many selves in a self. It all makes for a many-souled soul. [. . .]

Lots of Beat anthologies coming out, and I can't stand Ted Joans. He came to Paris and Venice and changed everybody's impression about Beat. He showing off his clippings and he says you say I keep all my clippings likewise, which is lie. And then tells people he go to see you in South America, then Kerouac in USA, then Bill in England, then me in Venice. A big professional spade and beatnik sickening, and I'll never forgive him for selling his no soul to people for 50 dollars an hour,[195] took him out of the anthology for that, he ain't no new beatnik, he been on the scene long long time, remember seeing him first Village years, old bohemian type come to bomb the new Esso building. Can sing, and is funny, and got much but no poesy, and can't stand his shade around because I feel like a freak—told him so! Always telling so. There, now you got my complaints, nice ones, mostly about people and friends, and all in all I ain't so hard or cruel on people.

But back to Beat anthologies, I like them all, the one from the Eighth Street Book Store [*Beat Scene*] has great photo of you, big face of hair and eyes. Lafcadio-one great, and the introduction is great. The Krim one is too Yiddish sounding, this "sweet un-kosher kid you," ugh! But he, Krim, seems very bright, sensible and the collection is good.

Is Jack's out? Please see if you can if he uses that letter of mine to change names, or something, because now looking at my letter to Don Allen in back of his anthology, its too weeping. I didn't mean it to be printed, I wrote it to him in 1957 when in Paris and Sura gone and I stole money and all that. Felt all doom, but it don't fit for now, can't stand tears, but it won't make any difference because I'm done with socializing, but before that it was terrible because people would always bring it up, and I'm not the sort to back away and keep quiet, I immediately would get involved. I learned one thing by all this, be proud and indifferent and care not what anybody says, for have I not poesy on my side? Is not a mountain an opinion of stone to me? Laughlin writes he wants to do another book of poesy, and I have much new poems, left them all in Venice though, must get them. Have *St. Francis, Orpheus, War, Man, God*, (where did you see *God*? because I don't remember what the poem is like, don't have copy, can you send me copy? Please?) and lots more, can't remember titles off hand.

Glad to hear your book is finally done, can't wait to see it. When will it come out? What think you of Ferls *He*? He, Ferl, always used to criticize me for using repetition like "Army army army army," "Explosions explosions etc." and he goes full blast out with "DEATH" at end of *He.* But he sure has changed in his way of writing, hasn't he? Much much better, how do you feel about his work now?

America seems in a terrible fix, really scary, something is drastically wrong. Where's the FDR nobility? He should be alive now, that's the kind of man we need. The whole American heritage, from Washington to Hamilton, all those guys were poetic statesman. We didn't have many poets then, all were in politics. A new country, all was purposeful. But now, bah! it's scary. The greatest country in the world and look—Eisenhower is really bad, isn't he? I mean, something is wrong with him, it is as though he weren't there, and everybody I see in American Express, the men women girls boys, all alike, all dead empty. Something is very wrong. I never felt this before about America. Never have I felt so patriotic in a way. Maybe it was because I felt America knew what it was doing and was strong and needn't examine it that closely. Now under examination, I find it completely bereft of greatness, no great statements are said, no great adventure or grandness done, no purpose, no nothing, but decline, defensiveness, all so unlike America. Yes, we dropped the bomb, we have hurt much, but I still feel we are better in our attitude than the Communists. This is a live or die situation, if we give in to the Communists, then Communism has it all. The same story from the beginning of time. The Phoenicians up, new ways, defended ways, victorious ways, no like Nazi who really had no world ideal or change. They lost, and so what? But communism has a world ideal. They are not looking for a country or their own country, they want to change the whole pattern of life. So in this case we are in a fix, because without war we may fall under, so what to do? I know what, we should find a better way, change our way, give up our system and find a new one, a grand one, one the whole world can look upon and revel in. Outdo Communism, that's the way, but no outdo it with evil intent or with intent of destroying their way, just find a NEW way. This could be possible were there such men as FDR or earlier Jefferson, etc., because what Jefferson had for his time was good for his time, but times have changed. Now we need something new. Kennedy in his New Frontiers, I'm skeptical about that, but at least its a right track, whereas Nixon still wants to retain the old tired way. I say we are doomed if we do not have a young Marx-like man in the Metropolitan Museum or the 42nd Street Library writing a new manifesto.[196] One that makes St. Francis of us all in a way. If Beat, (God I'm getting down on that word) but if Beat has done anything, I feel it has come close to that. But what Beat lacks is simply an all-out compassion. Beat stresses so much on individuality, that that's what it ends up being, every soul for itself, expression, etc., that all individual expressions (and this can be seen by the writing) becomes similar. Again I say I do not feel politics are to do with poesy, a no-politics politics can be a dangerous thing too, if not dangerous then a very powerful thing. I'd be for politics if I were in Jefferson's time, because then it was romantic and fire and a thing to live for. Today it is so systematic and dull. That is, two years ago it was dull, not today. Today something definitely is needed, and so with such feeling perhaps there will be that wild new birth of new revolutionaries to bring America to heaven. Strange to think of America having revolutionaries, who'd think it possible? But now it seems very possible. Imagine that when I was a child in classroom, America seemed so strong and faraway, as if Washington were still living. [. . .]

Good to be alive and watch it all, or do something about it? Indeed this is a time for God to show his face, or if not His face, His hand. But what has all this to do with the most important thing, Death? If one says but it is important how people live, then I say man is man, the greatest thing alive, the victory of life, he should go somewhere and wait to die, and while waiting think about it and wonder it and be glad that he is alive to wonder such. For I really think man has gone off track, has not followed the universe, he goes elsewhere and so all this world spin and trouble. That if man held to death he'd be very complete and meaningful. My attitude has always been this. Remember the time in Paris about the Hungarians and you threw the table? Well, I did have contempt for those who thought they were doing great, but such a life-like thing had nothing to do with the universe but with this small world, and so their meaning in life. [. . .] All right to have life as good and as simple as possible, everybody have enough to eat and all that, but then what would be needed would be love. For the man who shoots the communist to gain his freedom is no different than the communist who shoots. They all shoot. They are all freaks of this shooting. Man is great, I hold to that, ok, if he is great then he can do many things and be in soul filled with dreams and wonderment. [. . .] I tell you all this nonsense would end if all man suddenly stood as though struck by God and looked up in the sky and began to call or ask for some meaning or no meaning. That is, if they'd just get smart enough to ask the unaskable. Education is needed, a soul of poesy is needed. [. . .] It is all mixed up, because Communism looks to life, to the one thing, so does America, there is no difference really, they are both for life, how to live, a way in life, death they leave to religion and to fate. We take both, for if I felt it was just life that mattered, then I guess I'd be crying all the time about how life is really not that great and what a terrible predicament it is, and why do people persist in continuing, and if life is all, then why must man work or slave in it, and if life is all, then why doesn't he have everything? That we've had 25,000 years in which to acquire everything, then why is a blind man blind or why a child killed, or why death? Yes, I have contempt for Communism as I do for anything that masses up and seeks a way helplessly and hopelessly and humanly tragically seeks a way in life to eat and live and be satisfied and do well work well until death and final no more. Not that I feel there is another world after this. I do not know this, but I feel the ATTITUDE that there is something more, something far greater than this living greatness, something that will make sense of it all. That with the ATTITUDE I can be more than just a man caught in life's predicament and so helplessly live and gather for my need a way. O what a waste of manliness to cry about this short span. Yes, the span is made short by such tears. If ever I cried it was always with the ATTITUDE the wonder of elsewhere, no heaven. Not that, because often I feel this is heaven, and why not, did I not say heaven for all I know could well be a familiar place—and isn't it strange that we are here? So who is to say this is not heaven? NO—not another world, but the ATTITUDE of something more, that is what makes this span for me eternal, and makes life so great, and death so necessary. Were there just a mankind death, I think I would have welcomed it a long long time ago. When I saw cars as real, I meant that I saw death in a postage stamp. That if a car [is] capable of hitting and killing me, a simple stupid car, if it was capable of taking all my wonder and attitude away, then life indeed was a small thing, and not the real thing, and should no longer be my main concern, but that death should now be the concern. [. . .] For consider, can you ever really die? You, Allen Ginsberg? An example is George Washington. He is dead, but when we think of his death, we see another kind of dead, an almost deathless death, as though he never really died. Nor do I mean immortality of history, history books, no. It's simply the ATTITUDE again. Death I would say is undoubtedly the least strange, it becomes strange when the living view it. When the living view the dead, we, the living, make it strange, because we are strange. I say death runs all, governments, candy factories, all. Big classrooms on death, teachers on death. This is what I see for the future, and very necessary it'll be too. Life is hopelessly incurable. Nor is death the cure. Death is neither cure nor curable nor incurable. When Chessman took his last breath in the gas chamber, I know what he felt. He felt very strange, not scared. Strange because he suddenly realized that he Was Caryl Chessmen, and who IS Caryl Chessman? And his meaning in life? And not what is death, but what is LIFE?

Yes, Allen, What is life? In death there is no "what?" And so what I feel death is, death is knowing what life is. Chessman is a great example. Here was a man fighting death in the beginning, but at end what he realized was that it was not death he was fighting but life. Life is what most men think death is. Happily I would like to think visa versa.

Much love, and joy unto Peter and Laff, Gregory

Let me know what New York it like now, what is happening, and who why where and if you have any nice propaganda to show me, do I await your book, and Psalm, and wish I were there for the Yage, hadn't had anything like pot not anything like that in four months. Guess you can't mail me any liquid, but if you have chance for mescaline would love to have some, and how is Irving? I would very much like to hear from him, that photo of him in anthology is great, like early Russian revolutionary. *Partisan Review* sent me a silly article somebody wrote about me when on ship coming over from France in 1958. How basic stupid they've sunk, though I care not, for I felt true, have you seen it? Send me books to read, been much out of contact. All the cats gone? What you eating? Who new in friends? BJ still there?

Ok, but God wish you and Peter just hop on jet and come here and then we go off to Russia together, don't think alone there now for me. Warsaw yes, but Russia, not yet—and India seems farther and farther away from resting eyes on you again.

To James Laughlin Berlin
[late Aug.] 1960

Dear JL,

I am now on the right chosen path, not death, it never was that. Life holds the mystery, not Death. I am working on a long long poem—endless it'll be! Called *Man*, you have a fragment of it; other fragments are:

Spontaneous Requiem for American Indian. This you can get in anthology called *The Beats* ed. by S. Krim. This be the start of my Cantos, Paterson etc.—all Michelangeloian, sans philosophy, sans technique, sans everything but poesy and the obvious.

Humanity. I'll send this on in next letter. Keep all papers I send in folder called *Man.*

England and Autumn. Much of English history condensed to a flash! Still working on it.

America and Winter. Also in a flash, almost completed.

Greece & Summer. Now I need the *Greece* poem you have back, please return it, as I want to join it to all my other Greek writings on *Man*, if I see that it has nothing to do with *Man*, then I'll hold it as single poem.

Rome & Spring. Only outline for this, much notes. I have notebooks filled, all done since I left America second time. All this needs is typing notes. Plus *St. Francis* 400 line poem.

Prehistoric Man. This poem I left in Venice, will get it.

This will be not in chronological order, as I care not to have it that way—though first poem should be the fragment *Man*, and book should be called by that. Also lots of short poems, all those others are very long, (except *Man* fragment) on subject.

How to See the Strangeness in Man. In this poem I try to (hard to do) express the strangeness in him which he conceals.

Man: Fear Pain Death. In this poem I speak for Danger, holding it to be an uncontrollable force both outside and inside man.

Man in an Enchanted Grove. Not so much an Utopia, but a reflection, with all the elements hand maiding him.

The First Man & the First Death. This on his feeling, did he know? In poem I contend that in the life of him he knew death before death came—that death is with us at birth, always there—the first man knew. Ah, but what did he think about it? The inevitable. So Nature that exact, etc.

Man and Life. A run of likes and dislikes. "There are some who like you to your face and dislike you behind your back" etc., a little like my *Marriage* poem.

Friend. This poem is in the possession of Alfred Leslie, I have no copy. Can you have Ginsberg get it for you? I gave it to Leslie for his *Hasty Papers*, perhaps he can type up a copy for you, it is one page only. This poem belongs to the *Man* series.

Man In Body. Descriptions of all parts of body etc.

Greece, my fair Greece, brought me way down, yet a year later I find myself stronger and very certain of all I am and must do—or must not do—no must, but will do. A poem of this sort needs arrogance—I have not lost that. And book won't be complete until I'm dead! Now I know very well where I'm at! If anything Death showed me that. Life is much much more strange, and a tricker, using death to confuse the prober's trail.

My heart to thee, Gregory

To James Laughlin

Berlin
[Fall] 1960

Dear JL,

I have been re-working, enclosed find a new version of the *Love* poem, I suggest you throw away the old copy. I also intend to rework *Communism, People On A Day When I'm Happy, Queen Elizabeth, Good Goodbye,* and maybe *Humanity.*

The enclosed poems are dated. Some are very early, I think they should be dated in print. I will not rework those poems, not when so many years have gone by; re-working recent poems I'm all for, but when the poems go back to 1956 etc, no. These poems, by the way, were in Venice batch. If you like them, could they not go in section called simply EARLY POEMS? I seemed to have rested on my *Man* theme; was very set on it a month back; but I think this scatter of poems is best, and, of course, it is what I have. I have about another twenty poems to re-work, and send on; then I am done. Then I can go back to my prose; as I think it will take me years before I get it done. Whenever I set to write it, a poem creeps in.

Berlin seems so quiet, the world is quiet; I hope Mr. K [Khrushchev] and Ike are not playing this life for keeps. History does not allow deadlocks; yet something must break, no? What will set it all straight? Or has it ever been straight? I still hold it all depends on the young, if they be not replicas. The thought of God does encourage somehow. OK. and what if you like these poems (I think they are a nice loose collection so far, not as tight as *HBOD*) what to call the book? Another salable title list? No. When you have all the poems at hand I will come up with a flash title. How is *Happy Birthday* doing sales wise? Has the explosive cover proven a dud? Let me know all. And is Ferl's *She* [sic: *Her*] published? Can I have a copy? I wish you well.

Yours, Gregory

If you have any suggestions on any of these poems please don't hesitate to say; and if you think some could be worked over let me know; all is permissible. I send another batch soon; then the end; then I can travel on, maybe Warsaw, or Paris or USA, somewhere for sure, as of now you have with this batch, 41 poems; there are poems in *Big Table* 4 and *The Beats, Beat Scene*, and my *Triptych (Friend, Work, World)* that Al Leslie has for his *Hasty Papers*. Those, and with the next batch should make a very nice happy book. I will walk in the East today in hope that I can conjure a mad title, for the title must be free and new.

To Allen Ginsberg Berlin

[Sept. 12] 1960

Dear Allen, ballen, callen,

Been reading *Magic Psalm* over and over and was raised to height Shelley often lifts me to, the Desire-lift, Desire, which created me, desire, I hide in my body. Great timing and rhythm—no let down—a soft echoing, till a peak again in the "This is the Great Call, this is the Tocsin, etc." on and on to "Should my feet,—splatter my hairs, drape my head." And all the word use, imaging, joins in a herald. [. . .]

Great lovely inspired poems. Make sure if *Kaddish* is not printed yet, that that goes in, as is. No flaw but the flaw of love.

Yours, Gregory

To James Laughlin Berlin

[ca. Sept. 18] 1960

Dear JL,

After getting all my notebooks from Venice, I have the Greek books too, and thank God I have this life for reflection, because I am putting my Greek poem (very important to me) back in order, without timely hang-ups. So, get now in first Hermes delivery, my poems, some of Greece, some not, but more more to come. I just want to make sure what I send is satisfactory to me; I work much on some, on others, no. The Greece poem was a simple unhappiness that had nothing to do with poesy in a way, yet a lot too, because I am aware that what I write has to do with my life, no matter what. A good example or proof to myself was here, in Berlin, when I got to be good friends with a newspaper man, a young American working for the English *Daily Mail*. I met him his wife, been to his house, had great high talks about life and basketball; and then month late he was commissioned to interview me for CBC Canadian radio, and he didn't know what to do. He thought to plan it all before hand, but I said no, that it wouldn't be him I'd be facing at microphone, so do it cold; and cold I trembled and said what naturally comes. So the same for the poesy except that I am happy for reflection, as I think what I have done with the Greek poem so far is good, *The Poseidon And On The Acropolis*; sections; as they were almost originally in pen writing book.

I honestly write for myself, but as I say, I am also aware that what I write is printed, and lo, I then think to go stronger, and that strongness deadens me, yet, there comes a time, and these poems are example of it, that I think nothing but the joy that a man can revel in his small room away from all friends and love and sing. Accept these poems that way. I once told you I was a big fuck up, but I will never fuck up with poetry. NO.

Yes, and in biography for German anthology I call you a "human empire state building." Is that all right? The only thing I hated doing for that anthology was the biographies, I did a hash of it, told the publisher and Höllerer to get somebody else, what a mess. Yet I think I did justice to what I feel is poesy.

Ho illustrious giant, Gregory

To James Laughlin

Berlin
[ca. Oct. 1] 1960

Dear JL,

Here is another batch (I think the best batch so far) and will send more on, probably the last. I have the title: *The Victory Of Life.* As soon as I forward the last poems to you I guess I'll be off to Warsaw or Paris. If you feel I should not have a fat book, then omit the early poems.

Yours, Gregory

I still must revise *Communism. I* really feel this to be a fine batch. Also don't use Krim's *The Beats* poem, *Spontaneous American Indian*, it's too long, and has been printed before. That is, if you feel there are too many poems. Hard cover, soft cover? Or will you even take it? In any case, let me know. I never worry about these poems when they are at hand, but I do become anxious about them when they leave my hand.

To James Laughlin

Berlin
[ca. Oct. 2] 1960

Dear JL,

What think you of *Correspondence*, too silly? Found it in same notebook I wrote *Marriage* in, has the same tone in a way. I think I am going to hold off on fixing up *Written On A Day When I Am Very Happy* and *Communism*, so put them aside. Also, I will choose from, but if you feel as of now that you have enough for book, let me know. I have some Berlin poems I can send on. But you have all the main poems. Any suggestions? I think that if there are too many poems, then please omit the early poems; they can hold. How is everything? October is indeed a lovely month; I like it best in New England—that IS the month of New England .

Gregory

To Allen Ginsberg

Berlin
[ca. Oct.] 1960

Dear Allen,

You always know what you are doing—but I sing to you, dear lark, a song you well know. Once you take a stand, be it pro or con, for or anti-force, then you are in that air. A poet true stands on no side, but has all history before him to regard. Castro in manifold–be thou select–see him, regard all history, but do not with one hand hail him, and the other down whatever he downs. All is up where you're at. These men—Castro, etc.—all who are in political time, are henchmen of death, baby, their game is their life. Your game is life. Politics are always filled with complaints, there is no satisfaction, else if there were, there'd be no history to talk about. People who have nothing to believe in on their own, usually back up such heroes, Hitler, not to be compared to Castro, nonetheless is good example of political time, it is their singular world. Your worlds are many, don't fizz them out by selecting one world, their world. Now, of course, I can feel the truth of a Mayakovsky hailing a Lenin, Whitman a Lincoln, Swinburne a Mazzini.[197] Swinburne be your state, as his hero was alien. That is, there are many reasons why a person does and believes in things, and usually they are all good reasons—therefore I state no argument. I believe that whatever you do is done with bright conviction, and is intelligently weighed. It's just that I see your sorrow about America is valuable, not to side with Castro's complaint (sorrow, whatever) is bogus gold—no worth in it. Of course I speak as one who has not the political fire in him, as you have, and it is good as Americans—remember that, you are concerned and in love with America, Castro is not. Can Castro help America? You undoubtedly believe America should help Castro, or leave Castro alone, or what? Ah, but if [you] like Castro for outstepping himself as a man, for being the neo-revolutionary of the Americas, then great, I am with you. You recall in Chicago that we agreed it was sad that he executed all them those people—we even argued with Percy Heath about it? Well, I don't know just what I'm trying to get at. Why don't you let me know what you feel, really. I mean, what can I gather from you saying you're pro-Fidel? I neither like nor dislike the man. I like his youth and his achievement, dislike his executions, his bugging the giant in the apartment next door. But, outside of everything, he is a part of a new Marx Brothers era in neo politics. Not so much gloom there be when such as Lumumba,[198] Kasavubu,[199] Tshombe,[200] Castro, Khrushchev, yelp at roll and up and down. Life in the Western diplomacy needed a shot in the behind. These people do it. Life is funny, but remember, this clowns do hold stun guns. *Basta.*

Now, I will leave Berlin soon. I want to return to U.S. I sent off all my new poems to Laughlin, he has *St. Francis*, etc., go up office, see them, and let me know what thy wild eyes sees. Title will be *The Victory of Life*, if he gives me advance I will buy ticket passage. I can do nothing here no more. Europe has become like a self-inflated prison, I have done my penance for all the horribles I did in N.Y. etc. I do hope I can embrace you for Xmas. Take care of yourself, and I want you to know that whatever you do, I am all for. I do not contend thinking for myself where you're at—for whatever convictions I have are always subject for self-contradictions.

Peter, how is Lafcadio? Peter, I am become old-gray hair! yes! so sudden! so, you see, there will be a time in which I'll be a Geppeto.

Yours in this fine Octob'rian argosy, Gregory

To James Laughlin Berlin

[ca. Oct. 12] 1960

New address, American Express, Paris, France. I go there in hope that when I receive some money I can get boat at La Havre and return to USA, want very much to return. Am in top form, unlike two years ago when all was pinched and sprity and gnarled and owl and heap gloom. Maybe if you like all my soul-pourings you'll again advance me, for indeed the first advance sent me here, and now the proper return? Whatever, I'll be glad to be traveling on. West Berlin can't go to opera, only me, foreigners can, but Germans no. So I go girless to opera. Can you send me another *Happy Birthday*? I'm always giving it away.

Yours, Gregory

To James Laughlin Paris

[ca. Oct. 24] 1960

Dear J.L.

Greece poem is very bad. If you go thru new batch of poems you'll see that I put the Greek poems back in their original order, taken from the notebook. *On the Acropolis—Poseidon—Greek Notebook—First Dream of Greece.* Use whatever you like, I really don't know what to feel about such a poem, a year later. I can only hate it. Also omit emphatically from the poems you have—*A Good Goodbye, People On A Day When I Am Happy—Communism—Written When A Sad Girl Told Me Of Shock Treatment.* That's five poems. I may re-work them. Hope all this does not confuse you. Sometimes I feel I can write the worst poesy in the whole wide world. Happy about you and staff wanting to do another book. I swear to you it will be the last, so I would prefer if I worked over this book with some care.

Everything so lovely in Paris . . .

Yours, Gregory

To James Laughlin Paris

[ca. Nov. 7] 1960

Of course use *Greece* poem in anthology. I am very determined not to rush into print the poems you have at hand. I feel something unfulfilled and too condescending about the *Victory of Life* collection. So let us hold, I would like to go over poems again. How are you? Hope Kennedy wins, though I see no faltering in U.S. prestige, no hate for U.S.A. here, just good natured ridicule.

Gregory

To Allen Ginsberg Paris

[ca. Nov. 12] 1960

Dear Allen,

Am almost done with my novel (no sex) a fairy tale really and then I'll be able to return to U.S.A. Glad Nixon didn't make it. But tell lovely Bill de Kooning he need not send me ticket if Laughlin will advance me the poesy. Are they pooling together for a ticket? I don't understand, whatever the ticket should be an open end ticket.

Because I know not exactly when I will leave Paris, still getting into some trouble, but not as much as I used to—mostly with people who are evil in a way. I care too much yet what people think—hope I get off that. America scares me, the return that is. What is there but to see your face again? Let me know who will supply ticket, de Kooning has done enough for me—he did not have to.

Gregory

To Allen Ginsberg Paris

[ca. Nov. 28] 1960

Just finished great epic on *Man*—life, birth, death. Mr. Death, grand Achiever. Book is endless too—as there are no set rules for finality. My novel will add a star to Beat lit.

Yours, Gregory

To Allen Ginsberg Paris

[ca. Nov. 30] 1960

Dear Allen,

I was going to come to N.Y. especially to see you, Jack and Peter, as I think it would be good for us all to see each other again. Well, tonight a kindly soul Swede offers me round-trip fare to Sweden and to you—from U.S. to Sweden—to read as he says for the Swedes who could use us ones. I'm apt to agree and feel it be fine to see Sweden again. So, my dear poet soul, what say you? Will you meet me in Stockholm? As I feign to return just now to U.S.A. He be director of modern art museum there and looks like Charles Olson. Radio company pay all expenses, but what I want to dig most is living in those wonderful Bergman woods with snow, otters, and peace. What say you, Peter, Jack? Bobsled to Lapland from there? I been, as you know, to Sweden before and found it a very nice place. The inviter was amazed at my enthusiasm for what he termed "dead" Sweden, but I like that kind of atmosphere (never dead) at times. And now is time. So, he will contact you, this be opportunity paid for deal and I know we should meet now. It do both our cringy souls some good, no?

You will like my novel, it be undercover kids classic called *The American Express*.

I am determined to go to Sweden, the whole thing sounds wonderful and what joy to meet out in the country, with mountains, trees, and strange environs. Please weigh this carefully. Why it might hold the fate of poesy in the balance for all the confused muses know—no?

I ain't written a poem in eons and as it be the realty of youth, my lease may well be up poesy wise, sense way much fire remains now for Epics and painting. I seriously would like to do Michelangelo kind of gifts.

Please send me twenty pages on your feelings and impressions on Fuck, also Jack and Peter. I make anthology for Girodias, Olympia book. Be called plain FUCK and be sold in store windows. McClure sent me nice wild twenty pages. Quick, it be good, it be paid, it be wild, and the old sickness be gone from the word.

Love, Gregory

Get Jack to send me fuck piece, anything about WORD is permissible, all be worthy anthology.

Did you read my Berlin piece at Grove office, or did they print it? This be important, let me know. I did not give them the piece, though they gave me 50 dollars sight unseen. I sent to Ferl and he gave to Don Allen. I explicitly asked for it back, for late changes—they have yet to do so. PLEASE LET ME KNOW, send card, this is important. You rarely reply to this kind of stuff, as when I asked where you saw *Man* poem. I had good reason for asking—no sense going into it now, but tell me if my *Berlin Impressions* is printed or not. I have indeed written a kid's undercover classic. It be filled with birth, life, death and Burroughs-like midges of good and good-evil with lots of mini illustrations. I wrote book like madman, mostly dialogue, hardly description. Most poets, like Ferl for example, when they write prose they experiment and word blah. Mine book is straight old hat traditional prose—but in the great epic tradition. I got wars Tolstoian in three pages. I got conspiracies, quests, expeditions, love scenes, monastery scenes. The book be one big metaphysical detective story with my detective being Death. Overall meaning of book be clash between dream and reality, creation and the world or worldlessness beyond—all done in 183 pages—fast as a cheetah to read, sudden switches of emotion. I learned about prose writing it, and as is with poesy, the ellipse sense, it works well in prose for me. It be the most immaturely written, yet old cringy philosopher tone to it. It be called *The American Express*.

I have written to Laughlin he knows where I am. I asked him for fare home for new book he has of mine, he said yes, that's last I heard from him. But I don't like dealing with publishers anymore because in prose it be fun, but in poesy, it is too heavy a load. I am done with publishing poesy. I will yet write it, but I am done printing it. From now on it be vast paintings, prose, and plays for the public eye. I intend to make much money now, that be my concern. I have been noble with poesy—didn't abuse it too much, nor sought gold from it, but I will jump into that prose / painting market, and clean up. Prose is easy, and though I've yet to respect it; my prose is worthy of respect, in that I think I have brought it down, without gimmick writing, to its simplest meaning. Say what you got to say, and fuck the trimmings, or the acrobatics of syntax, etc.

The proofs be ready in two weeks; book be out in five weeks, Girodias fast and great, good man. He been giving me money for book a year now so don't think there will be enough to come home on. Maybe, but I wish it not from de Kooning, so if you see him say I am getting the money from my work, and to thank him very much.

I am Git-le-Coeur, so write me here. Mailer, yes, and life, yes, and it goes on and on. And no turkey for me, but a dish of oysters which I threw up on Thanksgiving Eve. Good about Kennedy—no? I would love to see you for Xmas—if so, please keep my arrival a secret. I wish no one to know, not even Laughlin or anybody, nor ANYBODY. Please do this for me, you will be only one to know, and thus I can set myself up somewhere, and cool things. Mushrooms alas, Johnny Nicholson came by and gave me some mescale with good pot and both were great. He very nice man, nice talks.

To James Laughlin Paris

[ca. Dec.] 1960

Dear J.L.,

I am now determined to make a lot of money, to have complete peace, the least bit of human disturbance as possible. I have decided against returning to U.S.A. I will off in the woods somewhere and write Tolstoian epics, and do giant paintings (I can paint). All for love <u>and</u> money. I will be rich and am determined to act in accordance to wealth, not socially, but as master of a castle. Now, can you help me make a lot of money? All those who have money rarely tell, like Getty, I bet if I got to him, something would rub off. Poesy is the property of youth and so I leave that piece of real estate. I am quite proud, in a detached kind of way, about every poem I ever wrote, but I shan't sit away a professional bard. If I am moved to write a poem I will keep it for myself. So, you have my last poesy—and from now on I'm going to make new friends, like Frank Yerby, and Taylor Caldwell, and all them there folk—because I want to and will be RICH.

So if you think I'm become an awesome monster, then all I can say is, don't talk to me when you see me at the Club 21. I just finished a fairy tale and so my debt to Girodias is paid. I think it be a book you will like and it is in the great tradition with a difference, an undercover kid's classic with big battle scenes, and conspiracies, and detective hunts. Overall meaning of book, (called *The American Express*) a saleable title for sure, [is] birth, life, death of a young man. Young man symbol of creations of the world. Anyway I can write prose. And it's what I want to do.

How's this for title of mine poems *Gregorian Rants*? *Victory of Life* to old man heavy heavy. Are you angry at me for coupling with Girodias contract? Don't be—I promise thee my great *Les Miserables*, I am now working on. You've been very good to me—or have you? Yes, you have. But you did not make me rich. The oldest existing piece of human writing sayeth—"Alas, things ain't what they used to be." Do you invest in stock? Can you invest some money for me? Are you good at it? Let me know- or if you can, can you send me some stock and bond literature? I am quite serious. I want to make millions—if not in America, then here. Do they have an international stock market?

How are sales on *Happy Birthday* doing? Strange mad review of it in *Partisan*. Gregory, the cannibal. God knows at times I feel that way, but he's wrong about me being rude to the broadcaster who kept a pet rat, as I never met the man. I think he was afraid of the book. A man does not want to be reminded of what lies ahead of him. Get a pest like me to go around spelling what perhaps might be there, can quite well as not weigh the heart down or lift it. Whatever, it certainly was never done with intent of cruelty or aggressiveness. But if I be in the field of gold, then I need be cruel and aggressive. I will make so much money everybody will become scared. I think I'll go to Germany and capture all their Marks! I know a way. Open up a series of chile con carne cafes there, all over the country—Gregory's Chile Con Carne Cafe. It should clean up. Now I need backing. Are you willing to invest in my star as a business man as you did in my poesy? You can't be my partner because that will cause difficulties. I got to run things my own way, but you will get double your investment back. Think about it.

I like Ferl's *Her*, but all poets when writing first prose go the way of Aiken's *Ushant*[201]—Experiment with words—as if to say—"see, even in prose, I'm still a poet." I passed that pitfall and done a straight *Peyton Place* kind of book with a difference. What that difference be of course is me.

Be good, Gregory

To Allen Ginsberg Paris
[ca. Dec. 14] 1960

Dear Allen,

I take first jet tonight to Greece! Sent only proofs back today. Book be out next month, I rush you copy. God how scared I was seeing proofs, got to dislike the whole thing. Then I get your letter with man being God, as I always since Greece did feel, and so immediately injected what you said in mouth of Carrol, special hero of book, who talks to Cardinals etc., saying they had nothing to do with the new consciousness. In fact that is what book is about; about the war between the old and the new. I give Hinderov the old, he lives incorporates American Express, sells bombs, distributes war, etc. But a nice funny sort too. And Mr. D. as Bill Burroughs, in a way, who seeks to give the new consciousness a new language, and so I have him go around seeking to buy one—and I give him victory at end of book. I have the wordman prevail. It be written grammar school like, no toying, and so I wonder, I do. No sound from Sweden yet, though they said they would let me right away know. If not I zoom back to USA, get boat and go. I think Girodias owes me two hundred dollars so I can get boat. Too bad about Berlin piece I wrote, it be already at printer. I no even see proofs; I wanted to change something and also add final impression as it was writ in beginning. I wish I had some mushrooms like you, it all sounds fine, and isn't it nice about the new consciousness, and beware the psychiatrists, not so much the church, but the Freudys. They no like idea AT ALL.

I zoom this off to you, motherfucker. I's going back to Greece, I be in Athens.

Love, Greg

Yes, I go back to Greece, not USA or anywhere but old Zeus land. Come see me there—it be new and great life.

To James Laughlin Paris
[ca. Dec. 14] 1960

Dear J.L.,

I is off to Greece at this moment by my first Jet. It be all in a wonderful re-birth. I go now no longer hung on my self, all is good and life is great that it can leave the door opened. I know I will now see mine Greece and then back to U.S. in Spring with my *Les Miserables* for you.

Love, Gregory

To James Laughlin

Hydra, Greece
[ca. Dec. 18] 1960

Dear J.L.,

I am here, all is wonderful, and if you could send me advance on book I'd be very happy, as I am wishing to obtain a small room on the isle of Hydra, and here rest and work. Could you send it to: Gregory Joseph Corso, Poste Restante, Hydra, Greece. I hope you can, I could use it now.

Hope all is well, Gregory

To James Laughlin

Athens, Greece
[ca. Dec. 29] 1960

Dear J.L.,

Merry Merry Zeusmas. I saw Hydra, had a nice calm time. Came back to Athens, had a nice Xmas and am living in Athens. So my address from now on will be American Express, Athens, Greece. I have been thinking that if I am holding on the book of poesy that no advance is due me—so excuse my urgency. Yet I am, of course, in dire need, and if anything is coming to me, I would be very happy to receive it.

Hope all is well, have a great New Year, Gregory

To Allen Ginsberg and Peter Orlovsky

Athens, Greece
[ca. Dec. 30] 1960

Dear Allen and Peter,

Come to Greece, I have a three room apartment right underneath the Acropolis. And only a few feet away, on both sides, from the Roman Agora, and Diogenes' gymnasium. It is a lovely place and an appropriate one for us to embrace by. Bring Lafcadio, he should not be denied Europe, and we will somehow manage gold-wise because I am sure mine novel will sell, though not commercial in content. I don't see how that title (*The American Express*) can miss. From here, there is all directions. Take a [berth] on the Greek freighter in Brooklyn straight to Piraeus [Greece]—an 18 day trip—a lovely one actually, even through I had some silly difficulty on it. Tonight is night before New Year's Eve, and I had so anticipated seeing you both tomorrow night—but instead of jet-ing to New York, I chose Greece. God only knows why, but I had to return to Hydra, and did. I went to the exact spot where it all happened. It's a long walk to it and this time I went with no sorrow but with heavy breath. And excitement. The place is the only truly deserted enclosure of the whole island. A ship grave yard in the crack of two huge mountains. Nothing happened. I looked for the black bird—no bird. The light was the light I had always known. I hurried back to the main part of the island—where all the people lived. It was seven in the morning. Raining. I turned the bend—and lo! a Norwegian girl dove into the sea. She had been drinking and was upset about her child. "Suicide! Suicide!" cried the fishermen, and the whole town rushed to where she had jumped. I was standing over her—where she dove from very shallow. She hit her head, she came up and held her head, "My head hurts." "Grab the iron rail," I said, as she swam to it and held on. Boats came to get her. "Great! Wonderful! Beautiful!" I cried, as she looked up at me in amazement. "I'm sorry, but I couldn't jump in after you because I would have been an embarrassing casualty as I cannot swim." I told her because I felt kind of guilty not jumping in after her. Anyway, that for my return to Hydra.

Rush me Fuck piece. McClure wrote a great one, this should be *the* anthology of 1961!!!

Love, Gregory

To James Laughlin Athens, Greece
[ca. Jan. 1] 1961

Dear J.L.,

Last year I wrote not to Ginsberg, who is very dear to me about an experience I hysterically embraced, but in blind letters to Ned Erbe and Don Allen, both of whom I was corresponding with at the time. They are strangers to me, yet it flowed to them. Well, I could never understand that, in fact it became more vivid in its address to me than the actual experience in itself, which I still to this day hold lightly because something in me tells me that I saw light because I simply opened my eyes. As silence can be heard, so light can be seen. Darkness is not seeing, nothing too extraordinary in that. Anyway I feel that Ned should know that I returned to Hydra and in the most comical fashion possible. I went with a pair of binoculars, really determined! Well, I did not see darkness, or extreme light. The spot is far away from the village in a deserted ship graveyard actually and seeing what I am oft accustomed to see, I sat down and with the binoculars looked across the sea, and felt wonderful about everything. I would like Ned to know this, also Don Allen too, but am wont to write him.

I did write something there and this was it. "What makes me see man as wonderful and victorious is in part my lack of seeing myself as so." Such self-put down was surely presumptuous, yet I feel I know what it means, and it has nothing to do with downing the self. I wrote it happily and proudly.

So a Happy New Year to Ned and to you.

Gregory

To James Laughlin

Athens, Greece
[ca. Jan. 2] 1961

Dear J.L.,

Enclosed find a letter I wrote last night, [the previous letter above] the morning tempts me to tear it up, if for no other reason than its penmanship. Anyway I send it on, and quite willingly at that because it does say something. That is, I felt I was saying something upon writing it. I just read [Alexander] Pushkin's *Egyptian Nights* for the first time, and God how at times I feel exactly as he did. Poets sure do enlighten me in that no one "poet" stands alone. Even if one feels one does.

If all goes well, if I make treaty with myself, I will have the second part of my "novel" (it's more a self-probe—a search of the present—therefore a truly endless work) in a few months, as I did set myself in Paris in a room and did do the entire first part (the part Girodias has) in a month's time, though the scheme of the work was long ago set out. It is also an exercise in creating for me, as I know myself quite well when writing poesy. Prose is something else, something I always had disrespect for, but having gotten into it. I find that I can make of it what I will, for I did fear prose was nothing but Woolworth art. *The American Express* is written in a downright grammar school way. I had much difficulty with the "he said," business, but have overcome that. And as it is too easy and false for me to undertake a poetic-prose style—the fault of most poets when undertaking to write prose. *Ushant* of Aiken's is a good example. I feel best at traditional prose, as I still feel the idea behind the word is more important. Words hinder ideas and lie, as often as not, the imagination.

Poesy I find also disturbs the flow. I really do not think there is such a thing as contemporary poesy—or, I do not feel it could go anywhere but to prose and when that happens (as I feel it happening to me)—then ways and wants, styles, and patterns, delivery etc. will lose their selectivity and become all poesy. I get the same feeling in this form of writing as I did in poesy, so I guess I am simply progressing rather than abandoning poesy.

I also feel that I have experienced a change in thought-process. I always wrote my poems with fire and I was never aware of that fire until Berlin when I coldly changed most of the poems sent to you. I had become aware, and such awareness does not allow for such fire. What I became aware of was that I was writing poesy. I questioned myself very much, wondering if I wrote for myself, or for mankind, or for man's entertainment, or for the want of love, and so on. Well, I know myself quite well, and I would say, all the questions were in a way true. If Shelley gave me anything it was a kind of nobility, an effort at plagiarizing the Gods as it were, and I think he would have liked me very much for seeing that in him. He's a pure angel-man, a great poet, and he wrote some awfully bad poems, and that too is enlightening. Not like Shakespeare who is all too perfect and inhuman, for Shakespeare and Christ—they both could be the Messiah—who would doubt Shakespeare that? Shakespeare himself and with good reason, too. He was much smarter than Christ because he well knew that everyman is the son of God. Actually, I guess, Christ knew that too, and in fact was what he was getting at. I'm reading St. Augustine now, *The City of God.* And it's the right time for it because mine *American Express* novel has much talk and questioning and actions of Christianity. I look very deeply into Catholicism, and see that it has no place in the new consciousness. That it will undoubtedly to keep its life jump into it. This jumping into something it had not conditioned is what I question. I see the church as something that gave light to dark, but that now gives dark to light. I call it a dark yet humane tribute to life.

For all my fuck-ups, I am coming very close to a wonderful intelligence, I can feel it near—and yet the laughable image of a nigger-Shelley looms before me—and that's not so bad because I can see that too, even if it's an image only unto myself. So, all this as prelude to a fast heart felt letter written to you last night.

I feel great, and cars, as Prévert would have it, "I dreamed so much of them, they've lost their reality." Enter the dream, see it as real and dream on. What a life!

Best to you sir, Gregory

To James Laughlin Crete

[Jan.] 1961

Dear J.L.,

Well, I finally got to Crete. As you can see by these cards, old Mr. Evans[202] was the Disney of archaeology—no? Actually I think the American Indian started it all. They migrated from the Americas to all parts of the world. One place they migrated to was Crete. Where else can such long black braided hair be found but in the American Indian? Also the red skin, the nose (that famous Greek nose) and the colors are very Aztec and the pillars are smooth totem poles. Yes, it is my belief that America is the cradle of all civilizations and that is why things are the way they are today. But I must do more research before I expound this fact. What a wondrous people these Cretans must have been. Also, all the designs, the rosettes etc., are just like those found on teepees. Yes, there is no doubt that Sitting Bull is descendent of Minos.

I guess there must be Atlantis after all. Why don't you sell all your ware, and with the money excavate the sea and have us find it—or do you feel it were better it were kept a dream? I often feel the later. No kidding, I really think the American Indian had a great civilization in the Americas before a weather change destroyed everything and scattered them throughout the world. That means of course that it could be possible that the first human beings were American Indians.

You are the first one I am telling this to, as I only came upon the illumination yesterday when visiting the ruins at Gnossus. At first I was greatly disappointed in Evans's Disneyland, then upon studying a real fresco of a Cretan youth, I saw the American Indian. I always believed there was something spooky about the American Indian. In short the whole glory of Egypt, Greece, India, China, etc. etc., is because of the vast migrations from the Americas many thousands of years ago. I will write an exact and scientific report on this (I will write it just like an archaeologist's) and will shatter all history books.

Yours in ever growing light, Gregory

I return to Athens this week and will continue mine novel. Also can you mail me all the poems to set straight. Make photos of them, as I have no copies. I want to look at them, get them in best order, and have done with them—o.k.?

To Allen Ginsberg Athens, Greece
[Jan. 12] 1961

I sat on throne of King Minos, and all the world be here because of American Indian, he having migrated to Crete, etc. Lovely land here at birthplace of Zeus. Are you coming? I have apartment, etc. Let me know, if not I go down to Egypt alone.

Love, Gregory

To Allen Ginsberg Athens, Greece
[Jan. 20] 1961

Dear Allen,

I just sent you off a 400 drachma telegram, (fifteen bucks), to hear quick if I should wait or not as I got boat ticket for 7th of February, 24-day trip. Hate to take it, won't if you are coming. If you ain't, then I go to New York, as I want to see you, no sense passing you by on ocean, unless you pirate mine ship. Anyway the fifteen bucks okay because I got one thousand dollars from the Poetry Foundation. What be the Poetry Foundation? Can you find out for me? Anyway they said, here's a thousand dollars for poesy 1960. I got it two weeks ago, and figured you were coming here with Peter and Laff, so built up house for you all, bought beds, rugs, pillows, books, record player, records, etc. All nice home things for your stay, back and forth from Turkey, Egypt, Athens. Be good stop place, like Paris be for Europe. Anyway spent much on them there goodies, then no heard from you, got disgusted with hominess, bought ticket for freighter going to New York, and am left with a couple of hundred now. So I hope you did rush a telegram back to me to let me know. I think either way is fine, if you stay, I come, if you come, I stay. Either way we'll meet.

What is it about junkies that need care? All a cheat and weak con, I say. And I said it to Burroughs' lovely face too, because I got on it [drugs] in Paris via Stern monster angel, and got it bad, but never went to hospital. What I did do was take jet to Athens, lock me in a room with St. Augustine, and lo, am all well–no hang-ups. It be because I take H [heroin] not because I am weak, but because it is there, and when it stops being there, or when it gets too much there, I take off to where it ain't. That is all. Why do they take it, if they be sick by it? I never really bugged anybody under such authority, as I would not let myself heed that authority. I think H depends upon the person and not the person on H, as in most cases. But it be a sick drug, a depressive, a real nothing drug. Your experiences, and lovely Harvard conspiracies[203] sound great! I knew Harvard had it in 'em, I did not have it as mine alma mater for nothing, no? I am writing vast play, all about J.F. Kennedy—wild, poetic, just like Shakespeare with King Henry, or Sophocles with Oedipus. Crete great, GREAT, the prince of lilies, lovely man, what height, they had heaven all right, but when man gets heaven he falls don't he? The young priest kind, all asplendor, our first Western heritage, and at Phaestus [Crete] I saw the Neolithic caves, all so wild and new, new in a way that life is so close and new, not old. No sir, it all happen right near, how strange and nice.

If you come PLEASE BRING ALL RECORDS, very expensive here. Remember, bring records. As for Laff, the money I get I will throw in with and for him. Also please rush me poor old shot up Parkinson's *Casebook on the Beat,* please. I'd love to have a copy, air it to me, thank thee.

Love, Gregory

To Allen Ginsberg Athens, Greece
[Jan. 24] 1961

BABY ANGEL,

Waited your word if you come or not, no wait now, but hope I don't pass thee by on sea, for I will return to USA now, in months time be there, go by slow boat. Time for rest think, and Amerique seem nice now, what with Kennedy somehow, and Paul Goodman's nice *Evergreen Review* piece, etc. All seems to open. Mine European beatniking forth, done. Whatever need be done, is done, and like old Yeats say, who can separate darkness from the soul? It be there always but it be nice to know that. Now for final help. I got no time or rush today to send Laughlin a letter to say don't send me back my poems, that I will return and therefore mend or unmend them there. Can you phone him right away? Thank you, and of course, it'll be great to see you again. Guess what? Ansen has been here six years, I am getting him back, he returns with me.

Yours yours, Gregory

To Allen Ginsberg

Athens, Greece
[Jan. 30] 1961

[telegram]
BABY JUST GOT YOUR LETTER HAVE BOAT TICKET TO USA ARRIVE MARCH 3RD DO I REFUND IT AND WAIT FOR YOU? PLEASE REPLY BY TELEGRAM AMERICAN EXPRESS IMMEDIATELY WAIT HERE BRING ME MUSHROOMS

LOVE GREGORY

To Don Allen

Athens, Greece
[Jan. 31] 1961

Dear Don,

I have written a great important American Universal play. The muse gripped me after not having written a poem in six months or more, during which time I wrote a grammar school cute novel which Olympia publishes this month—but the muse hath not abandoned her madman; and in three days, aye that much time, steadily, no food, only drink and peeing, I wrote mine play. You be first to hear this, and you be my hope for it, as I would like you to read it, let me know about it, and do with it as agent. Will you agent this for me? It would be best to show it first to the Becks of the Living Theatre, then whatever for possible publication—all this I leave in your hands—do you wish to hold? Let me know and I will send it straightaway to you, the play be called *President Kennedy*.

It be in the style of NOW and Sophocles—Shakespeare HENRY cycle, etc. I mean this, at least I feel it, nay I know it, for with such a work arrogance (long since having abandoned me) hath returned. I rush this, and expect a rush reply.

Yours with new light and love, Gregory

▼ [Don Allen replied a few days later that he appreciated the offer, but that he would not be able to be Gregory's agent for the play. He suggested LeRoi Jones or contacting Julian Beck at the Living Theatre directly.]

To Don Allen

Athens, Greece
[Feb. 13] 1961

Dear Don,

I'm all asunder, aye, a prophet of the most quacky sort; for today the Russians are on their way to Venus, when mine play has Mr. Kennedy aspiring there; yes, this is fact; and I am holding dynamite, but it must be flowery dynamite, and so I will hold the play for a while, then pounce upon it, and complete it in such fashion; unlike other things I wrote, this I wish to mend, hold, study, etc. So bear patience with mine enthusiasm in this case. As for publishing it, nay; as I must certainly ethically give it to James Laughlin and will; but as for it being performed; yes, and immediately because like all great silly plays it holds for the moment, and will, I feel, maintain that moment forever. Aye, it be that kind of play; and it could only have been done after my experience with mine novel. I got the fire of talk in me, and so I write it. I will send play to you, promise, near end of this month; when too you shall receive Olympia [*The American Express*]. I asked them to send you a copy toot-sweet; though what you read in *Transatlantic* is not in novel. The detective is, but the script not, as I deemed it a separate piece, and in the style of spontaneity, which I did not wish for mine medium; as I found that I could express myself equally if not better with concern; as say, a book written in the grammar-school style—old Neolithic caveman me. Anyway I think you will like the book, as its all about money, bombs, wars, castles, monasteries, boats, seals, carrots, Catholicism, ancient England, food, heat, and birth—and death—and the entrance and exit of a dream—and, ultimately, the victory of man.

Now what are you doing in S.F., or will you live there forever; or can't you stand Mr. Rossett's Galilean smile? But is Ferl's any less Galilean? Do you see him? If so, tell him I am firmly convinced that poesy and science must join; and that the time is at hand man shall KNOW the meaning of life. It has never been impossible—that hideous word, that delayer! I say it is possible. "I do not begin with a theoretical how and conclude with a theological why." This I have President Kennedy say; and I make my boy seek the meaning of life in the White House—there is no other way out for him; Laos, Congo, etc; these are earthly distractions to STAY man from FINDING OUT—finding out what? finding out if we see light, and light travels approx 180,000 miles per second; then it means WE SEE 180,000 miles per second! and if we see as fast as light, then we are unto light, and therefore light must <u>think.</u> This and other statements like it are the major concern of mine Jack F. Kennedy.

The only thing that swims in my head is the nearness to quackery a thing like this can lead to, ergo I must boost mineself up with renewed arrogance, and self-love; I must not lead the old lady across the street, I must brush her aside with my one tract cane—self; and thru self, I will find out just what light is thinking about. I end with poesy in a sense, and with it end the possible pretension of love—Christ love, mankind love etc. I can only look up, and hope that nothing straight ahead will distract me; earth must not be so cumbersome; it must not bore. Who cares about Berlin when there is heaven?

Whatever, I will keep you informed on any new discoveries I might make. As of now I am studying the possibility of light as a police force. For example, when you see dust slowly rising and falling in a sunbeam, look hard and see that the dust, countless thousands of particles, never clash with each other. Is light that regimented, or is it in the air, and light be it's spy? Whatever, I'm keeping my eyes opened. If I can't find a cause to defend, if I am uninterested in the pursuit of adventure on earth; then I must embrace and claim the over-all mystery until I die—*basta*. I hope I can be a benefit to that victory I call man.

I went back to Hydra with a pair of binoculars and laughingly saw only sea and sky. I was sure begging for a sign that year, what with my hang-up of death. I made death get the better of me, but it did not win, as I am far beyond that now.

This be a lot of me, and nothing about my good Sherlock. What are you up to? Do you want to join me in the quest (quite at hand) of life's meaning? If so send me important books on the Quantum Theory; or anything by Planck.[204] As of now all I got is Einstein's *General and Special Theory* and Defoe's *Journal of the Plague Year,* and *Dracula*—they don't be too much to go on. So if you ain't gonna be my agent, then be my aide, and if you prove Trasyllus' [Thrasybulus?] fortune book as self-evident, then you can be my partner in this wonderful search. As of now I remain your hopeful employer on matters of chance and probability.

Gregory N. Corso

To Paterson Society Athens, Greece
[Feb.] 1961

Find it so hard to write the how why and what about poesy at present. I find that whatever I say I usually contradict or eventually change. As of now I am of the opinion (belief) that poesy is layman's way of probing life and understanding universe. They say clouds of hydrogen gas, out of which new stars are spewed, is a <u>scientific</u> claim—the poetic claim be: "Stars spewed from some cosmic hole / a furnace womb / shooting out billioned life / Here these eyes by some divine cosmorama / will peel the supreme virus / and smile upon its Intelligence within." I think Science and Poesy must eventually meet, go hand in hand, and see what life, God, man, whatever, is all about, and I think this be soon too.

To Allen Ginsberg

Athens, Greece
[March 11] 1961

Dear Allen,

Just came back from one week car trip thru Peloponnese, my second trip to Mycenae Olympia Bassae Delphi in two years. Am all but wanting to do that again or remain here, as I wish Paris now, spring, newness, etc., and Bill is there. So why don't you get boat to Le Havre, and we all meet there? But if you want Greece I will wait, been here four months now, have had it, really. So rush me letter and let me know, what ever you decide I will abide by, though I do think it be shorter travel time for you and wiser to make Paris.

Love, Gregory

Allen the "Fuck" project for Olympia Press be in prose. I asked Kerouac, no reply, but the process going great guns. Yes, I think we should all join in Paris. Hurry, and get tickets, leave all behind, come and rest.

To Lawrence Ferlinghetti

Athens, Greece
[March 17] 1961

Dear Larry,

I got, I think, in November or December, here in Athens [a] check for 69 dollars. Is that the one? I hope not because then maybe I could have more money. Anyway, it is nice of you to give me all the [money] of Feltrinelli [an Italian publisher]. I live very strangely and continually without money, especially in this merchant-drunken-happy city of Athens. I hope to return to Paris soon. Who's going to India? You? Would you please send me *Kaddish* and your *Fidel Castro*? I have yet to get Allen's *Kaddish* book. When my novel *American Express* comes out I'll send you one. Am almost done with a play, then what? Get some chickens, a few goats, and die.

I think we all stink as poets, you most, Allen too, and me the worse, But ain't nobody more stinkier than Lionel Atwill.[205]

Yours with love love love, Gregory

To James Laughlin

Paris
[ca. April 27] 1961

Dear JL,

How wonderful to hear from you, but I felt very funny not hearing from you for so long, thought you were fed up with all mine rantings, and *American Express* book—so thought best not to write to you; am so happy that that was not so, nor did I believe it really, yet whirlwinds—Am back in Paris.

Greece is complete—that is done. It was fine, and did lots of reading there, and work on prose, which will be great, the *American Express* book taught me much about prose, its delivery, execution etc., I will do a great second book, one with more patience, that's what prose demands, and why not? Happy to be in contact with you again, been holed up in Athens, all by mine-self, reading lots of cosmic books, really know a lot about layman science; also books and records on the English plague year, Defoe's book, journals, grand writing. He is very good writer. Well the combination of science books and plague books took me over, and all my thoughts and talks had to do with those subjects, but not the sparse writing I've [been] doing, hardly any poems, but a verse play about Kennedy; was really inspired by his face his election campaign, etc.; so wrote first part of play, all in accord with him youth future America etc.; but now with that sad trek of his into Cuba, I don't know. It's tough, all of it. I mean Communism is BIG, and its anti-force, America, is BIG. It is not Afghanistan that opposes Communism, it is America. So fate; what to do but stick by one's heritage, no? Anyway I really have a funny feeling that nobody is going to either win or lose because nobody is nobody; and when nobody tries to be somebody, its all laughable. Also read quite carefully complete, two volumes, history of USA, from beginning to now, and found it so different from pure grammar school concept of holy America. In other words all I know is what I read—and little man in me says don't put too much store in that. Back in Paris to meet Allen, thank God for him, he be my oldest friend, and the talks we have are enlightening for me—gaps all filled, and for first time since I know him I feel quite serious and mature before him, and he treats me such. Thus we still do sillies, and all that. I will go to India with him, first I want him to come to Cannes with me to film festival, sun, swimming, girls, etc.; so that he can forget politics, Cuba, America, Anslinger, etc. for awhile. He's tireless old battler—and his *Kaddish* is really advance into soul-poesy; all so honest and good. Fine that poets are unlike novelists, in that the novelist who makes it with his first book always follows with a rank one. *Howl* tended to be an albatross round his heart, but he is an ever-poet, *Kaddish* proves so. Girodias just had a big cocktail party for me, for book, and it went off fine. Buchwald wasn't there, he sent his secretary who I know quite well and like. He did a column on the party, and I wrote him what I thought about it, said I was funnier than he because other two articles he did with me doing the talking was funny, but this one, all his own invention wasn't funny; something like that. But in publishing sense it be good for book, and I think that is why Buchwald did column, actually perhaps he meant it not to be funny because who's funny all the time, and he does like me very much and figured it be good for book sales. I will rush you a copy—do you like my drawings? Can I do some for poesy book? Am doing some on present prose venture; like doing the two together. This book I am doing now is hundred times better than *American Express*, and it will be done before *American Express* gets to America, so in all you can come out with that, and have whatever priority—and if Maurice [Girodias] doesn't send you book first then I will inform him that I find his action ungentlemanly, and threaten to cease being an idea man for him, as I have given him some very good ideas on a new magazine he is doing, 50 thousand copies a month, with digest from all his sex books. I suggested that he gather intelligent and honest essays from writers on the subject FUCK, done in the same spirit as Miller's essay in latest *Evergreen*, which I found very good. Also title of magazine *The Black Market Monthly*, plus articles on those crusading subjects, politics, drugs, etc. In short, a varied literary magazine, but not literary literary, not Genet all the time, but a magazine of interest, quick reading, etc. He would like me to edit it, and also he will give 1,000 dollars a month away to the best writing in magazine, which is wonderful. I would receive salary, plus percentage of sales. I could make lots of money that way, and make a pretty good magazine, but I am not of that responsibility, for a one shot deal yes, but to stick at it I don't know; but if I did, and did it with strength of thought, Julien Sorel-like,[206] great power, make it big important magazine; it would be funny. Nice that most anything like that would be funny.

By God, I will scream that I am serious even if it means cutting my throat. Actually I am completely in accord with myself and everything; those months in Greece did wonders for me. I am myself, but I am nobody, and whatever happens is good because it never happened before, and what happens to nobody is not important, so live on, and enjoy it all, even praise it, thus the continuance of poesy. That the biggest realization—realized that I could not go BEYOND death—but I could go beyond truth, God, etc.—and thought to go beyond poesy—did, and wondered if one who was aware of oneself as poet if such a one could ever honestly write the "I" again. Said to the muse, "I shan't have you cross me off your chart!" I will send that poem to you, it's quite revealing. So now that I am nobody, I fear nothing, in fact I feel deathless; so whatever I do is ok, like even doing that magazine. But Allen is going to India and India I will go—lo the offer! Girodias offered me apartment, office with secretary, plus big salary, and percentage. In year I could accumulate enough money to buy what I dearly need, a house with all my books and heavy doors and fireplace and cats, and music, and big curtains and eternity, just sit at big sunken wooden desk and write great big fat novels, what soul will be sold or lost by this? None, because I'm nobody; and so are you nobody; and we're the strangest because we are somebody. Well, the house will come, someday; and I will decline the offer, as the stipulation goes that I must remain in Paris in order to edit the magazine. I do think it is in a way a big offer, don't you? I mean I could maybe prove to myself or to people that I could create a practical big business industry. Remember how I felt about making lots of money, how I wanted that very much? Well, I don't feel that way now, but I do believe everything is opened for one, that one need not feel what is right or wrong for a poet to do; of course India is obvious, to shatter that and make a go of the magazine. I think I'll think about it, and whatever the enthusiasm of the day be when I have to choose, I'll abide by it. And will stand by it, too. I don't see how you find my letters interesting, this one is so muddled and rapid and further ventures in the life of Gregory Corso, no problem at all, and you with all them books to do, poor publishers really must have a time with their writers; and lo, considering how pesty and disobedient I was as a kid, you really got yourself something. I bet a publisher knows more about an author sometimes than the works of an author reveal.

Yes, please send on manuscript of poems. I'll have them so, and with some recent ones, a fine book indeed. I'll be off to Cannes soon, return to Paris in three weeks, so send it to American Express, Paris. I am glad we held back on book, actually rushed it off to you to keep my option now, though indeed *American Express* was rightfully for you. No getting out of that, but from now on I will direct all to you—don't get scared, as I haven't been writing that much. Doing things with great patience now. I do not downgrade my *American Express* but the first cake baked was so enjoyable to make the eating of it little mattered. What came of it was a better cake. *Basta*—all will resolve itself.

James Merrill's lover did a big lie about me in *Partisan* [*Review*]. I'm sure he was directing his cheap despair at me, for who else wrote *Hello Doom*, and I was the only beatnik they met in Munich. Actually I had a nice time, the two times I met Merrill, his friend I hardly said a word to. He implied that I took off my clothes to sleep with Merrill, that I failed, and that they threw me out naked and my clothes after me, calling me a creep. Now none of this occurred, at all—what presumption, and I ain't that literary fool to retort back and please them or *PR*—but I do think it was bad taste, and a lie. I don't mind my personality flaunted about when I do such things, and I do some pretty funny things, but when it is a lie, then I feel some kind of justice. Well I know what kind. Could I sue? I mean he is lying, but he called his article fiction. Does that exempt him? Granting it does, I have, as I've said, a reply. I will challenge him to a fight. No—when I see him I will sock him—yes! Because in said article he posed me as a delinquent, rough, etc. Well then, I will act in accordance, none of this literary dilly dallying, poets are human beings and some of them don't have to take any ratty falsehood.

If you haven't read the article it is in this or last issue by David Jackson, Merrill's boyfriend. Really rank that. I can stand on whatever I do—but will not on what I do not do. See how disturbing all this is? I really don't see how you can enjoy my letters. Saw Reuel Wilson, Mary McCarthy's [and Edmund Wilson's] son, and he said his mother thought the article a new low for *Partisan*. No, this must not go on unheeded. The word will be silent, it would be base of me to reply to it, but if I punch him, just once, I can hold myself and besides, he, the liar, is twice as big as I am, so it's not as though I were a bully. Their depicting me as homosexual (they themselves are) would of course, answer many things whereas their mental-scope is concerned. Well, I am no sex, yet do like going to bed with women, and only once with a man, and felt uncomfortable about it—no desire or need there. They just didn't like the idea of my saying I thought sex was unimportant and that I feel a poet can too easily be and so shouldn't. Quite silly on my part, but nothing so profane as to warrant such a disgusting lie. I really think Mr. Rahv ain't so bright having done that. *Basta*—there's so much more to be married to.

I will write soon, more, been a long time. Hope everything is O.K. with you and that what I write doesn't upset you, as I am not at all deeply affected by anything so small.

Love, Gregory

To Michael McClure Paris

[April 28] 1961

Dear Mike,

The f project [Fuck book] is dear and on the way. Money will be paid on publication which is this year. Please treat me only as idea man, not publisher which I ain't. Gave idea to Girodias, he crazy about it. I am thus done with it, except to suggest contributors. Know that your due will [be] allotted, especially for such a great lovely poem-essay snowfall. I hail thee and that's something, considering I don't often hail contemporaries. Only dead ones. If you see Whalen tell him I wrote a awful grammar school novel that might yet ingest goodies into prose's wheeze—O.K. I love you and I'm suddenly realizing there ain't no poet like none of us. I'm nobody, who is you?

Gregory

To James Laughlin Paris

[mid-May] 1961

Dear J.L.,

Am off to Cannes with Allen for rest and high talks. Just got appropriate check, thanks, glad to see *HBOD* wasn't a weight on you, good. That ain't so bad for poesy, is it? Am almost done with novel—will re-work it, then send it on. Please send poems to Cannes, I will work there. It should be a great book of poesy, as I have not written much since, but I feel that funny surge within once again. Girodias wants to get as much [as] possible for *American Express* so it's no sense talking with a business man, though other times he is really fine soul. I refused magazine offer, as India and self-work calls. Do you know I just found out that [Henry] Miller in *Colossus of Marousi* believes too that the American Indian is with the Minoan. Thus too simple a connection maybe, best to abandon that. Some nice man from Yale, a rare book buyer, bought my first draft manuscript of *Bomb* from me for 150 dollars—isn't that great? I think I should find a better title than *Victory of Life*—no? What about: *Gregorian Rants?*

▼ [Corso was just discovering that the actual manuscripts and notebooks of his work were worth more as objects to rare book dealers than he could earn through royalties. This lead him to begin selling his manuscripts, sometimes even before they were created.]

To Henry Wenning Paris
[mid-May] 1961

Dear HW,

Thanks for your letter and stipulation, all over 500 fine. You have been very kind to me, as the money is now going for the three of us to rest, a much needed one, in Cannes. I will send you *American Express* manuscript today if I can, as for money, anything you feel will be all right; look over manuscript, value it, and let me know. I think you a very fair and good wise man, so we can't go wrong. Just got letter from Laughlin today, New Directions publisher, and he said sales of my *Happy Birthday Of Death* was very good, and that I am one of the ten best selling poets in America. Wow, so I guess that *Bomb* manuscript won't be a dud.

I hope you read and like my *American Express*—I enjoyed writing it, had much fun, and got to learn and like prose by it. Ok, (how much is this letter worth?) Let me know when you receive the manuscript; whatever you can send me upon receiving it will be needed and appreciated. Ginsberg will get in touch with you soon; it's really good to see somebody who appreciates rare manuscripts.

I think my father has [copies of] early *Gasoline* and *Vestal Lady*, he needs money, and maybe you can write to him and propose an offer, he be a hard working man of whom I do not have much contact with, never had, but I will write to him, and say that I will give him newer copies, that he should sell etc. Ok, let me know if you write him, I will now.

Goodbye, Gregory Corso

To James Laughlin

Cannes, France
[May] 1961

Dear J.L.,

Happy anniversary of publishing!! Hail Céline, Eluard, Pound, [Dylan] Thomas, Nick Kenny,[207] and Gregory! Everything is fine. Yes—I will go to India, as soon as I get the fare. Allen and I will go, as of now I will remain in south of France. Am working, so please do air me poems, I promise you I will make a grand book for you. I feel a great change in me—thus. Again happy anniversary.

Best, Gregory

To James Laughlin

Tangier, Morocco
[June 12] 1961

Dear J.L.,

I am in Tangier—if you have yet to send me mine poems would you please send them here, care of American Consulate Tangier Maroc? Surely in the peace of this fine environ the master's touch will touch. Whatever, the calm of Bowles and Burroughs here just fine.

Best, Gregory

To James Laughlin

Tangier, Morocco
[ca. June 15] 1961

Dear J.L.,

Waiting dearly for them there poems to arrive, wish they were here as I want very much to WORK. Am waiting, why not air [mail]? It's all done—ok, it'll be a fine book, fine, yes. Wrote to Girodias, told him to rush you copy of *American Express*, did you get it? I found an ethical way out. You buy the book from him, don't let anyone else, you do it, and the money coming me from the sale I'll return to you, and so there, you have the book. That I think is only thing I can do thus to ensure ethics, etc. Also I have reworked much of book, as you know it was a rush job, did it in one month, though the idea boiled for years, the execution was rapid, and for a first jump into prose, wow. Only after it was in print, and only after not having seen book in many months, did I see all the flaws, carelessness, etc. A very simple matter to tidy it up, so if you like book and think it fine for your fine publishing house then great, all is saved, and I will be at hand to present the reworked and final copy. I feel it to be a fine book, and probably the dirtiest book he ever published considering there's hardly a kiss in it—such dire secrecy indeed should be banned from the face of the earth. Once I have this *AmEx* settled, good; the last of the big time fuckups. So let me know how you feel about all this, and I do hope you have received book by now. If you see fit to let this work, *AmEx*, go by, then that too will ease things. I guess there's no real problem here; and besides, in about six months I'll be done with the one I'm at, a definite sequel, as it were to *AmEx*. There's a lot to be answered in book, and this number two does just that. When they are placed entwined as one, I feel I would have written a unique shaky ideaful entertaining mind-twister, and easer. What say you of the drawings in book? Actually it would solve everything if you took book, you could entwine it with the one I'm at as one book, and we'll give it another title, as *American Express* means nothing to Americans there—and besides I would like the whole work to be titled differently. Now you can't say anything about this until you see what I have done on second book—so all I can say is, if you like first book, the second you'll like more. Is all this confusing, am I biting off more than I can chew, or you? What with the poems, and then this prose venture—actually it seems quite clear to me, and I will do everything I can to straighten things out. I would like to be a permanent author of yours, many reasons, the main one being you wouldn't print anything of mine you did not feel up to what I could do; and so all that would see print would be without regret or subject to change. I have received word from the only girl I ever loved in mine life [Sura] is back in America after three years in Yemen, and I haven't seen her in four years and would love to, so may return to USA just for that; so far I have a hundred dollars down on ticket, am expecting more soon, and might just do that and return, at least for awhile, then India to join Allen; also I would like to clear things up emotionally with family, get to be their friend and nice etc., and then go, clean of past, nostalgia, with everyone happy; it would be correct then, I feel, to go to India. I got to make up with my fellow man, I guess, the time is opportune, moving, even the trees outside my window seem to be passing by. OK, great about your ski-lift, worked on one in Manchester, Vermont, when I was sixteen, and learned how to ski in Plattsburgh in prison. The construction gang, to which I belonged, built when it snowed a great ski-lane, with small jump, from hill into courtyard, skis rented or bought from Sears Roebuck. What a place to learn how to ski! No?

Everything fine, and clear, and am hearing lots of talk of second coming, etc., all so damned secular, spiritual, subud, zen and all that jazz, when I feel the actual second comer will be a politic visitor, not a religious one. Whatever, it's all so wonderfully interesting; we are really living in a very strange time, expectation everywhere, what will happen? Must something? In it all, I, mineself, feel quite deathless—like it's going to go on and on—why I'm sure even your lovely aunt felt this to the last.[208] A new kind of faith abounds, an intelligent one, an awareness that no matter what, something rich and strange is surely ramparting us. That's why I've always distrusted Lazarus, he shouldn't have been so happy to come back.

How's your anthology? Will you use that *Greece* poem of mine? I looked it over again, and I like it the way it is, so won't change that, except for grammatics. Weighing all I have written so far I see that I'm really a cement mixer, patience would have me a diamond poet, I have written some real terrible poems, even shock me, who credits himself on knowing what is bad in poesy, guilty of bad poems. Ten years ago I would have shuddered to think I was so capable, and of course there are the good poems, no bother there; big trouble is when the bad and good make one poem, then patience, I say is all that is needed, time to reflect—as I often do; when I say I write spontaneously, I usually mark the poem so—spontaneous, why every thing written is spontaneous in a way, it's got to come out, it comes out. Anyway I have no set way with poetry, I do what I do, some, with effort, could be better, others, with fine study, could be torn away; and others, couldn't be better. The bulk of it, I feel, is yet to be, this I know; I know there is more to come, yet I do continue to claim poesy to be done and over, as something for youth, and that the true lyric will always remain, that the machine system of poetics will never hurt the lyric—The power of poetry lies not so much in the writing of it these here days it seems, like poetry is used now as magic, words are both dowser's wand and newt, all a playful alchemy. This is ok, gives man something to do, all variations looked after, the cut-up method, jumbling words together and making static sentences of them, measure forms like William Carlos Williams, and the ironmesh shirt tactics of Levertov, are riverlets; the main poesy is old as poesy itself, the soul's the ramifier, what flows from that is poesy, and no method can ever be exact when that flow's about. Therefore poetry, though going through its most dangerous battle and change since ever, will never die. What can cut-up the true felt emotion, idea, dream, vision, love? What measure, what science? Poets should write poetry and leave it alone, they who inspect the lyre, and I now definitely see Levertov, and even Ginsberg to an extent, messing with an alchemy that denies them lead into gold. Poetry was here before we came and will be here after we go, and if one can come and benefit it by systemizing it, by breaking or altering it, by contemporizing it, by bringing it to the consciousness of the times, fine; they paid their dues as poets—yet there's that in me suspects it all. Poetry is conditioned to its clime, poets are not, therefore they change it to their clime, and have it orderly there at—now all this shows one big terrible advance—poets today are aware of what they do, even non-poets are; these people are not poets to me, they are brilliant seers of poesy, they know everything about it, never would they be accused of one drop of weakness, they are bulwarks; their line their style their form their say stronger than the foreign legion. I can only speak for myself, I am in this poet guise in life, and I can't see it—but I usually end up seeing what I cannot see. Truth is, I read so much about the how why and what of poesy, I suspect a big hideous con. Poetry is a great lonely thing, and I confess to you that sometimes I feel I own it. Ha!

Get lots of sun, Gregory

▼ [Wenning had just complained to Corso about the manuscript he sent to him for purchase. Corso had discarded the handwritten copy and sent a typescript along to him, but it wasn't what he had bargained for and so he wrote that he was disappointed with the *American Express* manuscript.]

To Henry Wenning Tangier, Morocco
[ca. July] 1961

Dear HWW,

Ah, but Allen and I and Peter who are really broke here, at least until next week thought surely you came through; but I see why you hadn't. The script you have isn't so great or anything much but it is the only script extant. That is, I used to sit up at nights, (couldn't type then) and write out story in longhand. Next morning I'd type out what I had written nite before, that done I'd throw away hand copy. Alas I did not know of M. Wenning at time. So, for what it is worth, the typescript you have is only copy; there is no other, also if *American Express* is taken by American publisher, I will definitely rework it—was a rush job, done in one month. I see many things to be changed. So if that happens I will send on corrected proofs to you. Also New Directions, James Laughlin, has just written me that he is sending by post my next batch of poems (poems of which I have no copies, sent to him a year ago for publication) and I will surely pencil those poems up–haven't seen them in a year, it should be interesting, one year, things happen, lots changes–poets change, so do poems. Well, I could also give you them when done, so if all fails and or seems waterymilk concerning *Amexco* typescript, surely that batch of poems would do. So could you send on the gold token to me here, a bank check or two hundred dollar bills or whatever; and if you can't give it all at once, part will do–whatever. But we are in need here, living off Bill Burroughs and Paul Bowles for the moment. They too are poor old Arab souls. The Moroccans are truly another people; I used to think they outdid the West only by mental living; but their actual everyday living is quite extraordinary (for those who have some sort of income) they sit in sumptuous cafes drinking mint tea, reading the Koran, smoking kief, eyes far out across the sea. God knows what they think but, by their expressions, I would imagine they think that nice heaven the

Koran promises them. Whatever tis a splendid environ to find oneself in, at present. OK, I rush this off to you, hope all is cleared up; and glad you like mine *Bomb*, that it were no dud, and as investments go, quite safe, unless a literary Black Friday glooms a cloud over the rare book industry, but it'll be you jumping out the window not me. But then I would insist you don't sell short, but hold. That's what happened to the Burroughs adding machine fortune, they sold short. Or, and I much doubt it, a great big real bomb falls, then we're both out the window and all occasioned with us. Now I hope this cleareth up things. I'll repeat that *American Express* typescript is ONLY extant script, that New Directions is doing another book of mine poesy, and that if *American Express* script don't work out, that batch of poems will. I will not lay anything minor on you whatever. You have been, and are, very helpful to me, as I am quite often as not, slight of funds, and it is also nice to receive money for one's produce that would as it often had find itself indifferently disposed of—as I have no place to keep my things, as I carry all I write around with me, as I travel much, and carry little, I had no choice but to throw such valuables away. Now I don't have to, now they have a home, and a worthy one—so fine; all right sir, have a good summer, and excuse this rush letter.

Best, Gregory Corso

To Lawrence Ferlinghetti

Tangier, Morocco
[ca. July 15] 1961

Dear Larry,

This is my best poem in time and please print it as I labored especially for you and JL and surely it is indicative of your objective magazine, so. How you like it? I love it. You do too, or else I'll rat on you and tell the House of UnPoetry Committee what you're about and have you shot—ok. Great about your new baby real lovely of you that—true man of sensibility.

Gregorio

Fine about Kay Johnson,[209] she's a very good poesy. My female find actually, so I guess I can see sometimes. Love to J. Laughlin, I've yet to receive my poems from his ND [New Directions] - seamail takes time, waiting impatiently, raring to go. Actually you don't have to print that poem. I could see that you might find it a denial to take on position - but I would were one possible, y'know? And I feel the soap-box of Death is a select and worthy one. O.K.

To Henry Wenning Tangier, Morocco
[Aug. 7] 1961

Dear H. W., Mr. Wenning, Sir, Friend,

I am working on my book of poesy for Laughlin and when I have completed task will send the manuscript to you—all forms and variations. I will be off in two weeks to England, then expect to return to U.S.A. in winter. So maybe we'll meet there, perhaps I'll come up to Yale as I have friends there and present poems in person. O.K. best to you,

Gregory, Greg, G.C., Mr. Corso all

To Henry Wenning Tangier, Morocco
[ca. Aug.] 1961

Dear Mr. Wenning,

I intend to arrive in England broke and so could you extend your solid investment a cashiers check for 200 dollars good for any London bank to Joseph Gregory Corso, address US Consulate London England? This upon entire bulk that I will bestow upon you, this be quite urgent as I have received manuscript from New Directions and wish to work them over in London, in western clime, not here in Muslim land. I know they are poems you'll be happy to have. I would appreciate it very much if you could do this for me, and I hope I do not exercise your hospitality by such. Hopingly I await your decision on this.

Your friend, Gregory

I can also tell you that this batch of poems are to me my best.

▼ [Allen Ginsberg was traveling in Greece at the time and had just sent a letter to Corso in which he enclosed a typical tourist photograph of himself posed in front of the Parthenon. Since he was short on money, Ginsberg was hoping that Corso could repay him some of the money he had loaned him, but Corso was low on funds himself and it would be quite some time before he was able to begin repaying Ginsberg.]

To Allen Ginsberg London
[Sept. 6] 1961

Beautiful Allen,

So nice on Acropolis and surely have by now seen Mycenae, and I am sorely broke and no money from filmers or anything so how can I be responsible dependable but will hate across firey letters that I be responsible to thee and keep my commitments to you, ok as soon as soon I swear but all is not dark here except for place to live, been moving all about yet London is lovely the street names the pub names QUEENS HEAD and ARTICHOKE all like that, and met Colin Wilson[210] who I think is great, and so nobody else, saw

Archer[211] and he is broke and smarter than most folk and am keeping away from all else. Portman[212] is sick with replica BB. Always talks about Bill and Tangier and drinks thick sugary mint tea just to show what??? He's a bore, really thus, and when I arrived I went direct to Bill's and there in a smoky room was Mike, Ian[213] and Bill. Lo and behold, where do I fly to??? It was Tangier all over again. Awful that, sick and dead, and fled from there, but did come back to say goodbye to Bill who flew off to Cambridge, and he ain't a good man so much that William who leaves Sinclairs[214] and Michaels in his wake, a dead zombic junkie out to fuck all hoooman beans, really, and what for his sure fire style of speech and writing, he's a bore too, and I'll be a bore if I don't come across with that gold and laden you with what is deserved you. I rush this off to you and tomorrow will send press clippings from Ferl to you, and love, see and enjoy all you see. I'm sure you will and don't ever be sad and don't ever worry and I love you and we're deathless, yes, and you so nice on Acropolis, spread legs and Themistocles arrogance, yes.

Yours, Gregory

To Allen Ginsberg

London
[Sept. 13] 1961

Dear Allen,

Worlds fall on heads—only way I can make money to send you is by writing article about—about what? Anyway, will do so that I repay you, though I am literally broke, it distresses me that I have not repaid you. [. . .] Am all right and hate to ask Don Moraes[215] for money to eat and rent by—but do, much, and so life goes on until I finish film script (haven't even started). And N.Y.C. and where ever, where from there.

Love, Gregory

To James Laughlin

London
[Sept. 18] 1961

Dear J.L.,

Am almost done with poesy manuscript all are truly great—yes. There's a publisher here wants to do all my books in one—*Vestal Lady, Gasoline, Happy*, and the one now. So could you send me air one *Happy* (which they don't sell here). *Gasoline*, yes, but *Happy*, no). I will have him contact you after he sees book. I live on Oscar Wilde's street, Tite Street. London is wonderful, a relief after two years of alien tongues.

Gregory

To Allen Ginsberg London
[Sept. 25] 1961

Dear Allen,

This face gave me Greece when in jail, early days.[216] Wept upon seeing it, thinking mostly of you and how I wish I were by my dear friend's side. Yes, you can depend upon me, before the week is out I will send you some of the token you bestowed on me, not all but some. O.K.? Please take care of yourself and let me know if there's anything I can do.

Love, Gregory

To Allen Ginsberg London
[Sept. 27] 1961

I am off to Cornwall, to live awhile with Colin Wilson, who is fine young man. Have you heard from Peter? Please tell him to write to me or I'll cry cry cry—and what news? and darkness only heightens a love for going life. Yes—keep strong and don't miss the ruins around the vicinity of Phaestus.

The Black Hole was opposite side—long walk away from Seamens Academy, down by deserted ship building site. Here this card hails the loveliness of the human produce. I know you'll love Crete. I wish I could empower myself to fly there, meet you there and together witness climb, Mt. Ida [sic: Idi], the birthplace of Zeus. Do go to Phaestus—that is must!!

Love, Gregory

To James Laughlin London
[Sept. 27] 1961

Hi,

Everything is fine and I am really enjoying England and will, I'm almost certain return to N.Y.C., U.S.A., next month. I am off to Cornwall to stay with Colin Wilson awhile who I find to be a truly wise young man. Sure was odd after two years to talk to everyone English again, had to be aware of whatever I said all the time, whereas in Europe I got away with a lot of conglomerated *raisons.*

Best, Gregory

Will see Pollinger[217] tomorrow. Just received *HBOD.* Thank you.

To Allen Ginsberg London
[Oct. 13] 1961

Dear Allen,

Things might pick up ducat wise as publisher here wants maybe do omnibus of all mine poesies, fine that and also Girodias says Doubleday paperbacks Anchor is interested in *American Express*, and that will be florins galore, so I will deep mine responsibles to thee, and enclosed find something of sort. If Anchor Books takes then I must insist on revising grammar of book which was done in months time speed and heart soul but after months of rest, looking at it much, much has to be changed, so I will have my work cut out for me, but it is as should be.

England fine and restful and am almost done with poesy for Laughlin, as you can see I've been working, not so much revising as selecting, get very depressed from last year's depression by looking at last year's poems, bah. I will make this book *APPLES*, nice light bright little bunchy poems. Had fight with Mailer here at literary party, he insulted me by putting down beatniks and I called him on it and swung at him and people broke it up, etc. But he is jerk truly who has eaten from youth spirit and when that spirit gone journal flesh he joins in to partake of the carrion, can't be both corn and crow. No honor amongst thieves in this literature racket, alas. So the heck with high talk, fisticuffs tell more the man in some cases by God and me so thin and not strong am never hurt, not yet anyway, but the mind is sore and the soul the next day for such involvement. Colin Wilson pure ego and it is nice to see after all that GET RID OF YOUR EGO IDENTITY ETC. GANG, but I fear he's ego because he's got no other choice, pure boy they made big of him here freaked him then dropped him and so he must stand up, and I love that kind of stand in a man—and he's damn smart too; we got along, and I could go stay with him in Cornwall but I want to be alone. I am alone here, living near zoo, and go there often, big panda there, and ugly stork—my friends, of course. So you saw Mycenae, my homeland, my final resting place, I will go back there to end my days someday for sure.

Please see Phaestus in Crete, take taxi, have taxi stop you off at Grotyn [Gortyn], I think it spelled like that, old Roman town, on way, and a little beyond Phaestus go see the Neolithic caves by the sea, and see the old pillars left on shore by Romans, unbuilt—and at Phaestus there is only one hotel tourist bureau. The man will remember me with two blonde people, one girl, one boy, and he will take you to little idyllic Greek haunt near by, and go into town there of twenty five families and only saloon and see if my painting is still on wall, and feast your eyes upon the vast expanse and Mt. Idi in distance.

Sorry that Peter doesn't write and he should and will and maybe he is come upon something rich and strange. Should I yet write to him care of express in Istanbul? When Bombay? Snyder there and you and when? I still feel I should see America soon, I ain't no expatriate, as you well know. I been in Europe only to see Europe and isn't that part of a young man's upbringing? I truly feel I must get some more of USA in mine blood ere I lose my heritage, no? Have you heard from Jack? He still in America? He fat with heritage, him should grow thin, no, yes? Like come to Bombay and become as scrawny as an untouchable; why be a fat untouchable in USA when you can be a skinny one in Bombay? Ok, I rush this off to you and hope you can get nice important useful drachmas for what is inside, and here a poem for you: "*SEED JOURNEY* / There they go / and where they stop / trees will grow / / The nuts of amnesiac squirrels / will more nuts be / burr takes freight on animal fur / And pollen / the wind can carry / For some seeds / bread is death."

Be good and don't fall off a precipice and say hello to Zeus for me and did you see Olympia and have you met anybody with cars? Car is important in Peloponnese, and Thessaly. Surely [we] shalt encounter soon again, dear friend.

Love, Gregory

To James Laughlin London
[ca. Oct. 15] 1961

Dear J.L.,

Met Mr. L. Pollinger, and he is fine. Will take care of the dealings with publisher here who is interested in doing omnibus of all books of poesy, including the one I am almost done with for you. I will present it to Pollinger and he will see that you get it (nice that he'll take c/o the mailing etc.)

The main difficulty was in sorting out poems, not so much revising as I found I became terribly depressed looking upon last years depression via poems, so I put them ones aside, and you can expect a happy light bright book of little poems of which I'd like to call *APPLES*.

When if ever get the fare I'll return to my U.S.A.

To James Laughlin London
[late Oct.] 1961

Dear J.L.,

Would you believe it. Read my *The Apple Rustler,* it is true! Ha! Big shortage of apples here, so it should follow *Apples* poem as last poem in book. I truly think this will be a most wondrous book. I stand detached and see it thus. Enclosed more poems, I still have two notebooks to exhaust, so we'll have goodly size book, yes.

Best, Gregory

To Don Allen London
[Oct. 24] 1961

Dear Don,

Sherlock, your Baker Street is all a gloom, but with little and big shops that sell anything but scarlet. Anyway I'm coming back to USA soon and want that very much as I am not an expatriate but simply a young man who went for his European education, maybe leave in two weeks. Sorry haven't written sooner or anything about mine Kennedy play, subjects like that tend to weary me if I don't get it right out, and usually getting things right out get lousy—so I abandon all and go toward selectivity. Find enclosed selected poems from forthcoming book I will present to Laughlin next week, none ever published before, but you said that didn't matter, and also within find young Anselm Hollo who I feel is quite very good and he's a Finn and writes like George Washington—or if you don't like he will still admire thee and same for me. What means NEW POEMS 1? A series, etc.? That's real wonderful of Grove to phoenix poesy like the way they are. Don, if any of the poems you don't want you can give to Fred Jordan and perhaps he'll prefer those to that poem he has of mine.

I was working on English little girl sex crimes, very pastoral, but subject depressed me—get too affected by poesy sometimes, sometimes I feel poesy is nothing but mauling thoughts, or mauling thoughts ain't poesy.

Please let me know what you think about this cargo, and give Ferl my love and say I will write when I'm all done with what I'm at which is getting JL's book together, want it to be a wonderful light smart book, will call it *APPLES*, and it be the first book I've truly depended upon mine own selection. Selection is much more difficult than revision, ok, and things will always be nice, and smarter. Can you tell Ferl to air me *Journal for Prevention {of All Beings*] which I never got? I would love to see it.

Best to you, and if you're not happy with what is sent, let me know and I'll try to remedy it but I'm happy with what I sent. No, forget that *Bring Back The Dead* poem, that was two years ago with all its idea—gone, let it rest, please: and *Humanity* is nothing but a series of wordsettings, the poem that is, and have put that aside as exercise. What news?

Best, Gregory

To James Laughlin London

[late Oct.] 1961

Dear J.L.,

Hope you got my *Apples*, it's a book I'm very happy satisfied mature in and about, and the poem *Apples* says it a lot, and should go last in book, and it'll be a nice concise small book but with big print, yes? I want you to know I wrote you countless letters but tore them up because I wanted only this to say—I'm making you a book that you will be proud of –

As for Girodias, this—he says Doubleday wants mine *American Express*. I wrote to Carl Morse there and said explicitly on condition that I re-write it, and I have, and NOW it's a great book. One year on it and that too, I'm happy about. But working on mine conscience I am determined that nobody gets that book but you or nobody or if he, Girodias, goes ahead without my permission then I will let it go and not touch a penny of it, this I swear to you. I am insulted that he should not have shown you it first, and so I stand and if to be unethical, is there anything to stop me from giving you revised book? It's vastly different, ergo another book and let him sue. Your contract has option on next book, you are in clear, also conscience wise because it's your book, and I tell you, you'll love what I did with it. I'll bring it to N.Y. with me, should be returning in two or three weeks. Write me right away and let me know how you feel about this. I have screwiness by no intent, but also a hard stubborn core of ethics, yes. He cannot insult two fine poets as we, and that's that. Don't grow any taller.

Your friend, Gregory

To James Laughlin London

[Nov.] 1961

Dear J.L.,

I'll have another batch of poems for you. I had wanted to keep the *Apples* selections as is, but is it possible to supplement the forth-coming batch? Most [of] the poems I have are what I term "Poems that flowed in surreal writings." One, *Time Magazine*, was writ in Greece after that incident with photographer and is done in good taste but perhaps it may spoil as you correctly state, down-to-ness tone of *Apples*. Whatever, I'll send them on, and you decide—plus some more little poems for *Apples* collection, so we'll have a full book.

I wrote a play in 1954 called *In This Hung-up Age* and it was performed at Harvard in 1955 and was liked very much. Seven years later I get my hands on it, and it is a strange dynamite. I met Stephen Spender and he's truly fine, and he like play so much that he's going to put it in his 100th anniversary issue this Dec. 20th.[218] Now perhaps we could put play in book. I'll give you synopsis and have a copy for you as soon as possible.

1956 was the year San Francisco made any noise, but in 1954 I predict (in play) Beauty, Hipster, and Poetman go via Greyhound bus to San Francisco. 1956 was first mention in writing of Hipster as central character, my play's hero is called the Hipster. 1956 poesy started to wake up and my poetman in 1954 vows to renew poesy and the oddest thing, and most wonderful, is that I called my play, a 9-page one-act, a farce. Thus I made farce of what I saw coming. My Poetman has absurd social complaints, my Hipster is but a jive-talking juvenile delinquent, my tourist (the Square) is also perhaps the first definition of American Square. He and Hipster are truly comical antagonists, thus a document indeed. Predates all this serious Hipster social rebel nonsense of today. As soon as Spender sends me proofs I'll ask for typescript copy and rush it to you. Thus it be Harvard that first heard of the Hipster, truly funny this, and like Spender said, oddly prophetic. The year it was written and performed makes all the difference. The play ends with the entire bus getting stampeded by herd of buffalo—only one to live is Beauty. Hope there, yes, and the last line of play belongs to Hipster: "Man, what a draggy way to die." I'm very happy about this for it can show you how, when Hip fell into the hands of college social dissenters, serious the Hipster became. I christened him farcical, even the poets to come. I made their complaints inane yet true happy ones, it should enlighten Mailer no end.

I will leave on the Queen Elizabeth on the 24th and arrive in New York on the 29th. I can't wait, I've had my four-year European education.

Best, Gregory

To James Laughlin London

[Nov.] 1961

Dear J.L.,

Asked Spender as soon as possible to give me copy of play to zoom on to you. God knows why I feel play a "document" important that it might set things straight and that it is not meant to against mine friends; as Beat is Jack's (???) and all that there stuff. But as for FIRSTS, what matters it? Still I would like to write mine own epitaph as concerning social-rebellion. Enclosed find note that will precede play and mine full name which is Gregorio Nunzio Corso. Joseph is my brother's name, and (keep this to yourself of course) got passport under his name for fear that they wouldn't give me one because of prison record. Quite silly and impulsive that, but what boots it; if I ever get caught (not much chance of that, for who's to say I'm not Joe), anyway if I ever get caught, I shall say "I love my brother, and he is a hard working man with lots of kids and can't do traveling etc., so I went under his name, and pray that I have done it honor." How's that? So you see when I say I sometimes do screwed up, harmless things, that can become very big, and the world comes tumbling down; but I fear nothing. I've got love in my heart and know that everything day or night is all right.

Now about coming home; I'll come home and don't know anybody there, and don't want to live in Village, but maybe uptown, and if you could really do me the greatest favor in the whole world and with the 200 dollars you would like to bestow upon me get me an apartment, maybe two rooms, furnished or no, and give them the whole 200 in advance. Or this will drag you, won't it? But when I get off the boat, where? I'd hate to start off banging on ghost doors—and my father, I wrote him three weeks ago, a real true letter saying I want to come home and get to know the whole family and be a son and all that but no reply. I guess he's real sore at me for having writ some silly things about him, that Grove New American poesy letter in back of book where I say not-too-bright father. Damn Don Allen should have had the sense—*basta*. I hardly know my father, and he wasn't really great to me as a kid, but he is a good man and works hard and I would like to do something. Ginsberg told me long time ago, if you're going to love, you got to start at home. He's right; so maybe after awhile things will work out; I'll be straight with them, show them I'm a man, and life is good, and things like that always work out—so. So could you maybe get somebody to apartment inquire for me? Somebody who likes me and thinks I'm a big poet and would be honored to find me a domicile. This is short short notice, but getting off that boat with sole suitcase—I'd what? Yes, I'd get a hotel; and that's not so bad, so if you can't do anything like this for me, then that's what I'll do. Kerouac I'd ask but I don't think that guy's ever done anything for me but write about me, and always off base; so you see why I say I don't know what "friends" is; but Allen is, I know what friend in him is, and I'm very lucky to have such a funny Jewish duck like that for a friend; and he'll be the only one to break up happy over my funny claim to have been the first to define hipster accurately, and be advent of S.F. as Bethlehem. Tis all a farce, it is, a nice happy serious good farce; and who's to say I'm not endowed with Serious. Humor can make Serious cry wolf. Serious deems Humor the wolf.

Enclosed find some poems, just read the *TIME MAGAZINE* piece. I don't think it is worthy to go in mine bushel; and I didn't need Allen or anyone to help me with my poems, I am my own master.[219] All I gotta watch out for is impulse; and that "watching out for" is your fine selective insight into such a me; and that can only mean that I respect your know, sir.

Okay, and more poems will come, I have little notebooks and haven't gone through them fully, as I said I sometimes come upon truly depressing things written way back when I was depressed and it is painful to look back; but that's the poet's plight and no complaints, I think I'm gonna write an essay called: "The Haphazards of Poesy."

As for the misspellings, we'll work that out when I get back; you must realize that I am without dictionary; that I am a good speller but sometimes goof; and that you are right when you say sometimes the misspell is purposeful—also I can draw, and I would like to do cover for mine *APPLES*, ok?

And if you like the play, which you will, I'll bet all the steel bits in my room against your steel mills that you will; so if you do, it should go in as Supplement; other than it appearing in *Encounter*, it has never been printed in USA, and besides, we gave them a goody in *HBOD*, with *Bomb*, now we'll give them another goody.

Can you tell me exactly how many *HBOD*'s sold? And why didn't you send me some of the bad reviews it received? I read the one a couple of days ago in library here from *Poetry Magazine*, I loved that one. It made me out of a whole batch of books the villain; but he defeated his purpose in quoting me, the *Transformation And Escape* poem, never been too fond of it, but loved the fragment he selected to be critical about; "a gooey heaven, Dante's hang-up." I like Milton much better; really. Dante is that kind of Italian who is cocksure, smart, granite morality; and beautiful; but I like Milton better; the difference between a catholic and a protestant in depicting heaven and hell, I'd trust the protestant's define. Something about Dante has always irritated me, and I think I know why; his wit is sarcasm; a closed mind, the secret to itself, vaulted with sentience, opens to close. His vision was an opinion, *basta*. I have no doubts about Shakespeare, Homer, Milton; I doubt Dante.

Now what else? Nothing else, but that it'd be great to see you again; I'll keep in touch, bye bye.

Gregory

To Allen Ginsberg and Peter Orlovsky London
[Nov. 14] 1961

Dear Allen and Peter,

From all that hits and strikes home in me—seriously and honestly, I am most happy my two lovely companions in this here *Pull My Daisy* life we together and forever again. Peter, baby, I miss you and hope I can do whatever you wish me to do when I return a week from now to New York. Just ask me, let me know, and I'll do it. It's the least I can do for indeed a friend—and friends must fight sometimes, so? Yes, O.K., but no more. Allen, as for money, it be slow—I did all I could to obtain ticket, but when I get back to U.S.A. I'll try to sell some of my manuscripts and secure some gold for thee. I shan't rest until I repay thee, enclosed find five pounds which I hope comes in handy. How is Israel, and how are you honored there? Let me know, and this is the last time I make up with Peter who lacks what I have and that is never to remain mad at anybody for too long. This be fact, and no sense hiding it. I am not altogether to blame entirely for our dispute, good God. *Basta*. We are bonded together by forces more than me, and it be absurd to play against it. I hope, Allen, that Peter is O.K. and better than in Tangier where Burroughs did spook things a bit and I suddenly realize about Bill, he's no respect for us ever since his *Naked Lunch* and power mad. He has much to be humble and magnificent about, but I have lost faith in him because of his human con, though I don't think I'll ever encounter more genius and dignified type man, ever. He has bad tastes in his Gysin kick, and unlove for his replica-ing of Micky

Portman, who, a doll to begin with, is now absolutely batty. He takes apomorphine just because Bill says they're good for you! And everything he speaks about is Bill says this, Bill says that. His poor mother! I saw the whole sorry mess when I stayed with them, he's [a] downright bore! Well, he's off to Tangier, and I do hope he stays out of it, or with Sinclair Beiles again. And I once offered to aid Bill in everything, he telling me he was God, etc. He played with the wrong one. I'm just as sharp in some respects as he, if not sharper. It's [a] fact that I am of new school—he old Texan type—smelling of biblical vanity. I shan't go visit him in N.Y.C. until I write to him first. I find the world less a sinister hang-up sans him. He's a little like Norman Mailer. Poets become novelists! They hate poets—envy though a novelist just loves to be called poet, untrustworthy. I wouldn't trust Bill quite seriously, he betrays. And to his face I called him Will the Weasel. The man is everything and I wish him the best because he's had a hard sad life and is, as I say, a great man.

Allen and Peter, in 1954 I wrote a play called *In This Hung-Up Age*. It was performed at Harvard then, and is as far as I can tell the first writing about the original Hipster, the delinquent. Also the play has to do with Beauty and Poet among the passengers on a bus all going to San Francisco! Now this be 1954—quite a prophetic that—and I called play a farce! Which is the great thing. Mark revenge, of course. *Encounter* will publish it in their 100th anniversary issue, and I hope it sets this Hipster nonsense straight. I, as Beat, if that's my stigma, was first to depict the Hipster, only one to mention hipster is Holmes and he only once and in parenthesis, my hero is called The Hipster! Spender flipped over the play and said it was sure to cause some literary fireworks. I wrote note before play saying that the noise started in 1956 by late comers, Mailer 1957. It might bug Jack, but it's Hipster I'm at, and to show up Mailer who insults the Beats here in Albion quite falsely and creepy. He's *Partisan Review* nut, Allen, and not crazy crazy like some people think. He's ambitious traitor—he joined the Beat bandwagon and journal Hip as possibility to destroy Beat. He took from Beat, but the laugh is with me. He wrote seriously of Hip—I, premier, wrote farcically of it. Happy that life is funny, not dark sad like some would like it to be. Anyway I did funny note sure to bug everybody as setting myself up as originator of Hip. I don't believe I am, but did encounter Hipster and hip talk way back in 1943 in Tombs with spades. So I got good indoctrination and my Hipster is a Lower East Side delinquent who talks in "dese dem and dose—goil," intermingled with "man, crazy, cool, square, flip, etc." I think you'll love my play, and I feel I got my job to not lie down and take journalistic crap, Mailer, or anybody. I am just a poet, but it is not my life entire, I am also a being with social comment on my tongue though I could never really believe it. Fine, then if I down and laugh at some of the quirks of society, I can well expect a retort, and should be man enough to take it. Well, I have taken it, and have always brushed it off as lukewarm inferior rebuke. I have poetry, and that's unbeatable (pun?) yet I shan't be down and take it just because I dished it out. No, when they're wrong, I'll tell them so–so. But I do hope when I return to N.Y.C. I'll go unnoticed and live a select life. I'm actually weary of Beat Square holy love war etc. I'll go see your father Allen, and Peter I'll see Laff.

Love to you both, Gregory

To James Laughlin

London
[Nov. 18] 1961

Dear J.L.,

O.K. about advance. True I recall asking for it a way back, and you graciously complied. I have boat ticket in hand and some extra funds to hotel mine self. I am sending you some more poems today. Poems that should make *Apples* burst with ripey goodness. I feigned to include my *Humanity* and *Man* poem, but realize that it be very important to go with collection. It's a statement of my faith and makes the poem *Apples* all the more sensible. I wrote Ferl and told him my *Apples* will be best book of poesy since 200 years!

These poems I send on shan't be in English book, those have already been collected, thus the American *Apples* will be a complete book. I did the selection from my three books of poesy and Spottiswode was pleased with it. What think you my note to play? It was done with intention to irritate some folk but I don't think I bit off more than I could chew—no sir. O.K. see you soon,

Gregory

To Ted Wilentz

London
[Nov. 18] 1961

Dear Ted,

Thanks for books and for enlightenment as regarding Ted Joans, he then has something to fall back on with all that mockery he helped join in regarding Beat-mass-media. Though this absolves him—it is done goodly and intelligently. Though it seems now he goes to Hip bandwagon when he first went on Beat bandwagon (he didn't fare too well there). God only if he would have thrown all that crap on Mailer type hip. Still he and a lot of people got big surprise coming them in Dec. 100th anniversary issue of *Encounter.* In it will be a play I wrote in 1954, and had performed at Harvard 1955, long before anything was ever extensively writ about Hip or Beat. The play is called *In This Hung Up Age*, and quite prophetic and the main hero is called Hipster, and play is a farce. They were all so serious with it in 1956-57 (*White Negro*)—so it will be a bombshell, all right and underdoes Joans by seven years, Mailer by 3, and as when I was 13 in Tombs prison in N.Y.C. I learned all my Hip talk from spades (ten to one white) there, long before anybody (literally speaking). The play has been in the dark for seven years—now it comes out, and my Hipster is the first Hipster. Yet though Joans is late, he is redeemed, you just can't swap from Beat to Hip unless you are both—and Joans is neither. He is old-fashioned Bohemian, and that's all. He has done nothing to help man truly, but his Hipsters is not amateur, which he is. So I am very happy for him, but when it comes to <u>advents</u>, time is very important, and my play will reshuffle things somewhat. Things must really be bad for Beats there if a such like Joans gets off it. But fine—because one must sing his own song—thus when play shows that it was a Beat who first wrote about Hipster, Joans (Mailer more important) will have to find another bandwagon song.

Yours, Gregory

To James Laughlin London
[Nov. 22] 1961

Dear J.L.,

How lovely to have somebody meet me at boat, because only you know I'm returning, and like I said everything back there seems ghost to me, and good, I can live my life in peace in New York, unto myself, and will set to painting, as I am a good painter, and my first picture will go to you. I paint like Rembrandt, millions of dollars him, and what a lovely Rembrandt that is isn't it. Great, that should put them there abstract business men painters in their place. And also will do last finishing touches with that play I spoke about way back; now if I let you publish that does it mean you own rights to play because then what merits it me money wise? I mean I could get it produced first then it can be published, but as I ain't got no agent then maybe we could work something out, for I swear to you the play will be a smash. And as I have my *Hung Up Age* and four other little ones written about that time, you could do a book of my plays, five little one acts and one big one. The big one has to do like this: a great young man does nothing but stand on street corner. "Standing on a street corner waiting for no one is power." Well I go to prove it, in three acts! So it takes a lot of genius to keep people interested in a guy standing on a street corner, doesn't it, but God what possibilities, all the mad occurrences on that corner! So doesn't it sound nice? Your little book is lovely and straight and you got that very important thing in a man, childlikeness; that, without that, is great part of poet, and danger, how to use that lovely quality. I'm giving a lecture tonight a high class prep school here for Stephen Spender and son, and fifty young lord sons. I will show you lecture when I get back, and you'll see how smart I'm getting. You see, I come on with you as a son who wants to make his father proud of him, and don't let that scare you, I'm a million years older than you sometimes, so there.

And as I'll be off tomorrow there won't be anyway my knowing who'll meet me at boat, so you don't really have to have anyone there, because how will they know me? I've changed facially, and all that, but whatever you think best, and as for finding me a place to set up for a while, that would be a great benefit, and I'd appreciate it very much. I won't let you down as to exercising anyone's hospitality who would be so kind as to put me up. Saw Eyre Spottiswode here and he says when Pollinger gets things all straightened out he'll have contract ready so that'll be in New York, and he'll be in New York, the editor of Spottiswode in January, so you'll be able to meet him, a very fine man. I gave ND [New Directions] as my mailing address here, so you'll probably get letters for me, ok?

I have more poems for you, a batch called *Gregorian Rants*, funny light subject matters, and if possible maybe they could go as supplement, they must not go together with *Apple* collection. Here's a mystery, England has an apple shortage this year, swear to God. I anticipate seeing you, sir, good health to you.

Gregory

To David Meltzer London
[Nov. 24] 1961

Dear David -

Indeed you are a poet—a lovely one, a fine fine one, for to me a poet is one who alive is a poet and not a poem on a page. The poem is nothing without the poet. This I always believe with all my heart and your lovely Tina childbirth in Journal Protest [*Journal for the Protection of All Beings*] was assuring mine belief. The world will be wonderful if more fathers and mothers and doctors and nurses and babies be the world of yours. How can it miss?

Thank you, and let me be the spiritual God father of your child if by thought as it were because I feel something of mine property there, so oddly, bless you all.

Gregory

To Michael McClure London
[Nov. 24] 1961

Dear Mike,

You is genius, your Journal Protest great. Are you in New York? We must face each other, true, so I arrive in five days on Queen Elizabeth, perhaps on 29th of month. If Ferl can, for me, telegraph you in time, ain't got your address, hear you're in N.Y. Maybe you could meet me at boat? Will you? Ferl please rush this off to McClure or telegraph him to meet me, inquire just when Queen Elizabeth arrives in N.Y. I'll be on seas when you get this, so there's time for you to get in touch with Mike.

Best, Gregory

To James Laughlin New York City
[Dec. 11] 1961

Dear J.L.

Here are poems and your A-f man did enlighten me as to some changes and eliminations. As stands these 40 odd poems ring of all that is good and excellent. They, with play, can make fine book. Sorry you're not here for me to see other poems you think might fit in, but then I can come up during week. Tomorrow, Tuesday, I go to Yale for day. Will see you Thursday if you are here—or Wednesday morning. If you feel there are not enough poems, then let us select from old batch. I go to Allen's father's house, and there I am sure to come upon early poems, so perhaps some from that lot. BUT, as stands, the tone of book as is, holds well for me. Title: I would be inclined to have "New Poems" by G.C.—I wish not an entertaining salable title—but can suggest some. Here goes: *Full Acceptance—To Decalenderize—Everyone Faces Universe Alone—Long Live Man.*

Best, Gregory

To Henry Wenning New York City
Jan. 1, 1962

Dear Henry,

Just got your month old letters. Happy New Year and hope all goes well with you and family and life. I want to thank you for your ransom of Romeo to me. It came in handy, but I gave it all away to a father I don't know, a brother I don't know, and a grandmother I don't want to know. So I am again broke. Now be patient and ponder this. In Venice are *Vestal Lady* and *Gasoline*, about 14 books. I'll give them to you for the other 500 dollars and Alan Ansen has them there and he'll be back in Venice, April. So in April you'll have them and by March you'll have what is already owed you. That means if you give me the 500 now—needed now—I'll be in debt manuscripts 900 dollars. Wow! But I will comply, and can be trusted, as Gregory Corso cannot hide, alas. And if I die this letter is document as to what is rightfully yours.

So, sincerely, I am without a place to stay and all that, and the money would go into getting an apartment. I waste not. As I say, I gave it all to a family who never had any use for me, nor did I think to buy their love, their love is alien to me. *Basta*. Whatever you will—I will abide. Thank you, and hope everything will be o.k. with us. It will, because I hold honor to be a very necessary thing.

Best, Gregory

P.S. I promise to keep my end of this bargain.

▼ [During this period Ginsberg had been traveling extensively. After leaving Morocco he went to Greece, Israel, East Africa and finally India where he and Peter Orlovsky were to stay for the better part of two years. His letters to Corso are filled with the sights and impressions of these exotic places.]

To Allen Ginsberg

New York City
[Jan. 20] 1962

Dear Allen,

O you lucky angel of an adventurer—Pygmies! Elephants! And I bet the sky really cracks there with all sorts of sky-goodness. How was Greece? Disappointing? In a way it is, but the past holds firm there, doesn't it? and it makes all the difference. But great about your visit to Africa—that is good. I miss you and Peter, I do, I do. And please let me know how long you intend remaining in India—for I'll fly there, and be good, I swear. America, New York, I had to come back and see my dear old home again—but, alas, it dawns upon me that my maturing years were had in Europe—and lo, Europe seems my home and here, a strange land. Never did I think it would be, but it is. I feel I'm outgrown it. I stay indoors, in hotel, and write, and that is good. Sam, my father, brother and his kids—all politeness, but nothing to talk about, so I hardly go back to visit them. Saw your father and retrieved my papers there. Your Dad is fine, and I helped clean up his mind about your use of the word "fuck" in poesy. I explained to him how once I was called a dopey fuck, and both he and your new mother laughed, proving that the word can be other than what it is to them.

I wrote a little play for *Evergreen* with drawings and it will be in *Evergreen Review* 23. I wrote about a smart goofy soul who stands on a street corner all day helping people cross and talking with them, and says smart things about fallout shelters and bombs, all innocence. Then at end of play I break this innocent into pieces. I question him in form of tall academic man. I do it to myself ere anyone else can, quite unique and *charmantique*, you'll see. I really am very interested in play form, and hope to do a big one! Then money for us all in our old age! I still owe you gold and in next letter you'll have it, I swear.

Where's Bill? I want to write to him, have you heard? He's not in U.S., I don't think. Please send his address. Went to see Leary at Harvard weeks after I arrived. He's O.K. but I can understand Bill's not going along with the "game." Leary sees it all as "game," too collegiate thinking, that. O.K., don't get mutilated by some spears dear boy and never cease loving me, never. I am, as always, endeared to you. We is big growing men, so weak sometimes, so strong sometimes. I regret nothing, do you?

Be good, love, Gregory

To Lawrence Ferlinghetti New York City
[Spring 1962]

Dear Ferl,

I did not receive mine meager royalty check you sent to England. I wrote there for it, but they say it's not there. What do I do? How are things with you? It's been a long time. I seem to have lost my love for letter writing, I can write from Europe, but not from Amerique. Am finishing a book for Laughlin, poems from 1959 to 1962, I'm sure you'll like it. New York gets me down, everybody seems sad or cold or dead or on junk. I like indoors, or the space of Europe. O.K., my best to you, and when will we ever meet again?

Gregory

To Allen Ginsberg New York City
[March 9, 1962]

Dear Allen,

Been fluttering mentally soulfully about, out of contact, with contact, saw family of mine, said I'd get them out of their squalid neighborhood, then disappeared, never showed up again, what a fool they must think I am, anyway, can hardly care for myself. I do try, alas, and saw your brother, he's fine, and Jack too, but he not so fine, drunk, and can't talk straight with him. Wanted to, he just cares about his self and demands I respect that self, but I can't if he just sits about bubbling drunkenly how great he is and how bad who else is, so unreal, unrelated, that he truly bored me—and your brother did try to make sense to him about trial, his wife had him get blood test, and test shows that kid is Jack's, and Jack no want that baby.[220] He said she said: "Jack, I don't care if you're my father or not, (double negative girl) I'll still love you." Poor Jack, to hear something like that can break your heart. Anyway I was in no mood after three years of separation to hear his boring diatribes.

Thank you for your lovely letter and that strange African adventure, sounded real great, and how is India? Miss Rachevsky tells me you are not too happy there. I always laugh when I think of you entering India, I have two imaginary holy men sitting on rock, eyeing you as you leave gangplank, one saying to the other: "Boy, here comes a live one!" But I'm sure it isn't like that, but hot and dank and poor people, and surely life as never you saw it before, and perhaps hope for a treat of perhaps a touch of Amsterdam life, respite from that Africa trip. But what of the sunsets? They surely must be something, that's what I wonder about India, those amber sunsets.

So miserable and lost here and unable to write I resorted foolishly to drugs. Stanley Gould and Eager, those Mr. Deaths for sure. Began to lose all sense of love, body, self, spirit, dignity, that which you think I assume. But truly do not, but truly am serious and mixed up because of life, I lived it fast, Allen, and can't bear the slow down; but as is often the case with me, I come out quite strong when under stress; but as I grow older it leaves its mark. I've ceased drugs, and hate of self, and am now getting better, and soon Spring, and I have dreams of returning to Paris, to Git-le-Coeur. Three dreams of Git-le-Coeur so far. First one long time ago, when I dreamed Git-le-Coeur was decorated in gold, with red velvet and two weeks ago I dreamed I returned to Paris, went to Git-le-Coeur and Rachou[221] was no longer there, and met somebody who I corresponded with but had not seen ever. Then last night was there again—no thought of seeing Burroughs or Gysin at any given time. What means Git-le-Coeur? I woke after third dream with awful feeling that I missed out when I wrote *American Express*, that I should have written about 9 rue Git-le-Coeur. Perhaps I still can. If I can get back to writing. That's what I miss, working. Good news for you, New York passed narcotic law that enables junkie to be treated as sick person and not criminal.

What are your plans? I am seriously thinking of getting together enough funds to return to Europe. I miss the life of Paris, Italy, Greece. I've become accustomed to the life of Europe, New York is no longer mine. Hope Savage is in India, do inquire around for her please, and see her, and tell me all about her, your friend.

Love, Gregory

To Allen Ginsberg and Peter Orlovsky New York City
[April 13, 1962]

Dear Allen and Peter,

First of all, Allen, please rush me negative of that nice picture you sent me taken in Tangier by Lance of you and me on bed you with shirt off, me real dreamy, I want it for book cover; please hurry, dear friend. Been hard at work on book, all is done, and I am satisfied. *Basta* for publishing now, I have had it. I will disappear into no-name, no-sound, and of course will continue to write; it's my mean is it not?

Alas, alas, poor bright blond Harry [Phipps] is dead. Died yesterday, amphetamine, he never took depressive drugs, H and all that. Found dead in dingy hotel, needle beside him on floor; and he all of 30, and lovely wife, and two year old child. Dead and gone, and I saw much of him of late. He very nervous, strange, and I sensed it, I sensed something wrong, it was at time I was taking drugs, and in him I saw the horror, not in myself. His face was changed, no longer the bright blond fair golden rich boy, but a pockmarked pimply thin pale twitch of a face; and I did ask him what about heaven? I did go to him with the feeling that I could save him. I swear this was my feeling. I did say, without her asking, to his wife: "Don't worry, I'll see to it that he is all right." I did ask him about afterlife, death, heaven, God and all that, very quickly, excitedly, and he said: "All that was just human emotion." He said that heaven was a human emotion. He made sense, and I believed him. I renounced God, heaven, and all that. I believed him, but O he was sick and sad, and I had a sense of it and wanted to save him but only acted like a dope and got on drugs or asked him for money and so my downfall in that. My goodness down, no chance of it now, he's dead, and I wonder what emotion for him. He was a strange boy, much wiser than most people, and yet life seemed insufficient. He had everything, and it were not enough. My venture into drugs here in NYC has shown me the true horror and sadness of people here. I've stopped, not because I am ill or scared or whatever, I stopped because if I don't stop, nobody will, that's how I feel. Salute to Mr. H.O. Phipps, a fine young man, who I hope knows some sort of heaven haven whatever,

Have a good healthy time, all is well with me. I am saving money to come to India. All will be well, the best is yet to be, the world is getting better, yet is tragic tragic for many. What can be done? Maybe nothing, maybe something, but I swear to you, drugs are a filthy nurse.

Love, Gregory

To James Laughlin New York City

[ca. April 24, 1962]

Dear J.L.,

While cleaning up mine papers I came upon a batch of poems I forgot to work on and join to *Long Live Man* collection.[222] I feel these poems very important for book, so I'll zoom them off to you. I've dated them, place them anywhere (in date group) you feel like, except at end of each group. And now the book should be happy pregnant, no? And being that I'm omitting the *Ode to Old England* poem, there shouldn't be too much trouble—I hope. Anyway, I'd not disturb the collection again. All my things are packed away—I am poemless. I may stop off in Venice for a month before India. Speaking of Venice, could you please put "for Alan Ansen" as dedication to *I Where I Stand Poem*—thank you. I leave in about two or three weeks.

Best, Gregory

The poem about my asking the policeman to kiss me is fact. I thought it a poem to keep to mine ownself, but no, it's a damn good true sad funny poem. He was a young policeman, and when I am happy and have some drink in me I can talk gold. He listened and I spoke truth. Had I received such a kiss, good God, good God, I shy away from policemen, they truly scare me, but what fault be theirs? None. In him I saw some kind of absolvement, I guess. Anyway they're rare occasions, and I seem to come out of them unscathed. Could you imagine if he were some awful cop? O.K. Write to me as to how you feel about these poems, I'd like to know.

To Lawrence Ferlinghetti New York City
[April 24, 1962]

Dear Larry,

For a moment I thought you were in Italy, that Roman G, letter. Too bad, because I thought we'd finally meet, I am going to Venice, and from there India. I leave in about two or three weeks. God, but I'd love to see and talk with you. Want to know something odd? I'm lost for better works. Aye, and so are you, that inch of your soul on a little Italian letter. Didn't I give you in mine letter some things to write about, like how come I ain't got my royalty check, and how come I myself bought at least 30 copies of *Gasoline* and all I'm getting is 30 dollars? I think you spend it all on Chinese food. I think you should write a play about an alligator. And do you think it were wiser to be alive in a world of death than to be dead in a world of life? I asked that of your suicides, and of Mr. Burroughs—a powerhead. Everybody's a power-head but me, your D'Annuzio Castiglione, Cuban, O.A.S., Gaspar! I say do to politics as did Lycurgus[223] his harsh laws. Inject a music outside of poesy in your Ferlinghettian empire. As for me when I venture politics it ends up a Gregorian Rant, *basta*.

I love you, and have fallen out with the only good true minds of my time by simply jumping all over the European continent. I am beset by fools, and so deem it proper to stay indoors, or venture now outdoors. But as for letter writing, it's as difficult as poesy, if not more so. I refrain from writing letters because when I used to I wrote exactly what came from the heart, somehow I am wont to give that heart away because who wants it? Who needs it? Everybody's got their own heart. I make heart sound as though it were another word for "problem." Well, what else could be more problem? I got no factories to worry about, no gas and electric, etc. I only got my heart, and God knows I don't want to worry about that because it'll get that I won't be able to tell if I'm worrying or thinking. Worry poems are my great ignoramus poems. So I must tend my heart, never have I before. It was a smart sleep before, but

I know and know full well that I am getting old very quick, zoom! I'm in a tizzy - but when I reach my supposed correct age-stage I don't doubt I'll be the better for it - but during the rush zoom of it all - augh! I'm terrible, and scorn all and everything mainly myself. "The old light nurses it's dark wound with a filthy illegal flesh." This from my new Laughlin book *Long Live Man*, a book I think you'll like, Larry. Anyway, I just want you to know that I don't truly see the immediacy of death. You may feel I am a lack of manners or am bugged with you by not writing, but it's not so. Deep within I feel that I'll always embrace with a friend in this here life before either of us traverse the happy hunting ground. I think this life is endless. I'll see you in a million years. But O but O all around me, all who I know, are dying like flies, suicides, O.D's. All young. I can only say to them they die because they're afraid of death, but mainly it's because life is insufficient for them. Ah, I should be old Gregory who had contempt for those who beloved themselves failures to life. I like contradiction, suicide can't be contradicted.

If I were not Gregory Corso (in spirit) I would tremble to be square. Aye, that's what "square" means to me, a spirit that cries life insufficient, or itself failure, or suicides not it and makes the best of it in ten dozen loony bins. No, I've seen enough, and have been involved, I've seen enough to know there's a distinguishment as holds death. The lovers of life, with its joy and woe, are fit to die, and nothing is fit to die who sucks life either too much a bad thing, or too little a good thing. My good blonde $40,000,000 playboy friend, Harry O. Phipps, just died three weeks ago. 30 years old, lovely Countess wife, two year old child. He jabbed himself with cocaine, it finally killed him. When I came back to America six months ago I saw him, his face was another face. I knew and felt he had not long. I even told his wife I'll do something, she not even asking me, she not seeming concerned, but when I asked she lit up. If you know Zina Rachevsky or of her, she three months ago gave me an old Russian cross of a crucifixion. She had me swear I'd keep it because it was very dear to her royalty family. A week later I gave it to Phipps and wife, and only then did I notice that the Christ on the icon was a fair haired blond replica of the Phipps I knew a year before in Paris. Two days after I gave it to Phipps (his wife appreciated it, he no) I called him up. I wanted to see him. He tells me meet him in a hotel he kept around the corner from his home. I take a taxi there, and I swore to save him, this was upmost in my mind. I don't say Phipps was dying, nay, he was up and bouncy, and all that, but I felt something—something. So I get to his hotel room, and I'm a little sick because of my taking heroin, I say to Phipps: "Harry, do you believe in an afterlife, or God, or do you feel people just die and that's it." He replied: "After life is a human emotion, God fantasy, and yes you die and that's it ." He said it so convincingly and it sounded so logical that I became the saved. And as is my fate and taking self, I was broke and asked Phipps for money. He gave it and I didn't see him until a week before he died. I called him up and asked to come over, he said he was going out, and that people were over and he wished they were out too. I insisted, and he said, all right come over for awhile. I was tipsy drunk, I didn't go too heavily on heroin, sniffed it was all. When I got there his little daughter was upstairs, naked, two years old, I waved to her, Phipps got nervous. I think he resented my seeing his little girl naked. Anyway he was nervous, cocaine excitability, and after a while told me to get out and the others too. I said I would walk out but demanded courtesy. He pushed me, I stood there, said something and left. A week later Phipps was found at that dingy hotel room where we spoke of God and death, on the floor a needle in his side. O.D. of cocaine. Uncanny, uncanny, and it got uncannier. During that week, before his death, I began to use a needle—and lo, his death had me throw the thing away. And two nights after his death I dream I am being crucified, the spike going no in my hand but in my arm, the spot where junkies inject their needles - big spikes hammering into my arms. There were three of us on that field, and I was not the central cat. No the next day I do tell this to three guys who scored for themselves and me and I scared one enough that he gave it up. The next night I dream a man telling me that Christ wants to see me, he offers me the address and apartment number. I tell him I know the address, and run over to see Him. I get to what I think is the address, but am confused as to what apartment or if it was the building at all. End of dream.

This is only a small part of what I came back to in N.Y., America. I came back explicitly to see and make up with father and family. It was disastrous. They liked me, then wanted to see me, but I got uncomfortable and awkward with them. I've yet to go back to see them. The only truly good thing is I got a fine book of poems, three years work, in shape for J.L. here.

People only mean ill for me, dear old note, and of course there are those who don't, and maybe I'm ill for some too. Whatever, I just hope all this doesn't make me regard life in a clinical way. Something is indeed going on, something (because of ignorance) I feel to call strange—and being that I got good or whatever insight into things, I see the blur, something is there, and it don't bode joy. I am three weeks without a drug and have contempt for it in no uncertain terms. Not because I got sick, I wasn't even that far gone. I only felt hate and shame for myself when I took the drug, not pleasure. I pay my dues when served, perhaps my good fortune, I believe so. Anyway, I who have seen supposed horror when young, always saw life not death, even when death occurred. But these last six months in N.Y.C., my "City" had me discover something I never knew or believed about life. It's tricky, and people are implements of this dire trick. [. . .] In full, death abounds in this city for me. And though I fell, I got up. "They, that unnamable they, they've knocked me down but I got up I always get up. Only a mountain can unmove itself. They, I've long ago named them me." That poem is my power, and I blame no one falls because I'm a much stronger man that most, but I am human, that I am. What saddens me is life. It is, as President Kennedy says, "unfair." Why does it hurt man? Or why does man hurt it? *Basta.*

So when the letter is due it is due. I hardly write to mine Allen or anybody. And when I write it's either letters like this or short silly ones, both are indictments I'd rather blow to the wind. Gone. What means it but a true tale on one's mind set down on paper for a man I know I should commune with? Good, the time was opportune. J.L. asked me to write you. In his office, he handed me pencil and paper. I said I'd write you when I got home. I got home, and wrote you a long silly letter a la Papa Black Book. I sent instead the letter you received. This one is real, *basta.*

Be good, like me. And who's doing mine *Happy Birthday* in Italy? What about *Gasoline*, will they do that? How nice for Italia. How nice for me, for poesy, and for you. Hope you can make out mine scrawl, a sloppy letter, but the hand ain't as quick as the heart. Here's a nice poem for you, also a new book. "The astronaut was a Fulbright / A student of Italian painting, / and when everything became GO / up was not Tiepolo."

Gregory

To Allen Ginsberg and Peter Orlovsky New York City

[May 11, 1962]

Dear Allen and Peter,

I am leaving by Yugoslav boat to Tangier. From there I will decide as to whether I come to India or no—I still don't feel India or its demiGods or its man-strife and $ woe and save for the sunsets and the elephants and the east, what have I to do there? Aye, it best be I go to Czechoslovakia, Russia, Warsaw, for believe me I never was and is a dying thing, and maybe I should go see it in its throes, I don't know, but as I say I'm so Western inclined, that India don't seem to move me any. And well, but for seeing my two good friends again, and Hope, everything human contact I want is in India, friends, anyway I will decide whence on sea. I have funny desire to go live in lovely Florence—and write a nice book; and six months here in New York was sure an experience, by God. I had a dream I stuck up the Vatican; aye, with a shotgun, demanded the pope's gold. Lots of Christian dreams of late; what means it? I am all religious and none, I am my own Boswell, so I guess I must tell myself in mine sleep what I do not in my wakedness. The India article on you both was wondrous and good and true to form and honest and informative as to what you are about, but just what are you guys about? I mean, is it on earth? Or has it always been on earth, or what about me with all my myths and then mix them up with all their myths and what could it do but add, or lessen, or confuse, or to go to India and encounter Zina and Russ, augh, I mean they are looking too, and so go about it in way. Mystique just ain't my way, and mystique awarers bore me, and well, let the powers there be, I could see India just because it is there, and I should see everything, and yet would not dare to write hymns to Kali like you goons who don't know a damn thing about the Missus of Destruction with her necklace of menheads and swordy arms. You both sound like you're treating India like a coffee house, ha ha. But truly I think light is God and man has little light in him and he built up lots of light and so maketh God, and one million megaton holy father could well be it, but of course you know that God brings death too. I mean don't expect God and life, like life you already got, and if you want God you must take death, I think. Who knows? Not me, not you, not nobody but how nice to ponder, and so smartly too.

See much of Bremser, he takes amphetamine and what a lousy kick that; but all his own way, and he not sad, but enthusiastic about it and I always believe you could do anything so long you do it with enthusiasm. As for poems, he's doing much of that. Don't see anything of anybody else, and I think you both possess as grand Westerners much more than the East, and how wondrous it would be if you were to laugh at their gods and holy men and joy unto them to laugh at God, and lo unto them to dig it, but everybody goes there and treats their gods with newness and awe or ignorance or what, but I like the Catholic God best. I mean after silly Zeus, of course. I say in 32nd year poet, "32 and I've writ four thin wild mad bad wonderful books of poesy, the world owes me a million dollars." This after I state that I don't steal anymore, but do ask for money from strangers or near strangers. Anyway it be a fine book and I wrote it happy, aye, happy, this book, all books are happy. *Kaddish* is happy, but is Ganesh happy. By the way, years ago I drew a picture of a man with the head of an elephant. Never knowing Ganesh.[224] Peter, I don't go out to see Laff, why God only knows. I don't go to see family, just want out from them who I try to love, and trying fail. It be best, I stay away. I do, just couldn't bear to see Laff incarcerated, funny clodhopping Laff. No. Also I don't see any new poesy I like, and what means it but things are yet unanswered, and until they are answered then will poesy be in America again; deadlock, but too much of poesy is too much too, though I see 20th Century poesy American as being not message poesy or preaching poesy but as power poesy, that which can add to life, make life, give life, insight probe, and all that. All a benevolence I feel, but whence the true mean nasty evil poet? Ah, he will be a welcome, I dare say, or would be, I mean maybe he'll be like a Hitler and that ain't good, but still a real nasty one might just be the thing. If he'd be any good he'd have humor, and of course humor would make him a peaches and cream evil, so man is just stuck as being a nice sort of thing, silly, oafish, or tall thin and wise, still a man, a man—maybe something other than a man??? Yes, it's about time, about time we had something else, like when I went into grocery store and told grocer, why do you always sell the same food all the time? The same things, beans, meats, carrots, lettuce, milk, eggs, etc. etc.

So I'll be in Tangier on the 25th of May, back there! Whoa! From there I could to Marseilles and get a boat to India, I'll see. Must ponder this close and dear, will decide on sea, on sea will write you my decision, mail it in Tangier. So, keep up all the joy of thyselves, and may your hymns turn Kali bluer than her blue.

Gregory

To Allen Ginsberg and Peter Orlovsky New York City
[May 18, 1962]

Dearest funny angels of whom I am one,

I will try to get Jackie to fly away with me to thee, aye, but I am apt to get out soon. Allen you are right, horror has hung his hat here, and I knocked that hat off a couple of times for some by telling them true dreams I had and scared them. But not Stanley Gould who continues to die and did the dearth death of others. He's a fool, lost, done. I am strong, again, and ready to come to India and do right and well. Youth is gone, what remains is wise, nice, all of it good, and nice about Hope, thank you for that. I have 500 dollars, boat trip cost that much from here to there, and month time. Too much time, not enough money to eat by or live by, so will take plane. Yes, for 600 I can take plane, arrive broke, and lo, who cares. I will get some gold in sporadically, from various things and times, so can take care of mineself. I will let you know exactly when I leave by aeroplane, or whatever, but it be certain will come. What about you, how long you stay there, and will you meet me?

Phipps I saw much of him and he dies of overdose of C. He'd been taking amphetamine, and looked like hell, and I saw death in him like you smelled death in Elise,[225] so I went truly to save him but could not, he too overpowering, and wouldn't listen to somebody who also was dying. I was at time taking drugs and was in same boat, thus why should he listen to me? I will tell you more about it when I see you, suffice it to know that I asked him week before he died in that room he died in this: "Harry, do you think there's an after-life, God, is there anything after death?" He said it was all a "human emotion," like saying in effect, "it's something for the peasants." I was inclined to go along with him on that. It sounded so straight and logical and unemotional and more a real truth than a dreamy wish, and thus he died, and what emotion be there for him now? I dreamed two Christ dreams after that, week later. First dream three men were being crucified, I was not central figure, not Christ, and when they spiked me down, they put spike not in hand or feet, but IN ARM, junkie arm, alas. Next dream, night after, stranger. A man grabs me and says, "Christ wants to see you." And he hands me the address of Christ. I run away happily, refusing the address, saying "I know the address, you don't have to give it to me" and off I go and I find what I think is Christ's house, but when I get there, I don't know where to go or where I'm at. That dream is disturbing to say the least. Anyway I dream mad great dreams everynight Allen and remember them all and I feel something nice good great is afoot—and so. But the reason I mention these dreams of Christ is this. It has this to do with Phipps, a month before Phipps died, Zina Rachevsky gave me an icon, old one in the family long time. She gives it to me, after telling me about letter you wrote her. I go over to see letter, become friendly with her, she gives me this lovely old icon, saying, "You keep this Gregory, it's dear to me." Well, I go over two nights later to Phipp's house, see him, wife and child and present icon to Phipps, and then and only then do I see what the icon is. It is a crucifixion and the Christ is no dark black haired bearded soul, but a clean shaven blond soul, just like Phipps. You ask Zina about this, old man. Wow, o God, o what! I tell you I went explicitly to save Phipps, and shy, death weren't there, he wasn't sagging out, he was alive, vital, but something drove me that way, and all I asked for was money, so you see I hurt my powers by stupid need, from now on I forsake money, I am down on money, I care not about it, and when I take my vow of poverty I will take it with reason, Allen, is this not right? I have learned, and by learning I take my vow—not because I must. You know this. You have abided by it and have not been hurt and have remained beautiful, the only thing that gets me involved and in ugly scenes, all my life, has been money. Anyway I hope I cleared up some things about Phipps.

Ferlinghetti, who I haven't written to in years, I told him the whole thing. He wrote me nice letter previously, so it came out. It'll always come out. Bill is in England, says he hasn't heard from you, and I wrote him this, only note. "Dear William, a word from a master. I feel it wiser to be alive in a world of death than to be dead in a world of life." That should cool him, the man is way off base, and if you think you're gonna find a magic, bah, he's no magic, but Bill, and a genius, aye, but no magic. Thanks for the negatives, and did I tell you one poem I have in book of poems *Long Live Man.* It's best work I ever did, my swan song this book, really, and here is subject of this poem I wrote when I returned to New York, the second night, after three years, and it really happened. I was happy drunk, walking around the 80's and Riverside Drive having just visited someone, and I encountered a young policeman and I went up to him and happily and with gold tongue told him all about my prison days and how great the men were there and about Europe and I as straight and funny and he listened attentively and laughed, and all was well until I asked him: "All right, absolve it all, kiss me!" I actually asked him to kiss me, and he got scared, aye, he backed away saying "NO NO NO NO NO," and disappeared. So you see, I'm still a pain in the neck to man and society. Ha.

I don't see much of anybody, no Irving, etc., and LeRoi Jones and company. Bah, they're all editor type now, and they are what I call the second stringers, nothing happening there. Did I ever tell you about the 1,000,000 megaton Messiah? Well he began when everything began. He was benevolent and spread out all over to become what is the universe today, and now he want to get back together again, and the way he wants to do that it to become ALL-SOME LIGHT again. Yes, so who's to say the second coming shan't be of megaton stuff? It's LIGHT, ain't it? We can only get better not worse, believe me. Phipps is resolved, I'm sure.

Love, Gregory

To James Laughlin Tangier, Morocco
[ca. May 1962]

Dearest James,

Have arrived. Sorry I did not see you for last goodbye, so goodbye. I'll probably remain here until the tourist season is over in Europe and the rainy season over in India. It be either Europe or India come September. So I have plenty of time to decide and while I'm waiting I'll write my "potboiler."

Yours, Gregory

To Lawrence Ferlinghetti Tangier, Morocco
[ca. May 1962]

Larry,

I'll be, as usual, straight with you. I wrote a feeling letter to you, all that was on my mind at time, and much was on my mind. It was same kind of letter I wrote to Allen. I did not say I'll meet you a million years from now literally, man, you are as usual mistaken with me. Your only non-mistakes were *Gasoline, Bomb*, the rest, all wrong—mine fascism mine body afterlife, mine *Happy Birthday of Death*, mistakes. Well, this is not a sore letter, only a message to tell you I am not such a mystique that dreamed title for new great book of poems *Long Live Man* is, did not thee believe in man? I do and that's more heresy than God-talk. The trouble between us mind sense is this! Your way of thinking is very unlike mine. I heed to no poet, ergo when I write you it be only as friend, not as poet, which I tend to hail as soulful. Now don't go make anything out of my use of "soul." I long ago asked of soul. Are you but a white heart made of air? There's only one poet understands this Corso, that's Ginsberg, and one publisher, Laughlin. The trouble with some humorous folk is that they are serious where humor is directed to them. This I feel is both our failing. Mystique? Fascist? My *Happy Birthday* you insulted me by giving to that *San Francisco Review* mag? They to refuse all. All! It were personal that. Poor poems had to take the brunt. I asked you not to give them that and I admit when I write political I am Gregorian Ranting. What are you doing? I sound off to you because what good writing you letters when we neither of us understand each other? But my God your letters are mere letters, cold typewriter words. Who are [you] that I flow out so? Not mine mentor, that's for sure. I too have made mistakes, but not ones have I guessed where you were at, for pride is a deadly sin, then mark such sin a virtue. *Long Live Man* is the title and meaning of a great book that will make the hair grow back on your head, you silly man—*basta*. I do not expect no critique from you or anybody, but presumption is offensive to say the least. And if you care for me to write you, then write to me! or is it I am such a proven fool as to be wound up, and write at command? Was you who asked if I had any carbon's of that big letter I wrote Jack. You either are an innocent or ignorant and the latter you are not. If you were, then I could not forgive you. As again I say "ignorance is only excused when it is so." With you it is not so. So! And ah, another remembrance. Long ago when at *Gasoline* you wrote of poem *Visions of Rotterdam*, "why three 'explosions explosions explosions,' when one would do?" That silly critique made me suspect your ear as regards to natural ear. Not one bomb falls and yet you use in *He*, a zillion "death death death etc." How then am I to heed such critique? I'm a listener, and not that poet who would not change a word or a poem even, but good God believe in the poet you publish! Another memory—*Bomb*, you asked, "Do you really mean? 'You are due, and behold you are due. And the heavens are with you . . .'" Yes, I really meant it, and it's proven true, God by God. Due why this furtherment of tests, on and on. All this to tell you that what you have to say to me regarding my work rings a dull bell. I am not angry with you, merely bugged.

Gregory

And that Rexroth - he's a fool, I should never [have] given him my Shelley.

To Allen Ginsberg

Tangier, Morocco
June 12, 1962

Dear Allen,

If all be illusion, both, then both can be real too, and what is very real is fact that Tangier is become haven for Beatlies. Yugoslav boat, three a week, sails from New York, 120 dollars. So kids in Village who go to Village from all over the USA find that it takes just one step from Brooklyn to Tangier, a big ocean step, but that's all, so it is easy for them, and Tangier doth offer them tea [i.e. marijuana], and so the population of Tangier is *tres* Beat. It buggeth only the bar owners because these kids don't lush, and so they deem them riffraff, and when truth is that these Beat kids are considered quite much as holy men, and the chief of police said so to Paul [Bowles]. Besides [the] fact that young Moslem kids learn from these Beat souls, how to draw paint etc., and so they bring their Western class, the Western world, the best minds consciousness-wise for sure, and so the youth of Tangier doth benefit from these so-called "riffraff." In New York the Beat souls are unseeable, outside of the country they are realer and gooder and so all's well. We ain't made no Frankenstein though at times I've the funny mind to imagine we is Frankenstein makers, you, Jack, Bill, Peter, etc, but all is well and the world goeth its way and like the old Roman poet who said: "Death nibbles at my ear: Live—I am coming?" So do people and myself live and I can't wait to live real well in good surround with you Peter Hope in India. All that I want in life is there, true. Paul and Jane fine, and Paul is easier for me to get along with this year. He is truly fine gentle understanding being and is yet delightfully hampered and pecked by Jane who hath the wit of an Atlas Mountain. Tennessee Williams here and he is hung up on death as usual and when I suggested to him that I feel death to be an instant, he saith, "O no, death is forever!" But true, aye, but as he said it, he meant I'm sure, all dark, no more nothing woe gone is me. He is somewhat sad having broken up with his love, Frankie, and now has a young poet named Fred, who is quite nice, and so for the sun beach crowd. I can't really feel too at ease with Williams, but the man doth suffer, he does. Like an open nerve so sensitive alas. I like him very much, and when I see him I treat him like a southern gentleman, which he is, and say: "See any runaway slaves hereabouts?" Alan Ansen said he may come to Tangier, and Harold Norse is here and he gave me Krishnamurti to read. And this Murti fellow makes a lot of sense—clear, concise thought awareness, have you read him? Perhaps Hope is right, but I don't think I make conscious approaches, only want to be nice for old times sake. Don't mean no wrong no harm she still be my angel in this here love girl soul life and what more can I say who hath no seen or heard from her in so long a time. All my letter was was "HAIL DEAR ONE." Lesbian, no, but all changeth, so. Grove Press will give me 45 dollars a week for 22 weeks on premise that I will present them with novel, which I shall, and this be real wild funny good one, I feel great, and my surroundings are healthy, and I believe that if one is healthy and the surroundings be in accord with that health then the work will prove healthy and that's what I wish, a nice healthy work, why not? But ain't I always been healthy? I am poemless, all my poems are at Laughlin's for publication. I feel free. How funny, no poems, and freedom? India as coffee house? I pull your leg, wherever you go you exude sun, but I always like to tease you. Ted Joans here too, no getting away from the world of Pooh. He is funny though, and has been to Timbuktu and bought house there. He met Jacques Prévert, and said that Prévert said: "Mr. Joans, you got the sun in your belly and wherever you go you spread sunshine." That's nice.

Here are some things Krishnamurti saith that sounds downright fine: "As long as you remain as you are you shall not solve any fundamental problems." "Understanding yourself means—not the super-self, the Atman, the super-consciousness and all that—but understanding the ways of your own reactions, understanding yourself as you are, what you think, why you think, why you do certain things and say certain words. To understand is to be conscious, to be aware of what you are. You will find that is extraordinary difficult because most of us are unwilling to understand ourselves, we would rather believe, be told, pushed, persuaded, driven politically, economically, occupationally, environmentally. But to watch yourself in all your relationships whether with your servant, your wife, your husband, or others, to watch yourself when you get into a bus, to be aware when you look at nature, at the trees, the clouds, to watch all your own reactions and to be aware *** THAT, Sirs, is real meditation. Then you will go very far. Then you will not create for yourself any illusions." That sounds fine doesn't it? But what is awareness but being aware that you are aware, and that can be distracting? Anyway he says what I always felt and you and Bill, that the mind need change, that there must be a revolution in the mind itself, not merely a change at some partial level of human existence. The problem, true, is not static, it is ever changing, though we approach the problem with a static mind. A revolt in the WAY of thinking, not the choice of WHAT to think, or goal of right thought, but a revolt in the capacity itself, in the mind itself. A radical transformation of the mind itself. How can these happen for ALL of God's children? Well, I think poets do inform the way or the changing, so you is right when you consolve poet as priest. And surely then, we are very aware of ourselves. You do it finely, as me, well I am *tres* aware but don't often know how to apply the awareness, or find myself lost, lost to BOTH worlds, whether illusion or no. Makes no difference because lost is lost, and he be how lost. I believe the poet, the thinker, the mind changing worker, I believe he is in a tricky position, man is one step behind God, and the poet is a half step behind God, therefore a half step ahead of man, and poet wants to bring man closer to himself and there to God, but meanwhile poet might want to get so hung on God to get nearer that he gets away from man and suddenly finds himself miles away from man and miles closer to, what? He pays his dues for such travel, yet it be worth it if the mind be in the heart, aye, and so sometimes I find I am lost because I like to be not ahead of man but right with them and also right up there with whatever WHAT, and it makes all for an awareness that is that WHAT. Anyway GOD AS DEATH is so exact and true, of course, and who is afraid of God? So why fear death? The fear of death is minor, of course, and yet if one fears it and dies, then God will be sad that you were so afeared of him and all that, and so you'll feel like a fool before him for having been afraid, and to be afraid is to be afraid, and that stops life. So when death says: "Live?—I am coming." He, it, death, maketh good sense, no? Hart Crane said people kill themselves because they're afraid of death, which of course means life. Yet he too, Crane, maketh all sense. And Teddy Roosevelt saith: "Only those who do not fear death are fit to die and none are fit to die who do not live the joy and wonder of life." So Teddy too is sense. All man is sense, but alas, perhaps, I did wish to understand truth without. Still it takes hard work, and nobody wants to work hard, whether at home or in the office or in search of truth. Maybe hell be for the lazy? It all goes back to way back, Socrates, ah, know thyself. And thus without knowing yourself, how do you know what you think is true? How can you know of God, of death, without knowing yourself? Well, I found that if you have a sense of authority, a conviction, a belief, faith, if you have pigheaded stubbornness even, then can you <u>impress</u> those about you that you know yourself. But do you? To yourself? And how can you tell another what to seek or to do, even if you did know yourself? I ask myself this all the time, and like I say, it juggles me into chaos, meekness, stupidity. Aye, because trying to know myself I find I maybe don't and if I maybe don't then what is me and what is its meaning if it haveth no meaning, and so what is you Gregory? Such awareness is heavy heavy and lowers the mind to sullen countenance and melancholy, still I got poet's armor and am never sent to flipdom, only thing that sends me to that state is lush [alcohol], real life sillies, people, and as I realized what makes my dreams into nightmares are when the real everyday things enter the dream. I could dream a dream and when the real enters I wake up in a sweat. "To watch all your own reactions and to be aware. That, sirs, is a real meditation. Krishnamurti knows, but then how life if one is always aware, how chance, and chance is fortune, no? Then how surprise, and if not surprise in life, how dull, no? I mean to be constantly aware is the poet's chief self, and how pleasurable when he is not aware, when things come and happen, and of course the dues must be paid, such gamble doth bring in the horrors. If only I could cease to complain of the horrors, I willingly go into, then all will be all right, but I don't dig the horrors nor the suffering of others, myself, and so would that perpetual awareness. Why not? My age warrants it. My life surely and yet I've still the imp in me, and that imp, he don't much care for my watching over him like a matron all the time, he wants to go out and play. Allen, I think that if one does bad and has a conscience about it then that one will be open house for all the demons there be. The body is like Bill says, the host, the human host, for either demon or angel. Well I'm somewhat eased by the fact that I have not denied my house to either, yet them demons do leave a mess behind.

Anyway how can one understand oneself, if one doesn't examine oneself? And by God that is what I am at, and you. But like the simpleton who walks the correct path is always goofing, so is me, sometimes, sometimes. Please inform Hope that the man who has ideals cannot know love because he is enslaved in his ideals, or their concepts, and that my enthusiasm must not be mistaken for romantic idealism. Romantic idealism with me is merely obstinacy, it makes the heart flutter and thrill and good God I don't want to destroy that with strict mind. We are very much alike, but I don't talk that blue streak and anyway I love her high voice and flow. Maybe she should try to understand me in order that I might know of the correct "approach." She thinks perhaps I am a lost silly dreamy material earthbound creep. Ha! But I am more, no Allen? Anyway knowledge about real unreal is false, I feel, unless the mind is conditioned to what is real unreal, or—I know I am conditioned because I live in a real world and so my mind is "real." But what difference does it really make, I mean I think I'll go to my death bed not unhappy that it ever did make any difference. All I know is death is big, and life is big, and live, for death is coming, and if death be God and God be light, life, highmindthought, beauty, then how nice. As of now everything is good and the world is fucked up and people yelping like hurt dogs. It be sure sign all is not well, but for the selfish self all is well, and good, that.

I must write more often to you, Jack, ah poor Jack. I wish to hell he'd up from his life and off to us here, and please send me his address, I must write to him. That sad New York scene, no way of communicating there. I will try my damnedest to save up from the weekly salary to make the trip to India, because I want to see it with you there, you've broken the ground, and that can be a big help for finicky me. I know you and Peter are happy and deservedly so, and my heart goes out to you both and though I might curse and complain our state at times it only because I am a free spirit and can put you down when I feel too, and Peter too. In fact I reserve that right. But so do you. Yet I would not swap this life of mind with our friendship for anything, no Joe DiMaggio nor Kennedy nor centuries back and Shelley. [. . .]

Jane was asked [about Bill] when she, Paul and Norse were driving in car. She said, "O Bill is crazy, a beautiful crazy madman." And Norse asked her, was he mad? And she said, "A little," and then he asked is Allen mad? And she said, "No,

Allen is not mad." And this Norse told me, and of course I wonder what she thinketh of me? Yet I felt great when I saw how they felt about you—good God without your good sense where would we all be? My love, dear pretty Sanskrit above your dimply knees, let us be good, strong and full of vitals, that we meet in pure light, soon, on earth, here, now, aye, and what shant we be able not to do?

Gregory

To Judith Schmidt[226]

Tangier, Morocco
[June 18] 1962

Dear Judith,

I feel that by the rate I'm going the book should be all wrapped and bundled by 30 weeks the most, two months the least; that's the best I can do by that clause.[227] As for sending in what I have done as via carbon, well I just don't work that way. I write in long hand first. And what more can be added to that but that when I do type it, I will send carbon on, and I hope this is satisfactory with Grove. I can tell you that I am working like a bastard in this nowhere town. The sun and mosquitoes are too much. But the atmosphere otherwise is good for its lack of distractions. Work gets done. And I'm loving every minute of it. Also I asked for cashiers checks, not bank checks, which not only take two weeks to get to me, but I also lose five dollars by cashing such a check in bank and not on market, if it isn't too much trouble, it would be better to return to the likes of the first check, there is somebody here to cash it, or a cashiers check, but bank check is slow and moneys lost.

I also want to say I may at any time up and leave here, and when I do I'll let you know right away. Hoping everything is all right.

Gregory

To James Laughlin

Tangier, Morocco
[June 27] 1962

Dear JL,

I'm so happy you liked selections and translations of your poems,[228] and mine introduction which I beerly and schnappsly happily wrote. What was all that about Romance I was saying? But I am glad that I hit on the poesy as regards "change" "new consciousness", that I'll hold to. After all, we have come a long way from the proconsul, but I still don't like you thinking me a primitive because a primitive is always a primitive and to be always something is to be never nothing else. The old Indian guru says: "As long as you remain as you are, you will not solve any fundamental problems." Well I haven't any problems, but I always do want to be something else, better and better all the time, and eventually become respectfully aware of a lot of things, so

I did not sign English income tax form for Pollinger, instead said: "Dear Sir, I feel it were easier and, in a way, befitting that I heed the taxation of the United Kingdom, and besides, what country is more deserved of poesy's royalty." That of course means losing almost half of mine royalty—but I haven't made out an American tax form in years and so couldn't fill out form—will I go to Alcatraz? I owe America a lot and I will pay my dues, whatever.

I am working on novel, tentative title: *The Computer And The Centaur.* Can you rub out the last poem in *Long Live Man*? Put it elsewhere but not at end because that be my only game in book, and no games with this one. I am occasionally writing a poem, and how nice to be really poemless, I have no old poems, no poems, and when I do one I just hold to that one, and so future work will be hard done by. One night in my Tangier backyard, I have big sky over me, I looked up at the stars and READ THEM, yes, I sought out the only language I know, and saw the letters V I A; which almost means mine name; and so I can write a poem that way—get all the letters I detect and work them into words into lines into poem. Maybe one poem like that be nice.

I've come to the conclusion that I am of sound mind and healthy and so am able to enter my subconscious freely without being conscious of conscious state, and therefore enter subconscious and discover and write there from. I shan't get lost in there. The mind is truly a wondrous thing, and though it is possible to get <u>into</u> it quicker, but tricky, with drugs; I'd the poesy-herb, the thought of the muse, to quicken me there. The only thing that scares me is Kit Marlowe's *Dr. Faustus*; see what happened to him for entering that forbidden territory? Marlowe at end "Those fiendful fortune may exhort the wise. / Only to wonder at unlawful things / Whose deepness doth entire such forward wits / To practice more than heavenly power permits."

"ONLY TO WONDER," that was Faustus' downfall. Curiosity killed that cat, man. Well I don't go into it with wonder or curiosity because I've gone past wondering, past curiosity—it is what I am aware of, what I know, that I enter. At thought I am a master, at craft I am careless or careful, at writing I am beset by the world outside the mind; at conclusion the master-thought doth flow. So be happy for me for I am happy for you—and in your travels and daily life and all your encounterings please do let me know if you ever come upon a thought-shattering realization, because as you well know I do not keep mine secret, and know that I am as obstinate as they come when it comes to another's thought, though I believe all minds are one, one mind is all, and one mind is all I got.

I do hope now, for my mind is certain, that there is time for a dedication to *Long Live Woman*,[229] I would it: "For my father." And he is good and it would make him very happy.

So my best to you and Rhoda and Ned Erbe who I finally faced and to New

Directions, and is it true you are a steel man, Laughlin Steel? and if so, why did you let Kennedy admonish you? And if you are said steel man why did you sell that great Balthus, and why is everyone saying you're a tight Scotchman, and why should they care for surely they must have wanted more than their due, and when they receive such augmented token they seek more to receive, no? When it is told me that you are tight of gold I say the truth: "He's been straight with me and I have received my deserved due, and twice prematurely at my asking." Did you know this all about yourself? and don't ask me who is everyone, everyone is a few writers, some you've published, many you haven't. Williams loves you, I love you, and a so-called "tight" poet surely keeps poesy balanced and sane. Could you send me seven hundred dollars? I am doing all right and living by good means, Grove Press, I will give them my *COMPUTER & CENTAUR*, and they in turn send me $50 dollars a week for 22 weeks, which is wonderful, I may live and work, and no distractions. If it were not for all the trouble I get into by the need of money, if I had it not to bother me, then all my books would go first to you, so I am glad you left me that new option, I can write and do what I must. Am I going to have the swirling nebulous stars on the cover of book as I wished? And so, good day, fare well, and have a nice summer.

I leave for my accustom'd clime—Europe. I go to Florence, Italy, tomorrow. I hope to settle there until I complete book and if my "novel" makes it, (for *American Express* was young experiment) I'll take you to 21 Club when I return. By the way, you never took your author out for a gentleman's drink—that's why poets take marijuana!

Love, noble love to you, Gregory

I'm beginning to feel free speech is abused—and if the pen is mightier than the sword then the pen be more dangerous. I'm gonna write a nice poem about the truth of free speech, so guised in democracy, liberty—as: "Give me liberty to kill or kill me, Mr. P. Henry."

To Judith Schmidt Tangier, Morocco
[June 27] 1962

Dear Judith,

It amazes me that you still call the checks I received: cashiers checks. They were not cashier checks, they were bank checks, payable only at ONE BANK, and that bank, the bank of Maroc, takes years, as Africa is a yearsome slothy country, to cash–whereas true cashiers check is made out TO NO BANK but the bank that issued it, and such a check made out to cash, not Corso, can be cashed anywhere–but it's too late for that, and thank God anyway, because it would have had to change anyway. I find I work better in my Western heritage and clime, Europe, so I go to Italy, and ask you please to send checks to Florence Italy, American Express. I go tomorrow, and so please send mine token there, where I will settle down, one can make it all right there on 50 a week, rent, food, etc., and get done with my book which is going along like the NASA projects, some misses, lot of great achievements; it be a book, a poem, a play, a essay, a critique, a lampoon, a detective story, a romance streak, a horror story, a happy dippy story, a profound story, poet may never be novelist, true, for what I am writing is either something NEW in prose: idea and style; or something other than prose, dragon prose perhaps; whatever, one that will cork many an eye. So don't goof anymore and send me nice Grove checks, no trouble with a Bank of Maroc check today, before I leave, or if it is forwarded to me in Florence, I will send it back to you. Thus far for month of June I have received three checks, which is my due—all is well.

Best, Gregory

Also please make checks out to Gregory Joseph Corso, as mine passport saith such and would make it easier—love you for all this bother.

To Judith Schmidt Florence, Italy
[ca. July] 1962

Does Fred [Jordan][230] want a nice Florentine poem? In my new disconnect style? Will I see you when you come to Europe, perhaps this way? Yes, I left forwarding address in Tangier, that is if American Express ain't bugged with me for book. They'll forward. I have found quiet place in villa to work, 70 dollars a month—and tentative title for book! *The Centaur and the Computer*—which will be America's new beautiful book. Beautiful books just ain't writ today. So its up to me.

Love, Gregory

To Allen Ginsberg Florence, Italy
[ca. July 16] 1962

I'll stay in Florence until September or October when I have sufficient fare to arrive in India, will you be there? I need craftsy surround for awhile and Florence suffices. New York and Tangier the same mental air waves of hung-up folks. I need monks' calm—so I got it.

Love to Peter, Gregory

To James Laughlin Florence, Italy
[ca. July 16] 1962

I've discovered that rhythmic neatness proclaims the whole method of Florentine decoration (art). Could B. Berenson[231] discover better? I saw the

Italian translations of *Happy Birthday*, truly fine. It was in Florence I got *Happy Birthday*—perhaps *Long Live Man* will be received here too.

Gregory

To James Laughlin

Paris
[ca. July 17] 1962

Dear J.L.

I am in Paris to stay, how nice to be back. Here I do fine work—always—and I will write why I left Florence and what I think of the Italians! The French are the most civilized and respect poets. My address is: City Hotel, Paris. Nice place near Pont Neuf. How is my good friend?

Your fellow poet, Gregory

To James Laughlin

Paris
[ca. July 24] 1962

Isn't this a pretty stamp! How happy I am to be back in Paris. New York, indeed, seemed like a small provincial town to me. It's probably true, it's no longer big. Tangier even smaller, Italy awful. Paris, Paris is freedom. I hope you are well, and that you are happy.

Your friend, Gregory

They forgot to put Levertov in anthology.

To Lawrence Ferlinghetti

Paris
[ca. Aug. 8] 1962

Ferl,

Would you do a broadsheet I'm almost finished doing on Capital Punishment? I promised it to Grove for *Evergreen* and is part of a book I'm doing for them, but I'd have you do it first. As you know I probed thru poesy death and came to some clear sensibles. Sad as, "death is not property and yet he's built a vast Hilton there." It be like my *Bomb* poem, but now continued *Loved*. The bomb is sort of active death capital punishment is. It's more necessary to abolish that—the time is opportune. What with peace, smarter people, sit-ins, etc. Also I spoke often to an old man in prison who spent two years on death row. I never forgot what he told me, Ferl. So now I can do what I always wanted to do, get it abolished. Thus far I gave a shot in the ass to the capital punishment abolishment committee telling them to wake up. I've some young lawyer on my side in N.Y. who I told that of all youth in U.S.A., lawyers were the oldest the nothingest. I woke 'em up and my tract (for our broadsheet) should get the beards and non-beards to direct their misdirected cries. Capital punishment is my baby because of my experience, first hand, with death and prison and poesy. The only hate poem I ever wrote was because of capital punishment—Chessman. I found a loophole in this Crump case, that's what did it. He, because he was rehabilitated, was commuted. Ha! ha! Ha and again! Ha! When a man is sentenced to death he's given no choice of rehabilitation, death row ain't no rehabilitation center. He, Crump, capitulated as a "good nigger," whereas Chessman held some arrogance, but what education can do! Why death row is greatest school because who won't learn Swahili if it meant getting a chance to get out? He was lucky a friendly warden, a good press, convert to Catholicism, and the timing. America could show the world they are not barbarians. They commuted his sentence expiating Chessman. You'd think only two men were sentenced to death in U.S.A. And one, to boot, escaped the sentence—hypocrisy! Every week of the year men die, unheralded. They say the doomed man must pay his debt to society, not the courts, judges above, but to me, to you! Well, I want to stop killing people, me who is society. You'll be hearing from me,

sometimes cry baby Gregory

Who's a better poet, me or you? I am. Who's a better painter? I is. Who's a better soul? You is. Who is Gregory's good friend? You is.

To Lawrence Ferlinghetti Paris
[ca. Aug.] 1962

Dear Ferl,

Can I have some money, because I know some must be coming me? If not by sales of *Gasoline*, only 28 bucks, surely by foreign rights, Italy, England, and some reprints in America anthologies? So could you please give it to me now as I am in sore need? Remember that President Kennedy thing I sent you for *Journal*? Well, I fixed it up into something real nice. Also could you send me capital punishment piece back? Need copy, want to polish it up for publication, too mixed up crazy as is—no?

Paris is getting all cleaned up, buildings look like baby shit, awful. OK, Larry, other than this, I may end up marrying Miss [Sally] November, my loved one's name is November!

And if you can, can you let me know if you reprinted *Gas*, if you will, and when will the rights go back to me? With James Laughlin, after six months of no reprint I get book, also, I don't think you could have many on hand because most stores always seem to want some but can't get. I think I be fair always and mine own salesman like getting *Gas* for foreign publishers. Movies in back for you, you didn't do bad by me, nor I by you, so could you let me know where I stand in all ways in regards *Gas*?

Now that I'm going to get married I must care for my interests. You is married so I should now. Big bundle of love kisses to you. You look like a charley-pot on *Coney Island* cover.[232] Wait till you see what I look like on *Long Live Man* cover, like a mess! A pretty mess!

Love, Gregory

To Allen Ginsberg Paris

[Aug. 21] 1962

Dear Allen,

Enclosed check, hope you can cash it. It from my girl. I love her, love her more than anything, more than Hope ever. She great and loves me and will marry her, yes. So check is made out to you, you can cash it am sure. My *Apples* changed to *Long Live Man*, out in October, both in England and America. I know you'll like it.

Don't get sick man, or get in new atmosphere where disease is lax. Yes, for writing, something new is needed, and you will find it. Remember, you made big jump, from *Empty Mirror* to *Howl* to *Kaddish*, what now? I understand your plight. See Bill [Burroughs], he fine, not much of him but when I do we talk well. He off to Edinburgh Festival, writers conference. So, don't think I'll be off to India yet, don't know about India, am up in air, but glad you are happy there, and I will try to get loot, it be hard for me to come by, it be.

Ok, I rush this off, and what is there to say? We need see each other, or tend to write long flighty letter, whatever. Things are shaping up in mentaldom, no? Yes, a new form of writing, or just plain old writing. That is why I always believed the idea was more import than the way idea was expressed. Expression is best plain, compact, exact, but all else be iambic pentameter, yes, all else that makes a pattern of what you wish to say. Thing is WHAT IS THERE TO SAY? Well, that is something, and who wants to keep on spitting on City Hall steps? and capital punishment is thing to say, but that too is itself tiny. What big thing? It will come; it always came. Send me photo of you and Peter, like to see how you look. Ok, rush this off.

Love, G

To James Laughlin Paris

[ca. Sept. 4] 1962

Dear JL,

I've been thinking how nice it would be for both of us, and it could bring in some money for us too because it would sell more than poesy, and think I can sell still yet no; well, how about a book of my essays and little plays—as for fiction, you're right about that, I can't do it worth a damn, I'm just not that kind of writer, I'm best at real things, why couldn't fiction be a real thing? Anyway,

I have some nice essays and writings, and what with the plays, it should make a buyable interesting book. Here is list: Plays: *In This Hung Up Age, Standing On Street Corner, Pres Kennedy;* essays: *Berlin Impressions, Introduction To German Anthology Of American Poets, Impressions Of Museum Of Natural History,* (all have been published but *President Kennedy* which you have.) By the way I haven't a copy, could you please mail it to me for rework? By God that little play was kind of prophetic in that I had him poetic and moony, all he wanted was to get up into the stars, space race, etc. I gave it to Ferl but I still hold that that man, Larry, is one-sighted politically, blind in lots of respects, and that is why his *Journal for Protection of Beings* failed. He made it too one-sided. Also I have an essay called *Capital Punishment*; a dialogue called *The Year 2462*—and some other writings that I can gather up and send them on to you. It should make for a varied and interesting and fine little book, what say you? I know I can do prose, but I can't do fiction prose, and that is what I'm hung up with right now, for Grove, I got to find a new medium by God.

OK, JL, hope all this sounds fine to you; if you maybe want to see the entire manuscript, all things grouped in one, fine, I'll send what I have on to you; but please send me my *President Kennedy* back for re-work. Ferl said he gave it to you, or was it Grove gave it to you? O God, I hope it isn't lost, because I just got some bad news, it seems Alan Ansen, he had house in Venice, and he safeguarded my things and Burroughs' things, was kicked out of Venice and he negligently let the papers rest behind and I fear they are burned. Peggy Guggenheim and a painter friend of his were supposed to clean out his house for him of valuables but I guess they didn't think my papers valuable. Painter I encountered recently on street says he thinks they were burned as waste paper, that waste paper happens to be all letters sent to me during 1957 to 59; important years as concerns Allen G., Burroughs, Kerouac, I feel like suing those negligent scavengers of the arts, which she is, and Ansen is, damn. So you see why I need lots of ducats and florins, to buy a big house and a wife to keep all my things nicely kept and tied. It's truly a crime, those were very important historical Beat years, by God.

My best to you JL, your old friend, Gregory

To James Laughlin New York City

[ca. Sept. 1962]

Dear J.L.,

See how nice I completed *President Kennedy*! So—you have the *Hung Up Age, Standing on Street Corner*—three plays thus far with possible 4th—I send you in separate envelope a letter I forgot I wrote to Jack K., on exhibit at Brown University, they sent me photostat. Wow, I was amazed to see how clear and right a letter it was! Considering some of my letters! I feel you more than most know me as regards poesy in full extent. Therefore I know you'll like to see letter, writ in 1958. I would have it to go along with the plays, essays, and writings in proposed book—what say you? How can we do it without resorting to unnaturalness? It would seem as though I wrote it plainly for publication, though it seems I did have something of sort in mind, as it was information for Jack on article he was writing about me and Allen at time.

It would be fine if you gathered all and have them at hand as I will keep on sending in things, all carefully worked on, there for final selections together, O.K.? Thus far all have been published except for J.F.K. play which will be, *London Magazine* I think, plus this letter to Jack as regards my way with poesy, plus lots of little writings about things, other writers, Beat effects on the soul, etc. All which should make a gasser of a book I truly feel. What say you about *Fried Shoes* for tentative title? *Fried Shoes*, a collection of stuff—might as well make capital of that nice nonsense. Or how's about *Gregorian Rants*, a collection of plays and writings. Actually *Gregorian Rants* is my favorite. I feel it be about time I stand up and talk! I know how busy you are and all, but if I feel you have all the work at hand, it will save me lot of mental confusion as to gathering material at hand. If you do *Gregorian Rants* for me for this Spring, then the gods will unsinus you, and give Rhoda her back back.

O.K. Hope you like what I did to President Kennedy play, the ending came like a sledge hammer of inspiration. It makes play credible and pretty cute, sharp and knowing. I am now working on some essays I have had around for years. Could you let me know what you think about it all?

Your friend from the Big House, Gregory

To James Laughlin Paris

[ca. Sept.] 1962

Dear JL,

Every year the epitaph makers produce my demise. A few weeks ago the *Times Book Review* invisibled me. I would a fine almost personal favor from you, one I would gladly pay for, but feel it grander if you via New Directions were to announce my vital presence via an ad. Could you, though *Long Live Man* is due in November, give notice of coming publication? I mean a real nice big one. If it goes to a hundred dollars all right, just deduct from monies due me. How awful to have so many epitaphs thrown at one—and me a mere 32, and kicking as ever. I'd hate to get to that state that would have me gloat over the death of my epitaph maker, so many are making them, it could get to be a sick preoccupation, waiting. Please state I am very much alive, and that as poet I reserve the right to make my own epitaph, that I don't want no second rate poets or critics or literary gossips making it for me, like it scares my grandmother, she having to call my father to find out if it's true I'm dead. Of late I've noticed a lot of downright vicious unfairness given the Beats, not poets, but people, and it's gotten so I'm standing up for them all the way. If Beatnik is the name that describes me, then Beatnik I like, and Beatnik I'll defend. I see no thing in it to be ashamed of. Lots fled the Beat band wagon (poets) when they started to get mocked and laughed at. They themselves were of the mocking sort, and so joined the mockers of poor Beat. I myself welcome mockery, I invite it, for I too am a mocker, I can dish it out, and I can take it, and when I grumble about it, it only shows I'm not that idiot who enjoys being ridiculed. But I welcome it because it's vital electric and generates further truths, some laughable some nasty, but nothing dead. I feel that if any new poetry will happen [in] American poetry, it will be us doing it, and when we are truly epitaph'd, it will be poetry stemmed from us. That is one thing no one can do, make a poetry to replace a poetry that has bugged many a people. They can write the epitaphs, but not the poems. It's a funny business this. Take prose, after the likes of Hemingway and Faulkner, who today is the great American novelist? Poets there are a plenty, but the time nears when the wheat shall be separated from the straw. Now that Hem and Faulk are gone, does it mean that their work has gone with them? So for the Beats, the good few that there are, myself, Allen, Wieners, McClure, Ferl, Whalen,—when we go, will our poesy vanish with us? I find it hard to say it be the poet's life that keeps his poems alive. Of course when you're dealing with the Beats, you got to look at the epitaph two ways: who's vanished, the poets, or the generation? The latter I'd say was merely a changing of the consciousness, a mental evolution has happened [to] them, youth, in a way, and this will always remain, just like the physical evolution if a nose remains. The first, the poets, well, I feel that the Beats have broken new ground, made poesy kind of public in a way, put it on the map, with Columbus's death died not America. That! should go in ad, James, aye: "With Columbus's death died not America— / With the "vanishing" beat vanishes not / their poetic territorial gains," or something on that order. Anyway just something to herald the finest book of mine to date, *Long Live Man*, a premature announcement, an announcement two months ahead of time, ere two months from now it be regarded as a posthumous work. This is the only time I ever opened mouth on the countless epitaphs, begun way back. Can I have my say? Justice? I know somehow it'll come off correct and best via a ND [New Directions] announcement. "Our author is very much alive, and so are you as his new book indicates due etc. etc." I will be forever thankful to you, James. Right in the Sunday Book Review edition, you can quote of this letter, even say Corso's reply to his 20th epitaph. However you set it up, I know it'll be fine. Can you do this immediately?

Wonderful to see second edition of *Happy Birthday of Death.* I hope your sinus and things aren't bothering you—how's your annual getting along? What of mine goes into it? The England poem, with all those lovely names? Re-looking my Kennedy play, he just doesn't seem the type I created, thus makes play seem kind of naive. Sometimes naivety backfires on me, though character of Nixon comes thru. Could be Nixon has more character, something I'd never have believed before. O.K. Please hurry up and Lazarus me. I am Gregory from the happy hunting ground.

If you feel you can't set it up for me, then let me know, and I'll make the ad. Actually, all it has to say is: "This is to say Corso is very much with us, he has not vanished, and he will appear to all, full blast, come November."

But you're good at this sort of thing, James as *Happy Birthday of Death* and *Long Live Man* "blurbs" tell. Also I would you also do it as a New Directions announcement and I haven't any ready cash at hand, so would that you subtracted from whatever royalty will be due me. Let's go up to 200 dollars if possible for fine ad. Also state the lively presence of Ginsberg and Ferl and Whalen in your coming annual! After all I am not Beats, just Beat and Kerouac is OUT! He joins the epitaph makers in my book! I feel you can realize the importance of this James, and I am asking you in behalf of Allen and the goodly Beat poets to go all out for us on this.

G.

To Allen Ginsberg

Paris
[ca. Sept. 7] 1962

Dear Allen,

Don't know if my letter will get to you soon enough, didn't put enough postage and letter may come back, so I'll hurry this to you. Great, yes, I love Penguins[233] and it be first time we be together, and what about Jack or Bill? I could get Bill to gather 30 pages, I can put them in poesy style—or Jack. As for English publisher, why deal with him, he is doing selected poems due for October.[234] But by time this Penguin supposedly comes out, it'll not hurt sales any; and besides, they'll be 30 pages of new unpublished poems, so no publisher has tie on them, and this be not book but kind of anthology; so can't I just join you without having to write to publisher in England? Have contract in America, and am so lost and tied up with publishers don't know where I'm at, but God I'd love this joining with you, and being that you suggested me, then why don't I just send you 30 pages of poesy; all fine, and all that. Or must they be anthologized from old poems? Whatever, I will write to English publisher if it helps any, all he can do is say no. But can he say no to new poems, and poems not for book but for anthology, which the Penguin will be? *Basta*, you let me know. I rush this off to you as you asked, and tell you plain I am wont to write to publishers or ask them permission on anything anymore. I don't feel my old free self, they got me tied in a funny kind a way. I want out, I need be free this way or else I give up publishing. I am working hard and trying to see clear at all times, how bout you? and how about Jack or Bill for third soul? Ok, I zoom this off to you; hoping all works out well, and maybe you'll get my other letter anyway, but if not, here be this one. How is Peter, and the Indian world and the elephant sun?

Love, Gregory

To Allen Ginsberg Paris

[ca. Sept. 7] 1962

Dear Allen,

Third letter about Penguintocical offer. It be first time we be together; and I say Jack should go third poet, no? or Bill? or Peter? Aye, Peter, if he has enough poems, and my 30 pages can consist of poems that aren't in English *Selected Poems*, like *Power, Army, Bomb*, and from *Gasoline*, and *Vestal Lady* and new ones, so here be list: (none of these poems are printed in English *Selected Poems*, so that must leave me free, and *Gasoline*, as Ferl did not reprint is fully mine, but *Happy* must go to Laughlin's hands, that's what bugs me, he so much with red tape, and Czechs wanted to do me, but he Laughlin insists on being paid for William Carlos Williams first. Now what kind of deal is that? I wish you'd write him letter and state that it be important Czechs get mine work. Aye, he is slow, and my poetry is tomorrow come to bring today to me, ergo to tomorrow, and it be urgent. Aye—and these publishers with their options, like they hold you back. I will play it cool from now on; so Allen, let's see how we can work this out and without stepping on anybody's toes. *Vestal Lady* is mine, but not all poems in that ultra, and *Gasoline* is mine, but *Happy Birth* and *Long Live Man*, be Laughlin's. And in *Long Live Man* I got some real fine poems English publication has not. So maybe I write to Laughlin and see if I can get rush copy (no copy here) of *Long Live Man* manuscript, and select from that too.

But tentatively here be list, and approximate length of poems: from *Vestal Lady*: *Requiem For Bird*, about 100 lines [from] *Dialogues From Children's Observation Ward*, one page—*Dementia In An African Apartment House,* one page—the rest are in English publication. From *Gasoline*: *Ode To Coit Tower*, 2 pages, or 3; *Don't Shoot The Warthog*, one page, *Hello*, half a page; *The Mad Yak*, half a page; and from *Happy Birthday; Bomb, Power, Police, Army; Bomb* need not make broadsheet foldout; *Bomb* be about 4 pages, *Police* 3, *Army* 3. From *Long Live Man; St. Francis*, 3 pages, *Greece*, 3 pages, *Man*, 2 pages, and some others I forget titles, but real fine poems. And some new ones. So actually only business we got to deal with is Laughlin. But all in all I ain't lacking for poems, even though I be poemless for first time in eons, hardly no poems, been doing one or two with long care, trying out slow turtly poems, be master craftsman, eh.

I say we should really make bombshell, now that we got opportunity to be together, and now that we ain't lumped with others. I say whether Jack, Bill or Peter, the daddies, this be clear and exact then. And put in their places the others, those second stringers who are so damned lax. You may think my English publication of *Selected Poems* are slight because no *Bomb* or *Army* or *Power* be in it, but it is fine collection, Al. Yet I would have liked some loud poems in collection, as it is it seemth I be a Edwardian poet. True, and no screammouth rebel yebel, which I is, by God. How is the state of poesy with you? With me it's got up to a crisis in execution. I want to write a new poesy. I'm tired of my carefree old self, though it served well and did what I wished, the expression of idea, and no loss of idea thru form or measure. But now I want true craft power, but a new kind, am tired of hat play or juxtas or ellipses or green armpitry or ghost cheese, two word poems, or icals, like deathical. It be raw clear concise saythings, writings, with built in rhythm. I want now a new poesy, do you got one handy? I listen to you, only one I do listen too. I reject fine ole Bill's way, though he got way by God. But I still care about what is being said, I still want to say. I be inexhaustible when there is to say. [. . .]

What think you of Hollo's *Red Cats*.[235] Title great, but them poems seem kinda milky somehow. I mean no Blok or Mayakovsky[236] there, no advance, and advance should be the light no. Like they is just starting. That creep Alan Ansen, O Allen, this be sad. I think he burned all my papers in his Venice house. He was kicked out, given 24 hour notice, and he told Peggy Guggenheim and [Guy] Harloff to salvage all his things, which she did. But I saw Harloff and he hates me so I don't think he cared much for my papers, and I asked him about them and he thinks they were burned. O that negligent Ansen! That Guggenheim and Harloff! Scavengers of the arts they are! They have destroyed important history there. A crime it is, a true crime, and they should pay some kind of dues. A body can respect those artist and art lovers for such negligence, and Ansen swore he'd be guardian of those papers, he swore. And now I fear they are lost, that no poet, that disgusting faggot! I don't care about my poems or papers so much as your letters and Jack's and Bill's. That be the sorrow. I hate to tell you this. Didn't want to, but maybe they are rescued. Maybe they aren't burned. If only you could write Ansen and ask him to find out. We ain't on speaking terms. I'm miserable because of this, sickening sickening sickening and those fat Jews should be made to pay for this crime, what to do? How are you? No more sick? All India disease go away? And what is new in mind? I love mango eye, mango eye great India image. If you do that to India, then you got something great out of a land sucked dry of imagery. If your poems can indicate sans religious air. But the mango eye of the jungle, then great. Then I see India in your eyesenses.

Love, G.

To Lawrence Ferlinghetti Paris

[ca. Sept.] 1962

Good God man, so I had to close off everything and sit down and read your stuff. All that I had around, *Coney Isle*, German anthology, and see if what you said, how I felt about your poesy was true or no. I read it and I looked out on *stadt* [city], and I saw people walk by with their lives, and I compared your book to them and saw the wow of a difference, like you're at what I'm at in life. And there was no question whether I liked or not. Not one bit of a doubt had I as to your being as fine poet, you're a fine poet all right, but it stops there. I don't know you but for a short span of human contact and letters, letters which in the beginning flowed, and late dribbled. I lost you. And when Laughlin asked if I was sore or something with you for not writing, I was amazed as I was surely not, so I wrote you, but what an inopportune time! Hit by a N.Y.C. that so froze me, and a woe of a letter to what and for what I'll never know. I mean a letter should be contained of what is of import to both. And restrained of what is not. I tried to flow again Larry and the result was a letter of a cold piece of tin on a cold winter icy sidewalk, I regret such missives. Now I can not regret my last missive to you, though your reactions to it made me sad, sad that you truly misunderstood me entire, just like *Happy Birthday* manuscript and ugly "fascist." You see, it weren't as if I wrote you bugging you month after month for financial support, etc. All I wished at the moment of writing letter was some bread, and I felt some coming me. Perhaps I worded it wrong, but good lord man, must I beg please for my due? I'm sorry if it were a cold letter, it seemed to me quite straight but that it wasn't, what the heck, all I can say is, I'll wait your word on the whole matter, and never question my due. Sometimes it's nice to know where a man stands as regards his work, like with J.L. I know where I stand. I could easily know with you if you'd only tell me, that's all I ask. Thus I took the initiative and asked. Again, if I were persistent about it, then such a card were indeed my due, deservedly, but I have not bothered you, and saw no call for such due. After reading it, it were not whether I liked your poetry or not, but if I liked the poet or not. You picture me as a nose-picking kid. On the contrary I am 32 years old, and quite past that descript, please don't feel you're dealing with that description, it makes for who is writing to whom.

In all our years, I feel it was first letter that asked for report as to my standing with *Gasoline*. I wish not to mar such a fine occasion as it proved to be, your publishing it. If you feel it gave me national fame, then good God thank you. I was weighed with the horror that it was my wild crazy me, what with all the 1958-59 national publicity reading made me famous, but that that isn't so, that *Gasoline* made me famous is truly enlightening. Then it is as I always believed. I am famous for being the author of *Gasoline*, and not for being Gregory the Beatnik, Gregory of the Beat Generation. How to figure it out? It's driving me nuts! Because, after all, I am a poet first, a Beatnik second. I mean *Vestal Lady* came before the Beats, right? Well, just yesterday or so I get this letter saying in effect I should be honored to know I have been selected to rank of a *Who's Who*. Into *Who's Who* I go. Now I wondered why? Indeed I began to re-value myself, and all that. Was it because of my poetry? Well, then, if so, then it means that no matter who published me I would have had it made. Ah, and therein lies the rub. An "if." I wondered if Ferl hadn't asked for *Gasoline*, maybe nobody else would have published me. But what if somebody had? Oh, I would have made sure of that! I was not one to keep my poesy in a drawer. I was out for the world, by god! So if somebody else would have done it, it might have meant I would not be a gang poet, not a Beat poet, but a poet all by his lonesome, who stood outside the academic world and the Beat world. And you know what? I could have made it! Aye, my poesy is such would have made it. Consider if the stain of Beat were not on me, consider my status. Oh but "if" serves no remedy, I always say.

What is, is. And what is, I am very content with. Life has been exciting, it to me, me to it. And I am a Beatnik, I guess. Or maybe it is nameless what I have done (outside of poesy - nice poesy) what is called Beatnik, Larry, I am known as a Beat Poet, millions have heard of me as a Beat first, as a poet second. And consider if you hadn't printed me, consider if no one had. Where would I stand today with my poems? And especially when I was the first one to write things like *In This Hung-Up Age, 1954*, and *Vestal Lady*. Imagine how great it would be for me if I would have kept quiet and unpublished all these years, and then go to some publisher and show him the published *Vestal Lady*, and the play and the poems meant for *Gasoline Happy Birthday*. It would all make for a great romantic picture because I would have by-passed all the Beat mockery and abuse. So, I honestly feel I made myself, Larry—myself, plus a good part of what is called the Beat Generation. More, let's say, than Jack. He merely gave name to it. Was Allen and I brought it to the people. We gave it life, and you, you produced the goods, and poetry on your own right, but when it comes to true Beat poet, it be Allen and myself, no one else. Ergo when Jack and you and the epitaph makers say Beat is broken up, is aging, is dying—bah!

That Allen and I gave it life, so will we know its death. We know it not!

I do not say if we die Beat dies, or if Beat dies we die, or if, if. The facts be Jack denies he's a Beat and how could he possibly know who sits on his mother's ass writing all that shit to a people who have contempt for him, he telling them all about his big heart and cock. How unmanly and ratty! He should thunder at them, but no, he wants their love, their acceptance, he wants to be Hemingway loved by the people. I told him no when I saw him in N.Y. If Beat is the name given us, then by God I'll not be ashamed of what is called me. Kerouac is foolish to think he can join the epitaph makers so. If so then good, he's completely out of it now. Now is the time to separate the straw from the wheat. What a motley cowardly lot these Beats be. Well, I say then those who are out, stay out and shut up, if it's dead then make not of its carrion. Jack is a down right sell out. History will tell the true Beats, a name I'll make wonderful, by God, so will Burroughs, so will Allen. And you, if you still feel we ain't dead, because remember about poetry, if anything new is to be written who but us ones will write it? I dare say the epitaph makers will come and go, we'll watch em die. I can't wait to write Ciardi's epitaph—ha. Make it new? Aye, but better than that—make it ever new! If anything is to come after us, and I mean us, it will have to stem from us.

I couldn't nor wouldn't wish to see Joe DiMaggio be in a uniform other than a Yankee uniform, so the same for *Gasoline*, it must always stay with City Lights. I suggested not otherwise. What I did suggest was the rights. J.L. and Olympia Press, they give me let's say—out of 300 dollars, 200 dollars, a 1/3. Such I do not know about us, and I wanted to know. Also after so many printings I figure I get a raise from six percent to more. I mean there are some offers I get, not from big publishers, who offer me half-half. I believe in the poet getting all he can because what he gets is a joke. Out of 10,000 *Gases*, out of all that fame, *Who's Who*, did I get a thousand dollars? O.K., this implies nothing about cheating, it implies you can't get rich on poesy. Being as we had gentlemen's agreement, I figured I'd suggest as gentleman, now that *Gas* has fulfilled itself, that I get half the monies of the future sales. A chance for me to make some money on it, and 75 percent of European sales, if it seems unfair at this late date, O.K. Tell me so, but don't send me off packing to Abbes Abba [Addis Adaba] or wherever it was. You can't say I want dollars, because I never bothered you for dollars. But I can say I want dollars when I want to. Why not? I mean fine for fame but consider poor Cary Grant with no dollars, all that fame and no dollars. It means he'd have to go second class, ride subways, and all the people around his fame, no escape for him. He is doomed to their life, the envision of their income. Cary Grant could not last long thus, with fame, money is helpful and protective. *Basta*, *Basta*.

Allen wrote me about Penguin man saying he suggested me, now you write saying you suggested me. Dare I suggest myself ? Who's to be in it? Can you tell me who is to be in it? Anyway, what I wrote for I did not get—a check. When must I wait for it—the Spring of 1963?

Gregory

P.S. Squeaky American don't like Castro oil. When did I say I hated your poetry? Truth is, I don't like nobody's poetry but my own.

To Barney Rossett Paris
[Oct. 5] 1962

Barney,

Before anybody steals title, put it in contract: *The Great American Novel.* That puts an end to that! When it is asked who wrote the great American novel, why G. Corso, of course! It is a lovely book, and Columbia, the lady with the sparkling torch is the heroine. Girodias thinks title work of genius, so do I. For years the great, the small, have wanted to write it, well I wrote it. So please advertise it soon, so nobody steals it: *The Great American Novel*, by Gregory Corso. I go to Germany for a week on business. Sorry you no see me in Paris.

To Lawrence Ferlinghetti Paris
[Oct. 5] 1962

BOO! All poets are babies, you're a baby, baby. Gregory

To Lawrence Ferlinghetti Paris
[ca. Oct. 6] 1962

Dear Larry,

Forgive please my one tract'dness about *Gasoline* and it's royalty due me. What is cold silly obstinate (real?) letter it must have been. Surely it were worth no poet's time and sense, so accept mine apology for such a thoughtless letter. I think I goofed with J.L that way too. Not same subject, but some other impoetic crap, also sometimes me unpoetic, crap never.

45,000 copies! Wow, then you were correct in throwing away a chance to be a Who's Whoer.[237] Why consent to be what you already are. But mine measly 9,000 copies, good God man, could you blame me for answering the *Who's Who* people thus: "Who's Who? How nice." Alas, when ends the dragon? You, I always knew you to stand on its tail.

Your friend and fellow poet, Gregory

I will always love the soul who saw my work and me that sunny day in 1955 all the way from San Francisco to Cambridge, Mass. And impetus to go out to S.F. I'll see Allen again, differently and you for first time, unchanged.

To Lawrence Ferlinghetti Paris
[Oct. 13] 1962

Dear L,

Poets are also *Who's Whoers,* don't deny it. What udda scene you in? I love to be a *Who's Whoer.* Why me not? Yes, I write to Tony Godwin and say you, Allen and Kerouac best. Because I already be published in England. Second best I say is you, me, Allen. OK? I told Penguin: you, me, and Allen is best. I love Jack, but I don't love my temper. Thought he joined the epitaph makers about Beat. You see, I stand now for Beat, if Beat I is, then Beat I am. As for *Who's Who*, I told them, "how nice." So I guess no more noble poet me, but still chance. I and Penguin, no one, but you.

Love, Gregory

To James Laughlin Paris
[Oct. 13] 1962

Dear J.L.,

I will return to New York soon and will marry a most wonderful girl who I met when in New York last. If it were not for her I'd be a fallen man today, and boy I was fallin'. May I apologize for a stupid letter writ you in Tangier, writ under influence of pot. I could never write or be anything what I have been gifted with of any worth when outside the good clearness of my natural God-given head. I do hope you'll come to my wedding. I want lots of babies—three. I am your friend,

Gregory Corso

P.S. Her name is Sally November.

P.P.S. Though I shall remain here until I gather sufficient funds to return, thus whenever *Long Live Man*, please air it to me. *Long Live Man* is prelude to Abe Lincoln straightness and goodness in me. I ain't' gonna play around no more. I also owe Jack an apology to you, more than to him, in a way. I love Jack and dislike my impulsive temper. I truly felt he was denying Beat, and so what if he does? I denied it countless times. It's a hard thing, good Mr. Laughlin. You're a fool if you accept the brand; you're a fool if you pan it like all the others, is how I see it. After all, Beat people are human beings. Agreed they ain't (a good lot of them) the finest kind of folk (something repulsive there) but folk they are. I do hope that someday I'll be as wise and sure about it like an Abe Lincoln. God what a wonderful man he was, he cleans away all the stinking mystique weirdness I sometimes see man disrespectfully as. I am very happy about life, James, and I feel manhood sure. See how respectfully I behold you? Otherwise I'd not say such things. What wonderful legacy you are leaving to life, and I am proud (as I always say to you) to be part of it.

G.

To Allen Ginsberg Paris

[Oct. 18] 1962

Dear baby, gentleman, man, ultrahomo,

I me is yes going to get married in New York with my Sally November. She Jewish, family no like that, me not Jewish, me, who could have simulated the best to the best, but I respect the tradition, family ties, etc. But me Sally lovely, a true lady all the way, and shall have my baby. She now pregnant. We go to New York to get married, it's what I want, a life that shall bear life, produce in a funny kind of way. My poesy outlook has been getting too fanciful for so hard a real sad good world that I must join it and become it and then my voice shall find its right new way. The old way was new but is done and it ain't like me to be just one kind of thing, or to have found a medium and stick with it. I go beyond those angels Cavafy Apollinaire Lorca Mayakovsky Eliot. I go to tell the truth like them but I shall admit what they dared not. Me imagine admitting that poesy is dead? Aye Allen, for after me what can there be? No, it be not poesy any more, but something else, something maybe we can touch and bring out whatever. I cried upon seeing pictures of you looking like an Indian, like you always have looked, nice, good, and Hope so lovely. Truly her face is gotten great and fine, grown, womanly, wise, good good, and Peter, o funny Peter, how strange and fine he. Yes, all good there, in those pictures. I show them to Bill. He is at Git-le-Coeur wants to write you, says he's interested to see how you is after India. So I guess you did the right thing of course, hot like Tangier, something missing, now something found. I still hold myself distant with him, polite, not way out, he stop being way out. He no smoke pot even anymore. He like old professional writer, believes in it, in his work, no more magic with him, he no look at magic balls anymore, all is straight so, so, good and bad or, I don't know but I guess there can come a young wildsome and call him a deadhead, still his presence is awesome and demands respect, so. Yes Allen, I go that way, marriage, baby, all that, and will do it by God. I see what's ahead of me, some of it I can run from, but I stick it out and make that baby and someday I say aye, ah, and I of course look at the whole thing and interweave the poesy with it, I need a new poesy, a good timely voice, one that speaks not the outsider, but the in[sider] the knowing in, that is best, that is love, that is what is me, and so.

I enclose a fast picture of my love, she is school teacher, 23, and what a nice name, November, no? Give Hope my ever undying love, and to Peter, and when we meet, and I ask Girodias to mail you books asked, and I write to Penguin, use you, Ferl and Jarrell, or you, Jack and Bill, and that be a combine, or if nothing better me, you and Jack; so . . .

Love, love love love love, Gregory

To Allen Ginsberg Paris
[Oct. 19] 1962

Dear Allen,

Penguin Books did not get in touch with me, asking me for poems. Only by say of you and Ferlinghetti do they consider. And I wrote a post card telling them why not you, Jack and Ferl; why? My spoof of noble nonsense whatever. Then I get letter from Penguin and they say, "In view of what you say about being published in England already and also in view of arrangements which Mr. Godwin has already made with Ferlinghetti, I think perhaps we had better keep you for another day and put Kerouac in the present book. This may disappoint Ginsberg, who I know wanted you, but it seems the best solution all round, and I am grateful for your understanding attitude; with best wishes Prichard Newnham." So, how do I react? I write letter saying Jack is novelist, being that book is concerned with poesy then I feel I should be included—end of letter. Cold that, and somehow it didn't seem right, not after that post card I sent, so I set myself to do right. I sent Newnham another letter saying, "Allen, Jack and Ferlinghetti are a fine trio, why not four? If not four than I shall and should abide by my first feeling. It's just that I would have loved to be in a little Penguin, and that somehow I would feel left out. Is that an ignoble unpoetical feeling? I think, I am yours trying to do right, Gregory Corso." So it ends there. And what else? The more important—where are we going? Where have we arrived? I tend to marry, Allen. And she is already pregnant it seems sure. And so a child, and a life of wife and child. Will it change my outlook, yes, it will make me see clear, real clear, or I can run to India and embrace thee and Hope and sing and bang my head against the Indian temples for joy and forgetfulness and still want poetry or does that matter? It seems to have Bill. He stays in his room and writes writes writes writes. Somehow I know just where I am at Allen, as regards poesy and life, that is; through the state of poetry, where it stands, is how I measure life. Well, I see poetry as something finalized; rest is modern gimmickry, or simple honest talk, so true magazine, or won't it turn the world upside-down anymore? Can one sit in a room and depict what's bugging everyone or what everyone wants to know or why even direct to them? Who are they that the poet speaks to? You say poet takes over from priest. Yes, but that kind of poetry has reached its peak, now what? Where's the goods? It seems to be in the poet and that's it. He lives, he does, he experiences, he he he, and what he directs to goes on its clodsome way. Who do we attract? The literary! The literary, it ends up that way. I went to the Pommes Museum, where the Fantin Latour[238] Rimbaud is, the Impressionist and I sighed, "So this is where they end up!" Something so futile in that. Like it seemed to make dot of Cézanne

Monet etc. God knows what has that to do with anything but that paintings are new visions, but they end up being nice things to see, and some if you look deep [they] show that they saw and knew. But what is it they saw and knew? What do we really see and know, or attain? Does it matter? Is that the criteria? Maybe just live while you got the chance and don't question it so much or expect so much from questioning. But that's what poetry seemed to be, an asking, a wanting, a something like that, Allen. And now what? Surely I'm not that one to hold a woman so long as to cuddle and love and be a father all gooey and fine, no no no. But it seems a way I'm going in and so I look to my poetry, and how unaware I surely was. And yet a visionary yes, yes. I saw, and I saw not realizing I saw. Now I see, Allen, and such sight I have yet a poetry for it. Tell me something.

Gwegory, love love, Gregory

To Lawrence Ferlinghetti

Paris
[Oct. 19] 1962

Beat Penguin combines: you, me, Allen, because we three best noise nice true; or Jack, Bill, Allen; old buddies, or me, McClure, Lamantia. What do I prefer? I did you, Allen, me. You are in line with Cavafy, Mayakovsky, Apollinaire, so there. Now what about poesy ? I go for new poesy. Away from it, I marry, have babies, live alone in life, work hard, food good, simple. New poetry, only me can make it.

Love g g g g g g g g g

Penguin says no one—I say me, you, Allen. Jack is novelist.

To Judith Schmidt

Paris
[Oct. 19] 1962

Dear Judith,

Two things, first the check you said you sent to American Express Paris never arrived. Maybe American Express doing me in after that book I wrote? Second, I wrote a letter to [the] editor to *Evergreen* [*Review*], have carbon of it, and I don't dig letter. I mean it ain't necessary, so please see that it isn't printed. The rest is all wonderful and fine, the world seems to me, almost, as Abe Lincoln would have it. How's that? Let you in on something else, I am truly doing serious fine book for Barney and Grove, and that title *Great American Novel* hits me as jokesome, so. All I gotta do is keep my sights clear. Hoping for the best for the best.

Your friend, Gregory

To Allen Ginsberg Paris

[Nov. 3] 1962

Dear Allen,

Ferl, a while back writes me I don't dig his poetry. I write back he is a baby to think such, that I believe he is a seeing soul, but when it comes to seeing, JK has got it all over much of us ones. Yes, Jackie boy, you, me, and Jackie is realer and more exact because we wuz like that long time ago. So I hope it all works out, but whatever you do, don't back out, so long as your poems are there, what boots it who surrounds thee? Though I see your point, and fate will not deny Jackie's reward, which is immense, and he must bear the brunt of outward earthy unfame, it be so, bad boy, etc. And I always yelling at him but never denying his craft. Yes, he is a poet, and only as novelist invading poesy territory so easily I get bugged at him, remember, and have dreams of him that he is big fool who wants lots of gold and fame, then have dream of him so nice and lovely handing me figs and dates. God knows what it's all about? But the truth is, I do prefer his poesy definitely over Ferl, yet I do not deny Ferl. He is a seer Allen, he speaks straight, though he has some silly ideas, politic ones, and those absurd accusations calling me fascist and all that. Well he is extension of 30's Wobblies mind. As for poetry, well like I told him, in reply as to whether I liked his poesy or no, I said: "I like nobody's poesy but my own." *Basta.* Now listen, when I ask where the goods, I mean this. True, you is right. Poet is priest, prophet, etc. Yes, yes. But poesy's function is something more, and this I believe. If it can answer the whatall, if it hasn't got it that it need be wallowed in magic, or ritual relgios hashish whatever. If it can't get to what science will benefit by, then it ends up being the personal spirit recorded on paper for other spirits to observe. That in reply to uncontrolled communication forces. Allen, when Rimbaud had to resort to magic, when Bill cuts up the word, all this may benefit poesy but the direct DIRECT line to THERE or WHERE is, I find, NOT IN POESY. The fault lies not in poesy, but OUT THERE. So ply your magic on that, I say. Go to the source and work it into your expression which are words, etc. Yes, Bill is on right tract, but remember, Bill no ever listen to music, he is hard clinical, the joys of rosy-ass angels will never be for him. But what is for him is the old testament type prophets, the hard ones, almost cruel ones, he himself says all that out there, life, is a rotten mess, what a disgusting thing to do to man, etc. or how did his being ever get into this mess; same like Rimbaud. But what they both miss out on is that they are here saying that, wow, o wow, if they can't see that, they are the Godspirit here and now, that they be the only link to God, that without man God no be, then these powers will go unused in these souls. This I hold, and so to the spirit I hold, and now that this spirit is, as I say, full fledge, it seeks a new poesy

NOT IN POESY. I got it all right with the way I write, but speak! There is so much to talk about. Oh, well, time will tell.

I wish I could zoom to India and see you and Hope, and no baby for me. She bled the next day, but I was happy to think I might have a child. I see that as all right, long live man, so might as well help, and maybe I never marry if I don't do it on spur of joyous moment. Anyway what is truly important is poesy and nothing else. Never have I felt like this, I feel that it shall come greatly to me, for I don't go at it, never had to, don't know how to, it will come, and when it does, we will, you and I know well, because I know you see life as it is and have accepted it and damn the despair. Despair has cut the balls off many a poet, no? Here is how I end latest poem: "No, wormy Sibyl, I don't want your rosy-ass angels, I believe in the Flying Fish of Tyre more / God has become strange / His new Christ is not a likeable soul / distant He is, keeps alot to Himself / He doesn't like this world to much / calls the whole thing a lousy mess / What abstract? What magic? / This Almighty breaks my heart. . ." There, it be the God spirit in such as Bill that is distant, and not liking the world. All I can say is, "This Almighty breaks my heart."

That is apt to say he is unhappy, on the contrary, he is having a ball with his fold-ins.[239] The sufferer is not the disliker, aye, but the liker. Allen, just how long will you be there, maybe I try so hard to get a batch of money and fly down there, that I would, o how I would, so I try, let me know how long, ok? And send me some new poems, new parts or pieces of poems, and I send you mine.

Also realized that the Golden Age of Greece I loved so much was only for a select few, not for the masses. No golden age for the mass of man, alas. Anyway, I will from here on in write straight and make it, by God. We gotta meet before we get to heaven.

Love to Hope and Peter, Gweg

To James Laughlin Paris

[ca. Jan.] 1963

Dear J.L.,

Could you please not give me a "raise" boss, but can I have like I got on publication of *Happy*, the same 200 dollars for *Long Live Man*? It would help me get back to my country U.S.A. where I want to marry and have babies? Gregory, Jr.? Also am I due anything from second printing on *Happy*? Enclosed a poem I wrote in two minutes flat, inspired by the man I liked and saw in his face greatness on becoming President. Regard my JFK, the prophetic ending, also this poem was writ on the 23rd when everyone was worried about bombs. I saw the light, the goodness and result of good by his move. Everybody saw my way four days later, so I am a little kind of prophet and therefore I have come to a conclusion. Poetry, I thought something was wrong with it, well no, it's not in poetry, it's outside of it. That is, today, space age, etc., all is urgent, immediate, ergo poesy like that needs immediate publication, literary mags don't serve this function, newspapers do. As this "poem" more a feeling, sentiment, tells.

Can't wait to see *Long Live Man,* it is prelude to a new complete clear hard exact no-crap poesy. I wish there were a weekly called the *Poetry Express.* Anyway, youse is still my friend and that keeps me happy.

Joy, Gregory

To Louis Ginsberg[240]

Paris
Jan. 23, 1963

Ah, Louis,

How life-warming and opportune your letter; my best dearest friend in life has it his father look upon me with goodly eyes and heart. You carry the great Jewish tradition of wit on your person like a squaw carrying a papoose, it grows braver and keener all the time. In this day and age when one finds it hard to discern between wit and sarcasm, you're he such no one dare call corn, else you Sioux them, and give them something really to Crow about, so don't let any one buffalo you into thinking your wild wits is not a feather in your cap, it is.

I got a way of making a $ million. Europe loves the American Indians. I could open a restaurant and serve American Indian food! Indian pudding, wild rice, pumpkin, corn, turkey, sassafras, tapioca, deer, buffalo—and Tom Tom songs.

Anyway the Indian bit came out extemporaneously. I can match your smoke signal any day, see what you're in for? Son matches you in poesy, friend in wit. Won't let you monopolize anything, except the deserved pleasure you receive from a life you've given much to, as concerning young fold and their educations. Boy I wish I had you as a teacher. You don't pull ears, do you? only legs—good. My teachers used to pull my ears. I was really a problem in school. Never went to high-school though, straight A's except for penmanship and conduct.

I hold to you as a knowing Jew. I have a Jewish problem. I am [in] love with a Jewish girl and her family no like. They have yet to see me and I feel they'd rather not. Father is dead set on his daughter marrying a good providing Jewish boy (providing and Jewish go together, synonymous anyway). So she is all upset and if I had her with me she'd know what to do. I had her with me but her folks wanted her back. I sent her back, now she is with them and of course adds to her bewilderment. She's a school-teacher by the way, 23 years old, and an angel. I would readily wed her, but poets aren't very steady providers. So providing I either nip what grows full straight (my brother did so at 25, her family demanded it, he didn't care one way or the other). What is it with my family? My father re-married a Jew. My brother, and now it seems I may {marry a Jew}. When I lived with my father and step-mother we lived in a Jewish neighborhood. I would go out with Jewish girls, I truly suffered being a goy. I mean there is such a thing as a prejudiced Jew.

I am well aware of the father's position. I understand such feelings on his part, yet ever so fast the world and life and one should hold to that truth and not obstruct the fast livers, besides they never had a poet in the family, but *Time* magazine doesn't help. They read damaging things said about me and your son, calling us "spider-eyed." A sorry business. People are impressionable, and such phrases stick in the memory. God oh God but we ones had much dues to pay. I chalk it up as a matter of character, and one of the true heroics of the time, this antagonism between poet and society. One thing is certain, when it's time to go to the happy hunting ground, your son and I, and yourself, it holds for most poets, will secure satisfaction that life was best served by us. I too love life and am never the one to ponder as steady farewell to it. I am in a way a religious person, by default as it were, and of the things I hold as sacred life of course is topmost. Then must a poet above all be true! Yet honesty doesn't necessarily mean correctness, many status poets are compelled to be discriminate, they who write only that which serves them well. A tactful truth's quite often a clumsy lie. But as I say I feel more than truth is needed, that in itself it's not enough.

Anyway I feel I must go wisely and with good care as far as my future wife goes. I will not cause friction or hurt in her family by demanding she wed me with or without their say. She is 23, free to do as she wishes. I would rather it her father like me and agree, for us it is we'll have a tough go of it in setting up house, etc. I love her, and had it suggested her that if I knew someone else, someone of her faith, would be best for her, I'd say good-bye, but she threatened suicide, etc. if I did so. And yet she loves her family doesn't want to hurt her father who she is deeply attached to, all I can do is wait until I see her, that should make a lot of difference. I tell you this, Louis, for perhaps some of your goodly wisdom, as well as to show you what has been happening to me since I last saw you. If we get married in New York, you must definitely be there, can meet my father for the first time, maybe it can get Allen to return from the hinterlands the land of the violent peace.

I will return to U.S.A. in February, will see you then.

Yes, the German book came out and I am furious with it. The co-editor who worked on it with me, doing all the translations, etc., took it upon himself to exclude you among others, stressing only on the young loud mouths. I gave him the manuscripts in 1958 thereabouts and last time saw it in 1960, then in printed form in 1962. He left out some people who are easily hurt, who have never had a poem printed and who were very happy about their inclusion. When they saw that they were not, it hurt them sorely. I felt awful, and was powerless to do a thing except that if I ever do such a project again I'll make sure it holds as I would it. They excluded Miss Levertov, though they have her name on the cover. They put in poets I did not authorize. Anyway it's not such a vital book, done in less expensive way, only 3,000 copies have been made, and stands not as an indicative anthology. See I'm trying to let you not feel bad about your exclusion, though I do feel it was a wrong thing to have happen, still I do occasionally see your heart-words in *Herald Trib*, Paris edition and always give them special attention. As for myself I feel for the first time a sense of discrimination, as to what words to use, and added care to craft. Old belief that poesy is property of youth doesn't hold water—nectar. I myself get better as the years go on, though [I] write less. "Hey call you this snow? / What is this stuff, / I want to know! / 'Tis, my good man, / God's dandruff." I remember that last line as a kid—don't know who told it to me, or if I told me it myself—but it is cute. Maybe I'll settle down to writing nursery rhymes, real hard to do, you know. But I am actually working on what I always wanted to do and that be an epic. What about *The Everlasting Minute*?[241] What doth the hour tell?

Love, Gregory

To Sam Corso Paris
[ca. Jan.] 1963

Dear Dad,

In America they have a book called *Who's Who*, in it all the big deals go. Well, you are in it by virtue of me, being my father. Now this is something, isn't it, for they say only three out of 10,000 people get into it. That really makes us select, and for what? For some words I wrote? Surely I am probably the poorest soul in it, with hardly a cent to my name, but whatever I have brought the Corso name into such selective honor. The book will be out in the middle of this year. Now I wonder just what father I have honored, plus by dedicating my *Long Live Man* book to you. I have honored the man now, the person who I hardly know, and who I feel like a stranger to, but a friendly stranger. I honor the man who has been a good father to Jerry, and husband to Flo, and that is as far as it goes. I can not honor the man who was the father I knew. That man was a stupid cruel man, a man who mercilessly whipped with a strap the small backs of his sons, and I mean backs, not ass. I remember carrying the scars for months, and they have never quite disappeared. I remember only having that man for a father, one who abandoned me when I went to prison, who never sent a cent for either cigarettes or candy. Who never cared. How can I honor such a father? It was because of him I learned fear, fear of coming home to get another beating for having lied about wetting the bed—and I wet the bed most everyday! So every day I had to fear a beating. This has left its mark on me, this fear. I had no one to turn to. My father was my enemy, home was a dreaded place, never was there love and when I left my many jails and came home you immediately would say, "I hope you learned your lesson," just like a cop. Whereas a father would have embraced his son weeping and would have shown love. O he was truly a stupid cruel man, and I could never know why he hated me so. That is why I find it hard to see you now. I know you are a different man, time changes things, and yet, and Joe is like you, he too resents me, always has, just like you. You two were a pair, and both were ignorant, just physical strength was all you had, and you boasted it against brains. Well brains was helpless then, and brains could not hurt like a punch in the face like Joe gave and did threaten to give. All I can say sadly for my brother and such strength is that it has not honored the Corso name, it has not placed his father in honor, and it will grow old and weak and die. I say some of the old yet remains in you and him for when you visited me at Ginsberg's house, you both slyly looked the place over, you both examined things in your petty ways rather than behaving like close beings. I knew then you both yet resented me, and then I learned why, I finally learned why. It was because I was unlike you two, a million miles away. And when you left you and Joe both snidely said don't forget your name is Nunzio—well that night was like old times.

How could I ever forget Nunzio? That poor kid has been thru hell the likes you two God has spared. Nunzio means announcer, and he did just that. He announced to the world, to history, and what did he announce? Not his hell, but beauty, and the joy of life. Here then was Nunzio that was a man, a great man, one who saw the meaning of life. Everyone has their life to live, I live mine, you live yours, but I will die never having ruined a life. For you are lucky, Nunzio was strong, he did not die or rot in a prison cell like I am sure you thought I'd end up. But if I was that weak person then as sure as the sun is the sun his death would have been on your hands. I cannot say I can forgive and forget because Nunzio is not around any longer. Don't you know that he was an angel sent from God? That he suffered on earth thus to learn the sorrows of life and then to announce? He was all of 17 years old when he finished hell. He was 13 when he was put in the cruelest mad ward in Bellevue hospital. I say I, I am Gregory. Nunzio is gone. I only use Nunzio sometimes in my writings when I speak of that time and in *Who's Who* I put in Nunzio.

So I hope this makes clear of what Sam Corso I am referring to, when I dedicate my work to {him}. I cannot honor, out of respect to the memory of Nunzio, his father. But I can honor Jerry's father, and have. I let you know this to show that it is not easy to visit you. That you or the family don't get the idea it is disregard on my behalf, as Dotty implied when I saw her on last visit. She, like the rest, are ignorant of what has befallen me in the past and to have to think of only the present, fine. Then we are but strangers because all I know is the past, almost twenty years ago!!! So, Dad, when we again meet, it'll be on terms less rigid, with no promises, as I awkwardly made. I so sadly believed I had a family. I have no family, you are not my family. I am merely that strange son of yours who you only know from the past. When you see me you do not see a fine man, one who is a good poet, but Nunzio, the boy of the past. That is all you can see because you saw no other, nor I of you. I can only look at Jerry to know you have been a good father there.

And the same for grandma. When I saw her, all I could see was that not so kind lady who always gossiped and denied me and Joe, when we were 12-14 years old, one very snowy night a bed to sleep in. That was all I could see. I could not love her. The only way I could have been happy with the Corso's was if I were stupid. Well, I wasn't stupid.

Grandma saw my wife to be. The last time I saw her, I brought my Sally with me. Sally is a Jewish girl, and her family is not too keen on her marrying outside the Jewish faith, but with all their influence and money, they can't stop us from marrying. They would prefer it I became a Jew. Never. She will have to come on my terms, and shall.

To Ted Wilentz

Paris
{Jan. 24} 1963

Dear Ted,

Angels of light and white apples are beset me again. I will be home in February, finally. And am back in good shape again. So all is O.K. and again thank you for coming through. Is it cold there as it is here? Brrrr—I bought pretty stamps just in case your daughter saves them or if not, they're lovely in themselves. This is quick—just to let you know how things stand. I go back to London in a week and will sail from there. I'll see you soon.

Gregory

To Ted Wilentz

London
{Feb. 7} 1963

Dear Ted,

I have asked that my mail be forwarded to your store. How nice to want to meet me at boat but don't because it takes so much time and hassle with customs etc. It arrives in morning of February 15, the Ryerdam, but I feel it be better I get off, dispense my belongings in terminal locker, and see a place. I'll zoom right over to bookstore.

Yours, Gregory

To Allen Ginsberg

New York City
March 7, 1963

Dear Al,

Got a gassy electric typewriter lent me by friend goes fastzzzzzzip! Now heard about you getting kicked out of India.[242] Good God, maybe that China scare made them get middleclass or something like. Maybe they scared of you and your electric influence of the young like. Whatever I think it be time you come home. Really, like come home and we build big house, like Williams' is dead and so somebody must keep his homeside fort. True, listen to Gregory, his name is Gregorio Nunzio Corso. It means Greg, watchful; Nunzio, I was born on the annunciation, means announcer; and Corso means the way. [. . .] So bring Hope with you. Tell her I can't marry nobody but her, that I will die loving her, that she is my first and last love, that I can't stand no other female but her, and that be true. So there, so there. And tell her that I am her real poet not a dead one. She and I, we only liked the dead ones, you still didn't get *Long Live Man*? Well in it is a poem to Robert Frost in which I tell him that Poe is my American poet, and Shelley my teacher and Demeter my mother. And of the contemporary, Ginsberg's metaphor is all I care to understand, so like I raise thee high high up there, you balding Jew. You oldest friend in my life, you duck, you galaxical snob, you swivel, you gate, you SPQR.

Now really Allen, the time ripe for a return here and a meet with me. I think I got death by the balls really, and it comes very close to agreeing with your orgasm of universe, that void is perpetual orgasm that the earth is a baby, like a woman gets lots of come, the stars are dead come, void is cunt, void is endless because the orgasm is endless, that is why infinity, that is why. And so then take from there what means America. America is the second coming because Christopher Columbus means Christ bearer, his ship Santa Maria meant same, angels in his dreams told him to find America. America is the second coming and its destiny its meaning is to kill death. That is why me, Gregorio Nunzio Corso. But I feel I am a successful angel, but a fallen one like. Yes, alas, o woe, and you. I know what you mean but ain't telling until you come back home. I want you back. I swear that the scene here is cool, quiet nice, just right. Please take heed, India you had, good, but don't die there, don't [grow] old there. Please take hold and heed of heritage. Now that Williams is gone, take heed, home ground, America second coming, messiah is here. True God can be a plot of land not just a man you know and tell Hope, my John Alden, or was it Miles Standish who was told to speak for himself? Whatever, when you speak, I speak, when I speak, you speak—Allen. I am on to dreams. They tell me all, they tell me much, most every night. I dreamt Hope the other night, for the first time she was kind to me and loved me. What a great dream. I dreamt a while back that I was back in time, 1962 back to 1950, I met Jack and Bill, not you, but it was a quote of first line of *Howl* that convinced Bill that I was telling truth. Bill was great in dream, Jack no. Jack needs a lesson, I don't care what you say, his *Big Sur* at first I thought it all right but rereading it I see that he is lost, blind. He sees only his worthless skin, his woe his beatnik plight. That hang up I got rid of long ago. So did you in *Palante*[243] letter, but at least your letter was true and universal. His is small and fake and I tell you he needs help, a real good awakening or he is forever lost. Just don't say "aw good old Jack" because you won't be helping him much that way. I love Jack as much as you and know what Jack is and man is human and no one can be as perfect as we poets but they can be made to wake up by God. Read *Big Sur* and see what I mean. He is in Florida, I last saw him a year ago. He was obnoxious, drunk and yet his eyes betrayed him for indeed he is hurt and a good soul. I only wish we could be together again and help ourselves once. Like it seems lots get helped by us but when it comes to one of us, one of the boys, wham. Like Bull,[244] bull, Bill don't need no help he is ok, yet a little nutty. I swear, old alchemy man, him and word and poetry hating, bah. I am Captain Poetry and he is Savania, and I tell you he ain't got no chance. Poetry will live because Bill wants to live, wants to be like Swift, don't want to be mean man, he truly wants to be a committed soul. And he is, I got him to confess to the dignity of man. And he maintains such dignity but I told him don't forget his sources, not to forget his past.

Alex Trocchi[245] tells me that Bill comes over to turn on, takes a shot a day, I doubt this is true, but why would Trocchi lie? He jealous of Bill. To me big tragedy is Bill got real hooked, but I am glad that he isn't morally head down on nothing like then it makes him afraid of something and he should be afeared of no thing, should conquer all. Burroughs has changed because he finds that he is of worth. That his word is heeded, that the young adore him, that is why you saw a different Burroughs. But God, o God, I love you more than any man and don't want to see you fall prey to his poetry destruction. It be a kick but not for you, NOT FOR YOU. You made the man remember. You did much to make that man, much in the past, giver of light, remember, and don't think his work is all ALL. It is reasonable and good but not the ALL. Man is all we know, all who we have heard and learned from and by. Don't believe that any one man can hold the works, the gist of all. Gregory tells you that he, Gregory, has had deep contact with the forces in his dreams and that Bill is a very important functionary in the nether world but not the overall central boobugaboo. Burroughs has learned. From me, he has learned that death is a gimmick, a con. He uses that much. And he has learned from you and others. And he is not to be too trusted. How can he be when he don't trust no man, and his experience has hinted him this distrust. Yet it does not deny him the soul to understand and feel, for him writing him being concerned is a fine goodly almost extraordinary thing. But he be a writer from way back. He don't trust you or Peter or me or Jack but he does trust his lackey Portman, etc. because they don't infringe on his territory. Bill is a megalomaniac, too. In short, please please don't die because of him. That letter in *Palante*, I got bugged with you. I don't want my best poet friend adhere to no man on the face of this living earth. By God, Bill is great, but don't monster him by making him like he once told me that he was God. God is who claims it, but man is the result of that claim. Don't think that god is so straight as all that as to take a Bill form. Nay, nay, nay. god is lesser than man, I say. It be man who manipulates him, but it be God who keeps man sane, who makes man lovely, hopeful and good.

The years are rewarding us, we are highly respected all around, we are heroes now. True, people really think well of us. That makes me happy because I always thought well of people. I went to a Larry Rivers' party and an elderly lady upon leaving asked her husband is that Gregory? The husband admonished her for being so fan-like, he embarrassed. He led her away, they took elevator. I went down steps. I met them outside and I put my arm around the lady and said I am Gregorio and how are you and lo Spring is coming. And I said goodbye, it made both husband and her glow. I made them happy. I was admired by them, and I said hello to them. And that made me feel wonderful all over because here I knew that apart from creepy *Time* telling people that we is spider-eyed conspirators, we are in truth, the best people in the world. I say this in no high-handed way, well you know how down to earth I am. And how bugged in the long run I get by too many admirers, etc. Yet that elderly lady felt truly, and I felt it, and it made me be proud to be a poet, though I wish I could have gathered another gift besides the arts, like Williams and have been a doctor or something. I don't know maybe what is, is supposed to be. I can still do whatever I wish, but not now, now I need all the time I can get my hands on, I am writing epic poem, my hearts desire from way back, an epic, yea and yea for that. I am now doing it, and the form will contain every possible form I am capable of.

I'm asking you come back Allen. Yes, because here is your home and your source and here you can write your big mango-eyed epic. I want that our epics appear same time. Maybe we print them together. I say that there are only two poets in this here world today and they is you and me. I mean this because I am fair and I can't in my fairness find any poet worth a great big YEA YEA. But then again I don't read that much of the new stuff. Maybe you can suggest somebody who is better than us. I say this as the one who stands detached from us, from our work. Were I to say this as Gregory poet, then I'd perhaps be hesitant as to who is best or not, anyway what means best, not best. By God a lot. Yes an awful lot. Because man o man, poetry is not something to toy with, to dance with. Sorry, poetry is important like doctors are, and sickness is a serious business by God, so I ain't gonna feel terrible for saying we is the best. You know that I am no ego Allen, but I wish to hell those poets of power and in control of communication outlets were downright realer and gooder.

I'm writing this a million miles a minute, as fast as my thoughts can go. Ah, yes, Penguin. How wonderful, they go all over the world, don't they? Why they finally accept me? What happened? I gave them great selection. Had to, look who I'm set against. But Ferl is a funny kind of likable poet, no? He is wrong as to me, his political belief about me, and treats me like a thoughtless nose-picking East Side angel. Told him I was a man son, but I know he only means it in fun, yet wow o wow. How bugged he gets when I ask him for a royalty statement! He writes back that he isn't a publisher but a poet and that I should write to him as a poet, etc. etc. A real drag that, because he is a publisher by God, as well as a poet. Real touchy he be there. Maybe I should write to him as a poet. "Dear poet please give me the heavenly muse's royalty decree, mayest I knoweth what is comingeth me? etc. etc." Something like that. His poetry is well known and respected by the way, in Europe. I met many people who know of him and believe him to be quite important. He is straight, you know, and isn't phony. I mean he ain't the likes of a Micheline or a LeRoi Jones, who is real nasty. He bugged with me because I put down all them there Cuba poet enthusiasts. I think they did a humorless job on Cuba, Allen, and that they failed, these second stringers, to do anything really great, *basta*. I only say what I believe to be true and usually I'm right. Why not? I have a good youth experience to fall back upon. I can't help but know the innerings of life somehow. Though I do admit I am a little nutty in my outflow, that there is such a thing as commitments, and they are committed folk, *basta*. All will resolve itself. Saw *Guns Of The Trees*[246] What a bore, but I loved you. You were best, your voice when about suicide, Apollinaire Mayakovsky Crane, came over great. So this be my letter and I hope I have enough gold worth in soul with you to get you back home, because this be most vital time. I count the minutes, not much do I hold, so must I threaten you with my demise, you and Hope? I believe a meeting will be a revelation for us all, and of course assy silly goodly Peter too.

Love, Gregory

▼ [Gregory had stirred everyone up by having Kirby Congdon, a poet and friend, act as his literary agent. After offending all his publishing contacts, Corso had to write letters to all of them, mending fences.]

To Lawrence Ferlinghetti New York City
[ca. March 7] 1963

Dear Larry,

Kirby Congdon is no longer my agent. I don't dig agents, so disregard all his say. We keep going as we always have in regards on *Gasoline* and *Bomb.* But can't I ever ask for my royalties without you getting bugged? Glad about you not using mine rant, silly business. I got no material really. Heavy work on Grove Book, that's all.

Gregory

To Allen Ginsberg New York City
[ca. March 31] 1963

Dear Allen,

You are amazing. I find my treks and ferrets into what is what and how and why ends up where you've begun—every man is God. Because it will be some day America's belief that such is so. Then Columbus was St. John the Baptist, America Christ. You announce it. I joy in my having been born on the annunciation, and given Nunzio (announcer) for name. Therefore we fulfill Columbus's meaning. You are right, there should be one full hour of truth in all forms of communication. A grand result or madness will occur, and I don't hold to the fate of machines: i.e. bomb, computer, George Orwell, etc. And, I am driven to include, Communism. I don't like communists, their way of life, but I do like their struggle, their wanting to feed the poor, etc. South America as you well saw. But it is not the way. Old Europe, Russia, is given first crack at outer space. America first with the Bomb. What did the American Indian, do made him lose his Eden? It's ours, at hand. You can't tell India everyman is God, but you can America. If you saw, no, if I saw, blonde Iowa young *Time* magazine housewives burn on the pyre like the ones you witness in India [the burning Ghats]. I'd say it was like when I had pigeons. When one died the other birds were all nervous and wild-eyed. No form likes to see his form blaze and sizzle eruption of cooking blood out of melting nose. Blonde hair steaming white smoke. See where I am stuck Allen? I believe if the Egyptian believed he was going to another life whence death then he went. If the Indians see making logs of what Bill calls "the human host," then it be their way, and I would regard their way and not mind the roasting. But it says nothing of death and perhaps everything. Dead Americans should build pyres—O vain cemetery! It's because the body is what we are and feel we forget that we are mere radios to express godness. Turn off a radio, you don't turn off the program—right? So the Indians do go to wherever they believe—as sure as the Catholic gangster getting the electric chair. He is given a servant of the Catholic God [to] lead him into death and unto heaven. If the Catholic gangster believed he was going, he went, like Bill and you. I too have held death a con. Allen, I'd that hour of truth release God's hang up on the human host. Who else but God can watch its momentary skin slip into flames and yet shudder to see the skin blonde haired. Who else but God can announce He is God? Were there such a God separate from us I'd him cross-eyed, confused as to how it itself came into being. God was the dinosaur. God is even Howard Johnson's. Which is to say God is pretty sick, and you and I and Jack, yes, Jack, and Bill and many others want God made well. Or, if we're all puffs of divine emptiness, it still goes to say that no man has yet laid down the true story. Not Plato not Socrates, not Shakespeare, Shelley, Christ. No man has given the true way. Man has followed other ways and I can't gamble it they all found themselves facing the zenith like a sulking caveman facing a cave wall. That is why I death-think. I called, in *Long Live Man,* Death an instant! That's all, a wham, instant. The taking leave of the human host. No, not taking leave, it is always outside the host. We are pick ups. We are lots of times silent radios. God is not in us at all. Then lots of times God comes in us, our wonderful brain gives Him (it) (us) chance to get hip.

So thank you for dedicating a book of yours to me.[247] I hold it you are the only person I know longest. If Manny the Pony Stable Artist were my steady friend he'd be the oldest. He was great Allen, he was the true Bohemian, never serious about his art. The romantic artist who one day flipped because his art became a vision of time. He couldn't be today what he was then. Yes, we are changing, and at a reading I gave in Cleveland at Western Reserve a kid asked me to prove to him how the consciousness has changed in the last seven years. He did not experience the change because he merely grew into it, like it was supposed to be like that. I mentioned *Howl, Cancer, Naked Lunch*, as breakthrough—then a professor gets up and says Hemingway and others used the same words. Yes, I agreed. But they never spelled the words right, like fug, f. . ., frig, etc. Allen, I also read at the University of Buffalo, there and Western Reserve in a week. On my 33rd birthday I read at Western Reserve, at the Hart Crane Memorial, I did fine, but Buffalo, Buffalo was great! Over a thousand kids came to hear me read and we had great rapport. They dug the poems as straight talk to them. I read *Marriage*, and a new great funny poem called *Russian Dream* in which I have a flying rug poem, and I fly this over Moscow telling everyone I'm Pushkin, Mayakovsky, Essenin, etc. After all these years and all the epithets laid on us we have remained a curious funny lot. I brought in the greatest audience. I read in accordance to the occasion, easy, humorous, straight, hardly any heavy serious poems, the time just didn't seem right for heavy. Though I pondered the fact that three years ago when we read the word—serious was the tone. There's no need to call society's ills. The big important business is after the body. I no longer care to advise the body how to live. If I can give the body a sense of unbodiness—see beyond the body, then I succeed in what may be them there puffs of divine empty or whatever be the opposite. I hail your words my words. We hold to the same end result, fine. Rather we die uncertain than the Catholic gangster who sits on the electric chair with purified soul. We will die (if not sudden, unawares) with hopeful curious and your face will look as benign as it looked when you took laughing gas. I watched your face. I got scared, you remember. Well, I have now reached your rhythm of death sense. I was born and raised to die a Catholic, you a Jew. But we will die a Allen and a Gregory. Bill will die good too. The very very end of life is death. There is no realm of death, death is only the end of the life that vegetates and walks. See you on the farthest sun in space someday, or may pass you by unknown, like I might be passing the friend I knew as previous life which goes to hold that God is simply life and we've no part of that God when we die. So you and me in nothingness is got to meet and switch on somethingness again.

Whatever I hope you come to N.Y. soon, or else I'll come to India, finally. Am with my Miss November again, wife and child business. Yet I shy away to live a wifeless and childless life. I usually have made many goofs, the goof of impregnating a goodly girl won't be such a bad thing. I'd still be no being's mate. So were I in India I'd be just a lurking mind in a white suit. I bet you're turning the young sharp Hindus on. And I also bet no place in the world has the answer. Stein: "What's the Answer? Then what's the question?" I say the question is "what is this length, this Goddam stretch from dinosaur to Howard Johnson motel?" God will never cease to grow. Bomb won't hurt Him (it). Bomb can only hurt body because body is hurtable. Yes, I was on H and did nothing. Sat like a vegetable, couldn't write. Became a H body and H bodies find it hard to operate active God. Yet God gets on H too. Junkie bits of God as it were. All I got to say is, if God needs H, then something is missing in life and H takes its place. Is it the body or the God in the body feels the H? Both? Then whence death told may perhaps die too. The God that is in me and you may be the height of our Godsomeness. We perhaps are swinging Gods but doomed to the way of all gods. What dies then is God. If Life is God, if life dies, God lives and dies—endless. Ergo there is no death. What means final, no more, end all, the jigs up, etc. a death assumed by our human ancestors.

I go to go to sleep. Thanks for great lovely India letter and Peter has my pesty heart, he who discovered all those socks under my bed will relate it to his future Russian grandmother on the farthest sun in the cosmos. Ed Sanders of *Fuck You Magazine* is a corny poet but a funny editor. He and some others broke away from *Catholic Worker* Miss Day[248] to create and edit *Fuck You: A Magazine of the Arts.* I hesitate to give em a poem because somehow the title seems not vulgar but curse-like. Only kids say fuck you. Men in anger say fuck you. All American swear words got to do with sex. If it were called just *Fuck*, I'd give it my best though still feeling awkward about it. When poesy first came to me I never combined it with taboo words. I convinced your father and stepmother your necessary use of them there words. I told them you took the vile forbiddeness from such words. Ok, be good. I see Jack's *Big Sur* now. But never o never did I see Jack as the tragedy. Our Beat Bill you me mean. I thought oft that I'd be the goat, then fully thought Bill the goat, then you, Peter, now Jack. Jack, Allen, can write but Jack and good God I almost couldn't tell if it were Neal Cassady or Dean Moriarty. I can't truly believe either Carl Solomon (back in the bin) or Neal Cassady to be representative America. They are merely two different humans as are all humans. The man we never met who lives in Brooklyn has a great hero friend who fought in the ring, became champ, went blind, ended up selling newspapers. The other man we never met has a friend who helps all who need help etc. I dedicated *Happy Birthday* to Gould after long thoughts of you, Sura, etc. I immediately [thought] Gould because he is Anton [Rosenberg], [Bill] Keck, etc. who were the true hipsters. So I knew that you'd agree with my choice, so [would] Sura who knows Stanley. He was in jail when he found out I had dedicated a book to him. So *Long Live Man* dedicated obviously to father. Next work to my Allen. We dedicate to each other one time.

Kiss Hope on the nose for me, and tell Peter his drawing was incomprehensibly funny and eye-blurring. Peter, Sura too will be so dedicated whence future work.

Love, Gregory

▼ [Contrary to the previous mentions of his undying love for Hope Savage, Corso married Sally November at New York's City Hall on May 7, 1963, with Ted Wilentz and Lawrence Ferlinghetti acting as his best men and witnesses.]

To Ted Wilentz — New York City
May 7, 1963

Dear Ted,

Thank you for your goodly love shown to Sally and me. Our wedding was greatly enhanced by your help, and presence as best people as well as rescuing me from continuing delay. The most wonderful thing from a most wonderful day was seeing how it affected my Sally. My heart to you,

Gregory

The ceremony was heavenly easy and a tiny delightful odd—see?

To James Laughlin New York City

May 7, 1963

Gregory Corso's day of marriage with the make of life. Thank you very much for gracing my and Sally's wedding day. Larry, who I last saw in 1956, is a complete surprise to me. He is gentle and truly good poet human being, sometimes face to face is worth a thousand letters. I want to have a daughter so that I'd no son to give Gregorian rants as well as chants to. A wild boy can be hurt but a wild girl, I mean wondrously beautifully brilliant, can bypass such hurt. Besides a girl is hard to be. Yet girl or boy I'd be giving it a grip-less world, but I wouldn't have a child if I didn't feel it were quite possible to grip it and hold on to it, life, with thankful acceptance. If I hadn't seen you today I told Larry before the marriage ceremony to tell you that I'd you there with Allen foremost in mind. The ceremony was sans any kind of pie glue thought, it was mostly my joy to see how illumed and happy my Sally was. But I gotta make a million dollars.

My heart to thee, Gregory

To Allen Ginsberg New York City

May 7, 1963

Dear Allen and Peter,

Today I got married and Ferlinghetti and Wilentz were best men, though I'd you there as holy ghost best men. It was heavenly simple, the ceremony, and when the marrier asked if I promised to honor and cherish for my life, I replied, "I hope so." He let that pass. At end he said I was to say, "Yes," but my 'impasse' was so honest it had to hold.

I asked your blessing and I hope it makes both your hearts glad. I have, after all, married the maker of life, that which made you, that which made me. I enclose a lovely letter sent me by Hope's brother. Broke my heart. Please return it. Oh God, Oh me, Oh we, Oh death is dead for me.

Love, Gregory

To James Laughlin New York City

[July] 1963

Dear James,

Sally and I send you our loving thanks for your wedding present. In January I'll be a father.

Gregory

To James Laughlin New York City
Sept. 23, 1963

Dear Sir James,

I pray me and my cohorts didn't bug you too much. Thought they would have amused you. One a Persian prince for real, the other two a Chilean, and a Argentinean, the Chilean is a damned good painter, and is having a show tomorrow, until God knows when, the Feigen-Herbert Gallery and they never smoked a cigar before.

But mark ye well that I love my Sally deeply and am constantly at her side. This because I had the feeling that you thought I was a dopey, drunky cad. God knows I ain't, and I'm sure you know, too. Sometimes I go overboard, that's all, but a man has got to be his own scryer. Ted Wilentz, my best man, saw me drunk one night and wham, what a presumptuous lecture I got! Like, "Please be nice to Sally, poor Sally, etc." Like I was some monster or something. Then wham, he ends up breaking up with his wife, after fifteen years of wedded life. I'm telling you, peoples is alack of what they presume and hope for another, so I don't lecture him. All I ask is: "How do you feel when you come home at night and she's not there?" He replies: "I feel fine." Well, that I think is the only thing a smart person should ask. I know that I'd suffer were Sally not there, but who knows, maybe after fifteen years.

I am now looking for a job, perhaps a nite clerk, where I could maybe write whilst clerking. The baby will be supposedly born end of January; and our bank account is nil. Do you think Rhoda can set up a series of readings for me? I have no car but I can make it by train, the east coast colleges, and maybe as far as Chicago. $300 a reading is what I should get, what I have gotten. Sally will need me most during January and February, so March would be best, also April. I know Yale would like to have me read there, Mr. Pearson (?), I think that's his name,[249] a Pound man, and he's deformed. Ferl introduced me to him, and he sure is brilliant. Anyway, he said he'd like me to read there. So if I could get Yale and Harvard and Dartmouth, and Princeton, and Muhlenburg (here I am also wanted, Prof. Kinter asked me at the beginning of summer if I would read). I do have new poems, and that of course is very important; just can't read my old ones, because it's expected of me to give forth a new word, message, etc.

Now one last thing, and I pray it isn't so. Sally and I had 100 dollars in the bank, and she gave a check for 75 dollars and another for ten dollars. I did not know, nor did she about the ten dollar check, when I asked your book keeper to cash a twenty five dollar check for us. She couldn't, but Mr. MacGregor was kind enough to do so for us, her checking account being in Cleveland. It was hard for me to get it cashed here, except by the 8th Street Bookstore, and Ted [Wilentz] was out of town. So I pray the check doesn't bounce, we rushed

50 dollars to the bank, so I hope it works out. If it doesn't, please don't have Mr. MacGregor think unwell of me. I will quickly reimburse him. I fear checks, especially that time when I went to Greece, and I gave the shipping company a two hundred dollar check, and I had only 185 dollars in bank, forgetting that I had given out a fifteen dollar check earlier. I don't know if I told you about the awful experience I went through because of it. Whatever, I want very much to do right and hope good fate is on my side.

And did I tell you about being invited to a symposium on the state of poesy today at the YMHA? Well, it's for Feb. 2, and time of times! That is when my Sally should be giving birth. What I'll have to do is wait and see, and if it is impossible I will cable them and say, "Sorry, but the state of poesy today is an anxious pacing daddy to be." Sally sends her best to you.

As always, Gregory

To Allen Ginsberg New York City
[ca. Nov. 12] 1963

Dear Al,

Of course, my love is yours when you come to N.Y. There's so much for us to eye and silence about, but to grasp what must be seen. You—me—therein and silent, the awakening to hear. Yes, I am somewhat "down," but even happy at the drop of a plumed hat. Everybody seems to know what's up with me. Sometimes I get a funny feeling that I have been part responsible for the way people are today. Of course they're not as I would them be and if they ain't then maybe I had no part of what they is become. I used to be the youngest always in jail, in poetry, and now I'm the oldest. I guess we've changed a lot. It's been two years, no? I feel I've gotten less goofy, how's about you? And Peter!! Wham! Bill Burroughs is but a novelist! Didn't you realize this when you were pedaling *Junkie*? There are blind folk, one, bugged Jack, Bill is as sad a futility as any man, Jack is ever Jack. Novelists and poets are different but Jack does verge toward poeticness in being. Hurry.

Love, Gregory

To James Laughlin New York City
Dec. 10, 1963

Dear James,

I hope you think well of my *Vestal Lady* to publish it. There is a demand for it, and fortune will be with us I'm sure. My play *Hung Up Age* plus five or more poems written at the same period (they're in various magazines, not in any of my books) could all fit into it, thus making it a goodier *Vestal Lady.* I was wondering if you could make it a hardcover book, something real special, a book created for those who really care about my poetry or some other kind of format, different than *Happy Birthday* and *Long Live Man*? Of course you know what would be best, and being that you're still the best maker of books in the whole wide world, in my mind, I'll be happy however you decide, if you decide, to present it. Also the poems are very early and somewhat shaky; there are many changes I'd make, always wanted to whenever I look at the book, so maybe we could have it both old and new; thus again a very special book for those who really care about my work. It should clearly show how much I progressed with the craft, showing the original along side the altered—what do you think? As it stands the book is a collector's item, goes for thirty bucks, so I seriously feel that it should be done with stress on quality rather than quantity. My *Vestal Lady* means an awful lot to me, and it's all my own property. I can think of no better hands to bestow it to than yours. It's a book I know I can have published. The Czechs want it, so if you take it, please send them a copy, Dilla Company—by the way, did they publish *Happy Birthday*? If they want *Vestal Lady* then surely they must have come out with it by now. Will you please find out for me? The early poems are in *i.e.: The Cambridge Review*, I'll obtain them. Hope all works out okay.

Gregory

To Randall Jarrell New York City

Feb. 21, 1964

Miranda November Corso, born Feb. 13, 1964, 5:38 am. 7 lbs, 14 ozs., 20.5 inches.

To James Laughlin Shaker Heights, OH

[May] 1964

Dear James,

Sorry so long in doing this. What with change of scene and people. Also please ignore my thousand ducat demands the other collect call night. New Biography for *HB* [*Happy Birthday*]: "G.C. is 34, is wedded, and has baby girl, and must now support souls other than the muse. It should be fun or hell—all the muse needed was a poem—but a wife and daughter, a million dollars, plus careful love."

Hope this does it. Indeed I no longer sleep in English gardens.

To Don Allen

[ca. Aug. 27] 1964

Dear Don,

Thank you for considering me once again. Your faith in me is fine for the fated heart. As you see I deem your appreciations of what's what in poesy as tops, not merely because I happen to be of said "What's What." I'm in *Who's Who*, but I do not commend Mr. Marquis his Who's Whoring of me, or anybody. I commend thee because first of all you're fully educated as to compiling anthologies, clearly prophetic and empowerment with the same power a poet has, and that's being up in front, there, with the times, are fairly in touch, if not directly involved, with that common consciousness aswirl amongst thinkers and poets. Just thinkers, poets if they're worth anything are essentially thinkers, ergo it takes a thinker to know a thinker. So what am I saying? Maybe something to cheer you up because I do know my business, so from whom could you get it best? Gregorio of course, now I hope the poems are okay for you, they are part of my new book for ND [New Directions]. I am now in the process of compiling. So I picked at random what I feel to be my best of the best. Excuse the order and messiness, but I am pressed for time. Do send me back all copies please. Don't know if I have exact copies, even if I do they'll be different variations, so I do hope you have a secretary or something. Book is called *There Is Yet Time to Run Back Through Life and Expiate All That's Been Sadly Done.* A long title, but one that was necessary, considering the previous titles of *The Happy Birthday of Death* and *Long Live Man*. Be good and let me know what's up, and what you think, and write me in care of Ginsberg, 704 East 5th St., NYC.

From my heart, sir, yes, Gregory

▼ [On September 15, 1964, Sally Corso wrote to James Laughlin from Shaker Heights, OH: "I'm sorry to have to communicate the following news to you. Gregory writes me that he is not well physically and mentally, and that he is presently hospitalized for an undecided period of time—he can go home whenever he feels ready. It is better, however, as I understand it, that he remain for several weeks and be fully cured or rested or whatever else done for him that he so vitally needs done. This news is particularly painful for me to report to you at this time because I know you had so counted on his working to full capacity on There Is Still Time in order to make the printing deadline. Although I know the book is foremost in his mind now, what he needs now and is getting is complete relaxation. I hope and pray that he takes full advantage of this temporary respite, and hope you feel the same."

To James Laughlin [Buffalo, NY]
Nov. 27, 1964

Dear James,

I am all right, and resting. The sun (long climbing behind me) now drops before me. I owe your fine wife 100 dollars, which I will return shortly. My wife and child are ok. And our book shall be done.

Your faithful friend, Gregory

To James Laughlin [Buffalo, NY]
[Dec.] 1964

Dear JL,

Seems my sorrow was I just couldn't write, not even tailor my *There Is Yet Time* (because the poems were long since written) when in the midst of my wife and her family's house, she and they not really wanting me there, what without a job, etc. But I did have a job, a big one, and it was my book. So I am in Buffalo, where I have lovely friends, the main one being the conductor of the Buffalo Philharmonic, Lukas Foss, he and his wife are truly great and have been so enlightening to me. He composes real fine music and we have decided to do an opera, I the libretto of course, he the music. He has been commissioned by the Lincoln Center to do an opera, and feels that I'm the only one for him as for the words. So, as soon as I finish tailoring *There Is Yet Time*, I will get to work on it. How nice it is to be working again. Haven't worked in a year; and how great to get back to these poems, which are THERE all the way. God, I haven't felt so free and happy in so long a time. I figured all was done with me, but in heart I'm endless, ain't I?

Now for *There Is Yet Time.* This book of poems would do right if each poem had its own page and did not overlap, like our last two books, mainly because the poems are without titles, and also because the whole book is actually one poem; you know that all my poems are one poem, the poem of the poet, and of life, and what with cantos and maximus, they be mine epic; so I shall set poems up in their correct order and all those poems that are very short and impractical for a single page I shall put on one page; I shall specify the end of each page by putting CORSO under the poem; those poems that are more than a book page, the long ones, I'll number. If a poem is too long for a single page and what is left over too short for a whole page, then I shall either lengthen the lines thereby making it shorter, (can such a long lined poem go on the book page horizontally? If so I shall write on bottom of typescript page-poem, print horizontally) so the book shan't have empty space, empty space is waste, especially when you think of all the poets who'd like to have poems on them. Whatever, when I send you the poems, then we can really work it out—ok?

Buffalo is real nice, and I get the best seat in the music hall, by the conductor's wife! And speaking of wives don't be bugged with your lovely Ann, she came through for me when my wife wouldn't, which is something . . . to me, and so should be for you, my JL publisher poet and human empire state building friend.

Love, Gregory

To James Laughlin [Buffalo, NY]
[Dec.] 1964

Dear James,

You're right about horizontal business,[250] I'm working hard on poems. Also changed my mind about titles—poems should have titles. No? Did you see my Kennedy poem in *Poetry And Power*, Basic Books, it just came out? Get that for book. Also *Olympia Magazine* number 2, I think, where I have four poems in it. Also from Phoenix Book store, my *Mutation Of The Spirit*, these are poems for our book, and you have the two poems I wrote for my lovely daughter. This is gonna be a fine book, by God. I read to the kids here at Buffalo University, and they all dig the poems, so let me be for a couple more weeks and then we got it. Have a Happy New Year, and to your Ann say I said Merry Zeusmas.

Your friend, Gregory

To James Laughlin [Buffalo, NY]
[Feb. 26] 1965

Dear J.L.,

Believe me that *There's Yet Time* will make you proud and pleased, as I am proud and pleased. These poems are now broken from their storage, the cocoon, a lost sick and weary poet wove them in two years ago has been opened by that same poet, only now, found healthy and spirited. Buffalo has been good for me. I have my own apartment, I teach college seniors Shelley twice a week, I have good friends in the Foss's and their small children, and the painful worries of not being with my wife and child are become but extra hearts in me. Hearts that excite and inspire rather than worry and woe. So know that this little S.O.B. has everything in control and shall, of course, expiate all that's been sadly done.

Your ever fateful friend, Gregory

To Sally November Corso [Buffalo, NY]
[ca. March] 1965

Dear Mrs. Ex,

Just got your post card seventeen days late. I didn't think you would dislike those things I sent that much that you wouldn't make mention of it. Okay, what kind of books? French books? My books in Czech and Polish? Art books? How ship? Let me know, and I'll come through, but I just don't know what to send, your tastes being what they are, I'd have to rob a museum. Yes, that cultural swampland Cleveland. How right you are and that is the place where they almost quicksanded me. Indeed some lesser pridesome souls would deem they were quicksanded. Like that hideous Dr Jones. Doctor indeed! The bastard hated my guts. And he's the one that got me committed to the State Hospital. He's the one that pumped my belly, oh the nightmare of that! I was just high and about to sleep, same as old me. But I truly admit that I did black out on two occasions. Once in New York, you remember, St. Vincent's {Hospital}. What disgust or contempt you had for me, seeing me stretched out like that. I guess we're just different. Like I would have died seeing you so, but I guess that is what I love about you—your ego, your prideful ego. When I blacked out in the house on my angel's birthday; just overcome with joy, and fear. I couldn't face you alone without anything, but as for that "drug" I was done with that. I was using an amphetamine, that combined with sleeping pills sort of satisfied my miserable thirst. I must have looked pretty stupid again, stretched out like that. Though I would like to think I frightened you, than think otherwise. Else your calling the police or ambulance would be an act of overwhelming hate. As it was, I woke up soon after, all right and all that. But what a shock to find myself there with all them cops asking me questions about my needle, etc. Lucky I had a doctor in New York who was caring for me. Not old doctor on Fifth Avenue. In Ohio they put dope addicts away for fifteen years! But I held my ground, that pride again, even with that awful dirty needle in their possession. I held up my head and though the tears couldn't be held back when they fingerprinted me, and mugged me (photo) and heard my past record of yore (they electronically got a file on me from Washington, D.C. past record), it amazed the chief of detectives there. The others were crude creeps, but he was an educated man, and spoke to me with respect. That is, as much as was possible for him to be thus. While the others were wanting to lock me up, etc. They released me on a charge of being a "suspicious undesirable, disturbing the peace." Indeed what price to maintain one's equilibrium. A leap out of bed, a dash out of house, a plane, a kangaroo, baby and you, and wham! O but I would have died had they put me back in Cleveland Hospital! I mean, I might have rotted there—like two weeks is rotting there. So you could imagine when I went to bus terminal. Went? Was driven by detectives, like kicked out of town, not allowing me to go back home to see my baby's birthday, like "You don't live here says your wife." So I phoned you in my outcast state and damned you and child, and expected you to hang up as usual. I can't remember if you did. I just couldn't talk or curse anymore, just lost my voice. The sorrow, of course, was not being given a damn about by any of you there in Cleveland. Not a single soul. That wasn't the nicest feeling to depart with. So I buy ticket for bus one in morning, I fall asleep (normally now on bench) and wake up two o'clock. No more buses; so I call up train, plane, no dice; finally got a cab to take me to Buffalo. He got all the money you or baby or presents were supposed to get, but he got me out of there. That is all I wanted, out of there, of that quicksand. Bad place to get stuck in, even with people around, no one extends a helping hand.

So I get home seven in morning and would you believe it? The same time I left the morning before? Like did I sleep that, dream that, or what? I mean, Sally, life can be a nightmare on equal basis with dream, could stand up to the best of nightmare's dream could offer. Still, I did see her on her birthday; I did do that. So I paid for it, but at least I did do that. I guess I'm not telling you anything new, but what with it on my mind and not knowing just how you stood in the whole affair, like my not believing it was you who gave me Dr. Jones but that radio creep. He supplied me with some pills that nut; and me human pill dispenser takes any, or rather, took any that came my way. He had me write that like you say "stupid" blurb for him when I was listening to my Berlioz on hi-fi electronic sound, etc., high as a kite, happy and in love with world, so.

Surely that do me no good, though at time I feel they do, and that life in Cleveland was so boring and empty and in the air for me, I had to break out and drink or take something. It was no place for a convalescing body. I needed care, love, sun, peace, no in-laws, but I mean no being TRAPPED with in-laws, their house etc. And not knowing whose side wife was on, as if sides were needed! But they no did very much-a like-a me. Alas, shant moms and dads ever like me? All my life and none durst twirl my curly hair affectionately. Still it was brave of you to accord my being there, what with my ways, and talk, etc. I was bound to ruin it for you. Yet I do hope that I brought together your dad and his ex-partner relative with the boat goof-son. Usually I have an aptitude for such things, and it seemed that my "me" created a kind of bond of common sympathy for each other in regard to poor you or poor them, unite against the dread stranger in our midst! I always thought I would get along with them . . . since after all I presented them with a legit grandchild. Like their daughter could have done worse. She could have married a spade, or merely been knocked up by a "certain well-known beatnik" whom the daughter met in New York and had an affair with. But I was a man of honor and I married and then knocked up the daughter and even jumped into the supposed "hell" of beatniks: the Midwest—and Ohio is known to be the most insufferable circle of said hell.

I swear this, baby, it was writ of me in a magazine called *Writers* something or other by Sy Krim, before our even knowing each other or soon after, I remember it well: "It is [as] though Corso went to live in a typical mid-western community; could you imagine that!" In reverence to Thoreau—and I can recall feeling abashed by that, like what was I, some sort of spook or something? I was indignant to say the least! For had I not lived amongst the peoples of society before? And was I not a "credit to the community and the society in which he lived"? (this is about me in a Honorarium Americana Who's Who). So you can see what hypocrisy I am bombarded with, and with how other people expect and think of me, like I can't be myself, which is what I yearn for again, but seemed to have lost or been denied ever since I became some kind of public bad property. And did not the wife say to me: "I am as—." I forget, had something to do with my being something you thought I was, but when I wasn't . . . like I was to blame. That I was your hero once and am now but a fallen . . . what? Perhaps I never was that hero you dreamed or imagined or thought you saw. Perhaps you never had in me what you felt was there. Perhaps you married Marlon Brando and saw that he was just like Dopey Sid around the corner but worse. You do have this thing, you know, about "celebrities." But God only knows that I knew you to be a smart "chickie" and realized that a poet was not to be so marked as to be known. True he is ever-changeable, but that doesn't mean <u>he can be changed</u>.

And as for drugs, you married me knowing that. And I dare say you had enough belief in my strength that it would never turn out with me being weak; and weak where? But mostly physically, and domestically; as I can take drugs alone and not suffer it. Yet, I too would imagine one as being weak spiritually mentally et al. So when you saw that, you took upper hand. And what with baby, that put the lid on it. A strong body was needed and I didn't fit that bill.

When I was in New York last I happened by Stanley [Gould] and he said: "Man that woman of yours was something else." Before I could tell him I don't want to hear it, he'd out with, "Like she got you on your Catholic guilt so much it would have killed you more deadlier than any poisonous kicks." That got to me, for I alone I do not feel dirty or "bad" taking drugs. But with you, that was really hell. The drugs, not you. You, I believe were truly wanting the best for "your" husband. Your tears, after I'd suffer the day getting the precious money we so badly needed, the pain of getting that money, and then gasping for breath as there is no worse illness than that to find a "connection." And finding one after hours, he steals my money, giving me milk sugar instead. I knowing you are home and wanting so to be back, but can't because of the "need," so off for money again, and again. Times like that, then getting something at last, then coming home, and you threatening the police on me, calling me names, crying. If that wasn't hell, what is? And what I could not understand was why I ever came home to you, knowing what would happen? Again lesser souls would have gotten their mates addicted so as to keep a happy medium in household. Thank God, it never got to that. And that day of great sickness when I had my tools of misery in that room and you not letting me in, you knowing that I needed them. I begging for them. That was awful. That was a brokenness there. How could we ever be the same again? We two so pridesome ones. I couldn't expect you to know what the sickness is like and I knew what your "sickness" was like, but couldn't help you. My wife was drugs, and you resented that. It took away my sex, thus your sex. It was bought with the furniture, etc. We never had those. Drugs, yes, of course, you had every right to despise them. But hell is not an easy place to get out of, and since we were in it, since you married one so damned, it could have used some compassion, some selfless care, some patience, and much less despair. It should not have been used as a weapon to beat me with, to beat that pride so miserably down and battered. It was not an old junky you had there, as I was never in such a plight before, never hooked or sick or desperate as that. It was all new to me as it was to you. I too was an innocent amongst you and I guess that is why I was so susceptible to your getting on my "Catholic guilt" as funny Stanley puts it.

What it all amounts to is—what purge? I mean it is because of the bad behavior we exercised in hell that I found myself deprived of my wife and child. I mean literally deprived as to my feeling, I am not allowed to have anything to do with them! Can you understand this? It is for this reason I don't know what to do, or you for that matter. I tried telling you in that hell, since I am at least that wise as to know where I am at, at a time, that patience and care would get us, or rather me, out.

To Lawrence Ferlinghetti

[ca. 1965]

Dear Larry,

Me make it? Well for 2 1/2 months now, I've been abstaining, so I guess one could say, "He's making it." Yet it were no sweat—no doctor or hospital—on my ownsome. It was painful, but I'm conditioned for such askew physics. Only sorrow is the sorrow I caused [the] few good souls who worried over me, but as I told them: "Look, I never have hell down pat, so if it be hell again, okay. Yet deep down in me, there's that that assures me I rising again."

And other sadness was my not working on poesy when hellbound. Still I feel balanced, i.e. the creator has the child in him. Well, I began to feel uncomfortable childlike (childish) etc. So my past three year experience, plus lack of seeing child of mine, quieted me. Not solitary but observant rather then seeing. *Basta*. Anyway, I'm sorry I'm in red. I thought that since you re-printed *Gasoline* I was due, but I've been off [the] poesy scene quite some time, no? So, Ferl, I would truly appreciate if you could advance me on future royalties, as now I am without funds, and having some will maintain my attitude of new health.

Luf, Gregory

▼ [In order to teach at Millard Fillmore College in Buffalo, all instructors were required to sign a document known as the Feinberg Certificate, which contained a pledge of allegiance. One was mailed to Corso in mid-February 1965, but he would not sign it and as a result he was terminated on March 9, 1965.]

To James Laughlin

Milan, Italy
[ca. May 10] 1965

Dear JL,

Am living in Milan, working clear of mind but poesy mind. I hope all is well with you, it is with me. Send me nice news and I send you nice news. I expect to return to USA when our book is done done.

Best, Gregory

To Allen Ginsberg

Milan, Italy
[ca. May 10] 1965

Dear Allen,

Think you can drop by Milano and allow us to look into each others eyes? Or perhaps I could see you sometime before you return to U.S.A.? Hope I catch you in time. Am at rest, alas, thank Zeus.

Gregory

To James Laughlin

Milan, Italy
May 26, 1965

Dear James,

I have a brainstorm that could make us a "lot of money"! How can I be sure you won't make off with it once I've told you?

If you can get the rights to a Pound, a [Alfred] Jarry, a Rimbaud—you certainly should be able to get the rights to the great lovely dreamy American mythical comic-books of 1930-40 and you will have six or seven volumes of poetical longevity. Suggestive titles of real comic book myths some of which I'm sure you'll recognize: The Human Torch—The Flash—The Plastic Man—The Submariner—Henry—Daredevil.

Now let me tell you about them: The Human Torch, a good looking jr.-professor type, snaps into anatomical flame whenever evil lurks—The Flash (good-looking jr. exec.) speeds into invisibility whenever evil lurks—The Plastic Man can sit in his room and stretch with a lone finger wherever evil lurks—The Submariner comes out of faucets whenever evil—Henry is very strange—Daredevil's nemesis The Claw walks a gigantic-yellow man in a red cloak across the Pacific Ocean when always the Daredevil beats him. *Basta*, O.K.?

Yours as ever, Gregorio

▼ [June 1, 1965 Corso goes to Paris, Ferlinghetti invites him to read at the Albert Hall, Gregory plans to visit with Allen]

To James Laughlin Paris

[June] 1965

Dear James,

This batch of poems *Immutable Moods*, are each and select and yet an entire whole, just like my shuffle poems. Thus they should be printed as a group poem as I have numbered them. The next batch will be short (time wise) in coming. As my shuffle poem had but one title so do these.

I am seeing Larry [Ferlinghetti] here in Paree and he is truly gentle soul. We go to London to read with Ginsberg and Russian poet, the fine one, Voznesensky, plus Lamantia. So that should be something. I haven't read in years, yet when I read a smattering of our *There's Yet Time* I'm sure I'll make it, and at Albert Hall of all regal places!

Yours, Gregory

To James Laughlin Paris

[July 17] 1965

Dear James,

I am in Paris for good stay and get hard at work. But I guess I've become a stickler for par excellence. At any rate I am desirous that this volume of three years work should be representation of a poet's mind during said years. Indeed it be one long poem, this *There's Yet Time.* And I can tell you no matter what the tailored result it'll be unlike anything. I suddenly realized what my muse's name is: Principle. I used to think it was dignity, honor, etc.—but without principle a poet is nothing.

Be good, your friend, Gregory

To James Laughlin Paris

July 22, 1965

Dear James,

Finally I have book as I want it. I have set it in three parts. First part is *Mutation Of Spirit* series with extra poems not used in leaflet, also I tidied up the leaflet and numbered it, so ignore the copy you have. Second part is a series of spontaneous thought—fragments taken from notebooks and set up in exact order thus to show how the poet's mind jumps from idea to idea, thought to thought, image to image, all ranging mostly on two or three themes, thus it sustains and results in a unique whole. Third part consists of individual poems, each titled and dated 1962-1965. Mutation of Spirit is 1964—Notebook writings, 1963-64—And so the gap is filled. A difficult gap to satisfy, but I always prefer what I shall do to what is already done. I had three years of poetry with me, I never knew just where to start. And those three years were more than poetry, too. [. . .]

Gregory

We filled Albert Hall—a mad hodge-podge of poesy but did they mention it in America?

▼ [According to Ferlinghetti, Corso was in very bad shape drug-wise in Paris at this time. LF gave him $100 advance for *Vestal Lady*, which New Directions had found out was not owned by GC, but instead by the original publisher, Brukenfeld. Corso's life for the next thirty five years followed a pattern in which fewer and fewer poems were written and his prolific letter writing habit slowed to a trickle. As time passed he alienated more and more of his friends and his days were spent in the pursuit and use of drugs.]

To James Laughlin Paris

Sept. 6, 1965

Dear James,

The thing that held me up with book so much was the typewriter. It would stump me all the time; so instead I copied out poems in longhand; and thus have I completed said book. Now all that needs be done is my getting somebody to type the manuscript up, with my constant supervision as my hand is atrocious and I must be there to cipher the glyphs, so to speak. That means I am wanting to return to USA, to Buffalo preferably where Mrs. Foss can help me out. I need someone who understands where I'm at and would do such task as I ask, and she's the one. So can I once again ask you for the fare home? As I am clear of my debts to you, deduced from last royalty monies, could it again be possible to get an advance on next royalty due? A seven month loan it be and I'm sure that I'll at least make enough to cover that which I ask. I can buy a charter plane ticket, a return ticket from a student who has decided to stay for $180. Plane leaves Oct. 6, and I would like to get it as soon as possible before he sells it to somebody else. But as I once told you when I was enlightened as to capital investment, how a loan of 100 dollars is actually 500 dollars to the loaner if said loan is not paid, I shan't be disappointed if you can't make it for me; still I do hold off ever asking you until I really need it, and my returning home at this time is important to me, as well as getting the understanding help that I need. Also I may get the monies before royalty time and would see to it that you are re-reimbursed; since you do not make a habit of advancing authors on their eventual due I would assume it comes from your pocket. Whatever it would sure be a pleasure to receive it and return home.

Some good news money wise there for me too. I got a letter from a Miss Cheryl Crawford, Broadway producer, saying she had a "project" in mind and would like to talk to me about it. I can only surmise it means working on something for theatre, which I'm anxious to become part of. I can write a play, by God, but since poesy has been a full-time job its been hard. One thing about a play is that it results in a conclusion, and the reward is rewarding; whereas poesy is an endless task, and I'm in it for the duration. It never ends. Here I have three years work, and so what that I make a book of it. I still don't feel as if I have completed something. It is without respite poesy; without end, and the reward is only that which I make it to be. The monies be a pittance, surely not enough to support wife and child, enough the poet. But I've learned not to expect more than I get from it anyway. But a play, a real down to earth fine play might be just the thing.

Gregory Corso

▼ [Laughlin is distressed that Corso hasn't even typed up the poems yet. He does send him the money and warns him to be certain that the student's plane ticket can be used by Corso.]

To James Laughlin Paris

Sept. 15, 1965

Dear JL,

Thanks for advance, will take your advice and be careful as to ticket as I do seem to get in odd situations when it comes to money transactions. Speaking of money transactions, something I never thought to set straight, that be just in case of my demise I would all my royalties to my daughter Miranda. Also I would *Vestal Lady* and *Gasoline* (which have no contract for, and which in just such a case I'd rather you have the book, this be my right). Also, all my prose efforts, the one in book form, as well the published articles, two small plays, to you go the printing rights and to Miranda the royalties. As for my manuscript and letters how do I let it be known it be her property if happy hunting ground? Can I state it here, as proof? Gregory Corso

The reason why I can't get to typing the poems is not that I am bugged by typewriter but that those poems go back to four years, do you realize what a heavy burden it is to return to the occasions of those years of poems? It's like using my memory for a handball, to endure in an hour what I endured in a year. It can wreck a less sturdier mind I assure you. I mean, my mind is an old warrior, it can take a lot, and the prospect of reliving those battles grips the belly—but it must be done. Oh but how it must! Consider will you the damned poem *That Expiates All That's Been Sadly Done*. Who, what man can no one forgive today? Then if there be one such man, there be one such hell. I try, and o how against my grain, to find forgiveness for Hitler; I even rhyme the poem! and I swear to you he wants me to forgive him because I dreamed him kissing me, yes, just once, on the lips, like that, I woke up feeling awful accursed, until I realized the meaning of it. I who truly have no enemies, except for the moment, but never any that endure—how to cope with it? I figure the poem will pull me through, well we'll see.

Yes, it be the only logical step, if *Long Live Man*, then after it, it must be *There Is Yet Time To Expiate All That's Been Sadly Done*—if I can achieve thus via poesy then I would have concluded that epic poem which began with *Vestal Lady* and so ends with *There's Yet Time*. Finally a conclusion! for it has been an endless business this poetry; rewardless, and never the feeling of having completed something. The poetry that will come after this book—aha! I can't wait. And it shan't be the heavy labor it is now, nay, but into a play will I put such work, and thus God willing know respite.

Now while I am yet here I will begin typing poems. Your "disappointment" over their not being typed has encouraged me to get to it, since you came through for me, as always.

Your friend, Gregory

▼ [Randall Jarrell died in a car crash on Oct. 14, 1965. Suicide was thought to be a possibility. Corso wrote to his widow, Mary, when he heard the news.]

To Mary Jarrell

Paris
Oct. 21, 1965

Dear Mrs. Jarrell,

Know that my heart sank and the weight of the sorrow which caused it so stunned me I could but cry within like a piece of stone. You and Randall were so good and wonderful to and for me I have never forgotten. You were my only Xmas in life, I swear. Throughout the years I maintained the highest respect in regard to his name and his poetry. I can only hope that I had not been a disappointment to him; that he could yet see in me what he had nearly ten years ago in San Francisco. Oh, the good, the sad good, they go away; and when a poet dies, how barren the things of beauty become. That beauty which he added so much to. A poet can feel this when a "brother" dies, but it is to you, to the soul he loved, I pray a deep-embedded hope that all that we mean and are, that such is not for naught, for nothingness, that all will round itself out and prove the loveliness and the wisdom of a poet's living dream, proved real by whatever means the Gods there be allow, for the poet beyond the sleep that dreams, the dream itself, my battered and scarred soul of hope, grab hold of it. I offer you, good woman, as an expression of my appreciation for you and your loved one's niceness to me in this life.

I am, a friend of old, Gregory

To James Laughlin

Paris
[Oct. 26] 1965

Dear JL,

My return is up in the air, not literally though. My wife writes that she may secure a teaching post either here or Greece, so I shan't return if such happens. So it is just as well, as I am typing double space et al, the book. It must be done now. I can't put it off any longer. It is an immense job because the poems are immense, and I am fit for the combat.

I just finished my first poem in French. First thing I ever wrote in French, and I tackled a tough subject too. My kid brother is in Army and is due for Viet Nam having seen action in Santo Domingo already. My subject deals with that, with the marchers and demonstrators etc. People very much like me, yet would I march? If of course from what I gather the marchers are more intent on stopping USA from bombing Viet Namien civilians, than getting soldiers back, seems both State Dept. and marchers are more concerned with civilians. State says we are there to protect and not let down our friends the South V N. Marchers say stop the bombing—so where are the soldiers at? A seven-page poem, double space in three parts. First part I have an imaginary Viet Cong *mère*; mother. I tell of her plight with me, age 20, for 20 years of war, with no respite, war as old as me, my mortal playmate etc. I handle all the warring forces, Japs, Chinese, French, South Viet, and Americans; in pure imagery (since it is imaginary, ain't got no Viet Cong mom like). Then second part I have my brother, real live soldier, American. Thus I ask my mind who am I for, do I care more for imaginary mother, or real brother? For surely she is not his mother; and as Jerry is no beatnik-type, or the committed-like either, just a straight kid, he is sure prototype for soldiers there. But I claim he is no disemboweler, etc. Then third part of poem in Paris room, looking back on poem, realizing that a poet is for [everyone], damns war on both sides, but prefers brother, body blood same, whereas Cong is but shadow in a poem. Yet give up principles for brother? It ends with deadlock, meaning a war that shouldn't really be in first place. I'll translate it back into English, but by God, I really had a time of it, what with new words, etc. I may really go into it all [the] way someday.

Yes, please have my mail sent on, but air please. Last time it took fifteen days, what with some urgencies therein. Whatever the outcome with my wife securing position, or not, I will keep you in touch. As is I can't buy any student cancels, so I put it in with Icelandic Air open date, with 140 dollars left over, pretty cheap. My life here I would like you to know is one of indoors and work. A nice cheap clean hotel room, and all my poems. So things will result—no social life or anything like that. Can't wait to see my kid, she sounds great, just great.

How's Bob Kaufman's book doing? I lent it to some creep and he's now in Spain with it; like he raised his right hand promising to return it. I don't have many books so hate to part with any. Oh—yes about Spottiswoode, when I was in London (for that reading) many people asked where they could buy my books, any book? Seems no books of mine can be sold if any of poems are in the Eyre book [*Selected Poems*]. What a silly business? Especially when the Eyre & Spottiswoode book is not distributed, is a hard-cover, and all that. So I was quite pissed-off. And told or asked Eyre why no New Directions books, or *Gasolines* were allowed to be sold? He said something about contract that stipulates such, as not to hurt sales of his book. Hurt! He kept the book in the warehouse, not bothering about it, since it is already established that poetry doesn't sell and he had that "defeatist" attitude from the start. "Oh people don't much go in for this sort of thing, it'll go slow, etc." Well, fine, but let it go.

So in future I wondered were it possible for me to have a simultaneous publication, with your giving book to Eyre & Spottiswoode as is your fashion with European publishers? I had not said that I would give him a book of poems, he being sole publisher and all that. But I see now that that is what they would prefer and find worth it to make a paperback of it (their first in poetry—which Eyre promised he'd do for book). Thus book I had in mind is our tardy book. Gosh, I hope they're willing to make a nice thing of it even though it comes to them from a previous publisher. I want to keep Eyre as publisher, and would like to see him have something nice to put his teeth into, but getting it second hand ain't so hot, is it? Maybe I could reserve collected works for him, you don't usually make such book. If I can recall, poets have their books by you and their fatty by another publisher, but that's a way off from now. I could see how they misinterpreted it.

Basta, Gregory

To Lady Frankau Paris

[ca. 1965-66]

Dear Lady Franco [Frankau],

I have long heard about you, and the main thing I make in unifying it all is, you are quite straight and compassionate toward those who are in dire states, the heroin-addict foremostly. I have been one these last three years, though I saw much of it early in life I never ventured the taking of it until late in life.

33 years old is late when you consider youngsters galore take the stuff, and most American herioneers start in their teens. My reasons for taking the stuff are, I guess like most everyone's, kind of complex. Yet one thing I can apart myself with is, "I have taken the drug but I am not a drug addict." By that I mean, I take it not for kicks, nor did I become a slave to it because I started out for pleasure. As a poet I am already complex before I begin. Pitted against most junkies, I had and have all the reason to stay with life and not darken away from it to the womby air of drugs. I was a famous poet when I took steadily to it, and that made it all the more sadder and darker for me. Firstly, I had a strong sense of honor and pride, such cannot last long when you find your very blood dependent upon something that is soul-breaking and furtive, but I fought to keep myself a man.

I can honestly say that I have not refused a sick person, junkie, in need of some if I had it, though never has one ever given me anything, and when you are sick that is when they really relish in not giving you. The difference was: I was a poet not a junkie. Ergo as poet I could not refuse even though it meant taking away from what I desperately needed. Nor have I ever abused the amount that I took, never went over my quota. I kept a steady but expensive (in the long run) and dangerous habit. In New York City it's truly hell trying to keep from being sick, and since a steady "connection" is virtually impossible, it would mean my having to go out every day looking for one. That was not only dangerous whereas law was concerned, but it also meant my being taken in every so often. I'd receive milk sugar, etc. for my hard received six dollars. My tragedy was that I had just married when I began with the drug, not knowing that I'd be addicted to it. Thus after awhile, down went my marriage and down went my muse, and still I could not understand why I continued to take the drug or why in the first place. All I know is that I would be deathly ill without it. I managed to stop when the baby came, and thank God I never ventured to hook my wife (most do so thus to keep their wives). But I was far from well.

I still suffered from that "pain" that caused me to take drugs in first place. Only until I could learn what that pain was, could I then stand up and stop. Well, after three years, after losing wife and child, after giving up a talent that burned in me like a Christmas tree, I found myself still a poet and still a man. [I] have no sad memories of having hurt any sick person, "junkie," that is. I maintained an honor with them but that they hated. They figured everyone was alike, and by God they are, just like replicas. For that reason I have never lived with them or made of them my companions. Though I most necessarily meet them since I seek what they seek and thus our worlds meet. I have found out what that "pain" was. Simply it was like giving birth to a twenty year old

Up from my subconscious unknowingly came a me I had long ago put (fifteen years ago) out of my conscious mind. From birth to my twentieth year I was constantly in orphan homes and jails and when I left prison at twenty I entered the world a poet. The poet in a matter of years cast his name upon the world, and had been quite responsible for the social betterment of those my age. My cry was "beauty" though one would think to consider my past the cry would be "hell." But I cried "beauty" and truly believed I had had my hell.

At the height of my poetic abilities, I suddenly faced responsibility for the first time by marrying. From birth to twenty the state cared for me, from twenty to thirty one the muse and the companionship of fellow poets and myself cared for me. Then I suddenly found myself called "a leader of his generation." And since my name and fame spread constant and wide, my wife thought that my insistence that, "I shan't marry unless I have sufficient money, because marriage means having a child and I won't have happen to my child what happened to me." She convinced me that a poet, a successful poet, would be assured enough to maintain a wife and child. I took her word for it. I suddenly, willingly, did so because it was then I was suffering from that "unknown pain," that birth of that twenty year old me I had so long suppressed. And indeed my life is split in two, the two lives are so far and alien to each other. But of course I am all 35 years of me, no such thing as split-personality, since such a personality hovers back and forth. This is merely matter of living first twenty years without mother or father, instead with six different mothers and fathers before I was ten years old, and then the typical path led to jails and prison. I was never a tough person, but I never knew how to fend for myself, so I stole in order to keep existing. It was a constant sheer monotonous hell, since I'd spend a year inside, get out and find myself aged 14 with nobody and no money. So right back to stealing I'd go. Like kicking in tailor shop window to get clean decent clothes, or food shop to eat. I doubt I lasted longer than two weeks at any given time up to my 16th year. My life of jails began age 11, when [my] real father finally took me back "home" with his new wife. My real mother I never saw. He was worse than any foster-father, and he cared not for me as did the fosters. They had to make sure I went to church and they also had to live in nice places. Thus my father took me from them to the slums of the Lower East Side. In my tenth year began "hell," though the obstinate uneducated Italian mind of my father felt that I was grateful to be finally "home."

I feel I know first generation and early second generation American-Italians very well. They are or were the most stupid of the white minorities. I was never around a book to read in the house, I never heard classical music until I left prison. All I had were movies and comic books and they, thank God, served this inquiring mind well when it was young. So anyway this twenty year life I speak of, was most certainly a crushed thing of authority. But since I was the orphan, the alien one, since birth (put in orphanage age one), I never knew otherwise and therefore it did not suffer me. In short, I doubt it can be said I suffer an inferiority complex, since I never had a different complex to be made inferior. But I somehow began to suffer just such a damning complex when the twenty year old bore itself out of my subconscious mind. I was after all a poet.

I was looked up to, and I wrote with a chastising arrogance, too. I felt good to be recognized, but I was never egotistical about it since I had no time to be. What can be mistaken for humility is, in fact, inferiority. Thus the twenty year old stood before those who felt they were facing the poet. Suddenly it no longer felt good to be recognized. I became immensely shy and then at times wildly extrovert. The twenty year old and the poet were fluctuating back and forth, and alas, the poet knew not this sudden change in him to be the emergence of that necessary part of him that, I've no doubt, has always been of him but never unified. And in time if a poet be a poet he must become a unified being. So the lovely just ways of nature were working, but I had no idea of it at the time and such ignorance could only despair what was for the only years in my life the happiest of my life. From twenty to twenty five I learned all I had missed of beauty as a child: music, art, people, manners, and so forth. It is these five years that made the bulk of my poetry. I sang of beauty, as I say, when in fact I could have sung of my dark miserable youth. But how could I when I was happy?

Not to fall on to the mystique in what appears all too productive of a society, a society that was mainly responsible for the dire plight of my youth. Since I was given to it when an infant and became a ward in its heartless care. An example: being I was too young to experience the trauma of my mother abandoning me, I was given to a woman who I believed to be my mother and I was taken away from her aged two. That I felt and of course remember. Another example of the father. He told me a few years ago that she, this second mother, who I believed to be my real mother, had offered him ten thousand for me. He was a poor man and it was depression time, but he says, proudly, I refused her. And since he said to the orphanage people he should someday take me back, I could not then become too acquainted with any one mother. Well, this surely is the cruelest and most stupid thing to do to a child, is it not? Especially when you consider he took me back in 1940, aged 10, when after my third mother I lost all belief in mothers. And if he had a son perhaps, and a pregnant wife, he would not be drafted; so I say he took me back for his own selfish purposes and since he never showed me or gave me love (merciless beatings to cite the most common) and being that he and I only lived together for a matter of 1 1/2 years (the Navy took him anyway), I most conclude that he is or rather was, a stupid man. He denied me love, the second mother loved me. He and the orphanage saw to it that such would not come to me. And when he finally did take me home it was to hell and he himself cared for me only a year and a half. After that I was on my own, and have been ever since. I became of the streets, and from the streets into jail. When aged 13, I was put in Bellevue madhouse because of my constant running away from "no home." It was the lowest circle in that hell. I was put with human butchers, in a place where men in sheets seeked at walls like mice.

Ah—why do I tell you all this, why? I know why, only I pray it's not an imposition. I feel that my sincere openness perhaps will contend otherwise. Nor do I wish anything from you, like medicines. Just some of your feelings toward my present state, perhaps, and an admonishment of one of your young patients, an American, who today left Paris to go to London, so undoubtedly he'll be seeing you. I feel he should be "woken up." And I present myself as an example of his non-compassion, his no honor amongst junkies, so to speak. He had medicine from you. He was not desirous to use it, only when he could not obtain the drug thus to prevent himself from being ill. In short, he doesn't wish to stop. But I did. He knew that. I wished to stop because, as I say, I found out the cause of my "pain" and thus could not go on with the easing of that pain since the pain left as soon as I found it. I was cured by methadone in New York City, and though the pain still endured, I managed to keep off for four months. Since I've been in Europe, I have been on for six months, and now I want very much to stop. He had methadone (physeptone) ampules, ten of them. I said I would give him five pounds for them. He said all right. When he came over with them, he came at an inopportune time. I was waiting for a friend to return who cashed a check for me. He had to catch a train to London. I begged him to take a later train, to wait for my friend to return. He acted as though I wanted to buy a drug from him. It was merely a medicine, and he was going to a city where he could easily obtain it again. He could have been responsible for another human being, indeed a being he knew was a poet and therefore something fine to help because this poet needed it. And also this poet accepted him when he came to my home, though after much refusal (since, as I say, I did not like the company of junkies nor did I relish wanting to know them just because I took that which they took). They always assuming it meant a pass to acquaintance-ship and could not understand my not accepting said pass. But they insist all the time, and since the drug world is small here in Paris we in time became acquainted. Now I mention this to you because I feel that he should be chastised. That I who have no chance of doctors and who suffers a constant denial of the drug, want truly to get well, and have always bestowed my strength, what was left of it, to those who hadn't any. I almost childly cry that that young punk is off to make use of your good offices for kicks. He is heartless since he was no man to leave me the ampules he wanted to sell me. He could have asked me to send him the money in England, but he can't trust junkies, because that's the pattern. But I was asking for a cure, not for a bag of joy. I know that ten ampules could have taken me over the hill. All I need do is go three days without the drug and I've passed the physical worst. After that it would be up to my desire and faith as a man to make it. Well, now I have to make it cold, and I shall, but it shan't be easy. I suffer a lot, I just have that kind of condition. Were it a matter of paying my dues, then fine. But I've paid them, manifold and unlike those who take drugs for kicks, I never enjoyed the blood running down my arms, the holes in them. The poet cried much for that blood. The neglected twenty year old mess let flow. But I believe it all to have been worth it. I have to, for no passing fancy, but for good reason did I fall into living hell again. I now have my past as well as my present, and I face the future complete. This I believe, this I pray, and perhaps my words confirm it. The little fool's name is Roy L., mine is, Gregory Corso

To James Laughlin Paris

[ca. Jan. 1966]

Dear J.L.,

I have been trying to find out a way for a successful poet [. . .] to make, if not as much on one piece as much as any other successful artist, at least as much as a tradeless laborer. I am sitting before my book. Three years of such wrought pain accomplishment stress distress duress hunger and hurt of pride, self-respect in having to support a wife, and unblamable she couldn't allow such with child, nor could I, so separations, and all for a book. The hours of which can only be summed up as three years work, a book that will go on a book dealer's shelf—just another 40-percent-for-him book. A book say, sells 50,000 copies at $1.00 each in a period of three years, which is great but hardly probable. Fine—but great for whom? Surely money-wise not for me. Consider 40 percent for book dealer—$20,000 dollars. 54 percent [for] publisher—$27,000. Poet, six percent—$3,000 dollars. If I were a Marxist I'd holler exploitation since I am the maker of the product. You are the manager-employee who sees to it that the product which took me three years to make is reproduced thousand-fold and distributed to such places as sells the product. Who is most important here? [. . .]

So I hold that the poet most assuredly works the hardest of the three, next to publisher, then the book dealer. The only one with anything to lose is publisher. He invests in the poet. But the only one with anything to gain without having anything to lose is book dealer—and what a gain! Books in a bookstore should be dealt with <u>individually</u>. A best seller is different than a slow seller

[. . .] a book of poetry should be to the book dealer what it used to be to the publisher, a prestige bit. Usually put at a loss. In this way the book dealer doesn't really suffer much for he, remember, is not one, like you or I, he is many, thus six percent makes much sense here. [. . .] Something has to be done. Fifty-four percent [to] you, because you pay for printing, advertising, employees, rent, and personal effort. I don't think you are undeserved of it, but I honestly think [the] book dealer is, and that I deserve much more.

Can you imagine what it would be like? I'd get that which is due book dealer, it would mean that instead of earning a thousand a year (which I don't—$400 is more like it) I'd be getting seven thousand. That is worthy of a poet's effort, by God. Why publishers have allowed book dealers this outrageous unfair amount I'll never know. Isn't there any safe-guard, any protection for the author? Books is big business in America, but also is life. Since it be not the proletarian but the artisan that is so ignored and all, I swear that this "class" will create a holocaust one day. [. . .]

So you see it has nothing to do with you, it's the book dealer who does me in. Now, either they give in, and accept ten percent on books of poetry, or no poetry for them. Soon it's bound to hurt them since they'd not be able to boast such stock. You, James, who have claim to some of the best poets, surely can do something to press them to this. It can be told these book dealers that book stores who do agree will catch all the customers, or a good deal of them. I mean, it can work as a prestige commodity.

[. . .] There are worse things one could do, like begging for money, like selling one's manuscripts to vultures, like filling out grant forms, or applying for welfare checks. Since I'm not inclined for any of it, I'll probably get a job again, and put off what I most want to do. Like I've had it—but not without having touched the spot that caused it. Assuming I sold since 1958, 70,000 copies of all my books, at one dollar, forty percent of it, $3,000 a year, would have kept me in step with my accomplishments, my wife and child, and poesy and me. And fuck that crap, this is the lot of poets! A poet is a man by God! And if he becomes public property then that public pays for it and no book dealer should eat that painfully earned cake.

Gregory

To James Laughlin Paris

[ca. Jan. 1966]

James,

I met lovely Marianne Faithfull, top English pop-folk singer, a 19 year old beauty with fine voice. She said she'll make me lots of gold because she'll sing my lyrics. So since words are become the most important thing in teenage songs today, I'm sure I can make it, at least I'll try. I feel I can't fail if I stick to straight where-its-at honesty. She is best friends with talented Paul McCartney, the Beatle. He writes the music and she said he digs my poetry and would musicfy mine lyrics, but I backed out of that saying I'd rather she sing the lyrics almost like speaking, stressing down the musicality, according to how words make her feel. More real like that. She thinks idea wonderful. So that's why I don't ever make big money which Paul McCartney surely would have commanded, but I'm a slave with a zombic obedience to the spiritual edict of the muse, alas. Thank God.

See you soon with the best poetry of 1963-64-65-66—ergo with the Pons Asinorum of America's labor, giving birth to its promise, but from what a tight stupid dry creepy cunt. I shed no tear for the death of the deliverer. God death so saddens all the time, its about time it performs a service. I respect your head of poetics to dig what I mean, so need no explain mine explanation. They say an asteroid's gonna hit earth and kill millions come 1968. "They," astronomers, are told in very small print thus not to panic masses. Do I believe it? Not if I believe your saying there'll be millions of poets to come, though my *There's Yet Time* be a lid on poesy, by unconceitedly God! Once again I am your insanely sane friend.

Gregory

If Marianne Faithfull digs singing a poem from one of our books, then of course I'll refer her agent to you. Yet if I only get six percent out of it! I'm dead set on writing especially for her, sole possessor of work, which I intend to do anyway. But if from our book which I'm sure will be so, then let's both make money. We have children to feed after all, but I want a fair deal from you. Let me know. She sells 500,000 discs.

▼ [By now, even the normally even-tempered James Laughlin was losing patience with Corso. Laughlin had written trying to prod him into working harder on the next book by reminding him that people would forget who he was.]

To James Laughlin

Athens
[Spring] 1966

Dear James,

As for people forgetting Gregory Corso, since Gregory Corso is no longer in public eye, all good and well. A poet is not a movie actor whereby he needs make a picture a year thus to be remembered. Old grows a movie actor and he's had it, not a poet. I could think of Tennyson who stayed from publishing twelve years and I amongst many hath not forgotten Tennyson. But I do agree that these times are quick and if a poet has what to say he best say it when said. What then has happened to eternal poetry? That verse which stands for all time? Alas—poets today are become eventful and topical, prophets indeed, merely roseate journalists, if you ask me.

Anyway, I do have a book, and I know it will be a bright departure from my last work. I have, in fact, enough for a book, but I hold off. Why? That I seem to answer unto myself, sufficiently somehow. Yet I can't answer it for you. I think I am waiting to see what is astir in the minds and acts of my peers, thus far I see nothing. Ginsberg is one long poem, his cast is set, all know where he's at, thus it becomes virtually impossible for him to hit upon the unknown, the new, the different. That is what happens when the poet settles into his public identity. Aside from Allen—who else is there? [. . .] I alone, well I know, am yet unpredictable. The next word I voice may only be attributed me by what craft I enflower it. And yet again all has been too much with poetry these last ten years, a hiatus is due. I shan't think the muse would flaunt and abuse me by jutting me into the public ear and eye constant.

Know as I know that when I feel the time due to reappear via poesy, it shall be the time. I am never uncertain whereas poetry and myself are concerned. Why are you concerned? I could frankly assume it be for the profit I, as a good selling poet, bring in. Or I could kindly believe you would me be well and content and my producing lots of poems would indicate I am. Well, I hope I am all things to all hopes and wishes. Worry about my lack of gold, I say, but never about my golden goose. Athens is 100 years behind the times. Something new and wonderful could happen here or something creepy and sad.

I am, as ever, Gregory

To Allen Ginsberg

Athens
May 23, 1966

Ah Punjab Allen,

[. . .] I'm not down on Leary or LSD, outstep yourself as man, man. It be the whole evolutional process, ergo chance, change, mutation, etc. But his saying the war is won, that man has mutated (those who took the ride), is a little too powerhead far-fetched for me. [. . .] As for his getting 30 years, then by God, I'd fight that. And as for his being, I feel it too be sad since he has only LSD to his credit. He has nothing else to fall back on. And you, my dear bogomil, you are poet insighter prophetman. I can understand defense, [but] I can't see you making LSD your sole defense. There are, like the Wichita poem,[251] lots of areas, indeed all acreage (if they be to your heart) to stand by. In other words, always have alternatives. Remember when you said about me, "He could write anything from mothballs to atom bomb"? Well there's it.

You're right about my static state regards my long due book of poesy. The poems are all done, all I need do is put them in form. But with past illness, and despair, I couldn't get at it. And what with war, I felt what's the use? And what with that title, I was at a loss as to what I meant. Surely not an apologetic meaning and "expiation," what expiate? Mine life? By the look of my poems, I'd say no. Expiate my fellow man? Nay; then what? And why such a loaded word, so religious like? Well, after a while it came clear to me. I know what [the] title means, thus I am free to get to work. As for the past poem, well, I do think of that, but it be no bother, as you say, deathbed will take care of that. Like if I go the way of all health I have at least twenty years to go, so.

As for doing anything for me, well, I am at ducat end. I don't get upset about not having any, but it does pose a distraction. I am in a state of repair, two months and half now sans anything nod wise. So whatever I can get regarding bread helps me maintain my restoration of health, and self-respect, that is, care.

I live alone, see only Ansen, read alot, read the first epic, writ in early Sumner, the epic of Gilgamesh. Real fine—plus old testament—and for first time Nietzsche. I like *Thus Spake Zarathustra*, but don't dig his use of word Superman. Not because of Nazi superior bit, surely Hitler and Mussolini got him all wrong, but because I would it Human Victoria, in regards to attaining evolutional summit. Also didn't dig his *Ecco Homo*, but on the whole, I was amazed to see lots of my thoughts and ideas therein. Good that I picked up on him at this stage of life. I prefer reading influencers at an uninfluencial time of life.

My daughter is truly lovely, I received a photo of her and she looks terrific! What else to say other than I hope to see you face to face soon. And thank you very much for the money, and I hope another check won't crab thee. I would not ask if I did not need. By the by, can you send me the latest mags, plus ask [Ed] Sanders if he'll send me a batch of past and present *Fuck You's*.[252] Ain't nobody seen anything here. Again don't be despaired of me not signing Leary petition. I don't think I need explain, I feel you know why.

Your friend meeting the on-rushing years, and ne'er a turn of the head,
Gwegory

If anything e'er happens me I bequeath my only child to you as to her welfare, education, etc. I feel a friend is ethically moral as concerns such things, but something tells me I'll see you off to heavendom. But just in case. Also if so, I want to be buried in Potters Field, after being cremated, of course this I demand, Potters Field it be.

To Allen Ginsberg Athens
[June 16] 1966

Dear Allen,

I am going to live like a monk for month, high up on a mount on the isle of Moni, in a German outlook post. The isle is uninhabited 'cept for peacocks and wild goats. Lovely Miranda Rothschild has secured it for me. It will take half an hour to climb up to it; I will bring with me all my work of the past four years, and shall thus finally put together my book. Plus I shall truly regain mine health there, I'm hopefully sure. You wouldn't think I went thru what I did these past four years by the look of me, yet beneath that look is a pretty much purged skin of blood. Still it was something I had to go thru with, as I first realized, and as I hoped you would have understood. Like I learned bitterly that I had not hell down pat. What I poesyly learned will, I pray, come out in mine book. I not only saw myself the wreck of a wrecked childhood, who in manhood was unable to live the life denied me whence birth; constant punishment cannot be relieved by those few wonderful years (1950-1960) I took to be a lifetime. I blindly believed myself the essence of that decade, with no contact with the Nunzio Corso of 1930-1950. I was, so I felt, that Gregory Corso, poet and bohemian, who in a matter of ten years lived a full youthtime and speedy age. God only knows where I got the drive and ego (if such can be so termed, being I was always living in an environ that knew not the liberty of the ego). Nor was I so desperate as to "make" of my past, a present, and a future. I cut off the past, lived the present; and when the boom was lowered, I faced the future with no real history to present it with . . . other than that one I had cut off, so it came back to me and hard. Like I said months ago, it was like giving birth to a twenty year old crushedness. What womb is there could plop it out painlessly? I knew to write "Marriage," but little did I know how prophetic the subconscious past could be—and what with me dutying the muse with hopeful predictions of the future, I was in a most dire predicament. The boom came when I realized I could not husband be, nor father. The ten year old poet could not cast off the father of my own past. Indeed I was mother and father and child, and none could trio it, a sad helpless split left mine spirit a cold and frightened thing. Thus the "filthy nurse" was secured me in the infirmary of hell, and from that hell I fell. When one gets knocked down that low, one either stays down for good, or mutates. Well, I feel that I have mutated into the only thing I could understand and live with . . . a thing familiar to me all my 36 years, that realistic dreamer, that stuff called "spirit"; and once I knew this to be so I thanked the Gods there be that I might yet live AND evolve.

This is of my experience, and it is the subject of my latest works. I am grateful for whatever science I can make of it, and to do myself and the muse justice I can only hope that I offer my spirit accordingly, to science that is; for as pre-man into man evolved, so hath spirit genetically grown and aspiringly climbed. Some reach it by the same route (in one lifetime, like the caterpillar become the butterfly) and some, like the slow change of the reptile bird into the feathery bird, not in equal route and single lifetime. I remember a dream I had when in prison of seeing myself lying dead on the wayside while I walked on the highway. That dream makes a lot of sense to me now. It told of the divisionality of the spirit and the body, the mind was it that told, when it was as is my good fortune so realistically dreaming.

Then I bid you hail for you are right, it is up to man, and not natural chance, to change. Nietzsche had it almost but goofed with the idea of "Superman." What he couldn't grasp was the fact that the mind alone could only power the will to thus mutate. I prefer the word evolve better, and that it would be a spirit change, and not so much a mind, mental, change. Ergo LSD would seem to help those who are of one lifetime one unit; this is "the creature born of itself" you so clearly and long ago envisioned.

Some sort of purge, some kind of expiation, is needed to divide this trapped unit. I guess the terrible wonder of such a drug fits the proscribed bill. I say this as one who made his journey not by said drug but by route the chopped eel would manifoldly take. The analogy is precise I feel, both in the painful sense and in the division—if I am correct in assuming that this is what such a drug as LSD can provide the "sinking ship" that is embodied spirit, then I must hail your belief in its blessedness, and as well wholly agree with Dr. Leary.

I do not say I am completely healed. For I still have to make strong my will, as I would still fall for that filthy nurse, and she is always around. Well, she won't be when I go to mine retreat. There I shall be entirely alone, except for the heavens of Zeus, and the whole of the past four years scored on paper before me. I go there not for any spiritualistic savior, but that I have not had such solitude ever, for even in prison I was yet with conditional life. [. . .] I need the peace, the rest, the quiet, and the self-certainty of a clear head and soul. For it will not be a newspaper I will bring with me but the past four years, years of terrible de-unification. I have no doubt I shall overcome the weight and pain and, hopefully, the freaks of said mutation; like no more myths, no more straw (as compared to the wheat, the essence of those years). I would like to achieve in the coming month a stop to cigarettes and meats. I would like to practice breathing exercises. I will ask Zina for her Yogi system, for what I would of it all is a re-empowered body, as I hail the evolve of the spirit, I know full well that the butterfly could not be but for the caterpillar; only in this body is it possible for the human spirit to change and gloriously grow. I know that this seems kind of late and somewhat naive to come to, but will allow the newborn his ignorance . . . which is, after all, but an innocence . . . and now do I realize what I meant by the title of my next book: *There Is Yet Time To Run Back Thru Life And Expiate All That's Been Sadly Done.* I now know what "expiation" in what context etc., means. So I'm off, and I will pick up my mail when I leave the Mt. once a week and go to Aegina—address will be Aegina, Post Restante—Greece.

Ah, Allen, so it does matter all this, it does change, it does mean, and how nice to wake up to it, and feel it, and live it, and progressively, i.e. evolutionally, be.

Love to you, Gregory

To Allen Ginsberg [ca. 1967]

Dear Allen,

Do not take this as Gregory gonging some kind of alarm—I merely want you to know a few things time, fate, and faith (blind) has prevented me from telling you. It would seem that since Tangier, before your trip to India, and mine to Miss Filthy Nurse, we were able to communicate, as I am sure we still can, but we have grown up these past four years, and the best of friends blossom away. I want you to know that I love you as my dearest friend and as a fellow poet, and that you have stuck by me and have encouraged me almost to a point that I couldn't expect otherwise. That night at Albert Hall, aye, I did read awfully, but please take solace in the fact that I was nonetheless real in what was perhaps my first lousy poetry reading. You well know how I used to wow 'em, Allen, and though I had much of the ham in me, it was not fake ham, it was a happy kid who had something to say, and who said it in poesy. I claim no loss of trueness to myself as poet-dreamer incapable of being unreal! An unreal me would have badly tried to "wow em" that Albert Hall eve, so I say to you, take solace in the strange wonder of a poet who is your muse-mate in this here life, who has yet to feel himself false to his dedication. To you I will give a soul-true synopses of my five books of poetry—hoping that thru me and mine you'll maybe glimpse at you and yours. Though my four books are quite unlike each other, this fifth one is wholly different. I feel the same will be true of your next important work. A work, without any hint of pessimism or gloom, well purposed to be the last, but dreamy gloops like me always feel their last behold is at hand. Okay, here is where I was and am at—

Vestal Lady On Brattle, was never less real than the actuality of a child-man's imagined sad loneliness, repeated themes of feet and mothers clearly chant an unknowable passion awkwardly compassionate. In short: poems composed before the poet.

Gasoline, a haughty poet's happy acclaim of the self bursting with new insight humorous and optimistic though never wholly blind to that burning eye's hurting light. In short: poems composed by a new-born poet.

Happy Birthday of Death, of bombs, cars are real, of fear of death, of ambitious attempt to poetize in turn subjectize death, yet of humor, of lost hair death, and marriageless death. Secret hope that subject would make me a man as well as make people see me as man. Poet I was thus, cared not to prove it, but as for being a man, I had exaggerated doubts. I still don't know what is or isn't a man in a manshape. In short: poems composed by a maybe "great" poet.

Long Live Man, a hope and certainty somewhat desperately heralded, didn't dig rut of prophet of doom tag, a scrapbook in comparison to *Happy Birthday*. A book writ overnight, poems of no longer laughing defiance, a sort of refugee from the muse. In short: poems that could mean either dead end or delicate respite for poet, All Depending on His Next Book!

And, Allen, that next book is 80 pounds of crumpled folded dirty torn papers the clutterage of three crumpled folded dirty torn years. Having long since titled it *There's Yet Time In Which To Run Back Thru Life And Expiate All That's Been Sadly Done*—I for the life of me, couldn't understand why I wished so finky sounding a title. Surely if I believe to ask to whom can a poet go to, then to whom can a poet go apologize to? Well, obviously my Catholic strain entered my allegiance to poesy. I felt I sinned against poetry whenever I took a shot. I'd literally get nauseous if I dared to mix junk and poetry together. Thus Miss Filthy Nurse was in fact Miss Death of Verse. Still, it wasn't all junk those three hard, hard years, and I managed to write 80 pounds worth, but oh to look at them is to look at those years, those days and weeks and months. How I suffered Allen, how I suffered, and still will I suffer until I get back to the muse, until I run back and expiate all these sadly done poems. Poems? I can't call them that. And then I am yet retained with the gift of seeing myself and my whatever hang-up from my God-perch and lo all becomes so simple and clear. Just dump them 80 pounds of goopy years on the likers (and dislikers) of Gregory Corso's poetry via the Laughlin network and have done with it!

When someone said a poet dies a little with each poem, I'd it: Poems die when the poet partakes of alien charge. Ah, Allen, well you know that though poetry is the cause of much of a poet's suffering, he, the poet, never condemns it. For, like you say, if the poet is shapely, the poem will be shapely. Therefore if poetry suffers us, it is because the poet, for reasons he and the muse alone knows, is insufferable. Thus it was not junk saddened my Sally and child, but poetry. A poetry that kind of died with *Long Live Man*, a poet whose spirit did indeed mutate, thus drugs did nurse this poet when this poet fell from hell, and in limbs did nod and agony, bleeding arms, filthy as a dull rusty bent needle is filthy. Oh, Allen, Allen, is it enough my cry that poets have not spilt blood in all of history when my poet arms spill and yet spill? I believe I must believe that none of this is done in vain or downright stupidity. I am not a stupid man, but if I am then I am a stupid poet and my poetry a stupidity. How odd that I do not fear death at all, and yet fear O awfully fear the sad stupid death of an

O.D. or some junk death. The only death I fear, the only death I call a bad death, the only death I know will diminish all my hopesome words of beauty and heaven and no more sad hearts, and yet do I flirt with it, aye, like a crazy hot rodster kid. God knows I don't dig this cheap psychological fact of flirting with the anti-muse, and should have it suffice me to stop forever, and anticipate the surprise of some unforeseeable demise while living a good smart life. Here the crux, Allen, here the poet shaping up the poem. My old chant of the importance of dying good. Here do I then know my bad death, for poetry has told me. Alas, it does seem simple for me, doesn't it, Allen? Surely you'd it simpler than Jack's breathing fate. But no, I see to all as incredible. Why should we be so damned? What wrong has Jack done but to weep for man's pain? What wrong you who craves the love of God life men with an insatiable heart? What wrong Bill and Peter who finally know to love each other? What wrong I who has it in him to make so many so happy and a sad temper caused by early hurt? We are none of us mean awful people. We have voiced aloud our direst ill, no dark devil-fact lurks secretly within. We are poets, Allen, and our poems are example of a gentle, as well as temperamental, humanness. If you did howl and I did hate old poetmen, it was a real cry and for that the lack of compassion were no eternal damnation.

True some fine people have suffered all their lives and were I to suffer unto death it wouldn't mean that I had bad in my heart soul. But how can I poetry this life if this life contends such endless senseless misery? It's life has got to make the poetry, not poetry life.

So, Allen, we are yet young, middle-aged, though I swear we look and feel the same as years ago. And we have come a long hard real strange historical holy way, haven't we? And be we rebels then by God we have won the revolution because all we did was write poetry and behave with honor and professed love so much so that we could admit being spooked by all that "love" gobbledygook. We always laughed at ourselves, and we took a lot of punishment and some of it truly hurt, but we are still around and Sorbonne professors treat us as if we were something new on the scene.

Peter is a poet and is bugged at me for once saying he wasn't a poet. And that because I felt he should have a acknowledged me his teacher. My poetry's way can only be followed by such as Peter and I, so anyway I didn't dig him cutting in on my territory, which is silly early me. I hope Peter can realize it for what it is. Jack's bugged with me and yet hails me. I do not like the Corso of his novel, but then again no many-sided soul such as Corso likes to be represented by one side only, especially if it's a goopy side. Allen can't say that I ever really did something to hurt him. Gregory can say that Allen shouldn't have ignited a Corso Fund well knowing Corso's wop pride.[253] Burroughs is like the best I knew in prison, but he no should have God-ed me or Gysin-ed me. And I, I should have kept him a human being in my otherwise practical eyes, but did oft oblige him his "Invisible Hombre," his outer space elsewhereness. But we were all kind of mad in those early cut-up Git-le-Coeur days. Though some of my finest times with him was working with him on first cut-ups. Gysin just the opposite. He tried to tell me he from far away elsewhereness and I no never believe, like to this day I begrudge a man his artistry simply because he partakes in art. So, who else? Ted Wilentz—I hope he hasn't lost all faith in me. And Sally, I hope she falls in love and finds the joy she so deeply deserves. And my daughter—Oh, God, my daughter, all she is, is a photo to me. I hope a great wonder can happen that I'll be able to care for them both, and of course myself.

So and thus, Allen. Here be by first missive to thee in eons. Please keep me near and dear as I shall you, and surely India will be anew when you venture it with me. Don't fear whatever fate America hath in store for you. Keep healthy and maybe I should say America don't fear whatever fate (faith) Allen G. hath in store for you.

Gregory

To James Laughlin Woodstock, NY
[March 29] 1968

Hello,

This will be my new address starting now for the rest of my life, if I can help it. It's lovely here and just the place to put the finish to my Sisyphusian book. Like it's already over the hump. And this is what I have finally decided to call it: *SPACED.*

SPACED means many things just like my book means. You may wonder what took so long, well it's not the poems, they have long since been done. It's the form that I put all the force of my shouldery-brain to. I feel that I have succeeded, that I have taken poetry a step farther. I just hope that you [will] be able to publish it (for it is publishable). Perhaps I'm wrong to think that what is unconventional is more costly, dollar-wise that is, but it is most imperative that the book be done according to my presentation. I could give in to only one content, color. If you feel it is too costly, but I mean really feel it, and that you couldn't afford the sacrifice, then I shall afford it, though color is a very great part of the whole. It would make me so happy, James, and it would truly make the muse happy, were you to go full blast ahead with what took much out of my spirit. I put all my energies into the poem these past years, though I was often taunted by the events of the day, pressed as to whether or not I was doing the right thing by not going out into that day and stand a true active son of revolution full and utmost. And then where and what and who would mind and care for the fort? Ginsberg, [LeRoi] Jones, et al were off to wars. Those inside the fort were old and immutable. Nobody young seemed to be riding brightly toward said fort, so I stayed, and minded it. I did the right thing because I couldn't do otherwise. My wishes of years ago (as seen in essay *Berlin Impressions*, and poem *The American Way*) is come fulfilled; youth is arrived. I called for the young to come and set it all straight. In the poem I awkwardly prayed that youth rise and slay the dragon once and for all. If I had the poem I'd show you. [. . .]

I've always said that man, since the awakening, has taken as mighty a leap today as when he first awoke, and that today's young were the proof of it. They are man of tomorrow clashing with man of yesterday who has a iron fist on today. That is why the day is revolutionary, why the generational gap is so pronounced. Hard realist me knows there can't be a happy marriage, that only death can make tomorrow livable, and this death is not revolution's kind which is quick, but time's kind which is slow. Unlike revolution of old which brought about change, today the change is already so. That revolution is behind us, it came and went bloodlessly overnight. Here I feel that I as manstuff have played some part, having lived up to my name which means announcer, I think I sounded the changing via poetry; thinking back on those poems now makes it seem so. What else was there then for me as poet to do? Writing about topical stuff wasn't my speed really, though I found a way to make it come into my poetry bag, consider *Bomb*. Critiques on social ills and all such seemed to bring my poetics into some kind of street argument, like the sacredness of language, the magic of the word, was not where I was at, and of course that is exactly where I was at, or wanted to be at, a pox on the rest. Thus I moped about feeling that I lost the word, that my spirit was no longer spirited, that I fouled the tongue that spoke the sacred language, and God knows what else self-recriminations. I found myself traveling the western world now neither revolution's son nor the muse's standard bearer. I tell you they were heavy awful years James, I found I couldn't even write a letter anymore. In short, I, not the word, was lost. When I found myself, well I found the word, and mine tongue again.

Spaced deals with the discovery, the lost experience was something to go through and had nothing to do with the making of the poem, only the poet. As in the past, say my wild childhood and prison life which weren't poemed, served as ladders which I climbed, and having reached the top I wrote about what I saw from there, and not from whence I came. Though I will of course fill in those periods, as I have been [doing] via autobiographical prose.

So you can see now what took me so long in coming up with a book. The truth needs be lived first before it can be stated. That is why poesy is so sacred a business, it demands much. Creation is no easy thing and cannot be toyed with, and that is what the poem is all about, creation, which is never completed, all is ever creating. Were creation a completion then creation would cease.

This I learned and more. The mind cannot fully know the mind; were it able to then it would know all mysteries. It would comprehend what man terms incomprehensible, thus if I desire to know the meaning of time, energy, space, if I would know or were able to conceive infinity and eternity, I must know the mind to know, say, time. To further comprehend and conceive I must know the extension of thought; a cosmic-consciousness depends upon the extent of one's consciousness and not upon the extent of the cosmos. [. . .]

My book is a feast of combinations. Who knows but that one might open an unknowable, though it isn't something I went after? My intention was simply to make poems out of the sacred language of spacestuff, which hath made the stars and us ones. I'm in the right place to conclude my work; with a considerable amount of money, made from my notebooks which I sold. I rented a house in the midst of 30 acres of trees and mountains above, and in such peace of nature I photograph my consciousness on the page. I wish to wait publication for two months. I must be fully satisfied with the form these poems shall be set in. *Basta.*

I bought a car; and I learned how to drive the moment I got behind the wheel. I feel I have arrived. All impossible obstacles have been passed. Have a good summer.

Gregory

To James Laughlin Cherry Valley, NY
[Dec. 11] 1969

Dear James,

Why I hadn't realized the following sooner is beyond me. The poems I would like to see come out in book are on tape and are slowly being transcribed. By [the] time I put it altogether, another bunch of years will have elapsed. I can't afford anymore years, though mine vision-agent deemed the past years not worth the sight. A time of no word it was, a time of Beatle simplicity and song, a time of assassin and unpoetry. In 1964 I said at YMHA poetry is in abeyance. And thus, unlike my fellow ones, I frequented the all too real Puerto Rican Mafia streets for a desperate score for a desperate ill. Looking back I could see no other way for one such as a me. Allen's way was long ago intended, Burroughs' way was made and fortuned by his confession of a past way, and Kerouac's way came to a halt by the obvious, death. Yet he was not unfulfilled, he did the work he set out to do, full and beautiful. Allen and Ferlinghetti are active and constantly write on, if not poems, journals. It will never be said that their work was cut short. And Burroughs', well, one *Naked Lunch* is the work of a lifetime, all he can do now is create, innovate, magicianly. Since my poems are very much the result of my living day and Grand Central height of traffic hour mind, I find it increasingly difficult to put such mindful day down on the page. [. . .] Only the hard mind-blowing events of the historic day sets such mind to disregard the pillow; events either topical or personal, like JFK's and or Jack's death, like the mutation of the spirit.

And I have these poems, and they give sign of my constant activity, for poems I have written. Their publication with goodly New Directions I have not had. The problem is manifold. First that title. It could have hung me up, took me much time to figure just what kind of poems I meant to give in the name of what "expiation." Also getting bogged down with the harsh reality of wife and child, so easily answered in the poem, so insufferably unanswered in the home. Only recently have I been eased on that account. She having remarried, thank God. For the sake of her life, and the welfare of mine daughter, laden with the guilt of a failure father, I could not see myself speak or be father to that generational America we, the prophetical bards of Beat, gave birth to. And at a time when I lost whatever God it was I held faith to. Losing as well, contact with my fellow fathers, losing and nearly lost, the very self, the very spirit, and therefore the muse. Yet never dimmed the mind, but more vivid became, and so was denied the mercy of insanity. For indeed what is insanity but some direly sad haven? [. . .] Yet mine's a good fortune, alas. How in the awful fragility of thing do I survive? Whether I continue to is a toss-up. I take my chances, often carefully, never with bad intention. For as far as I'm concerned, I've a full life, indeed many lives, and what is yet allotted me is but extras. I'm eased with the hopeful thought that once again I may wake up and joy in the dawn; that "from hell none e'er fell"; and that the muse is yet with me and I with she. All guilts be abolished, for there's only one thing I shall never be guilty of, and that's fucking-up with poesy. For though I hold that poet and poem are inseparable, and that the poet suffered the self-inflictions of the body, the mind did keep, and the poem is marked with experience with no scars of experience to tell.

So rather than wait for that volume of clear-cut verse, realized of stolid truth and wisdom's insight, as though, as Larry [Ferlinghetti] put it' "I was waiting for the definitive answer of the universe or and of existence." [. . .]

Whatever I want to get on the stick and do something, it's been too long, and it quite hampers me in many respects. So I'll quickly see what I can do about sending you Xeroxes of the first six long poems. They may well be in themselves enough to make a book. Thus far I've yet to receive any of the poems I had on tape, three tapes which are being transcribed by secretary of an English

Professor at Albany; in return I give them tapes plus something money form for the secretary. So rather than wait for them to come to light, let's work on the poems I already have. Hope you feel as do I that this time a book there'll be.

Your faithful poetfriend, Gregory

To James Laughlin San Francisco

[ca. Feb. 8] 1970

Dear James,

This book of poesy, very important as to content and as [to] how it is set up. For instance, *Indian Requiem* is 1958 and should go early in book, plus dated. All poems when I get galleys will be dated. If someone reads a poem I wrote in 1961 like *American Way*, undated, it will seem like I'm writing dated stuff, not to say for prophetic content. In poem I state, "Oh that youth might set it straight, etc." and such has come to be or they is trying. And I want most poems to represent title, therefore *Geometric Poem* must go in. I gave Pivano that poem, as poem, not as book, because she knew I was in contract with you for book. I said it's okay to book the poem but I will have to publish it with you when my book is together. That was way back in 1965. She agreed to do only 300 copies. If she hasn't got rid of 300 copies in all that time, I feel she has had more than ample time and chance; ethics and all. I don't imagine you'll print it like her with pictures? So it will be in print not in my hand; it will be two wholly different works. I gave her poem out of good grace, she is not doing fair by me now. Well, I have no contract with her; at least don't think I do. Anyway it is IMPORTANT for book and must go in. You write her and tell her that I can't wait until she is ready, and state what I have stated. Also, Bob Wilson has copy of *Mutation of Spirit*, I think I have more poems in it than ones I gave you. Ask him to Xerox the Death Press edition. He will, he was very obliging to me when I asked for other poems.

Yes, I didn't think you'd rush it so fast, but being that you are, I must keep eye open to see that it is done my way. I know what I want and envision a real fine work. You are concerned about amount of pages and would fill book with just anything, but I demand order, even though I sent them in disorder. I decided that I could write you as how I wished poems to be included and in what order, but [there is] no time you say. Okay, then I either have to do it when I get my galleys or now. I say we have a book; we don't have to clutter the pages, we could make larger print, more spacious. When I think of the cargo it could be, by God, don't destroy it with allotments to time and space and excess matter. The poems we have for book is far more a cargo than most books I see—the Indian poem, the American Way poem, the Kennedy poem, the Mutation of Spirit poem, the Geometric poem, the Kerouac poem, plus some others, I can't recall. I had those things on tape, was asking to get the important ones for book, but no time. These poems are long poems, and should be read slowly, and should not be cluttered, but given room and size. I could have waited longer for book to you, as the tape poems is the book, but I thought it would be nice to do this little venture with you, and I would it were appreciated in that light.

But when I heard about Pivano, by God, I gave her work out of kindness, not out of money, there was no monies involved. Now she talks like monies, and you sound as though you would bury my intent for precious cargo I had in mind. Granted I gave you list to help me track down poems, but I did the tracking, and the poems I sent you were the ones I wanted as selection for book. But you speak of 64 pages. I am a poet, not a page filler, James. You are an honorable publisher, but I have the feeling you do not think I know what is good for me, like thinking either Ginsberg of Ferl has to make my book. Nay, I make my own books, always have, all Ferl supplied was office, typewriter, and help in tracking poems down. It is the way I work; I get a book together when I see a book. With the Kerouac poem I saw my book, I saw the title *Elegiac Feelings American* in the poems I had written and were not in book form. I saw the form and have filled it with said cargo. If I feel that there are some poems you wish included that fit to order of book then fine, I'm willing. I have never been difficult this way, always listened to reason, most often complied. I did a lot of work in three weeks at Ferl's because I suddenly was felt to do so. I have not been idle these years, I have much work, and just because no publishing did not mean I was not producing. I produced lots. But when what I have produced is finally volumed complete before my eyes, then I sit down and put it all together. I do not set out at offset to make a book when I write a poem or poems; the poems come first, book later; pure science. That it took me eight years to come up with a book is no fault of mine, I do not make books, I make poems. How these poems are presented is of great import to me, and I never minded when I gave you past two books how you presented them, just that they were dated (another important fact and an order I insist upon). I would like to see a poem, especially a long one, presented and concluded without another poem following so close on its heels.

I always liked you because I felt you served the poet first, then the public second. But pray do not disappoint me and present it reversed unto me. I have a great book on those tapes being transcribed, if I am made unhappy by what I have asked and then it is the end for us. I really am to be taken on my own force and style, not on anybody else's. This book is unlike the two books I previously gave you; it has a purpose as a book; the previous books had purpose as just so many poems. We cannot treat this book that way. Only those poems I feel fit up to the title are fit for my cargo. [. . .] If I can't have the book I want then I want no book at all. I gave you this book because I felt I owed it to you though your book was on the tapes, which I was getting on paper. Please let us do well by what I write, I swear nothing makes me so unhappy as my work presented in bad light, even though it may seem in good light to presenter, and meant meaningful like I know you mean to do well by me.

I am, Gregory

To Allen Ginsberg Buffalo, NY
[ca. Oct. 26] 1970

Dear Allen,

How I would like to maintain good beingness. For assuredly I get myself all enmeshed in awfulness, like it's a bummer that doesn't have to be. How painfully absurd I am unto myself, and I know I don't have to be. Like some bizarre stupidity I can't shake off, yet oh, how I hope to. I make my peace, I cannot bear this self-hellishness, I would peace. Yet all I seem to generate is bad karma, drek memories for one's olding age. The heart craves peace, good encounters, sweet occasions. The blame lies within me, and the vulnerability I host invites the disruptive. I get beat, hurt, and it never seems to end. I am bruised my old friend, and I am unable to bemoan my state, for when I did, I took to such as drug-sleep and my state got sorrier, stupider. I would in urgency to some sort of strength, a salvaging strength, whereby to live in this life and this head of memories so as to leave a good taste in one's self and in those one encounters. Yes, yes, how so very right and smart your "if the mind is shapely the poem will be shapely." I know I would do well and enjoy my doing (the poem) were I to make life enjoyable for myself and others.

I don't want to be fucked-up, Al. I never wanted to be. My soul cries out to cease this constant blowing, I just want to do right by all my living days. You, my friend, have seen me in my drunken sorry fucked-upness; and how piteous it must seem to you. I can only ask forgiveness for such behavior and hope, deeply hope, to come to grips with myself and life by each and every second of it. Time is growing short for this actor on the life stage, the stains weigh heavy on my trail, Allen. I would the stains cease and I make marks of light before I depart the set. Hurt begets hurt. I lash out at being hurt and cause more hurt. I cannot envision myself as a complete loss, a blow out; for I am able to talk softly and do gentle. To be constant thus is my deepest desire. Indeed this be the heaven and hell of it. Hell is sure here for the making and what a lousy downright deplorable structure I've built myself. [. . .]

There's Yet Time To Run Back Thru Life And Make Up For All That's Been

Sadly Lousily Done. I couldn't write that book, nay, that's a book to live. The shapely life. How so very important this life suddenly seems to me and it's not death what's to hear, but the blowing of one's life spooks me. Not that some future Judgment Day awaits the result of one's lifetime, but that there be the judging of the present, the self-judgment, of what one's peers makes of each and every second of our lives. Its not hard at all to live good and kind, good souls are not judges, but how can a bad one be judged otherwise? If I'd resign myself to the belief that good and bad abound in the human condition then not enough to hope the good outweighs the bad. That the bad is so painfully so it bests one to act strongly determinedly at being good. Control, and drinking makes such a drunken driver of me, out of control, crash, and to the casualty reflects himself to be a mess of a life thing. How I wish to get myself and life all together, and if I put away stupid chances it shouldn't be all that difficult to become that wish. No one has to be doomed. I feel the option is there, that one is yet for the salvaging. I would try try to make, finally, a good go of it, such that one would regard me not as trying but as being one's true self. My truth is good, Allen. I envision a good truth; that's always been with me, for some kind of sake I feel deep deep within me I gotta make the effort—wish me luck, I know you do.

My love to you, Allen. The fold, the good bright fold, how I yearn to return to it. The separation is dark and cold.

Love, Gregory

To Allen Ginsberg Buffalo, NY

[ca. Dec. 11] 1970

Dear Allen,

Wrote you a long funny letter about the state of poesy. Since if the seas die, poets die, and that will make us the last poets. Whitman for sure will die, and the fall of Rome will really fall. So I decided instead to write you about now and its essentials. Sorry to have blacked out there, hear Maretta [Greer] was funny calling me [to] take a stick of grass from her. Went to your doctor friend, [. . .] he gave me one tranquilizer for all my effort. Medicine can help, but I chance life, Allen. Whether take a car trip, a walk, or shoot dope. The pain of life did drive me to the pain killer of life, and that killer hurts when it's forsakened. The thing here is not whether to ease the pain of life but how to ease the pain of the pain-killer. A fix, aye, seemingly so, yet that is my lot, and damn that ignorance geniused in me. I am what I've become and what I've been I hardly remain.

Allen I'm to father another child soon. Belle [Carpenter] is pregnant with my seed. She wanted a child by me, considering my first child, also wanted. I feel like some prize stud. The cow stays by the calf, the bull not. As I wrote when I found out (her ex-husband told me). "Where are my children? / Fled with their mothers / Abandoning me, the father / As did my mother my father and me." Well, two children when you consider the population meat increase is enough if not two too many. If I live on and I encounter them, all grown and selved, will I seem a stranger to them who'll be strangers to me? Well, if they so choose they can check me out by my poeminess. Gives one the desire to create real sharp smart shit for them to dig. Like my intro of you said: "Here's your daddy—and wise fucker" was correct appellation to give you.

I guess you get exasperated with some of the news you get about me, or with my presence. Well, I'm sorry about that, but what has it all to do with you really? I say we're friends because we were. Poetry made for bondship and as revolutionaries of a new consciousness, so are we linked. Yet my presence is not wished for at the farm,[254] and I can surely understand why. I find you old poet and authoritative over me and thus speak not of poesy to you because of it.

If you've your house in order and I've mine in disorder such should not differentiate us since I've no house and only seek order outside, true and harmonious order. Your orderly house is in an outside totally in disorder. What I'm trying to say is, if we're anything as poets, we're apt to be very unlike one another. Who's better or worse has nothing to do with it. I think I know what differentiates your work from mine, yet we've always had a common energy of spirit, and though my living self may not indicate it, I too would life were a blessed joy unto peoples. I take life, living, the whole shot, as something sacredly wondrous and serious indeed. [. . .] So be of good cheer towards old Gregory, he still makes laugh, and loves and knows wisen the lyre.

And if I even die, don't you excuse the car crash that didn't die me if a drugged fall does. The moralist on life is a fool on death. Nonetheless, I love and respect your way of life, you who so chanced death by being the first being I saw take a shot of dope back there in Mexico, Garver and all. I got hooked, you did not. And I was 31 when I first started, quite late in life, and now I'm 40 and I can take it or leave it. No matter what I claim to be intact. So much for me, there are so many people, and so many more to come, yet for the life of me, I can't see the poets to follow us. Will they yet discover the unknown knowables, and yet generate the consciousness anew? [. . .] The task seems to be easing the injustice and iniquities what exist. Go to it sweet Al, ease the pain, and teach the truth. I haven't given up mine selfsame task either.

If Gordon[255] has contact with Belle, he should tell her not to worry about me, have the child she so desired without my being confusing her and disturbing her. I promise not to seek her out, that she'll have it as she so desires. And so, Allen, the creators of the first A-Bomb, the DuPonts,[256] have the child of the poet, the Corso, who wrote the first *Bomb*, maybe like the first poet the first Bomb will die with me.

Love to Maretta, Peter, Gordon and all else.

Gregory

To Belle Carpenter San Francisco

[ca. 1970-71]

The essentials: I promise never to encounter your friends, path, home, phone. I am needed here, perhaps for reasons you may someday understand. I was never meant for woman, thus both woman and I suffered for such sad action. I hope you didn't have it all that bad. My birthday present was a diamond, not a sick girl. Yet you made it appear so and if it were jealously then I risked my love, you, and my friend, Bill, and lost. If she doesn't thank you for your care, as she thanked me not, then she surely must have been hurt terribly by life. I don't know her, so I can't tell too much about her. Yet I've known such, and they cause trouble for joy. Please read this letter to end when you feel you can because it might help enlighten you about my sorry state and police thing.

Firstly, Ferlinghetti will ask what charges are directed toward me, since I was in sorry state at time. Yet you refuse to believe it. I have proof police charged me with attempted robbery. I was going to buy you classical music, as you once desired. The joke being, [I am strange looking] not only to Sears but also to others. I was straight as a hatter. Mrs. Clarke can tell you about Hilton Hotel, whereas because of my "looks" I was forcibly thrown out.

Sorrow cut deep into me when you believe the arresters and not me. After all, I am not blameless when it comes to losing my balance. So like always I pay at wrong time as well. For were I truly a fuck-up, I could not have done the things I should be doing. Only you bring me unhappiness and pain, such is love. But since God is Love, then goodbye love, like goodbye God. Death I long ago overcame. All only by comparison of two who loved. You are not without stain and I always fore-sensed the day of your betrayal, as you did in the past with past lovers. I cannot say I am guilty of such. I had asked for marriage so that I might be free to work and do for us and child life. How insufferable to be so suspended, never knowing when the axe would fall. Sure I was constantly ill, those dreams of you no more, how true! And you once offered to wed me only because of Tasha[257]—use of me, that's all. The indignation of having not to answer phones, of having to duck in cars, did you never feel how shamed I must have felt? How low? And what was I but a hurt soul from angeldom, ever lost and alone in this world?

The indignity of having to go and live where you so choose, never asking me where I'd like to go or never coming to where I'd be. If you loved me like you claimed, then anywhere would be heaven. The way you placed Tasha in it all too. A child is a part of the parents, not parents part of child. Where it was home for us, it would be home for her. Never was I meant to feel as part of the family, you see I've been insighting all this. I looked upon our present state, and our past, with a fairness to both of us. And I realized you could have saved me from further suffering, but instead only increased it. I am quite a serious man, one who has been thru the mill so to speak. Ergo, I couldn't be your constant clown, make you laugh at will.

Of course it had to come to this. You being ashamed of me, afeared that I'd be seen in a Ratner's[258] by a mother. Me like a kept cock or head entertainment. What with my ailing with drug need, and depending upon you for love and bread. How I came through from such insufferability I'll never know. For truth has it, I looked not for you for dependency, [but] looked for drugs to ease my unimaginable pain. And always I had to feel inadequate because sick, I could not do much. If you would have loved me truly, you would have had a healthy man. How? By marrying me, allowing Tasha to heed my word as she'd yours, living whence it befitted all of us, depend upon me for support, give me the chance to care for my family, and once I worked, having cause to work, I would have not rushed to drink, to drug, to sorrow.

You are delicate, yet never saw me in such light. Tonight I read [at a] benefit for Indians, and the poem I read joyed and warmed all. [. . .] I will no longer give myself wholly to any one soul, because only a fool does such a thing. Easy for you to take up with another, not I. I, though my actions might not indicate so, hold soul in high esteem.

To Lawrence Ferlinghetti Buffalo, NY
Jan. 11, 1971

Dear Larry,

Thanks for your nice understanding letter. You and Allen are really coming through that way. Yes, it be right I give you my next book of poesy. I wrote you over twenty page letter trying to explain just what was up with Sally and me, once I felt you were opened for understanding. You see I couldn't years ago, not to you or Allen because I felt I was closed book in both your eyes. Now he, Allen, has realized that I have suffered too much, but in hell one never suffers enough. Belle, whom I truly love has given me nigh the death blow but I sustained, survived, and good for that. She just gave birth to my baby, a girl, name Indica, for middle name I gave her Egyptian ank [symbol], since nobody uses middle name but for initial, that be the best initial there is. Belle wants me to see kid, since I've been denied her pregnancy. She plumb disappeared on me.

Then on birth day she checks me out and asks for forgiveness. I readily gave it, because I still love her. I have been keeping away from junk, dehydrated death shit, for year now, but am run out of methadone pills, doctor in Frisco won't send me no more. I can get some here; but it cost two bucks a pill. Fifty pills is all I need to keep me going for fifty days, important days to keep me in tip top shape whence comes Belle with daughter to see me come end of February; so, yes. Since I shan't be getting any royalties from City Lights, owe so much I guess, but at least I'll be paying off mine debts. I think you should really give me nice advance on my new book of poesy. It be a breakthrough this book. In long letter I explain it; in short it has to do with the golden calf. Like we ones did Moses the young out of the land of Old, and then they got stuck in desert and worshipped the golden calf, Leary, Dylan, Joplin, etc. And we were not guiltless, while they worshipped, so did Ginsberg chant around it, so did you think that they was the new true poesy, which they wasn't, so did I nod under that calf. Well now is time to get them away from them calf's calf. All gold all right, the calf done up and left with its gold self. Now what's left is the Moses ones from the beginning. It be our task to lead them straight to the promise. Tis a time of shaky quiet, they are waiting, we shall give them the word again. All this my new book will point out. It will be the culmination of years of hell, but whenever I go to hell I Virgil myself, and come out singing joy not despair, like *Gasoline, Vestal*, were all the produce of an ex-con. So send me contract and a fair advance, I'd say $500 would be fair, and the poems I will send on to you as I perfect them. They are done, but I must make them perfect. At 40 I have gained wisdom. Let me know what you think and if you want that long letter, okay, but I feel I might have been too unfair to Sally, though it be the honest truth. She hated beatniks, and madly believed she'd save squareland by destroying me, in tone and image. Well, anyone who voted for Nixon in 1960 like she did, I had no right marrying, but she cried for it and I soft hearted fool fell for it, and fell hard. So I'm a father twice now, and the miracle I seek is for Belle to accord me chance to be father. I know I can be a fine one, teach em all the glorious wonders truths beauties.

Let me know, I got the letter, I got the poems, they should be really all set after I see my new-born. Right now I am too nervous; and want very much to be in best shape when Belle decides I either come to her or she to me with child. I'll need independency for hotel payment and food, and clothes to look the man I is. I got a beard finally. If I promise to give you best book of verse I know I have, then you should hold faith in me.

Yours, fatefully, Gregory

To James Laughlin Buffalo, NY
Feb. 2, 1971

Dear James,

I hope I wasn't too shaky on phone, get that way sometimes when I drink alot. Thank God I don't drink alot of late. Indeed don't do much of such of late, which be good because I've truly lots of work to catch up to and do. Am giving a series of readings since I've two young daughters now, and even though my first Miranda, be well off by Sally's second marriage; and even though my Indica be very well off with very well off mom, Belle Carpenter, I still want to support them because I want to be their daddy, if not now, as fate seems to have it, then by future date. So I will work out something, somehow, that I claim them both as dependents and a very good number for this will be in my willing them each a fine manuscript of verse, stipulating that they be published when girls reach certain age. In this way I can also venture into future by writing such things as I would feel would be indicative for said future time. In year 2000 Indica will be 30; I sure would like to have something to say then, but who knows, maybe a funny me will make it to 70 years of age in this here life on planet earth? Yes, I do recall that long letter I sent you from Frisco imploring almost that I receive galleys which I never did receive; and thus what happens but that our book is full with inaccuracies and wonted changes. For instance, there's about three poems you already published in previous books; also my wanting certain if not all poems dated was a most very important desire; for instance, *America Politica Historia* was published in 1960; yet nowhere is it specified; and this poem reeks with allusions of things to come; but were it writ 1970, bam, gone the whole shot. Not only that, but it maketh me seem old hat, and sadly a-want for themes.

Anyway, it shouldn't be too difficult a thing to remedy; I suffer that thing all poets suffer, the printed page as final. Well, being I go thru many printings, we can save this book. I do like it, want to like it, can like it, and never again shall I rush myself into anything. Like I always said, there is yet time . . . . . and the time must be opportune, always. I say we can make it a book, a book of to-date, if we get rid of the already published poems, if we shorten down some of the long ones (too repetitious) and include some of my finer recent ones.

So let me know how much time I have ere *Elegiac* [*Feelings American*] goes into print again. I swear to you, it can be that book I envisioned. True, I was sloppy in giving it to you, but I did feel that when I got the galleys, all would have been taken care of. It still can be. Allen G. tells me I'm up for National Book Award. Well that's thanks to Allen, but God how much thanks to me to thee if I was only in love with that book? All them political poems; how awful I am at political poems. The only reason I thought they'd have it made, however slightly, was by what they prophesied; yet take their dates away, and what have you? No, the 1970 Corso is not the 1960 bad Corso (else why didn't I include them in *Long Live Man*?) I am a hit and misser; in 1960 I hit well, but the baddies I just didn't bother with. Then comes along an eight year self-afflicted drought, and wham, all the old baddies get in. No, something wrong and messy here. So please let this constant self-Lazarus do his task, no matter how belated. Be good, but not like me, AND then again, why not? Your ever fateful friend,

Love, Gregory

▼ [Corso continued traveling to and from Europe over the years. While in Paris in 1975 he married Jocelyn Stern, who he would frequently refer to in his letters as Joss. She became pregnant within a short period of time. Corso continued his love/hate relationship with drugs.]

To Allen Ginsberg Paris
[Oct. 9, 1975]

Dear Al,

How's things? What news? Hope your face is what it used to be. I miss you, as always, dear friend. Paris, is Paris, after ten year lapse. But great news is I finally have my own home, Jocelyn's mother willed it to both of us, a lovely place, real classy, and comfy, a poem-factory for sure. Don't give my address to debtors, please. And if my cats get rabies shots and wait the necessary time, they can be flown to me without quarantine. Are you in anyway bugged with me? If so, you're wrong for being so, because I'm a good soul, I am. How's Pete? Bill's in Geneva, tried to find Gysin, can't, hear he be cancer colon sick.

Jocelyn is 4 1/2 months with child. We are happy. We have a home, rentless, and beautiful! You are welcome anytime. We got pictures of you on our wall, do you have one of me? No!! How's Harry Smith?[259] Out of hospital, I hope, please let me know. I am writing love poems. Please get laid before you answer this. I know what it does to your attitude—ha!

Love, Gregory

To Allen Ginsberg Paris
March 6, 1976

It's a Boy—March 6—2:20 40" in name: Orfeo-Max Corso. Am very happy.

Love you, Gregory

To James Laughlin Paris
April 16, 1976

Dear James,

Great to hear from you. Paris ain't what it used to be. So am I, I guess, but the place is quite oppressive; indiscriminate police searches, queries, etc. Gives the Queen city a kind of fascistic tinge. Poets and artists rare now. Paris used to be a great inspiration to me but now that I have a son I care only for his welfare and joy. I know I'll be a good father to him, my two daughters rightly belong with their mothers, a father should rear his son, a mother her daughter.

Hope your health is okay. I am working hard on our next book, *Heirlooms from Future*; both trying to make an heirloom and poems like fine exquisite Armenian rug; plus contain montage of images from past experiences and imaginings and memories, all to be wove into a conceptual picture of what I believe shall befall us humankind in the coming of days. I intend this work to be of my very best, thus I shan't rush it. I have all the material I need (encyclopedic) in my head. I've hit upon the one illusive problem, that of new style. I think I have that down pat, though it took years of experimentation, as my notebooks can attest.

I am as ever, Gregory

▼ [Jocelyn Stern turned out to have problems of her own and abandoned Corso's son, Max. A friend of his living in San Francisco, Lisa Brinker, soon became Max's surrogate mother, much to the delight of both Gregory and his son.]

To James Laughlin San Francisco
Oct. 25, 1978

Dear uphill skier,

Enclosed find a piece by McCabe,[260] who drinks in same bar I do, he real smart fellow. Also find poem for anthology, I read it in Marin with Ginsberg and everybody seemed to like poem. I wrote it fast, it be a theme I would like very much to deal with simply and intelligently. Enclosed also find an asking for 200 dollar advance if it be possible. As always I never feel bad if it can't be done. Also another asking: could someone in office please send me anthology with my play *In This Hung Up Age* within. I spoke to Ferl about my four plays, mostly written in mid '50s. He said he'd like to do a book of them—is it all right with you? I think recalling that I had mentioned a play, my first, about 12 pages, *Sarpedon*, 1954, in verse. [It] was an attempt to replicate Euripides, though the whole shot be an original. Like the great Greek masters, I took off where Homer left an opening (like Euripides did with the fate of Agamemnon). My opening was found in the *Iliad*. Sarpendon, son of Zeus and Europa, died on the fields of Troy, and Homer had him sent up to Olympus with no complaint from Hades, who got all the others what died there. Thus I have Hades complain, demanding from his brother Zeus, the dead, all the dead, from said fields. It being only equitable, since Poseidon, another brother, sided with the Trojans, and Zeus with the Argives, via his daughter Athena.

Oh, why don't I just send you the play, I will after I Xerox it, ok? Anyway don't give up on me, poetry is truly a blessed business, can't sneak the miracle. I need first feel to write; when I try just for the doing of it, nothing wondrous happens. I know full well that I haven't lost my feeling or shot my load, as (they) say. If anything, I am more the wiser than yesterday, though my eyesight suggests I get glasses. Now my son wants to type, okay enough I tell him, he understands, yet can't say a complete sentence. He be a real good boy, I mean very loving to people, he embraces their knees, nobody's a stranger to him. I love him like I never loved another human being, James.

It be important that I finally get our book done, because, among other reasons, once it be done I can then finally work on an autobiographical prose work. I have in mind my relationship with a wondrous brilliant girl name Hope Savage, who truly was an angel without wings, who taught me so much, and who also taught Allen mantras when he first arrived in India. She was the girl who had me print and post "Revolution is the solution" on an "I got my job from the *NY Times*" ad in the Fourth Street subway, 1954. Of all the wise heads I knew in the early 50's, she was of the best. A girl of 17, hers is a sad yet beautiful story; in the early 50's, in upper middle class USA, children were getting shock treatment. Her parents thought they were doing her righteously, since they were paying 50 dollars a day for her "care." Of course the bastard shrinks wanted to keep her until she got "well." All they did was kill a poet and good she was, too. At nine she got prizes like Rimbaud for Latin verse. Oh so many things so sad so beautiful about her, I know I can do her justice, with a short crisp solid biography. In the whole "Beat" clique she was the only girl, and Kerouac so loved her, too. She went to India in 1957 and no one since 1961 has ever heard of or from her. Gary Snyder has fond memories of her.

I am your poetfriend, Nunzio Gregory

To Allen Ginsberg

San Francisco
[Feb. 7] 1979

Dear Allen,

Thank you for your understanding C.O.P. situation.[261] Yes, I will try to set up reading for us here. After all, we've ain't' read together in San Francisco in at least 22 years. Let me know when it will be convenient for you. As for Naropa,[262] I know that you would want me there but for my behavior, I'm sure

Naropa too would want me. I do think an invite like say a reading and a class or two a couple of weeks, should be enough time to blow their minds on how nice I can be. Say something on level of a Kate Millet or [Ken] Kesey attraction. I got some nice new poems too.

Everything's all right, except for occasion of drinky poo. I try, I really do, to keep together, considering. Max and Lisa are fine. I don't know about giving Ferl my plays, in that all he'll advance me is 200 dollars. Perhaps another publisher. I am working hard on Hope book, should give me a chance to put some of 1954-1957 thru her about Kerouac and you.

I got Medi-Cal,[263] went to get glasses, and doctor tells me I might have the makings of a Milton or Homer. Another doctor tells me my lungs are a mess. Alas, so I now only smoke ten cigs a day after two or three pack a day habit. If you hear any bad news about me—believe it, I guess, since drinking doth rob me of my good meaning self. Neeli[264] and Raymond[265] are very helpful in inspiring me to get my book of poems finally out. I think I have a good chance of entering the 1980s with a sizeable gem pack of three. Book of Plays, Poems, and Hope's Story. Who knows, I might surprise even myself?

I love you two guys and don't feel that I've been declined what isn't there. Things will work out and even better if I put mine energies to it. Lisa's mother pays rent, and its a blessing, yet I have to sole card this one. That is why I will try to earn a fair token from my work, Ferlinghetti can't fair me. Perhaps you can suggest a publisher? New Directions I will give a try, but they want the poesy. My last play, *The Magic Fink* is a lot of fun, know you'll like it.

Well, good friend what more can I say but that I got in the *Village Voice* too—a picture of me and Max. How's Peter's fine book doing?[266] For a long time I haven't done what I do best (writing). It's an almost now or never situation as far as Gregory Corso poet goes, I think you know what I mean. I realize how much <u>time</u> I've truly wasted, yet if my health doesn't suddenly grab me with all those junkyard years and lay me low I should, as I say, enter the 1980s alive and well, with some works [that] all who like me can be happy about.

It's hard to make house messy. Lisa, Dutch, likes clean, yet never does she admonish me, ergo I try to keep as neat as possible. Bob Wilson of Phoenix has spread word about me to all manuscript buyers here.[267] Thus no one will buy what probably will be my finest book of poems. There's Max's future to consider, thus I will do best by him if I bequeath him my manuscripts.

So as you can gather, I'm okay and willing. In our long friendship I feel there's been glowing occasions worth the remembering, so don't regret my having been. Nobody's perfect it's said, and me, well, I'm still alive, and have love and I know that I'm always welcome at your door. Who knows but that if I stay clean [. . .] the Hope prose work might just make me kind of prosperous? Who knows but that I could well have a Corso Poetry Fund for the worthy needy? Anything can happen and oft does. *Basta*—be well, and, of course, think well.

Love, Gregory

To Allen Ginsberg Bologna, Italy [Oct. 1] 1979

Dear Al,

Am in Bologna, a beauty of a city. Saw Patti Smith[268] here and she took me, Max and Lisa on bus to Florence. She said I was king, and gave me her room, treated me nice. Julian [Beck][269] called, said you decided against reading with he and I. Too bad because I got three readings already set up, one in Ravenna, the others [in] Venice [and] Florence, and great certainties of Naples and Palermo. Great chance to see my homeland. You said you would like to read with me, especially if I was O.K. health-wise. I'm feeling great. Julian said you preferred Spring. Spring too late for me since I'd be back in Frisco, the cost to carry this bulk o'er the ocean again. Lisa and Max leave for Frisco October 5 [and] I go to Amsterdam and read the 6th. I'll be able to support myself and hopefully make some monies to send Lisa for to get a pad in Frisco.

My book is finally done! I feel you'll really like what I did with these poems of ten years. What a nice way to start off the 80's! Whatever, if you care not to do these readings with me (and Julian) [its] your choice. Just take care of yourself, for indeed I do love thee. [. . .]

Be wiser, love, Gregory

To James Laughlin San Francisco Dec. 22, 1979

Dear James,

Am back a week now, am looking for apartment, meanwhile staying with my lovely wife's mother and sister. I have a friend's place in which to work, that is, type, the major work as I have said to be done. I think perhaps I'd best send you poems every other day until we have the book. I feel that that process will help serve me best. As I type each day from my score of manuscripts, I will mail you the day's effort, keep for myself the Xerox. This process will enable me to send you the very best I have right at the start, and I will continue sending you the very best until I cease sending. That would indicate that I'm not necessarily out of "very bests" but that I would be less sure than I was to begin with, which means that at least I did send off the poems to you rather than holding them and holding them until I felt I had all the very best at hand, that would take years again, and like I said I would like my book out in 1980.

The readings in Europe really went over great, it took Allen by storm. He really was amazed and at [the] expense of him feeling that his poems were not as successful. I told him that was because he reads so often, that the poems become kind of tired for him but not for those who hear them. They being new to the new ear. We really read well together and he wants to do more of the same here in the states. Wonderful, but I told him it would be best if I had my book out already, then it would help ensure me an audience. New work, finally, after ten long years, the poems will show that I have not been sleeping for ten years, but working at my craft incessantly, plus making two lovely children.

I am in great health, had my blood computerized, cost $200 and nothing wrong with me, no bad liver, no bad nothing. [I] asked the doctor why, said to her that I hadn't been too considerate with mine flesh and blood, what with years of drinky-poo and dopey-poo. She said that I must have good genes. Well, it all goes to tell me not to over abuse, that is, don't depend too much upon goody genes. After all, all are just poor simple human bones. Boy o boy, is my son growing! and how he talks! and he is truly a delight to behold. He looks a lot like Caravaggio's Angel, the one in West Berlin museum. So I am yet a fortunate man, and I feel great about this batch of poesy. I know they be each one of them gems. That is what years of work brought about. In the past I hardly ever worked on what I had jotted down, this time I did, and I don't regret it, not even the long delay. The only sorrow being that some people wrote me asking to see my new work ere they die, and some had. But being I'm the one who doesn't believe life ends with death, all is okay.

Love, and good cheer, Gregory

▼ [Kaye McDonough, poet and writer, whose book *Zelda* was published by City Lights in 1978 met Corso around this time in San Francisco. They lived and traveled together until she gave birth to Corso's last child, Nile.]

To Allen Ginsberg

Paris
Dec. 4, 1983

Al,

A fast, loving note to you dearest of friends. Since 1965 something happened to our friendship. I don't know if you can remember that time in Paris, at Whitman's bookstore. You were off to America, I was staying. I was once known to be a charming fellow, after Albert Hall, *Mutation of the Spirit*, people shied from me. Bereft of poetry, I am nothing. Indeed without my great store of beauty, I am worse than pitiful, I am like some monster thing, a fool with a face looking like a pile of shit. Ugliness becomes me not, dear friend. So the filthy nurse, heroin, helped me die for a respite. Then came my beloved son Max Orphe. Hark the awful redundancy. His mother drops him age one, my mother same shit. I run up to farm, junk sick, I kick cold. I clean his ass, I feed him, I had to watch him every waking second, I did not sleep for two weeks. Frazzle! I had to make it! My father put me in the dark rooms of seven or eight foster mothers. I can be an arrogant tough fucker, as you know, so I mothered that boy. And while Orlovsky planted his baby trees, I raised a baby. His trees died, my baby is as beautiful as his father was when a child. And debonair he be. And loved! Lisa and her mother are devoted to Max. He's theirs! And anytime I wish to take him on a trip, like say to Santa Fe to see his sister (Belle's) I'm daddy! So I feel my son saved me from total demolition.

The methadone program in New York sucks—they treat you like a convict. And especially the one in Queens, a supposed "poet" runs it. Comes along L. B., his friend. She offers me the world if only I allow her to love me. Me I don't have to love her. That was her offer. I asked for money for dope, she gladly complied. Thus began my biggest habit, and most hellish nightmare of my life. Remember when you came over I whispered to you, "Al, I'm in hell." But I lost you twenty years ago. You couldn't help me, no one could have. I'd sit on that couch day after day for six months. Every morning copping $100 worth of dope. I'd wake up sick, that was when she'd say, "Gregory let's talk." I cried that I was in pain, that I needed a shot—fast. She says, "I don't want to give you money to hurt yourself. Haven't you anything to sell?" "Yes, I've my manuscripts, ten note books, and all my papers of *The Golden Dot.* "Well, my son loves your poetry—he'd buy your manuscripts." Bullshit, she no fool, knew that if I didn't get any money for my habit I'd leave her. So she buys each day a book, then all my papers. Then the bomb fell! She like all poets whose ambitions are worse than Hollywoodians, starts bitching about my never offering to read with her. This she demands, always in the morn before the obtaining of what was now a medicine. The junk was yuk, no high, no relief or reward for having sold the spirit of the muse. Every morn I am ill, and the danger! Cops all over the place. Rivington Street is infamous! I told her, "Look, let me buy enough for a week, one of these days I'm gonna get busted!!!" She knows that her hold over me will loosen if I have enough for a weeks supply. She'd have me write notes saying, I was her boyfriend and that I felt she was the best chick poet I ever met! And I grant you some of her poems are good. It appeared that I was living like a king! I did three paintings for a watch, which she got back. Either I was a very ill man, or desirous of death. There was no love.

My son was in California. Kaye, my true love, came to New York because I begged her to free me from myself. She couldn't support my $250 a day habit.

I decided to put myself in Bernstein Hospital to kick. She, L., said I was lying, that now that I sold all my manuscripts I was going to run back to Kaye in S.F. Then all hell broke loose! She said she bought manuscripts. Said I was a bum living off old books of poetry. I can't recall the worst, all I know is I grabbed all my new poems and threw them down the incinerator. Then I begged her to please drive me to N.Y.C. and leave me. She said she had no money for gas. I suddenly got scared, I really thought I was going to kill her. I begged for bus fare, no money. Then a blessedness showered the little orphan boy whose love was murdered age one. I phoned Kaye's father in N.Y. asking him to please pay a cab from New Jersey to his N.Y.C. apt. He tells me Kaye is with him, that she's all packed to leave for Amsterdam in five hours! The rest is beautiful history, we are together and very much in love .

I'm a strong man, in good shape, down to fifteen mil of methadone a day. Bill takes 60. So I can dwindle down to zero in a month or less. I was very upset with you because I felt you no longer loved me like the brother I always felt you were. I'd get pissed when I'd hear that you told people, "Poor Gregory, what am I to do with him?" Or like you grabbing a glass of wine away. Like at Yoko Ono's yelling at me, angrily telling me if I fucked up on stage at Passim's[270] you'd kick me off. And all I did was be on my best behavior! What hurt was, you did it in front of strangers. So I guess that's why I put you down a la *Herald Tribune*, etc. picking on your Buddhism of all things! Forgive me that, Al. I wish I had a Godly path to embark upon.

Yes, that's it—remember I used to believe in God? It was when I rid myself of God I rid myself of all that was worthwhile in life. How empty life is when the great void filler, Monsieur Absolute is evicted from one's spirit. There's hope for me, Al. I feel I've a good sense of Godness, of life, of meaningfulness. I mean what good my son if God were black? I tell him God is all that is good and beautiful. It's what I feel. What need have I of faith? A poet for almost 40 years knows a few things by jingo. Life is beautiful, bad, ugly, wondrous, mysterious, poetic, strange, violent, sunny, ad infinitum, just like me.

I never lied to you. When I took your book manuscripts I told you.[271] I paid heavily for that fuck-up. People hold that against me quite meanly. Granted it was a shitty thing to do, but that's all I ever did real bad to you. Also will you please clear up people's heads about our sex life? That creep H. [. . .] tells people at S.F. parties that we were lovers until Peter came along. All I remember, sex with the young man I loved like a brother, was when I came home all bloodied having had a fight with a black man, my prison experiences were such that any black who'd order me about would have a tiger in his midst. So I came home bloodied and sad that I had struck a man. I could have blinded him! I broke the beer glass in my hand and smashed it in his face?

I was due for death, he screamed Geronimo! And came after me. The Minetta Tavern knew my uncle Rocky, so the bartender saved me. The next day I go to Washington Square Park, brave me! Yuk—I go looking for him and him big black book mine friend, and tough ex-con talking to me is a pip-squeak. I see him with three other blacks, his face is bandaged in about ten places. Thank God his eyes were okay. I go up to him and put out my hand. "Sorry, man, but I just got outa prison, and let me tell you the blacks were very hard on me. The police and white law was hard on them, so it's all a fuck-up. I'm a poet. I don't like hurting people. I'm real sorry. Can I buy a lunch or something?" That's the best I can recall. Anyway, let's get back to that night. I was bloody and in tears, you get angry at me for doing such a thing. You helped wash the glass from my hand. I couldn't stop crying, you came on like big papa. You took me to bed and sucked my dick, then you tried to ram your dick up my ass. I thought you were being sweet and kind to me. A big trauma just happened me. I didn't get a hard on. Your dick was fat and limp and my virgin asshole suddenly realized your sweetness, kindness, was a sneaky fagotty trap! There was me, poor me, all bloodied and crying, and all you could feel was sex! Al, I love you and you are one tough son of a bitch! If ever I wanted a man, it'd have been you. And had you fucked me, I'd consider it an honor, not something shameful. You were my first great friend in life. I had no body. I was never loved. You loved me. Can't you realize how life suddenly became a pleasure to live? Damn it! I imagine if I were your lover, today I'd be rich, all the poetry readings would have been you and I. The farm, mine! Your undying love, mine!

Anyway, that's all I remember about our love life. If you remember anything else, pray enlighten me. I'm a 53 year old man. I don't give a fuck what people think, all I care about is *veritas*. Ah, Allen, Allen, what 's life, eh, what? How fortunate we were blessed with poesy. If there were no you I'd be scared, two fine poets are better than one. As I oft tell thee you're [the] only poet I respect and feel peer to. As a poet (human being) I feel I fucked up a lot, the memories are sad. But I got time, don't I?

Without the gentle love of the ladies: Hope, Belle, Lisa, Kaye, I'd be the most lonely miserable human spirit in all Galaxies. So I ask forgiveness for all my dopey troubles, as I forgive you, your yenta heart laid bare. [. . .] Soon Bill will hit the big 7-0, you the 6-0. Everyone's gonna write something for the occasion, my shot on you shall apothegm thee.[272] Good, all the more to spook you by.

See how nice I can be? But can I be trusted? Can I be a constant? Would you buy me a home if I weren't a poet? Is there an old poets home?

Love, G.

▼ [After Corso's repeated requests for money for his book, *The Golden Dot,* the editor at New Directions, Griselda Ohannessian sent back a short letter to Corso telling him that he had "scraped the barrel dry" and suggesting that a new book would be just the thing to refill the coffers. Her sentence, "Seems to me now that it was a waste of what cash you had to toot off to Europe and come back to the same old story," no doubt angered him. She referred to him affectionately as her "Peck's Bad Boy."]

To Griselda Ohannessian San Francisco

Feb. 6, 1984

Love,

For the life of me I cannot understand this letter. When I phoned it was not for the asking of monies but to herald the coming of my fourth child by my Kaye. She be three months pregnant, made in Paris, city of love, wherein I wrote 13 love poems. Know that I was never in the habit of rushing a book out and what with such a doomy presumptuous title as *Golden Dot*, I feel I had better have that dot golden. I am not a lazy man when it comes to poesy, I take exact care even though the poems may appear dashed off. Know that I am well into the volume, one that I wish to be happy about. Once printed that's the ballgame, and it is in me to hit homeruns, indeed.

I am sorry that I appear to be what you deem me to be. I am in good health, taking care; no fool am I, if anything I'm the fake-fool. Just hold in there with me. I want very much to come out of this heavy task, poetry, a blessed gift given me wholly perfect. I will dot this one, for sure. Every night I tailor a poem to fit exact where mine spirit stands old of raiment. You'll see, for indeed have I yet to fail? A fuck-up I am, granted, your Peck's Bad Boy number. Yet I blast the ear with each stitch of the cloth, this I feel profoundly. Soon it shall go to the presser, I make life. Life is all I know, not death. When doling on that subject I only seek to learn how it can lessen the pain and sorrow people feel towards it. Mine is an honorable quest. I do not, know not, to try to explain the non-existent unknowables. James [Laughlin] would not have held such faith in me were I stuck so. So be of good cheer towards me, know that I am not ill-fated; that I do, like I say, fuck-up at times, yet out of it all, I feel goodness on my side, that I am a good man, and that I shall be that poet I believe myself to be. Neither major nor minor, just a poet who has written and will write, both major and minor.

No, that monies was not wasted. I am cured, and have created another life asked for. That night when I lay with her, she 40, she never having had a child, wanting one desperately. So it was to be, just like my other three. They were asked for. I wrote down the date, November 11, 1983, that very morn. I tell you the Gods are with me, so not to worry, angel, not to worry.

Love, Gregory "Peck"

To Griselda Obannessian San Francisco
Nov. 16, 1984

Dear Griselda,

[. . .] I've a lovely three month old son and he's indeed a gift from the Gods that be; never question a divine gift, just make good use of it, right? Maybe he'll become a seal trainer and support me in my old age. Just received card from Allen in China, he says the Chinese students understand my verses though they regard humor with great profundity. Allen is the most beneficial poet unto poets and those of poetic soul. If anyone is deserved of the Noble Prize, he by Augustan right is. Me, I'm another story, I have to be me, else who'll keep the hectic honest? If I'm to be credited with anything let it be my steadfast obstinate tumbling sojourn in *Till Eulenspiegels* fashion, meaning no harm to others or self; like Catullus saith: the true poet needs only be chaste unto himself, his poems are free to be otherwise. Me, I'm the opposite; a pop of haywire springs in a body struggling to be of chaste sensibility, writes poems under the banner of goodness, light, righteousness.

The *Golden Dot* means, and the book will make it clear to all, that all my poems since poem day one unto this book to come, is a serial of a life—an autobiography as it were—of a poet named Gregorio Nunzio Corso. When I put the dot to it, I'll have my *Paterson*, my *Canto*,[273] my epic. I knew that was my fate, to follow Calliope,[274] yes, and the *Golden Dot* will fill in all the important gaps. [. . .] There are three occasions of events in a being's life. There's the here and now, awake. There's sleep, dream. And there's imagination: daydream, fancy, thinking, surrealing, poetrying, illumination, creating. And where cometh vision, apparition, hallucination? Well, drugs for hallucination. I'm hard pressed to depict where from vision. I know I had one big one in life, and I was not drugged, not drunk, not asleep, and aged 20, my head was well with me. As a child I saw things, but children are susceptible; dreams are a wonder. I saw Paris before I ever went there; saw the Eiffel tower, the streets, etc., great architecture builds the dreaming mind. So if my poems bespeak of here and now events, or dreams, or imagines; all are of me, ergo all be autobio.

I see now why people write to James asking when my next book; it's like a serial, they want to know what happens next. Will I make it; will I die; will I be saved, will I see God, will I answer death; will I write a great poem already? Ha! Seriously, as I grew and grow, so do my produce. [. . .] I've written some outlines on how I wish to present *Golden Dot*; my venturing to poem those occurrences that so marked my life, indelibly, unforgettable; by poetry to portray what makes me tick, what I feel myself to be, to ask "Who am I?" then answer who I am. All will be worthwhile. It benefits another to see, to learn something about themselves, for surely if I learn then they'll learn. Poetry is more than portraiting the poet; though there be no one like you or me in life, each of us select and unique like a fingerprint, are nonetheless a common lot. Language binds us; emotions emit from likewise two stimuli. Nobody's too far apart—revelations that might be in store, who knows?

It's early Sunday morn, my son is talking to his mother; and I'm talking to myself via you. I'll see if I can find my other notes on *Golden Dot*, my plans for it; since I do have all the poems, what's needed is the format; I want to do something new; and consider, no autobio has death make the dot.

Please send my apologies to James and his wife for not appearing at their visit to City Lights. When the frenzied wanta-be-published poets heard he was coming they piled me with their manuscript to hand to him. I told them all to go stand under Pegasus's ass and leave me alone. So I thought it best to stay clear—though I did want to see James, and his wife, who was kind to me, who I don't think I ever met. Oh, well, there's yet time.

Most disobediently yours, Gregory Gregory

▼ [Allen Ginsberg was constantly trying to hook his friends up with lucrative deals. He and Hanuman Press editor, Raymond Foye, were acquainted with the contemporary Italian painter, Sandro Chia, and they suggested that an expensive art and poetry collaboration with Chia and Corso might be interesting and profitable.]

To Allen Ginsberg and Sandro Chia San Francisco

Nov. 8, 1985

Dear Allen and Sandro,

During my haphazard lifetime I've know both the high and lows. The highs I took for granted like water. The penalty of hubris unbeknownst to me began to pile up, the avalanche would come when I no longer had youthful arrogance to dam the flow; the time came for payment all at once. I no longer had the up from the down in me. I found myself overwhelmed, unable to call out for help. Those that would come to my aid, my oldest and dearest of friends and loves, all had been burned out. The band of drug addiction tired my loved ones, even beauty became a tired beauty. These past three months, what with the loss of my beloved Kaye and our year old boy broke me. I found myself locked in an old nightmare, a fallen soul on the street I feared to fall on. Grant Street of North Beach, birthplace of beatnikry. I, one of the major Beats, open to humiliation and danger. I'd drink to drown, drunk and out of control, my head was witnessed hanging off the curb of Grant and Green, a booted foot kicking it, over and over.

In the past I would call the only one I knew to call, not my beloved Kaye, not my 21 year old daughter, but Allen, my older brother in life. But somehow something stayed the budge of my heart's cry for help—I thought best to depart, just up and walk away without aim or direction, walk until I'd collapse. I once did such as a runaway child, I got caught and was sent back "home." Being 55 and a mite less strong than I used to be, the world and me finally became a wearied of each other. Death seemed a mercy. The pain of it was the incompletion of my devotion to the only good thing that blest me in life—my poetry. For the past three months I've been living on miserable people's miserable floors. Not one hour was I able to snatch that I might vie for completion of what I feel to be my best book, my *Golden Dot*. Then strange of strange! As I headed toward that aimless trek, I stopped at lawyer friend's office to advise him to see to it that my son Max receive all my papers and whatever future royalties the years might insure. He informs me that you, Allen, were trying to reach me. I asked him if he knew why and he said no. I asked him if he told you of my miserable lot, he said no, though he suggested I ask you for assistance. I told him I had about depleted any further extension of the hand of friend. Then emotional me cried, wailing that if it were Kerouac, Bill, or Allen, plighted so, I'd rush to save my friend, no matter what sad occasions of past. I promised to return your call, I tried for three days.

Then I get a letter from a 32 year old Minnesota nurse, mother of four, straight as an arrow, saying she was my daughter, and I remembered having known (biblically) her mother in L.A. in 1952. One knowing and month later she tells me she's pregnant and that she'll give baby to rich couple, childless, assuring it a fortunate future. I agreed, and signed a paper. Well, she, Sheri [Langerman], says 16 years ago she went thru her mother's papers, and saw my name on telltale paper. She never thought to connect the G. Corso she read in school with the G. Corso on paper. She said she contacted ten or more G. Corso's, and all said they have tons of my mail. Her letter to me reached me on that desperate day of decision getting away from North Beach at all costs. She came for two days, I hid not my downfallen state. [I] told her it was more important she find her father, than I finding her, as I have children, she only one father. That were she my mother, then that would have been something. Whatever, she couldn't help me, I couldn't ask for it, were she able. All it succeeded in doing was make me more miserable. [. . .]

I reasoned that all my fuck-ups came when drunk or in need of a fix. That sober and on the methadone, I was a good man, one who felt that thru his God-given gift of poetry could benefit the great pain of life. I reasoned that Christ wasn't the only one who suffered the hurt of life, that all, most all of us, suffer, and that the best one could hope for was the understanding of another. I had finally become humbled, I stopped in my tracks toward nowhere and hurried back to my poems. I would use the library. I would finish my book. Screw the

"Golden" I admonished, put the "Dot" to it. At least that, or surely as owls be owls there be a hell for poets who dock with insufficient cargo.

And fate of fates! O joy! O good, good life and friends. My true dear friend whom I so Judased. I went back to lawyer to retrieve my poems and his words turned my sky of stone back to that great expanse of air, breath in Latin, breath be spirit. "Gregory, Allen says [Sandro] Chia would like to work with you, that you should come to New York, he'll see to it you'll have a place to stay, a respite is offered you." I held back my tears, I smiled that weak smile of mine. I knew that 55 years of poetness just couldn't go down the tubes just like that, that what I have can't wait another 55 years for some one else to replace it. So I made a trembling vow there unto myself, vowing to work for whatever is bestowed me, vowing to never needle again, to take my Darvon's and Valiums to see me thru methadone withdrawal. That I shan't burden thus drag you timely uplifters with my sickness. That I finally be mature, that all I ask is have faith in me. Aye, for I swear it all seems as though I were given a reprieve of sorts.

I have nothing, Allen and Sandro. What I've lost I can, if I keep true, quite possibly regain. My Kaye and son, my Allen, and my Muse's love. All I ask is to be alone and at peace with myself. My goal is to regain whatever health I've lost, and whatever time wasted. My *Golden Dot* will aright me with those who've held to me all these past terrible years. Gentlemen, that I grow to become 70, I would love to have the coming fifteen years be years of fond memories. You've extended your hand to me, I humbly grasp it.

Love, Gregorio Nunzio Corso

It's lonely when there's no God to go to, yet far lonelier when there's no friend to commiserate with. I miss your friendship terribly so.

▼ [Corso learned that his old friend Peggy Biderman was dying of cancer, and he began writing one of his lengthy confessional letters to her.]

To Peggy Biderman

New York City
Nov. 3-5, 1990

Only yesterday I wrote after having had another dream of Kerouac, how beautiful his nightly visits, beautiful because he was beautiful, and that thought saddened me. Me thinking myself not so beautiful, that who'll dream me with such claim? I chalk it up, this mean-spiritedness in my life, to having had a loveless childhood, stunted at six, so behaviorists say. Deep inside me I know I'm essentially beautiful, and proof of it is in your claim of it in me—as soon as I get a batch of monies I'll come out there. I've some things in the fire of hope, miss Max, miss you, Lisa, ah, my good Lisa, how I saddened such a nice bond. She truly loved me. Blind me took it for granted, thinking I'd be loved forever. Terrible it is to be a dumb poet, for poet I am, this I know. What I did not know was poet don't mean nerewithal without the smarts of love. So in a sense I've failed. I don't believe in hell but I do feel you pays for your inexcusable ignorance—in a way, like you, I too am dying. The spirit does show signs of getting better, but how so little time there really is. You, you need no time to cure an ailing spirit, the strength of yours is what's keeping you going. I know now what salvation means. I can, I pray, I hope, I know, I can get over this soul-sick and when comes my time to unform I shan't unform so pointedly lost. O I wish to be so lucid on this. You see, my feeling about death is quite childish, first the fear of the hurt and the unknown. Second, the belief that there's no such thing as death a la finality, but that of change, because I am not my name, given me, I am not my looks because I don't look like yesterday nor will tomorrow, so neither name nor looks, how describe me? The measure to a friend or a simple acquaintance could well be the personal history of one, of one's unity of being, of one's acts of behavior, of the good, the harm, done. Am I but memory named and fleshed? [. . .]

I write letters, then re-read them, and tell myself, this you don't throw away. I write letters often, but never post them. Lost? It's because of that lostness I spoke about, having contact with no one, having no loved one to confide to; but I'm a grown man am I not? There's no time for self-condescension. Let it flow, open the heart, and pray it lightens yours, my dear old friend. I wish I was God, all powerful, come take you, buy you an Eskimo coat, and take a trip on a luxury liner along the coast of Queen Maud, way up there, warm in the arctic in our warmth. Or not even a god, but a rich man, hire a plane and go. You ask if I yet loved Greece, Vermeer? There'll always be someone to romantically love them. No, not really as much as I used to, all has grown thin, life has but few rare gems, and I've paid homage to them all. Only a woman can be loved forever—unlike Greece, Vermeer, who cannot return such love. [. . .]

I have a new nice book of poems ready, all I need do is type em up; and that, that can take years. Once I write the poem, what's the rush? Would you believe it, after re-reading Whitman, I see that I'm more in line in heart and flow [with him] than the claimer heirs who merely do the long line. Oscar Wilde went to visit him [Whitman], when he came to the States, and Wilde never wrote of what they spoke. Only that old Walt's private room was filled with stacks of reviews of his book. All Walt said of him was, "I like that Mr. Wilde."

Imagine, in the beginning Mesopotamia, today USA and Mesopotamia.[275] Beware Shamash, Tiamat, Bel, Marduk![276] Heavy Gods them. If war comes it'll only mean dead bodies in the sands that blanket the resting oil like bedcovers a child; what legacy the dinosaur has left us; and the fern that once bloomed there—well, what has the world to look forward to? In the past, the heroics of war; war doth regenerate, but at what price? We'll be leaving a world that hasn't changed much; that there could well be faint chance it'll never really change, then maybe we'll evolve into choosers of our destiny on this planet; like making no more babies (fodder) for war. If the time chances an Adam-Omega, surely by select intelligence, choice, there'll be an Eve-Alpha, and together start the human business all over again anew; with no expulsion this time, with foreknowledge of beingness, with gentle nature, and all such etc. blessed wished for things—there's so much, and then, so zero, just here one hundred years and gone eternally. [. . .]

Miserable street walk with Bob Rosenthal (we stayed with him in Chicago when I read at theatre calling all Chicagoans dumb! Recall?), he alright, but the sounds, zounds! Fire engines, ambulances, drills, and thought of you, thought of you and he, Rosenthal telling me the woes of Peter and Allen, the love what was made in heaven. What yuk. Allen's romance always did have a cold humorless straightness to it. I mean he never loved a faggot, so what does he do? He gets a straight guy like Orlovsky, keeps him by getting him girls. Peter obliges by giving himself to Allen. Just bring on the [good] times, the farms, the girls, the power, the whole scene. Disgusting, because now Peter is in looney bin and Allen is complaining, telling people how sad he is because of Peter's condition, what a cunt Ginsberg be. When I consider how dopey I was ever to confide in that loud mouth, when I think that one time Lisa and I spent but one night in his house (I'm truly hurt by him). He next day on phone screaming to people, "I've got Corso and his wife and child to care for!" One day! But he told the world! The creep. He loves but himself true, he needs love, he always told me he just needs love and then he'll reward the world by saving it. How sad, sad that I see it all so. Now Peter is in nut house, maybe a year, and Allen is seeking sympathy. The fool, didn't he know the ego of souls? That he bringing Peter on stage as poet, lover boy, Peter had to be at least poet, and face it, Peter's poetry is the best any human being can innocently do; which is saying a lot, like so what, people write poetry. Allen's lover boy writes, gee whiz, while all the while in the dark shade of the stages hovers Allen to whom all have come to see and hear. The joke is it could seem he replaced me with Peter. Thank Zeus at least I know what's poetry to be poet. What a finality, Peter in Looney bin, Allen flying jetting about with his tired word; it's over, love, over and sad, well Vincent [van] Gogh didn't have it as fine as he. I bet in 50 years he'll be read but not inspirational. Not like his love Walt [Whitman], and even Walt today is silent in the leaves. When I lost Lisa and with her Max, I wildly got Kaye and Nile and when I lost them I cried. I finally realized that life wasn't every day. Had all, lost all, so when in Rome, recall

I told you earlier I lost something there? I receive these countless letters from Al about Peter, his woe about Peter. I write one back, truly heartfelt and broken, about my losses, and he replies "Stop being such a cry baby!"

That told me I had no one, no one to connect with, give soul hurt talk to. Whatever, thus am I truly alone. I thought Ginsy might hold, not cash in his chips, because he I knew longest, he had better sense, so I thought, and perhaps, perhaps he saw that note, I was asked to write something for his sixtieth year. A book celebrating him.[277] I wrote [that] I wish it were he and not Kerouac had died. Of course, I never sent it, but I kept it in my suitcase at Naropa. He gets someone there to Xerox my papers because of my losing things so oft. Perhaps he read said note. Wow, well, what a hurt indeed! Still, it were not meant for him or anyone but the sadness of my friendship in life. [. . .]

Alene Lee is dying.[278] Yep. Yup. She too cancerian kind. She who broke the heart of Kerouac and me just because I wuz just outa jail and never got laid and laid her and wow, *Subterraneans,* that book that has me like a creep who fucked his best friend's girl. I didn't know Jack well then, that is a sadness, indeed. Future folk think I fucked my best friend's girl. I met them together. Jack and I became friends afterwards. Why I wrote a twenty-two page letter to him telling him of its untruth, plus he ends *Subterraneans* killing me yet! I saved him there, told him don't want to kill no Gregory. My God—I'll never write a biography, so the only way I'm gonna set things aright is by letter writing. [. . .]

Went to see *Goodfellas,* wop mafia ignorant Ginszo pain hurt and hardheadedness, true to such false life. Glad when I left prison I made friends with Bohemians, not hoods. Can't bear dumb talk. Even in prison, the hoods I knew were the head guys, with the smarts. The pic I'm in *Godfather 3*[279], for all I know I could end up on cutting room floor, a tragic business that. Everybody expecting to see Gregory come on [as an] unruly stockholder. Still I got a million lira a day, for four days. He, Coppola, knew I was broke so maybe he was just aiding me, he does that for people, helps them, good heart. But I did give my best, even Al Pacino said I was a natural. They'd blow it leaving me on cutting room floor; the poet can enhance magically the film. Well, I'll wait and see [. . .] Hate to think of Max going and waiting to see his dad and sees no dad. See my problems? And that's only on the blind side. I got all these kids I love and only hear from Max; the mothers forgot me; Kaye the worst never tells me about Nile. I did them no harm, indeed gave her a joy to get old with. [. . .]

Belle, I love like I love Hope. Sally, no love there. Joss [Jocelyn], no, it be Max. Kaye, Kaye saw her doomed father in me, spooky, she believes she got her wishful insight. Thus she takes from me what they took from him. I can only hope she speaks truth of me to Nile; I did not monstrous wrong. It was the wrong they deemed me capable of, so to spare me such horror, regret, etc., the flee to Egypt. Many you see, was *deja vu,* my mother left me, his mother leaves him. Thanks [to] Lisa and her mom, he suffered not my fate, no can love Joss for that. Can't love Kaye for her selfishness, her assuring herself she did the right thing. Not once having the kid [write] a holiday card, "Hi Dad!" Not one sign, guess she would it so, and I comply, I leave them alone though it breaks my heart, though they reverse it saying "See, he doesn't care!". How care? I've no address of them, no phone. They have mine. Belle same way. I never went to see them, for it would have been a bother to her, though not for my beloved Cybelle. She's 19 and what I hear saddens the heart; her ex, Godfrey something, made film on Hopi Indian Hokosanni. Met him in Rome, and he tells me she's like a child, and innocent angel. Her being denied me hasn't softened her to whatever hardness this hard life will come truthing down upon her. As for Miranda, gone, too far gone, 25, she's her mother, not likeful of me, hardly know the girl but mother sure made a dire beatnik bum out of me to her. I hurt to see her. I see the mother. I hope Kaye has better sense—and to think it was I who asked for the lives of these children. They are not accidents. Now you see why Max is my true heir. Besides the girls and Nile are of well-off mothers. What confusion, only occasionally Max writes. [. . .]

Just came from street, where I been thinking, that recent time in Rome where I went through something, a change, a kind of death. And I'll let you in on it because it be both physical and spiritual—but before that I'm gonna write an interlude to Allen Ginsberg. I could do it on a different paper, but I want you in it, I want the whole shoot in it. All you gotta do is make sure one day he sees it, if he dies before you, better maybe he don't, then he'll probably deny me the pittance I beg from him. Here he calleth me greatest poet, and yet grants thousands to lessers, though they be gay and not in drug need.[280] Hah, Jack Smith[281] yet druggie, no he'll then excuse it by saying he gets grants a la [American Academy of] Arts and Letters. No, last one came from Jean Stein, she told me he had nothing to do with it, though he acted as though. He cleans up on money by photos of me, nude, sold in postcard stores, I don't get the price of a fig leaf. He forgets I was one of the big four. He snuck his lover boy made in heaven in, Peter got the monies; Jack was set, Bill too, but not me. I just wrote poetry and you and he knoweth poetry don't make for a family man, me so silly wanting to be one. I could have been it for him, Al, cause Peter couldn't give him, but no, I give it to you, to you I can give soul to. He no, he so hung on his, that truly hurt. Recall all those letters I said I got in Rome about his plight with beloved Peter? And me writing only once because I truly felt I was dying in Rome. I wrote him what was to be this kind of letter; but only two pages. He writes back, "Don't be such a big cry baby." Loss of all my children, and their mothers three of whom I loved, kids all. See, I don't want to have to set me down and write to him. I just don't anymore. I'd rather it here, you be my lovely ear, understander, relater, vault of all I feel gypped out of, of all the untruths, since surely I'll never write the autobio. [. . .]

Love, Gregory

▼ [For the last decade of his life, Corso lived with old friends, Roger and Irvyne Richards on Horatio Street in Greenwich Village. Richards was a rare book dealer whose shop had been frequented by Corso and other Beat writers in the early 1980s. Around this time Corso came under the care of a patron, Hiro Yamagata, a wealthy Japanese artist who had been deeply influenced by the writings of Beats. He provided a monthly stipend that helped support Corso.]

To Allen Ginsberg New York
[May 1] 1992

Dear oldest and firstest poet and truer brother than mine own blood-fleshed one,

Here it is: this be poet speaking, thus no lie, no bullshit, no sudden decision, sober as the settled dust round the bones of Errol Flynn. It shall be the old that'll have dreams, the young visions, no? I dream much Allen, the unforgettable ones are worthy of remembrance. Dreamed I was in a room not mine, I screamed a cry that sent Irvyne running to me. "Gregory, you all right?" she asked—I WAS STILL DREAMING! "They're all on the roof," I told her. "Allen, Bill, Jack, Peter, my children and their mothers, my growling father, my holier than thou brother, and others. None of them are looking at me!" I cried. "Gregory are you okay?" Gradually my room became noticeable, her voice undream sounding. "O Irvyne, it's you! and I'm back in my room!" "You were crying in your sleep, now, go back to sleep." I told her I was sorry, and that was that.

I [know] what to make of it, all my rooms are alien, I cannot communicate with my loved ones, not that they are deaf or cashed in of chips. You dear friend wish to help me, and yes, as the years pass, and illness is ever so nigh, I had better lay bare what I wish to do, complete. And life, finally I have in steady hold—death awaits the drug router, "death follows like a loyal dog." Twenty mil of methadone a day would relax this tired heart. I know I can get it in Rome in the Vatican, they know me. From thence I may travel. Here I love not, the drug program wracks the spirit, I'm looked upon as Mr. Shit here, here where the arbiters of morality replaceth the dope dealer. In Rome, I'm Professor Corso, a good but screwed-up man of creation. If only I could have a minutes time of Moses' God. I'd have opened the hearts that hold the key that opens the door to the American Academy there. I have my book, *DOT*,[282] all ready to tailor and the final draft my Singer machine, the typewriter. Stitch together the words of our beloved language and voice the poetic spirit the finest cloth, too, as befits our good birther, momma muse, the raiment a-swaddle, the new born, the babe, as is called poem.

This be my first true heart letter to you in eons; don't carry the Judas of my having seen a skinless light, claiming Bill saw it but not yet you. I need accept methadone, I tried 28 hellish days, need accept my illness-self-esteem. Can't die a junkie. I've no leisure to be cocooned in drugdom, my work is not yet done. True, a few good poems deems a poet undeniable, yet my task is the poem human. I so feared reality I refused to enroll in its university; what the surer; the drunk dreamer in life or the sober realist in dream? Gotta get weaned off the illusory teat of motherlessness and birth myself; all the estranged years with you denied me the understanding ear I so needed, so lacked. I cursed you for changing, growing up, your attainment of manhood. The clown lost his trickster; the world snatched you up; you became just another abandonment. This olding face and body is merely a stunted orphan, crying for a love full grown. [. . .] Orphaned, divorce of families, bereft of dearest friend, Godless, there had to be a way other than suicide.

One day it'll be too late; the circle of loved ones shrinks into a dot. I ask not for much; I am not afflicted with a deathly ill; I can travel, settle, and work; again I'm not at leisure to die. NYC is no longer for me, there's Rome, the hospital will not deny me my medicine. Drugs are rare, too expensive, and truly I'm wearied of 'em. If only Hiro [Yamagata] could grant me a year or less in Rome. I've so much work to do; as of now I'm doing a series of drawings of Edgar Allen Poe, pure imagination; I've my *DOT* to stamp fini; I know I can get a show of my water colors.

I know no labor but that of art. Love, I haven't held a human being since Kaye fled with my Nile. Whether you believe it or no we were on the best of terms. She saw her alcoholic father in me, true, I was a mess, the horrid need. So perhaps her decision was correct, yet some show of compassion is due me, a letter, a photo. I hear nothing about my little boy. There's so much to do, with my other three, but I am not summoned so I let it be, leave them in peace. Only Max holds near and dear.

In the '40s you, Jack, Huncke, Bill saw from your Hector's[283] windowed perch, and teenster, me. I left that scene 1947 to do Dannemora [prison]. Too bad for quirks of fate, you could have grabbed hold of me—was my desperate turf—1942, 43, 44, 45, 46—that gap, 1947 to 50, served as my prep-school; blest be that respite 1950 to 54 dear old romantic Greenwich Village, you, Jack; then Harvard and back to you, Jack and heavy duty Bill.

I cannot seem to measure time, world after world is soon gone. Biographies say the same bullshit. Stuff I oft incorrectly informed, but never said I,

"Randall Jarrell taught me most I know." What a joke! Bigger joke, that I nigh loved his verse, [*The Death of* the] *Ball-Turret Gunner* okay, but *basta*! Music, you and Hope gave me. Introductions to some poets, you. Philosophy, Harvard deans and students allowed; nobody gave me you but me. Jack and Bill were choices of taste, I got good taste. Peter took me a length, then I awoke to his profound simplicity. There wasn't much I missed. As for me, truly, I never cared to be the choice of anybody. I knew poet I was, what to deter me? Calabrian hard head, *testa dura*, me knew me, that's why swearing never to be a hypocrite allotted myself, of all peoples, the least love. This truncation was not yet fit for the love I know I can quite wisely give. Well, that you know; you must have thought me blind or a retard or doomed hopeless. I couldn't understand how you could respect the poetry and not the poet, since, for me, both were inseparable.

I asked Hiro, "Why?" "Because I like your poetry," said he. Perhaps I shall write to him, tell him I'm incurable, but not a bottomless pit. That I can live where drugs are rare and where the hospital doctors allot me methadone without having me bark like a dog. Tell him, true, that my drinking is seldom, a beer here, a beer there. The Hazeldon[284] medical report has it, heavy drink fortifies the red cell army, leaving the white cell battlefield defensively weak. Ah, Allen, why war? Our own bodies are at battle since birth. Many enemies hath our fleshedness. [. . .]

Jack doesn't know how to sneak outa heaven and hip us to what's a-foot. No denying transportation; five times have I seen him, spoke to him, via dream transport. [. . .]

Bull, I love this span called life. I love my kids, and that damned father of mine, so loveth he I and I'm not playing it safe; told you, opposite of poesy is hypocrisy.

Gregory

To Allen Ginsberg

New York
Sept. 17, 1992

[. . .] Poems are complete, all is needed is the "tailoring" final draft, should take three weeks most, that is if I do not have to be ill one day, well the next, ill, well, etc. I have a $100 per day habit. When I have nothing, a bag will ease the pain, but the fear of the oncoming need is part of the daily horror. I will venture to cut down, $100 for three weeks comes to $2,100. After that, I will put myself in detox, which is available at Smithers, then Hazeldon [Drug Treatment Center] if Peter [Orlovsky] is accepted. As I understand it, Hazel will take alcoholic but not dual diagnosis. No sense swearing to you that this is it, but my options and life grow shorter. I am, believe it or no, a fighter.

If you have doubts, I'll ask sweet Nikolas to occasionally look in on me, or phone. I don't have to go to street to get stuff, it's brought to me by a guy who likes my poetry. The poems I complete each day will be Xeroxed and sent to you, thus to insure my fruits of labor. This is the straightest I can be. I see no other way out for me, at least I'll have my book done. This sounds like the most sensible plan to me. All I am on is heroin, I cannot take cocaine. I'll call G. and find out if I can detox with him or face the fact that I'll be on methadone rest of my life. Can't work on methadone, it drives me to boredom, thus drink. I can't swear to you; can only pray that all will turn out as I would it, you would it, the powers that be that would it.

Love, Gregory

It always confused me. I knowed you all my life, and felt you were so non-understanding of me, that I inferred it as non-love, understanding = love. Yet when I consider the burden upon your Allen shoulders, I suffered the cost of a peer, a brother. Lost a lot in life—mothers, children, friends, peers. I won't fuck up this benefit, just to complete my book, over ten years now. It worries me, it takes the desire of life out of me.

▼ [Corso lived in a self-imposed hermitage for the next decade, living next door to his friends, Roger and Irvyne Richards, on Horatio Street in the West Village. He gave readings only on rare occasions and usually only at Ginsberg's urging. He watched his old friends die one by one over those years. When Ginsberg died in 1997, Corso wrote a moving tribute for his memorial service. He was still unable to break his old habits, though, and purloined some of Ginsberg's books during the wake, just as he always had done during Ginsberg's life. Burroughs passed away later that same year and Corso became the last of the major Beat figures on the East Coast. His life wasn't without a few bright moments, though. Through the efforts of Gus Reininger and Hiro Yamagata, who were making a film about Corso, his mother was discovered. Although he hadn't seen her since he was one year old, she was still very much alive and well and living not far from New York City. A reunion took place and at last Corso had an extended family.]

To Griselda Ohannessian New York

May 18, 2000

Dear Griselda:

I'm in St. Vincent's Hospital right now and won't be able to read over the letters until I'm let out—in four or five days. [...] I hope there's an index so that young people and students can find Ginsberg, Kerouac, and so on.

I'll get in touch as soon as I get out of the hospital. I have no qualms about letters asking for money—in that respect I'm in good company — Mozart, Wagner, James Joyce and many others. I want you to publish this one too. If I had known my letters were going to be published I would have endured whatever hubris had befallen me. Ginsberg and Kerouac knew they were writing for posterity — the lucky sons of Angels!

Love, Gregory!

▼ [As Corso's health began to fail due to cancer, his eldest daughter, Sheri Langerman, took him to her home in Minnesota where he spent his last days. A funeral mass was given for him in the parish church where he had been baptized and his ashes were taken to Rome and placed at the feet of the poet, Percy Bysshe Shelley.]

NOTES

1 MacLeish, Archibald (1892-1982). Pulitzer Prize winning, American writer, poet and dramatist who held the post of Librarian of Congress from 1929 to 1944.

2 Charleston, South Carolina. Corso was staying in a small town near Charleston with his girlfriend, Hope Savage and her family.

3 Chatterton, Thomas (1752-1770). English poet who committed suicide by drinking arsenic.

4 Orlovsky, Peter (b. 1933). In December 1954, while living in San Francisco, Allen Ginsberg fell in love with Peter Orlovsky. They were to remain companions for the rest of Ginsberg's life. Peter's brother, Lafcadio (frequently called Laff by Corso) was mentally handicapped and lived with them in San Francisco for a year.

5 Fictional characters in the works of Fyodor Dostoevski.

6 Rosenberg, Anton (1927-1998). One of the original Greenwich Village hipsters and artists described by Jack Kerouac in his book, *The Subterraneans.*

7 Marlowe, Christopher (1564-1593). Early English poet.

8 Unamuno y Jugo, Miguel de (1864-1936). Spanish poet and philosopher.

9 Holmes, John Clellon (1926-88). Friend and author of the first "Beat" novel, *Go.*

10 Carr, Lucien (b. 1925). Columbia University classmate of Kerouac and Ginsberg.

11 Merims, Robert. Early Columbia University friend of Ginsberg.

12 Parker, Helen. Girlfriend of both Allen Ginsberg and Gregory Corso during the early 1950s.

13 Ansen, Alan (b. 1922). Poet and longtime friend of Ginsberg, Burroughs and Corso. He was once the secretary of W.H. Auden.

14 Keck, William. One of Kerouac's quintessential Subterraneans. He figures prominently in Ginsberg's masterpiece, *Howl.*

15 Moreland, Dusty. Another girlfriend of both Allen Ginsberg and Gregory Corso during the early 1950s.

16 *Vestal Lady on Brattle*

17 LaVigne, Robert (b. 1928). Painter and friend who introduced Ginsberg to Orlovsky.

18 *Siesta In Xbalba,* a long poem by Allen Ginsberg that he self-published while on board the ship to Alaska.

19 Whalen, Philip (b. 1923). Poet and writer, author of *Self-Portrait from Another Direction* and *On Bear's Head.* He and Gary Snyder were two of the first Beat writers to seriously study Buddhism.

20 McCorkle, Locke. Friend of Philip Whalen and Gary Snyder who shared their interests in Eastern philosophy. His cabin in Marin County was a frequent gathering spot for the San Francisco Beat group.

21 Witt-Diamant, Ruth. Founder and director of the influential Poetry Center at San Francisco State College.

22 Rexroth, Kenneth (1905-1982). One of the greatest of the poets and critics who formed the nucleus of the San Francisco Renaissance.

23 McClure, Michael (b. 1932). Poet and playwright, author of *Dark Brown* and *The Beard.*

24 Moricand, Conrad. An astrologer; writer and friend of Henry Miller in Paris, the title character in Miller's 1956 story, *A Devil in Paradise, The Story of Conrad Moricand.*

25 Solomon, Carl (1928-1993). Author and friend of Allen Ginsberg, to whom the poem *Howl* is dedicated.

26 Novalis was the pseudonym of the German poet Friedrich von Hardenberg (1772-1801).

27 Wackenroder, Wilhelm (1773-1798). German writer and a leader of German Romanticism.

28 von Kleist, Bernd Heinrich Wilhelm (1777-1811). German poet, dramatist and novelist.

29 Donlin, Bob. Friend portrayed as Rob Donnelly in Kerouac's *Desolation Angels.*

30 Gumps. A large department store in San Francisco specializing in Oriental objects and artworks, such as those by the Russian-born American artist, Ben Shahn.

31 Bufano, Beniamino (1898-1970). Italian-born artist and long-time San Francisco resident.

32 Moloch. Allen Ginsberg had a vision of the face of Moloch, the terrifying Phoenician God to whom chil-

dren were sacrificed, one foggy night while looking at the upper floors of the Sir Francis Drake Hotel.

33 Institute of Asian Studies. More precisely, the American Academy of Asian Studies, then at 2030 Broadway in San Francisco. Alan Watts, the author of *The Way of Zen* was the director until he was forced to resign later that same year.

34 Du Peru, Peter. One of the denizens of the lumpen world of San Francisco, a friend of Ginsberg's and Kerouac's.

35 C.F. Macintyre's translations of Rilke in 1947 were considered to be the best at that time.

36 The publisher of City Lights Books, Lawrence Ferlinghetti, had asked Gregory to put together a group of poems for what would become *Gasoline,* number 8 in the Pocket Poets Series.

37 In 1956, Hungary and Poland were in the news due to the Communist military suppression of uprisings.

38 Boswell. Daughter of Randall and Mary Jarrell.

39 Corso was still hoping to make it to Washington in time for the football game that they have bought tickets for.

40 Ezra Pound was being held as a mental patient in St. Elizabeth's Hospital in Washington, DC, in lieu of being charged as a traitor for his support of Mussolini during World War II.

41 Laughlin, James (1914-97). Owner and publisher of New Directions Books.

42 As the Poetry Consultant for the Library of Congress, Jarrell was involved in collecting tape recordings by poets to be added to the library's holdings.

43 MacGregor, Robert. Vice President of New Directions and James Laughlin's right-hand man for several years.

44 Laforgue, Jules (1860-1877). French poet whose importance is due more to the effect his early death had on his contemporaries than to his own poetry.

45 Corso was worried about getting a passport since he had spent time in prison. He used his brother's name to get one and carried that passport with him for much of his life. It frequently caused problems for him when he tried to cash checks, etc.

46 The Open Door was a popular jazz nightclub in New York City's Greenwich Village.

47 Parker 61, a style of fountain pen.

48 San Remo Bar, at the corner of Bleecker and MacDougal in Greenwich Village was a favorite hangout for writers during the 1950s. Portions of Kerouac's novel, *The Subterraneans,* were based on events that took place in the San Remo.

49 Williams, Oscar (1927-66). The editor of the influential *Little Treasury of Modern Poetry* which was published in 1952.

50 Eberhart, Richard (b. 1904). Pulitzer Prize winning poet and critic.

51 Shapiro, Meyer. Art critic and sometimes poet.

52 Ferlinghetti had received a notice from Railway Express that books were being held for Corso. Gregory would later regret that he didn't claim the copies.

53 Irrgang, Robert Harrison. Robert LaVigne's friend and roommate during this period.

54 Breit, Harvey. *New York Times Book Review* (Jan. 20, 1957) p. 8.

55 Harmon, James. He and Michael McClure edited *Ark II, Moby I,* a San Francisco-based little magazine.

56 Gould, Stanley. New York doctor and friend of Corso's.

57 Whitman, George. Owner of the English-language Mistral Bookshop in Paris, which later took the name Shakespeare and Co. after Sylvia Beach's famous store. Whitman was one of Lawrence Ferlinghetti's oldest friends.

58 Olympia Press, whose publisher Maurice Girodias frequently paid cash to legitimate authors to write porno for this press using pseudonyms. He was a flamboyant publisher who had a taste for great modern literature by authors like William Burroughs, Vladimir Nabokov and J.P. Donleavy but he found that x-rated books sold better than anything else. He invested the profits from his publishing company in a nightclub/restaurant that didn't last long.

59 The Cellar. A basement bar in North Beach, where an early series of poetry and jazz readings was held. One session with Ferlinghetti and Rexroth was released as a popular recording by Fantasy Records.

60 Stock, Bob. An anarchist trumpet player who hung out in San Francisco at the Co-Existence Bagel Shop.

61 Reginald Bunthorne was a character in the Gilbert and Sullivan opera, *Patience.*

62 Ponsot, Marie. City Lights Books published her book, *True Minds* in 1957.

63 Baldwin, James (1924-87). The well-known author of *Giovanni's Room,* he was living in Paris at the time.

64 Lawrence Ferlinghetti was arrested for selling Ginsberg's poem, *Howl*, and government authorities were quoted as saying that you wouldn't want your children to read it, hence Corso's comments.

65 Allen, Donald (b. 1912). One of the most important editors of post WWII American poetry, his *The New American Poetry 1945-1960* introduced many of the Beat poets to the public.

66 Artigas, Joan Gardy (b. 1938). Artist and favorite ceramicist of Picasso and Miro.

67 *Partisan Review*, vol. 24, no. 2 (Spring 1957) pp. 296-298.

68 Note that in this variation of the story, Gregory attributes the remark to his "friend."

69 Corso mailed the manuscript of *Gasoline* along with this letter.

70 Ginsberg had suggested that Corso send poems to John Wieners for his *Measure* magazine as well as to Don Allen at *Evergreen Review*.

71 The publisher is Maurice Girodias of the Olympia Press.

72 Pomerand, Gabriel (1926-1972). One of the first members of the Letterist group, author of *Symphony in K*.

73 For the publication of *Howl*.

74 Corso is again referring to Jarrell's job as Poetry Consultant to the Library of Congress.

75 Garver, Bill. A Times Square hustler and friend of many of the Beats, he was most famous as an overcoat thief and drug dealer.

76 *Poets Hitchhiking on the Highway* appeared in the Spring-Summer 1957 issue of *Coastlines*, a little magazine published in Hollywood, CA.

77 Bellevue. A large New York City hospital noted for its psychiatric ward.

78 Tombs. A New York City prison.

79 *In the Baggage Room at Greyhound*

80 Kallman, Chester (1921-75). A longtime partner of the English poet, W.H. Auden.

81 Magister Theodoricus. Czech court painter for Emperor Charles IV.

82 Ungerer, Joy. A beautiful Indonesian artist's model who was Corso's girl friend for a time and hung out at the Beat Hotel.

83 Corso is referring to the von Weber opera, *Der Freischutz*, of 1821. The hero of the story, whose name is Wilhelm, not Kasper, makes a pact with the devil and accidentally shoots his wife with magic bullets.

84 Marshall, Edward (b. 1932). American poet and student of religion associated with the Black Mountain School of writers.

85 Loewinsohn, Ron (b. 1937). One of the younger poets of the San Francisco Renaissance, his first book *Watermelons*, was published by Totem Press, and included an introduction by Allen Ginsberg.

86 Corso, with Allen Ginsberg's help, had written an article, "The Literary Revolution in America" for *Litterair Paspoort* (Nov. 1957) in which he praised the members of the Beat Generation and San Francisco Renaissance, and was highly critical of those he considered more academic, such as Ashbery and Koch.

87 Guggenheim, Peggy (1898-1979). Millionaire patron of the arts, whose *palazzo* in Venice is one of the world's great museums of modern art.

88 *A City Winter and Other Poems*, by Frank O'Hara.

89 Yage. The common name for a tropical vine, Ayahuasca, which produces psychedelic effects.

90 Burroughs, Joan (1924-51). Wife of William S. Burroughs, she was killed by her husband in a shooting accident in Mexico City in 1951.

91 Jones, LeRoi (b. 1934). Poet and editor of *Yugen* magazine, he later became Amiri Baraka and was prominent in the struggle for Black equality.

92 Guggenheim, Pegeen. Peggy Guggenheim's daughter.

93 William Carlos Williams' book, *Kora in Hell*

94 Ginsberg had given a clover leaf from Percy Bysshe Shelley's grave in Rome to his father, Louis Ginsberg.

95 Corso must be relying on his memory here. Sherlock Holmes lived at 221B Baker St., and Oscar Wilde lived at 16 Tite Street, but he was very close in both cases.

96 Watson Taylor, Simon. English surrealist and translator of Alfred Jarry's *Ubu*.

97 Ponystabled - Corso and Ginsberg first met around 1950 at the Pony Stable Bar, a lesbian hangout in Greenwich Village.

98 Corso is referring to an emergency grant from the American Academy of Arts and Letters for $250.

99 Allen Ginsberg had insulted Peggy Guggenheim on his earlier visit to Ansen in Venice. He and Peter Orlovsky narrowly missed hitting Guggenheim when they threw a wet towel across the room at each other.

100 Two bookstores in Paris.

101 Thomas, Sheldon. An American poet who joined Burroughs and Gysin in psychic experiments at the Beat Hotel.

102 Creagh, Patrick. A friend of Corso's who he would later stay with in Rome.

103 Postell, Thomas. A troubled young poet to whom LeRoi Jones addressed his poem, "For Tom Postell, Dead Black Poet."

104 Harloff, Guy (1933-89). A Dutch artist who introduced the Beat writers to what became the famous Beat Hotel in Paris. Harloff was also a close friend of Peggy Guggenheim.

105 Alain Bosquet was editing *Trente-Cinq Jeunes Poètes Américains* at the time.

106 Balf, John. A friend who also lived at the Beat Hotel in Paris.

107 Silverman, Herschel. A poet who owned a candy store in New Jersey.

108 B.J. Carroll was a would-be actor, who caused an unwelcome commotion one drunken night on a boat in the Seine with a much more famous actor, Errol Flynn.

109 de Angulo, Gui. Daughter of Jaimie de Angulo, a California eccentric and Native American expert.

110 Mayakovsky, Vladimir. Russian poet.

111 Benn, Gottfried (1886-1956). German nihilist poet and essayist.

112 Peter Orlovsky was working as an orderly in a local hospital.

113 Glassman, Joyce. Kerouac's girlfriend at the time, later as Joyce Johnson she wrote *Minor Characters,* a memoir of her life in New York City during the 1950s.

114 Jones, Hettie. Co-publisher with husband, LeRoi Jones of *Yugen* magazine and author of *How I Became Hettie Jones.*

115 Peret, Benjamin. French artist and colleague of Duchamp and Ray.

116 Neal Cassady was sentenced to prison for possession of a small amount of marijuana.

117 Sublette, Connie. An old friend of several of the Beats, Connie Sublette was killed on the streets of North Beach.

118 Bremser, Ray (1934-1998). A poet who had served prison time in Bordentown, NJ.

119 Ginsberg's "mother poem" is a reference to his poem, *Kaddish.*

120 Mistral Bookshop's owner, George Whitman, wanted to publish books like his friend, Lawrence Ferlinghetti, but the idea never got off the ground.

121 Schwartz, Jerry. An American artist living at the Beat Hotel.

122 Turnbull, Gael (b. 1924). A Canadian poet living in England much of the time.

123 Hart, Howard. Poet who gave an early series of poetry and jazz readings with Jack Kerouac and David Amram.

124 Stern, Jacques. A young intellectual and friend of Burroughs and Corso. He was a victim of polio and needed aluminum crutches to move around. He was extremely wealthy and interested in both the avant-garde and drugs.

125 Appel, Karel (b. 1921). Dutch painter and member of the COBRA Group.

126 Francis, Sam (b. 1923). American abstract expressionist painter.

127 Boyle, Kay (b. 1902). American writer, member of the American Academy of Arts and Letters.

128 Goodie's Bar. A very large bar on Sixth Avenue in Greenwich Village, an old-time neighborhood hang-out, actually spelled Goody's.

129 Shattuck, Roger (b. 1923). An instructor at Harvard while Corso was living in Cambridge, he was also an editor and the author of *The Banquet Years.*

130 Read, George Herbert (1893-1968). English art critic, editor and poet, also the author of *The Green Child.*

131 Phipps, Harry. A young American millionaire, who frequently traveled with Jacques Stern.

132 Roditi, Edouard (1910-92). American Jewish art critic, translator, and poet, author of *Dialogues on Art* and *Magellan of the Pacific.*

133 *Akzente.* A German literary magazine that published many of the Beat writers.

134 Rosenthal, Irving. Editor of *The Chicago Review* and later *Big Table.*

135 Feinstein, Elaine. The editor of the *Cambridge Opinion.*

136 Dr. Dent was a London physician who helped several of the Beat authors including Burroughs. He recommended an apomorphine treatment for drug addiction much favored by Burroughs.

137 *Laughing Gas,* Ginsberg's poem describing the effects of the drug, see his *Collected Poems,* p. 189-199.

138 Rahv, Philip. Editor of *Partisan Review.*

139 *First Poem* was actually published as *Frist Poem* to accentuate Orlovsky's unique way of spelling even the simplest words.

140 Don Allen had asked Corso to write a short autobiography for his anthology.

141 Mardou Fox was the fictional name that Kerouac gave to the lead character in *The Subterraneans,* love interest of both Kerouac and Corso are in love with.

142 Ginsberg had put an ad in the *Village Voice* asking for money to get Corso back from Europe and several people contributed to the fund. Corso was happy to get the money but embarrassed to be the object of such publicized charity.

143 Trelawny, Edward (1792-1881). English writer and friend of Shelley and Byron.

144 After Corso's own death in 2001, his ashes were buried at the foot of Shelley in this same cemetery.

145 Jones, James. Author of the bestseller, *From Here to Eternity.*

146 The Loewinsohn's were expecting a baby at the time.

147 Steve Allen had sent a contribution to help buy a ticket home for Corso. Allen was the host of the Tonight Show and a supporter of Kerouac and other Beat writers.

148 Suetonius (69-122 A.D.). Roman historian and court bureaucrat who recorded the lives of the Caesars.

149 Ferlinghetti bought a cabin retreat along the Big Sur coast, south of San Francisco.

150 Forest, Lee. An American fashion model who occasionally lived at the Beat Hotel.

151 Greenberg, Sam. A poet who had a great influence on Hart Crane. James Laughlin suggested that Corso should look into his work since he thought they had much in common.

152 Phrygia was an ancient country in Asia Minor.

153 Corso had suggested the title *Cars Are Real* for this book, but Laughlin didn't like it.

154 Schwartz, Delmore (1913-1966). American poet and writer, editor of *Partisan Review* and *New Republic.*

155 Willard Maas was a critic, poet, film director and teacher, and Corso was writing to his students.

156 Kerouac and Corso had read at the college.

157 Ferlinghetti had just sent him a copy of the third printing of *Gasoline.*

158 Corso is referring to the fact that some of Ferlinghetti's ancestors were Sephardic Jews who had roots in the Virgin Islands.

159 Brody, Iris. A long-time friend of Ginsberg's and a painter of mystical landscapes. She died of an overdose in the mid-1960s.

160 Blok, Alexander (1880-1921). Russian poet.

161 Hesse, Eva. A friend of James Laughlin that he suggested Corso look up during his travels.

162 *Pull My Daisy,* a classic Beat film, produced by Alfred Leslie and Robert Frank with a narration by Jack Kerouac. Corso, Ginsberg, Orlovsky and others acted in the movie.

163 *Hotel Wentley Poems* by John Wieners.

164 Lebel, Jean-Jacques. French poet, writer, artist, theater director and translator of the Beats. Corso shared an apartment with him in Venice.

165 Villiers. The printer in England that set the type for many New Directions and City Lights books during the 1950s.

166 The Salute is a beautiful church on the Grand Canal, more formally named Santa Maria della Salute.

167 Corso is referring to the picture on the postcard he has sent to Ginsberg.

168 De Kooning, Willem (1904-1997). Dutch abstract expressionist painter.

169 Connolly, Cyril (1903-1974). British writer and critic, founder of *Horizon* magazine.

170 *Her.* A surrealist novel by Lawrence Ferlinghetti, published in 1960 by New Directions.

171 Erbe, Ned. The publicity and promotion manager for New Directions at the time.

172 Crosby, Harry. The publisher of the Black Sun Press who killed himself and his girlfriend in 1929 in a famous murder/suicide that scandalized the avant-garde.

173 Kerouac's article "Roaming Beatniks" appeared in the October 1959 issue of *Holiday* magazine.

174 Copacabana. A famous New York City nightclub.

175 Ginsberg had just sent him a copy of his poem, *Death to Van Gogh's Ear.*

176 Carnera, Primo (1906-1967). American boxer who was the heavyweight champion of the world in 1933-34.

177 Ferlinghetti had just sent Corso a copy of his poem, *The Great Chinese Dragon.*

178 William Burroughs and Brion Gysin discovered a method of writing that they called "cut-ups." By slicing up existing texts and gluing them back together randomly, they created new juxtapositions of words and phrases, often with interesting results. At first Corso was enthusiastic about the method, but then he began to see it as a danger to creative writing and original thought.

179 *Pull My Daisy.*

180 LeRoi and Hettie Jones had just had their first of two daughters, Kellie.

181 Adar is a month in the Jewish calendar year.

182 Ciardi, John (1916-86). American poet and critic and author of the influential 1959 book, *How Does a Poem Mean?* Corso refers here to Ciardi's article "Epitaph for the Dead Beats" which had just appeared in the Feb. 6, 1960 issue of the *Saturday Review.*

183 Pivano, Fernanda. The first Italian translator for many of the Beat authors and a close friend to Corso, Ginsberg and Kerouac.

184 Ned Erbe, at New Directions, had just written asking Corso if he would mind having his palm print read by a reporter who specialized in the palmistry of celebrities.

185 Caryl Chessman became a cause célèbre during the mid-1950s. He had been sentenced to death and spent 11 years and 10 months on death row. On Feb. 18, 1960 he received his eighth stay of execution, which Corso is referring to here as the good news, but in the end he was executed on May 2, 1960 which Corso will also comment on in later letters.

186 For years Ginsberg and Corso talked about traveling to India together. It wouldn't be until 1962 that Ginsberg and Orlovsky would go there, but Corso never made it, although it was a long time dream.

187 Gary, Romain (1914-1980). French novelist, born in Russia.

188 Seberg, Jean. Actress in such films as *A Fine Madness* and *Lilith,* and her title role in *Saint Joan* which Corso refers to here.

189 Ferlinghetti's poem, *He,* is a long poem about Allen Ginsberg.

190 Wilentz, Elias and Ted. Brothers who owned the Eighth Street Bookshop and also published books under the imprint of Corinth. *The Beat Scene,* edited by Elias was one of the important anthologies of that press.

191 *The Beats* was edited by Seymour Krim and sold as a mass-market paperback by Gold Medal Books, hundreds of thousands of copies were printed of this anthology.

192 Quasimodo, Salvatore (1901-68). Nobel Prize winner in literature.

193 Joans, Ted (b. 1928). One of the few African-American poets in the early Beat Generation group, he spent much of his later life abroad in Europe and Africa.

194 Veidt, Conrad. Actor and star of movies such as *Suspicion* and *All Through the Night.*

195 During the height of the Beatnik craze in the 1950s, photographer Fred McDarrah organized "Beatniks" like Ted Joans to attend and entertain at parties of the very wealthy who wanted to appear "hip." They called the business "Rent-a-Beatnik" and advertised in the *Village Voice.*

196 This is a reference to the well-known story of Karl Marx working in the British Museum Library while perfecting his social philosophy.

197 Mazzini, Giuseppe (1805-1872). Italian patriot.

198 Lumumba, Patrick (1925-61). First prime minister of Zaire.

199 Kasavubu, Joseph (1910-69). First president of Zaire. He ousted Lumumba in a political coup.

200 Tshombe, Moise (1919-69). President of the Katanga Province.

201 Aiken, Conrad (1889-1973). His book *Ushant* was a fictionalized autobiography.

202 Evans, Sir Arthur John. The British archaeologist who excavated the palace of Knossos on Crete.

203 Ginsberg had met a Harvard professor by the name of Timothy Leary who wanted him to take part in psychological experiments with newly discovered drugs such as LSD, at first for scientific purposes, later it would develop into the psychedelic revolution.

204 Planck, Max (1858-1947). The German physicist who formulated the quantum theory.

205 Atwill, Lionel. A classic horror film director, with credits such as *Son of Frankenstein* to his name.

206 Sorel, Julien. The main character in Stendahl's book *The Red and the Black.*

207 Kenny, Nicholas (1895-1975). A poet and columnist for the *New York Daily News,* who used his own sentimental verse in many of his columns.

208 In his previous letter to Corso, James Laughlin had just told him about the death of his elderly aunt.

209 Johnson, Kay. An American poet and painter who also lived at the Beat Hotel in Paris for a while and worked under the name "Kaja"

210 Wilson, Colin (b. 1931). The author of *The Outsider* and one of the writers that the press grouped together as "The Angry Young Men," a British version of the Beats.

211 Archer, David. A young British book dealer who showed Ginsberg and Corso around Oxford when they came there to read for the first time.

212 Portman, Michael (1940-1983). At the time he was a young, spoiled, British aristocrat who fell under the spell of William Burroughs' and Brion Gysin's teachings, to the point where everyone thought Portman had become a clone of Burroughs.

213 Sommerville, Ian. A young follower of Burroughs and Gysin, very much like Michael Portman. Sommerville, a Cambridge educated mathematician, helped Gysin develop his "Dream Machine."

214 Beiles, Sinclair. A South African writer who worked with Maurice Girodias at the Olympia Press and helped Burroughs organize the manuscript of *Naked Lunch.* Later with Burroughs and Gysin, he developed the cut-up method and co-authored the book *Minutes to Go* with them and Corso.

215 Moraes, Don. A British writer.

216 This note was written on the back of a postcard showing the head of the statue of Demeter in the British Museum.

217 James Laughlin suggested that Corso get in touch with the agent Lawrence Pollinger before entering into a book contract with Eyre and Spottiswoode for a book that would become his *Selected Poems.*

218 The play appeared in the January 1962 issue of *Encounter* magazine, edited by Stephen Spender.

219 Laughlin had mentioned that Corso might want to ask Ginsberg to help him edit his poems for publication since it was taking him so long to send the final versions.

220 Jack Kerouac's wife, Joan Haverty, had a baby girl whom Kerouac refused to acknowledge as his own daughter. He hired Allen Ginsberg's brother, Eugene Brooks, to defend him in the paternity suit.

221 Madame Rachou was the *patronne* of the "Beat Hotel" at 9 rue Git-le-Coeur and a very understanding landlady.

222 During discussions with James Laughlin at the New Directions offices, *Long Live Man* was picked as the new title for his book. Originally Corso had planned to call it simply *Apples.*

223 Lycurgus (390-324 BC). An Athenian orator.

224 Ganesh. A Hindu deity with the head of an elephant.

225 Cowen, Elise (1933-62). A woman who was madly in love with Allen Ginsberg. Ginsberg always said that she reminded him of his mother, Naomi, and smelled of death.

226 Schmidt, Judith. An editor at Grove Press who was assigned to Corso's book.

227 Corso had signed a contract with Grove Press for a novel, but it was never completed.

228 In Corso's *Junge Amerikanische Lyrik.*

229 Probably just a little word play as the title was *Long Live Man.*

230 Jordan, Fred. One of the editors at Grove Press.

231 Berenson, Bernard (1865-1959). An art historian and critic who spent much of his life in Italy studying the Italian Renaissance.

232 Corso is referring to one of the first lines of Ferlinghetti's poem "Away above a harborful / of caulkless houses / among the charley noble chimneypots ..." Charley Noble pots were funnel vents on the decks of ships.

233 Penguin wanted to do a book of poetry with Allen Ginsberg and two other poets.

234 Ginsberg had raised the question of whether there might be contractual problems with the British publisher of Corso's *Selected Poems.*

235 Anselm Hollo's translations of the Russian poets Kirsanov, Voznesensky and Yevtushenko had just been published as *Red Cats* by City Lights Books.

236 Alexander Blok and Vladimir Mayakovsky were earlier Russian poets.

237 Ferlinghetti had written telling Gregory that he had thrown his letter from *Who's Who* on the floor.

238 Fantin-Latour, Henri (1836-1904). French painter.

239 Fold-ins were an outgrowth of the cut-up method, made by folding the paper like an accordion instead of cutting the paper into strips.

240 Ginsberg, Louis. Allen Ginsberg's father. He was a high school English teacher and a poet himself. He was also a great lover of puns which Corso is mimicking in his letter.

241 One of Louis Ginsberg's books of poetry was titled *The Everlasting Minute.*

242 After a year in India, the authorities became suspicious of Ginsberg and Orlovsky, who were living like poor Indians, rather than typical American tourists. Their visas weren't renewed, but after a few appeals they were allowed to remain in India.

243 Corso is referring to a letter by Ginsberg which was published under the title "Prose Contribution to Cuban Revolution" in *PaLante* (May 19, 1962).

244 Burroughs was frequently referred to as "Old Bull Lee" by his friends.

245 Trocchi, Alexander (b. 1925). Author of *Cain's Book,* a very influential first novel which plumbed the depths of drug addiction.

246 *Guns of the Trees.* A 1962 film made by Jonas Mekas which featured Allen Ginsberg reading his poetry.

247 *Reality Sandwiches* (City Lights, 1963)

248 Day, Dorothy. Social activist and founder of the *Catholic Worker* newspaper.

249 Pearson, Norman Holmes. A scholar and literary critic, who among other things was H.D.'s literary executor.

250 James Laughlin did not like the idea of printing the poems on the page horizontally as Corso had suggested, he felt it would make the book difficult to read, and Corso agreed.

251 *Wichita Vortex Sutra*, by Allen Ginsberg.

252 Ed Sanders' mimeo magazine was called *Fuck You: A Magazine of the Arts.*

253 Corso is referring again to the fund that was set up by the *Village Voice* ten years earlier asking for money to get him home from Europe.

254 Corso lived on Ginsberg's farm in Cherry Valley, NY, for a while.

255 Ball, Gordon. A film-maker and the manager of Allen Ginsberg's farm in Cherry Valley. Ball edited several of Ginsberg's books after becoming a college professor.

256 Belle Carpenter was from a family that had strong ties to the DuPont chemical family.

257 Tasha was Belle's daughter by another marriage.

258 Ratner's was a famous Lower East Side delicatessen.

259 Smith, Harry (1923-91). A film-maker, folk music anthologist and self-proclaimed alchemist who was occasionally supported by Ginsberg.

260 McCabe, Charles. A columnist for the *San Francisco Chronicle* was a regular at Gino and Carlo's Bar on Green Street, also one of Corso's haunts at the time.

261 The Committee on Poetry (C.O.P.) was a non-profit organization founded by Ginsberg through which he could give money to writers and friends down on their luck.

262 Naropa Institute in Boulder, CO, was the first Buddhist college to be accredited in the United States, it was founded by Chögyam Trungpa, Rinpoche in the 1970s. He asked Allen Ginsberg and Anne Waldman to co-found the poetics department which they named the Jack Kerouac School of Disembodied Poetics. Every summer Ginsberg arranged for his friends to teach and give readings at the school.

263 Medi-Cal was the California medical assistance program.

264 Cherkovski, Neeli. A friend and poet living in San Francisco, the author of many books including biographies of Lawrence Ferlinghetti and Charles Bukowski.

265 Foye, Raymond. A friend who worked for City Lights Books and edited several important works of poetry including those of Bob Kaufman and John Wieners.

266 Peter Orlovsky's book *Clean Asshole Poems and Smiling Vegetable Songs* was published by City Lights books in 1978 as part of their Pocket Poets Series.

267 Wilson, Bob. Owner of the legendary Phoenix Bookshop in Greenwich Village. He discovered that Corso was creating manuscripts, notebooks and letters solely for the purpose of selling them to rare book dealers. Whenever Corso needed money he would sit down and write a notebook, then take it to Wilson and sell it, blurring the line between a working notebook and a commodity. Due to this practice, several "original" manuscripts of poems such as *Bomb* are known to exist. It presented a problem in the rare book trade. Were notebooks created for such sales are less valuable than those created for the writer's personal use?

268 Rock singer and poet, Patti Smith gave her farewell performance in Florence to an audience of 70,000 fans.

269 Beck, Julian (1925-85). Co-founder, with his wife Judith Malina, of the revolutionary, avant-garde Living Theatre.

270 Passim's was a nightclub in Cambridge, Massachusetts, where Ginsberg frequently appeared.

271 Corso is referring to the fact that he often stole Ginsberg's books and manuscripts and sold them in the rare book market. Several times he told Ginsberg about it after the fact, and Ginsberg went to the dealers to buy back his own books.

272 Corso was asked to write something for a festschrift in honor of Ginsberg's sixtieth birthday. It was published by the Lospecchio Press in *Best Minds: A Tribute to Allen Ginsberg,* edited by Bill Morgan and Bob Rosenthal, 1986.

273 The reference here is to William Carlos Williams' *Paterson* and Ezra Pound's *Cantos.*

274 Calliope. The classical muse of epic poetry and eloquence.

275 A reference to the 1990 Gulf War, which took place in the ancient land of Mesopotamia.

276 These were ancient Babylonian gods.

277 *Best Minds: A Tribute to Allen Ginsberg,* mentioned earlier.

278 Alene Lee was the real-life name of Kerouac's character, Mardou Fox in *The Subterraneans.*

279 Corso was asked by Francis Ford Coppola to appear in the movie *Godfather 3.* They were filming in Italy at the time and Corso played in one scene.

280 Reference is again to Ginsberg's Committee on Poetry as a source of funding.

281 Smith, Jack (1932-89). Underground film maker, whose *Flaming Creatures* was censored in New York City.

282 Corso had planned to call his next collection of poetry, *The Golden Dot.* He was given several advances from his publisher, New Directions, for the book, but it never appeared.

283 Hector's was an all-night cafeteria on Times Square where many of the Beats hung out in the 1940s.

284 Hazeldon was a drug and alcohol treatment center where several writers including Corso and Peter Orlovsky sought help.

INDEX

Lightning Source UK Ltd.
Milton Keynes UK
UKHW012331070422
401246UK00001B/1